Also by G. J. Meyer

A World Undone: The Story of the Great War, 1914–1918

THE
TUDORS

THE
TUDORS

The Complete Story of England's
Most Notorious Dynasty

G. J. MEYER

Delacorte Press
New York

Published in the United States by Delacorte Press,
an imprint of The Random House Publishing Group,
a division of Random House, Inc., New York.

DELACORTE PRESS is a registered trademark of Random House, Inc.,
and the colophon is a trademark of Random House, Inc.

Map and family tree copyright © 2010 by Daniel R. Lynch

Library of Congress Cataloging-in-Publication Data
Meyer, G. J.
The Tudors : the complete story of England's most notorious dynasty / G. J. Meyer.—1st ed.
p. cm.
Includes bibliographical references and index.
ISBN 978-0-385-34076-2
eBook ISBN: 978-0-440-33914-4
1. Tudor, House of.   2. Great Britain—History—Tudors, 1485–1603.   3. Great Britain—
Politics and government—1485–1603.   4. Monarchy—Great Britain—History—16th century.
I. Title.
DA315.M477 2010
942.05—dc22   2009040032

Printed in the United States of America on acid-free paper

www.bantamdell.com

4 6 8 9 7 5

Text design by Virginia Norey

For Rosie

Contents

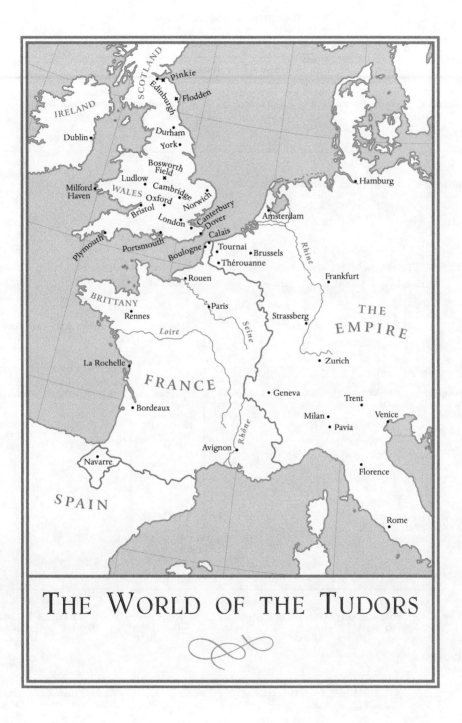

THE WORLD OF THE TUDORS

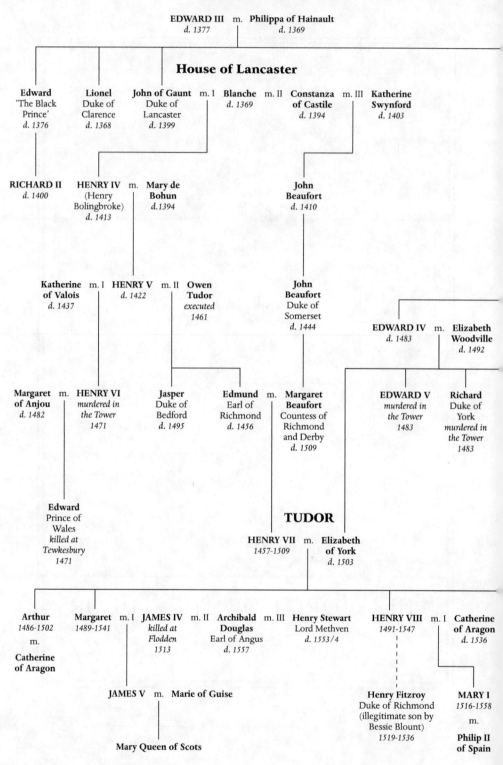

PLANTAGENET

EDWARD III m. **Philippa of Hainault**
d. 1377   *d. 1369*

House of Lancaster

Edward **Lionel** **John of Gaunt** m. I **Blanche** m. II **Constanza** m. III **Katherine**
'The Black   Duke of   Duke of   *d. 1369*   of Castile   Swynford
Prince'   Clarence   Lancaster   *d. 1394*   *d. 1403*
d. 1376   *d. 1368*   *d. 1399*

RICHARD II **HENRY IV** m. **Mary de** **John**
d. 1400   (Henry   **Bohun**   **Beaufort**
               Bolingbroke)   *d.1394*   *d. 1410*
               d. 1413

Katherine m. I **HENRY V** m. II **Owen** **John**
of Valois   *d. 1422*   **Tudor**   **Beaufort**
d. 1437   *executed*   Duke of
                                         1461   Somerset
                                                         d. 1444   **EDWARD IV** m. **Elizabeth**
                                                                              d. 1483   **Woodville**
                                                                                                 d. 1492

Margaret m. **HENRY VI** **Jasper** **Edmund** m. **Margaret** **EDWARD V** **Richard**
of Anjou   *murdered in*   Duke of   Earl of   **Beaufort**   *murdered in*   Duke of
d. 1482   *the Tower*   Bedford   Richmond   Countess of   *the Tower*   York
               1471   *d. 1495*   *d. 1456*   Richmond   *1483*   *murdered in*
                                                         and Derby   *the Tower*
                                                         d. 1509   *1483*

Edward   ## TUDOR
Prince of
Wales   **HENRY VII** m. **Elizabeth**
killed at   *1457-1509*   **of York**
Tewkesbury   *d. 1503*
1471

Arthur **Margaret** m. I **JAMES IV** m. II **Archibald** m. III **Henry Stewart** **HENRY VIII** m. I **Catherine**
1486-1502   *1489-1541*   *killed at*   **Douglas**   Lord Methven   *1491-1547*   of Aragon
m.   *Flodden*   Earl of Angus   *d. 1553/4*   *d. 1536*
                                1513   *d. 1557*
Catherine
of Aragon

                    JAMES V m. **Marie of Guise**   **Henry Fitzroy**   **MARY I**
                                                           Duke of Richmond   *1516-1558*
                                                           (illegitimate son by
                                                           Bessie Blount)   m.
                    Mary Queen of Scots   *1519-1536*
                                                                               Philip II
                                                                               of Spain

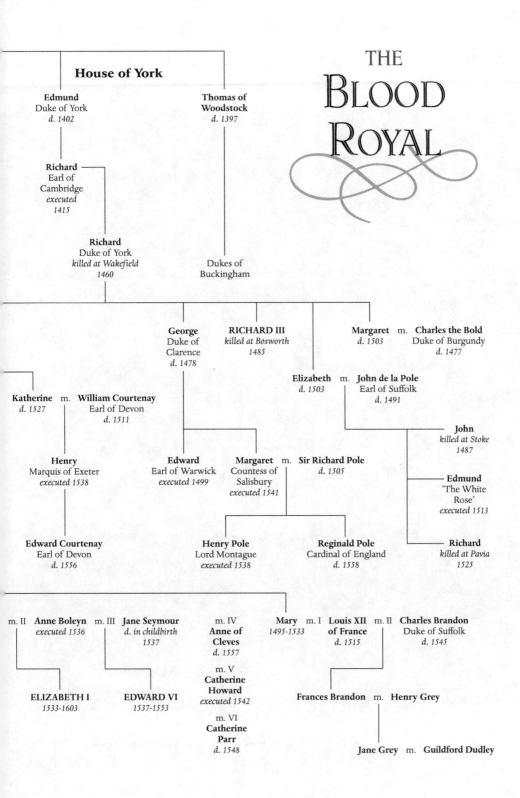

House of York

THE
BLOOD
ROYAL

Edmund
Duke of York
d. 1402

**Thomas of
Woodstock**
d. 1397

Richard
Earl of
Cambridge
*executed
1415*

Richard
Duke of York
*killed at Wakefield
1460*

Dukes of
Buckingham

George
Duke of
Clarence
d. 1478

RICHARD III
*killed at Bosworth
1485*

Margaret m. **Charles the Bold**
d. 1503   Duke of Burgundy
         d. 1477

Elizabeth m. **John de la Pole**
d. 1503   Earl of Suffolk
         d. 1491

Katherine m. **William Courtenay**
d. 1527   Earl of Devon
         d. 1511

John
*killed at Stoke
1487*

Henry
Marquis of Exeter
executed 1538

Edward
Earl of Warwick
executed 1499

Margaret m. **Sir Richard Pole**
Countess of   *d. 1505*
Salisbury
executed 1541

Edmund
'The White
Rose'
executed 1513

Edward Courtenay
Earl of Devon
d. 1556

Henry Pole
Lord Montague
executed 1538

Reginald Pole
Cardinal of England
d. 1558

Richard
*killed at Pavia
1525*

m. II Anne Boleyn m. III Jane Seymour
     executed 1536   *d. in childbirth
                  1537*

**m. IV
Anne of
Cleves**
d. 1557

Mary m. I **Louis XII** m. II **Charles Brandon**
1495-1533   **of France**   Duke of Suffolk
         d. 1515   *d. 1545*

**m. V
Catherine
Howard**
executed 1542

ELIZABETH I
1533-1603

EDWARD VI
1537-1553

Frances Brandon m. **Henry Grey**

**m. VI
Catherine
Parr**
d. 1548

Jane Grey m. **Guildford Dudley**

A Tudor Timeline

1457	*January 28*	Henry Tudor is born to Lady Margaret Beaufort, thirteen-year-old widow of Edmund Tudor, Earl of Richmond
1485	*August 22*	Tudor is crowned Henry VII of England after defeating Richard III in the Battle of Bosworth Field
	December 15	Catherine of Aragon is born in Spain
1486	*January 18*	Marriage of Henry VII to Elizabeth of York
	September 19	Birth of Arthur, Prince of Wales
1491	*June 28*	Birth of future King Henry VIII
1494	*September 12*	Birth of future King Francis I of France
1495	*April 27*	Birth of Suleiman I, Sultan of the Ottoman Empire
1500	*February 24*	Birth of Charles of Hapsburg, future Emperor Charles V
1501	*November 14*	Catherine of Aragon is married to Arthur, Prince of Wales
1502	*April 2*	Death of Arthur, Prince of Wales
1503	*February 11*	Death of Elizabeth of York, Henry VIII's mother
1509	*April 22*	Death of Henry VII
	June 11	Henry VIII is married to Catherine of Aragon
1513	*June 30*	Henry crosses the Channel to take command of the campaign against France
	September 9	Scots army is destroyed by the Earl of Surrey's English force at the Battle of Flodden
1515	*December 24*	Thomas Wolsey becomes chancellor of England
1516	*February 18*	Future Queen Mary I is born to Catherine of Aragon
1519	*June 15*	Birth of Henry VIII's illegitimate son Henry Fitzroy

1527	*May 21*	Birth of Philip of Hapsburg, future King of Spain and husband of Mary I
1529	*September 22*	Thomas Wolsey is stripped of chancellorship, replaced by Thomas More
1532	*March 30*	Thomas Cranmer is consecrated as archbishop of Canterbury
	May 16	More is allowed to resign after the submission of the clergy
1533	*January 25*	Henry VIII is quietly married to Anne Boleyn
	April 13	Anne is proclaimed queen
	May 28	Cranmer's court declares Henry's marriage to Anne to be valid
	June 8	Parliament extinguishes papal authority in England
	September 7	Birth of future Queen Elizabeth I
1534	*April 20*	Execution of Elizabeth Barton, "Nun of Kent"
	April	Thomas Cromwell is confirmed as Henry VIII's principal secretary
	November	The Act of Supremacy establishes Henry VIII as head of the church in England
1535	*June 22*	Execution of John Fisher
	July 6	Execution of Thomas More
1536	*January 7*	Death of Catherine of Aragon
	March	Dissolution of monasteries begins
	May 19	Execution of Anne Boleyn
	May 30	Marriage of Henry VIII to Jane Seymour
	July 1	Mary and Elizabeth are declared illegitimate
	July	Ten Articles assert reformist religious doctrines
	July 22	Death of Henry VIII's illegitimate son Henry Fitzroy, Duke of Richmond
	October 8	Start of Pilgrimage of Grace in Yorkshire
1537	*October 12*	Birth of future King Edward VI
	October 24	Death of Jane Seymour
1539	*June*	Act of Six Articles returns the church to a more conservative position
1540	*January 6*	Henry VIII is married to Anne of Cleves

1540	*July 9*	Cleves marriage is dissolved
	July 28	Henry VIII is married to Catherine Howard; Thomas Cromwell is executed the same day
1541	*May 27*	Execution of Margaret Pole, Countess of Salisbury
1542	*February 13*	Execution of Catherine Howard
	December 8	Birth of Mary Stuart, future Queen of Scots
	December 13	Death of James V of Scotland
1543	*July 12*	Marriage of Henry VIII to Catherine Parr
1544	*July 14*	Henry crosses the Channel to make war on France
1547	*January 28*	Death of Henry VIII
	February 20	Coronation of Edward VI
	March 31	Death of Francis I of France
	September 10	At the Battle of Pinkie English forces commanded by Edward Seymour, new lord protector and Duke of Somerset, defeat the Scots
1549	*July 8*	Start of Kett's Rebellion in Norfolk
	September 5	Execution of Thomas Seymour
1551	*October 11*	Arrest of Edward Seymour, Duke of Somerset; John Dudley, new lord president of Edward VI's council, is elevated to Duke of Northumberland
1552	*January 22*	Execution of Somerset
1553	*May 21*	Marriage of Lady Jane Grey to Guildford Dudley
	July 6	Death of Edward VI
	July 10	Jane Grey is proclaimed queen
	August 3	Mary I enters London in triumph two weeks after being proclaimed queen
	August 21	Execution of John Dudley, Duke of Northumberland
	October 30	Coronation of Mary I
1554	*February 12*	Execution of Jane Grey and Guildford Dudley
	April 11	Execution of Sir Thomas Wyatt
	May 19	Release of Elizabeth after two months of confinement in the Tower
	July 25	Marriage of Mary I to Philip II of Spain
1555	*October 16*	Execution of Nicholas Ridley and Hugh Latimer
	November 12	Death of Stephen Gardiner, chancellor

1556	*March 21*	Execution of Thomas Cranmer; Reginald Pole becomes archbishop of Canterbury
1558	*January 5*	Fall of Calais to France
	April 24	Marriage of Mary Queen of Scots to future Francis II of France
	November 17	Deaths of Mary I and Reginald Pole; appointment of William Cecil as Queen Elizabeth's secretary of state
1559	*January 15*	Coronation of Elizabeth I
	May 8	Elizabeth signs Act of Uniformity
	September 18	Mary Queen of Scots becomes Queen of France with accession of Francis II
1560	*December 5*	Death of Francis II
1561	*August 19*	Arrival of Mary Queen of Scots in Scotland
1564	*September 29*	Robert Dudley is created Earl of Leicester
1565	*July 29*	Mary Queen of Scots weds Henry Stuart, Lord Darnley
1566	*June 19*	Birth of future James VI of Scotland and James I of England
1567	*February 10*	Murder of Darnley
	May 15	Mary Queen of Scots is married to James Hepburn, Earl of Bothwell
	July 24	With Mary a prisoner, her son is proclaimed King James VI
1571	*February 25*	William Cecil is raised to nobility as Baron Burghley
1572	*June 2*	Execution of Thomas Howard, fourth Duke of Norfolk
	August 24	Start of St. Bartholomew's Massacre in Paris
1584	*June 9*	Death of Francis, Duke of Alençon
	July 10	Assassination of William of Orange
1585	*August 20*	With Treaty of Nonsuch, England commits to sending troops to the Netherlands
1586	*January 15*	Earl of Leicester takes the oath as governor-general of the Netherlands
1587	*February 8*	Execution of Mary, Queen of Scots
1588	*July 27*	Spanish Armada arrives off Calais
	September 4	Death of Robert Dudley, Earl of Leicester

1593	February 25	Robert Devereux, Earl of Essex, becomes a member of the Privy Council
1596	July 5	Robert Cecil is appointed secretary of state
1598	August 4	Death of William Cecil, Lord Burghley
	September 13	Death of Philip II
1599	April 14	Earl of Essex arrives in Ireland as lord lieutenant
1600	June 5	Arrest of Essex
1601	February 25	Execution of Essex
1603	March 24	Death of Elizabeth I

Introduction

The Tudors ruled England for only three generations, an almost pathetically brief span of time in comparison with other dynasties before and since. During the 118 years of Tudor rule, England was a less weighty factor in European politics than it had been earlier, and nothing like the world power it would later become. Of the five Tudors who occupied the throne—three kings, followed by the first two women ever to be queens of England by right of inheritance rather than marriage—one was an epically tragic figure in the fullest Aristotelian sense, two reigned only briefly and came to miserable ends, and the last and longest-lived devoted her life and her reign and the resources of her kingdom to no loftier objective than her own survival. Theirs was, by most measures, a melancholy story. It is impossible not to suspect that even the founder of the dynasty, the only Tudor whose reign was both long and mostly peaceful and did not divide the people of England against themselves (all of which helps to explain why he is forgotten today), would have been appalled to see where his descendants took his kingdom and how their story ended.

And yet, more than four centuries after the Tudors became extinct, one of them is the most famous king and another the most famous queen in the history not only of England but of Europe and probably the world. They have become not merely famous but posthumous stars in the twenty-first-century firmament of celebrity: on the big and little screens and in popular fiction their names have become synonymous with greatness, with *glory*. This is not the fate one might have expected for a pair whose characters were dominated by cold and ruthless egotism, whose careers were studded with acts of atrocious cruelty and false dealing, and who were never more than stonily indifferent to the well-being of the people they ruled. It takes some explaining.

At least as remarkable as the endlessly growing celebrity of the Tudors is the extent to which, after so many centuries, they remain controversial among scholars. Here, too, the reasons are many and complex. They begin with the fact that the dynasty's pivotal figure, Henry VIII, really did change history to an extent rivaled by few other monarchs, and that appraisals of his reign were long entangled in questions of religious belief. It matters also that both Henry and his daughter Elizabeth were not just rulers but consummate *performers,* masters of political propaganda and political theater. They created, and spent their lives hiding inside, fictional versions of themselves that never bore more than a severely limited relation to reality but were nevertheless successfully imprinted on the collective imagination of their own time. These invented personas have endured into the modern world not only because of their inherent appeal—it is hard to resist the image of bluff King Hal, of Gloriana the Virgin Queen—but even more because of their political usefulness across the generations.

Henry, in the process of forcing upon England a revolution-from-above that few of its people welcomed, created a new elite that his radical redistribution of the national wealth made so rich and powerful so quickly that within a few generations it would prove capable of overthrowing the Crown itself. No longer needing or willing to tolerate a monarchy as overbearing as the Tudors had been at their zenith, that new elite nevertheless continued to need the *idea* of the Tudors, of the wonders of the Tudor revolution, in order to justify its own privileged position. It needed to make the mass of English men and women see the Tudor century as the supreme forward leap in England's history, a sweeping away of the dark legacy of the Middle Ages. (This whole "Whig" view of history requires a smug certainty that the medieval world was a cesspit of superstition and repression.) It demanded agreement that the Tudors had put England on the high road to greatness, and that to say otherwise was to be not only extravagantly foolish or dishonest but actually unfit for participation in public life. Centuries of relentless indoctrination and denial ensued, with the result that England turned into a rather curious phenomenon: a great nation actively contemptuous of much of its own history. One still sees the evidence almost whenever British television attempts to deal with pre-Tudor and Tudor history.

It was not until the second half of the twentieth century, really, that historians of some eminence in England and the United States began, often slowly and grudgingly, to acknowledge that the established view of the Tudor era was essentially mythological and could never be reconciled with a dispassionate examination of the facts. Not until even more recently was the old propaganda pretty much abandoned as indefensible. Tudor history remains controversial because, quite extraordinarily for a subject now half a millennium old, its meaning is still being settled. The truth is still being cleared of centuries of systematic denial.

With the academy still bringing sixteenth-century England into focus, we should not be surprised that much of the reading public and virtually the entire entertainment industry remain in the thrall of Tudors who never existed. Whether this will ever change—whether the cartoon versions of Henry VIII and Elizabeth I that now shine in the celebrity heavens alongside James Dean and the Incredible Hulk will ever give way to something with a better connection to reality—is anybody's guess. Perhaps such a change is no longer possible. It is certainly not going to happen as a consequence of this book. I do entertain the more modest hope, however, that a single volume aimed at introducing the entire dynasty to a general readership might prove useful in two ways: by helping to show that the true story of the Tudors is much richer and more fascinating than the fantasy version, and by showing also that the whole story is vastly greater than the sum of its parts. That it contains depths and dimensions that cannot be brought to light by focusing exclusively on Henry VIII, Elizabeth I, or any other single member of the family. That if it is as deeply tragic as I believe it to be—as I hope I have shown it to be—the extent of the tragedy can become clear only when the five reigns are joined together in a narrative arc that begins with Henry VII building a great legacy out of almost nothing, moves on to his son's extravagant abuse of a magnificent inheritance, and follows the son's three children as, one after another and in their joltingly different ways, they attempt to cope with what their father had wrought. If a writer should have an excuse for adding to the endless stream of Tudor literature, I therefore offer these: that not enough has been done to deal with the Tudor dynasty as a continuum, a unity, and that popular perceptions of the family have fallen so far behind scholarly understanding that it is necessary to try, at least, to narrow the gap.

I disavow any claim to competing with, never mind replacing, the many splendid biographies of the Tudor monarchs and their spouses, agents, and victims that have appeared over the last half-century or so. To the contrary, I have drawn heavily on many such works in assembling the facts with which to weave my story, and I am not merely in their debt but could scarcely have even begun without them. And I am mindful that my approach carries a price: dealing with five reigns obviously makes it impossible to provide the depth of detail available in (to cite just one distinguished example) J. J. Scarisbrick's magisterial *Henry VIII*. But it seems fair to question whether so much detail is necessary or even desirable in a work aimed at a general readership, and in any case forgoing it brings a gain too. The story of the whole dynasty is not only bigger in obvious ways than any biography—encompassing more personalities, more drama, more astoundingly grand and ugly events—but also, if paradoxically, *deeper* in one not-insignificant sense. The story of any one Tudor becomes fully rounded only when set in the context of what had come before and what followed, with causes and effects sketched in.

Not being a work of scholarship in anything like a strict and academic sense—not the fruit of deep tunneling into original source materials—this book is not intended for professional Tudor scholars. I can only express my gratitude to the members of that community, most of whom will be familiar with my facts and my arguments and some of whom (any still attached to the old conception of the Tudors as "builders of England's glory," certainly) are likely to reject my conclusions. In any case those conclusions, based on years of reading and reflection, are my responsibility entirely and not to be blamed on anyone else.

I am indebted to my editor, John Flicker, whose suggestions unfailingly prove to be perceptive and helpful (even and perhaps especially the ones I don't welcome at first), to my agent, Judith Riven, for her unflagging support and encouragement, and above all to my partner, Sandra Rose, who cheerfully shared and endured the whole years-long, life-devouring process.

G. J. Meyer
Goring-on-Thames, England
June 2009

THE
TUDORS

Prologue

August 22, 1485

I t is an astonishing fact, and a measure of how much the world has changed in five hundred years, that of the thousands of men who were present at what would come to be called the Battle of Bosworth Field, not one left us a description of it. By any reckoning it was one of the great events of English history—even a glorious event, assuming that your idea of glory is broad enough to embrace the firing of arrows into the bodies of living men and the breaking open of their skulls with axes. It was the blazing sundown of the Middle Ages: men in armor, gleaming blades, banners waving in the summer breeze. It would bring the last charge by mounted knights ever seen on English soil, the last death of a king of England in battle.

But because we have no eyewitness accounts, nor even any accounts written while memories of the battle were still fresh, we know far less about it than historians have traditionally pretended.

We know of course that King Richard III was on the scene—a tough little man with reddish-gold hair, only five foot four but a seasoned warrior, awesomely courageous, the hardened veteran of many bloody fights. We know with certainty that he was there, because he was within minutes of his famously nasty death. We can be sure that he wore a sword, the familiar tool of his trade, and that he carried it as easily as a carpenter carries his hammer. His armor would have been covered with a tunic, made of silk, probably, bearing the colorful symbols of his Plantagenet ancestry. We are told that his horse was white. Being the king's, no doubt it was a majestic horse; feel free to picture it snorting and prancing. That Richard wore a lightweight crown, a coronet, over his iron helmet also is plausible, as his purpose that day was to defend his possession of the crown. With him was his standard-bearer, his old comrade-in-arms Sir Percival Thirlwall, holding aloft a staff from which streamed a long standard displaying Richard's emblem, the blue boar.

And of course Henry Tudor was there—a good distance from Richard, necessarily, but not quite so far away as to be out of sight. As it happens, he too was astride a white horse, one he had been given at some point in the previous two weeks as he and his ragged little army of French and Breton mercenaries and English runaways made their long trek across Wales. No doubt people would have been surprised to learn that, at twenty-seven, Henry was only four years younger than Richard; he was so unknown, had so much less experience and apparent *substance,* as to seem a boy by comparison. So far as we know, he had never been in a fight of any kind. He had never commanded soldiers or ruled anything. Until that month he had not set foot in Wales in almost fourteen years, and the time he had spent in England could be measured in days.

Richard could trace his descent in the male line back through three hundred years of royalty—he was a shoot of the same family tree that had produced Richard the Lion-Hearted and any number of other legendary heroes. Beyond that his ancestry reached to William I's granddaughter and so finally to the Conqueror himself. By contrast, Henry Tudor was the grandson of a Welsh commoner who had had his head chopped off in a town square, and this at a time when most Englishmen regarded the Welsh as a scarily alien race. And yet here he was, presuming to call himself the Earl of Richmond, come to the gentle green hills of the English Midlands for the declared purpose of making himself king.

That he might ever be able to launch even a semicredible effort to take the throne would have seemed impossible just thirty months before. Until 1483 he had been living an idle, pointless life at the court of Duke Francis of Brittany, whose guest and political pawn he had been for nearly half his life. He had been adopted, by then, as the focus if not necessarily the real leader of England's Lancastrian faction—as the man who would be king if somehow the House of York could be overthrown, though increasingly that seemed an empty honor. The leader of the Yorkists, Edward IV, was a strong king in secure possession of the throne, the picture of boisterous good health at age forty, if soft and overweight after almost a decade and a half of peace. He also had a large brood of daughters and sons, the eldest of them just entering adulthood. There was every reason to expect that he and his descendants would rule for generations—and that there would be no place in England for the likes of Henry Tudor.

But then in March 1483 King Edward suffered something like a stroke and within a few weeks was dead. His heir, another Edward, was only twelve and therefore not possibly ready to rule, but that should not have been a problem because the boy had uncles—men of proven loyalty and talent—to govern on his behalf and guide him to maturity. On the paternal side was the dead king's youngest and last surviving brother, Richard, Duke of Gloucester, still barely thirty but deeply experienced in the arts of war and governance. Opposite him was Anthony Woodville, Earl Rivers, eldest of the numerous ambitious brothers of Edward IV's widow, Queen Elizabeth. There *was* a problem, however: bad blood between Richard (who was supported by many of the old noble families) and the upstart Woodvilles, who were resented bitterly because of the wealth and power that had come to them for no better reason than the fact that King Edward, while still a very young man, had impulsively married the obscure if powerfully attractive widow Elizabeth Woodville Grey.

Duke Richard, it is clear, saw the situation as fraught with danger for himself. Earl Rivers had a close relationship with their nephew, whereas Richard, who for years had been far from court governing the north as his brother's representative, scarcely knew the boy. The duke need not have been paranoid to fear that if the Woodvilles could maintain custody of young Edward V—hardly an improbable development, considering that the child's mother was the most prominent Woodville of them all—they could also control the government and destroy their rivals. Whatever his motives, whether he was driven by ambition, hatred, or fear, Richard struck first, setting in motion a series of atrocities that would not end until eight of the last ten legitimate Plantagenet males, five of them boys too young to marry, had died violently. He came down from the north and ordered Rivers to bring their nephew to him. When Rivers did so, both he and the boy were taken into custody. In short order Rivers was executed along with young Richard Grey, Queen Elizabeth's son by her first marriage. Edward V and his ten-year-old brother were sent to the Tower, and Duke Richard had himself crowned.

Convulsion followed convulsion, and with each new upheaval the existence of Henry Tudor became both more significant and more precarious. The princes in the Tower were heard of no more—it was impossible to doubt that they had been murdered—and many of the men who had figured importantly in Edward IV's regime left England rather than support the new King Richard III. Ineptly and for reasons that remain obscure, the Duke of Buckingham, probably the richest noble in England and a man whose royal blood gave him a claim to the throne, raised a rebellion not in his own name but in Henry Tudor's. Francis of Brittany gave Henry a tiny fleet and army with which to invade England, but it was scattered by storms. By the time the ship carrying Henry hauled alone into Plymouth harbor, Buckingham had been defeated and executed and the rebellion was over. Richard's agents met an advance party sent ashore by Henry and, by reporting that the rebellion had already succeeded, tried to lure him ashore. He learned the truth in time, however, and made his escape. Fresh storms then drove him into port in France, and with great difficulty he managed to make his way overland back to Brittany. When on Christmas Day the English exiles who had gathered in Brittany assembled at Rennes Cathedral and pledged to support Henry, their oaths must have seemed nearly meaningless. Equally empty was Henry's promise, made that same day, to marry Edward IV's eldest daughter, Elizabeth of York, then in sanctuary at Westminster Abbey with her mother and four sisters.

Worse soon followed. An exiled bishop with sources of information at the English court sent word that the Duke of Brittany was negotiating an agreement by which he would be richly rewarded for delivering Henry to King Richard. Henry opened communications with the French court and, upon establishing that he would be welcome there, laid plans to get himself and his followers across the Breton-French border. This ended in high drama: Duke Francis's soldiers were hard on Henry's heels as he galloped to France and safety. From that point, however, all his luck was good. The French king, Charles VIII, was a boy in early adolescence. His older sister, Anne of Beaujeu, headed the government as regent and badly needed to make trouble for Richard III, who was attempting to encircle France by allying himself with the two autonomous duchies of Brittany and Burgundy. (It is worth noting, in this connection, that Charles and Anne would have regarded young Tudor not only as a useful political tool but as a near kinsman. Henry's grandmother Catherine of Valois had been their grandfather's sister.) They added to the money coming to Henry from England to provide him with the means to again assemble some ships and hire a mercenary army. The resulting invasion force sailed out of Honfleur in Normandy on August 1, had good weather all the way this time, and made landfall at Milford Haven in the southwestern corner of Wales just six days later. It is said that Henry had to set one of his ships afire to prevent some of his more fainthearted troops from returning to France.

Richard, meanwhile, was experiencing much misery. His son and heir had died early in his reign, and when his wife died not long afterward, it was widely rumored that he had had her poisoned in order to free himself to marry his niece Elizabeth of York. The rumors became so damaging that he was obliged to take the humiliating step of denying them publicly. His subjects, evidently, were prepared to believe anything of him so long as it was sufficiently horrific. He made efforts to shore up his base of support—raising John Howard to Duke of Norfolk, for example, and giving offices and lands to the Stanley family—but the estimated number of his troops, when they came face-to-face with Henry Tudor's on August 22, suggests that he should have done more along that line, done it sooner, and been more careful in selecting the beneficiaries.

We don't know the size of the armies that faced each other that day. Henry must have had about five thousand men: several hundred displaced Englishmen who had made him the centerpiece of their quest for revenge, a few thousand thuggish soldiers-for-hire contributed by the regent of France, and a disappointingly small number—no more than a thousand or two, surely—who had joined him after he came ashore in southwestern Wales. Richard may have had twelve thousand, possibly ten, possibly fewer than that; the estimates vary, and there is no way of choosing among them. Whatever Richard's total, it would have been cause for concern. It was pathetic compared to the thirty-five thousand or more troops that his late brother Edward IV had taken into the Battle of Towton on Palm Sunday in 1461, or the army of fifty thousand Lancastrians that Edward's men had shattered that day. Richard had known months in advance that an invasion was being prepared. He had learned on August 11 that the invaders had landed four days earlier, and he had sent out summonses for the nobles of England and Wales, all of whom had been put on alert weeks before, to muster their soldiery and join him at Leicester. No more than one in every five had done so. It was unsettling evidence of how little support Richard had, and of how badly the old feudal system had decayed.

Strangely, ominously, there was a third army on the field; it might even be accurate to say that there were four. These were the forces of the Stanley clan, raised to the nobility less than twenty years before but already a major power, the greatest landowners in the northwest and de facto rulers of the Isle of Man. The Stanleys had remained loyal to Richard in 1483, when he seized the throne after his brother's sudden death and the Duke of Buckingham raised a rebellion against him, and they had been richly rewarded for doing so. The head of the clan, Thomas Lord Stanley, had been made constable of England and steward of the royal household. His brother Sir William was chamberlain—governor, in effect—of Chester and North Wales. Upon receiving word that Henry Tudor was ashore, Richard had ordered the Stanleys to join him with their liegemen. They had done so, but more slowly than Richard could have wished, and their behavior had become increasingly suspect. Much earlier than Richard himself, they were in a position to intercept the invaders as they emerged from Wales. Instead of doing so they had continually fallen back, allowing the advance to continue. Now, with the showdown clearly at hand, they had some five thousand men with them, separated into two groups, each commanded by one of the brothers. Nobody knew whose side they were on; apparently they were pretending to be on both sides while not yet knowing themselves what they were going to do. Their first loyalty had always been to themselves, and they had long ago demonstrated that they would betray even kings when doing so was more or less certain to be to their advantage. Richard, aware of their history and fearful of their power, was holding Lord Stanley's son hostage. It is said that he threatened to have the son executed if the Stanleys failed to join their forces with his, and was told by way of response that his lordship had other sons. It is said also that when Henry Tudor asked Stanley to join *him* on the morning of August 22, he was told to mind his own business.

One of the more bizarre aspects of this story is that Stanley was

Henry Tudor's stepfather, the third husband (or fourth, if one counts a childhood marriage that ended in annulment) of his mother, Margaret Beaufort. It was a purely political marriage—the contract stipulated that the bride's chastity was not to be compromised. Though it is almost certain that Henry had long been in secret communication with the Stanleys and was counting on their support, he could not have been confident of getting it. The brothers were hanging back, Sir William with his men in one place and Lord Thomas with his in another, watching the situation unfold. If they could be counted upon to do anything, it was to wait until someone was winning and then strike at the loser in order to be in on the spoils.

The detailed descriptions in countless books notwithstanding, we have no way of knowing how the various forces were arranged. We don't even know where they were, except somewhere within a circle with a diameter of several miles. When the earliest account finally was written, presumably drawing on the testimony of participants, its author was an Italian retainer at the English court who had good reason to want to please his Tudor masters. He tells wonderful stories: That Richard was uneasy all through the night before the battle, and that the little sleep he managed to get was punctuated with horrible dreams. That he rose while it was still dark (which means that he must have been up by four A.M.), inspected his lines, and ran his sword through a sentry who was sleeping on duty. That he wanted to hear mass, but the only available priest was unable to find the necessities. That when he called for breakfast, it too proved to be impossible. And that the most powerful and dependable of his henchmen, long-faced old John Howard, Duke of Norfolk, awoke to find a handwritten verse fastened to the entrance of the house where he had slept:

> *Jack of Norfolk, be not too bold,*
> *For Dickon, thy master, is bought and sold.*

"Dickon" would be Richard. For "bought and sold" we would today say "sold out." We are told that Richard's army was melting away like snow in springtime, some of the deserters joining the rebels, others running for home.

These stories have come down to us at second or third hand, selected by a writer who was a propagandist at least as much as a historian, and any or all of them could be inventions. We can't even be certain that the Battle of Bosworth Field was fought at the place called Bosworth Field, which is now a popular attraction with walking tours and a visitor center and all the paraphernalia of the tourist trade. Richard is supposed to have positioned his forces there, atop a high point called Ambien Hill, from which he could look out and see his enemies approaching in the distance. Henry Tudor would have been accompanied by his standard-bearer William Brandon, who hoisted a banner on which was displayed the red dragon of Wales. They would have been surrounded by a life-guard of pike-wielding foot soldiers and mounted knights.

Supposedly the battle began when the main body of Tudor troops, commanded by the dashing Earl of Oxford, recently escaped after ten years as Richard's prisoner, started up Ambien Hill. Perhaps it happened that way, but students of the battle now living claim that the two sides collided not at Ambien Hill but on flatter ground some distance away. The evidence they offer is complicated but not easily dismissed. The author of the present work can attest, after visiting Bosworth and walking its length and breadth, that the landscape as it exists today does not make the traditional version of the story particularly convincing.

This we do know: at some point after the first clash of troops under the command of Oxford on one side and Norfolk on the other, with the situation stalemated and the Stanleys still hovering like vultures on the sidelines, Richard made a decision that would lead to one of the most dramatic climaxes in the history of warfare. He decided to forget about defeating the invader army with his army and instead settle things personally, in something very close to single combat, himself against Henry Tudor. In the absence of sources, it is permissible to imagine him summoning his lifeguard of perhaps a hundred knights to gather round, unsheathing his sword and pointing with it in the direction of the red dragon, and shouting for his men to follow while spurring his charger into a headlong gallop. Something like that has to have happened.

Why it happened we can never know. Possibly Richard acted out of desperation: apparently Norfolk had been killed by this point (taken by an arrow in the throat by one account, executed on the spot after surrendering to Oxford by another), and if indeed his troops had failed in an initial assault despite their superior numbers, this must have been deeply unsettling. Or perhaps Richard saw a target that was simply too tempting to ignore: the tiny far-off figure of Henry Tudor, as passive as the king in a game of chess, remote from the action and not that strongly protected. If Henry's guard could be penetrated—and why not, if Richard himself brought a phalanx of heavy cavalry down on it like the blow of a mace—killing him would become a simple matter. It would no longer matter what the Stanleys or anyone else did. The Tudor cause would be decapitated, the whole invasion rendered pointless.

What ensued was a poetically fitting end to three centuries of rule by Plantagenet warrior-kings. The last link in that long royal chain, sword in hand and blue boar unfurled above his head, thundered across the battlefield with his knights just behind, the hooves of their chargers throwing up fat clods of earth. Richard crashed headlong into the first defenders to come out to meet him, laying about him with his sword, bringing down the banner of the red dragon by instantly killing William Brandon, and sending the biggest of Henry's knights crashing to the ground with a clang of armor plate. His horsemen hit like a wave of flesh and iron, driving into the melee with lances lowered, hacking away with clubs and blades. Whether any of them got close enough to engage Henry personally is not known, but the onslaught had to be terrifying. It is to Henry's credit that, despite never having experienced anything like this, he did not turn and run. Nearby, perhaps steadying him, was his uncle Jasper, as tough and fearless an old campaigner as anyone on the field that day.

For a long moment things hung in the balance. In one recent treatise on the battle, the writer claims to have found evidence that Richard's assault was foiled by a tactic he had not encountered before: French pikemen, forming up in a square around Henry and planting the butts of their weapons in the earth to create a wall of iron points that no cavalry could penetrate.

To return to what we know: suddenly, from the side or rear, scores and then hundreds and finally thousands of men in red tunics came pouring in, swamping Richard and his band. These were William Stanley's men, wearing the Stanley livery. In the moment of crisis—perhaps as soon as it became clear that Henry was not going to die—Stanley had seen his opportunity and gone in for the kill.

Richard was swept back and unhorsed. Shakespeare, more than a century later, would have him crying out for a fresh mount: "My kingdom for a horse!" Older accounts say something very different: that one of Richard's companions urged him to flee, offering him a horse. If that happened, the king refused. Again we can only guess at his thinking. He could have had little hope of assembling another army if he managed to escape, and perhaps he could accept nothing but victory or death. He fought on as, one after another, his men were cut down around him. The faithful Thirlwall held the blue boar aloft until his legs were chopped from under him. Finally it was Richard's turn: men he could not get at with his sword, Welsh troopers, jabbed at him from all directions with their long-handled points and hooks. He screamed defiance, cursing them as traitors. It must have been even more like butchery than most battlefield deaths in the Middle Ages, the pikemen probing for the seams in the king's armor. Without question it was a brave death; even those who depict Richard as a monster have always acknowledged that. When it was over his body was stripped naked, thrown over the back of a horse like a sack of grain, and hauled off for public display. Those of his men who were not dead or captured ran for their lives. Lord Stanley's son was still alive. In the confusion no one had remembered, or bothered, to kill him.

The whole thing must have seemed a dream or a nightmare, depending on which side one was on. In seconds Richard had been reduced from a king at the head of an army of thousands to a mangled lump of dead flesh. Henry had been vaulted from adventurer to conqueror. Survivors must have stumbled about the field, trying to absorb what had happened.

It fell to the ever-resourceful Lord Stanley, who had played no part in the battle even after his brother went in, to focus the moment. Someone retrieved the crown that Richard had lost in the moment before his death. The legends say it was found in a hawthorn bush. Sober historians have dismissed this as a romantic fabrication but fail to explain why, not many years after the battle, a crown in a thornbush became a royal emblem. In any case, Stanley arrived on the scene while everything was still in confusion and took possession of the crown. Putting himself at the center of a great occasion that he had done nothing to bring about, he placed the crown on his stepson's head and led the assembled company in a hearty round of cheers.

At which moment, in a turn of fate as improbable as any in history, Henry Tudor became King Henry VII of England.

PART ONE

An Excess of Good Fortune

1485–1532

1

The Luck of Henry Tudor

None of the events that have made the second Henry Tudor the most famous king in history happened in 1534. Henry VIII divorced no one that year, married no one, killed no eminent person. But the year was a milestone all the same, arguably *the* great turning point in his stunningly eventful career. When it began he had deteriorated only enough to be the sort of person you would hate to be seated next to at a dinner party: arrogant, opinionated, a bully inclined to self-pity, invincibly confident of his own charm, and certain that he knew best about everything that mattered. Before the year ended he had become what he would remain for the rest of his life: a full-fledged tyrant in the strictest sense of the word, a homicidal monster, absurd, pathetic, mortally dangerous.

A person in Henry's predicament, a man whose pride has walled him up in such impregnable isolation, becomes incapable of an emotion as healthy as gratitude. Certainly he cannot see himself as merely lucky. His fate, he thinks, is coterminous with divine will. Everything good that befalls him does so in fulfillment of God's great plan for the universe. Every disappointment can be traced neither to God nor to some failure on his own part (that is impossible; he could never commit a serious error) but to something outside himself that is cosmically out of joint. Nonetheless, lucky is what Henry was—one of the luckiest human beings who ever lived.

Much of his good fortune he owed to his father. In the quarter-century between his victory at Bosworth and his death in 1509, Henry VII had made the English Crown more secure and powerful than it had been in generations. He had filled the royal treasury with gold and accustomed his subjects to the benefits of peace. He is today a remote and elusive figure, a king about whom most people know almost nothing, and he appears to have been much the same in his own time. Though his life before Bosworth had been studded with moments of high drama and hairsbreadth escapes, little of the excitement had been of his choosing. Mainly his early years had been spent waiting. Even what we know of his part in the fight that won him the crown suggests that it could have been played by a deaf mute, a mannequin. Henry was attacked, Henry was defended, Henry was crowned—every episode finds him in a passive role.

And yet something tremendous was achieved, and the achievement *was* Henry's. None of it would have been possible if, even in his youth, there had not been something about him—something not quite explainable at a distance of five centuries—that won the support and even the affection of the Duke of Brittany, the ruling family of France, and one after another of the older, more experienced men who had fled England after Richard III became king. Nor could he have succeeded if, whenever enemies appeared to be closing in on him, he had not had the courage and resourcefulness to outwit them. However colorless he may seem to us, however much the contemporary chronicles fail to make him a fully three-dimensional figure, the one thing that always comes through is his unfailing *competence*. In temperament he appears to have been more like a modern corporate executive of remarkably high caliber—coolly savvy, demanding but amiable enough, a good judge of risk and reward—than some swashbuckling medieval warrior-king. He always had himself firmly under control, and he seems always to have been somewhat inscrutable.

He took the one great chance that fate offered him, pulled it off, and devoted the rest of his life to the careful consolidation of his winnings. He was disdainful of military glory, and though he sought and won the respect of the continent's ruling families, he displayed no wish to cut a particularly great figure among them. If he left almost no mark on the world's imagination (biographers have taken little interest in him, perhaps in part because they could never be confident of understanding him), his reign is important all the same. It built the stage upon which his son and then his granddaughter would be able to show themselves off for almost the whole of the century that followed his death.

The most impressive thing Henry did after reaching the throne was to establish himself securely on it. This was no small achievement: to grasp its magnitude it is necessary to remember the hundred years before Bosworth, with their tragic succession of Plantagenet kings and claimants clashing and killing and being killed. Henry, his dollop of royal blood inherited from a bastard line that even when legitimized had been excluded by law from succession to the crown, could not have been given good chances of lasting long when he became king. But step by slow step, in his methodical and undramatic way, he made it clear to England and the world that he was a real king and a strong one and not to be taken lightly. He did so carefully, confiding in only his oldest friends, never moving so fast as to provoke reaction, watching for opportunities to eliminate rivals and seizing those opportunities as they arose.

The death of Richard III had left only one legitimate male Plantagenet still alive: the boy Edward, Earl of Warwick, the orphan son of Richard's suicidally troublesome elder brother George, Duke of Clarence. Immediately after Bosworth, Henry sent a lieutenant to find the child and lock him in the Tower, out of reach of anyone who might hope to make him king. He then fortified his own claim to the loyalty of the Yorkist party by fulfilling his pledge, made when he was still in exile in Brittany, to marry Edward IV's eldest child, the twenty-year-old Princess Elizabeth. The marriage made it impossible for anyone to oppose Henry on grounds that the crown rightfully belonged to Edward IV's descendants. Significantly, however, Henry delayed the wedding until months after his coronation. In this way he underscored his claim to be king in his own right, by right of conquest as well as descent, rather than thanks to his wife. He was as shrewd about chronology as about most things, dating his reign from the day *before* Bosworth so as to make everyone who opposed him there guilty of treason.

From Rome Henry procured a papal declaration not only that he was the rightful king of England but that anyone who refused to acknowledge him would be subject to excommunication. This was no mere formality: it meant that the kingdom's bishops, with all their wealth and influence, could find no basis for opposing him. As his counselors and ministers he chose trusted cohorts, men who had shared his dangerous years on the continent and fought for him at Bosworth. The Earl of Oxford, his ancestral lands restored, became admiral of England (land and sea warfare not yet being distinct disciplines). John Morton, who had been bishop of Ely under Edward IV and an exile during Richard's reign (it was he who had warned Henry that the Duke of Brittany and Richard were plotting against him), was not merely restored to his see but elevated to lord chancellor, archbishop of Canterbury, and cardinal. Morton and two other former exiles, Bishop Richard Fox and the layman Reginald Bray, would remain the king's chief administrators for nearly twenty years. Their services helped Henry to limit his dependence on, and need to share power with, the nobility.

His apparent vulnerability during the early years of his reign—the inability of some subjects to accept the emergence of such a nobody as king—gave rise to two of the most ludicrous rebellions in English history. Just two years after Bosworth a youth of lowly and obscure birth named Lambert Simnel (he may have been a carpenter's son and may have been from Oxford, but little about his origins is certain) was put forward as Edward, Earl of Warwick, and therefore as the boy who should be king. Simnel was the tool of John de la Pole, Earl of Lincoln, the royal nephew whom Richard III had named as his heir after the death of his own son and who had been with Richard at Bosworth. Lincoln, like Warwick, had been imprisoned after the battle, but Henry soon freed him and restored part of his patrimony. Disgruntled and ungrateful, the earl left the country, found support in Europe and Ireland (where Simnel was crowned King Edward VI), and invaded England in the pretender's name. Met by Henry's troops at Stoke in Nottinghamshire, he was defeated and killed. The dupe Simnel was captured but not punished. In perhaps the most attractive act of his life, King Henry gave the youth a job in the royal kitchens. Later he would be promoted to falconer.

In the early 1490s another false Plantagenet appeared: a young Frenchman called Perkin Warbeck, the handsome servant of silk merchants, chosen by disaffected Yorkists to impersonate Edward IV's son Richard, Duke of York, the younger of the two princes who had disappeared in the Tower. The threat this time was more serious, and it simmered for years. Warbeck, like Simnel, found much support in Ireland, always a hotbed of Yorkist sedition. He was recognized as king by James IV of Scotland (who gave him a young woman of high birth as his bride), by Charles VIII of France (now Henry Tudor's rival rather than his boyish admirer), by Maximilian the Hapsburg "king of Rome" (a title borne by sons and heirs of Holy Roman emperors), and even by the dead princes' aunt Margaret, the embittered sister of Edward IV and widow of the Duke of Burgundy. Things threatened to get out of hand when taxes levied by Henry to provide money for military operations in the north sparked an uprising in Cornwall. The insurgents, marching on London, declared their support for the pretender. They were defeated at Blackheath less than a day's march from Westminster, and after further misadventures Warbeck was captured and hanged. At the same time charges of conspiracy were concocted against the Earl of Warwick, who was twenty-four years old by this time and had been a prisoner more than half his life. Though guilty of nothing and apparently mentally impaired (whether congenitally or because of the miserable conditions of his upbringing cannot be known), he too was put to death. Thus did the first judicial murder of the Tudor era extinguish the last Plantagenet. It was the darkest act of Henry VII's life.

Along the way—this was perhaps the greatest of his gifts to his heir—Henry VII brought the nobles to heel. His whole reign was a prolonged exercise in stripping away their autonomy. First he marginalized them, making room on his council for those he did not actively distrust but excluding them from offices of highest importance. The few nobles who dared to oppose Henry, especially but not only if they had royal blood, were destroyed. The death of John de la Pole at Stoke was followed in 1506 by the return of his brother Edmund to England, in chains, by the Hapsburgs. He was promptly locked away. With the passage of time Henry found it possible to move against more and more of the nobles, even the strongest of them. Sir William Stanley, who had saved him at Bosworth, was put to death after being implicated in the Perkin Warbeck affair. His possessions, including enough land to generate the stupendous sum of £1,000 annually, went to the Crown. Other members of the Stanley family, including the king's stepfather, the Earl of Derby (the former Thomas Lord Stanley, promoted after Bosworth), were required to pay heavy bonds as a guarantee of good behavior. Bonds and recognizances of this kind proved an effective way of neutering mighty subjects and were levied against more than half of England's nobles during Henry's reign. Half-forgotten laws—statutes, mainly, that the nobles had found it convenient to ignore when the Crown was weak—were dusted off and used to cripple great families financially. Henry was so unwilling to create new peers that their number shrank from fifty-five at the start of his rule to forty-two at the end. A substantial number of the 138 persons that he had attainted were nobles, and the resulting confiscations of land played a major part in making him richer than any previous English king. That he was able to do all these things without provoking the nobles to rise against him testifies not only to his political skill but to just how much the peerage had been reduced in power—how negligible a factor it would prove to be when his son's reign entered its revolutionary phase.

Henry milked the church too. As much as at any time in the history of the kingdom, more than at most times, bishoprics became a reward for service to the Crown. Thus the ecclesiastical hierarchy came to be dominated by administrators and politicians accustomed to serving the king and aware of owing their positions to him; this would have momentous consequences when, a generation after Henry VII's death, the bishops found themselves having to choose between submitting to the Crown or defending their church. Henry regularly transferred bishops from one see to another for no better reason than his own financial advantage: each new appointment required the payment of substantial fees to the Crown, and the revenues of vacant bishoprics went to the king as well.

Henry avoided war in spite of the fact that the nobility, generally not understanding that the kings of France were no longer as weak as they had been a few generations before, were eager to loot and pillage on the continent as their grandfathers had done and perhaps even recover their families' lost possessions there. He took an army across the Channel only once, in the early 1490s, and then mainly to demonstrate his objection to France's absorption of Brittany. He was pleased to return home after little more than a month, as soon as Charles VIII agreed to pay him handsomely for doing so and promised to stop encouraging Perkin Warbeck. War, as Henry knew well, was risky. Even worse from his perspective, war was expensive. He was satisfied to do nothing about the time-honored but now meaningless claim that kings of England were also rightfully kings of France. By the end of his life only the oldest people living had any memory of the bloody conflicts of the past, or of their costs. As for the continental powers, they could see no profit in meddling in the affairs of a distant island kingdom that was no longer meddling in theirs.

Sadly, it is probably his reputation for greed, for being willing to bend the law in every feasible way to relieve his wealthiest subjects of as much of their property as possible, that stands today as the most vividly remembered part of Henry VII's legacy. This reputation is not entirely deserved. Henry was not *merely* a miser, certainly—he cheerfully gambled away substantial sums, and spent lavishly to impress subjects and foreigners alike—and a full treasury was undoubtedly the best form of security at a time when the Crown still had no standing army and the old practice of depending on the nobility for fighting men in times of need was in an advanced state of decay. Still, the lengths to which Henry went to increase his revenues, and the glum and solitary figure that he became after the deaths of his queen and several of their children, made him so unloved that his death, when it came, was received with more gratitude than grief. By then he had accumulated so much wealth in gold plate and jewels—certainly no less than a quarter of a million pounds, possibly twice or even four times that amount—that his heir was free to spend as much as he wished without giving a thought to the consequences.

Henry's unpopularity in the last years of his reign was his last great gift to his son. By the end, in a kind of foreshadowing, he appears to have become not only a miser but something very like a tyrant, the joyless ruler of a joylessly submissive realm. In his final illness he is said to have repented—to have vowed that if he recovered, his subjects would find him a changed man. There was no recovery. He was barely fifty-two when he died but seemed very old. England did see a new man, but it was not Henry VII restored to health. It was his son and namesake and heir, the dazzling boy who ascended to the throne like the dawning of a new day. The seventeen-year-old Henry VIII arrived on the crest of England's first uncontested transfer of power in almost ninety years—a transfer that itself testified to how much the dead king had achieved. He was greeted with shouts of joy and was filled with joy himself.

There had never been so good a time to be king. The emergence of artillery was rendering the dark and cold stone fortresses of the Middle Ages, long essential for defense, vulnerable and therefore obsolete. At the same time the new big guns, though primitive in their technology and as difficult to move as they were treacherous to use, were giving central governments an unprecedented advantage over anyone inclined to rebel: rebels might have swords and lances and even handguns, but they were unlikely to be able to buy or build many cannons. Old castles were rebuilt or abandoned in favor of a new kind of royal habitation, a kind intended less for defense than for ostentation and pleasure, rich in windows and therefore in light and designed to provide the ruling families of Europe with a degree of luxury that would have been unimaginable just a few generations before. In all of Europe there were few more impressive examples than Henry VII's huge and sumptuous Richmond Palace—so named because he and his father had both been earls of Richmond—which now of course passed to his son. The new royal lifestyle was apparent even in Richmond's tennis courts.

Henry VIII was blessed with more than a secure throne and the wealth that came with it. Nature had endowed him with a fine intelligence, a six-foot-two-inch frame that was as strong as it was handsomely proportioned (broad shoulders tapered down to a waist that in his young manhood measured only thirty-two inches), robust good looks (though his eyes were small and he had a puckered little rosebud of a mouth), and even better health. He was the third of the four children of King Henry VII to survive childhood; his sole elder brother, Arthur, Prince of Wales, appears to have been a frail runt and died, in all likelihood without achieving sexual maturity, at age fifteen. Henry's parents and his imperious paternal grandmother, Margaret Beaufort, had seen to it that he was splendidly educated—able at an early age to converse easily in Latin as well as French—and taught to be a faithful son to Holy Mother Church. No one ever overburdened him with duties and responsibilities. Through the first decade of his life, as a younger son, he was free of the pressures and expectations commonly brought to bear on heirs being prepared for rule. Thereafter, in the seven years between his brother's death and his father's, he was the king's sole surviving son and therefore too precious to be exposed to risk. He was kept in almost monkish seclusion, rigorously protected not only from the many fatal diseases of the time but even from the stresses that might have accompanied a serious apprenticeship in governance. His mother died when he was eleven, and by all accounts his contacts with his father were neither frequent nor notably pleasant.

Such a cheerless and constrained life must have been intensely frustrating for a youth of Prince Henry's vitality and capacity for enjoyment. When he entered upon his own reign, suddenly not only free but ruler of the whole kingdom, he was without preparation or experience. He was also less interested in ruling than in having the best possible time. He liberated himself from celibacy by marrying almost immediately, even before he was crowned. Such speed was possible because he had close at hand a young woman who was not only pretty and accomplished but unquestionably suitable: his late brother's widow Catherine, daughter of the mighty King Ferdinand of Spain. Henry and Catherine were quietly married at the church of the Franciscan friars in Greenwich on June 11, just fifty days after the old king's death. Thirteen days after that, bedecked with diamonds and other precious stones, the two were anointed king and queen of England in a lavish ceremony at Westminster Abbey. By then the royal court, a dark, dour place during the last years of Henry VII, was being transformed into a scene of music and dance, games and laughter.

At the court's center were the royal couple, both of them all but swooning with happiness. The young king was besotted with his wife, who was at least his equal in intelligence and education and, with vastly more experience of how hard even royal life could be, much more mature. For Catherine even more than for Henry, this new life was a deliverance, a rescue that could hardly have been more unexpected or welcome. And she more than most women was equipped to make the best of it. Her late mother, the formidable warrior-queen Isabella of Castile, had schooled her almost from the cradle to become a worthy consort, capable, supportive, and submissive, to some king as great as her father, Ferdinand. Upon being sent to England, however, she had found only marriage to a boy who could not or in any case did not consummate their union, early widowhood followed by illness, and years of mistreatment at the hands of her increasingly mean-spirited father-in-law. All this had ended, to general astonishment, with the sudden decision of the new king, who was six years her junior, to fulfill the old

king's half-forgotten pledge by making her his wife. As Henry VIII gathered around himself an entourage of high-spirited and fun-seeking
courtiers, Catherine assumed a role even bigger than that of bedmate
and partner. She appears to have become a kind of indulgent and approving mother figure, one in whose eyes he could find confirmation of
everything he wanted to believe about himself and loving acceptance of
his every self-indulgence.

There was, however, a kingdom to be ruled and a government to be
run, and during the two and a half decades of Henry VII's rule England
had become accustomed to a very personal style of management, one in
which the king's household directly controlled everything of real importance and nothing significant was undertaken without the king's knowledge. Such a system was scarcely workable under a new king who had
no intention of submitting to the tedium of daily administration. Except
when dealing with matters that engaged his interest in some personal
way, Henry was willing to talk business only during morning mass—evidently he was not an attentive worshipper—and just before retiring at
night. He disliked having to read official documents, generally insisting
that they be read aloud to him, preferably in abridged form. And he regarded it as a nuisance to be asked to put his signature to things, so that
such orders and approvals as he issued were often done by word of
mouth. It was a recipe for disorder, but again Henry was lucky. From the
start of his reign he was served by the same loyal and capable men—
prelates of the church, mainly, headed by William Warham in his dual
capacities of archbishop of Canterbury and lord chancellor—who had
been the government's senior ministers during Henry VII's last years.
They looked after whatever required attention, freeing their new master
to pursue interests that ranged from hunting to music and dance (he was
a talented instrumentalist and composer of songs), from jousting and
gambling to tennis and the collection and improvement of palaces.
(Eventually he would have fifty royal residences, more than any English
monarch before or since.) The people, meanwhile, knew nothing of
Henry's work habits and could not have cared less. After years of dreari-
ness they were delighted by what they could see of the eager and energetic youth who now wore the crown. A new day seemed to have
dawned for all of England.

The previous reign still cast its shadow, however. One of Henry VII's most detested innovations, the so-called "Council Learned in the Law," had become an all-too-effective way of compelling the wealthy to disgorge land and gold for the benefit of the Crown. The functioning of this council was the responsibility of two of the late king's most trusted lawyers, Edmund Dudley and Richard Empson, who had amassed considerable personal fortunes in the course of doing their work and thus made themselves the most hated men in England. Dudley was president of the King's Council, the first layman to hold that exalted post, Empson was chairman of the Council Learned in the Law, and both must have expected to play major roles during the transition to the new reign and thereafter. Instead, as a way for Henry VIII and other councilors to show that a new and better day really had dawned, the two were arrested even before Henry VII was in his grave. After sixteen months, when it became clear that resentment against them was not abating, they were attainted of treason (which meant they were stripped of everything they owned) and put to death. Their execution was a cynical act of judicial murder, done purely for political and propaganda purposes: ruthless and grasping Dudley and Empson certainly had been, but they had done nothing without the approval of the king and are likely to have been following his instructions. It is impossible to know whether it was young Henry or his council or both who wanted them dead. Whatever the case, the episode added an ominous background note to the jubilation that accompanied the accession of the new king. Henry himself learned a memorable double lesson, one that he would find ample opportunities to apply. He had been shown how easy it was to deflect blame for unpopular policies onto servants of the Crown—and how the anger of his subjects could be dissipated through the extermination of those same servants.

The ministers inherited from the previous reign satisfied Henry's needs for only a few years at best, and their dominance lasted no more than five years. Although they relieved the king of the mundane routines of governance, as a group they were unable to share his enthusiasm for adventures on the international stage. Even before the end of his adolescence, Henry displayed an almost desperate hunger for glory. He wanted to become a hero-king, a conqueror, a great romantic figure in the pattern of Richard the Lion-Hearted and his own great-grandmother's first husband, Henry V, the victor of Agincourt. And so he turned his attention to the place where his most honored predecessors had most often won their fame. He wanted to fight in France—not only to fight there, but to turn the long-standing English claim to the French crown into a reality. But the old men of the council could not be persuaded. They were bishops, many of them, churchmen not generally disposed to embrace war. And they had learned statecraft under Henry VII, who taught them to regard involvement in Europe's wars as a fool's errand, risky and wasteful. They exasperated their young master by raising such tiresome questions as the cost in gold and silver—never mind the likely cost in lives—of taking an army across the Channel. Henry had no patience with such quibbles. Like many people who are wealthy from birth, he regarded his riches not as a stroke of good fortune but as part of the natural state of affairs, what he was entitled to. He saw in himself the potential to become not only one of the major figures of his time, the equal and perhaps the leader of the greatest continental monarchs, but one of the giants of history. It could have made no sense to him to draw back from such a destiny because a gaggle of quibbling old celibates didn't want him to spend *his* money.

What Henry needed was new management, and again he was fabulously lucky. As if on cue, there stepped out of deep obscurity one of the last and most remarkable products of the medieval English church's meritocracy, an Oxford-educated butcher's son named Thomas Wolsey, a tightly packed bundle of talent and drive with a sharp eye for the main chance. A priest from age twenty-five, Wolsey had escaped the schoolmaster's life for which he seemed destined by securing appointment as one of several chaplains in the household of the archbishop of Canterbury. From there he moved on to become chaplain to the governor of Calais, England's last foothold on the coast of France, and then somehow at the court of Henry VII himself. Thus he was in royal service when Henry VIII took the throne in 1509, and that was all the advantage he needed. The new king first made him almoner, dispenser of charity, and then in 1511 appointed him to the council, the circle of royal advisers.

When in the fourth year of his reign Henry wanted to invade France—his opportunity to do so came in the form of an invitation from Pope Julius II to join a so-called Holy League against King Louis XII—he got no encouragement from the two dominant members of his council,

Archbishop Warham and Bishop Fox. This was Wolsey's cue to rise and meet his fate. Almost forty years old now, he offered the twenty-two-year-old king not only approval but a willingness to take responsibility for the logistics of the entire French campaign—a tremendously challenging assignment. Again Henry was freed, first to pursue his dreams of military greatness without actually having to do very much, and then, after he had landed in France, to indulge in jousting and festivities rather than subjecting himself to actual combat or, worse, the hard toil of keeping an army in good order on foreign soil. As a precautionary measure, before leaving England Henry saw to the execution of his cousin Edmund de la Pole, who by then had been a prisoner in the Tower for seven years. In strict legalistic terms the killing was justified: de la Pole, younger brother of the John de la Pole who had masterminded the Lambert Simnel affair, had committed treason by claiming the crown for himself. By the time of his execution, however, he had become an impotent and even pathetic figure. In practical terms the execution was simply another Tudor murder.

This was Henry's first war, and like all his European campaigns it turned out to be sterile militarily, financially, and diplomatically. The old-timers on the council had been entirely right in attempting to discourage him. The king's partners in the Holy League made a fool of him. His father-in-law Ferdinand of Spain betrayed him not once but three times, the Holy Roman emperor Maximilian and the Swiss mercenary army whose services Henry had purchased at immense expense once each. The bill, including both direct costs and the subsidies that Henry had naïvely paid his faithless allies, was nearly £1 million. This wiped out everything inherited from Henry VII and plunged the Crown into financial difficulties from which it would emerge only intermittently over the next century and more. But Henry returned home convinced he had achieved great things. Together his troops and those of Emperor Maximilian had captured the towns of Thérouanne and Tournai, successes of some value to Maximilian but none to England. At one of the few points of real drama English horsemen had put the French cavalry to flight in what was jokingly named the Battle of the Spurs, a skirmish of no consequence in which Henry played no part. In fact, though he loved to play at jousting and was big and strong and well equipped enough to be successful at it, Henry would never in his life face an enemy in battle. But he heaped upon his fellow campaigners rewards that might have been excessive even if something of consequence had been accomplished. Many were knighted, and Henry's boon companion Charles Brandon, son of the William Brandon who had carried Henry VII's banner at Bosworth and been cut down by Richard III, became Duke of Suffolk. More fittingly Thomas Howard, Earl of Surrey, who had fought on Richard's side at Bosworth, was restored to the title that his father had lost there along with his life: Duke of Norfolk. To his chagrin Howard had been left behind when Henry crossed over to France, but therefore had been on hand to take an army north when James IV of Scotland tried to take advantage of Henry's absence by launching an invasion. The victory that he achieved at Flodden, killing not only the king of the Scots but much of the Scottish nobility, overshadowed everything that happened on the continent.

Badly as things had gone in France, military operations were not Wolsey's responsibility, and what he was responsible for had been managed exquisitely well. When the fighting was finished, he took on the job of negotiating a settlement, thereby launching his eventful career in international diplomacy. He managed to put the best possible face on a miserable situation by working out a treaty in which Henry would receive a "pension" in return for staying out of France and was allowed, mainly for face-saving purposes, to retain Tournai as his trophy. The only lasting effect of the entire episode, Henry's emptying of his treasury aside, was the discovery in Wolsey's person of an ideal royal instrument: an able, intelligent, inexhaustibly hardworking minister who was prepared to take upon himself the whole burden of running the government but was always careful to understand what his king wanted and focus relentlessly on giving it to him.

The rewards were dazzling. In 1514 Wolsey was made bishop of Lincoln, then archbishop of York. In 1515 he replaced Warham as lord chancellor and, at the king's request, was given the red hat of a cardinal by a pope made desperate for friends by the failure and disintegration of his league. Somewhat less willingly, Pope Julius agreed also to make Wolsey his legate or representative in England. This last honor contributed to making the new cardinal's stature within the English church greater even than that of the official primate, Archbishop Warham.

As Wolsey gathered more and more reins into his own strong hands, the council declined in importance, Henry remained free to hunt and gamble and otherwise keep himself amused, and nevertheless the government operated at least as effectively as in the past. But the international political landscape began to change dramatically as the warrior-pope Julius II died and was replaced by one of the Medici of Florence, Ferdinand of Spain died and was succeeded by his (and Emperor Maximilian's) grandson Charles, Louis XII died after just weeks of marriage to Henry's beautiful sister Mary and the French throne passed to the vigorous and ambitious young Francis I, and James IV's death at Flodden left Scotland in the hands of his widow, Henry's elder sister Margaret. It fell to Wolsey to deal with all these changes, and he did so with his customary energy. Onlookers marveled at his ability to stay at his desk hour after hour, turning his attention from subject to subject without pausing even to relieve himself. He shared Henry's zest for international power games, for winning for England (and Henry, and of course himself) a place in those games that the kingdom's size and economy did not really justify. Being a player, however, involved him in an unending struggle to extract from a small, simple economy the money needed for a seat at the table. In taking all this upon himself, he made many enemies. He rarely disappointed his royal master, however, or gave him cause for complaint.

Even in the most intimate dimensions of life, Henry VIII could have found little to complain of. His wife Catherine had through two decades of matrimony remained an exemplary consort: capable, virtuous, admired by the people, and unfailingly loyal. If the years and numerous pregnancies ending in dead babies gradually drained away the queen's beauty and youth, Henry was free to divert himself with mistresses. And in his and Catherine's one living child, their daughter Mary, he had a bright, attractive heir who naturally adored her formidable father. By virtue of her position, Mary was growing up with the most brilliant marriage prospects in Europe. She seemed fated not only to wear the English crown but to become, like her mother and her grandmother Isabella of Castile, the wife and partner of some great prince. Her children, Henry's grandchildren, were likely to rule more than England only.

On top of all his other blessings, Henry had the inestimable advantage—one that fit beautifully with his increasingly grandiose conception

of his own place in the world—of happening to rule at a time when the
curious idea of the divine right of kings was becoming fashionable
across much of Europe. The emergence of this notion was understandable as a reaction to the bloody instability of recent generations, and as
an expression of the widespread hunger for law and order and therefore
for strong central government. But it gave crowned heads a justification
for turning themselves into despots with no obligations to anyone. It fed
Henry VIII's inclination to think of himself as a quasi-divine being
whom heaven intended to be all-powerful and had endowed with the
wisdom to decide all questions. He did not have to look far, in the first
decades of the sixteenth century, to find scholars eager to assure him
that it lay within his authority to overthrow centuries of law, tradition,
and precedent.

The effects of so much good fortune were, perhaps inevitably, tragic.
Henry remained lord and master of everyone around him for so long,
and became so accustomed not only to doing whatever he wished but to
making everyone else do as he wished and being applauded for doing it,
that he lost contact with the commonplace realities of human experience. Power corrupts, as Acton famously said, and a generation into
Henry's reign there was beginning to hang over him the stench of corruption, of something like spiritual death. He was slipping into the special realm of fantasy reserved for those deprived too long of the simple
truth even—or especially—about themselves. In ancient Greece or
Rome he might have declared himself a god. Living in Christian England on the threshold of the modern world, he had to settle for being
treated like a god.

Throughout the first half of his reign, from the 1513 war in France
onward, the Crown's worst problems had been financial. To some extent this was a function of the times: revenues were inadequate to needs
in all but the most prudently managed kingdoms, and as a rule Henry
was little worse off than the kings of France, his wife's father in Spain,
or even the imperial Hapsburgs. In any case his blithe assumption that
the whole wealth of England was his to dispose of as he wished, that
somehow money would always be available for whatever he wanted to
do, meant that in practical terms the state of the treasury was not his
problem but Wolsey's. Time after time the cardinal had to search out
new ways of keeping Henry and his wars, his diplomatic intrigues, and

his many amusements afloat. When the seemingly endless demands for new taxes reached intolerable levels, popular anger was always directed at Wolsey, never at the king.

But as the twentieth anniversary of his coronation approached, Henry found himself up against a problem that had nothing to do with money and that he could not possibly ignore because it was entirely of his choosing. It would become the defining challenge of his life and his reign—would come to be known, with good reason, as "the king's great matter." There were two elements to it, and there is no way for us to know which came first. One was the sad fact that Queen Catherine had become a rather dumpy little middle-aged woman whose childbearing years were clearly behind her. The other was Henry's passionate infatuation, obvious to the entire court as early as the spring of 1526, with the dark-eyed, swan-necked young Anne Boleyn, whose years as a lady-in-waiting at the court of the French king had given her an elegance and self-assurance that not even the grandest noble ladies of England could rival. Soon Henry was confiding to certain intimates, and then to anyone who might prove helpful, that his conscience—his regal and therefore exquisitely sensitive conscience—was suffering painful doubts about whether Catherine was actually his wife. Perhaps these doubts first entered his head because he wanted Anne and she, having seen her own sister become the king's mistress only to be discarded, would not give herself to him. But it is not impossible that Henry's doubts came first, and that they were not in fact doubts at all but a growing conviction that he had no queen and therefore was free to choose one. At which point he would have looked around until his attention settled on his former mistress's sister, now lady-in-waiting to his wife and as bright a jewel as his court had ever contained.

However it began, Henry's struggle with his conscience soon ended in what was, by his reckoning, a victory for truth and justice. What settled his mind was what Leviticus said in the Old Testament: "If a man shall take his brother's wife, it is an impurity: he hath uncovered his brother's nakedness: they shall be childless." That seemed conclusive: Henry's marriage to Catherine had violated the law of God, and ever since the two of them had been paying the price. If not precisely childless, they were certainly sonless. God was displeased not because of any wrong that Henry had consciously committed but because in the innocence of childhood (he had been thirteen when his father arranged his betrothal to Catherine) he had been made the victim of others' mistakes. It was not his right but his duty to put Catherine away. She could remain a member of the royal family as Dowager Princess of Wales, honored and comfortable and freed from the horrors of incest with her loving brother Henry. If their daughter became thereby a bastard ineligible to inherit the throne and possibly unmarriageable—well, such an unfortunate situation was bound to have regrettable consequences. The important thing was that he had uncovered the truth while there was still time to put things right.

Certain formalities had to be attended to first. Henry's marriage to Catherine had been made possible by a dispensation issued by Julius II. Everything would be resolved if the current pope, Clement VII, declared the marriage null. There seemed no reason to expect difficulties; relations between the English and the papal courts had long been excellent, and annulments of royal marriages were, if not exactly common, far from unheard of. Wolsey, when he turned his attention to the situation, focused on the prospect of marrying his master to a French princess—on the part that such a union could play in achieving the great pan-European peace that had long been the overriding objective of his diplomacy. On a more personal level, Wolsey had reason to want to be rid of Queen Catherine. She had long criticized his grandiose style of living—palaces more immense than those of the royal family, platoons of uniformed retainers, pomp and ceremony everywhere he went—as so inappropriate to his clerical state as to constitute scandal.

Inevitably, and for all we know to his complete satisfaction, Wolsey set about to make it happen.

THE ORIGIN OF THE TUDORS

WHY HAD HENRY VIII FOUND IT ADVISABLE, BEFORE GOING off to make war in France, to pull his cousin Edmund de la Pole out of prison and have his head cut off?

Because de la Pole had royal blood, obviously. And because his claim to the throne was quite good enough to rival Henry's. (He was the grandson of the Elizabeth of York who had been Edward IV's sister, whereas Henry was the son of Edward's daughter of the same name.) But could Henry, with his mountainous self-assurance, really have been *that* insecure about his hold on the throne? Could his bluster have been a mask behind which a very ordinary and frightened man was keeping himself hidden?

If it is perhaps a little too easy to say so, it is also not impossible. Especially if Henry knew the story of the strange path by which his father had come to the throne, as he certainly must have.

One of the threads out of which that story is woven goes back to 1422 and the premature death, of natural causes, of one of the most brilliantly successful of all the Plantagenet kings, Henry V. He was the second king in the so-called Lancastrian branch of the Plantagenet dynasty—his father, Henry IV, had overthrown their cousin Richard II—and in nine years on the throne he had risen to the heights of achievement and prestige. The most famous of his triumphs, the one that put him among England's immortals, came at Agincourt, where his outnumbered invasion force defeated the armies of France so conclusively that the French king acknowledged him as his heir and gave him his daughter, Catherine of Valois, in marriage. All this became the seedbed for decades of tragedy when, at age thirty-four, Henry suddenly died, leaving a beautiful widow with all the normal appetites of a healthy twenty-one-year-old woman and a son who, at the age of nine months, became King Henry VI.

This is where Wales becomes part of the story and the Tudors enter

English history. Wales was, at this time, less an integral part of the king-dom than a conquered territory—a remote, alien, somewhat mysterious, and definitely distrusted province. Only those few Welshmen whom the English occupiers deemed to be sufficiently loyal were allowed to hold office, carry weapons, or even live in towns. In the years before his fa-ther's death, while holding the title of Prince of Wales and spending time there, the future Henry V had seen that this state of affairs could not con-tinue. He began to take selected Welshmen into the royal service. Among those so favored, we know not why, was the young squire Owain ap Meredudd ap Tudur—Owen son of Meredith son of Tudor. The word *squire* indicates that he was regarded as being of gentle origin, which in fact he was, his family having been important in North Wales until its participation in a failed rebellion brought it to ruin. Almost nothing is known of the early manhood of this Owain, who might have been ex-pected to take the anglicized surname Meredith but somehow became Owen Tudor instead. It is possible though not proved that he served with Henry V in France and even fought in Greece. After the king's death he was kept on as a member of Queen Catherine's household staff, and what happened from that point forward makes clear that his was an adventuresome spirit.

The paternal uncles of the infant Henry VI, governing in his name, de-cided that allowing the nubile dowager queen to remarry was out of the question. If she took a husband of inferior rank, the dignity of the House of Lancaster would be compromised. Any bridegroom from the higher nobility, on the other hand, might become dangerously powerful simply by virtue of being Catherine's husband and therefore stepfather to the king. And so they decreed that any man who dared to marry Catherine before her son was old enough to give informed consent would be de-prived of his lands. This removed from contention all those members of the nobility who might have been pleased to take the queen to their beds, but not at such a price. The field was left open to contenders as ob-scure as Owen Tudor, who owned no land and therefore had nothing to lose. By the late 1420s he was a member of the queen's inner circle, holding the suggestive title of keeper of the wardrobe. His position must have made him a familiar, if unimportant, face at court.

No one knows how it happened, but at some point around 1430, when both were about thirty years old, Owen and Catherine married.

Their union was kept secret, at least from the powerful men who dominated the boy-king's Council, until Catherine's death in 1437. (The cause
of death was described in Catherine's will as a "long grievous malady, in
the which I have been long, and yet am, troubled and vexed by the visitation of God." One cannot but wonder if this mysterious affliction, so
ambiguously but intriguingly described, may have been the mental illness that had figured importantly in the life of her father, King Charles VI
of France, and would recur in her son Henry VI). By the time of Catherine's death, she and Tudor had had four children. One was a daughter
who died young, her name unknown to history. Another was a boy who
bore his father's name, entered the church at an early age, and would
live and die in deep obscurity as a member of Westminster Abbey's community of Benedictine monks. The two other sons, the eldest, were
named Edmund and Jasper.

The widowed Owen had to flee when he was discovered to have broken the law by marrying the queen. He was captured and incarcerated
in Windsor Castle, but after a year he was released and a comfortable
place was found for him at court. Obviously there were no hard feelings
on the part of his stepson the king.

Rather astonishingly, Henry VI's uncles now had in their care two
boys who on their father's side were Welsh commoners, on their
mother's were related to the royal family of France, and were also, and
more important, half-brothers of England's king. The pair had no inheritance, no place in the world in spite of their lofty connections, and the
council must have had some difficulty deciding what to do with them.
For five years after their mother's death they were raised in a convent
whose abbess was a member of the de la Pole family. Then, at about the
time when they must have been entering adolescence, they were
brought to court, where they continued to receive the kind of training
and education appropriate to the elite. What happened next pivoted on
the fact that Henry VI, himself a young adult now, was a remarkably
sweet-natured individual (a saint in the opinion of some) who had grown
up without siblings or a father and throughout childhood had seen little
of his mother. He embraced the Tudors as brothers and made himself
their patron. Eventually he did more than that. In 1552, as they were
coming of age, Edmund and Jasper became the first Welshmen to be
raised to noble rank in England. The former became Earl of Richmond,

the latter Earl of Pembroke. Extensive holdings of land and castles came to them with their titles.

King Henry's next gift to his brothers would prove to be even more momentous. He gave them—and that is not putting the matter too bluntly—the girl Margaret Beaufort, still a child, an orphan of royal blood and the richest heiress in the kingdom. Like her cousin the king, the little Lady Margaret was a great-grandchild of that John of Gaunt who had been one of the numerous sons of King Edward III, bore the title Duke of Lancaster, and became the progenitor of the Lancastrian Plantagenets when his son usurped the throne and became Henry IV. In addition to a succession of wives, John of Gaunt had a mistress, Catherine Swynford, with whom he produced a litter of bastards called the Beauforts after the castle in which the first of them had been born. After being widowed, Gaunt married Catherine. Their children were legitimized by King Richard II, whom Henry IV would one day dispossess, imprison, and probably murder (most likely by starving him to death). The Beauforts, though specifically barred by Richard from ever inheriting the throne, made good use of their lofty antecedents: the only daughter became the wife of an earl, one of the sons became a cardinal of the church and for a time the most powerful man in the kingdom, and the offspring of another son would include a queen of Scotland, the dukes of Somerset, and (the only child of one of those dukes) Lady Margaret Beaufort.

Among the brutish aspects of life among the English nobility in the Middle Ages was the practice, hallowed by custom, according to which the minor heirs of deceased nobles became wards of the Crown. In theory this was a way of protecting orphaned children and preserving their inheritance until they came of age. In practice it was an opportunity for plunder. Kings could keep all the income from their wards' estates, which almost inevitably, the kings being chronically short of money, led them to maximize short-term revenues and do nothing to maintain the value of the property in question. Alternatively, kings could sell or give wardships to third parties, who would likewise be motivated to squeeze as much money out of them as quickly as possible. Worst of all, wardship brought with it the right to give—which often meant to sell—an heir or heiress in marriage.

Her enormous inherited wealth made an extremely valuable commercial asset of Lady Margaret, who was not quite one year old when her father died, a probable suicide. When only a few years old she was "married" to John de la Pole, the almost equally young son of the powerful Marquess of Suffolk. Suffolk was later accused of plotting to put his son and Margaret on the throne—striking evidence of just how potent and dangerous a possession the child could be. He was murdered in consequence of this, and the marriage was annulled when Margaret was nine. Some two years later the king made her the ward of Edmund and Jasper Tudor jointly. Rather than merely looting her estate or selling her off to the highest bidder, the brothers quickly made maximum use of this opportunity, and of the king's friendship. Margaret became Edmund's wife. (Her onetime fiancé de la Pole went on to marry a daughter of the House of York, with tragic consequences for his descendants.) The wedding took place no later than 1455, the year of Margaret's twelfth birthday. Rather horribly, she was pregnant by the middle of 1456.

Because Henry VI was not only weak, passive, and inept but at times deep in the grip of psychosis (for months at a time he would speak to no one and have to be carried from place to place), the young Tudor earls had little opportunity to enjoy their good fortune. The king had a Plantagenet cousin, Richard, Duke of York, the descendant of yet another son of Edward III, who was the richest and most powerful magnate in the country, ambitious, aggressive, suspicious, and easily offended. This cousin clashed not with the king (it appears to have been nearly impossible to rouse Henry out of his serene indifference even during his periods of sanity) but with Henry's French queen, Margaret of Anjou, a tigress every bit as ferocious as York himself. They fought not for the crown, which York never claimed for himself until the final weeks of his life, but for custody of the king's person and therefore control of policy. Their struggle sparked the long conflict that Walter Scott would, centuries later, name the Wars of the Roses (the red rose being a symbol of the House of Lancaster, the white rose representing York). By the standards of history it was not a terrible conflict. Towns were not destroyed and only rarely pillaged, the countryside was not ravaged or the economy greatly disrupted, and most of the population was left entirely undisturbed. Though the fighting went on for decades it was only intermittent, with far more days of peace than of war, and though there were savagely bloody battles they were usually limited in scope. But it was a

time when barons and dukes and even kings were still expected to lead
men into battle, to kill and be killed. All the branches of the royal family
were inexorably drawn in, along with the nobility, and the toll on their
numbers was cumulatively painful. Ultimately the great Plantagenet
dynasty would annihilate itself in a long orgy of fratricide.

The Tudors were involved from the start, and prominently so. By
1455, long-standing conflicts for dominance in Wales had become part
of the national struggle. Edmund Tudor, the Earl of Richmond and husband of Margaret Beaufort, was dispatched to Wales to take control on
King Henry's behalf. He was almost immediately engaged in fighting,
capturing Carmarthen Castle, being taken prisoner in the autumn of
1456, and dying suddenly (possibly of wounds, possibly of disease)
shortly after his release. Three months later, at Jasper Tudor's big stronghold of Pembroke Castle at the southwestern corner of Wales, Margaret
gave birth to a boy who was given his uncle the king's name and inherited his late father's title of Earl of Richmond. The birth was not only difficult but damaging to the young mother, leaving her incapable of
bearing additional children. She was all of thirteen years old.

The next quarter-century was turbulent, and the two earls—first
Jasper, but then his nephew Henry while still a child—were involved in
the turmoil. Within a few years of Edmund's death, Jasper helped to
arrange his sister-in-law's marriage to Henry Stafford, second son of the
Duke of Buckingham. Somehow it came to pass that Lady Margaret left
her son at Pembroke Castle when she went off to her latest husband.
Jasper by this time was established as what he would remain as long as
his half-brother lived: the king's and queen's most resourceful, energetic,
and passionately faithful supporter in a conflict with the House of York
that grew ever more savage as the cost in lives mounted. From start to
finish it was a seesaw affair, and immensely complicated. The Duke of
York was driven out of England in 1459, taking refuge among his parti-
sans in Ireland. The following year he returned at the head of an army at
the same time that his young son Edward, Earl of March, was leading
an invasion of his own from France. King Henry was captured by the
Yorkists in 1460, Margaret of Anjou fleeing first to Wales and then to
Scotland, but on December 30 of that year York lost his life in a skirmish.
His head, mockingly adorned with a paper crown, was put on public
display.

This might have been fatal to the Yorkist cause if not for the fact that the duke's eldest son and heir, Edward, not yet twenty years old, was already a bold and determined military leader with no hesitation about carrying on the fight. On February 3, 1461, at Mortimer's Cross in the Welsh borderlands, this new Edward, Duke of York, thoroughly whipped an army, part of which was led by Jasper Tudor. Among those fighting on the Lancastrian side was Jasper's father, Owen, still soldiering in spite of being sixty years old or more. He was captured and taken to the town of Hereford, where, upon learning that York had ordered his execution, he was heard to say that "that head shall lie on the stock that was wont to lie on Queen Catherine's lap." After his death a madwoman placed his head at the top of a set of stairs in the market square, washed off the blood, combed its hair, and surrounded it with more than a hundred lit candles. Jasper, having escaped, made his way back to Wales. Early in March the Duke of York took possession of London and was proclaimed King Edward IV. Immediately thereafter he set off for the north, gathering as many men as he could along the way. At Towton, just south of York, nearly a hundred thousand men fought one of the most terrible battles of the late Middle Ages. Defeated, King Henry and the queen fled with their small son Edward to exile in Scotland. All of England and Wales thus fell into the hands of a new Yorkist king who was still only nineteen years old.

Jasper, already in exile, was soon attainted as well, meaning that he was deprived of his title and all his properties. Many of his Welsh possessions were given to the Yorkist Sir William Herbert, and along with them came custody of the fatherless, essentially motherless four-year-old Henry Tudor. The child was taken into the Herbert household, where he would spend the next nine years. The Herberts raised him as a member of their family, eventually making plans to marry him to one of Sir William's daughters. He was in fact a prisoner, however, and his estates had been given to King Edward's greedy and unstable younger brother George, the Duke of Clarence.

Jasper spent the 1460s trying without success to organize invasions of England, staging guerrilla-style raids into Wales where his family history and outsize personality made it easy for him to muster support, and conducting a kind of shuttle diplomacy on behalf of Margaret of Anjou and her hapless husband King Henry. Jasper's stature as brother of the exiled king of England and grandson and nephew of French kings assured him of a respectful reception in the courts of Brittany, France, and Scotland. His tirelessness and willingness to take risks—he would come ashore in secret, muster enough men to capture and burn a Yorkist outpost, and then disappear before the authorities could respond—made him the kind of folk hero about whom ballads were sung. Nearly a decade of this, however, accomplished nothing. All the leading Lancastrians remained exiles, dependent upon the willingness of foreigners to support them in a cause that seemed increasingly hopeless.

Then, with astonishing abruptness, everything changed and changed again. In 1469 the mighty Earl of Warwick, the head of northern England's powerful Neville family and known to posterity as "the king-maker," broke with Edward IV. He and the king's chronically dissatisfied brother Clarence defected to France, where they won King Louis XI's support for an invasion that in 1470 caught Edward badly off balance and forced him to flee to the continent. Henry VI was freed from the Tower of London, where he had been in confinement since being captured four years earlier, and restored to the throne. Almost overnight Jasper Tudor was again Earl of Pembroke and a rich and powerful personage. He retrieved his thirteen-year-old nephew from Wales and is believed to have taken him to Westminster for introduction to his namesake the king and the mother he is unlikely to have seen since he was a small child.

But the high chief of the Lancastrian cause, Margaret of Anjou, was inexplicably slow to return to England and consolidate the victory, and she still had an implacable and able enemy in the exiled King Edward. In March 1471 Edward launched an invasion from Burgundy, where his sister was the wife of Duke Charles the Bold. He landed in the far north and, after a month on the march, met near London an army commanded by his onetime ally Warwick, whom he defeated and killed. Edward's frontline troops had been commanded by his youngest brother, Richard, Duke of Gloucester, then eighteen years old. Immediately the brothers set off in pursuit of Queen Margaret, who was trying to assemble a new army while simultaneously moving westward to rendezvous with Jasper Tudor and the men he was hurrying to muster. They caught up with her at Tewkesbury, achieving a smashing victory with young Duke Richard again leading the Yorkist van. King Henry's son and heir, the eighteen-year-old Edward, Prince of Wales, was taken prisoner. When questioned, he spoke defiantly and was beheaded on the spot. King Edward and Richard returned to London to reassert Yorkist control there, and within hours of their arrival the helpless and harmless King Henry, a prisoner once again, was murdered. Margaret of Anjou, her fires extinguished by the killing of her son, would spend four years in the Tower and then be returned to France, where she eventually died in poverty.

Jasper fled back to Wales with the Yorkists on his trail, taking his fourteen-year-old nephew with him and trying to make a stand first at Pembroke Castle and then in a smaller stronghold at Tenby. There was no way to avoid capture except by running. The Tudors set out in a small ship for France, but storms forced them into a fishing port in Brittany, at that time an autonomous duchy coveted, and therefore threatened, by the kings of France. Brittany's ruler, Duke Francis II, had had to spend his life in an endless struggle to find counterweights to the pressure exerted by Paris, trying to maintain alliances with England, with the Duchy of Burgundy on France's eastern border, and indeed with any potential source of help. It was established English policy to help Brittany remain independent of France because its north coast was directly across the Channel. Not surprisingly, Duke Francis received the Tudors with every courtesy and display of hospitality: two very useful bargaining chips had fallen into his hands as if out of the sky. King Edward of England wanted Jasper and Henry. Therefore Louis XI of France, a man so devious he was called "the universal spider," wanted them also. The duke saw immediately that, as long as he retained custody of his unexpected visitors, he would have leverage both in England and in France.

The military convulsions of 1470 and 1471, and the battlefield deaths and murders to which those convulsions gave rise, drastically changed Henry Tudor's place in the political firmament. With the killing of King Henry and his son, the House of Lancaster was extinct in the male line. So was the Beaufort branch; Henry's mother had been its last surviving member since her uncle Edmund was killed in the Battle of St. Albans in 1455, her cousin Henry was executed after an unsuccessful raid out of Scotland in 1464, and Henry's brother Edmund was among those executed after finding themselves on the losing side at Tewkesbury. (This litany of bloodshed is typical of what happened to more than a few noble families during this period.)

As Lady Margaret's son, Henry was now the only living adult male who could point to his ancestry in claiming leadership of the Lancastrian party. It was a thin claim all the same, one that for a long time appeared to mean almost nothing. Not even the Tudors themselves—not Margaret, not Jasper, certainly not the boy Henry—could possibly have imagined that in another decade and a half *they* would be England's royal family. Their highest political aspiration could only have been to somehow recover the titles and property that King Henry had bestowed upon them. Until the unexpected death of Edward IV, there would have seemed little chance of even that ever happening.

2

The King's Great Matter

In setting out to end his long marriage, Henry VIII enmeshed himself in an impenetrable tangle of political, diplomatic, religious, historical, and even philosophical complexities. In trying to cut his way through that tangle, he found himself in conflict with what must have seemed almost the whole world: a pope willing to do nearly but not quite anything to avoid offending him, his nephew-by-marriage the Holy Roman emperor Charles V, a thousand years of English tradition, a great many of his best-known and most respected subjects, and indeed a very large part of his kingdom's population. It was by plowing forward in the face of this opposition, by gambling that no one could stop him and responding to every setback by raising the stakes, that Henry had such an extraordinary impact on the world.

For the king himself, the question of his marital status was not difficult at all. The facts of the case were certainly simple enough in his eyes. When Henry was still a mere boy, his father, wanting to preserve an alliance with the royal house of Spain, had arranged his betrothal to his dead brother Arthur's young widow, Catherine of Aragon. Everyone recognized that such an arrangement raised questions—under canon law, sexual intercourse created a blood relationship and marriage to a sister-in-law was tantamount to incest—but these questions had been settled with a papal dispensation, a decree to the effect that in this case the prohibition could be set aside. But Henry had decided, no later than

1527, that the law against marriages like his to Catherine was not man-made but divine, God's own law, set down in the Bible for all to see. It was entirely consistent with Catholic belief for him to assert that not even popes could nullify the explicitly stated will of God. Therefore he and Catherine were not married and never had been.

Only to Henry and the most loyal of his supporters, however, was the situation that simple. Everyone else saw questions, complications—problems. First and most fundamental was the mystery of whether Catherine had actually *been* Prince Arthur's wife. There had been a wedding ceremony, of course, but that alone was not enough, under canon law, to constitute marriage. Physical consummation was required, and the question of whether the union of Arthur and Catherine had in fact been consummated was shrouded in uncertainty. After the wedding festivities the two young people had with great ceremony been put to bed together at Baynard's Castle, an old royal residence in London. Soon thereafter they were sent off to live as man and wife at Ludlow Castle in Shropshire, where Arthur was to prepare to become king of England by participating in the government of Wales, and where he died. From her earliest widowhood until the end of her life, Catherine not merely said but swore under oath—no small thing for a person of her character and strong religious convictions—that she and Arthur had never had intercourse. Not even Henry's most ardent champions ever attempted to deny that Catherine at all times and under the most trying circumstances showed herself to be a person of high integrity, and her credibility is reinforced by the little that is known about her young bridegroom. Arthur is a faint figure in history—the very fact that his contemporaries had so little to say about him raises the possibility that his appearance may have been a delicate subject—but he is reported to have been on his wedding day half a head shorter than Catherine, herself well below average in height. A question inevitably arises as to whether Arthur, who was born at least a month prematurely and appears to have developed slowly thereafter, had reached puberty by the time of his death. On balance it is improbable at best that he ever "knew" Catherine physically.

There were problems, moreover, with the biblical passage to which King Henry attached so much importance: "If a man takes his brother's wife . . . they shall be childless." One of the mentors of Henry's youth, the learned and revered John Fisher, bishop of Rochester, pointed out that nothing in these words indicates that they refer to a *dead* brother's wife. On the contrary, a reader's natural inclination might be to assume the opposite. As for the warning about childlessness, nothing could be more obvious than that Henry and Catherine had a living child, Princess Mary. Henry, clutching at straws, suggested that a mistake had been made when Leviticus was translated from Greek into Latin, so that the word *liberis* ("children") had been incorrectly substituted for *filiis* ("sons"). In an age when all educated people shared a knowledge of Latin and no one could have claimed to be a theologian without mastering it, this argument got him nowhere, having no basis in fact. Leviticus was in any case a peculiar foundation upon which to construct arguments about how Englishmen were supposed to conduct themselves in the sixteenth century. It included many rules, some of them intended for Hebrew priests, to which no one paid the least attention: instruction in the proper way of killing chickens, for example, along with prohibitions against the eating of rabbits and the incorrect trimming of hair and beards. The church had long taken it as settled that the relevance of Leviticus did not reach far beyond the time, place, and people for which it had been written.

Even worse for Henry's case, Leviticus was directly contradicted by another Old Testament passage, one from a book written later and therefore arguably preemptive. Deuteronomy 25:5–7 declared it to be not only permissible but *obligatory* for a man to marry the childless widow of his dead brother: "He shall go in unto her, and take her to him to wife." Failure to do this would mean that the dead brother was "put out of Israel," a deplorable fate, and therefore severe punishment was prescribed for those who did not comply. The straw that Henry clutched this time was the notion that the kind of marriage prescribed by Deuteronomy had been a mere ceremonial matter, and that in any case the Jews themselves had abandoned such practices many centuries before. About this, too, he was proved wrong.

No one saw more problems, or had better reason to see them, than the pope, Clement VII. He is too easily thought of as a kind of immovable and impersonal force against which Henry VIII threw himself uselessly—a sort of oriental potentate on a high golden throne, hurling anathemas down on all who displeased him, too insulated from reality and immersed in his own arrogance to respond understandingly to the needs of mere kings. In fact he was nothing of the kind, and undoubt-edly would have been amused to see himself depicted in any such way. Almost fifty when word first reached him of the English king's marital difficulties, the former Giulio de' Medici had been pope for four years and had spent those years sinking steadily deeper into an ocean of trou-bles the likes of which Henry had never experienced—troubles that must have made him regret ever having been elected. A member of Florence's fabled ruling family, son of a father who had been stabbed to death in his home city's domed cathedral months before his birth, he had been raised by his uncle Lorenzo the Magnificent and grew up to become not only an intelligent and conscientious cleric but, at least by the standards of the Renaissance papacy, a model of responsible behav-ior. As cardinal-archbishop of Florence he had made himself a force for reform, during the reign of his incompetent cousin Leo X he had been a constructive influence on the papal court, and he then became a sup-porter of the virtuous Dutchman Adrian VI after losing to him in the election of 1522.

Elected following Adrian's death in 1523, just as the Treaty of London with which Wolsey had hoped to establish peace across Europe was falling apart, Clement was immediately caught up in a war between the emperor Charles and Francis I of France for control of northern Italy. (Not even the best-intentioned popes could keep out of such contests, because as rulers of the so-called Papal States they were themselves among the leading players.) Schooled in the Byzantine politics of Re-naissance Italy but not nearly as shrewd or decisive as he needed to be, Clement made the mistake of allying himself with France and therefore shared in the disaster that followed Charles's great victory at Pavia in 1525. The consequences included the most savage sack of Rome in the Eternal City's long and bloody history, the humiliation of the papacy, a rearrangement of alliances, and finally the resumption of war. Until Henry VIII sent his request for a judgment on the validity of his mar-riage, England had not been a problem for Clement at all. Even after Henry filed his suit, it must have seemed an almost minor matter com-pared to the multiple nightmares that now faced the papacy: disorder al-most to the point of chaos in Italy, the Ottoman Turks' conquest of Hungary and threat to Christian central Europe, and the upheavals re-sulting from the successes of Martin Luther and other radical reformers.

The Vatican was in desperate need of friends, England had been among its best friends as long as anyone living could remember, and Clement had no reason to want the relationship to change.

King Henry, even as his doubts about his marriage hardened into a determination to be rid of Catherine, tried to conceal from her his plans for securing a divorce. (Henceforth we will follow convention in using the word "divorce" although, strictly speaking, that was not what the king sought. He was asking not for the termination of his marriage but for an annulment, a finding that he and the queen had never been married. Canon law contained no provision for divorce: marriage was forever. But annulments—findings to the effect that a couple had never entered into a valid union—were not at all rare.) The secret, inevitably, was soon out, and when the queen learned of it she was angrier than she had ever been in all the years of her marriage—angrier, even, than when her husband had raised his illegitimate son Fitzroy to the highest rank of nobility, possibly positioning him to inherit the throne. Court and clergy began to pull apart into two camps, one supporting the dignified little woman who after a quarter of a century in England could be faulted for nothing except her failure to produce a living son, the other rallying to the king. The dispute, at this point, was about the marriage only. It had not yet metastasized into an epic struggle over bigger issues.

Henry, characteristically, thought himself entitled to everyone's support because right was so obviously on his side. Cardinal Wolsey, as chancellor, was with the king from the start—from the point, at least, at which it became clear that Henry was not going to relent. Catherine blamed Wolsey for everything, believing that the idea of a divorce had originated with him rather than with the king, and that his motive was revenge for her criticism of his lavish way of life. About this she may very well have been wrong; in years to come Henry and Wolsey would both state publicly that it was the former who had first raised questions about the Spanish marriage. Though both would have had reasons to lie (Henry to assert his independence, Wolsey to show that he was never more than the king's good servant), it seems unlikely, all things considered, that they did so. Henry was neither a habitual liar nor a very good one, appearing rather to believe his own most outlandish untruths, and his years in royal service had shown Wolsey that he had little to fear from the queen's disfavor. He would have needed no better reason to go along with the king than simple self-interest—his expectation that a divorce could be obtained without great difficulty and would please his master. It is entirely plausible that he simply saw an opportunity to turn the king's latest brainstorm to political advantage. He would be stunned to learn that Henry had already decided on a second wife, and that his choice was a member of Queen Catherine's entourage.

Behind all these intrigues stood the slender figure, still fascinating and more than a little mysterious after four and a half centuries, of Anne Boleyn. It is of course impossible to say, especially at such a remove in time, just why the king had fixed his attention on her of all the women available to him both in England and abroad, but her allure is entirely understandable. Though less than classically beautiful, Anne had striking dark eyes, a magnificent mane of dark hair, and an elegant carriage crowned by a long white neck. Her father Sir Thomas Boleyn's position as one of the king's most trusted diplomats had made it possible for him to place Anne first at the celebrated Brussels court of Margaret of Austria, widow of Catherine of Aragon's brother and now Hapsburg regent of the Low Countries, and then in the service of the queen of France, whose friend she became. This background, coupled with Anne's considerable intelligence, set her apart from the other women of Henry's court when the threat of war between England and France made it necessary for her to return home in 1521. She was about twenty-one years old by then, accomplished as a singer and dancer and instrumentalist, by the standards of the English court a paragon of fashion and taste. "No one would ever have taken her to be English by her manners," one observer wrote, "but a native-born Frenchwoman." As for her own aspirations at this point, too little is known to provide a basis even for responsible guesswork. In time she would champion ecclesiastical reform to the point of making herself an enemy of Rome, but this would happen only as it became obvious that she had no friends among the religious conservatives at court and the papal court was not going to clear the way for her marriage to the king. In the early going she was not so much Rome's enemy as Wolsey's, using her growing influence to cut off the cardinal's access to the king.

Her own allurements, combined with her status as granddaughter and niece of dukes of Norfolk, meant that Anne had no shortage of suitors. Her best chances for an advantageous marriage, however, had misfired one by one. A proposed union with the Earl of Northumberland's son and heir, Henry Percy, was blocked by Wolsey for complex political reasons having nothing to do with Anne herself. The cardinal may or may not have been acting on the king's instructions, but in any case his intervention caused Anne to distrust him forever after. By the mid-1520s Anne had seen her sister Mary become the king's mistress only to be pensioned off after a few years, had witnessed her father's elevation to the nobility as Viscount Rochford (whether in recognition of his services or as a reward for providing a royal mistress can never be known), and had found herself crossing the border into spinsterhood. But in 1526, just at the point when Henry was being overtaken by doubts about his marriage to a queen who no longer interested him, he suddenly fixed his attention on Anne to the exclusion of every other woman. In one of the many letters he sent her—letters rendered all the more extraordinary by the fact that throughout his life Henry almost never wrote to anyone else—he confessed to having been "struck by the dart of love." Setting aside the fact that in the eyes of the church and the law he was still a married man, he would not appear to have made a foolish choice. Anne was no giggling girl but a mature and accomplished woman, as worldly-wise a woman as the king had ever known. Nature had endowed her with an acid wit, a razor tongue, and a bold willingness to use both even with the king. Henry, long surrounded by fawning sycophants and female courtiers of limited experience and education, is likely to have found such a woman irresistible.

Be that as it may, from early in the relationship Henry wanted not only to bed Anne but to marry her, to make her the queen and mother of a royal family. It has generally been assumed that their relationship remained unconsummated for years because Anne, having seen in her own family how limited the benefits of becoming a royal mistress could be, refused to yield to Henry's advances. It is entirely possible, however, that he was as reluctant to proceed as she. Despite his posthumous reputation as a bluebeard, Henry was never a man of exceptional sexual appetite. His opportunities vastly exceeded the number of his mistresses, which was almost negligible compared to the tallies run up by other monarchs of the day. Anne herself, when their long courtship was over, would joke unkindly (and dangerously) about Henry's inadequacies as a lover. Where the king's greatest hopes were concerned, it would have been a disaster if Anne had become pregnant before he was free to marry her. At best that could have led only to the birth of another royal bastard. What Henry needed, what Henry wanted, certainly, was a *legitimate* son.

Consideration had been given, in the beginning, to having England's primate, the archbishop of Canterbury, declare the royal marriage null. The archbishop, William Warham, had long been close to the king and was likely to be amenable. But such an approach might not have been found acceptable either in Rome or at the court of Catherine's nephew, the emperor Charles, and in any case Henry wanted not just an annulment but the world's acknowledgment that he was entitled to an annulment. And so in 1527, on Wolsey's advice, he proposed that a special court be convened—in England, though by the pope's order—to consider and rule on his suit. This had to be a legatine court, meaning that the men sitting in judgment would be representatives of the pope, authorized to act with his authority. Henry proposed two such judges. His first choice was all too obvious: Wolsey himself, a logical candidate insofar as he had long been both papal legate in England and the kingdom's only cardinal, and a safe candidate because he was unquestionably the king's man. His second, seemingly almost as safe, was Wolsey's longtime friend Cardinal Lorenzo Campeggio, who was based in Rome but had been made absentee bishop of Salisbury in recognition of his services in representing the English Crown at the papal court. That Pope Clement readily agreed to the appointment of two men so obviously predisposed to favor Henry—that he did so in spite of his own sympathy for Queen Catherine as an entirely innocent victim—is early evidence of just how far this trouble-plagued and uncertain pontiff was willing to go to accommodate the king. Though a Medici and pope, he had little inclination to try to force his will on anyone.

Henry was not slow to give signs of just how far he was prepared to go to get what he wanted. As early as 1527, with Campeggio still months from arriving in England, the king was saying threateningly that he might, if not given the justice he knew he deserved, repudiate papal authority and thereby break the ancient connection between the church in England and its continental roots. The situation was not unique—there had been bitter struggles between kings and popes in the past—but Wolsey knew his master well enough to be alarmed. Both directly and through his agents in Rome, he began warning the pope that Henry was in dead earnest, and that if he were not placated the results could include the ruin not just of Wolsey but of the church in England. "I close my eyes before such horror," he would tell Clement in a pages-long, almost hysterical letter in 1528. "I throw myself at the Holy Father's feet." His appeals must have been one reason Pope Clement continued— though in ways so convoluted and hesitant as to be ultimately self-defeating—to do everything he felt he could to avoid offending the king.

As he waited for Campeggio, Henry began a campaign to get all of England on his side. He was savvy enough to understand that, however invincibly right he knew his position to be, in order to have any hope of carrying his subjects with him he was going to need the cooperation of men whose opinion the people respected. Catherine was a popular queen, much loved for her kindness and generosity and admired for the fortitude with which she had borne the disappointments of her life. Word that she was to be put away because Henry wanted a new, younger wife was already in wide circulation, and it was not being well received. The judgment of learned and esteemed Englishmen could change public sentiment if anything could, and so Henry turned early to two men to whom he had long been close, a pair known not only in England but across Europe. Bishop John Fisher had in the reign of Henry VII been confessor and counselor to the king's formidable mother, Margaret Beaufort, Countess of Richmond, who shortly before her death had urged her newly crowned young grandson to keep Fisher close at hand and heed his advice. Henry VIII himself, early in his reign, had boasted that no other ruler in Europe had a bishop to compare with Fisher—though the fact that in the following two decades the unpolitical and stubbornly independent Fisher was never promoted to a more important see than Rochester suggests that the king's enthusiasm may have had limits. Thomas More was younger than Fisher but already one of Europe's best-known thinkers and writers, author of the sensationally popular *Utopia,* a lawyer-politician whose company the king enjoyed and who had long since risen high in Henry's service. He was a friend of Erasmus of Rotterdam, the greatest exponent of the "new learning" sparked by the Italian Renaissance and a biting critic of clerical misconduct.

Asked for their views on the divorce question, More and Fisher responded characteristically. The cautious and lawyerly More declined to offer an opinion, asking to be excused on grounds that he was not qualified to judge such a matter. This was not the answer Henry wanted, obviously, but he accepted it with good grace. The answer that Fisher gave, on the other hand, must have ended any hopes that Henry might have had of getting through this business without a fight. Catherine was Henry's wife, the bishop declared. To claim otherwise was outrageous. If there had ever been reasons to question how the marriage was contracted, three decades and Catherine's many pregnancies had emptied those reasons of pertinence. This was definitely not what Henry wanted to hear. From that moment John Fisher was the king's most conspicuous adversary and a marked man.

Henry now entered upon the momentous part of his reign. It began with a slow sequence of years—it must at times have seemed an eternity—when all his energy and all his power as king were focused on securing the annulment but were not enough to make it happen. Everything seemed to conspire against him, both at home and abroad. May 1527 brought the previously mentioned pillaging of Rome; Clement VII took refuge in the ancient fortress tomb of Castel Sant'Angelo and soon found himself the prisoner of the emperor Charles, who had neither approved the destruction of the city nor even known that it was happening but did not decline to reap the benefits. On the face of it this was the worst possible news for Henry: the one man recognized across Europe as having the authority to free him from Catherine was now at the mercy of the one monarch who, in addition to being the most powerful on the continent, had committed himself unreservedly to her cause. Nothing connected with Henry's great matter was ever that simple, however. The rape of Rome, though not the emperor's doing, gave Clement abundant reason to hate him. It also underscored Clement's need for allies, and England, lacking as it did the means to pursue territorial ambitions in Italy, had always been a more dependable friend to the papacy than France, Spain, or the German states. Clement's need for support became all the greater when, toward the end of the year, he managed to escape from Rome only to find himself and his court living without furniture in three rooms of a derelict palace in the town of Orvieto. Historians have sometimes assumed that, after Rome fell into Charles's hands, Clement had no choice but to do the Hapsburg emperor's bidding. This is far from certain, and the opposite is not impossible. Clement, when his fortunes were at their lowest, wanted nothing from Charles except his removal from Rome and if possible from all of Italy—above all from Florence, the hereditary domain of the Medici.

No easy solutions were open to Clement. If he overruled the dispensation by which Pope Julius had approved the union of Henry and Catherine a generation before, he would compromise the authority of papal dispensations generally. If on the other hand he failed to do so, or to find some other solution, he risked losing nearly the best friend he had in all of Europe and compounding the problems rising out of the Lutheran revolt in Germany. From the beginning of the divorce case until his death, Clement repeatedly weakened his own position, risking betrayal of the principles by which justice required that the case be judged, in a fruitless effort to placate Henry. In the end the rupture between the two was caused not by obstinacy on the pope's part but by Henry's relentless escalation of his threats and demands even as the weakness of his case became more obvious. That weakness was so fundamental that—regardless of how much fear Charles V may have been able to arouse in the pope's breast—any ruling in Henry's favor would have been an act so transparently cynical as to constitute an indelible scandal. It would have seemed to confirm the worst things that any Protestant firebrand ever found to say about the papacy and its ways.

It was October 1528 when Campeggio arrived in England at last and preparations for a formal hearing could begin. The cardinal had moved northward from Rome in excruciatingly slow stages, so disabled with gout that he could travel only in a litter, in such pain that at times it was impossible for him to travel at all. He was a remarkable man, a legal scholar who had taken holy orders only after the death of the wife who had borne him five children, and an authority on canon law, a qualification rendered especially important by Wolsey's lack of background in the subject. He was known to be honest, fair, and wise in the ways of the world, and if he had often served England as an agent in Rome he had done so without compromising his integrity. The highest possible testimony to his stature is the fact that both sides in the divorce case—Henry and Wolsey as plaintiffs, Catherine and Fisher and others on the defense—initially welcomed his involvement.

Not all the cards were on the table, however. The king and Wolsey were privy to a secret not shared with Catherine and her advisers: Campeggio had brought with him from Rome a document declaring the case to have been decided in Henry's favor. Knowledge of this document, presumably to be disclosed at some propitious moment, bolstered Henry's confidence that everything would soon be settled to his satisfaction. To complicate the situation even further, however, Campeggio also had unwritten instructions, confided to him by the pope in person and not known to Henry or Wolsey. Clement had told him to search for a compromise solution that would make a formal hearing unnecessary and, if no such solution emerged, to delay a final decision by every possible means. With this in mind, Campeggio met repeatedly and at length with Henry, with Catherine, with anyone who might be able to influence Henry or Catherine or help him to do so. He tried every imaginable gambit, starting by assuring the parties that the pope would be pleased to issue a new dispensation correcting any flaws in the one that had permitted the marriage in the first place. This was obviously the last thing Henry wanted. Campeggio suggested to Catherine that she should enter a convent, take religious vows, and so free her husband to marry; the queen replied that she would do so as soon as Henry agreed to enter a monastery. Some of the things that Campeggio allegedly proposed could only have come from a desperate mind. He is supposed to have invited Henry to take Anne Boleyn as his mistress with a promise that Rome would legitimize their children— and to have suggested that Henry commit bigamy, marrying Anne without dissolving his marriage to Catherine. (Martin Luther, opposed to the annulment, would offer the same idea.) He is even supposed to have encouraged the king to ensure the Tudor succession by marrying Princess Mary to her half-brother, the king's illegitimate son Henry Fitzroy, an act of incest that would have stunned all Europe.

The whole affair seemed at times to be in danger of sinking to the level of farce. Henry sent a new petition to Rome, one distinct from the annulment suit, asking for a dispensation permitting him to marry Anne Boleyn in spite of the fact that her sister had, some years before, been his mistress. The issue here was the same as in the divorce: "consanguinity," a supposed blood relationship created by sexual intercourse. Canon law said that, because of his past relationship with Mary Boleyn, Henry was linked to Anne in a brother-sister relationship as real as the one that had joined him to Catherine before their marriage—*assuming that* Catherine's marriage to Prince Arthur had been consummated. If there had been no consummation, the barrier blocking Henry from marrying Anne was actually bigger than any between him and Catherine. It is curious, not to say ironic, that Henry would request a papal exemption in the Boleyn case while adamantly insisting that no pope could grant a similar exemption where Catherine was concerned. Clement quickly and cheerfully granted the king's request, at the same time rendering his own decision worthless by noting that the dispensation could be put to use only if the marriage to Queen Catherine were found to be invalid.

In another irony, that same year Henry's older sister Margaret, widow of King James IV of Scotland and mother of the young James V, secured an annulment of her second marriage in order to enter upon a third. Instead of congratulating her—instead of observing a disapproving silence, for that matter—Henry boiled over with indignation, accusing Margaret of violating the "divine order of inseparable matrimony." It is probably unfair to accuse him of hypocrisy in outbursts of this kind. Whatever his own behavior, however much the standards he applied to others diverged from those he applied to himself, he does appear to have sincerely regarded himself not only as a model of uprightness but as qualified to pass judgment on his inferiors—a category into which he would have put virtually every living human being.

Even so, making every possible allowance for the blindness produced in Henry by his limitless self-satisfaction, the performance he now put on for the benefit of a number of the kingdom's leading personages was nothing less than astonishing. In November 1528, annoyed by public demonstrations of support for Catherine (she was so loudly cheered whenever she appeared that Henry banned the gathering of crowds wherever she was in residence), he summoned to his court an august assembly that included members of his council, representatives of the nobility, and the mayor, aldermen, and other leading citizens of London. To this group he delivered an address much of which was devoted to praise of Queen Catherine, "a woman of most gentleness, humility, and buxomness," as Henry described her. "Yea," he added, "and of all good qualities pertaining to nobility she is without comparison."

"If I were to marry again, I would choose her above all women," Henry declared. "But if it be determined in judgment that our marriage is against God's law, then shall I sorrow, parting from so good a lady and loving companion." This was Henry VIII in one of his least attractive, most shameless manifestations: Henry the virtuous, the entirely innocent, ostentatiously shedding tears as he stated his determination to do what was right (and coincidentally most convenient to himself) no matter how deeply it pained him. It is difficult not to find him guilty of rank hypocrisy in this case.

He told the assembled dignitaries that he was prepared to accept the decision of the upcoming tribunal whatever that decision turned out to be—good evidence of his certainty that Campeggio and the pope were going to give him what he wanted. At the conclusion of his monologue, suddenly angered by no one knows what—a skeptical or sardonic look somewhere in the audience, or a sudden stab of fear that the tribunal might not end as he expected?—Henry began shouting about how he would respond if contradicted. "There was no head so fine," an ambassador observing the proceedings reported him as saying, "that he would not make it fly." This side of Henry would not be much in evidence for another five or six years but would thereafter become dominant.

The last little farce of 1528 came when Henry turned again to the thankless task of trying to make Rome and England and the wide world understand that his position was above rebuttal or reproach. He circulated among the kingdom's leading men—the nobility, the senior clergy, other persons of quality and note—a kind of petition stating that his suit should be granted because his marriage was void.

When it came back to him, it bore exactly three signatures.

One was that of the Duke of Norfolk. He was Anne Boleyn's uncle.

Another was that of the Viscount Rochford. He was Thomas Boleyn, Anne's father.

And the third was that of Anne's brother George, still a very junior courtier.

It was a humiliation, but Henry did not react. Perhaps he thought it didn't matter all that much. The new year would bring the tribunal at last, and the result of that, surely, was in the bag.

THE SPANISH CONNECTION

WEARING AS HE DID A CROWN TO WHICH HE HAD ONLY the most questionable of claims, from the start of his reign the first Henry Tudor had reason to worry about the place of his new dynasty among Europe's royal families. Acceptance was essential and could not be taken for granted. It was therefore a great coup, a breakthrough, when just a few years after the Battle of Bosworth Henry's diplomats were able to arrange the betrothal of his little son Prince Arthur to a daughter of the royal house of Spain.

The arrangement offered Henry a connection to one of the most brilliant political partnerships in history, that of Ferdinand II of Aragon and Isabella of Castile. Their 1469 marriage had united Spain's leading Christian kingdoms, and they spent the years that followed in a hard, ultimately triumphal campaign to drive the Moors—Muslims originally from North Africa—out of the southern kingdom of Granada. (Less gloriously, the pair also used the Inquisition to expel all Jews and Muslims who refused to convert.) Ferdinand and Isabella both belonged to the ancient house of Trastámara (and were also, incidentally, descended from King Edward III of England through his son John of Gaunt). At the time of their wedding Ferdinand was king of Sicily (which his father had given him) as well as Aragon, and in due course he began competing with the kings of France for domination in Italy.

Isabella was the most impressive woman of her time. She was a strong, skillful ruler and an active field commander in the war for Granada, along the way giving birth to the son and four daughters with whom she and her husband planned to perpetuate the Trastámara dynasty and link it to other important kingdoms. Having secured for their son and heir no less a bride than the daughter of the Holy Roman emperor, and having compounded this success by arranging to marry one of their daughters to the emperor's son and heir (two other daughters went to the Portuguese royal family), they could afford to send their youngest child, the Infanta Catalina, across the water to England. It was of course a strictly political arrangement. For Ferdinand and Isabella it was a way of keeping England from allying with France, their archrival. For the Tudors it was a confirmation of legitimacy.

More than a decade had to pass, however, before Arthur and Catalina would be old enough to live together as man and wife. Both children received superb preparation for the careers that lay ahead, but hers was the more impressive. In 1492, the same year that Christopher Columbus came upon the New World during a voyage to India financed by the Spanish Crown, the six-year-old girl rode with her parents and sisters and brother into the newly conquered city of Granada. The reunification of Spain being thus complete, Isabella was able to give full attention to readying her youngest child for a future as queen of England. The result, when the time came for Catalina to journey to her new home and become Catherine, Princess of Wales, was a refined, strong-minded young woman who knew the classics, knew history and the works of the church fathers, could converse easily in Latin, and had been taught by her mother to take her duties seriously and always be loyal to her husband and the church.

During the years of waiting Spain had gone from strength to strength. Its vast New World empire took shape with astonishing speed after Columbus's first voyages, promising to generate fabulous quantities of wealth. In 1494 the Treaty of Tordesillas drew a north-south line down the length of the Atlantic Ocean, conferring all the non-Christian lands on one side to Spain and those on the other to Portugal (which thereby acquired a Brazil that was probably not yet known to exist). King Ferdinand continued to pursue his ambitions in Italy, having so much success that in 1504 he added Naples to his string of kingdoms. All this was rendered nearly meaningless, however, by the death of his and Isabella's newly married son, John, at nineteen. The prince's bride was pregnant at the time of his death (which the royal physicians blamed on too much sex, the actual cause probably being tuberculosis), but the child was stillborn. Suddenly everything that Ferdinand and Isabella had built, the glorious legacy of the Trastámara, stood to be inherited by the family of their eldest surviving daughter's husband. For Ferdinand in particular, the thought that the fruits of his achievement would fall to the German Hapsburgs was almost too galling to be endured.

When the ship bearing Catherine arrived in England in 1501 at the end of a grueling four-month voyage through heavy seas, Henry VII insisted on violating Spanish protocol and having an immediate look at her face. He was delighted by what he was shown: an exceptionally pretty and self-possessed little lady, nearly if not actually a storybook princess, obviously a fitting progenitor for a mighty line of kings. He spent heavily to make the wedding a grand public event, a declaration that the Tudors had arrived. Throughout many of the festivities Catherine was escorted by her bridegroom's precocious brother Henry, who at age ten was Duke of York, earl marshal of England, lieutenant of Ireland, and warden of the Scottish marches and appears to have attracted far more notice than Arthur. Shortly thereafter the newlyweds were sent to their new home at Ludlow Castle, where Arthur, still only fifteen and destined to remain forever an indistinct presence in the chronicles of his time, died within a few months. The cause of death was possibly a mysterious disease called the sweating sickness that had only recently appeared in England, or possibly tuberculosis or influenza. Catherine, too, became gravely ill but recovered to find herself a widow—by her own testimony and that of her principal lady-in-waiting a virgin widow—at sixteen years of age.

Life became difficult for Catherine. She wanted to return home, but her father-in-law did not want her to go. Henry VII was on bad terms with France at the time, and fearful of losing his alliance with Spain. Never a man to part lightly with money, he had no wish to return the half of Catherine's considerable dowry that Ferdinand had sent with her. And he continued to be impressed with Catherine herself—so much so that he applied to the pope for the dispensation required for young Prince Henry to marry his deceased brother's wife.

By the time the dispensation was delivered in 1504—the year of Queen Isabella's death, which deprived Catherine of her best source of support and counsel—relations between England and France had improved. Now it was Ferdinand who, afraid of an Anglo-French alliance, was determined that Catherine must remain where she was and wed the

English king's son. King Henry began to regard her as a nuisance and to treat her disgracefully. She wrote home to complain that she had lost her servants, her clothes were in tatters, and she barely had enough to eat. When Prince Henry became fourteen, the age of consent under canon law, he signed a repudiation of his betrothal. He did so, we can be sure, on the instructions of his father, who had become interested in marrying him to a Hapsburg. Wherever the repudiation originated, it was a blow to Catherine, whose health began to fail. She was making preparations to depart England when, in the spring of 1509, the king sank into his last illness and died. In short order—it must have seemed a miracle—the new king declared his intention to marry her, possibly on the advice of his Council but just as possibly because he was a youth of healthy appetites, had no experience of women and no other marriage prospects, and preferred taking an attractive bride whom he already knew over waiting for whatever his diplomats might bring home from the international matrimonial sweepstakes. He was almost eighteen, Catherine twenty-three.

It was a good marriage for a long time. Catherine showed herself to be a devoted wife, sometimes begging Henry to change his mind but never defying him and certainly never speaking ill of him. She even personally embroidered his shirts. He for his part was clearly delighted to have a partner who was fully his equal in intelligence and learning and had far more knowledge of the world. To the extent that there was trouble, it came from Catherine's father. Ferdinand by this time was a sour and scheming old man, devoid of any reluctance to exploit and deceive even his own daughter's husband. In 1511, taking advantage of Henry's eagerness to make war on France, he allied their two kingdoms in the Treaty of Westminster. He joined the subsequent invasion of France only long enough to grab the little Kingdom of Navarre for himself. Having accomplished that, he made a separate peace, leaving Henry alone, exposed and looking like a fool.

Back in England, meanwhile, Catherine was serving capably in the post to which her husband had named her before his departure: that of "rectrix and governor of the realm." Not long after Henry's return, when four hundred Londoners were on the verge of being executed for rampaging in the streets and pillaging the homes and businesses of foreigners, she remained on her knees in front of the king until he granted clemency. In such ways, and with her piety and unassuming demeanor, she was becoming a beloved public figure. No one had ever heard of her doing a dishonest or cruel or selfish thing.

In spite of her father, her family connections were growing in value. Old Ferdinand, a lifelong lecher and father of many bastards, remarried late in life in the hope of generating another legitimate son. He succeeded, but the child lived only hours. And so in 1516, when Ferdinand himself died, the Kingdoms of Aragon and Castile and Sicily and Naples, plus New Spain in America and much else, all passed to young Charles of Hapsburg, the son of Catherine's apparently insane elder sister Joanna. When Charles's paternal grandfather, Maximilian of Hapsburg, died not long afterward, Catherine found that her nephew now loomed over Europe as ruler of the Spanish dominions *and* Holy Roman emperor.

She had only one real problem: children, or the absence thereof. In the first year of her marriage Catherine gave birth to a daughter, but the newborn died. A year after that she gave birth to a son, named Henry after his father, but after fifty-two days he died too. There followed in short order a miscarriage and then another short-lived boy. In February 1516 Princess Mary was born, a healthy girl with her parents' red-gold hair. She was followed by one or possibly two more miscarriages, the last of them in 1518, at which point Catherine entered her late thirties overweight and menopausal, the girlish beauty of her earlier years a memory. Henry by contrast was barely thirty, a fountain of vitality. In 1519 his dalliance with a woman named Bessie Blount resulted in the birth of a healthy boy. In traditional fashion the child was named Henry Fitzroy—Henry son of the king. Though his mother was sent off into a respectable arranged marriage, his royal father took pleasure in having a son at last.

He took pleasure in his daughter, too, an appealing and clever child, small like her mother, eager to please her mighty sire. There is little to suggest that the king was, at this point, greatly troubled about not having a legitimate male heir. The succession problem, to the extent that there was perceived to be one, appeared to be solved in the early 1520s when Princess Mary was betrothed to her cousin the emperor Charles. It delighted Henry to treat the Holy Roman emperor as his son, to give him advice (unwelcome though it may have been) on statecraft, and to think that one day, as a result of this glorious union, some grandchild of his would rule much of the world. It came as a shock to Henry and Catherine when, in 1525, Charles withdrew from the engagement. They should not have been surprised: Mary was only ten years old, Charles twenty-five. He had decided to marry another of his first cousins, the daughter of the king of Portugal. She was grown and brought with her a big dowry that he desperately needed.

Henry, in his anger and disappointment, lashed out at his wife and his daughter, using Fitzroy as a weapon. At age six the boy was brought out of the shadows, shown off at court, and made Duke of Richmond (that old Tudor family title), Duke of Somerset, and Earl of Nottingham. He was given lands commensurate with his new status, and there was talk that his father intended to make him king of Ireland, perhaps one day even king of England.

Now it was Catherine's turn to be furious, and for the first time in a decade and a half of marriage she allowed the court to see that she was angry with her husband. Henry was untroubled. What Catherine thought had never mattered so little to him. Their marriage was dead, England's connection to Spain and the Hapsburgs dead with it, and the stage set for all the troubles to follow.

3

Frustration and
Embarrassment

Getting rid of Catherine of Aragon was far from the only thing that
Henry and Wolsey had to worry about as the 1520s drew to a
close. They had a kingdom to manage and a not very happy one at that.
Its propertied classes were fed up with the Crown's incessant demands
for money, and the population at large was staggering under the effects
of several consecutive bad harvests. Relations with the continent required a good deal of attention as well. From January 1528 on into the
following year, England in alliance with France was at war with the empire of Charles V. It was a peculiar conflict in the way that most wars of
the time can seem peculiar to us: a tentative, distinctly limited affair in
which England sent no soldiers across the Channel to do any actual
fighting. But the stakes were not trivial. One of the ideas behind allying
with France and helping to finance its armies was to isolate Charles and
force him to join in the great pan-European peace that had long been
Wolsey's dream. Less loftily but no doubt more importantly from
Henry's perspective, the alliance was intended to weaken Charles to
such an extent that the pope need have no fear in annulling the king's
marriage. Thus much of Europe was at war at least partly because of
Henry's "great matter."

But alliances and treaties meant so little in sixteenth-century Europe
that one almost wonders why anyone considered them worth making.
War against Charles V meant war with a Hapsburg empire extending

from Hungary to Spain and on to the New World, but where England was concerned the most important part of that empire was the Duchy of Burgundy, which included the so-called Low Countries or Netherlands, today's Belgium and Holland. In the 1520s, the empire having grown far too unwieldy for any one man to manage, Burgundy was ruled by a regent, Archduchess Margaret of Savoy. Margaret, like Catherine of Aragon, was Charles V's aunt. But she was the sister of Charles's late father Philip the Handsome and therefore a true Hapsburg, whereas Catherine was the sister of Charles's mother and therefore without Hapsburg blood. In her youth Margaret had been married briefly to Catherine's brother, the short-lived Prince John. A bond of affection had formed between the two women; the archduchess supported her sister-in-law unreservedly and thereby made herself one of Henry's most troublesome adversaries. But money can talk more loudly than family ties, not least when whole national economies are at risk. Margaret and her imperial nephew found themselves faced with the hard fact that England, a leading source of wool for Burgundy's textile industry, was indispensable not only to the duchy but to the empire. North of the Channel, Henry and Wolsey came up against the other side of the same coin: if cut off from its markets in the Low Countries, a worrisome part of England's economy would be in danger of collapse. The situation posed political dangers as well: merchants, manufacturers, and workers were not likely to passively accept the loss of their livelihoods for the sake of a distant and arcane war with little real meaning for any of them (if indeed it made much sense in any objective way). Nor could the royal treasuries on either side afford to lose the revenues brought in by tariffs on the wool and cloth trade and the taxes that the industry generated. A deal was quickly cut to permit the wool and cloth trade to continue as if there were no war. The leading powers of the time never indulged in total war. The defeat of the enemy, not his total destruction, was always the point.

King Francis of France, as charmingly amoral a rogue as was to be found in all of Europe, was prepared as usual to pursue whatever opportunities he could find regardless of alliances or declarations of war. He had reason to hate Charles V, who had imposed a humiliating peace after destroying his army in the Battle of Pavia in 1525 and taking him prisoner. Charles still held Francis's two sons as hostages, and the strength of the Hapsburgs in Italy remained the one great obstacle to the expansion south of the Alps that Francis would lust after all his life. Nevertheless Francis now saw advantages in trying to come to terms with the empire, if only for the time being. If doing so might involve the betrayal (not for the first or last time) of his old friend Henry of England, that was a price that Francis, even more than most of the rulers of the day, would never hesitate to pay. And so by early 1529 representatives of France and Spain (Francis's mother and Charles's aunt Margaret prominent among them) were meeting to negotiate a peace. The English were not invited, and Wolsey was alarmed at finding himself excluded: the treaty being discussed would unite the two great continental powers, leave England without allies, and mean the ruin of everything he had been trying to achieve. Henry was little less troubled: by making peace with France, Charles would escape his isolation, and would be free to make himself the ally and patron, if perhaps not quite the master, of the pope.

Henry's only hope was to secure his annulment before France and the Empire came to terms. A new field of opportunity suddenly appeared to open up when, in February, word arrived of the death of Pope Clement. Henry went quickly into action, instructing his agents in Rome that everything possible should be done to secure Wolsey's election. He had attempted this same thing on earlier occasions; long before deciding to repudiate his marriage, he had seen the advantages of placing an Englishman on the throne of St. Peter. That Wolsey himself felt any compelling desire to become pope is not at all clear; his exalted position in England appears to have satisfied even his voracious appetite for power. But things had never gone as badly for him as they were going in 1529, and he seems to have sensed that unless he seized the papacy his career, even his life, might be over. So he prepared to campaign as never before. Henry, meanwhile, was telling his agents that if Wolsey's election proved impossible, they were to prevent the election of any of the several possible candidates answerable to Charles V. But then fresh news arrived: Clement was not dead at all, but only very sick. Several weeks passed before he recovered sufficiently to resume his meetings with England's representatives in Rome. The senior member of the embassy, Stephen Gardiner, was a youngish priest-courtier of the sort that had for centuries played a central role in the government of England. Earlier

Gardiner had served as Wolsey's secretary and had won the king's favor by energetically supporting the case for the annulment. Now, having traveled to Italy on Henry's behalf and accomplished nothing, he was desperate for a success of some kind to report back to England. To the papal court he repeated Wolsey's warnings that Henry, if thwarted, might ally himself with the reformers who were tearing the church apart in Germany. Audaciously, he urged Clement to consider the consequences for his own soul should he die without having given Henry the justice to which he, as king, was entitled. The pope, as he unfailingly did when pressed in this way, offered sincere but useless assurances that he wished to be as helpful to the English monarch as it lay within his power to be.

Henry and Wolsey were growing desperate too. Blocked in Rome, and frustrated by how badly their proxy war with the empire was going (the supplies of gold they were sending to France were not preventing Charles from winning one military victory after another), they once again focused their hopes on the tribunal for which Cardinal Campeggio had been sent from Rome months before. All was in readiness for the hearing—the trial—that Campeggio was still under secret orders to delay by every possible means. The king's case had long since been ready. Catherine, too, with the assistance of English advisers including Bishop John Fisher and canon lawyers sent from Flanders by Margaret of Savoy, had made extensive preparations. In the course of doing so, however, Catherine had lost whatever hope she originally had of receiving an impartial hearing. From Wolsey she could obviously expect nothing. And Campeggio, she now feared, was so eager to accommodate the king and had been so entangled in Wolsey's machinations as to be no longer capable of independent judgment. And so, early in March, arguing that the tribunal lacked the authority to hear the case and could not be expected to proceed without bias, she sent a letter asking Clement to recall the question to Rome. The pope, around whose neck the case now hung like a rotting corpse, did nothing in response. Catherine's appeal had no effect on Henry's determination to move forward, Campeggio could offer no justification for further delay, and on May 28 a license for the tribunal to begin its business was issued under the king's Great Seal.

The tribunal met for the first time three days later at Blackfriars

Abbey in London, a full seven months after Campeggio's arrival in England. It remained in session for a month, producing drama of the highest order. On June 18, the first day on which Catherine's representatives were expected to appear, the queen arrived in person. She repeated the complaints that she had already directed to the pope, telling the legates that their proceedings were inherently illegitimate and she herself was at a hopeless disadvantage, and that she therefore intended to offer no defense. She demanded that Wolsey and Campeggio send the case back to Rome.

When she and Henry were ordered to appear on June 21, both did so, the king no doubt eagerly and with high expectations, the queen under protest. The few accounts of that day's proceedings differ as to whether the king or the queen spoke first, but they agree about what was said. Henry delivered an oration, a reprise of the things he had said earlier to the dignitaries assembled at his court. He had asked the pope to commission a tribunal, he said, not because of any fault in Catherine—again he rhapsodized about what a good wife and queen she had always been—but because the promptings of his conscience left him with no choice. Perhaps because he knew he was rumored to be a mere pawn of Wolsey in this matter, more likely to assert Wolsey's ability to serve as an impartial judge, he claimed that from the beginning he had proceeded not on but against the cardinal's advice. To the extent that he had followed the counsel of anyone, he said, it had been that of his confessor and of certain learned (but unnamed) bishops in England and France. He repeated his transparently absurd assertion that nothing would make him happier than a finding in favor of the legitimacy of his marriage, saying again that he intended to accept the tribunal's decision whatever it turned out to be.

Wolsey's contribution that day was to announce that he and Campeggio had found against Catherine's protest, so that the case would not be returned to Rome—not, at least, by them. He assured all assembled that he was in no way prejudiced against the queen and wanted nothing except a just resolution of the case. Campeggio must have struggled to follow the proceedings; his knowledge of English was so limited that since his arrival he had had to communicate in French and Latin.

At some point, possibly before Henry gave his speech—though it makes a better story to assume (as Shakespeare later would) that she acted in response to what the king had said—Catherine rose from her chair, crossed the room to where Henry sat, and dropped to her knees before him.

"Sir," she began in the accent that had not left her in a quarter-century in England, "I beseech you to pity me, a woman and a stranger, without an assured friend and without an indifferent counselor. I take God to witness that I have always been to you a true and loyal wife, that I have made it my constant duty to seek your pleasure, that I have loved all whom you loved, whether I had reason or not, whether they were friends to me or foes. I have been your wife for years. I have brought you many children. God knows that when I came to your bed I was a virgin, and I put it to your own conscience to say whether it was or was not so. If there be any offense which can be alleged against me, I consent to depart with infamy. If not, then I pray you do me justice."

It was at least as much a challenge as an appeal. Catherine waited for a response, but Henry said nothing. Finally she stood, a short, stout woman, aging and careworn but totally in control of herself, her dignity anchored in the knowledge that she herself was descended from kings of England and was the daughter not only of a powerful king but of a great queen. After bowing deeply in Henry's direction she made for the exit. When an attendant attempted to call her back, she paused and spoke again. "I never before disputed the will of my husband," she declared to the silent chamber. "I shall take the first opportunity to ask pardon for this disobedience." With that she was gone, ignoring further demands for her return. Neither on that occasion nor at any other time did the king attempt to contradict Catherine's assertion that she had been a virgin on the day they were wed.

Catherine refused all future summonses to appear or to send representatives, and the tribunal declared her "contumacious" for doing so. The hearing therefore unfolded as an entirely one-sided affair, with the king's attorneys arguing his case and receiving no rebuttal. Basically that case rested on three main points: that the marriage of Arthur and Catherine had in fact been consummated (unproven at best); that the dispensation permitting Henry to wed Catherine had been obtained under false pretenses (the evidence for this complicated claim was even less impressive than the witnesses who testified to Prince Arthur's alleged boast, the morning after his wedding, that he had spent a hot night "in the midst of Spain"); and finally that a document produced by Catherine to prove that her father had known her first marriage to be unconsummated was a forgery (extremely improbable, and if true not possibly decisive). Weak as the king's position was, the fact that his was the only case being presented must have heightened Henry's expectation that the matter would soon be brought to a satisfactory conclusion. Poor Campeggio, largely dependent upon Wolsey and others to explain what was being said by the attorneys and witnesses, must have wondered how he was going to avoid making a final ruling. He wrote to Clement, plaintively adding his voice to those asking for a recall of the case to Rome.

On the mainland of Europe, meanwhile, the ground was shifting in ways that Henry could not have welcomed and must have cost Wolsey sleep. On June 21—the day of Catherine's challenge to Henry—the forces of the empire met a French army at Landriano and routed it. This was the second time in four years that Charles had inflicted a devastating defeat on Francis in Italy, and it convinced the French king to push the talks then in process forward to completion. The resulting Peace of Cambrai, signed on August 3, left Italy under Hapsburg control. The triumphant emperor, a canny diplomat as well as one of the best generals of the day, wisely began dealing not only gently but magnanimously with the pope, allowing his return to Rome and the rebuilding of the city's ruined defenses. Clement at this point had every reason for wanting the friendliest possible relations with Charles, who had never been less than respectful in his dealings with the papacy and was its strongest, most dependable ally in the endlessly difficult struggle with the Protestants of Germany. Among the forces drawing pope to emperor was the fact that Charles, once again master of Italy in the aftermath of Landriano, had it in his power to decide whether the pope's Medici kinsmen would be allowed to rule in Florence. Clement declared, not surprisingly, that he was now a committed "imperialist."

Therefore it was probably for a grab bag of reasons—the appeals not only of Catherine and her supporters but of Cardinal Campeggio, the complexities of the case and questions about the authority of the legatine tribunal, the shift in the continental balance of power in favor of the House of Hapsburg—that the pope signed an order recalling the case to Rome. Time would show, however, that this order did not signal any readiness on Clement's part to find against Henry. In any case, the order had not yet reached England when Campeggio adjourned the tribunal and, using the rather far-fetched excuse that the papal courts would not be in session until October and he and Wolsey must adhere to the Roman schedule, announced that it would not reconvene for nearly three months. This fresh delay intensified Henry's and Wolsey's frustration, but it became irrelevant as soon as they learned of what the pope had done.

Henry's life had turned into a series of setbacks and embarrassments. Even before being adjourned, and even in the absence of a defense by Catherine's counsel, the tribunal had failed utterly to advance his agenda. On June 28, one of the several occasions when the queen refused a summons to attend, there occurred an exchange that was almost as damaging as her last appearance to Henry's hopes of winning public opinion to his side. The king himself was present that day, and in the course of the proceedings he asserted that all the bishops of England had affixed their signatures and seals to a document calling for a formal inquiry into his marriage, thereby showing that they regarded the validity of that marriage to be questionable at least. When this was confirmed by Archbishop Warham, John Fisher angrily denied that it was true. "No, my lord, not so," he told Warham. "Under your favor, all the bishops were not so far agreed, for to that instrument you have neither my hand nor seal." Warham, pressed, admitted that he had signed for Fisher and used Fisher's seal, claiming that he had done so with Fisher's consent. "No, no, my lord," said Fisher again, "by your favor and license, all this you have said of me is untrue." He was ordered by the king to say no more. The impression left with onlookers was that the king and the archbishop had resorted to forgery in order to misrepresent Fisher's position, and that when caught out they had denied him an opportunity to put the record straight. In all likelihood there had been no intent to deceive. Old Warham, a man of good character and certainly no clumsy forger, had probably misunderstood Fisher's position before signing for him. In any case the public contradiction of the king's claim to the unanimous support of the bishops did his cause no good.

Fisher himself was deeply frustrated, and before the end of that same day's session he erupted. Henry had said that he wanted a just resolution of the question at issue and had asked his subjects to shed whatever light they could on it; therefore he, Fisher, owed it to the king to state openly what he had learned in studying the matter for two years. He felt obliged to do this (so Campeggio wrote to Rome a day later, describing Fisher's speech as "appropriate" and with that one word revealing a great deal about his own sentiments) "in order not to procure the damnation of his soul" and "not to be unfaithful to the king, or to fail in doing the duty which he owed to the truth, in a matter of such great importance." On the basis of what he now knew, he said, he was prepared "to declare, to affirm, and with forcible reasons to demonstrate to them that this marriage of the king and queen can be dissolved by no power, human or divine; and for this opinion he declared that he would even lay down his life." He described himself as prepared to die just as John the Baptist, in the New Testament, had sacrificed his life by condemning the marriage of Herod and Herodias. These were shocking words, especially from a man of Fisher's stature, a prelate long associated with the royal family. By unmistakable implication, the bishop was drawing a parallel between the king of England and a despot complicit in the death of Jesus. It is especially striking to see Fisher, at this stage in his long conflict with Henry, already speaking of his own death as a possible consequence of that conflict. Evidently he knew the king well enough to understand where this drama was likely to lead.

The time had not yet arrived, however, when refusal to believe what the king believed could result in death. That time would come, but just now it was Wolsey, not Fisher, whose life was in danger.

ENGLAND THEN

A CONSIDERABLE EXERCISE OF THE IMAGINATION IS REQUIRED, even of people who live in England today, to get a sense of what the kingdom was like during the reigns of the first Tudors.

It was economically simple, almost backward, even by the standards of its time. It had little manufacturing aside from the cloth and leather-goods industries that had arisen as offshoots of England's huge numbers of sheep (vastly greater than the human population) and the extraction, still on a minuscule scale, of its rich reserves of coal, tin, lead, timber, and stone. An overwhelming majority of the population grew its own food on land that it did not own, living in cottages that we would regard as hovels. Almost no specimens of the homes of ordinary people survive from the fifteenth century or earlier, because they weren't built to last much longer than their occupants. The walls, typically, were made of webs of interwoven sticks coated with mud or clay. Few houses even had chimneys; smoke from the cooking fires had to escape through holes in the thatched roofs.

Foreigners commented on the filthiness of English homes. The great humanist scholar Erasmus, who as an honored visitor from the continent would likely have entered few houses except those of the privileged, observed more than a generation after Bosworth that "the floors are made of clay and are covered with layers of rushes, constantly replenished, so that the bottom layer remains for twenty years harboring spittle, vomit, the urine of dogs and men, the dregs of beer, the remains of fish, and other nameless filth." The quantities of alcohol consumed (in the form of beer and ale mostly, wine being too expensive for the majority of people) also provoked comment. Bathing was scarcely feasible much of the year, but its absence does not appear to have been much lamented. In England as elsewhere, May was a popular month for weddings because, with winter well past, brides and grooms could be given a scrubbing without undue discomfort or perceived risk. Any odors not removed by a plunge into the nearest stream could be camouflaged, or such was the hope, behind a wedding bouquet.

As with so many aspects of life at the end of the Middle Ages, the extent of literacy is impossible to measure. Schools as we understand the term were uncommon except in cathedral towns and the larger market towns (a category that included any community with a few thousand inhabitants), where reading and even writing were often part of the training of choirboys. It would be a mistake, however, to conclude that illiteracy was nearly universal. The fifteenth century saw a great increase in primary education; it was provided by the parish churches to be found in all but the tiniest villages, by clergy connected with "chantries" (chapels, commonly attached to parish churches, established primarily to provide prayers for the souls of the families that endowed them), and the numberless guilds to which people throughout the kingdom belonged. By the first Henry Tudor's time, elementary schooling of this kind, a grassroots phenomenon neither promoted nor supported by the central government, was widespread. Grammar or secondary schools, though less common, also were spreading and attracting increased numbers of students not preparing for careers in the church.

Nothing worthy of being called medical science existed. The wealthiest classes probably had the worst of it, because they had the misfortune of being able to afford the services of university-trained physicians, whose education was focused on the works of ancient authorities and on acquiring a mastery of astronomy (it being considered essential to understand how the stars and planets affected various sicknesses and the efficacy of remedies). These worthies commonly prescribed without ever seeing their patients, depending instead on the examination of urine specimens. Below them were the surgeons, essentially craftsmen with no more education than, say, carpenters or stonemasons. In 1518 London's surgeons joined with one of their peer trades to incorporate as the royally chartered "Masters or Governors of the Mystery and Commonalty of Barbers and Surgeons." Even their services were generally beyond the financial reach of mere villagers, who were required to make use of folk remedies of which little is known; in all likelihood they were better off for it. Life expectancy was short. Thirty was the portal to middle age, and those who lived to fifty had reason to think of themselves as fortunate—and as old.

It is easy, and a mistake, to think of medieval society as static and unchanging. In fact it underwent steady, sometimes convulsive change. England, from the fourteenth century, was literally transformed by disease. Like all of Europe, but for some reason more than many parts of the continent, England in the late fifteenth century was still staggering from the effects of the demographic catastrophe known as the Black Death. This was not a single epidemic but a series of outbreaks that first struck in 1348 (when it may have wiped out a third of all the people in England), returning in 1361, 1369, 1375, and six more times between 1413 and 1485. It was not one disease, almost certainly, but a combination of bubonic plague, pneumonic plague, septicemia, and finally yet another mysterious and fatal affliction, sweating sickness or "the sweat," which arrived in England in the same year as Henry Tudor's invasion force and may have been brought across the Channel by it. The population, which in the year 1300 had reached a total of approximately six million, fell to about a third of that by 1450 and to perhaps only three hundred thousand in all of Wales. (By way of comparison, more than sixty million people lived in the United Kingdom at the start of the present century.) By 1485 the population was again growing, but as plague, smallpox (never seen in England until 1514), and pneumonia continued to return at unpredictable intervals, the rate of increase was held to perhaps three percent per generation. The deserted remains of hamlets in which everyone had died were still scattered across the landscape, and towns were studded with long-abandoned houses.

Occasional famines, too, were an inescapable part of the experience of the common people. When the population peaked toward the end of the thirteenth century, it did so in part because it had reached a Malthusian ceiling: the agriculture of the day was incapable of feeding more. Even after the demographic collapse, many people lived on the margins of survival, vulnerable to going hungry or even to starving when not enough rain or too much rain caused crops to fail. They responded by deferring marriage until their mid-twenties or even later (the same pattern of behavior would occur in Ireland centuries later, in the aftermath of the potato famine), and this too contributed to keeping the population down.

The consequences were dramatic and far-reaching. Wages rose as labor became scarce, and landowners suddenly faced a shortage of tenants. Serfdom disappeared without being formally abolished: families that for centuries had been bound to the land by the old feudal obligations found it possible to pack up and go, moving to wherever they found opportunities to rent vacant land at attractive rates. Suddenly if temporarily, upward mobility became widely possible. Onetime serfs became free laborers and even tenant farmers, the most industrious of their children could rise to become yeomen, and within a few generations grandchildren of yeomen would be sufficiently prosperous to claim the status of gentlefolk. Landowning families, meanwhile, began converting acres traditionally used for growing crops into pastures for sheep, which required little labor. They found themselves profiting handsomely as a result: Europe, the cloth-making centers of Flanders especially, proved to have an insatiable appetite for good English wool.

Great fortunes were made in the wool trade, but for most people the good times were short-lived. As more and more arable land was given over to sheep and the population slowly resumed its growth, good farmland would again become scarce, wages would fall, and the "enclosures" would become a cause of instability as resentful rural communities demanded that they be stopped or even reversed. The old iron law of population imposed itself once again; agricultural output proved sufficient for the exporting of grain only when harvests were bountiful, and when harvests were sparse those who suffered nothing worse than months on short rations could count themselves lucky. The Crown found itself occupying an uncomfortable middle ground, unable to ignore protests about the enclosures but also unable to balance its books without the income that the tariffs on the wool and cloth trade provided.

The political and economic life of the time is incomprehensible without some understanding of how rare money was, and how valuable. In the fourteenth century the imposition of a poll tax of twelve pennies per person gave rise to the Peasants' Revolt, because twelve pence equaled many workers' monthly wage. Things were not greatly different in the early sixteenth century: more than a decade after Henry VII's death the richest noble in England, the Duke of Buckingham, had a total annual income of £6,045. The incomes of most lords—and there were only about fifty in the entire kingdom—were little more than a fifth, even a tenth, of Buckingham's. The kingdom's five hundred or so knights received on average less than £200 per annum from their lands, but that was usually enough to make them the richest men in their localities. The thousand or so "esquires" (no more than one such personage existed for every ten villages) averaged about £80 annually. Landed income of £10 was enough to keep a family among the gentry, itself only a tiny part of the population. The wages of working people continued to be measured in pennies per day—a *few* pennies per day, and even less when a meal or two came with the job. Cash was universally necessary, however, if only in the smallest denominations. Most houses lacked ovens for baking bread, few people made their own clothes or beer, and so small exchanges of pennies for goods and services were essential to the functioning of even the remotest districts.

As had been true throughout the Middle Ages, land continued to be the primary source of wealth and political power and was concentrated in very few hands. The king had so much land scattered across England and Wales that his income from it, when combined with the duties collected on foreign trade and the fees generated by the royal courts, was expected by the wealthiest prospective taxpayers (who, being human, had no wish to pay any taxes at all) to cover the costs of government except in time of special need—which meant in time of war. The church, taken as a whole, owned even more land than the Crown, possibly as much as a third of all the acreage in England, with most belonging to cathedrals, parish churches, colleges, hospitals, and the like—not, as is commonly believed, to the monasteries. The extent to which this ecclesiastical wealth can be considered scandalous varies with the uses to which it was put, and those uses covered a broad spectrum. Much church income went to provide the population with the only semblance of a social security system then in existence—meals and shelter for those in need, stores of food for distribution when harvests failed, lodging for travelers, care for the sick—and to support a network of schools that included the nation's two universities. Conspicuous sums also went, however, to support those men at the top of the ecclesiastical hierarchy who chose to live in princely splendor.

England was hydrocephalic, its economic, political, and cultural life concentrated in London. By the late 1400s, thanks to its access both to the sea and to the exceptional prosperity and productivity of southeastern England, London had a population in the neighborhood of forty thousand and was one of the leading commercial centers of northern Europe. It was also growing fast. By the standards of England as a whole (only Norwich and Bristol had as many as ten thousand residents), London not only seemed to brim over with wealth but was uniquely cosmopolitan, crowded with Flemings, Germans, Italians, French, and Spaniards, merchants and bankers and tradesmen most of them, who had come to England to do business. For reasons that are obvious today but baffled the physicians of the sixteenth century, disease ravaged the city even more severely than the rest of the country. But despite the appalling mortality rate, London continued to grow as people displaced from the countryside were drawn to it by the magnetic power of money.

For most of the people of England, London must have seemed scarcely less remote and mysterious than Rome or Constantinople. Going to the big city meant going to Exeter, or Leicester or Leeds or York, and for many even that was a rare adventure. To have seen London and returned home was to have something to talk about as long as one lived. The great outlet for those who yearned to see something of the world remained the pilgrimage routes, of which there were several famous examples in England. The days of traveling all the way to the Holy Land, however, were as gone as the High Middle Ages.

Though vast inequality of wealth and power was one of the defining characteristics of the whole society, differences were narrowed by the fact that even the elites lacked comforts and conveniences that today are taken for granted throughout the developed world. The landless (and literally almost penniless) peasantry was, aside from the largesse extended to it by the church, simply ignored. "The people here are held in little more esteem than if they were slaves," a visitor from Italy observed. "There is no injury that can be committed against the lower orders of the English that may not be atoned for by money." That the two million people lumped together at the bottom of such a society might be tempted to protest when their situation became desperate is hardly surprising. But they were expected to know their proper place and accept it. Life had inured them to hardship, and any who even appeared to threaten the status quo could expect to be quickly and brutally cut down.

4

Radical Departures

I f the recall of his divorce case to Rome was an infuriating setback for
Henry VIII, it did have one advantage. It could easily be blamed on
Thomas Wolsey. Easily but unfairly, because the king had given the cardinal a weak case to work with, at crucial junctures had gone around
him in trying to influence the papal court, and had refused to consider
compromises that might have put the entire matter to rest.

And if the Peace of Cambrai was a disaster for English foreign policy,
one that turned France from an ally of England into an ally of the Hapsburg empire and closed the breach between empire and pope while leaving England isolated, that too was easily blamed on Wolsey. And more
fairly this time, because it was Wolsey who had overreached and
Wolsey's ambitious strategy that had failed.

What was worst for the cardinal, he was nearly without friends. That
Queen Catherine held him responsible for the king's rejection no longer
mattered, but Anne Boleyn and her family had, with even less reason,
persuaded themselves that Wolsey was not only failing to pursue the divorce with all possible vigor but secretly undercutting Henry's efforts.
The nobility had always despised and resented Wolsey for being not
only a lowborn upstart but an insufferably haughty one, while the people at large, conveniently for the king, believed him to be at fault for the
financial burdens imposed by Henry's wars. In 1525, when Wolsey attempted to levy what he laughably called an "Amicable Grant" to pay for

a new continental campaign that the king was determined to launch (it was not a grant at all, of course, but a proposed confiscation of between a sixth and a third of the incomes and movable goods of almost every subject clerical or lay), protests came so close to turning into rebellion that Henry called off both the campaign and the levy. In doing so he pretended that the whole thing had been Wolsey's idea and that he himself had known nothing about it, cheerfully allowing the cardinal to take the blame. Later Wolsey drew both the king's wrath and that of Anne and her family by blocking the appointment, as abbess of the ancient convent at Wilton, of a Boleyn in-law named Eleanor Carey, a woman notorious for sexual promiscuity. The post went instead to the choice of the sisters of Wilton, an old woman known to be "wise and discreet." By doing the right thing, however, Wolsey had given the Boleyns fresh reason to regard him as their enemy, and by allowing the issue to become a royal domestic dispute he had deeply annoyed the king.

As for the world on the other side of the Channel, if the cardinal's many years in command of English diplomacy had won him any real friends there, those friends were, in the aftermath of Cambrai, unable or unwilling to do anything for him. On the contrary, all across Europe there were influential people who, if they were not exactly his enemies, could see little reason to lament his fall.

He had become eminently dispensable, a wonderfully convenient scapegoat. But for Henry, somehow, it was not enough merely to dismiss the man who had served him so faithfully and in most ways so effectively for two decades. The king wanted Wolsey's humiliation—his public humiliation and total ruin. On October 9, 1529, the day the cardinal was opening a session of the Westminster court over which he presided as chancellor, he was suddenly charged with several dozen crimes. Most strikingly, he was accused of violating the laws dealing with what was called praemunire, the interference by foreign courts—which in practice meant the papal court—in English affairs. These laws had been passed in the second half of the fourteenth century, mainly during the period when King Richard II was embroiled in a conflict with the pope, and after Richard was deposed they were almost never invoked though they were also never repealed. By making them his weapon as he now did, Henry underscored what would have been obvious in any case: that in throwing the book at Wolsey he was attacking not only the pope's legate but the papacy itself. He was taking a step the meaning of which could have been apparent only to those few English people who had any real knowledge of what Martin Luther and other reformers were doing in Germany. He was moving toward the separation of the English from the universal church. The fact that he was also destroying the most hated man in the kingdom, a man whose existence had become an inconvenience and whose ruin would deflect criticism away from the throne, was in the great scheme of things almost incidental.

The praemunire charges against Wolsey were true in a strictly literal sense but also absurd. Obviously the cardinal, by accepting his appointment as legate and then using his legatine powers, had made himself officially the pope's man in England; that was the very definition of the job. But all of it had been done with the king's knowledge and consent and often at the king's insistence—Henry had nagged at Pope Leo X to make Wolsey his legate, and at Leo's successors to renew the appointment and finally to make it permanent. For the king to now criminalize the very career that he himself had made possible was little less than an outrage. The cardinal would have had no difficulty in mounting a strong defense, had he chosen to do so. But he knew better than any man that he could have no hope of saving himself by opposing the king. He understood his sovereign's mind, and that resistance could only inflame the royal wrath. And so he surrendered immediately, without hesitation or argument, confessing himself guilty as charged. As the king demanded more and more of him, he continued to give ground. He handed over the Great Seal, and with it the office of chancellor, on October 17. He gave up the Bishopric of Winchester, and the handsome income that went with it, at about the same time. He also gave up his position as abbot of St. Albans, the wealthiest monastery in England. At the king's orders he withdrew to a rural manor house distant from any center of power.

For years Wolsey had been diverting part of his immense income to the creation of a college at Oxford (Cardinal College, it was to be called) and a grammar school in the town of Ipswich, where he had been born to a butcher's wife some fifty-five years before. In 1528 he had asked Pope Clement to permit him to shut down (to "suppress") twenty-nine small and presumably failing monasteries and use their revenues (mainly rental income from farmland) in the endowment of these projects. Assured that the monasteries in question were places "wherein much vice and wickedness were harbored," and eager as always to show as much friendliness to Henry and his chancellor as possible, Clement assented, cautioning only that the displaced monks must not be cast adrift but placed in other monasteries. In a seemingly trivial step that would have vast consequences, Wolsey gave responsibility for closing the monasteries and diverting their income to a resourceful new member of his retinue, a self-made lawyer named Thomas Cromwell. Soon after Wolsey's fall, the seized properties along with the other assets of his schools, which were to have been his legacy, were confiscated by the Crown. Cromwell moved with them as manager, thereby benefiting rather than suffering as a result of the cardinal's disgrace.

And so entered the service of Henry VIII the most remarkable figure of the entire Tudor era. Thomas Cromwell was sui generis—his own creation, like nobody else, about as self-made as it is possible for a human being to be. Born around 1485, the son of a blacksmith who was brought before the local authorities in his home village of Putney so many dozens of times that he must have been a troublemaker and probably was a drunk, young Thomas had grown up without connections, money, or much in the way of education. For reasons unknown he left England while still an adolescent, joined the army of the king of France and went with it to Italy where he may have been in a battle, and got himself hired by a banker in Florence. Later he worked in the cloth trade in Flanders. By the time he returned to England, aged about thirty, he spoke several languages, was an experienced businessman, and apparently had made enough money to set himself up in London and marry a widow of some means. He traded in cloth, became an agent for other merchants, and dabbled in moneylending and the providing of legal counsel. He must have made a powerful impression, because by 1523 he was a member of the House of Commons and a year later a fellow of Gray's Inn, part of the inner sanctum of the legal establishment. What most set him apart was his brainpower and his willingness to try anything. Once, on a business trip to Rome (where he inveigled an unscheduled appointment with the pope and supposedly used a gift of candies to win from him a favor sought by his client), he filled tedious weeks in the saddle by memorizing the New Testament in Latin.

He did not need long to get the attention of the king. His opportu-

nity came when Henry, in attempting to take over the revenues of the
suppressed monasteries, ran up against a legal complication. The pope
had allowed Wolsey to seize those revenues only on condition that they
be used for the endowment of his schools. By any reasonable interpretation of the law, the king had no right to them at all. Cromwell, characteristically, simply swept the problem aside, declaring that he had
"discovered" that Wolsey's agreement with the pope was in violation of
the praemunire statutes. Thus it was the cardinal who had no right to
the money, which therefore—somehow—became the property of the
Crown. As legal theory it may have been nonsense, but it satisfied the
king and no one dared to raise questions. Building on his strong start,
Cromwell began acting as liaison between the disgraced but still formidable Wolsey and the king, showing himself to be adroit enough to
avoid offending either party. Soon he secured a seat in the Parliament
summoned to meet for the first time in November 1529—the one that
would become forever famous as the Reformation Parliament. In short
order he was handling all the Crown's land transactions and overseeing
its many construction projects. His access to Henry attracted clients
eager to pay for his advice and support. There were complaints about his
methods—people said he extorted backroom payoffs whenever he
could—but if he was guilty it did him no harm.

As Cromwell rose, Wolsey continued his decline, surrendering one
by one all the things he had accumulated during his decade and a half of
power. Several years before, in a timely response to mounting criticism,
Wolsey had voluntarily handed over to the king the magnificent palace
that he had built for himself at Hampton Court. This palace was so
much grander than any of Henry's own residences that it had become
an embarrassment, a too-vivid example of the grandeur in which the
cardinal lived. Now, in giving up nearly everything else, he hesitated
only when ordered to sign over London's opulent York Place, soon to be
renamed Whitehall and to provide adjoining apartments for Henry and
Anne Boleyn. He explained that York Place was not his property but the
church's, belonging to the Archdiocese of York, so that he had no right
to give it to anyone. Told otherwise by the king's legal scholars, he
yielded with wry good cheer. "Inasmuch as ye, the fathers of the laws,
say that I may lawfully do it," he said, "therefore I charge your conscience and discharge mine. Howbeit, I pray you, show his majesty from

me, that I most humbly desire his highness to call to his most gracious remembrance that there is both heaven and hell."

Those were bold words to be addressed to Henry VIII, especially by a man who remained desperately hopeful, throughout his final tribulations, of being restored to royal favor. Henry encouraged Wolsey's hopes, periodically sending him little tokens of goodwill. Perhaps he was merely playing with his victim, as a cat will toy with a mouse. Perhaps, in spite of everything that Anne and her father and her uncle the Duke of Norfolk were doing to poison his mind against Wolsey, Henry was not yet certain that he could spare the cardinal. When he learned that Wolsey had fallen ill, he dispatched three court physicians to attend him. "God forbid that he should die!" Henry said. "I would not lose him for twenty thousand pounds."

But Henry had learned many things from Wolsey over the years, and now he was learning from Wolsey's destruction. He was even learning how to get along without Wolsey while making full use of his example. By achieving domination over the administrative machinery of church and state alike, the cardinal had demonstrated how the secular and ecclesiastical dimensions of English life might be pulled together into a single entity entirely subordinate to the Crown. By closing monasteries as a way of filling his coffers, he had demonstrated—Cromwell would soon show that he had understood this lesson best—how to tap a reservoir of seemingly limitless wealth. By not defending himself against ridiculous charges, Wolsey had shown the king how potent a weapon the praemunire statutes could be. By yielding without argument to the king's every demand, he had given Henry what must have been a deeply gratifying demonstration of how infinitely more powerful he was than even the mightiest of his subjects.

Henry was by this time developing a lofty conception indeed of the extent of his authority. On October 26, in conversing with an ambassador newly sent by Charles V, he concluded a monologue about the need for church reform, and the responsibility of rulers to effect reform, by stating that the clergy had no power over laymen except the power, through the sacrament of penance, to forgive sins. It can be difficult to grasp just how astonishing an assertion this was in the Catholic Europe of the 1520s. The word of the church had long been accepted as final in many areas of life, and in an age when religious faith was so nearly universal as to be taken for granted, those areas were widely regarded as more important than the ones under secular jurisdiction. The result was a division of power between church and state, a balance that by Henry's time had been in shifting and sometimes precarious equilibrium for hundreds of years. It had been sustained less by raw political (or military or economic) power than by an enduring consensus on how and for what purposes society should be organized. The papacy if not the church itself would have been extinguished many times over, between the end of the Roman Empire and the start of Henry's reign, except that an overwhelming majority of Europe's people were content to let it continue. Part of the consensus was an understanding, more often assumed than asserted or discussed, that the church must be free to govern itself, and that it was the church's responsibility to bring God and God's word to the people. Henry's comment to the ambassador provides a glimpse into a mind that was ceasing to believe such things, that wanted to move the boundary between church and state drastically in the state's (meaning in his own) favor. Over the centuries many European rulers, in England and elsewhere, had wanted something similar. Virtually all had failed, often paying a high price for their failure. None of those who succeeded had done so to such an extent as to overturn the ancient consensus.

But the world was changing. The foundations of the old equilibrium had grown brittle, and were more eroded than most people imagined. In the north of Germany the revolt of a single Augustinian friar, Martin Luther, had been enough to bring the whole traditional structure crashing down. Timbers were creaking in France and elsewhere. Everywhere people expressed discontent with the wealth and power of the church and its departures from its own standards, though the breadth and intensity of that discontent and the extent to which it was justified are impossible to measure. Throughout Europe, and for varied reasons, the general tendency of the sixteenth century was toward strong central governments dominated by monarchs who inevitably regarded the church skeptically, as a dangerous rival needing to be subdued. In country after country the church was on the defensive, and it would have been so even if the conduct of the clergy had been above reproach. It was under attack both by increasingly powerful princes and by religious reformers of many different kinds with widely differing aims.

Inevitably two of the great issues of the day, the condition of the church and the nature of kingship, became entangled. From an early age Henry had displayed an exceptionally keen appreciation of the powers and prerogatives of kings—exceptional even for the time, and even for a ruling monarch—while simultaneously making a great show of his Catholic orthodoxy and loyalty to the pope. As early as 1515 during a dispute with the clergy, he had angrily declared that "kings of England had never had superiors but God alone." Wolsey had defused that crisis by leading his fellow bishops in submission to the king, and by dissolving a Parliament that was raising unwelcome questions about the mysterious death of an accused heretic while in the custody of the bishop of London. But the idea of limitless royal authority to which Henry had briefly given voice continued to simmer not only in his own brain but in those of the most alienated and ambitious reformers. It also had the enthusiastic approval of some of the most powerful nobles in England, men who hated and feared Wolsey and after his fall directed their hatred at the ecclesiastical system that had produced him. In London and at Cambridge University and port cities like Bristol, those lawyers and merchants and scholars who were embracing the Lutheran ideas coming out of Germany supported this idea as well.

By 1529 those ideas were bursting into print, a still-novel phenomenon made possible by Johann Gutenberg's invention of movable type almost a century before. The year before, two remarkable works had been widely circulated and much talked about in London. The well-named *Obedience of a Christian Man* by William Tyndale, one of the first translators of the Bible into English, claimed for the king as much authority and as much right to the unqualified loyalty of every subject as any tyrant could have wished for. "God hath made in every realm [the king] judge over all, and over him there is no judge," Tyndale wrote. "He that judgeth the king judgeth God; and he that layeth hands on the king layeth hands on God; and he that resisteth the king resisteth God, and damneth God's law and ordinance." To justify these words, which would have raised the eyebrows of anyone familiar with English law and tradition, Tyndale invoked the example of the priest-kings of the Old Testament, chosen by God to rule Israel. Henry read Tyndale's book, possibly with the encouragement of Anne Boleyn, and of course was charmed. "This," he is supposed to have said, "is a book for me and for all kings to read." Tyndale's time as a royal favorite would be brief: within a year he infuriated Henry by condemning his efforts to rid himself of Catherine, dismissing the divorce case as the work of the papist archfiend Wolsey, and rejecting items of church doctrine that the king was determined to uphold.

Out of Antwerp there came at the same time *A Supplication for the Beggars* by an English lawyer named Simon Fish. It was a depiction of the abuses of the church so impossibly exaggerated as to be self-defeating where credibility was concerned. England was crowded with paupers, said Fish, because its wealth was being drained away into the church. England was flooded with women turned into whores by a lascivious clergy. The orders of friars that supported themselves by begging were draining £40,000 pounds or more out of the economy annually. (This utterly impossible number rivaled the regular revenues of the Crown.) Fish's diatribe was of course welcomed by those willing to use any stick to beat the church, but what particularly pleased Henry was his insistence that all these terrible abuses must be corrected *by the king,* the church itself being too sunk in corruption. Henry is said to have summoned Fish, extended assistance to him and his wife, and shielded him from prosecution.

The ideas of Tyndale, Fish, and other reformers represented a radical departure from traditional political thought in England. Certainly kings had always been exalted above mere holders of high office. Their coronations were quasi-sacramental occasions, centered upon an anointing with holy oil that made the person of the monarch almost, if not quite, sacred. From 1066, when William the Conqueror sailed from Normandy to win the English crown, to the first Tudor's capture of the same crown at Bosworth Field in 1485, successful claimants had offered the fact of their success as evidence that God wanted them to succeed. Those who never had to fight for the crown similarly regarded their possession of it as proof of divine favor.

But none of this was the same as saying that kings were God's unique representatives on earth and must be obeyed in exactly the same way that God must be obeyed: absolutely, at all times, and in all things. What the Tyndales and Fishes were preaching, what Henry and other princes were eagerly professing to believe, required the repudiation of the prevailing thought of the Middle Ages. If it had roots anywhere in the

Western past, they were to be found in the despotism of the Roman Empire and perhaps (as the most zealous reformers liked to claim) in the kings of the Old Testament. It is hard to know what could have motivated it except a burning hatred of the old religion.

For an expression of what was still Europe's living tradition, the tradition that the most radical of the new thinkers wanted to cast aside, one need look no further than to the man Henry chose as Wolsey's replacement in the office of lord chancellor. (The king's great friend the Duke of Suffolk had wanted the post, but the jealous opposition of the Duke of Norfolk made his appointment seem inadvisable.) Sir Thomas More was a prominent exponent of the so-called "new learning" but a traditionalist in every really deep sense—a man who loved and revered the church, England's heritage of individual rights under the common law, and the whole ordering of society that had taken shape in medieval times. He embodied nearly everything that the radical reformers sought to reject. For centuries he would be cast, throughout most of the English-speaking world, as the defender of precisely those things that had to be jettisoned in order for what is best in the modern world to emerge. Henry, by contrast, would long be seen as the man who had liberated his people from those same dark things. Today the truth appears to be very near to the reverse.

Henry, whose opinion of himself had always been grandiose (early in his reign he had boasted of not being able to see "any faith in the world, save in me," so that "God Almighty, who knows this, prospers my affairs"), was by 1529 arriving at the conviction that God intended him to have dominion over every aspect of the lives of his subjects, and that in ruling his kingdom he required the consent of no one other than God. But when on November 3 a new Parliament opened at Westminster, its members heard an opening address by More as chancellor that did not sit at all easily with what the king was coming to believe. Indulging the interest in philosophical questions that had already helped make him one of the best-known humanist thinkers in Europe, drawing upon ideas that he had earlier developed in his famous book *Utopia* and in a biography of King Richard III that would not be published in his lifetime, More invited his listeners to consider the question of where the princes of the world derive their power. His answer, which sounds startlingly modern, was based solidly on the mainstream thought of the preceding centuries. Genuine and legitimate power, More said, comes to the prince not from above but from below, from the community that is governed, "so that his people make him a prince." Society functions as it should when a prince, a monarch, acts in harmony with the will of the people. When on the other hand a prince acts at cross-purposes to what his people believe and want, the result is disorder.

These words were not thrown down as a challenge to the king, who stood at More's side as he spoke them. On the contrary, much of More's speech was a tiresomely commonplace exercise in political flattery. It praised Henry for his wisdom, his mercy, and most pointedly (if perhaps somewhat ignobly) for his ability to see through the schemes of Cardinal Wolsey and cast him aside. Henry loved flattery and easily mistook it for truth, and there is no evidence that he even noticed what More had said about the true source of his power. Nonetheless that part of the speech stands as an unmistakable early signal of just how far apart were the tradition represented by More, a tradition embodied in the Magna Carta and Parliament and indeed in the established relationship between church and state, and Henry's increasingly ambitious view of his place in the world.

It was a clear signal that, even at the start of his chancellorship, More was too far out of step with the king ever to become as powerful or even as useful as Wolsey had been. That the gulf between them was so wide that it would have been better for both if More had never become chancellor.

THE OLD CHURCH

THE ENGLAND OF 1530 CONTAINED SOME NINE THOUSAND parish churches, each a center of community life for the people living nearby. Each church had at least one resident priest, and attached to many were chantries, chapels with their own endowments for the support of additional clergy.

These parishes, along with those of Wales, were organized into twenty-one dioceses, each headed by a bishop or archbishop and supporting a cathedral with its chapter of canons and other clerics. The dioceses, in turn, made up two separate provinces: York in the north with only three sees, Canterbury with eighteen.

Additionally, nearly ten thousand monks and sixteen hundred nuns lived in more than six hundred monasteries scattered across the landscape. Nearly two hundred other houses, many of them situated in cities and towns, were occupied by the various orders of mendicant friars.

The kingdom's only universities, Oxford and Cambridge, were ecclesiastical institutions, administered by churchmen and dedicated chiefly to the education of clerics (many of whom, upon completing their studies, found employment in government or the service of leading men). The church operated an overwhelming majority of the lower schools and virtually every "hospital" (a broad category covering not just treatment of the sick but many charitable functions). Its courts had responsibility for everything from matrimonial law to the probating of wills.

The church was, in short, a massive and all-pervading institution, an essential and conspicuous part of England's public and everyday life. It was so big and so diverse, changing constantly as the society and economy with which it was intertwined changed, that evidence can be found to support almost anything said about it, whether in support or condemnation.

Was its leadership corrupt? Anyone wishing to say so need look no further than the greatest churchman of them all, Thomas Wolsey, archbishop of York, lord chancellor, cardinal, and papal legate. He had a bastard son, Thomas Winter, for whom he secured appointments as dean of Wells Cathedral, rector of several churches, and canon of still others. Together these offices generated annual income of £2,700, more than that of most bishops and many barons. And all while Winter was still a child. But to portray Wolsey as *only* corrupt would be an injustice. We have already seen him intervening to prevent a well-connected woman of bad character from becoming head of an important abbey. He spent years making the law courts more accessible to ordinary subjects and less biased in favor of the wealthy.

Nor was Wolsey's corruption typical. Other men, William Warham and Richard Fox among them, spent long years at the pinnacle of church and royal court without a whiff of scandal, cheerfully leaving the king's service as soon as they became free to do so and devoting themselves exclusively to their ecclesiastical duties.

Was the church the enemy of progress? Did it try, for example, to bar the door against the so-called "new learning" coming northward out of Renaissance Italy? This has often been alleged, but few charges could be more absurd. That the church contained conservatives who felt threatened by innovations such as critical analysis of the ancient sacred texts cannot be denied and is hardly surprising. But such men were not only balanced but outnumbered by the many prominent churchmen—Warham and other bishops among them—whose encouragement and support and own writings caused Erasmus to call England the great hope for the future of European scholarship.

Were the parish priests, especially those in the poorest and remotest districts, an ill-educated and brutish lot? Were the denizens of the convents and monasteries lazy, self-indulgent, and sexually licentious? Human nature being what it is, and considering that we are speaking of tens of thousands of people living under almost infinitely varied conditions, it would be a miracle if some were not. For centuries after the Tudor era it was taken for granted that many or even most were, but the writers who encouraged that assumption had axes of their own to grind. More recent scholarship, the kind that became possible only when sectarian passions cooled, has shown the reality to have been considerably less horrifying.

Anyone relying on movies and television for a depiction of England's bishops and abbots before the Reformation could come to no other conclusion than that their lives were devoted to oppression and denial, to forcing obedience to the most rigid orthodoxy on an unwilling but impotent people and crushing any departure from discredited ways of thinking. But it becomes clear, when one looks closely, that life in England before the 1530s could not have felt like that at all—certainly not for the vast majority of the people. "Heresy" was feared not only by the hierarchy but by people generally. It was feared because it appeared to threaten not just the prerogatives of the institutional church but the structure of society itself, even the meaning of life. But until the religious convulsions of the sixteenth century raised such fears to an unprecedented intensity, extreme measures for the punishment of heresy remained rare. Few English churchmen in positions of authority went out actively looking for trouble, at least where arcane questions of theology were concerned. One way in which Wolsey *was* typical of pre-Reformation English bishops was his lack of interest in searching out, never mind punishing, possible cases of heresy.

The documentary record—even the archaeological record—suggests that the people of England were strongly attached to their church in Henry VIII's time. The era was remarkable for the number of people remembering the church in their wills, endowing chantries, hospitals, and the work of the friars. Ordinary people contributed on an unprecedented scale—and, it must be said, voluntarily—to the improvement and adornment of their parish churches. The guilds that were an integral part of parish and therefore community and family life were not only active and prosperous but growing increasingly so.

Perhaps the most alien thing about England of the early sixteenth century, from a twenty-first-century perspective, is the extent to which almost the whole population believed—really *believed*—what the church taught. The result was not just consensus but something very close to unanimity, with all the advantages (a feeling of security, an immensely strong sense of community) and disadvantages (smugness, intolerance rooted in fear of the unfamiliar) that unanimity can bring. The "one true faith" encompassed not just every walk of life throughout the British Isles, not just all of Europe, but every past generation back to where history dissolved into legend. Few things could be more foreign to the sensibilities of the world we live in now.

England was not intensely anticlerical or anything of the kind. The church saw itself, and taught the faithful to see it, as a family of sinners rather than saints, of pilgrims making their way along the winding road to salvation. Its members generally accepted that in the family of faith, no less than in families of blood, there were drunken uncles as well as loving ones, that some uncles could be loving as well as drunk, and that even when their behavior was unacceptable, even when something had to be done about it, they were still part of the family. This is the spirit that suffuses *The Canterbury Tales:* some of Chaucer's clerical characters are absurd and some are unworthy of their positions, but they are not hated and the disappearance of their kind would be unthinkable. Such an attitude still prevailed in early Tudor times. England was not simply formally Catholic, affiliated officially with Rome; it was a deeply Catholic *culture.*

That culture came early to Britain—rather astonishingly so, considering the island's remoteness from the Holy Land and even Rome. At the end of the sixth century, when Pope Gregory I dispatched missionaries to Britain, he did so less to convert the inhabitants—he knew that many of them had been Christian for hundreds of years—than to make sure that the church already established there did not lose its connection to his own. That almost aboriginal church (sometimes called "British" by historians, more often "Celtic") had first taken root in the third or even the second century, when much of Britain was still a thriving province of the Roman Empire. During the generations following the departure of Rome's legions at the beginning of the fifth century, Britain's first Christians were able to maintain only informal, mainly commercial contact with the outside world. And though they clung with an odd stubbornness to ideas of their own on such questions as the proper dating of Easter, on essential doctrine they appear to have remained entirely orthodox. Recognition that the church was a unitary international community, and that the bishop of Rome was its leader, seems never to have been an issue: Britain was sending representatives to ecclesiastical councils on the continent even when the so-called Dark Ages were at their darkest. After the arrival of Gregory's missionaries, the indigenous church (which was especially well established in southwestern England and western Wales, the places most easily reached by traders sailing from the Mediterranean) was absorbed by gradual stages into the structures introduced by Rome.

By the time the future Henry VIII was born, Roman Christianity extended from the islands beyond Scotland to the islands of the eastern Mediterranean, and from the Atlantic Ocean to the western border of Russia. It was an essential element in Western civilization's understanding of itself, and England had been part of it much longer than it had been a kingdom, longer in fact than it had been "England." The first English diocese had been established in the year 597 at Canterbury (there were dioceses in Wales much earlier), which thereby became the home of the national church. Other dioceses soon followed—London and Rochester in 604, even York in the far north as early as 625.

It was a church with firm core beliefs, but it offered many different ways of living those beliefs—ways expressed, for example, in the very different rules of the various religious orders. It claimed to have been founded by Jesus Christ himself. It taught that Jesus had charged his apostles and their successors with bringing salvation to all the peoples of the world; that the bishops were those successors with the bishop of Rome as their chief; and that, as the instruments of salvation, Jesus had instituted seven sacraments—seven means by which the saving grace of God was conferred upon the faithful. One of these, the sacrament of penance or confession, was anchored in the belief that priests were empowered to forgive sin. Another, the Eucharist, was believed to return Jesus physically to Earth in the bread and wine that only priests could consecrate during the "sacrifice" of the mass. The church taught—and as the sixteenth century advanced would be reviled for teaching—that human beings were endowed with free will, so that they could accept or reject salvation, and that acceptance entailed earning divine favor by doing good and avoiding evil. It taught, too, that even most of the saved were at death not yet worthy of union with God, that to be made worthy they had to undergo purification in a process called "purgatory," and that the process could be speeded by the prayers of the living. It taught that the Bible was the word of God but not the only way of knowing God's will—that the core traditions of the church, teachings passed down orally from the apostles, carried comparable authority.

Of course, none of this could be "proved" on the basis of empirical evidence. All of it lay beyond the reach of scientific inquiry. It could be dismissed as pure invention, even as a conspiracy by which a cynically self-serving clergy had betrayed Christ and gained control over the minds and pocketbooks of Europe, and in due course it would. In the England of 1530, however, almost no one was prepared to see it in any such way.

Not that there was no trouble. There had always been trouble—how could there not be, with the church exercising so much authority at every level of English life? But the worst of it had generally occurred at a high level, with hierarchy pitted against Crown and the beliefs and practices of most people not affected. This happened in the twelfth century, with the murder in Canterbury Cathedral of Henry II's onetime friend and great adversary Thomas Becket. It happened later and in different ways under Kings John, Edward III, Richard II, and Henry IV. These episodes demonstrated that pushing the church too hard could be dangerous, but overall the monarchy more than held its own. Thus it came to be accepted that the king selected England's bishops, subject only to the formality of papal approval. And that the rules for the clergy of Canterbury and York were set neither by Rome nor by the Crown but by the convocations of the two provinces—regular clerical gatherings, divided like Parliament into upper and lower houses and usually dominated by friends of the king.

When Henry VIII set out to obtain the nullification of his marriage, there were already many points of friction between England's religious and secular authorities. Most of these involved old and even tiresome questions: whether cases of slander and libel really belonged in the ecclesiastical courts, whether it was necessary for the church's calendar to allow working people quite so many holidays, whether even holders of minor orders should be able to elude punishment by the civil authorities, how much priests should be allowed to charge for conducting funeral and other services. It can easily seem outrageous, today, that any church should have so much authority over so many things. There is, however, another way of viewing the subject. Twenty years into Henry's reign, the church was the only element of English society with any real possibility of opposing the Crown. Only it stood between the king and absolute power.

As for the king's subjects, no doubt many of them felt aggrieved. Many of them may have thought—and justifiably so—that it no longer made sense for the monasteries to own quite as much land as they did. Probably many of them resented the amounts of English money— amounts that tended to be comparatively trivial, actually—sent every year from England to a distant pope about whom they knew little and cared less. Those living in parishes where the rector was never seen would have understood that the practice of "pluralities," of granting one churchman the incomes of many offices, was much too widespread.

But any notion that the whole system was rotten at its core or was seen as such, or that England's people were eager or even willing to throw it off and start again with something radically new, is without basis in fact. In religion as in politics, the kingdom was in nothing resembling a pre-revolutionary state. A religious revolution, if there was going to be one, was going to have to come from the top down, not from the bottom up.

5

Another Way Devised

It is not at all clear why Henry VIII summoned a Parliament in December 1529. Such assemblies were not routine or regular events in those days. To the contrary, they were extraordinary: Parliaments met only when ordered by the Crown, and kings and their ministers rarely summoned them except when in urgent need of what only Parliament could grant—an emergency infusion of revenue. Under ordinary circumstances the Crown was expected to get by on the money generated by the king's own lands, the courts, and the tariffs, and so there was nothing resembling an annual tax on income or wealth. The calling of a Parliament was invariably a signal that the king was about to do what kings preferred never having to do: *ask* his subjects for cooperation. Such requests always created the danger that Parliament might make itself disagreeable by asking for something in return. Kings generally regarded themselves as fortunate if they could go for years, even decades, without having to deal with Parliament. Members, for their part, could have been excused for responding to a summons with a sense of dread.

Henry was seriously in need of money at the end of 1529, but that had been his usual condition for years, and it soon became clear that he was not intending to ask for more. Instead he and his agents began bullying the Lords and Commons to forgive the loans that Cardinal Wolsey had extracted from them in 1522 and 1523 to cover the costs of Henry's military adventures in France. All together these loans had totaled some

£352,000; that was a crushing sum, and it had fallen most heavily on the merchants and landowning knights and gentry from among whom the membership of the House of Commons was mainly drawn. The members of that house were not happy, naturally, when they learned with certainty what many of them had long suspected, that Wolsey's "loans" had not been loans at all but a confiscation; they were never going to see their money again. But the king's lieutenants had taken care, as usual, to assure that Commons was dominated by pliant and cooperative men— Henry's new lieutenant Thomas Cromwell probably conspicuous among them—and to exclude those who might prove resistant to the Crown's demands. No doubt the members were relieved at not being asked to vote new taxes or loans. In due course Henry got what he wanted: the loans were written off the books.

None of this explains why Parliament had been called. The king didn't really *need* a formal forgiveness of the debt he owed his subjects; he could more easily have simply continued to decline to repay. That he had something more in mind became apparent when other items of Crown business were brought to the members' attention. In the six weeks that it remained in session, after much disputation and considerable difficulty in the House of Lords, Parliament was presented with and ultimately approved three statutes laying down new rules for the clergy. One put limits on the fees that could be charged for the probating of wills, a traditional responsibility of the church's courts. Another specified how much could be charged for funerals. The third imposed restrictions on "pluralism" (the holding of multiple assignments or "livings" by a single churchman), on "nonresidence" (failure to be physically present at a living), and on the involvement of the clergy in trade and farming. Stern and unfamiliar penalties were imposed: a fine of £20 (a sum exceeding the annual income of many gentry families) for obtaining from Rome a license of the kind that traditionally had made nonresidence lawful, of £70 (plus the surrender of all income from the livings in question) for even requesting a dispensation to hold more livings than the new law permitted. These measures were entirely appropriate, being aimed at the correction of real abuses, but the bishops and abbots who made up a substantial minority of the Lords found them deeply objectionable. The problem was not that the hierarchy refused to acknowledge the need for change; many bishops and abbots were by this time imposing reforms of their own where they had the authority to do so, and the Canterbury Convocation was in the process of tightening the traditional rules. The problem, rather, was constitutional: the fact that the secular government—Parliament and the king acting through Parliament—was intruding itself into what had always been the business of the church.

In practical terms, the effect of the statutes would be limited, almost trivial. But the principle upon which they were based—that Parliament could set the rules by which the church operated—was potentially revolutionary. And because the kinds of dispensations that were being turned into crimes came from Rome (the reason for punishing those receiving the dispensations, rather than those who issued them, was that the recipients were within reach of English law), the ultimate target was the papacy. Though we do not know where the idea for this legislation originated—whether in a Commons venting its frustration with clerical practices, or with Henry and his advisers—it could not have been enacted without the king's consent. Frustrated by the failure of his divorce suit, he had been threatening for months to retaliate against Rome. Now he was doing so, albeit in a distinctly limited way that involved almost no risk. As soon as the statutes were approved—certain controversial provisions had to be removed to get them through the Lords—he sent Parliament home. He did not end it, however—rather, he "prorogued" it, declaring an intermission but leaving himself the option of recalling it whenever he wished without having to arrange another election. This suggests that he expected to be needing it again before very long—that he had something more in mind. It suggests as well that he was satisfied with the current membership of the Commons, which had shown itself willing to do his bidding.

Statutes of such limited immediate effect cannot have been intended to precipitate a showdown with Rome. By touching on fundamental constitutional issues, however, they demonstrated that Henry's threats were not empty. He was simultaneously asserting and testing his own strength, taking care not to overreach: when the possibility of closing some monasteries was raised in Parliament and drew a fiery response from Bishop John Fisher, the idea was quickly withdrawn. Meanwhile the king began applying pressure from other directions as well. He got a promise of support for his divorce case from Francis I of France, who had seen early on that it would be better for him if England's royal house ceased to be connected by marriage to the Hapsburgs. Henry's objective continued to be nothing more radical than the nullification of his marriage and the freedom to make Anne Boleyn his wife and with her produce children whom the world would accept as legitimate. When he learned that the emperor Charles and Pope Clement were together at Bologna—actually sharing the same palace, drawing together in the afterglow of the most recent expulsion of Francis's armies from Italy—he dispatched envoys to join them and try to achieve an accord that would include the annulment of his marriage. The talent that he put into this delegation suggests either that his hopes were high or that he was determined to leave no stone unturned to bring the pope around. At its head was the Earl of Wiltshire, who in addition to being one of the king's most experienced and trusted diplomats happened to be the father of Anne Boleyn (which explains why he had recently been promoted from viscount to earl). With him went the new bishop of London, chosen for that post because he had proved himself dependable on the divorce question, along with a clutch of legal scholars and lesser clergymen. One of the most obscure of these would soon emerge as a leading figure of the Tudor century.

This was Thomas Cranmer, an archdeacon and former Cambridge academic who just months before had been living quietly as a tutor and scholar. When Henry had made a visit to the abbey at Waltham and accommodations there were found to be limited, two court officers, the king's secretary Stephen Gardiner and his almoner Edward Fox, were lodged in a nearby house. Gardiner and Fox were priests (we earlier encountered the former as leader of one of the king's embassies to Rome), and at this point both were deeply involved in trying to help the king persuade the pope and the world that he was entitled to an annulment. When they fell into conversation with Cranmer, who happened to be living in the same house, he made clear his support of the king's position and offered an idea that caught their fancy. He suggested that, to bolster his position, Henry should get statements of support from university theologians. When Gardiner and Fox mentioned this idea to the king, he ordered that Cranmer be brought to him at Greenwich. When he had heard Cranmer out—heard his proposal for a shift from the arena of law, where Henry was making no headway, to that of academic debate—the king declared that here was a man who had "the sow by the right ear." At age forty Cranmer suddenly found himself vaulted from rural obscurity into royal service, assigned first to searching for texts supporting the king's suit, then to the Earl of Wiltshire's mission to Bologna. Thus was launched a career that would catapult Cranmer to the top of the hierarchy, change the character of the English church more profoundly than Henry himself could possibly have intended, and take many a strange turn before coming to its literally fiery end.

Thomas Boleyn and his retinue took with them to Bologna a rich array of offerings for the pope if he would see reason as King Henry saw it. From the start, however, things did not go well. Boleyn's suitability for this mission had been questioned—as Anne's father, he had a peculiarly intimate interest in the issues under discussion—but Henry had insisted that no other man could be so motivated to help him achieve his goal. Arriving at their destination, the Englishmen found pope and emperor ensconced together in friendship, Clement's outrage of a few years earlier buried and apparently forgotten. The pope showed himself, as always, to be not only friendly toward the English but eager to offer his cooperation. The generally good-humored emperor, by contrast, was stiff-necked and unyielding. He appears to have been motivated, throughout the long conflict over the divorce, less by affection for his aunt Catherine or concern for the honor of his extended family than by a visceral dislike for Henry, who over the years had shown himself to be a tiresomely overbearing and patronizing uncle-in-law and (during the period when Charles was betrothed to Princess Mary) prospective father-in-law. It is scarcely plausible that Charles cared enough about Catherine in any personal way to put himself permanently at odds with England for her sake; aunt and nephew did not know each other well, he having paid her little attention during his youthful visits to the English court. Throughout his life the long-faced, lantern-jawed emperor showed little inclination to be sentimental about his relatives on either side. When another of his aunts was cast aside by her husband the King of Denmark, he did nothing for her and took little interest in her case. Nor for that matter would Charles show much interest in Henry's continued bad treatment of Catherine after he divorced her and married Anne Boleyn. In fact, the vehemence and persistence of Charles's objections to Henry's divorce are somewhat mysterious. Pride may have been part of it: once he took a position, an emperor could not have wanted to be seen as backing down. The fact that during the years when the divorce was a live issue he had the upper hand over the nettlesome Francis of France, and so had no pressing need for the friendship of England, must also have been a factor. In later years, when his need was greater, Charles would actively curry favor with the English court. Henry for his part would respond positively to Charles's overtures whenever doing so suited his own interests.

Whatever his reasons, when faced with the visitors from England Charles assumed the mask of cold and arrogant emperor. He was offended by the presence of the delegation's leader, the father of the very woman—the "concubine," as Charles's ambassador to the English court called Anne in his reports—who was the cause of all the trouble. When Boleyn tried to speak, Charles brusquely cut him off. "Stop, sir," he said in French. "Allow your colleagues to speak. You are a party to the cause." Boleyn answered in the same language. He had come to Italy, he said, not as a father seeking favor for his daughter but as representative of the king of England, who hoped for the emperor's support but would continue to seek justice whether he received that support or not. In return for his friendship, he told Charles, Henry was prepared to pay him 300,000 crowns—the sum that had come to England as Catherine's dowry—and to support Catherine for the rest of her life in a fashion appropriate to her birth and her status as Dowager Princess of Wales. This proposal gave Charles a new excuse to take offense. He answered that he was not a tradesman and his aunt's honor was not for sale; that the divorce case was now before the pope where it belonged; and that he intended to accept the pope's judgment whatever it proved to be.

Things went more smoothly but no more productively with Pope Clement. Henry had authorized his envoys to offer Clement not only a substantial amount of money—at least as much as they had offered Charles, surely—but England's participation in a crusade against the Ottoman Turks. This last was no small point. Just months before, Sultan Suleiman the Magnificent had carried his penetration of central Europe to the very gates of Vienna, where he had been turned back after encountering not only masses of troops commanded by Charles and his brother Ferdinand but—what may have been more decisive—outlandishly bad weather. It is essential to keep in mind, in tracing the endless intrigues of Charles and Francis and Henry, that they took place at a time when the Turks, having overrun first Constantinople and then the Balkans and finally Hungary, seemed entirely capable of breaking through into Germany, possibly of overrunning the whole of central Europe. Clement was not the first pope to attempt to create a confederacy with which to oppose the Turkish threat and he would not be the last, but it had been generations since such an idea had had the power to pull Europe's leading powers together. In 1530 in Bologna it lacked the power to pull even the pope where he felt he must not go. Boleyn and his troupe returned to England with nothing more substantial than fresh assurances of the pope's goodwill.

Henry meanwhile was pursuing Cranmer's idea of showing learned opinion across Europe to be on his side. His agents, supplied with their master's theological arguments and abundant supplies of cash, were dispatched to the universities of Italy, France, and Germany. What ensued reflected badly on everyone, not least on Henry himself. Even in England, where to his offers of money the king could add an unrivaled power to make good on promises and threats, getting a favorable opinion out of the theology faculties of the two universities proved an awkward business. Fights broke out in Cambridge, and the women of Oxford stoned three of Henry's men. In Italy, where at Henry's request Pope Clement had issued a "breve" urging anyone who was consulted to express himself freely, the search went no better. In the end Henry claimed to have received the support of the universities at Bologna, Ferrara, and Padua, but the process had been so stained with bribery, and the reality of the support was so dubious, that no impartial observer could possibly have taken any of it seriously. In Germany the response was if anything worse: not only the universities in Catholic southern Germany but even the leading radical reformers declared against the divorce. Martin Luther himself, while insisting that the marriage of Henry and Catherine was valid beyond question, suggested that Henry might follow the example of the patriarchs of the Bible and take a second wife. (Even the pope at one point floated such a proposal, later conceding that he lacked the authority to approve any such thing.) None of this was of the slightest use, or interest, to Henry.

The great academic battleground turned out to be France, which had fourteen universities and a king who could always be depended on to fish in troubled waters. Henry's agents had spread out across the landscape, dispensing money as they went, while Henry himself sought ways to put Francis's support to the fullest possible use. Francis professed his eagerness to help—what he really wanted, as always, was to keep Henry and Charles at each other's throats—explaining however that he dared not act too boldly so long as his two sons, who had been Charles's hostages since the French defeat at Pavia four years earlier, remained in custody in Spain. This was, in effect, an invitation to bribery. Charles wanted two million crowns in ransom. And, Francis having broken virtually every promise he had made in securing his own release, Charles demanded payment in cash. Two million crowns was more than the French treasury contained or could raise. Henry obliged by sending Francis 400,000 crowns (it was a loan, presumably) and allowing him to postpone indefinitely the repayment of a previous 500,000-crown debt. With this Francis got his sons back and, as good as his word for once, he joined Henry in seeking a favorable opinion from the theologians.

But even two kings applying pressure could accomplish little. In Paris months of struggle culminated in the issuance of a supposedly scholarly endorsement, but it was of highly questionable validity. Having been drawn up not by the theology faculty but at Francis's instructions, it had little impact anywhere. Similarly ambiguous results were all that could be extracted from the universities at Orleans and Toulouse, and a final humiliation occurred when a decree favorable to Henry was issued under the name of the university at Angers but repudiated by that institution's theologians. When it was all over, the king claimed to have a number of universities on his side. But the squalid means by which his support had been won were known to everyone, including the church authorities in Rome, who knew also that all the arguments in Henry's favor began with the assumption—unproved, unprovable, and denied by the queen—that Catherine's first marriage had been consummated. Nor were the other side's hands clean: Charles had spent heavily to neutralize Henry's bribes. The episode of the universities petered out in March 1530 when the pope, weary of the squabbling, ordered that nothing more was to be written about the English royal marriage. The scholarly judgments obtained at so much trouble and expense were so compromised that Henry never even sent them to Rome.

Blocked everywhere he turned, Henry by midyear was showing signs of deepening discouragement. According to one of his confidants, he complained of having been deceived into pursuing the divorce and said he would never have done so had he foreseen that it would bring him to this pass. Probably he was missing Wolsey at this juncture and finding himself badly in need of a strong new chief minister. Soon, however, he rallied—not only the Boleyns but the champions of radical church re-form had good reason to fear the consequences if England and Rome were reconciled, and so they urged him on. By late summer he was again on the attack, possibly with Cromwell pointing the way. He some-how conceived or was given the idea, for which there was only the murkiest evidence, that a proper understanding of history revealed that no Englishman could rightly be made subject to a foreign court, even the papal court. In September he instructed his agents in Rome to in-form the pope of this revelation and search the papal archives for sup-porting documentation. The ambassadors had never heard of any such principle and so were reluctant to present it to Clement. Their search for corroboration turned up nothing. Henry, meanwhile, the bit in his teeth now, issued on his own authority and without the involvement of Parliament a proclamation forbidding anyone in the kingdom, cleric or layman, to "pursue or attempt to purchase from the court of Rome or elsewhere, nor use, put into execution, divulge or publish any-thing . . . containing matter prejudicial to the high authority, jurisdic-tion and prerogative royal of this his [Henry's] said realm." Possibly this proclamation was intended to prevent anyone from protesting to Rome the statutes that Parliament had enacted late in 1529. Possibly it was in-tended to provide grounds for punishing those bishops, John Fisher most prominent among them, who had already sent such protests. Most certainly it was an act of defiance aimed at the pope, a gesture of a kind not seen before. Vague as it was in referring to "matter prejudicial" to the "prerogative royal," its implication that the church in England was independent of the international church was unmistakable. Not coinci-dentally, just at this time Henry began to assert that England was and had from distant times been no mere kingdom but an *empire*. He wanted to be regarded as equivalent to those Christian emperors of Rome—Constantine the Great foremost among them—who were supposed to have exercised absolute dominion over state and church.

At the end of September Henry took an even more shocking step. He instructed his attorney general to charge fifteen notable members of the English clergy with having violated the praemunire statutes by dealing, in the discharge of their ecclesiastic duties, with Cardinal Wolsey. The concept of praemunire had always been somewhat vague, and in the century since their passage the statutes had almost never been applied. Therefore the accused must have had difficulty understanding precisely what crime they were charged with. The general idea, however, was clear enough and brutally simple: Wolsey had broken the law by serving as a legate accountable to the papal court in Rome—his literal guilt could hardly be questioned, he himself having admitted it as soon as he was accused—and therefore anyone who had done business with Wolsey as legate had to be equally guilty. By extension, anyone involved in the administration of England's ecclesiastical courts was now subject to punishment in spite of the fact that those courts had been, for clergy and laymen alike, an integral part of life in England as far back as the records reached. In terms of simple justice the whole proceeding was even more ridiculous than the original praemunire charges against Wolsey. Even if there were reasons for eliminating the ecclesiastical courts (not even the king was suggesting any such thing—the courts performed essential functions and would continue to do so long after England's separation from Rome), to retroactively criminalize their operations was contrary to common sense.

The shabbiness of the whole proceeding was further apparent in the fact that almost all of the accused men (eight bishops and three abbots among them) were conspicuous opponents of the divorce. John Fisher was one of them, at the center of the fray as always. Being charged in this way must have been frightening all the same. Praemunire was a weighty offense: lesser treason, punishable with loss of freedom and possessions. And the difficulties of presenting a defense, already overwhelming with the king driving the prosecution, were compounded by Wolsey's decision, almost a year earlier, to throw himself on the king's mercy and hope for the best. In fact, Wolsey *was* treated with something like leniency after he submitted. Though expelled from the government and deprived of his most richly remunerative offices, he remained archbishop of York, traveled to York for the first time since becoming the city's primate a decade and a half before, and was making plans for a grossly belated but grandiose consecration ceremony there. But his acceptance of guilt created a presumption that his colleagues must also be guilty.

At least some of the accused—Fisher without question, probably others as well—would have defended themselves rather than follow Wolsey's example. And their defense would have been substantial, even if not successful in terms of the final judgment produced. Perhaps for that reason the matter never came to trial. Cromwell, in corresponding with Wolsey, reported that a trial was not going to be necessary because "there is another way devised." This is intriguing: another way had been devised for accomplishing *what*? The answer, almost certainly, is that by this point, October 1530, Henry had decided not to fight the church on the issues but instead to undermine its ability to resist. The way to do that—hit upon, in all likelihood, by the increasingly influential Cromwell—was to frighten the leaders of the church so badly that they became incapable of resistance. Convicting fifteen clergymen of lesser treason for doing nothing more criminal than carrying out their traditional duties would have been an impressive step in that direction. But before the fifteen could be brought to trial, someone—no one knows who with certainty, but again Cromwell is the best guess—came up with a more ambitious idea, one whose breathtaking scope would give it vastly greater impact. *The kingdom's entire clergy*, the church itself in effect, would be accused of praemunire. The idea appears to have been settled on by October, but then set aside to be sprung on the churchmen in the new year. Meanwhile Henry was postponing and postponing again the reconvening of Parliament. It was obvious to all that he had *something* in mind but wasn't yet ready to act. Fisher and his fellow defendants were let off with heavy fines.

Also in October, in a step providing further clues to his thinking, Henry called together a number of leading lawyers and clerics and presented a question for their consideration. The background to his question was a recent action of the pope's. Clement, warned repeatedly that Henry was prepared to act autonomously unless Rome nullified his marriage and no doubt weary of being bullied, had issued an edict stating that no one was to do anything about the divorce or a possible royal remarriage until the papal court issued its decision. To the lawyers and clerics he had assembled, Henry now posed the following: in light of his recently improved understanding of history—the insights enabling him to see that popes had long ago usurped rights belonging to English emperors and that no Englishman should ever be accountable to any external authority—would it not be permissible to ignore the pope? Couldn't the archbishop of Canterbury, primate in England for nearly ten centuries, proceed independently to set aside Henry's false marriage and allow him to take a legitimate wife?

The assembly discussed the question, which it must have found unsettling. Then, evidently assuming that it was being consulted in good faith by a king seeking to do the right thing, it delivered its answer. No, it said, Henry could do no such thing, and neither could the archbishop. This response was inherently uncontroversial: it arose in straightforward fashion from what virtually every European had understood for centuries about how Christendom worked and was organized. When the laws and governance of the church were at issue, the last word belonged to Rome.

Again Henry was blocked. And this time he was blocked not just by a faraway pontiff whom he had never seen but by some of the most learned and respected men in England. His options were narrowing. He could accept a humiliating defeat and yield, abandoning the idea of taking a new wife. Or he could teach his subjects to take him more seriously. Again it came down to a question of fear. If he were to get his way, people had to be afraid to deny him. He had to give them reason to be afraid.

That has to be why he embraced the idea of charging the whole clergy with praemunire. It also has to be why, more than a year after Wolsey had been exiled to the north of England, he was suddenly arrested, charged with high treason (a crime punishable with death), and ordered to return to London and meet his fate.

THE ROYAL HORN OF PLENTY

ONE THING ABOVE ALL ELSE WAS ESSENTIAL TO ANYONE WHO wanted to make his mark in the England of Henry VIII: *access*. Access to the king himself. Intelligence, courage, ability, sound judgment—such gifts were no less important than they are today, but they could have only a limited effect unless displayed before and approved by the man who wore the crown. Access, in turn, was rarely possible unless one went where the king lived, which meant to court. This was true whether one wanted to rise in the government, in the church, or in military service. Without access to the court, nothing out of the ordinary was possible. Thus the desperate lengths to which men would go, the sacrifices they would make, to get positions at court for themselves or for their children.

The power of access is demonstrated by the improbable importance, in the second half of King Henry's reign, of the office of groom of the stool. The core responsibilities of this position seem ridiculous to the modern eye: not only to assure that his majesty always had a "sweet and clear" place for his daily evacuations, not only to collect what he expelled and deliver it to the court physicians for examination, but to wipe the royal backside (using, for the purpose, small triangular pieces of paper). But performing such intimate services required a degree of access that not even the king's senior ministers and private secretaries could equal. Grooms of the stool were so close to the king that they became some of the most influential and therefore envied people in the kingdom. They were made, in effect, general managers not only of the king's toilet but of his private quarters and of everyone employed in those jealously guarded precincts: the knights and esquires of the body (also prized appointments) and the grooms of the chamber. They were entrusted with substantial amounts of Crown money and even, to a considerable extent, with the organization of the king's private life. If they were ever scorned or ridiculed for the nature of the duties that gave their job its name, it is unrecorded.

Access mattered so much because the whole political system was powered by royal largesse. It was the king (along with those to whom he listened) who bestowed the highest offices, the gifts of land, financial favors ranging from annuities and monopolies to exemption from the payment of tariffs, wardships like the one that had brought Plantagenet blood into the Tudor family, and pardons for virtually any kind of offense. Such gifts were the means by which the king built a following and rewarded faithful service. To be eligible for them one had to be known to the king or his most trusted friends, and there was little chance of becoming known except at court.

Admission to the court as most broadly defined—to the crowds that gathered wherever the king was resident—was not difficult. It required little more than a reasonably respectable appearance (meaning the attire appropriate to a gentleman), a plausible claim to have business with the Crown (anything from wares for sale to a dispute in need of resolution), and a sufficient supply of ready cash (bribery being routine). Merely being at court, therefore, was of limited value. Men spent years, even decades, hanging around the court and angling for preferment, only to see little of the king and come away empty-handed in the end. The trick was to get lifted out of the herd; this could be accomplished through good connections, an ability to charm or to make oneself useful, simple good luck, or some combination of these things. The goal was to become one of the lucky few likely to come to the royal mind when lucrative offices needed to be filled or patronage was available to be disbursed. Getting there could take years.

It is estimated that, at the start of Henry VIII's reign, there were at court some 120 positions that ambitious men of good birth could regard as worth having if only because they offered the *possibility* of visibility and advancement. By the end of the reign this number had increased by more than half. The bottom rungs on the ladder of upward mobility were entry-level positions for boys of good family—jobs as pages, for example—and though the ladder extended upward to the Royal Council (and yes, to the groom of the stool), relatively few of those who stood on it received a gentleman's living wage. All the same, at every level vacancies were hungrily fought over, because they could lead to almost anything.

Success at court—by no means always the same kind of success—propelled the careers of virtually every major figure of Henry VIII's reign including Thomas Wolsey, Thomas Howard, Duke of Norfolk, Thomas More, Thomas Cromwell, and Thomas Cranmer. And of yet another successful Thomas, Anne Boleyn's father. The story of the Boleyn family, in fact, illustrates just how fruitful access could be for people who knew how to use it. And how dangerous it could become when the political weather changed.

The Bullens or Boleyns were an old family, farmers in Norfolk for at least two hundred years, and by the early fifteenth century they were established in the capital and rising fast. Geoffrey Boleyn made a fortune in the cloth trade, married a baron's daughter, served as lord mayor of London, and acquired the kinds of rural estates necessary to be upper gentry. In the next generation William Boleyn lived as a country gentleman and married the daughter of an Anglo-Irish earl. By virtue of his wealth or family connections or the two things together, he got his young son Thomas admitted to the court of Henry VII.

Thomas, born in 1477, clearly was intelligent and must have been ambitious as well; he is not known ever to have wasted an opportunity. While still in his early twenties, he took a long step up the social pyramid by marrying a daughter of Thomas Howard, survivor of Bosworth Field, Earl of Surrey, and future Duke of Norfolk. Howard had an abundance of marriageable daughters and is likely to have been pleased to place one of them with a family as prosperous and respectable as the Boleyns. His son-in-law soon began to leave his mark in the records of the court: in 1501, probably the year of Anne's birth, he was present at the wedding of Arthur, Prince of Wales, to Catherine of Aragon, and two years later he was a member of the party that accompanied the young Princess Margaret Tudor northward for her marriage to King James IV of Scotland. As an esquire of the body—proof of excellent access, the body in question being the king's own—he became part of the circle of well-bred young gallants that gave the court of the aging and widowed Henry VII what little luster it retained. When the king died, Boleyn was among the favorites selected for knighthood by his successor. His penetration of Henry VIII's inner circle is not difficult to understand. He was skilled at things that Henry VIII admired—horsemanship, jousting, hawking, and the game of bowls—and by all accounts was a man of exceptional charm.

Sir Thomas, as he could now style himself, was fluent in both French and Latin. This was an essential credential in the world of diplomacy, and early in the new reign he was launched on the series of foreign missions that would punctuate his career. His widening horizons opened up opportunities, too, for his children, Mary, Anne, and George. When the king's younger sister, Princess Mary, embarked for France and marriage to King Louis XII, young Mary Boleyn joined her as a lady-in-waiting. Anne, barely an adolescent, was sent to Brussels in the service of Margaret of Austria, Hapsburg regent of the Netherlands. This last was a particularly coveted posting, as Margaret was a daughter of the Holy Roman emperor Maximilian and her court was among the richest and most elegant in Europe. Both girls were thus positioned to get the kind of continental finish that, when combined with their father's wealth and stature at court and the dash of royal blood that had come to them through their mother, could make them valuable commodities on the aristocracy's marriage market.

Anne had her father's ability to make use of whatever came her way, but her sister did not. The sketchy available information suggests that Mary Boleyn was not a model of chastity even when very young, and that while at the French court she acquired a reputation for easy availability. Whether for that or for some other reason, her sojourn abroad turned out to be short. When the decrepit Louis XII died just weeks after his wedding, his beautiful young widow impulsively married Charles Brandon, one of her brother Henry's closest friends and son of the William Brandon who had died carrying her father's standard at Bosworth Field. When the newlyweds prepared to return to England, it was decided that Mary would return with them and become a lady-in-waiting to Queen Catherine. Anne meanwhile had received high praise from Margaret of Austria, who had overseen the continuation of her education along with that of the four Hapsburg youngsters who were her wards at the time. At this point her father was able to arrange Anne's transfer from Brussels to the French court, where she became close to Francis I's Queen Claude. She remained in France for some six or seven years, until King Henry's 1522 decision to go to war with France made it impossible for her to remain. She took back with her to England a degree of sophistication that gave her a confidence bordering on brashness, arriving at about the same time her sister became the king's mistress. Anne was firmly established as the court's principal adornment when, a few years later, Henry returned Mary to her husband with grants of land as a gesture of thanks. Mary had not exactly been seduced and abandoned, but her example would not have impressed Anne with the benefits of yielding when the king sought a lady's favors.

Anne very nearly disappeared into Ireland. Her father had long been in a dispute with a noble Anglo-Irish family called the Butlers, with both sides claiming the Earldom of Ormond (which had belonged to Thomas's maternal grandfather). King Henry and Wolsey, grasping at a possible solution to this tedious but troublesome squabble, offered Anne to Sir James Butler as a way of uniting the two families and making it possible for them to share the inheritance. The Butlers refused, evidently because they expected a dowry bigger than Anne would provide. And so she remained at court—an exceptionally dazzling lady-in-waiting to Queen Catherine, a model for anyone wanting to keep abreast of the latest fashions—passing through a flirtation with the poet Sir Thomas Wyatt and the indignity of being kept from marrying Henry Percy by the interference of Cardinal Wolsey.

Thomas Boleyn, the value of his diplomatic talents augmented by the king's wish to make him a grateful rather than a resentful father, was ennobled as Viscount Rochford in 1525 and raised to the English and Irish earldoms of Wiltshire and Ormond in 1529. His son George had virtually grown up at court, taking part in the Christmas revels at age ten, becoming a page at twelve and the recipient of offices and even a manor while still barely grown; when Thomas became an earl, George, in his twenties by this time, already an esquire of the body and a junior diplomat, assumed the Rochford title. When the king entered into full pursuit of Anne, the Boleyns became for all practical purposes more the king's family than Queen Catherine and Princess Mary. All the Boleyns were heaped with honors. That their success may have gone to their heads is suggested by their attempt, thwarted by Wolsey, to secure the appointment of a disreputable sister-in-law of Mary Boleyn's as abbess of the convent of Wilton.

In the months just after Wolsey's fall, a triumvirate made up of Thomas Boleyn and the dukes of Norfolk and Suffolk stepped forward to fill the resulting power vacuum. Together the three became the king's most influential advisers, but only briefly; none of them had the political skill or the force of character to hold such a lofty position for long. It mattered little to Boleyn, who by this point had bet everything on his daughter. He and his son could hardly have been less eager than Henry himself for Anne to become queen and produce a royal heir. That would make them the grandfather and only uncle of the next king—positions from which they might aspire to almost anything.

6

A Revolution in the Making

In the weeks following his fall from power, Wolsey took up residence in a community of Carthusian monks not far from the royal palace at Richmond. Ever hopeful that the king would restore him to favor, he seemed determined to stay as close to the court as possible. He had reason for optimism: Henry would occasionally send him gifts, rings usually, and encouraging little messages. Seeking support among the king's peers, royal personages with whom he had dealt regularly while in high office, Wolsey wrote to Francis I and to Francis's mother, to the emperor Charles, and even, at some risk, to the pope. At the same time he involved himself in an apparently serious way in the religious life of his new companions, who "persuaded him from the vainglory of the world and gave him divers hair shirts to wear." He appears to have made a real effort to become a better priest, but the old hunger for power and pomp continued to gnaw.

His chances of rehabilitation were reduced by the number and influence of his enemies at court. Almost everyone with access to the king's ear—Anne Boleyn and her father and brother; Anne's uncle the Duke of Norfolk; Charles Brandon, Duke of Suffolk—detested Wolsey, had no use for the connection with Rome that he personified, and likely would have suffered grievously if he returned to power. Anyone friendly to the cardinal, on the other hand, would have hesitated to say anything in his favor in such an environment. The king is unlikely to have heard anything good about Wolsey, or to have been encouraged to do anything but distrust him and keep him at a distance. That Henry did distrust the cardinal is apparent in the government's interception of Wolsey's correspondence and the questioning of his physician by agents looking for evidence of disloyalty. The discovery that he was writing to foreign royalty did him no good.

It is hardly surprising, therefore, that in the spring of 1530 Wolsey was ordered to pack up and move north to remote districts where his chances of crossing paths with the king would be virtually nil. He went for the first time in his life to York, there taking up with unexpected earnestness the ecclesiastical duties that he had so long ignored, visiting country churches every Sunday and holy day, dispensing alms to the poor, seeing to the repair of decrepit properties, and making it his special interest to counsel troubled families. But in his letters he described himself as profoundly miserable. That he continued to be regarded as one of the most important men in the kingdom—possibly *the* most important after the king himself—was evident in June, when an official letter demanding nullification of the royal marriage was prepared for delivery to Rome. This document, addressed to the pope and intended to show that everyone of importance in England supported the king, was sent to Wolsey before anyone else had signed it, so that his name would appear on it first. It is in the Vatican library in Rome today, dripping with ribbons and seals, Wolsey's name atop all the others. Notable by their absence are the signatures of John Fisher, of other bishops who would soon be complicating the king's life, and of Wolsey's successor as chancellor, Sir Thomas More.

Wolsey made elaborate plans for the ceremony in which he was to be formally installed as archbishop on November 7. On that same day, he ordered, the Northern Convocation (the assembly representing that part of the English clergy under the authority of York rather than Canterbury) would also convene. It was to be a great occasion, an echo of the cardinal's days of glory. But on November 1 a rider set out from the king's palace at Greenwich, bound for York with a warrant for Wolsey's arrest. It charged him with high treason—with engaging, presumably because of his wide-ranging correspondence, in "presumptuous sinister practices." Wolsey, upon being served with the warrant, understood that this was the end. He stopped eating for a time, saying that he preferred a natural death to what awaited him in London. His health was bad (he was afflicted with edema, or dropsy), and though he set out under guard as ordered, traveling on muleback, he made only slow progress. Near Shrewsbury he came down with dysentery and was unable to continue for two weeks. When he reached his next stopping place, the abbey at Leicester, the end was at hand. "Father Abbot," he said upon arrival, "I have come to lay my bones among you." He was put to bed, and a day or two later he opened his eyes to see a familiar face, that of the lieutenant of the Tower of London, who had been sent north to escort him to prison.

"Master Kingston," said the cardinal to this gentleman, "I pray you have me commended to his majesty, and beseech him on my behalf to call to mind all things that have passed between us, especially respecting good Queen Catherine and himself, and then shall his grace's conscience know whether I have offended him or not. He is a prince of most royal courage. Rather than miss any part of his will, he will endanger one half of his kingdom, and I do assure you, I have often kneeled before him, sometimes for three hours together, to persuade him from his appetite, and could not prevail. And Master Kingston, had I but served God as diligently as I have served the king, he would not have given me over in my gray hairs. But this is my just reward for my pains and study, not regarding my service to God but only my duty to my prince."

He died a day later, sixty years of age. He was buried in a nearby church, coincidentally next to the tomb of King Richard III, thereby creating a curiosity that the local people would come to call "the tyrants' sepulcher." In Wolsey's case at least, the name is unfair. He was a gravely flawed man, vain and proud and in love with power and its trappings, but his legacy was far from black. Over many years he had tried repeatedly to bring peace to a Europe endlessly troubled by futile wars, and more than once he had risked his own position in doing so. He had done much to improve the delivery of justice, and he had tried without much success to curtail the enclosures of farmland that were depriving rural families of their livelihood. He had served one of the most willful and self-centered monarchs ever to draw breath, and if the difference in Henry's conduct before the fall of Wolsey and after is any fair measure, Wolsey deserves to be judged, for all his weaknesses and failures, a force for good.

Whatever Henry had planned (a show trial leading to a public execution, probably), the cardinal's passing deprived him of it. If Wolsey had lived to speak in court as he had spoken on his deathbed, he might have given the king cause to regret calling him back from York. Be that as it may, a new year was approaching and the king was laying plans for bigger things than the destruction of his old lieutenant. His time of uncertainty, the period of some three years when he acted by fits and starts and sometimes reversed himself and often seemed paralyzed, was drawing to a close. It had begun with Henry wanting the annulment of his marriage and the freedom to take Anne as his wife. It would end when he showed himself to be openly and unambiguously set on separating his kingdom from the ancient communion of Europe and on making himself a kind of national pope, the supreme spiritual authority over England and its people. Historians disagree as to exactly when Henry stopped wanting just the first thing and started wanting both, which is another way of saying that no one can say for sure. It seems reasonable to conclude, however, that by the time of Wolsey's death, he was seriously considering, if not yet quite committed to, a break with Rome. This would explain the severely hard line that he now began to take, setting out not only to destroy a sickly and ruined old man who almost certainly wished him no harm and could not have done him harm if he did wish it, but to destroy whatever independence the English church actually possessed. A hypothesis in three parts—that by the end of 1530 Henry had decided to separate England from Rome; that he thought it necessary first to break the English hierarchy to his will; and that until the clergy had been subdued, he wanted to keep the divorce proceedings in Rome from moving to a conclusion—makes his actions at this time more intelligible than does any other explanation.

It explains, among other things, the otherwise curious fact that by late 1530 (probably even before the Boleyn delegation's visit to Bologna was known to have ended in failure) Henry's strategy had shifted from trying to get Pope Clement to issue a favorable ruling to trying to keep the pope from doing anything at all. Delay, long a source of frustration, now became an objective. His success in achieving it is reflected in Pope Clement's response to the appeal for action sent to him with Wolsey's signature preceding all the others. This petition, composed before Henry changed tactics, complained that the postponements, equivocations, and evasions of the papal court were depriving England's king of the justice to which he was entitled. It said that Rome's failures could expose England, in the event of the king's death, to the dangers of a disputed succession (his daughter by Catherine of Aragon now being, by the king's reckoning, a bastard). It accused the pope of being biased in Catherine's favor, and it repeated the by-now-familiar threat that the Crown's only recourse might be to proceed independently. By the time this missive reached the pope, Clement was able to reply that he was entirely ready to bring the case to trial, that he had not yet done so because Henry had not appointed anyone to represent him in court, and that the Boleyn party, in departing Bologna, had asked not for action but for more time. All these things were true, and they shed interesting light on the question of who was actually responsible, by this point, for the failure to proceed.

The case remained unsettled as 1531 began and the king put into motion the plan that had taken shape the previous autumn—the threat to charge the whole of the English clergy with violations of the praemunire statutes. The Canterbury convocation was in session at Westminster, and news of the king's threat threw the churchmen first into confusion, then into frightened and angry debate. They had before them the uninspiring example of the late cardinal, who had submitted without complaint when faced with the same charge and in doing so had left them all vulnerable. And they were being urged to submit by their own leader, William Warham, a respected figure after almost thirty years in the see of Canterbury. To his threat of prosecution, Henry added a demand that convocation, as the embodiment of a church that had caused him so much undeserved trouble, should reimburse him for the expenses of the divorce case (all of which had been incurred, as he saw it, because of the pope's refusal to do what was right). It was to do so by repeating a subsidy of £100,000 that Wolsey, in desperate need of money because of Henry's war on France, had wrung out of it in the early 1520s.

After days of debate, convocation offered Henry, in effect, a deal. It would pay him the £100,000 that he demanded (another £18,000 was being extracted from the much smaller York Convocation) in five annual installments, there being no tolerable way of coming up with such an immense amount of cash at once. In return Henry was asked to do two things. First, he was to issue a general pardon so that the praemunire charge would not hang over the heads of the churchmen forever, and provide a written explanation of just what praemunire was, so that in future they would know what actions to avoid. Second, he was to reaffirm the traditional liberties of the church as previously upheld by the Magna Carta and other precedents reaching even further back in time: the clergy's right to operate their courts under their own system of laws, for example, and to provide sanctuary to fugitives.

In the message that conveyed their offer and request to the king, convocation's leaders referred to Henry as the "protector and highest head" of the church in England—generous words, one would have thought, in light of the church's theoretical freedom from secular control. Henry soon let it be known that this was not enough. He wanted to be called "*sole* protector and *supreme* head of the English church and clergy." Here was a revolution in the making, and the terms this time were far more portentous than any mere quibble over pluralities or the cost of funerals. Henry was demanding what no king of England, no monarch of any European kingdom, had ever dared to claim. And there was more: he wanted an acknowledgment that he had "cure" of the souls of his subjects—that responsibility for delivering those souls to God rested not with the bishops, not with the pope, but with him. This was an entirely new theory of kingship, one that turned upside down what every Englishman had been taught about the relationship of church and state.

Four days after Henry made these demands, convocation accepted them in a way that left everything shrouded in ambiguity. In its final form, the clergy's message to the king described him as supreme head "as far as the law of Christ allows." It would have been just as clear if it had declared that the king is supreme head except if he isn't; its meaning depended entirely upon what "the law of Christ" was, and that of course could be a matter of opinion. It is unclear whose words these were. If they came from John Fisher or someone like him, they must have been intended to neuter the king's flamboyant claim without being unnecessarily combative. If they were Thomas Cromwell's words, or the words of some other member of Henry's inner circle of advisers, they were a subtle way of trying to seduce the clergy into abandoning a thousand years of tradition. Possibly they were the work of someone like old Archbishop Warham, someone not definitely on one side or the other, in which case they were simply an attempt to avoid or at least postpone a showdown. On the whole, the result appears to have been something approaching a victory for the clergy in all respects except financial. The king got his £100,000, but his new title of supreme head had been so hedged as to mean anything or nothing. Other changes left him with less than the cure of souls—convocation's final draft, accepted by a silent king, restored that responsibility to the clergy—and some of the things that he had demanded were omitted altogether.

In the end Henry granted the requested pardon. In doing so, he explicitly approved the continuing operation of the ecclesiastical courts, thereby confirming the lawfulness of the very activities for which the churchmen had been threatened with prosecution. Significantly for the future—the omission must have seemed ominous—he ignored convocation's request for a reaffirmation of its traditional rights and liberties.

The churchmen, if confused and frightened, had not been entirely cowed. They had shown themselves to be unwilling to yield to whatever the king demanded. Cuthbert Tunstal, a bishop known for his learning and virtuous personal life and so high in the king's regard that he had recently been promoted from London to the wealthy northern diocese of Durham, sent Henry a letter in which he pointedly objected to the royal claim of supreme headship. He argued—with the evidence of history overwhelmingly on his side—that the kings of England had always been masters in the temporal realm, never in the spiritual. Departure from this tradition, Tunstal warned, would destroy the unity of the Christian world. The king responded cordially but in startling terms. Of course I am not the head of the church, he said; Christ is the head of the church. I as king merely have jurisdiction over the church in England in Christ's name. Specifically, Henry said, his supremacy gave him final authority over the election of bishops, the property of the church, and the "courts Christian." He blithely assured Tunstal that there was nothing revolutionary in any of this, that he was simply stating what was obviously true: that "we and all other princes be at this day chief and heads of the spiritual men." Tunstal must have been taken aback. Though almost from time immemorial England's kings had enjoyed the right to nominate bishops, in principle such appointments were the pope's business, and no one chosen by the king could actually be consecrated until the necessary approvals were received from Rome. And though over the centuries innumerable disputes had erupted between Crown and church over property and jurisdiction and other matters, not even the most ambitious kings had ever claimed to be able to overrule the pope on every question. Henry, in his letter to Tunstal, was expanding his role in nearly the most radical way imaginable.

The churchmen understood that, though they had survived a skirmish, further and probably more dangerous struggles lay ahead. A letter signed by seventeen members of the Southern Convocation's lower house provides a rare glimpse (it survives only because Charles V's ambassador to England procured a copy and sent it to Spain) into how unsettled the situation of ordinary members of the clergy had become by this time. The letter takes much the same line as Tunstal's, affirming the independence of the church, the authority of the pope, the traditional arrangements between the temporal and spiritual powers, and the importance of preserving unity. The seventeen signatories say that, in conceding to Henry the title of supreme head, they had intended no repudiation of tradition. They conclude, oddly and rather pathetically, by disavowing in advance anything that they might later say or do to repudiate what they are here affirming. Any such later words or actions, their letter says, will be the work of the devil or the result of their own weakness. Such sentiments could have been put into writing only by men of passionate conviction who were almost desperately afraid both of what lay ahead and of how they themselves were likely to respond to retribution. That their fears were justified soon became clear: several were arrested not long after their letter arrived at court, and all who survived imprisonment (some did not) ultimately accepted all the king's claims.

Though Henry had accepted the insertion of the words "so far as the law of Christ allows," from the start he either ignored them or interpreted them in his own favor, displaying more and more boldness in his approach to religious issues. He fancied himself a majestically knowledgeable theologian, loved to engage in discussions of doctrine and dogma, and invariably concluded such discussions by proclaiming the truth to everyone involved. Soon after his exchanges with the Canterbury Convocation, he attended and actively involved himself in the heresy trial (such proceedings, historically rare in England, would occur with increasing frequency in the superheated environment of the early

1530s) of a preacher who had got into trouble by echoing the beliefs of the German reformers, most of which Henry abhorred. Examining a list of the accused man's alleged heresies, Henry saw at its top the statement that the pope was not the head of the whole church. "This proposition cannot be counted as heretical," Henry declared, "for it is both true and certain." Paying no attention to the rest of the list—it would inevitably, being Lutheran, have contained many items that the king regarded as intolerable—he ordered the lucky man set free. Thus did he exercise his new authority and shed a confusingly distorted light on the kinds of opinions he was and was not prepared to approve. For the first time in history the king was defining heresy and deciding who should be punished for it.

With similar aplomb he refused to allow a French abbot of the order of Cistercians to enter England for the purpose of visiting and inspecting the houses of the English Cistercian monks. The abbot's mission could hardly have been more routine: it was to determine whether his order's strict rule was being sufficiently observed and whether corrective measures might be in order. Such visitations had been a familiar and essential element of monastic life since the time of Saint Benedict early in the sixth century. The fact that the English houses were to be inspected by a French abbot reflected the international character of the order and indeed of the church, and it was mirrored by the use of English monks to inspect houses in France and elsewhere. But now Henry declared that no foreigner could have jurisdiction in his kingdom. If anyone was going to pass judgment on English religious houses, it would be Englishmen acting on his authority. It was yet another way for him to broadcast the fact that the old rules no longer applied, and that the new rules would be of the king's making and entirely in his favor.

The success of every such gesture demonstrated to Henry and to his subjects lay and clerical that he could do very nearly whatever he wished. The absence of serious resistance must have added to his growing self-assurance and to his willingness to go further. Rome offered no objections because Pope Clement—irresolute by nature and faced with the near-disintegration of the German church, plus the Turkish threat in eastern Europe and the Mediterranean, plus the ongoing conflict between Charles and Francis—still hoped to avoid provoking him. Henry had quieted the English clergy—which was receiving no leadership, not so much as a word of guidance, either from Rome or from Warham—by alternating between intimidation and confusion while casting an artful veil of ambiguity over his own intentions. As for the people at large, little had happened thus far to cause them serious concern. Squabbles between the Crown and the pope were a centuries-old story, and thus far they had always left the traditional order intact. This latest unpleasantness—which in any case had had no impact on everyday worship or on what was taught by the parish priests—could be expected to end in the usual way.

Suddenly the tide was running strongly in Henry's favor. In a stroke of sheer good luck for the king, a remarkably high number of bishoprics were now becoming vacant, thirteen between 1529 and 1536, along with the position of abbot at several of the most important monasteries. Any pope would have hesitated to deny any English king his choice of candidates to fill these positions, and Clement was still looking for every opportunity to make Henry think of him as a friend. And so Henry encountered no difficulty in filling the sees of England with men who had proved their loyalty to him. Stephen Gardiner, his secretary, became bishop of Winchester. Edward Lee, his almoner, replaced Wolsey as Archbishop of York. The dependable John Stokesley became bishop of London, and so forth. These and the king's other nominees applied to Rome for the traditional bulls signifying approval. When the bulls arrived in England, Henry accepted them without comment. Here again the interested parties must have been confused. Henry was already claiming, as he had done in his response to Tunstal, that as a matter of principle he had the authority to appoint England's bishops. But he was continuing to follow the old forms. He was either unsure of how to proceed—which would have been justified, considering the consequences that a conclusive break with Rome might bring down on his head—or simply biding his time.

Things were also turning in Henry's favor on the continent. If he was in fact determined by this time to break with Rome, he was also, necessarily, considering the possibility that such a step would lead to war. As a schismatic king, he could expect to be excommunicated, and as an excommunicated king he would be fair game for invasion by whatever forces the pope and the emperor Charles and possibly Francis I might send against him. He had good reason to be grateful, therefore, for the friendliness that Francis was continuing to extend. He could rejoice that Charles was adrift in a sea of troubles, so threatened by the Turks and overextended in Italy that he was forced to make peace with the newly Lutheran princes of northern Germany—heretics, as the Catholic Charles saw them, badly in need of being disciplined.

Henry became forty that year—still a strong, hearty man but past his physical prime. He was troubled now with the thigh ulcers that would plague him intermittently, at times causing excruciating pain, for the rest of his days. He was also suffering from severe headaches. Though his treasury continued to be painfully low in funds—the Crown was able to meet its obligations only because of the money extorted from the church and the "pension" that Francis was once again paying to keep the English out of France—Henry still regarded all the money in the kingdom as his to do with as he chose. His extravagance was remarkable: he wore a jacket that cost as much as a farm; bought a thousand pearls in a single day; lost thousands of pounds betting on cards, dice, tennis, dominoes, and bowls; and was building and expanding more palaces—Whitehall, Richmond, St. James's, and many others—than any king could possibly have needed or even used.

At the center of his life was Anne Boleyn, living though supposedly not sleeping with him. (This can strain credulity, considering that they had by this time been waiting for the divorce for four years and were at a level of intimacy that had Henry rhapsodizing about kissing Anne on her "pretty dukkys"—her breasts.) She was a high-spirited, temperamental woman, beginning to feel the strain of the king's long struggle to become free to marry, so uninhibited in her arguments with Henry as to reduce him to baffled exasperation. He complained that Catherine had never spoken to him as brazenly as Anne did, but he remained in her thrall. Through the first half of 1531 Henry and Anne and Catherine all lived under the same roof, Catherine stubbornly following along as the court moved from place to place. Anne found this intolerable, not surprisingly, and treated Catherine and her retainers with excoriating contempt. Anne was given lavish living quarters adjacent to the king's and allowed to spend freely. She could not have dominated the court more completely if she were already married to Henry and the mother of a royal son, but she was popular neither with the public (rumors circulated that gangs of commoners were plotting to murder her) nor with those members of the court who were not part of her family-centered, ardently antichurch faction. The comptroller of the king's household, Sir Henry Guildford, earned a small share of immortality when Anne became angry with him and said that when she became queen she would have him dismissed. Guildford replied that he would save her the trouble and quit on the spot. He refused to relent even when Henry asked him to pay no attention to "women's talk."

Early one morning in July Henry rode off from Windsor Castle, leaving Catherine behind and not saying goodbye. They would never meet again. When she wrote, he became apoplectically angry, shouting that she should be ordered not to send any more letters. But if this was a nerve-rackingly tense time for the king, for his subjects it was becoming dangerous. Anyone whose beliefs did not conform exactly to the king's was likely to find himself in trouble. To continue believing things that all Englishmen had been expected to believe since Christianity first came to their island was suddenly to put oneself in jeopardy, because the king no longer believed all those things and was determined that everyone should follow his lead. On the other hand, to repudiate too many of the traditional beliefs was to risk another kind of trouble, because the king still believed strongly, and would continue to believe strongly, that most of those things remained true and whoever denied them should be subject to the penalties prescribed for heresy. Anyone with serious religious beliefs of any kind would have needed nerves of iron not to feel unsettled.

No one's situation was more difficult than that of the man who had replaced Wolsey as lord chancellor, Sir Thomas More. He had not wanted to become chancellor, understanding from the start that his thinking about the divorce was irreconcilable with that of the king. But Henry had assured him that their differences on that one subject would not matter and prevailed on him to accept. But it *did* matter, as did More's conviction that without the old church Christian civilization would dissolve. He had never been a fervent papalist; early in his public career, when Henry was writing enthusiastically in support of the pope and against Luther, More had cautioned him to be more restrained in his language. In addition to being head of the church, More had observed, the pope was the ruler of a state and therefore a potential adversary. But More was a committed Roman Catholic all the same—Henry did not yet know how committed.

Because he was completely lacking in Wolsey's craving for power and also out of step with the king's thinking, More as chancellor never achieved a fraction of the influence that his predecessor had long wielded. By late 1531 he was not even part of the king's inner circle and barely had a voice in the making of policy. He focused instead on the judicial responsibilities of his office—the chancellor was a judge among other things, and More's background equipped him superbly for the bench—and on doing what he could to turn back the flood of heretical ideas that had been coming across the Channel since the advent of Martin Luther. Those ideas, as More saw it, were putting millions of souls in danger of damnation.

His role as a suppressor of heresy put More further at odds with the king because their views on what constituted heresy were diverging radically. And Henry compounded his chancellor's difficulties—we can only wonder if he was acting with malicious intent—by requiring him to present arguments to Parliament that More himself did not accept. More did as instructed, but he did it in a coolly impersonal way, refusing to answer when asked for his own opinion.

It was an impossible situation, an explosion waiting to happen.

WINDOWS OF OPPORTUNITY

THAT THE ENGLAND OF THE LATE MIDDLE AGES WAS A society of rigid class distinctions is hardly a secret. The nature of those distinctions, however, is considerably less obvious. Though a baron was not the equal of an earl, and a yeoman was not quite the same as a farmer, differences of this kind were subtle and of limited importance. Basically there was just one great line of separation, but it was a chasm so deep and wide, dividing the population into such grossly unequal parts, that the people on the two sides might almost have been living on different planets.

At the pinnacle, below the royal family but above everyone else, were the fifty-odd holders of hereditary titles. Dukes were highest of all (the name derives from the Latin for "leader" and was long reserved for the sons of kings), followed in descending order by marquesses (so called because they were supposedly responsible for governing marks or marches or borderlands), earls (an Anglo-Saxon word, the equivalent of count), viscounts, and finally mere barons. The proudest of these dignitaries were those with Norman forebears who had come to England with William the Conqueror (the Percy earls of Northumberland, for example, and the de Vere earls of Oxford) and those whose family trees had been injected with royal blood via marriage (the route that carried the Howards from obscurity to the Dukedom of Norfolk in just a few decades).

Below the titled nobility, but not always far below in wealth or even status, were the landowning families that made up the local elites ("lords of the manor" in spite of not actually being barons) in every part of the kingdom. They called themselves the gentry—people of "gentle" birth— because they thought of themselves as having, and in fact often did have, antecedents quite as good as the titled families; many were descended from the daughters and younger sons of nobles. This is a crucial fact about English society not only in the Tudor era but for centuries after: the closest thing to a middle class identified with—regarded itself as related to and descended from—those above it on the pyramid of rank. This was true even of those families that had climbed to wealth through the window of opportunity that opened briefly when the Black Death wiped out half the population, and of families that got rich in business and (like the Boleyns) used their winnings to buy country estates. Such families wanted no reminders of their origins and would have recoiled at any suggestion that they might ever have had any connection with the masses of landless workers. The word "gentleman," accordingly, carried a potency that it has long since lost, at least in America. It bore no necessary relation to wealth or position or even to having good manners (though all those things were prized). Rather its use was a claim to being special by birth, special in ways that only ancestry made possible.

This was the great divide: the line separating not just the rich from the poor or the powerful from the weak but the few who were inherently superior from the many who, having no family at all by the standards of the time, did not matter. To achieve a position of prominence in public life, it was not necessary to be noble—nobles were far too few for that much exclusivity to be possible. But it was *absolutely* necessary to be "gentle." Without that qualification, all the best doors remained shut.

With one conspicuous and important exception: the church. For centuries, and well into the reign of Henry VIII, it had been the one ladder by which young men of virtually any background could rise even to positions of the greatest power.

The pattern was set early, if not in the most appealing of ways. Ranulf Flambard began life in Normandy as the son of a simple parish priest (marriages of clergymen still being arguably lawful) but rose to become the strong (and brutishly ruthless) chief agent of King William II as well as bishop of Durham. Roger, bishop of Salisbury, had origins so obscure that no one knows where he was born, or when or to whom; but in the twelfth century he became Henry I's chancellor and most trusted adviser. Thomas Becket grew up as the sports-loving son of a London tradesman and took holy orders only after his father's financial ruin made it necessary for him to find employment, and he, too, became both chancellor and archbishop.

There is no mystery about the rise of men like these to heights that were utterly inaccessible to laymen of similar background. For centuries after the Conquest, education remained almost exclusively the domain of the church: even the universities were founded by clerics and operated by clerics mainly for the purpose of training more clerics. The aristocracy, by contrast, continued to live by a code that exalted martial values above all others; in their world, education beyond the rudiments long seemed to have little point or purpose. It was in the church alone, therefore, that kings could find the levels of literacy and intellectual sophistication needed for diplomacy, the creation and functioning of a system of justice, financial management, and general administration. And priests offered the further attraction of not having to be paid, no small consideration as money was always in short supply; they could be rewarded with appointments to ecclesiastical livings, any number of which might be held by a single churchman. The most valuable of the king's servants could be made bishops, which had the great advantage of putting the church itself, with all its wealth and influence, in the hands of men whose loyalty to the Crown rarely had to be doubted.

The church, for its part, kept the ladder of mobility in good working order by offering nearly unlimited opportunities, first in education and then in educational and ecclesiastical management, to the most able and ambitious of its recruits. Noble and gentle credentials were useful, inevitably, but rarely to the exclusion of talent. Communities of monks and nuns even elected their own leaders, commonly making their choices on the basis of merit. The almost egalitarian character of many of the church's institutions must have been rooted at least in part in the belief, integral to Catholic doctrine, that no human being is more or less a child of God than any other and the mighty have no better chance of salvation than the destitute. In part, no doubt, openness to the advancement of the lowborn was also a function of institutional self-interest: both the church itself and the Crown obviously benefited when talent was given the fullest possible scope. Aristocratic resentment at the rise of clerical leaders with roots in the peasantry, to the extent that it existed, was tempered by the clerical commitment to celibacy. An archbishop might dispense more money than a duke, but neither his title nor his wealth could be made hereditary, even if he had children.

As the amorphous phenomenon known to us as the Renaissance burst upon Italy and spread north, the scholarly apparatus of the church became the conduit through which it was introduced to England. And it found fertile ground there, thanks mainly to the ecclesiastical meritocracy. The most respected English bishop of Henry VIII's reign, John Fisher, became a member of the King's Council, founded two colleges at Cambridge, and by the time of the king's separation from Catherine of Aragon was known throughout Europe as an advocate of reform from within, a champion of the new humanist learning, and a man of impeccable probity. All this after starting life as the son of a Yorkshire cloth merchant. England's first great scholar of classical Greek, Thomas Linacre, was one of a number of eminent scholar-churchmen of whose family background virtually nothing is known. As for William Warham, the man who headed both church and government just before Thomas Wolsey's emergence, we know his father's name but nothing of his occupation. We know only that the family included a carpenter and a maker of candles.

With all this as background, there could be nothing truly astonishing about the emergence of the butcher's son Wolsey as chancellor of England, archbishop of York, member of the College of Cardinals, candidate for the papacy, and master of international politics. He was in fact a familiar kind of figure, having received his first degree at such a precocious age—fifteen—that he became known as "the boy bachelor," proceeded from there to an M.A., to ordination at twenty-five, to doctoral studies in theology (an unusual choice even then for a young cleric hoping for a career in government, suggesting that the young Wolsey had no such aspirations), and finally to the obscure jobs that led him into royal service. It is impossible to doubt that every step of his rise had been the result of ability and hard work.

If Wolsey was a great manager and administrator, he was certainly not the first churchman of whom that could be said. If for more than a decade he exercised so much power as to be called *alter rex,* the other king, again he was not unprecedented. If he became a great patron of education and the arts, if he showed serious commitment to the improvement of the justice system, and if he even tried to address abuses of the church's prerogatives (an area in which he was gravely handicapped by the burden of his own bad example), in all these things he was typical of the English church's hierarchy at the time. That hierarchy included many men of talent and learning. If few were as saintly (or as pugnacious) as John Fisher, virtually all set a better example than Wolsey.

It was his flaws, his failures, that really set Wolsey apart. His way of life was magnificent on a scale never before seen in England. It centered on a court of some five hundred persons (his kitchens alone employed seventy-three men and boys), and it shifted back and forth between palaces at Hampton Court and York Place that surpassed any of the royal family's homes. His every public move became a procession, a display of opulence, with gentlemen and nobles carrying before him the gold and silver emblems of his great offices and waiting on him at table. Some of this was appropriate to the king's chief minister in an age when royalty was expected to offer constant proofs of its wealth and power, and a man in Wolsey's position *needed* an army of assistants to deal with an unending stream of visitors and all the business of church and state. But inevitably it drew mutterings from almost every direction. And some of Wolsey's indulgences were simply indefensible. If it was not scandalous of him to hire an Italian sculptor to build his tomb—and to insist that that tomb surpass the one in which the remains of Henry VII and Elizabeth of York had been laid to rest in Westminster Abbey—it was not far short of being so.

Nor can anything be said in defense of Wolsey's private life. He had a mistress and children, and on his son and namesake, ordained a priest before he was grown, the cardinal lavished a cornucopia of church livings. When he vacated the rich see of Durham in order to become bishop of Winchester and abbot of St. Albans (grabbing the latter plum in defiance of canon law, which barred nonmonks from becoming abbots), he did so partly in the hope of inserting his son as Durham's new bishop. But even he was unable to get away with that.

Perhaps his ultimate failure grew out of his chief strength, his brilliance as an executive. In the king's name Wolsey ruled virtually alone, refusing to share power, reducing the council to a shadow of what it had been before his rise. This further inflamed the resentment of those members of the higher nobility who already hated the cardinal for his arrogance, for his constant rubbing of their noses in the outward signs of his greatness, for the intolerable presumption of this escapee from the wrong side of the class divide. Wolsey alienated everyone. Those loyal to the old church—Catherine of Aragon most visibly—regarded his way of life as a disgrace. Those drawn to the ideas of Luther and other radical reformers—the Boleyns and their faction at court, for example—pointed to him as proof that the whole Roman connection was corrupt beyond hope of repair. Wolsey had left himself with no powerful friends except Henry VIII, surely the least dependable and most dangerous friend in all of England.

By 1530 England had changed to such an extent that it no longer needed Wolseys. Education was no longer almost exclusively the province of the church. Laymen such as John More were becoming eminent jurists, and in the next generation lawyers such as More's son Thomas were among Europe's leading humanist scholars. A few years at university were now a rite of passage for sons of the nobility and the gentry, and some were even using those years to get educations. Only once after Wolsey would a power in the government become a power in the church as well, or vice versa, and that sole exception would be Wolsey's onetime protégé, Stephen Gardiner. With the old ladder of mobility destroyed, England's class divisions would become more rigid, more impermeable, than ever.

7

A Thunderbolt Falls

A crisis appeared to be near as 1532 began, but it was impossible to know for sure. Everything depended on the king, on what he intended to do, but the signals he was sending were so self-contradictory as to be indecipherable. That the king himself knew what he wanted is unclear.

In the year just ended he had given numerous indications that he no longer hoped for a favorable judgment from Rome, that his sights were on something much bigger than a mere annulment. But now he sent a delegation of nobles to Windsor Castle to call on Queen Catherine, to offer yet another solution to the old deadlock. The idea this time was that the divorce question should be referred to a panel of eight men, four lay lords and four bishops or abbots, with the understanding that whatever judgment they rendered would be final. It is not known whether her visitors informed Catherine that something very similar to their proposal had already been floated in Rome, that Pope Clement had responded positively, but that in doing so he had added that no such arrangement could be acceptable without the queen's assent, as it was she who had appealed to Rome. What they were offering, Catherine's visitors told her, would be of great comfort to the king's troubled conscience. "God grant him a good conscience," she replied. "But this shall be your answer: I am his wife, lawfully married to him by holy church, and so I will abide until the court of Rome, which was privy to the beginning, shall have made thereof an end."

She was ordered to leave Windsor for a smaller, more remote residence where there could be no possibility of her intercepting Henry and Anne as they made their royal rounds. "Go where I may," she said, "I shall still be his lawful wife." In the months that followed she would be moved again and again and would not be allowed to see her daughter. She wrote often to the princess, always advising her to honor her father and be properly submissive.

And so the king's great matter hung in the air unresolved, a vexation to everyone it touched, a force powerful enough to push even the queen to the outermost periphery of public life while drawing others toward the center against their will. Among those others were Henry's cousins the young Pole brothers, grandsons of that Duke of Clarence who had been the brother (and was killed on the orders) of Henry's maternal grandfather, Edward IV. Being of royal blood was a very mixed blessing in the England of the sixteenth century; the tenuousness of the Tudors' claim to the throne inclined them to see kinsmen as potential threats, which is why Henry VII had had Clarence's harmless son put to death. The Poles (a family entirely distinct, by the way, from the king's other and more obstreperous cousins the *de la* Poles) were already acquainted with the cutting edge of Henry VIII's distrust and anger. In 1521 their mighty relative the Duke of Buckingham, a man all too haughtily proud of his Yorkist blood and conspicuously unwilling to curry favor with the upstart Tudors, had arranged the marriage of his son and heir to Ursula Pole. Henry reacted to this union of two families that had plausible claims to the throne with unexpected savagery. Buckingham was convicted of treason and executed; Ursula's mother, Margaret, Countess of Salisbury, lost her place as lady governess to little Princess Mary; and the countess's two eldest sons were imprisoned in the Tower. Later the family won its way back into favor, Henry Pole achieving a prominent place at court as Lord Montague, but they lived with the knowledge that careless displays of ambition could prove fatal.

With this history—his grandfather put to death by one of the last Plantagenet kings, his uncle killed by the first Tudor and his sister's father-in-law by the second—it is hardly surprising that the youngest of the Pole brothers, Reginald, grew to adulthood with no wish to be involved in the court or its politics. In spite or perhaps because of this, Henry VIII took a fatherly interest in him, providing five hundred crowns a year for his education. In five years at the University of Padua, the bookish and unambitious youth won favorable notice for his devotion to his studies, his pleasing manners, and his excellent moral character. After two years back in England, during which he took up residence in a monastery and continued his preparations for a career in the church, he was permitted by the king to return to the continent for further study at the University of Paris. In departing he turned his back on the certainty that, had he remained at home, the king would have showered him with offices and other signs of favor.

Pole's quiet life in France was first interrupted when Henry set out to get support for the annulment of his marriage from the continental universities. Considerable intellectual gifts, excellent contacts in the academic world, and a growing reputation made Pole a potentially valuable agent in the king's campaign, and he received instructions to become involved. When he claimed to be too young and lacking in experience to be of any use—much later he would write that his real reason for begging off was discomfort with the king's position—he was ordered home. There the Duke of Norfolk, England's most powerful magnate as well as Anne Boleyn's uncle, confided to him that Henry had marked him out for a high place in the church but expected a clear statement of where he stood on the divorce. (The Archbishopric of York, Wolsey's old sinecure, was still vacant when this conversation took place and is almost certainly what the king had in mind. It would have been a surprising and even inappropriate appointment in light of Pole's youth and the fact that he was not yet even an ordained priest, but the pope doubtless would have given his assent even if Pole had not been so favorably regarded in Rome. Clement would soon be accepting from Henry an at least equally surprising nominee for the even more exalted see of Canterbury.)

When Pole confessed that on the basis of what he then knew he was unable to support the king, Norfolk advised him to take a month to learn more about the issues involved. In the weeks that followed he studied the relevant commentaries on Scripture and canon law and discussed the matter with scholars. Finally, perhaps in part because of his brothers' fears of conflict with the king, Pole announced that he had thought his way to a position that Henry was likely to find acceptable. He was summoned to see the king, who was eager to receive him as an ally and ready to reward him. Once in the royal presence, however, Pole found the arguments he had constructed in his mind collapsing under the realization that he was not being honest even with himself. He tried to explain why, to his own intense regret, he could not agree with Henry on the divorce. The king, furious, walked out on him, leaving him in tears. Lord Montague and Sir Geoffrey Pole, too, were furious when they learned what their brother had done. They accused him not only of destroying his own prospects but of putting the whole family at risk. Reginald wrote to the king, trying to explain why he had found himself unable to be more helpful and asking permission to go abroad once again. Lord Montague, expecting the worst, went to see the king to say how much *he* regretted his brother's conduct.

"My lord," a surprisingly good-humored Henry told Montague, "I cannot be offended with so dutiful and affectionate a letter. I love him in spite of his obstinacy, and were he but of my opinion on this subject, I would love him better than any man in my kingdom." This was the king at his magnanimous best, and a demonstration of Reginald Pole's ability, which only a tiny number of men would ever possess, to somehow bring out that best. Pole was allowed not only to leave England for Italy—where he must have hoped to stay well clear of the king's matrimonial troubles—but to keep his allowance. His brothers and their mother, all of them descended from kings stretching back to William the Conqueror, must have breathed easier when he was gone. But if they thought the worst was over for any of them, they could not have been more wrong.

When Parliament and the Southern Convocation assembled yet again in January 1532, no one outside the king's innermost circle had any way of knowing what to expect. That something extraordinary was in the air, however, must have been made obvious by the selective character of the royal summons. Cuthbert Tunstal, the bishop of Durham who had disputed Henry's claim to be supreme head, was not present because he had received no call. John Fisher, the scrappy old bishop of Rochester, was among the others not summoned, but he traveled to London all the same. The general sense of anticipation had sharpened his readiness for a fight.

Henry remained impossible to read. Pope Clement, who a year earlier had forbidden the king to remarry while the divorce case remained unsettled, received a letter from Queen Catherine reporting that she was no longer allowed to be under the same roof with her husband and asking for a ruling on the marriage. This prompted him to write to Henry and tell him that he dishonored himself in treating his wife as he did. He added that reconciliation with Catherine would be the greatest favor that he, Henry, had ever done for the papacy. Henry scoffed at this as he had scoffed at an earlier order from Clement to send Anne Boleyn away. The pope was giving signs of running out of patience, and the king was responding in kind.

On February 8 Henry showed his hand. He had sixteen clergymen and six laymen, all of them men in positions of considerable authority, indicted on charges that required them to explain to the King's Bench by what right or authority—*quo warranto*—they claimed to be able to appoint coroners, take possession of discovered treasure, and supervise local trading in bread and beer. Here again the clergy (the inclusion of six laymen in the indictment remains unexplained) found themselves accused of breaking the law by doing things that men in their positions had been doing for centuries. It made no sense except as harassment and intimidation, an attempt to add to the pressure applied earlier through the threat of praemunire. What was stunning was the identity of those indicted. The list began with the name of William Warham, a dignitary of unimpeachable reputation and unquestionable loyalty to the Crown. Also listed were a bishop and the heads of seven monasteries and several colleges. Obviously no one was safe from the king's displeasure.

These indictments seem almost childishly petty today, and probably they seemed so when they were issued. The supreme oddity, in any case, is that the charges were never pressed and no bill was ever proposed in Parliament for the criminalization of the acts—the supposed offenses—that had been the basis of the indictments. Instead, Henry changed course and delivered a different, harder blow from an equally unexpected direction. His agents in Parliament introduced a bill abolishing annates, one of the principal means by which England and the other countries of Europe had for centuries provided financial support to the papal court in Rome. In accordance with ancient practice, whenever a new bishop was appointed to a vacant see his first year's net income went to the pope as an annate—payment of what was called "first fruits." The sums involved could amount to several thousand pounds in a single year, especially when the wealthier dioceses were involved. It was not difficult to rouse the taxpaying knights and gentry of the House of Commons to a state of indignation over the sending of this money out of the kingdom at a time when the financial demands of the Crown had become so burdensome.

The scholars whom Henry had put to work searching for historical evidence of his supreme headship had turned up documents indicating that annates had originated as a way of providing the papacy with the means to defend itself against the barbarian invasions that followed the collapse of the Roman Empire. The transformation of such presumably temporary assistance into an eternal entitlement, the king and Cromwell now argued, was an example of how the bishops of Rome had, over the centuries, taken things to which they had no right. The annates bill was the most radical attack yet on the prerogatives of the church, and its introduction may have reflected Cromwell's growing influence and his willingness to push the king to new extremes. As originally proposed, it would have required any bishop who paid first fruits to Rome to forfeit everything he owned and the income from his diocese for as long as he remained in office. It would have established a new procedure by which any bishop-elect whom the pope refused to approve could be consecrated by his archbishop or two other bishops, and it would have ordered that anything attempted by the pope in the way of retribution—anything up to and including excommunication, which had always been the papacy's ultimate weapon—was to be ignored.

Such a bare-knuckles assault on ancient practice was too much for the bishops of 1532 to accept, and they along with several of the abbots who sat with them in the House of Lords declared themselves opposed. The bill was too much even for many in the Commons, where resistance proved formidable. Clearly rough tactics would be needed if the bill were to have any chance of passage. Henry showed himself ready to use them. He made three bullying visits to Commons, finally going so far as to order the members to divide themselves physically into two groups: those who supported his bill were to line up beside him on one side of the room and those opposed were to withdraw to the other. Even this exercise, intimidating as it must have been for country gentry, proved to be not enough. Henry did not secure passage until the proposal was considerably softened. Most important, it was made provisional: it would not take effect until Easter of the following year, and even then it would not become law unless Henry issued the letters of patent necessary for implementation.

The king's position remained ambiguous. In its original form the annates measure had been without precedent, overturning every Englishman's understanding of the kingdom's connection to the see of Rome and imposing ruinous penalties on anyone who attempted to maintain the old ways. But by delaying implementation for a year, thereby giving the king ample opportunity to change his mind, Parliament left a door open for reconciliation with the pope. Probably the king accepted this compromise less because he still harbored hopes of reconciliation, or would have accepted reconciliation if it became possible, than because doing so was the only way of getting the needed majorities: Parliament had not yet been pummeled into docility. Cromwell at this point had neither won Henry's full confidence nor brought Parliament under control, and he may have been trying to move faster than either king or Parliament was prepared to go. Henry, for his part, appears to have been adopting some but not all of Cromwell's ideas, trying them out, measuring the reaction.

Even as the king hesitated, however, Cromwell was helping him to see Parliament in an entirely new light. In the first twenty years of his reign, Henry had followed his father's example, doing his best to govern without Parliament, summoning it only in times of dire necessity. Wolsey had certainly favored this approach, all the more so as his money-raising expedients earned him the hatred of both houses. For two years Henry got little out of the Parliament first summoned in 1529, the one destined to be remembered as the Reformation Parliament. But then Cromwell, once his star had risen and his genius had ripened, showed him how to transform Parliament from a nuisance, an obstacle, into a tool of immense value. Together the two of them began using Parliament, at first almost against its will, to spread a canopy of legitimacy, of legal propriety, over their most radical initiatives. They maneuvered it into approving, or at least *appearing* to approve and sometimes even to initiate, the things they wanted done. By this means they could claim to be doing nothing beyond what the people of England wanted. It was in opening such new vistas to the king that Cromwell, a self-described onetime "ruffian" who even at the height of his power never lost the savage instincts of a backstreet knife-fighter, first showed himself to be one of the most brilliant political operators that England has ever produced.

Transforming Parliament required meticulous and skillful management. It required carrots and sticks—a balanced application of the Crown's power to reward and its power to destroy. Above all, in the beginning especially, it required creating the illusion that Crown and Parliament were in agreement even when a majority in Commons could not be depended upon to vote with the king. Thus even more attention had to be paid than in the past to finding the right kinds of men to sit in positions of leadership in Commons, and to culling candidates who were not likely to conform. Luckily for Henry, Cromwell was not only as painstakingly careful a manager as Wolsey had ever been but also, where Parliament was concerned, far more adroit. He was also more ruthless and much less inhibited by established law and custom. Once again Henry had been blessed with a lieutenant into whose hands he could confidently place full responsibility for the achievement of his own most urgently desired objectives.

If Cromwell was still learning early in 1532, he was learning fast and becoming capable of dazzling moves. On March 18 Parliament formally presented to the king a document called the Supplication Against the Ordinaries (an "ordinary" being, in ecclesiastical parlance, a bishop or archbishop—someone with jurisdiction over church courts and administration). It was a supplication in the sense that, after making numerous complaints about the church hierarchy's abuse of its rights in such areas as the handling of heresy cases, excommunication, and fees and tithes, it asked the king to take corrective action. It was radical in looking, contrary both to law and to tradition, to the Crown rather than to the church itself for correction of the alleged abuses. Although supposedly a spontaneous work of Commons, in actuality it was mainly Cromwell's doing. (Several early drafts, all in Cromwell's hand and dated before March 18, are among his surviving papers.) By having his allies in Commons offer the Supplication as an expression of popular discontent, Cromwell was able to raise Henry above the fray. Now the king, rather than attacking the church and challenging the traditions of the realm, was being called upon as an impartial judge. He was asked to consider the grievances of his people against a church that had, presumably, conducted itself so disgracefully as to give rise to deep and widespread unhappiness. Henry was no longer in the position of having to prod Parliament to act on his instructions; Parliament in presenting the Supplication had taken the initiative, and Henry was free to respond if and as he chose.

It was a neat trick, and Cromwell had pulled it off in spite of the fact that serious discontent with the church or its hierarchy was *not* widespread among the people or even dominant in the Commons. Resentment certainly existed, but with nothing like the intensity found in Germany, where a church immeasurably more entangled than England's in secular politics had in many places made itself the object of burning popular hatred. Anticlericalism in England was centered mainly in London, especially among the lawyers and merchants of the city's growing middle class. It was the representatives of these professions, together with Londoners serving as members for boroughs far from the city, who had pressed their complaints about the church in the Reformation Parliament's first session at the end of 1529 and been satisfied with a small number of limited reforms. It was those same men who now, under Cromwell's firm direction, asked the king to give his attention to the Supplication's fresh complaints. By involving the speaker of the house—an appointee of the Crown—Cromwell was able to create the impression that the Supplication represented the thinking of the majority. In fact, the membership at large had been given no opportunity to express an opinion.

Henry forwarded the Supplication to convocation and invited it to respond. On the face of it, this was an eminently fair and reasonable thing to do. But it was also tactically astute. It put the hierarchy in the position of having to acknowledge the accusations of some of its most intemperate critics, and to dignify those accusations with a reply to the king.

Though the Supplication complained of many things, its focus was on the ecclesiastical courts. It echoed Henry's claim to "imperial jurisdiction" (evidence of Cromwell's domination of the drafting process), arguing that Englishmen could not be held to account by any authority beyond the cliffs of Dover. It thereby delivered a fresh challenge to the old idea of a universal church and to the leadership of the pope. Initially, possibly because it believed itself to be responding to Commons rather than to the Crown, convocation displayed a determination to yield no more ground. It delivered to the king a Defense of the Ordinaries, much of which was written by Stephen Gardiner, who was Henry's secretary as well as bishop of Winchester. It offered one significant compromise, agreeing that during Henry's lifetime any new laws passed by the hierarchy would be subject to royal approval. Otherwise it rejected all the Supplication's complaints and claims. It reiterated the old idea, familiar to all, that the church had been given its authority by God and that not even a king—or an emperor, for that matter—could interpose himself between it and God. No part of this response could have surprised anyone; it was the settled orthodoxy of Catholic Europe. In saying anything else, Gardiner and his fellow bishops would have been repudiating beliefs that lay at the core of their clerical vocations. They would have been declaring unconditional surrender in their unwanted struggle with the king.

Nor should anyone have been surprised, however, that the king was unhappy with convocation's response. But he held his fire, passing the Defense of the Ordinaries to the speaker of the House of Commons with the wry comment that "we think their answer will smally please you" and asking the bishops to amplify on some parts of what they had written. That was where things stood, with Commons and clergy apparently entering upon an exchange of arguments as sterile as the endless dispute over the divorce, when suddenly a thunderbolt fell.

It came on May 10 in the form of a royal demand surpassing anything the king had thus far attempted. Convocation was given not a question to discuss or a complaint to answer but an ultimatum, and it came not from Parliament but from the king himself. The churchmen were ordered to give formal assent to three things. They were, first, never again to enact ecclesiastical laws except with the approval of the Crown—and not just during Henry's lifetime but ever. Second, all ecclesiastical laws then in effect were to be reviewed by a committee of thirty-two members, half clerical and half lay, all appointed by the king. Finally, even those laws found by the committee to be acceptable would remain without effect unless the king gave them his personal approval.

The climax had arrived at last: the moment, so long feared but so slow in coming, when the clergy were left with only two possible courses of action. They could stand up to the king, insisting on the rights that had been handed down to them through generations beyond numbering, or they could relinquish those rights forever.

PARLIAMENT

THE FIRST THING TO BE UNDERSTOOD ABOUT PARLIAMENT in the time of the Tudors is that it had nothing to do with democracy and was a "representative" body—representative of a substantial part of England's population—only in a sense so broad as to be practically meaningless.

Parliament under the Tudors remained what it had been since its origins three centuries before: an instrument of the Crown first, and then of regional, local, and commercial elites. It was closed to all but the king's wealthiest and most influential subjects, with limited room for individuals who were neither wealthy nor powerful but enjoyed royal favor. It had always been a malleable institution, used for different purposes at different times, and in the sixteenth century it evolved into something radically if not at first obviously new. By using it to cast a cloak of legitimacy over Henry VIII's unprecedented expansion of royal power, Thomas Cromwell not only established Parliament as an essential element in England's government but laid the foundations upon which, a hundred years later, it would become more powerful than the Crown.

Parliament had grown out of simple political realities: even the most powerful rulers find it easier to govern if they have the support of their most important subjects, if they provide some mechanism through which such subjects can be involved in the formulation of policy, and if they at least pretend to have the consent of the people they tax. Even William the Conqueror, whose victory in 1066 made him literally the owner of virtually every square foot of England (even the greatest of his nobles were merely his "tenants in chief"), found it advantageous to create and confer with his Magnum Concilium, or Great Council. It was made up of the mightiest of William's barons, the magnates, and its role was limited to settling disputes and managing whatever the king instructed it to manage. Its members—as well as the members of the Curia

Regis or King's Court, made up of individuals (often senior clergy) better qualified than warrior-barons to deal with challenging legal questions— were chosen by the king and could claim to represent no one beyond themselves and possibly their fellow lords. The existence of council and court signified very little beyond the obvious fact that William himself could not do everything.

Power as nearly total as William's could never be sustained, and after a century and a half his great-great-great-grandson King John took a great fall in trying to sustain it. The result, famously, was his signing under duress of Magna Carta. Though not exactly the birth of liberty that it is often represented as being, it did shift power away from the Crown in favor of the higher nobility. It committed the king to levying or collecting no taxes except with the consent of his council. Thereafter meetings of the Great Council and the King's Court began to include, if only occasionally, knights chosen by the leading families of every county. The idea of a Parliament (a "talking") made up of the king and his council, the barons and bishops, and representatives of influential (meaning wealthy) families of less than noble rank gradually began to take shape. Any notion that the non-nobles represented the people at large, however, would be grossly anachronistic. Just to vote in parliamentary elections one had to own property worth at least forty shillings, a threshold so high that in some counties fewer than a dozen men qualified. To sit in Commons, a "knight of the shire" needed an annual income of £600, and "burgesses" or townsmen needed £300. These were enormous sums.

John's son Henry III, too, found himself at war with the barons. The issue, as before and since, was money, and the conflict arose out of Parliament's new importance as the vehicle for approving royal requests for taxes. The leader of the baronial party, Simon de Montfort (himself not only a magnate but married to the king's sister) broke new ground in 1265 by summoning a Parliament without Henry's approval. He invited each county to send four knights and each borough to send two burgesses, thereby placing the Commons on something approaching an equal footing with the baronial Great Council. His aim was to use wide participation as a way of building support, and to use Parliament as a medium to communicate with all parts of the kingdom. A generation later Henry III's son Edward I (the first king since the Conquest, incidentally, to bear an Anglo-Saxon rather than a Norman name) followed

Montfort's example in recognizing Commons as a part of Parliament. His motive was not to weaken but to strengthen the Crown, using Parliament both to fund his wars and to demonstrate that he had the support of the kingdom.

As long as true feudalism lasted, with the barons able to function almost as little kings in their own domains and to demand military service of their subtenants, struggles for power were waged almost exclusively between the nobility and the king. The advantage shifted from one side to the other depending upon the personality of whoever happened to occupy the throne at any particular time. The main point of contention continued to be money: the kings' military adventures imposed a heavy financial burden upon the nobles. Important precedents were set as nobles and Crown alike paid lip service to the role of Commons in their efforts to attract support. A turning point as important as Magna Carta came early in the reign of the weak and pleasure-seeking Edward II, when the baronial party took control and issued the Ordinances of 1311. Whereas Magna Carta had taken the form of a royal proclamation, thereby recognizing the authority of even a gravely weakened king, the Ordinances were issued as the work of the barons, who merely claimed to be acting with royal approval. Having been driven to rebellion by the costs of the first Edward's wars and his son's reckless generosity to his favorites, the barons reasserted their right to limit the collection of taxes and control appointments to important royal offices. Though Commons was given no active role in any of this, the Ordinances enhanced its legitimacy by requiring the king not only to summon a Parliament annually but to include the lower house. Edward II, when he later repudiated the Ordinances, did so on grounds that they had been enacted without the approval of Commons. Thus both the Ordinances themselves and the grounds on which they were set aside helped to entrench the Commons in the government.

It came to be accepted that Parliament had three elements: the king and two houses, Lords and Commons, that met separately and were jointly responsible for raising the money required by the Crown. Parliament was also a mechanism for redress of grievances—the Ordinances of 1311 had asserted the right of subjects to appeal to it—and it came to be understood that any "petitions" (later they were called "bills") that both houses approved became the law of the land if accepted by the king. Thus Parliament continued to develop as a legislative body even as the judicial functions that had come to it through the Great Council and the King's Court were gradually taken over by other institutions.

By the time the first Henry Tudor became king in 1485, no one questioned the need for parliamentary approval of taxes and legislation. Indeed, it was accepted that Parliament could deny the Crown's requests for money if it chose to do so—something that it had already shown itself capable of doing when a king refused to consider its wishes. Like his predecessors, therefore, Henry VII preferred to do without Parliament, summoning it only when financial necessity left him with no alternative. This remained true through the first two decades of Henry VIII's reign, though his foreign adventures made meetings of Parliament far more commonplace. Both the Lords and the Commons remained the domain of the landed aristocracy, along with representatives of the wealthiest residents of the cities and largest towns. To Cardinal Wolsey, they were unavoidable evils that had to be placated in order for the Crown to pay its bills.

Everything changed with Henry's claim to supremacy and Cromwell's emergence as the man responsible for giving him what he wanted. That Henry was likely to be able to overpower the leaders of the church and bully the nobility soon became clear. What he lacked, and urgently needed, was a basis for claiming the *right* to overturn the traditions of a thousand years. Cromwell's genius was to use Parliament as it had never been used before. He coopted such authority as it had accumulated over the generations, driving it to pass statutes that acknowledged the powers that Henry was claiming for himself and thereby giving tyranny a footing in the law. In doing so he crushed whatever autonomy Parliament might have claimed to possess, arranging the election to the Commons of enough men under his (and the king's) control that later, when his innovations finally provoked an uprising, one of the protesters' complaints would be about the number of Crown employees and dependents sitting in Parliament as members.

Part of Cromwell's craft was to use Parliament without empowering it: in drafting his bills he was careful to include language stating explicitly that Parliament was not itself conferring powers on the king but merely recognizing that the king possessed the powers in question by divine right. The preambles to his most revolutionary statutes assumed the truth of propositions that were at best debatable: that England had long been an "empire," for example, and therefore could be subject to no external authority, ecclesiastical or otherwise. Cromwell has been credited with being the father of parliamentary government, in which sovereignty came to be shared by Crown and Parliament. The lengths to which he went to keep Parliament submissive while using its prerogatives to achieve a radical expansion of royal power, however, make it difficult to believe that he intended any such thing.

Whatever Cromwell's intentions, his actions permanently transformed Parliament's role. He would call it into session seven times in eight years, changing it from Wolsey's regrettable nuisance into an indispensable part of the machinery of government. What perhaps mattered most, he prepared the way for Parliament itself, Commons especially, to see itself in a new light. When he was finished, it was no longer the king who was supreme in England but "the king in Parliament"—a subtle distinction, but ultimately an epic one.

8

Submission

By the time King Henry delivered his ultimatum to convocation, almost everyone with a connection to his court was tangled in a web of hostility and dread.

Old friendships were being sundered by the tension. Even Charles Brandon, Duke of Suffolk, close to the king from boyhood and now his brother-in-law, was ordered to withdraw to his country home and take his family with him. Suffolk himself was loyal enough, but his wife, Henry's sister Mary, was too open about her contempt for the Boleyns.

The Tudors were not the only family being torn apart. Thomas Howard, Duke of Norfolk, though he kept his place at court, was compromised by his wife's outspoken opposition to the divorce and tormented by the angry outbursts of his high-strung niece Anne Boleyn.

Careers were being made and ruined. Stephen Gardiner, royal secretary and bishop of the rich diocese of Winchester, had damaged himself irretrievably by insisting, in his response to the Supplication Against the Ordinaries, that church law was above the reach of the secular authorities. He was now an outsider, still officially secretary but no longer trusted. The eagerness of Thomas Cranmer to find scholarly support for the king's every act and desire, by contrast, had lifted him into the bright sunshine of royal favor. He was back on the continent now, taking up new duties as Henry's ambassador to the court of Charles V.

Strange things were happening. One morning the whole household of Bishop John Fisher became violently ill. One of the bishop's servants died, as did an indigent woman who had come to Fisher's door for that day's distribution of free food. The bishop himself escaped, saved by his practice of not eating until the beggars had been fed.

It was discovered that the morning's batch of porridge had been poisoned. According to some of the surviving accounts, someone had given a powder to Fisher's cook, one Richard Roose, who thought it was a laxative and put it into the porridge as a practical joke. By other accounts Roose claimed complete innocence, saying that he knew nothing about any powder and that if anything had been added to the porridge, it must have been done while he was away from the kitchen, possibly by a nameless stranger who had shown up that morning and later disappeared. Rumors arose to the effect that the poisoning had been arranged by the king, whose motive would have been to put an end to Fisher's unceasing criticism, in writing and in person, of his pursuit of a divorce and his attacks on the church.

What is most interesting is the king's reaction to these rumors—a reaction so extreme that it stirred up further suspicion. He visited the House of Lords and delivered an impromptu speech on the evils of poisoning, a subject of which he appears to have had a deep horror. He then hurried through Parliament a bill that made the use of poison an act of high treason, and he had Roose attainted (a step, to be much used in the years ahead, that made it possible to punish and even execute a suspect without holding a trial). The unfortunate Roose, whose degree of complicity can never be known, became the first person to suffer the penalty prescribed for poisoners. He was deep-fried alive in a cauldron of boiling oil.

Next Henry himself became a target, though of words only. On Easter morning he attended mass in the church of the Observant Franciscans adjacent to the royal palace at Greenwich. The Observant friars, so called because they were stricter than other Franciscans in adhering to the rule laid down by their order's founder, Francis of Assisi, were respected throughout Europe as a model of how men in holy orders should conduct themselves. They had been invited into England by Edward IV, Henry VII had taken them under his patronage early in his reign, and their connection to the royal family remained strong. Catherine of Aragon had always been especially devoted to the Observants, choosing John Forest of the Greenwich friary as her confessor. Henry VIII on more than one occasion had written to the pope to commend their blameless way of life and their "hard toil day and night" to bring souls to God.

The preacher at this year's Easter mass was William Peto, former warden of the order's house at Richmond (another place where a Tudor palace stood side by side with an Observant friary), newly elected head of its English province and onetime confessor to the king's daughter Mary. Henry must have been expecting an edifying homily appropriate to the holiest day in the liturgical calendar and attuned to his lofty understanding of matters theological. What he got instead must have stunned him; it is difficult to believe that he would have set foot in the church had he known what Peto was intending. The friar addressed him directly, personally, telling him in so many words that he had no right to end his marriage, that there was no way to do so except by proving, contrary to what the queen continued to swear, that her marriage to Prince Arthur had been consummated. Moving into even more shocking territory, Peto compared Henry to Ahab, the Old Testament king who had been enchanted by the wicked Jezebel, was seduced into thinking himself above the law, and so had come to a terrible end. "I beseech your Grace to take good heed," Peto said in conclusion, "lest if you will need follow Ahab in his doing, you will surely incur his unhappy end also, and that the dogs lick your blood as they licked Ahab's, which God avert and forbid." Henry showed impressive sangfroid, not only sitting stoically through what must have sounded to him like incredible insults but staying behind after mass to talk with Peto, hoping perhaps to win him over with the royal erudition. Peto proved immovable, however. He warned the king that all England was restless because of his actions and that if he persisted he could put his very throne in danger.

Within the next few days Peto departed Greenwich for a general conference of the Observants' English province. As soon as he was gone, Henry issued instructions for one of the royal chaplains, Dr. Richard Curwen, to preach the following Sunday at the friars' church. This was irregular because Curwen was not a Franciscan, and it was unwelcome because he was known to be willing to do or say anything to win the king's attention and favor. Henry Elston, warden of the Greenwich friary, objected but was ignored. Curwen appeared on Sunday as instructed, and as he rose to speak the king was once again in attendance.

Things did not go according to plan. Curwen, knowing what was expected of him but going perhaps a bit far in his eagerness to please, not only repudiated Peto's words of a week earlier but denounced him as "dog, slanderer, base, beggarly friar, closeman, rebel and traitor." The friars in his audience absorbed this in silence. The king did the same, no doubt with considerable satisfaction. But when Curwen went on to accuse Peto of being absent out of cowardice—"not to be found, being fled for fear and shame as being unable to answer my arguments"—a voice called out from the loft above the king. "Good sir," said Elston the warden loudly, "you know that Father Peto, as he was commanded, is now gone to a provincial council held at Canterbury, and not fled for fear of you, for tomorrow he will return again." Elston declared himself ready to "lay down my life to prove all those things true which he hath taught out of the holy scripture, and to this combat I challenge you before God and all equal judges." Noisy confusion ensued, and quiet was not restored until Henry himself ordered everyone to be silent.

Peto and Elston were called before the King's Council. There they were roundly chastised, the Earl of Essex exclaiming that they deserved to be bundled up in a sack and thrown into the Thames. Elston was not impressed. "Threaten these things to rich and dainty folk who are clothed in purple, fare delicately, and have their chiefest hope in this world," he replied. "For we esteem them not, but are joyful that for the discharge of our duties we are driven hence. With thanks to God we know the way to heaven to be as ready by water as by land, and therefore we care not which way we go." The two were taken into custody, and Henry petitioned Rome for license to have them tried by the compliant provincial of a different order, the Augustinians. Before anything came of this they were sent into exile on the continent. They went to Antwerp, where they took up the production of books rebutting Henry's claims on the divorce and supremacy. Their persistence did nothing to encourage the king to allow those who disagreed with him to leave England and remain at liberty.

Just days after Elston's clash with Curwen, an outbreak of violence showed that tension was reaching dangerous levels even inside Henry's court. The dukes of Norfolk and Suffolk were by this point less influential with the king than the upstart Cromwell, and were disgruntled and perhaps even fearful as a result. The pressure they were under put them and their followers at odds to an extent that soon threatened to get out of hand. One day, after an altercation of some kind, one of Suffolk's retainers took refuge in Westminster Abbey to escape pursuit by a group of Norfolk's men. The abbey was a recognized place of sanctuary, but the pursuers entered anyway and killed Suffolk's man. When Suffolk learned of this (he was back at court, though without his wife), he assembled an armed gang of his own and headed for Westminster in pursuit of vengeance. The king was alerted in time to dispatch a messenger with an order for Suffolk to stop, and the duke and his men were obliged to swear that they would refrain from violence. They did so unhappily, and their mood was not improved by news that the murderers of their comrade had been let off lightly.

This was the atmosphere that hung over the Southern Convocation as it struggled uncertainly to respond to the king's ultimatum. The bishops in particular were in an excruciatingly difficult position. Most of them held their positions less because of any special piety or wisdom or devotion to the church than because over the years they had demonstrated an ability to make themselves agreeable to the king. They were better trained in obedience to the Crown than in loyalty to a distant, unseen papacy, they had more reason to fear their prideful and determined king than a pope who sometimes must have seemed little more than an abstraction, and if any of them had looked to Rome for guidance since the start of the divorce crisis the only response had been a troubled silence. Archbishop Warham, who since the fall of Wolsey had stood alone at the top of the hierarchy, only added to the confusion. Many years before, he had expressed doubts about the propriety of a marriage between Catherine of Aragon and her late husband's brother, but of course he accepted the pope's decision on the matter and even presided at the wedding. From the start of the crisis he had seemed lost in irresolution, sometimes questioning but at least as often appearing to accept the king's arguments. Not long before Henry delivered his ultimatum, Warham had publicly criticized some of the king's more aggressive initiatives. But after receiving the ultimatum and getting a taste of the Crown's hard tactics, he withdrew into silence.

Convocation as a whole, however, was showing signs of willingness to resist. The lower chamber especially, less accustomed than the bishops to the compromises required for political preferment, displayed an angry understanding of what was at stake in this latest confrontation. Henry, aware of its restiveness, reacted indirectly but pointedly, summoning a group of his most dependable parliamentary supporters. Among them were thirteen members of Commons, the king's handpicked speaker among them, and eight lay lords. Their function that day was to provide an audience for a theatrical performance in which the king would play not just the starring but the only role. "Well-beloved subjects," Henry told them (it is easy to imagine him expressing innocent surprise followed by righteous indignation), "we thought that the clergy of our realm had been our subjects wholly. But now we have well perceived that they be but half our subjects—yea, and *scarce* our subjects!"

This would have been the listeners' cue to feign astonishment and indignation. How was such a thing possible? How could the clergy not be true subjects of their glorious king? Henry then revealed the supposedly shocking truth (which of course had been obvious for centuries): "All the prelates, at their consecration, make an oath to the pope, clean contrary to the oath that they make to us, so that they seem to be his subjects, and not ours. The copy of both the oaths I deliver here to you, requiring you to invent some order that we be not thus deluded of our spiritual subjects." The opacity of the king's second sentence is likely to have been intentional: it leaves unclear exactly what Henry was threatening, but there could be no doubt that he was accusing the bishops of something serious, something smelling of treason, and that he would welcome the involvement of his friends in Parliament. In delivering this little talk, however, he may have been bluffing; it would have been far from clear at this point that Parliament as a body was prepared to support his most radical demands. If his words were a bluff, however, the bluff worked. Two days later convocation offered a compromise that had been hashed out between the bishops and the lower chamber, with the latter continuing to show more firmness than the lords of the church. The response to the king's ultimatum conceded much of what he had demanded, promising that the clergy would not legislate without royal permission. However, it repeated a familiar qualification along with a familiar request. The new rule was to be effective only during

Henry's lifetime (the bishops had been willing to make it permanent, but the lower house would not agree), and as before, the king was asked to confirm the traditional liberties of the church.

Again Henry was not satisfied. Having no further need for Parliament at this point, and probably not wanting its more restless members to remain together at Westminster as he pushed his conflict with the clergy to a climax, he sent it home. Convocation was told that it, too, was to adjourn—not quite immediately but in twenty-four hours—but that he wanted a better answer before it did so. He sent envoys including the Duke of Norfolk and the Boleyns, father and son, to make certain that the churchmen understood that he meant business—that failure to cooperate would bring consequences.

Thus it was that May 15 became one of the most significant days not only of the Tudor century but in English constitutional history. It was the day on which, in the person of Archbishop Warham, the clergy of the Southern Convocation utterly, absolutely, and forever surrendered such independence as their church possessed to King Henry VIII and his heirs. In doing so, they abandoned rights and immunities that reached back into the dimmest early years of Christianity in England, prerogatives that their predecessors had fought repeatedly and sometimes sacrificed much to maintain. The question that arises is how such a momentous surrender could have happened so quickly and apparently so easily—how the stewards of an institution rooted so deeply in English society and culture came to agree unconditionally to even the most extreme of Henry's demands less than a week after he first made them.

The answer is that it didn't happen that way. The whole process of surrender was little more than a sham. In fact, only three members of convocation's upper house—three out of all the bishops and leading abbots in England and Wales—signed the document of submission without adding reservations. Two refused outright, and more absented themselves from the proceedings than showed up either to sign or refuse. The lower house was even less cooperative; so many members refused to vote that there was no way even to pretend that the king's demands had been accepted. When the "submission of the clergy" was presented to the king, therefore, it bore the signatures of only a tiny minority of those men whose positions gave them at least some right to act on behalf of the church. As an expression of the will of the hierarchy or the whole clergy, therefore, it had an extremely dubious legitimacy. This fact appears to have troubled the king not at all. He had what he needed: an official document, bearing the signature and seal of the archbishop of Canterbury and a few others, that proclaimed him to be the ultimate master of ecclesiastical law in his kingdom. He still did not have a divorce, and difficult questions about the relationship with Rome remained to be resolved, but Henry had won one of the great victories of his life. He held in his hand a basis for claiming that the clergy now lay prostrate at his feet. That this is what he had wanted all along—that he had no real interest in a comprehensive revision of canon law—is clear in the fact that though Warham's submission agreed to the creation of a review committee, no such body was ever appointed. As for the troublesome fact that most of the clergy had not *really* submitted, that detail could either be corrected later, if necessary, or simply forgotten.

On the day after Henry received the submission, the Duke of Norfolk escorted Thomas More to the gardens of York Place, the great London palace that had previously been the residence of Cardinal Wolsey and was now home to the king and Anne Boleyn. There the chancellor met briefly with Henry, handed over the Great Seal that symbolized his office, and quietly ended his career in government. It is natural to suppose that More had decided to resign upon learning of the submission, realizing that he could not serve a monarch with whom he was in deep disagreement about matters of such great importance to both of them. But in fact May 16 was merely the day on which More, after an extended and unhappy wait, was at last *allowed* to resign. His position had become untenable long before, first because of the lengths to which the king was going in pursuit of his divorce and then because of his threats to the unity of the church. More had recruited Norfolk, with whom he had maintained an uneasy friendship in spite of the duke's impatience with the idea of papal authority, to ask the king to allow him to resign. For a long time Henry turned a deaf ear. He could not permit his subjects and the whole world to see the highest-ranking officer in his government quitting in protest of royal policy. Such a spectacle was especially impossible at a time when the king was seen to be locked in conflict with convocation and Parliament and neither could be depended upon to obey his instructions.

But now the annates battle was won, the hierarchy had surrendered if only in a formal sense, and neither Parliament nor convocation remained in session and capable of raising protests. If More remained in office, he could only be an awkwardness, and if he were still in office when Parliament or convocation reconvened he might become a figure around whom others could rally. It was the right time to let him go. The king accepted the Seal, and More withdrew gratefully to his home in Chelsea, saying that he hoped to spend whatever time remained to him preparing his soul for the hereafter.

OTHER REFORMATIONS

IT SEEMS AN EXCEEDINGLY STRANGE COINCIDENCE THAT the greatest turning point in the history of the church in England, the crisis after which nothing would ever be the same, occurred at almost precisely the same time that the religious life of central Europe was also being violently transformed. What is strange is that these two simultaneous revolutions happened independently of each other, rose out of radically different circumstances and causes, and ultimately unfolded in distinctly different ways.

Certainly at some deep level having to do with the spirit of the age, this wasn't a coincidence at all. Be that as it may, when Martin Luther fastened his ninety-five theses to the door of Wittenberg Cathedral in 1517 he set off a powder keg of a kind that simply did not exist in England. His revolt was neither the cause of nor the inspiration for the upheaval that Henry VIII put in motion a decade and a half later. Henry in fact loathed what he knew of Luther, and loathed many of the defining ideas of Luther's theology. Long before declaring war on the pope, Henry made himself the avowed enemy of Friar Luther and *his* war on the pope. For the book in which he responded to Luther's heresies (he had help in writing it, especially from Thomas More and John Fisher), he was rewarded with the title Defender of the Faith by—it would become the ultimate irony—the pope in Rome himself.

Luther repaid the king in full. First he declared in a book of his own that Henry was a villain and fool and tool of the Antichrist, a "damnable rottenness and worm." Later he denied that Henry had any right to divorce Catherine of Aragon, suggesting instead that he commit bigamy.

And yet, though both would have been pained to think so, Henry and Luther were intimately linked. Such intellectual support as Henry found for his revolution came largely from Englishmen whose thinking had been strongly influenced by Luther's. And Luther's impact could never have been as widespread as it finally proved to be if not for the resources that Henry's revolt made available to the Protestant cause.

There is irony in all this. From the beginning of his reign to the end, Henry thought of himself as not only a good Catholic but literally the best and most orthodox of Catholics—better than the pope, in the end, because better connected to God. Hence his revulsion toward the books, written in Latin mainly and reproduced in great numbers thanks to the recent invention of movable type, that Luther was turning out with dazzling speed and spreading to every corner of Europe as his dispute with the papacy escalated into schism. His beliefs as they matured—that man is so corrupted by original sin as to be incapable of acting freely, that therefore he can do nothing to merit salvation, that therefore faith alone can "justify" him or free him from the consequences of sin, and finally that acts of charity and self-denial and prayers for the dead must all be without effect—added up to a blunt repudiation of Henry's very Catholic views. Luther insisted that the Bible is the sole source of truth, that baptism and the Eucharist are the only valid sacraments and priests have no more power than any layman, that people are predestined to salvation or damnation and can do nothing to alter their fate—ideas no less offensive to the English king than to Rome. They were no more consistent with Henry's expanding view of his own role than with the most ambitious assertions of the popes.

Luther's first moves onto radical theological ground were viewed with enthusiasm, even with excitement, in a Germany where many people had long regarded Rome as an alien force, remote, exploitive, and corrupt. The accusations that he leveled against the institutional church received so much support and encouragement, even from powerful nobles and influential members of the clergy, that Luther himself must have been taken by surprise. Certainly he was emboldened to carry his attack further. When the emperor Charles tried and failed to silence him and even had him outlawed without effect, Luther found himself free to follow his ideas wherever they led. What he found, in developing them, was release from agonies experienced during years of struggle with an intense sense of his own sinfulness. The resolution at which he arrived, the conviction that neither he nor anyone could do anything to merit salvation but salvation was possible all the same as an undeserved gift from God, persuaded him that his struggle had always been not only futile but unnecessary. He thereby brought that struggle to an end. But this answer also reduced to futility his monastic vocation, which he had always pursued so rigorously, so self-punishingly, that his Augustinian superiors had warned him against excessive scruples. In fact it rendered the church itself futile—left no place for the church as it then existed. Thus it left no place for a pope. The gulf that opened between Luther and Henry VIII never narrowed even as Henry changed from one of the pope's most dutiful sons into one of his most implacable enemies. Luther, having crossed swords with Rome and emerged not only unharmed but a German national hero, became contemptuous of the very idea of ecclesiastical hierarchy. He decided that the papacy must be the shadowy enemy of Christ that the New Testament's Book of Revelation calls the Whore of Babylon. This took him down paths where the king of England had no intention of following.

One trait that Henry and Luther shared was a conviction that the whole world should agree with them, reinforced by an expectation that it would. The resistance that both encountered should not have surprised them but did. What was worst for Luther, what enraged him because it made a mockery of his determination to construct a new religious unity on the ruins of the old, was the way the reform movement itself began to fragment and fragment again as men who had begun by rejecting Catholic doctrine went on to reject Lutheran doctrine as well.

The first aberration was the most dangerous, and the most horrible in its consequences. By 1524, only seven years after Luther had first challenged Rome's practice of selling "indulgences" (which were rather like get-out-of-Purgatory-free cards), common people across Germany were inspired by his example to mount challenges of their own not only to the ecclesiastical authorities (hated in Germany to a degree unimaginable in England) but to the secular rulers as well. The result was the Peasants' War, as large an uprising by an underclass as Europe had ever seen. The aims of the rebellion were more secular than religious—an end to enclosures of farmland long held in common, for example, and a restoration of the feudal rights of the peasantry—but the rebels looked to Luther as their natural leader. This put him in a severely awkward position. The peasants were doing what he himself had done: not only questioning but defying traditional authority. But if he endorsed their rebellion he would alienate the many princes who, by separating their domains from Rome and confiscating church lands, had helped to make his revolt a world-changing event. He took the safer course, condemning the rebels in the most hateful terms imaginable and urging their rulers not only to suppress but to exterminate them. What followed was the butchering of an estimated one hundred thousand people, many of them armed only, where they were armed at all, with farm implements. The idea that Christians owe unqualified obedience to the state became at that point deeply implanted in Lutheranism and therefore in the psyche of Protestant northern Germany. What was implanted in southern and western Germany and Austria, where the rebellion had been most widespread and the reprisals most savage, was a deep popular antipathy for the whole Lutheran phenomenon. In Switzerland, too, where the reformist leader Huldrych Zwingli had supported the rebels, the Peasants' War opened up new divisions.

Zwingli would have been lost to Luther in any case, because in Luther's eyes he went too far in his rejection of established dogma and practice. Luther believed, in almost the same way as Catholics, that the living Jesus really was present in the Eucharist, holy communion; Zwingli believed that the Eucharist was merely symbolic. Luther believed that religious art—paintings, statues, crucifixes, stained-glass windows—fostered piety and should be encouraged; to Zwingli such things were idolatrous. Zwingli separated himself from Luther on the question of free will, arguing that with the help of God people are capable of choosing to live in accordance with the commandments. Luther believed no such thing: in his view, Scripture offers its admonitions to do good and avoid evil only to impress upon believers how impossible it is for them to do either, so that they will put all their faith in God's undeserved mercy and attach no value to the actions of their unworthy selves.

Thus did reform separate first into two main branches, German Lutheranism and a more austere, puritanical Swiss variant, and then, after surprisingly few years, into a multitude of sects. The most notorious were the Anabaptists, so named because they rejected the ancient practice, which Luther had retained, of infant baptism. Some of the Anabaptists were radical to the point of lunacy. In 1534 they seized control of the German city of Münster from the Lutherans who had recently expelled the local Catholic bishop. Under the leadership of a man named Jan Beuckelson, who declared himself king of the new Jerusalem and said he was following the example of the Old Testament patriarchs in taking sixteen wives, they announced that the second coming of Jesus was imminent and that it was the duty of believers to make war on their oppressors. They were considered such a threat that Catholics and Lutherans joined forces to take Münster back from them, after which Anabaptists everywhere were ferociously suppressed. Those who fled to England were rounded up and jailed, and those who refused to recant, Henry had burned.

As it broke into divergent and even warring factions, the evangelical movement—a name signifying elevation of the Bible over other author-ity—lost the momentum of its rapid early growth. The violent rise and fall of the Münster Anabaptists worsened the fear of innovation to which the Peasants' War had given rise. Even in England, as early as 1531, a king already at loggerheads with Rome was putting evangelicals to death. Thomas Bilney, a popular young preacher who attached more im-portance to Scripture than Henry found acceptable, was burned at the stake at Smithfield. John Frith, another young evangelical with many ad-mirers, met the same fate for his Zwinglian views on the Eucharist.

Luther and his followers had long entertained hopes of winning over Europe's leading humanist and scriptural scholar, Erasmus of Rotterdam. They had reason to do so: like Luther a disaffected Augustinian friar, Erasmus was for years a vocal and influential critic of a church that he saw as badly in need of reform. But he had not left the church, and for years he did not respond to appeals from evangelicals and traditionalists alike that he enter the fray on their side. When he finally did so, it was in a way that gave Luther fresh cause to be furious. In an austerely scholarly treatise, carefully limiting himself to only one of the issues separating Luther from Rome and to evidence taken from Scripture because he knew that Luther would accept no other authority, Erasmus argued that the father of the Reformation was wrong—that man does have free will. It was a restrained testament to say the least, but it put an end to any thought that the greatest humanist of the age would be joining forces with the greatest reformer. Protestantism continued to split into so many factions over so many issues that it seemed, in Luther's words, to have "nearly as many sects as there are heads."

As for England, from where Luther sat it must have been a very hard place to understand. The church of Henry VIII was not evangelical and it was not Roman Catholic. No one in either camp could have imagined that in the next three decades it would become first the former, then the latter, and finally go off in a third direction of its own devising.

9

Consummation

In August 1532, three months after receiving the submission of the clergy, King Henry learned of the death of William Warham. He must have been pleased with the news. Though both as primate of England and as onetime chancellor Warham had long been a friend to the Crown, his great age had reduced his ability to be useful even when he wished to be so, his swings of opinion since the start of the divorce case had brought his dependability into question, and his unhappiness with the direction of royal policy was becoming increasingly worrisome.

His passing meant that Henry was now free, assuming that he met with no interference from the pope, to fill the highest clerical office in the kingdom with a man of his own choosing. He would not have been slow to appreciate the potential benefits.

But Warham's death was an even bigger stroke of luck than Henry appears to have realized. The archbishop had been a man of exceptional abilities and great learning, with doctorates in civil and canon law, and his early performance in the royal service had caused him to be singled out for advancement by no less demanding a judge than Henry VII. And unlike Wolsey, who eventually succeeded him in the chancellorship (possibly but not certainly by elbowing him aside—Warham appears to have been genuinely happy to focus exclusively on his ecclesiastical responsibilities), he had always maintained the highest standards in both his professional and his personal life. Erasmus, an unsparing critic of clerical politicians, called him "a man worthy of the memory of all posterity." Though age had diminished his ability to provide consistent and decisive leadership, he remained a formidable potential adversary, and after his death it was discovered that he had been preparing to speak out. He had been drafting, presumably for delivery in the House of Lords when Parliament reconvened, a speech invoking the example of his most celebrated predecessor in the seat of Canterbury, the martyr Thomas Becket. A canonized saint whose tomb was a pilgrimage site that drew thousands of visitors from around England and the continent, Becket had been murdered in 1170 by a trio of knights who thought, probably mistakenly, that they were carrying out the wishes of King Henry II. Becket and the king, once the closest of friends, had come to be bitterly at loggerheads over the latter's insistence on trying clerics in his own courts and blocking appeals to Rome. The reaction to Becket's murder was so powerful that Henry, one of the most forceful and dynamic monarchs of the English Middle Ages, was not only defeated in his challenge to the church but forced to do public penance. The veneration in which Becket was held explains why such an extraordinary number of fifteenth-century Englishmen had been given the name Thomas. His legend was a potent one for Warham to draw upon.

Warham's draft referred also to other kings who had tried and failed to challenge the rights of the church, and it ended on a note of defiance. At the time of his death Warham had hanging over him a praemunire charge laid against him earlier in the year—another of the king's acts of harassment, this one accusing the archbishop of having failed to obtain royal permission before installing a new bishop in a small, obscure Welsh diocese. (The difficulty Henry's researchers must have had in finding a "crime" in Warham's past is suggested by the fact that the alleged offense had been committed a decade and a half before.) In his undelivered speech, Warham declared his refusal to pay the bond that was being demanded of him in connection with the charge. The Crown had no right to make such a demand, he wrote, or to take action against him for refusing to comply: anyone who arrested or assaulted a bishop committed a mortal sin, and any kingdom where such a thing happened could be—as England had been after the murder of Becket, until Henry II begged forgiveness—placed under an interdict forbidding the exercise of the sacraments. Implicit in these words was the threat that, if Henry continued on his present path, he too might be excommunicated. Had the archbishop lived to utter them, they might have had a powerful impact on churchmen whose refusal to accept the document of submission had shown them to be hungry for leadership. Their effect on the people, and even on a king still hesitant to complete the break with Rome, could likewise have been immense. Excommunication and interdiction had, in centuries past, stopped ambitious monarchs in their tracks. No one could be certain whether they retained their old power, but Henry had reason to be concerned. It was a boon to his cause that Warham went to his grave when he did.

The prestige of the see of Canterbury made finding the right replacement crucial. If Warham had died just a year earlier, he probably would have been succeeded by Bishop Stephen Gardiner, an early and vigorous champion of Henry's divorce suit. (An interesting sidelight on Gardiner is an old assertion, utterly unprovable, that he was a son of Jasper Tudor's illegitimate daughter and therefore Henry VIII's second cousin.) But Gardiner's part in writing the bishops' response to the Supplication Against the Ordinaries had been, in the king's eyes, an act of betrayal. Other likely candidates presented similar problems. Edward Lee had been chosen to replace Wolsey as archbishop of York after helping substantially with the preparation of the king's divorce case, but thereafter, while never daring to defy his royal master, he had become a halfhearted and almost grudging advocate. Cuthbert Tunstal was among the most respected bishops in England, and Henry's decision to promote him from London to Durham in 1530 had been widely applauded. But by now he too was out of the question, having put himself on the side of Catherine of Aragon in the divorce controversy and objected in writing to Henry's claim to be supreme head.

Other bishops had proved more pliant than Gardiner or Lee or Tunstal, but for one reason or another none seemed quite satisfactory. Thus the king's attention turned to a man who was not a bishop, had never before been considered for a bishopric, and was unknown even by reputation to most of the clergy of England. Henry appointed a new ambassador to the court of Charles V and ordered Thomas Cranmer to return home, where his opinions and willingness to cooperate could be given a final examination. All the auguries were encouraging, certainly. Cranmer came with the endorsement of the Boleyns, who had sponsored him earlier in his career and encouraged his membership in that circle of Cambridge clerics whose reformist ideas extended as far as a questioning of Catholic doctrine including the authority of the pope. The king himself, by this point, had had considerable opportunity to observe Cranmer and take his measure. He had used him as a researcher, an envoy to the universities, and finally a diplomat. He had found him to be intelligent, learned, industrious, and conscientious, and to give no evidence of seeking either to enrich himself or to push any personal religious agenda. Instead he seemed happy to embrace the king's objectives, and to acknowledge that the setting of priorities was the king's province exclusively. If Henry was hoping to find a lieutenant who could be as useful to him in the ecclesiastical sphere as Cromwell was proving in the council, he should have seen the emergence of the amiable, unassuming Cranmer as his latest stroke of good fortune.

There was an obstacle, however: in contravention of his clerical vows, Cranmer was married. During his time as Henry's representative in Protestant Germany, where his reformist and antipapal inclinations had been reinforced by exposure to leading Lutheran thinkers, he had made the acquaintance of a Nuremberg theologian who called himself Osiander and had won fame by persuading the head of the religious order of Teutonic Knights to break with Rome. This Osiander, himself a married former priest, persuaded Cranmer—who appears to have needed little convincing—that his vow of chastity was papist nonsense. Thus liberated, Cranmer married Osiander's niece; it was actually his second marriage, an earlier wife having died years before, thereby making it possible for him to resume his career at Cambridge and in the church. Cranmer kept the German marriage secret, and with good reason: King Henry was, and all his life would remain, rigidly insistent on the celibacy of the clergy, forbidding matrimony even to the monks and nuns released from their vows of poverty and obedience after the destruction of their monasteries. Eventually there would be stories— one hopes that they were the invention of his Catholic adversaries— about how, when Cranmer returned to England, his wife accompanied him upside-down, hidden in a trunk into which airholes had been punched. A decade would pass before Cranmer finally confessed his marriage to the king. There is no better evidence of Henry's unique affection for him, an affection anchored in the certainty that in Cranmer he had found an absolutely loyal servant, than his decision to allow him to keep both his job and his spouse so long as the latter remained secret.

As the end of 1532 approached the pace of events began to accelerate. The king's divorce case and his attack on the church, which until now had been distinct battles fought on separate fronts, came to be inextricably entwined. Barely a week after Warham's death, Henry raised Anne Boleyn to the high rank of Marquess of Pembroke with a suitably munificent income (land worth a thousand pounds per year, plus an annuity of another thousand pounds exacted from Stephen Gardiner's diocese of Winchester) and the right to pass title and wealth to the "heirs male" of her body. Never before had an Englishwoman received a noble title other than by inheritance or matrimony. Perhaps Henry's sudden generosity was intended as an inducement for Anne to surrender at last; it provided some assurance that, even if she and the king never married, she would be handsomely provided for, and that any son born out of wedlock would be heir to a title and a fortune. The title she was given had had special meaning for the Tudors ever since Jasper was made Earl of Pembroke three-quarters of a century before and the future Henry VII spent most of his childhood at Pembroke Castle.

Not coincidentally, Anne's title enhanced her suitability to serve as the king's companion at a meeting with Francis I in northern France. Both kings had been eager for this meeting, which took place in October first at Boulogne (which belonged to France) and then at Calais (English), because each wanted to make sure that the other did not enter into an alliance with Charles V. Henry in particular had to be concerned that a conclusive break with Rome might cause the pious Charles to want to invade not only to avenge his aunt's honor but to rescue England from schism and heresy. The gathering was a grand occasion, as such events invariably were. The new Marquess of Pembroke (she did not have the female form of the title, marchioness, because she held it in her own right rather than as a spouse) had the satisfaction of dancing with Francis and later of receiving from him the gift of a costly diamond. To be presented to the king of France as the king of England's all-but-wife was no small thing, and it must have added to Anne's confidence that she was in no danger of being cast aside. The only disquieting note was the failure of any of the female members of the French royal family to appear: evidently they found the relationship between

Anne and Henry insufficiently respectable. Concerns on that score were not assuaged by the refusal of Henry's own sister Mary, herself a one-time queen of France, to join the festivities in Calais; she remained infuriatingly loyal to Catherine.

The substance of the conference had less to do with Charles V— Henry and Francis were satisfied for the time being with reaffirming the defensive alliance that already bound their two countries—than with the recalcitrant Pope Clement. Francis professed sympathy with Henry's anger and frustration. When Henry proposed that the two of them call a general council of the church as a way of overriding and neutering the pope, Francis was not enthusiastic, perhaps out of fear of Charles's possible reaction. He offered excuses: a council would be too difficult, would take too long to arrange, would be unpredictable in the final result. As an alternative he said that he was attempting to arrange a meeting with Clement in the new year, and he offered to include Henry in this meeting and use it to try to effect a resolution of the issues dividing England and Rome. Henry agreed; the thought of the French king meeting separately with the pope, of his possibly being drawn into an alliance with Clement and Charles, would have given him severe discomfort. He promised to do nothing in the meantime that might make reconciliation with the pope impossible. Francis for his part pledged not to proceed with a plan to marry his second son to the pope's niece Catherine de' Medici until Clement nullified Henry's marriage. Henry and Anne then returned home by slow stages, making leisurely stops along the way.

It was at about this time that Anne, if she had never done so previously, admitted Henry to her bed. We know this for the best of reasons: she was, by late January, incontrovertibly pregnant. Several things could have caused her to yield at this point. Her prominence during the visit to France, and her new status in the upper reaches of the hereditary nobility, obviously would have served as positive inducements. On the negative side were the French king's unexpected offer of a meeting with the pope and Henry's alarming (from Anne's perspective) acceptance. This raised the spectre of a rapprochement between England and Rome, a development that could mean ruin for Anne, her family, and their whole following including the religious reformers with whom the Boleyns were allied. If Henry decided to abandon the divorce—that could not have seemed likely, but no one knew better than Anne how unpredictable he could be—everything that had come to them with the king's favor would likely be lost. On the other hand, the promise of a royal son could secure the future for all of them.

Anne's pregnancy further accelerated the pace of everything the king was doing. It immediately gave rise to a need to ensure that her child, the king's son, would be legitimate. This led to an impromptu wedding at York Place early on January 25. The ceremony was performed by one of the royal chaplains, Rowland Lee, who as he hurried to the palace's western turret that morning knew only that he had received an unexpected order to go to a specific room to say mass. When he arrived, he was surprised to find waiting for him King Henry, Lady Anne, and a lady and two gentlemen of the court. Told that Henry and Anne wished to be married, Lee, mindful of the unresolved state of the divorce case, expressed concern about whether he was free to proceed. The king assured him that the necessary papal permission was in safekeeping in his privy chamber. At best, he was referring to the bull with which, long before, the pope had set aside the impediment created by the king's affair with Mary Boleyn, granting him permission to marry Anne *if* the marriage to Catherine were found to be invalid. At worst, Henry was simply lying. Lee, whether or not his mind was put at rest, had little choice but to take the king at his word.

The wedding was kept secret so that, later, it would be possible to fudge the date and make it appear that Anne and Henry had been married when their child was conceived. Anne's father, however, was sent across the Channel to inform Francis I, who did not abandon his hopes of including Henry in a meeting with the pope but did feel free, now that the English king had broken his promise, to resume negotiations for the marriage of his son to Pope Clement's niece. Under other circumstances a Medici might not have been considered an acceptable bride for a prince who was second in line to the crown of France. But Francis, obsessed as always with his ambitions in Italy, would have sacrificed more than family pride in order to keep pope and emperor apart.

Henry now had the wife he had craved, and she was delightfully pregnant. The only remaining need was for the marriage to be declared valid, which would remain impossible until the marriage to Catherine was nullified. As he had no hope by now of getting the pope's help, he had to find another way, and quickly. Inevitably, his attention and Cromwell's focused on the Archbishopric of Canterbury. More than five months had passed since Warham's death, and the two had used that time to work out a plan of action more detailed and ambitious than anything they had thus far attempted. Cranmer was central to that plan and, in the days after he arrived home from the continent, had shown himself to be as eager to assist as Henry and Cromwell could have hoped. In mid-January the king dispatched riders to Rome with a politely submissive request that Thomas Cranmer be appointed to Canterbury. A heavy curtain of secrecy remained in place around Henry's marriage to Anne and her pregnancy so that the papal court would have no idea that something new was afoot. To further ensure the pope's good will, he continued to be sent his traditional share of England's ecclesiastical revenues. He like the king was of course unaware that the candidate had a wife.

The nomination of an obscure archdeacon to such a high post would have raised eyebrows in any case, but Cranmer's candidacy provoked alarm. Well-placed Catholics on the continent and even in Rome had had dealings with Cranmer, whose assignments had taken him at one point to the Eternal City. His doctrinal inclinations were therefore fairly well known if his marital status was not, and Clement was warned not to agree to his appointment. The pope, however, lived in fear of a break with England as damaging to the church as the Lutheran rebellion that had already engulfed half of Germany. Though he was satisfied that Henry's marriage to Catherine was valid, and though he was mortally sick of the king's ham-handed attempts to bully and cajole him, he remained willing to do almost anything short of approving the divorce to heal the breach between them. Knowing little of who Cranmer actually was and nothing of the uses to which Henry intended to put him, Clement dispatched the documents required for the new primate to be consecrated exactly as his predecessors had always been.

Henry and Cromwell's plan was to have Cranmer, as soon as possible after he was installed, declare the king's first marriage null and his second valid. It was a simple plan as far as it went, but there was one complication. Catherine was certain to appeal to Rome, just as she had appealed years earlier. This would lead to delays even more intolerable than those the king had already suffered, and there could be no hope that Catherine would be denied. The legitimacy of the prince whose birth now approached would be compromised, and Henry would stand in increased danger of being excommunicated, his kingdom put under an interdict.

Cromwell was ready with an answer, and as usual his solution was to cut the Gordian knot. Long before the end of 1532 he had had in preparation a draft bill that would become famous as the Act in Restraint of Appeals (not to be confused with the Act in Restraint of Annates). Once approved by Parliament, it would use England's supposed status as an empire and the English king's consequent autonomy as a basis for forbidding any of his subjects to ask any foreign power (the bishop of Rome most emphatically included) to overrule him on any question. Cromwell revised his draft and revised it again as he waited for Cranmer's bulls of appointment to arrive from Rome, and sought advice on how to maximize support in Parliament. As soon as the bulls were in hand, he was ready to move. The years-old deadlock would be broken at last.

The next necessary step was to consecrate the new archbishop. This happened on March 30, and it happened in a way so peculiar that it might not have been possible had Cranmer not already shown himself to have a relaxed view of vows. The ceremony for installing bishops had always included the taking of an oath of loyalty to the pope. Until Henry turned this oath into a weapon with which to charge the bishops with praemunire, this procedure had never posed a problem. Except on those few and usually brief occasions when kings had clashed with the church over questions of jurisdiction, everyone had understood the distinction between royal and ecclesiastical authority and accepted the legitimacy of both. But Cranmer came to his new position with no such understanding. On the contrary, he believed sincerely that neither the king nor he nor any Englishman owed anything to the bishop of Rome, and that where religion was concerned the monarch's wish and will provided the answers to all questions.

The papal oath, therefore, presented Cranmer with a problem of ethics. He resolved that problem, just minutes before his consecration, by taking four selected witnesses and a notary aside to a place where they could hear him privately declare that, although he was about to complete the traditional formalities, nothing that he swore publicly should be construed as an intention to violate the law of God, disobey the king, or fail to do whatever must be done for the good of the church in England. The installation ceremony then began. Cranmer took the very oath that he had minutes before repudiated, an oath in direct contradiction to the work he was preparing to undertake.

That work was multifaceted but went forward with lightning speed. Six days after Cranmer's consecration, with the new archbishop presiding, the Southern Convocation approved a resolution declaring that the king's marriage to Catherine of Aragon had never been valid. This victory was easily won; many churchmen had never been strongly opposed to the divorce, and many who had been opposed, faced now with the demoralizing presence of Cranmer as their ostensible leader, saw no point in resisting. Two days after that, in spite of stubborn resistance, the Restraint of Appeals bill was passed by Parliament and became law. After another six days Anne's marriage to the king was announced in such a way as to create the impression that it had occurred in mid-November, before the expected child was conceived. By all accounts the news was not well received; at one London church on Easter Sunday, upon being told that Anne was now queen and asked to pray for her, the entire congregation got to its feet and walked out. The lord mayor was ordered to make certain that there would be no more such displays of discontent, and the city's professional guilds were told to keep silent on the subject and make their apprentices do the same.

The stage was now set for the final act, an ecclesiastical hearing at which Cranmer and a selected panel of his fellow divines would hear arguments on the validity of Henry's marriage to Catherine and pass final judgment. The result was a foregone conclusion. A procedural difficulty arose, however, in connection with Henry's new status as supreme head of the church: with the pope out of the picture, so that Cranmer could not claim to be acting in the name of any higher ecclesiastical authority, on what basis could he *order* the king to appear before the court and allow his case to be judged? Seeing that there was no such basis, the archbishop prudently decided not to order but to beg. But when he wrote to the king saying that "most humbly on my knees" he requested permission to convene his court, his words were found to be insufficiently abject. In the final version of his request, poor Cranmer described himself as "prostrate at the feet of your Majesty."

On May 23, to the surprise of no one, Cranmer's court declared that Henry and Catherine had never been married. Five days later, equally unsurprisingly, it declared that Henry and Anne were very married indeed. Just three days after that, at huge expense and amid great fanfare intended to inflame the enthusiasm of a public that in the event showed no enthusiasm at all, Anne was crowned queen of England at Westminster Abbey.

All of it had gone almost exactly according to plan, and everything continued to do so. On July 11, the same day that Henry signed the letters needed to implement the long-deferred Act in Restraint of Annates and terminate all payments to Rome, Pope Clement declared Henry's marriage to Anne invalid and warned him that unless he recognized Catherine as his wife he would be excommunicated—but not until the following September, and only *if* he failed to mend his ways. Henry responded with a fury that must have been fueled in part at least by fear, recalling his envoys and cutting off communications with the papacy. His participation in the planned meeting between Clement and Francis was now out of the question, but when that meeting finally took place in September Francis remained hopeful of somehow effecting a reconciliation. He had little difficulty persuading Clement to delay the excommunication again. In fact it would never be promulgated, so that neither Henry nor Clement ever found out whether it was still a weapon that could hurt.

Only one thing remained for the scenario to be complete. Anne still had to give birth to her son.

The child, when born on September 7, was named Elizabeth, after Henry's mother.

PART TWO

Monster

1533–1547

10

First Blood

Two dams broke in 1534. One was in Parliament, where resistance to the Crown snapped at last under Cromwell's relentless pressure and a torrent of revolutionary new laws began to change the character of English government and society. The other was inside the mind of a monarch who, perhaps swept away by the ecstatic realization that in the whole kingdom there was no force capable of keeping him from doing exactly as he wished, threw off all restraint and showed himself ready to destroy not only anyone who opposed him but anyone withholding approval of whatever he wanted to do.

The first victim, both of the newly docile Parliament and of the newly savage king, was a twenty-seven-year-old nun named Elizabeth Barton. Possibly epileptic, Barton, while a servant girl still in her teens, had been mysteriously healed of some affliction and begun falling into trances, having visions, and predicting the future. This caused her to become famous first locally, in her home county of Kent, and then more widely. She came to be revered as the Holy Maid of Kent and then, after she entered a convent, as the Nun of Kent. By all accounts she lived a blameless life and made a favorable impression on practically everyone who met her, including skeptical clergymen assigned to question and report on her. But, tragically for herself, eventually she was making pronouncements on the king's efforts to divorce Queen Catherine and warning that evil would befall him if he did not desist. She sent a message to the pope, saying that he too would be cursed if he did as Henry asked. The attention that she attracted is evident in the fact that at various times Cardinal Wolsey, Archbishop Warham, Bishop Fisher, Chancellor More, and even the king himself all met with her. All who had firsthand exposure to her and left a record of their impressions said that Barton seemed virtuous, humble, and possibly even holy. Even Henry was favorably disposed until she began to talk about the divorce.

Barton's fame, and the increasingly inflammatory nature of her opinions, made trouble inevitable. Cromwell's power and confidence were in full flower by this time—he had been given a seat on the Royal Council before the end of 1532 and made chancellor of the exchequer the following April—and in July 1533 he had Barton arrested. He and Cranmer questioned her at length, after which she was confined in the Tower along with a half dozen of the churchmen (an assortment of parish priests, Benedictine monks, and Franciscan friars) who had made themselves her supporters and, so it was said, her manipulators in the national debate over the divorce and the king's claim to ecclesiastical supremacy. The idea, clearly, was to discredit Barton and make her a frightening example of the price to be paid for opposing the Crown.

In November the Nun and her adherents were put on public display, made to listen to a preacher who ridiculed and vilified them, and finally, according to accounts left by people in the pay of Cromwell, required to confess that her entire career had been a fraud intended to mislead the gullible. It is not certain that these reported confessions actually occurred; no record of them was left by witnesses who can be considered impartial. Even if the accused did in fact confess, the men in whose custody they had been for months were quite capable of using torture to get what they wanted. Barton's own confession, as recorded for posterity, was obviously not the work of a barely literate serving girl but of a ghostwriter of some sophistication.

The confessions were not the end of the story, in any case. An effort was mounted to convict Barton and her companions of high treason by establishing that she had prophesied the death of the king and so had effectively threatened his life—and to draw in other, bigger prey on grounds that anyone who had encouraged her or even listened to her without reporting her words was guilty of treason as well. This effort came to nothing. The king's judges reported that the case was too weak even for them—there never was a shred of evidence that Barton at any time encouraged anyone to oppose the king actively or to use violence for any purpose—and there was at this point no basis in English law for charging someone with treason because of what he or she had said. Treason was still an *act*. Remarkably, some of Barton's judges were reported to have declared that they would die themselves rather than find her guilty.

Cromwell responded by finding yet another new way to make Parliament useful to the Crown. At his direction both houses approved a bill of attainder that declared Barton and her six closest associates guilty of high treason. Six others, Thomas More and Bishop Fisher among them, were attainted for misprision of treason—that is, for knowing of another person's treason and failing to report it. From the king's standpoint, this simplified everything beautifully. Not only Barton and her cohorts but several of the most eminent personages in the kingdom could be disposed of without the inconvenience of a trial, attainder being a legislative rather than a judicial device. The fact that no one including Barton herself could possibly have committed treason as the word was then understood in English law became irrelevant.

More and Fisher defended themselves, or tried to. More requested permission to appear before Parliament to address the charge against him. Upon being refused he wrote to Cromwell and the king, explaining how, in his meetings with the Nun of Kent, he had refused to hear her opinions of political matters and had advised her to share those opinions with no one. He told them also that when visited by admirers of Barton who wanted to discuss her visions, he had not allowed them to do so. Cromwell advised Fisher to throw himself on the king's mercy—good advice where saving his own skin was concerned, as Henry was always most likely to be generous when his victims submitted abjectly—but predictably the bishop refused. He said, sensibly enough, that he had been told by men he trusted (Archbishop Warham for one) that Barton was an honest and virtuous woman, and that his willingness to believe them, whether wise or foolish, could not possibly have been a crime. He said he had talked with Barton on three occasions, but only because she visited him uninvited. He had not reported Barton's dark predictions, he said, because he knew for a fact that she herself had already shared them with the king.

None of this had any effect on Henry, who obviously was interested not in the guilt or innocence of the accused but in their elimination. His friends, however, saw that he was in danger of overreaching; in the end More's name was removed from the bill of attainder, but only because Cranmer, Cromwell, and the Duke of Norfolk literally got down on their knees and implored the king to permit its removal. The three were willing to beg less because they wished to save the former chancellor than because, as they warned Henry, even a supine Parliament could not be depended upon to destroy a man of More's reputation on such thin evidence.

Fisher's name remained on the bill, and after its passage he was imprisoned. After a while, however, he was allowed to pay a fine of £300, the yearly income of his little Diocese of Rochester, and set free. Barton and five others—two Benedictine monks, two Observant friars, and Barton's confessor—were taken to the royal killing ground at Tyburn. There Barton, perhaps because she was a woman and allegedly confessed to being "a poor wench without learning" and having fallen into "a certain pride and fantasy with myself," was shown the mercy of simple death by hanging. The priests endured a good deal more. They too were hanged, but then they met the full fate of traitors: cut down while still alive and brought back to consciousness, they had their genitals cut off and stuffed into their mouths, their intestines torn from their bodies and thrown into a fire, and their beating hearts pulled out of their chests and held up where they could see them. Finally their bodies were cut into four quarters for display in different parts of London, their heads boiled and put on stakes. As they had never been tried, it was impossible for anyone to know how, exactly, they had committed treason, or whether, given the opportunity, they might have been able to establish their innocence. The public was left free to conclude that they had died for displeasing the king. The king, no doubt, wanted it to conclude exactly that.

Henry, meanwhile, was occupied elsewhere. The future of his dynasty was a question that never went away, the birth of the baby Elizabeth had done nothing to answer it, and now that he was in his forties the king was giving evidence of being more seriously concerned about his lack of a male heir than he had ever been before. The previous November he had married his only living son, the illegitimate fourteen-year-old Henry Fitzroy, to Mary Howard, who as a daughter of the Duke of Norfolk was also Anne Boleyn's cousin. This was another coup for the Howard family, another joining of its blood to that of the Tudors, potentially of vast importance because of the possibility, which had been in the air for years, that Henry might choose in the end to make the playful young Fitzroy, on whom he doted, his heir. By January, however, Anne was pregnant for the second time. As preparations began anew for the arrival of a crown prince—Henry was always touchingly certain that his next child would be a boy—the king took as his mistress yet another young Boleyn cousin, a girl named Madge Shelton. The magic was going out of the royal marriage by this time; the increasingly insecure Anne upbraided her husband for his dalliances, and Henry turned his back on her in mute disbelief. The situation was not improved when Anne miscarried. This happened in the middle of a remarkably busy spring, when the Nun of Kent was being readied for execution, the papal court in Rome was taking up the divorce case at last, and Parliament was pouring out laws that would have been unimaginable a few years earlier.

Pope Clement, under pressure from Charles V and provoked into action at last by Henry's taking of a second wife without being released from his first, assembled a council of cardinals—a consistory—to consider the divorce case. On March 23, rather to the pope's surprise (he knew that agents of the king of France had been lobbying hard to line up support for Henry, spending the English king's money freely), nineteen of the twenty-two assembled cardinals voted to deny the annulment, uphold the validity of Henry's marriage to Catherine, and declare that Catherine had been dealt with unjustly and should be restored to her place as queen. The remaining three voted not in Henry's favor but merely for further delay, at which point, after so many years, the king's great matter was settled even in Rome. But Clement, his hopes of somehow avoiding a final break with Henry being practically inexhaustible, postponed issuing a formal judgment.

Rome was no longer relevant, however; things had gone too far in England for papal rulings to matter. By coincidence March 23 was also the day on which Parliament, with Cromwell issuing the instructions, passed an Act of Succession that not only gave the force of civil law to Cranmer's nullification of the king's first marriage and validation of his second but erected around the archbishop's findings a protective barrier of punishment for anyone who failed to assent. The act's assertion that Henry was to be succeeded on the throne by the children of his "most dear and entirely beloved lawful wife Queen Anne" (the sheer number of adjectives heaped upon the lady's name is suggestive of royal defensiveness) could have surprised no one by 1534. Its failure to mention Princess Mary, implying that she was illegitimate and therefore excluded from the succession, would have offended many but surprised few. Much more startling, for anyone who knew the law, was the act's broadening of the crime of high treason to encompass anyone acting or writing in defiance or rejection of the Boleyn marriage. Even speaking against the marriage was made misprision of treason. With these provisions the king closed the loopholes—it would be more accurate to say he destroyed the protections—that had made it impossible to bring the Nun of Kent's case into a court of law.

The Act of Succession did not stop even there. Not satisfied with forbidding criticism, Henry had added a requirement that every subject "observe, keep, maintain and defend the act and all the whole contents and effects thereof, and all other Acts and Statutes made since the beginning of this present parliament"—since, that is, December 1529, when the king had ventured his first hesitant attack on ecclesiastical privilege. To ensure compliance, every subject was to take an oath of loyalty not only to the king but to his heirs by Anne, and refusal to swear was made treason. Conveniently, Parliament neglected to specify what the words of the oath should be. This left Henry and Cromwell free to put it into whatever form best pleased them and even to require different people to swear to different things.

This was not the only law approved by Parliament in furtherance of the king's agenda that spring. An Act for the Submission of the Clergy gave statutory form to, and therefore enhanced the legitimacy of, the submission so dubiously wrung out of convocation two years earlier. An Act in Absolute Restraint of Annates removed the conditional aspects of the earlier annates legislation, diverted the payment of annates from Rome to the Crown rather than eliminating them as might have been expected, and laid down curious new rules for the selection of bishops. The king would henceforth send the name of his nominee to the clergy of the diocese involved. The clergy would then be accorded the privilege of approving the king's candidate. If somehow such approval was not forthcoming, the royal choice would take office anyway and the clergy of that diocese would lose the honor of being consulted in future. Yet another act took the awarding of dispensations away from Rome and gave it to the archbishop of Canterbury, assigning two-thirds of the fees thus generated to the Crown. Anyone appealing a ruling by Canterbury was to turn henceforth not to Rome but to the King's Chancery Court, and of course it was no longer heresy to refuse to recognize the pope—the bishop of Rome, as he was now to be called—as head of the English church. Those monasteries which until now had been under the jurisdiction of the orders with which they were affiliated rather than their local bishops were put under the authority not of the bishops but of the Crown.

What it all added up to was a wholesale chopping away of the English church's traditional connections to Rome and their replacement with new obligations to the king. Henry was creating, not a church free of domination by any external power, but a church that he himself would dominate totally. Parliament, too, was being made newly subordinate to the Crown. Cromwell continued to take care, in preparing the latest statutes, to make clear that Parliament was merely recognizing the king's supremacy rather than conferring supremacy upon him. The king's authority was acknowledged as coming directly from God, not from any earthly source and certainly not (as Thomas More had dared to suggest years before, in his first public appearance as chancellor) from his subjects. To oppose the king was to oppose God. This was the highwater mark of royal authority in England, the opening of an era—it would not last long—in which the Crown claimed, and for a while actually possessed, mastery over the lives, the property, and even the consciences of its subjects. Cromwell's reward for making it happen was to be appointed, that spring, King Henry's principal secretary. He would turn the position into the most powerful in the government. From it he would reach out to control both houses of Parliament, the courts, and the council.

The destruction of ecclesiastical authority was final: after the 1530s the bishops as a body never again played a major role in the political life of the kingdom. It is arguable, some would say certain, that this and the other changes of the spring of 1534 were an improvement over traditional arrangements. Most of them were, in any case, irrelevant to the everyday lives of the overwhelming majority of English men and women. Few of them could ever have had occasion to appeal to Rome or even to Canterbury, to request a dispensation or become involved in questions of heresy. Aside from being required to take an oath that must have struck many of them as more odd than important, most people would have had little reason even to be aware that new laws had supplanted the old. Parish life, the age-old Latin Mass, the seven sacraments, beliefs that had been part of the heritage of every man and woman in England through more centuries than most of them had knowledge of—none of this had been altered at all.

Still, the popularity of Catherine of Aragon and the widespread sense that she had been dealt with unfairly ensured that the Act of Succession would not be well received. And many, almost certainly most of the best-informed and most influential of the king's subjects, those who had some sense of the significance of the new laws, would have been uneasy at least about what was happening. The making into treason of things that had never been treason before—had never even been crimes before—would have unsettled any reasonable mind. The requirement that everyone swear to defend and uphold innovations condemned by some of the best men in the kingdom could easily have seemed an outrage. Henry was discarding beliefs and customs and understandings that his people had been raised with. To require those people not simply to accept his changes but to champion them, to swear that they believed them to be right, was an assault on the integrity of the individual of a kind never before seen in England. It was inevitable that the people would be skeptical. Outbreaks of popular discontent, too, were probably inevitable, though they would not be quick in coming.

Further initiatives by the king *would* be quick in coming. The butchering of the Nun of Kent and her group was barely the beginning.

THE TOWER

MAKE A CHRONOLOGICAL LIST OF ALL THE NOTABLE ENGLISH men and women who were ever imprisoned in the Tower of London and then put to death there, and a remarkable fact leaps out: such executions were overwhelmingly concentrated in the Tudor era, with few happening afterward and even fewer earlier, during the supposedly terrible Middle Ages. There is no better measure of just how big a deviation from the norm the Tudors were—of how much more savage their politics were than anything seen before or since.

Though the Tower had loomed ominously over London for four and a half centuries by the time Henry VIII had Elizabeth Barton and her associates locked up in it and then killed, throughout almost all of its history it had not been a particularly bloody place. In its earliest manifestation it was an improvised motte-and-bailey affair—a wooden stockade on a hilltop—hurriedly erected shortly after the Norman Conquest of 1066 not as a defense against possible invaders but to intimidate the Anglo-Saxon population of the adjacent and still tiny city of London. After ten years William the Conqueror decided to rebuild it in stone and began work on the massive keep that came to be known as the White Tower. It, with the four "onion domes" added by Henry VIII in 1530, became the centerpiece of a complex of surrounding fortifications and remains one of England's most familiar landmarks down to the present day. Here as elsewhere the Normans built for eternity: constructed of stone carried by ship from northern France, the White Tower was ninety feet high with a 118-by-107-foot foundation and had walls that were fifteen feet thick at the base and eleven feet thick at the top with towers at each corner. The entry was well above ground level, and the stairs leading to it were removable in case of attack.

When completed by William II in 1097, the Tower was by far the most impressive structure ever seen in London. Though its location near the lowest bridgeable point on the River Thames would make it increasingly important as a defensive stronghold in case of invasion, as the twelfth century began its prime purpose continued to be to give the Normans an impregnable base from which to dominate a subject population. From the start it served multiple purposes—fortress, royal residence, place of worship, armory, prison—and as the generations passed so many kings expanded and altered it in so many ways that it became, as it remains today, a kind of museum of medieval castle architecture. Three generations after the completion of the White Tower, King Richard the Lion-Hearted returned from the Third Crusade with new ideas about defensive stoneworks and ordered the construction of so-called "curtain walls" around the original tower. Even more extensive additions, the most important by Richard's nephew Henry III and Henry's son Edward I, extended the perimeter out farther and farther until finally what was still called "*the* Tower" covered eighteen acres and included twenty-one distinct towers, all behind two concentric walls of overwhelming height and a broad moat filled with water from the Thames. There was no more powerful fortress anywhere in Europe. It retained all of its original functions, becoming an increasingly opulent home for the royal family, and also provided a virtually impregnable home for the Crown jewels, the mint, the government's records, and even a royal zoo complete with lions.

Though its radically increased size and strength made the Tower an ideal place for the confinement of important prisoners, it remained remarkably free of political violence for almost four centuries. Within a few years of the White Tower's completion and King William II's death, his hated minister Ranulf Flambard (Ranulf the Torchbearer) was imprisoned in it, but he escaped by climbing down a rope smuggled to him inside a wine cask. Richard II was forced to abdicate in the Tower in 1399, but his death took place elsewhere. The climactic years of the Wars of the Roses brought the Tower's first major eruption of mayhem: the 1471 murder of Henry VI; the 1478 execution of Edward IV's and Richard III's brother George, Duke of Clarence; the 1483 killing of Edward's chamberlain Lord Hastings by Richard; and the disappearance of Edward's two young sons in that same year. Things were again quiet for a decade and a half until, as we have seen, Henry VII had both the imposter Perkin

Warbeck and Clarence's son the earl of Warwick taken from their cells and put to death.

The Tower was still a royal residence when Henry VIII was a boy (it would remain one into the Stuart dynasty in the seventeenth century), and he must have known it well while growing up. When he was not quite six years old, he and his mother, Queen Elizabeth, took refuge in the White Tower when a force of rebels professing support for Warbeck came out of the west and threatened London. Six years later Elizabeth died in the Tower shortly after giving birth, and her body lay in state there before being taken to Westminster for interment. A year after Henry inherited the throne he reached into the Tower to deliver to the executioner his father's hated henchmen Dudley and Empson, and three years after that, before leaving England for his first war in France, he did the same with his cousin Edmund de la Pole. But then quiet returned for two decades—the last bloodless decades that the Tower would know until the Tudors were no more. The change came in 1534, when Elizabeth Barton and her five associates were sent to their deaths and replaced in the Tower by Sir Thomas More, the onetime lord chancellor, and John Fisher, the bishop of Rochester. From then on, to be a significant character in the Tudor story—even to *be* a Tudor—would be to run a high risk of being sent first to the Tower and from there to a gruesome death.

11

Supremacy

King Henry was driven—by his compulsion to dominate, by his hunger for admiration and approval, and by the dangers into which his needs were drawing him—to become an early practitioner of the art of political propaganda. What he was demanding was obviously not going to be easily achieved, and the price of failure was potentially high. Discontent could turn into rebellion, and Henry's new status as an outlaw in the eyes of the Roman church could become an encouragement for the continental powers to invade. His survival might very well depend on the acquiescence of his subjects, for whom he seems to have felt little except contempt.

Those subjects had to be won over. Where they could not be won, they had to be frightened into conformity. In the spring of 1534 Henry undertook to do both things: to convert his people and to terrify them. A national propaganda machine was erected for the purpose: instructions went out for churchmen, on Easter Sunday and thereafter, to preach the new truth—that the pope was an imposter and a usurper, and that in religious as in secular matters there was no authority higher than the king. Cranmer, free at last to give vent to the hatred of Rome that appears to have been boiling deep inside his otherwise placid nature nearly all his life, showed the way by telling his congregation at Canterbury Cathedral that the bishop of Rome was "the Antichrist of the Apocalypse." Such words would have shocked and offended many of the clergy whose leader Cranmer now was, not to mention his conventionally Catholic lay listeners. That his example was not followed as widely as he wished is apparent in the fact that he soon resorted to the novel idea of requiring all the priests in his archdiocese to obtain licenses to preach, suspending the licenses for a year, and instructing all the bishops of the Southern Convocation to do the same. Everything possible was being done to silence a recalcitrant clergy, but resentment became almost palpable. A monk who laughed at Cranmer, calling him "a fool archbishop," was thrown into prison; it was reported that guards were needed to ensure the archbishop's safety when he was in Canterbury. Justices of the peace around England and Wales received instructions to arrest any preacher who spoke in favor of papal authority. Propaganda was reinforced with the police powers of the Crown.

In the days following Easter the royal hammer began to descend on anyone whose words, acts, or omissions might, in the opinion of the king or his ministers, serve to encourage disobedience. The Crown's principal weapon was the oath prepared for use under the Act of Succession. In the form approved for general use, this oath acknowledged that the king was right about the divorce, his marriage to Anne, and his imperial authority—about everything. Agents fanned out across the kingdom, to the universities and to distant villages, seeing to it that the oath was taken everywhere. Some targets, however, had higher priority than others. Anyone in a position of authority, anyone whose decision was likely to become known to substantial numbers of other people, was automatically a prime target. Any such person likely to be perceived by the public as not in agreement with the king received an even higher priority. No one had higher priority than Thomas More, who had left the chancellorship rather than assent to the king's supremacy and had since then maintained a silence that was obviously heavy with meaning, and John Fisher, who from the start had been anything but silent and was all the more dangerous because so widely admired.

Both Fisher and More received summonses to appear at Lambeth Palace, the London residence of the archbishop of Canterbury, on Monday, April 13. They knew what to expect. More spent time with his family before leaving home that morning, telling them that he was likely bound for prison and might never return. Upon their arrival at Lambeth he and Fisher found themselves in a long procession of men being

marched one by one into the presence of Cromwell, Cranmer, Thomas
Audley (the nonentity who was More's replacement as chancellor), and
the abbot of Westminster. All were asked, when their turns came, to
sign the succession oath. Almost all did so and were sent on their way.
Fisher refused and was escorted to the Tower. More asked for time to
read what he was being asked to sign and, having done so, observed that
by signing he would be accepting not only the succession rights of
Henry and Anne's offspring but the ecclesiastical supremacy of the king
in England. He too refused. When asked to explain himself, he declined
to do that as well, saying only that in signing he would be violating his
conscience and thereby endangering his soul. Clearly he had already offended the king, he said, and in giving his reasons he could only give further offense. Even when standing on principle, he remained the crafty
lawyer.

More was told that every member of the House of Commons had
sworn the oath. He was shown the signatures and asked how he could
oppose his conscience to those of so many others. He answered that he
had no quarrel with those who elected to sign, but that he himself could
not do so, and that he had on his side most Christians living and dead.
After that the discussion had nowhere to go. More was put under arrest.
He spent the next four days in the custody of the abbot and then joined
Fisher in the Tower. The two were kept apart in fairly comfortable accommodations (More was allowed to keep his manservant), and in the
days following both offered to swear to the succession. The king and
Parliament had the right to decide such matters in whatever way they
chose, More and Fisher said, and they could have no difficulty in acknowledging that right if they were not required at the same time to repudiate the authority of the pope and, by extension, the international
community of Christians. Cranmer looked favorably on this offer. He
urged the king to accept it, and to make much of the fact that More and
Fisher had done as he required while ignoring their refusal to do *everything* required. Cromwell, however, was opposed, and Henry agreed
with him.

Faced with the grim consequences of refusal, and receiving from
Rome no word of guidance or encouragement and from Canterbury
firm instructions to conform, most of the clergy subscribed. Where resistance appeared, it was generally hesitant, isolated, and susceptible to

modest applications of pressure. The exceptions, those instances where resistance was bold and not quickly dissolved by threats, brought down the full wrath of the Crown. Those who resisted were seen as both a danger to the king and an opportunity for him and his henchmen to show that they would not be defied. From this followed, with a speed that might have surprised even Henry himself, the extinction of the Observant Franciscans, as respected a religious order as any in England.

The Observants, the reader will recall, were the order of William Peto, the priest who, from his pulpit at Greenwich, had dared to chastise King Henry on Easter Sunday 1532. Founded a century and a half earlier by a breakaway group that believed the Franciscans were becoming too lax, the Observants won recruits and admiration for the austerity of their lives and their dedication to their preaching mission. Invited into England in the early 1480s, they soon had six flourishing friaries. Henry VIII himself had been baptized in one of the friars' churches, as were the short-lived son to whom Queen Catherine gave birth in 1511, Princess Mary, and—rather surprisingly, considering all that had transpired by the time she was born—Anne Boleyn's infant daughter.

Not surprisingly, considering this background, the Observants' refusal to accept the divorce became a major source of annoyance for Henry. The diatribe that Friar Peto directed at him, and Friar Elston's withering treatment of the preacher sent to answer Peto, had been startling acts of defiance. Observants from the order's house at Canterbury had been involved with Elizabeth Barton, too, and a pair of them died with her at Tyburn. The frequency with which Observants denounced the king's innovations in their sermons, along with the writings being sent across the Channel by Peto and Elston from their place of exile, made it inevitable that the Crown would move against them.

By the spring of 1534 Henry and Cromwell had no reason to delay. A special version of the succession oath was prepared for the friars' exclusive use. It was even more comprehensive, and from the conservative perspective even more objectionable, than the version that More and Fisher had been unable to accept. It required the Observants not only to swear allegiance to Henry and Anne and the offspring of their union (none of them disputed the king's right to require that), not only to recognize the king as the supreme earthly authority under whom they followed the Franciscan rule, not only to deny that the bishop of Rome had more authority than any other bishop, but to pledge themselves to do everything possible to persuade others to do likewise. In demanding so much, the king was requiring that the friars actively repudiate much of what they had vowed in becoming Franciscans.

To humiliate the Observants and underscore his unhappiness with them, Henry ordered that the oath be delivered to their six houses by visitors selected from other, more cooperative orders of friars, the Augustinians and the Dominicans. This too was provocative. There being, inevitably, a degree of rivalry among the orders, sending representatives of one to make demands of another came close to being an insult, all the more so as the original encouragement of the Observants in England by Edward IV and Henry VII had implied dissatisfaction with the orders already established there, the Augustinians and Dominicans included. The results of the visits were, in any case, infuriatingly unsatisfactory from the king's point of view. At the Canterbury friary, a house traumatized by the ghastly killing of two of its members with Elizabeth Barton, only two members of the community refused to take the oath. But at Richmond, though the prior was willing, almost all the friars refused. At Greenwich, the Observant establishment with the closest connection to the royal family, refusal was again almost unanimous. Overall the results were ambiguous; at some houses a solid majority was opposed but after much persuasion agreed to let four senior members decide for all. The one thing that would satisfy the king, unanimous acceptance, the Observants could not be induced to give him. And so Henry settled for second best: another chance to show just how high the price of refusal could go.

One day in June two carts loaded with friars were seen rumbling through the streets of London en route to the Tower. Others followed, and by the end of August every one of the order's houses had been emptied out and some two hundred of its members were in prison. They did not get the gentle treatment accorded to Fisher and More. Many were chained to the walls of their cells, many were tortured, many were starved. Some fifty eventually died in confinement. After several years, the king's attention having moved on to other things, those still alive would be permitted to slip away quietly to exile in France, Scotland, and Ireland. There has never been evidence that any of them had been involved in sedition, in attempting to overthrow the king, or in encouraging others to do anything of the kind. Not one was ever charged with any crime. The extermination of their order was simply an eloquent demonstration of the king's power, and of his willingness to use it.

The lesson was not lost on the bishops, none of whom followed Fisher's example. Several were clearly unhappy with what the king was doing, and some would eventually regret their failure to resist. The reason for that failure lies partly in the starkness of the choice that Henry laid out for them: they could do things his way and prosper, or they could be locked away. It also lies partly in the bishops themselves. They had been chosen for their positions not by the pope, not by other ecclesiastics or any other element of the clergy, but by Henry or (as was true of a few of the oldest of them) by Henry's father. And most had been chosen because of their service to a Crown to which, in consequence of how they had been rewarded, they felt a heavy obligation. They were administrators and diplomats. They had political skill. They lived in a time increasingly dominated by the idea that princes ruled by the grace of God, and that to disobey one's ruler was akin to disobeying God. Nothing in any of this had prepared them for martyrdom, and few of the decisions out of which they had shaped their careers had shown them to be inclined in that direction.

Even so, some of them had to be wrestled into submission, and some paid a price for resisting as much as they did. Cuthbert Tunstal appeared for a time to be destined to follow Fisher into the Tower. When at the start of 1534 he set out for London and the next session of Parliament, he received an order from the king to turn around and return home— not the first time his criticism of the king had made him unwelcome at Westminster. It was not until the parliamentary session had concluded, with its flood of statutes cutting off England from Rome, that Tunstal was summoned. He arrived in London to find Fisher in prison amid reports of the killing of Elizabeth Barton, and soon his London residence was invaded and ransacked by Cromwell's agents. At this point Tunstal capitulated. He took the oath of succession, supposedly with reservations that have been lost to history. As usual the king wanted more. He made certain that Tunstal was not merely subdued but made to crawl, requiring him to visit Catherine of Aragon in company with the archbishop of York and explain that he no longer believed her marriage to be valid. Catherine of course was hurt and angry, all the more so because at about this same time she learned that her former confessor, the Observant friar John Forest, also had taken the oath. (He was in prison at the time.) For Tunstal the experience must have been excruciating. He was allowed to return to his ecclesiastical duties but was never again trusted by the king.

It was much the same with Stephen Gardiner. Though originally one of the most active supporters of the king's campaign for a divorce, Gardiner was deeply conservative, and he had immense difficulty in leaping from a simple belief that the king's marriage was invalid to the vastly bigger idea that the papacy had no right to the authority it had always exercised. After being passed over for the see of Canterbury in 1532, Gardiner got back into line and tried to show himself to be the king's man first, but he did so too late. His expulsion from the court's inner circle became official when Cromwell replaced him as secretary.

November brought news—accurate this time—of the death of Pope Clement. Surprisingly in light of the lengths to which he had already gone to put an end to papal jurisdiction in England, Henry ordered one of his agents in Italy, Gregory Casale, to go to Rome and do what he could to promote the election of a candidate likely to be friendly to his cause. He could not have been disappointed by the emergence of Cardinal Alessandro Farnese as Pope Paul III; before his election Farnese had expressed his eagerness to bring the English monarch back into the fold, and soon afterward he was asking Casale for advice on how to make that happen. He was unable to grasp that Henry would no longer consider conceding anything—that though he would have been delighted by papal acknowledgment that his marriage to Catherine was null and his marriage to Anne valid, he had no intention of undoing any of his anti-Roman statutes. Thus the new pope, like Clement, continued to nurse empty hopes.

The sterility of those hopes should have become obvious even as far away as Rome when Parliament reconvened in November and in short order passed three more momentous laws of Cromwell's devising. The Act of Supremacy was, strictly speaking, nothing new. It summarized and put into statutory form much of what Henry had previously and successfully claimed for himself: supreme ecclesiastical jurisdiction including authority over convocations of the clergy; the power to issue injunctions to which the clergy were obliged to conform; and the power to declare, through Parliament, what his subjects should and should not believe. Like the statutes passed in the year's first session, this one conferred no powers on the king; instead it acknowledged the powers presumably conferred on him by God. Its importance, Cromwell's reason for drafting it and pushing it through to approval, lay in the simple fact that statutory expression of the king's authority gave Parliament a basis for punishing anyone who denied that authority. Thus it became impossible—or less possible, at least—to accuse Henry and Cromwell and their agents of acting unlawfully when they killed or imprisoned the likes of Barton, Fisher, More, and the Observant friars. Such acts would henceforth be in accordance with the law.

The king's powers having been thus laid out systematically and in some detail, all that remained was to establish what exactly the king's subjects owed him in this connection and what kinds of behavior would put them in violation of the law. This was accomplished by a new measure that extended the state's definition of treason into areas that even the Act of Succession had left untouched, fundamentally changing that definition for the first time in 182 years. If the Supremacy Act was little more than a codification and legitimization of things that Henry had previously done, the Treasons Act of 1534 was without precedent. Until it was passed, no English man or woman could be found guilty of high treason and therefore be made subject to a penalty of death except as a result of attempting to end the king's life, making war against him, or allying with his enemies. And there had had to be at least two witnesses to the commission of treason. But now, and most ambiguously, it was made treasonous to deprive the king, the queen, or their heirs of "the dignity, title or name of their royal estates." To be guilty of high treason, it was no longer necessary to try to do harm to the royal family but only to "wish, will or desire by words or writing, or by craft imagine" such harm. Mere words, even mere thoughts, could now be punished with execution, and only one witness was required. Finally and absurdly, the new law made it a capital offense to call the king a tyrant (or for that matter a heretic, a schismatic, or an infidel).

Though records of the parliamentary proceedings of this period are sparse and often of questionable accuracy, these provisions appear to have shocked a good many members, and to have moved some to resistance. This probably explains the insertion into the bill, at two places, of the word "maliciously"; Cromwell is believed to have had to agree to this in order to get the bill passed. It meant, presumably, that one could wish to deprive Henry and his queen and children of the "dignity" of their "royal estates," or even call the king a tyrant, so long as one did not do so with evil intent. It was another unfathomable ambiguity, and it would prove to be no check on the king as he went about bending the law to his purposes.

The third major statute passed by this session was a stone that killed two birds. It conclusively cut off the flow of money from England to Rome, not only diverting it to the Crown but increasing it substantially. It was called the Act of First Fruits and Tenths—first fruits because it required anyone appointed to an ecclesiastical office to give the king the year of income previously sent to the papal court; tenths because it gave the king, for the first time, ten percent of the income of every "archbishopric, bishopric, abbacy, monastery, priory, archdeaconry, deanery, hospital, college, house collegiate, prebend, cathedral church, collegiate church, conventual church, parsonage, vicarage, chantry, free chapel, or other benefice or promotion spiritual, of what name, nature or quality soever they be, within any diocese of this realm or in Wales." By this single stroke the Crown's income was majestically increased, and the supposedly unconscionable burden that Rome had long been imposing was abruptly made bigger. The numbers are impressive: the average amount sent to Rome annually between 1485 and 1534—£4,800—was replaced by payments to the Crown of £46,052 in 1535 and £51,770 the year after that.

In 1534, for the first time in a decade, Henry asked Parliament for taxation. He was given a traditional levy: two "fifteenths and tenths" (percentages of certain assets of different classes of subject) and also a subsidy. When everything was taken into account, therefore, the year brought the Crown a massive inflow of gold. It was not enough, however, to remove the financial difficulties that Cromwell now had the duty to manage. The king's gambling, his many luxuries, the expansion and improvement of Hampton Court Palace and Whitehall and his other residences, the building of the new St. James's Palace in London—taken together, these things were almost more than the treasury could bear.

The year had brought astonishing things: proof of Henry's ability to make Parliament deliver practically anything he demanded, the enshrinement of his ecclesiastical supremacy in the law of the land, the crushing of domestic opposition, a conclusive repudiation of Rome, and a great deal of badly needed money. But all of it seemed merely to whet the king's appetite. He wanted more. He became more determined than ever that everyone in England was going to conform to his will and embrace his definition of the truth.

Queen Anne, tragically, was failing to conform: her second pregnancy ended in miscarriage. Henry was still hopeful, still trying, still sleeping with the queen for whom he had waited so long, but he was becoming weary of her tantrums and her jealousy and her failure to produce the expected heir. He began to wonder if something was wrong—not with himself, of course, but with Anne, or with their union. He began to suspect that his second marriage must be as displeasing to God as his first had been. Evidently he also—as Anne would be heard to complain— began to have difficulty performing sexually. A long time would pass before Anne became pregnant again.

Fisher and More were still refusing to conform. Maddeningly, they sat in their stone cells in the Tower and under the closest scrutiny said nothing and did nothing that could make it possible to have them put to death. Henry therefore resorted to what was becoming a favorite way of destroying those he saw as his enemies when they were not within reach of the law. He had them attainted for misprision of treason, and this time the penalty would be no mere fine. Attainder provided a basis for keeping them in prison for the rest of their lives if that was what the king wished, and for confiscating everything they owned. More's Chelsea household, which included a large extended family, was reduced to destitution. More himself was no longer allowed visitors or access to the Tower gardens.

As one of his last acts of the year, Henry appointed Cromwell to serve as his vice-regent, empowered to administer the church on his behalf. Even the most reform-minded of the bishops, the ones most antagonistic toward Rome and most eager to cast off the old ways, found this hard to accept. Suddenly they were subordinate not only to their king but to a rough upstart commoner who had never taken holy orders at even the lowliest level and had no training in theology or canon law or anything of the kind.

Cromwell and Henry, of course, knew exactly what they were doing.

They were positioning themselves to use for their own purposes a power that traditionally, virtually from time immemorial, had belonged to the bishops and the heads of the religious orders. This was the power of visitation—the right and responsibility to enter the religious houses of England and Wales, examine their operations, and impose such corrective measures as might be found necessary.

For the first time in history, thanks to the parliamentary enactments of 1534, this power now resided in the king.

And the king had in his vice-regent a man who understood what kinds of opportunities this created, knew how to exploit them to the full, and would feel no hesitation in doing so.

Cromwell was now ready, as one of the most momentous years in the history of England came to its end, to begin using the king's new powers in ways that the king himself may not yet have imagined.

MONKS, NUNS, AND FRIARS

FOR AT LEAST FOUR CENTURIES AFTER HENRY VIII'S DEATH, British conventional wisdom insisted confidently that his assault on the religious orders and their houses was not only justified but little short of imperative. The people of England were taught that by the 1530s monasticism was dying, was sunk in a moral decay too awful to be discussed in mixed company—fabricated stories about secret tunnels connecting the sleeping quarters of nuns and monks had become part of the national folklore—and needed to be put out of its misery.

About one thing, at least, this national mythology was right. Monasticism in England *was* dying when Henry decided to kill it—in fact, it had been dying for centuries. But that is only part of the story, and not the most interesting part. What is equally true, and more significant because so greatly at variance with what is commonly believed, is that England's monasteries had also been reviving, reinventing, and renewing themselves all through the centuries of their decline. Which is simply to say that the institution of monasticism, in the sixteenth century no less than in the fourteenth or the twelfth or long before that, remained a living, multifaceted, endlessly changing thing—a *dynamic* thing. If in some ways it was not entirely healthy when Henry launched his attack on it—and it certainly was not—in others it had rarely been more robust. Some parts of it were withering even as others flourished, and up to the end it appears to have been changing for the better in at least as many ways as it was changing for the worse.

It had always been so. Recurrent, frequently radical reform had been one of the main threads in the history of European monasticism from its beginnings. Monasticism had arisen out of an urgent impulse to create something new—to find a way by which people in pursuit of the transcendental might organize themselves into supportive communities—and naturally it was the seekers themselves who did the creating. The waves of reform that followed one after another were almost without exception the work not of some disapproving outside authority but of the monks and nuns themselves. There should be nothing surprising in any of this. The monastic vocation being almost by definition a way of life for men and women wanting something not easily found in ordinary experience, it is only to be expected that some of the people who enter it will be dissatisfied with what they find and that some of those will insist upon going deeper. It has always been inevitable that the very success of different varieties of monasticism would spark a desire to experiment with other, newer (and sometimes older) forms.

Britain's first great experience of monastic reform came as early as the tenth century, the time of the Anglo-Saxons, when the perhaps two hundred small monasteries then functioning on the island agreed to organize themselves in a new way and subject themselves to a new system of discipline. Throughout the preceding four centuries, during what later times have named the Dark Ages (they were distinctly less dark north of the English Channel than on the European mainland), the monasteries of England and Wales and even more so those of Ireland had been very nearly the only institutions in all of Western Christendom to preserve the cultural and intellectual heritage that had collapsed with the Roman Empire. Many of these earliest monasteries were, in addition to unique centers of learning, bases from which parties of monks set out to carry the gospel, and with it literacy, to barbarian tribes on the continent. Each was organized and governed according to whatever system it had worked out for itself or borrowed from some convenient source. Each adopted whatever practices and purposes it chose, and the differences between houses could be extreme and controversial. Through many generations there was no widely accepted answer to the question of how religious communities might best manage their affairs, and the extent of dissatisfaction with this situation can be inferred from the readiness with which a remedy was embraced as soon as a potentially workable one became available.

What crossed to England in the tenth century was the so-called Rule of St. Benedict, a system of monastic governance that had been drawn up by an obscure abbot in Italy fully four hundred years before. This set of regulations, rigorous but not fanatically severe, proved to be the most workable of many early efforts to show people wanting the religious life how to form communities that would not fall apart under the strain of human interaction. Benedict of Nursia's plan met so many needs so well that it was adopted throughout Italy and from there spread north. Eventually it became so universal a standard that, for a time, nearly every monastery in Europe was "Benedictine." In 970, at a church synod at Winchester, the abbots and abbesses and priors and prioresses of England accepted Benedict's system as their "one uniform observance." A form of monasticism that would remain familiar across the island for the next five and a half centuries began to take shape. It was a simple system and not easily abused. Men and women were strictly segregated. The members of each community elected their superiors, who exercised absolute authority but could be removed for unsatisfactory performance and were adjured in Benedict's writings to consult with the members before making decisions. The monastic day began at two A.M. (three A.M. in summer, when darkness fell later) and was divided into periods of prayer, labor, and study. The schedule varied only with the seasons and the demands of the liturgical calendar of "feast days" and fasts. There were two meals a day in summer, when more daylight hours were available for work, but only one in winter, and only the sick were allowed meat. All visitors were to be offered food and shelter, and providing for the local poor and sick became a primary responsibility of every house. This was not a life likely to attract anyone without a serious commitment to spiritual pursuits. A system of periodic visitations by authorities from the outside helped to ensure fidelity to the rule, and in the centuries following its adoption there were strikingly few grave or systemic failures of discipline. Problems did not go unaddressed. A typical problem, one characteristic of the time, was the practice, carried forward from pre-Benedictine days, by which wealthy families not wishing to divide property among multiple heirs would deposit their surplus children at the abbeys, presumably for life. The worst consequences of this were removed by a rule forbidding anyone to take monastic vows before reaching the age of consent, which was usually eighteen.

Success bred prosperity and complexity. Some of the houses grew large and rich: forty-five (eight of them communities of women) were important enough to figure in the public records of 1066, the year of the Norman Conquest, and the Normans in their turn endowed new establishments on a sometimes lavish scale. The Benedictines—now formally an international order—grew increasingly sophisticated. The abbots of the greatest houses sat in the House of Lords. It came to be the norm for the monks to be ordained as priests, whereas Benedict himself had not regarded monks as being clergy in the strict sense, and when the first universities were founded one of their primary purposes was to educate young men sent from the monasteries. The religious observances of the houses became so elaborate that little time was left for work or solitude. A growing perception that all this marked an unacceptable departure from the spirit of the rule led first to discontent and then to the establishment, in France initially, of the breakaway order of Cistercians, whose garments of unbleached wool caused them to be called the "white monks" in contrast to the black-robed Benedictines. (The "black monks," not pleased with this implicit criticism of their presumably more comfortable attire, accused the Cistercians of making an ostentatious display of humility and austerity. Members of different religious orders were not above jealousy and resentment.)

The emergence of the Cistercians was a real revolution, and from their arrival in England in the twelfth century they attracted astonishing numbers of recruits. They settled in wild and unpopulated districts, set out to support themselves by draining marshland and converting it to pastures for sheep, and gradually grew rich by doing so. Within a generation the order had almost a dozen English houses. Its growth was only part of what is called the twelfth century's Monastic Renaissance, during which more than 250 new houses for men were opened in England along with more than 100 for women. Among them were the first English houses of the so-called canons regular and also of the Carthusians, a hybrid order of hermits-in-community that would grow to nine houses, only to be singled out for early destruction by Henry VIII and Cromwell. These and other orders—Norbertines, Bridgettines, the English Order of Sempringham, Knights Templar, and Knights Hospitalers—adhered to orthodox doctrine (though disputes about how well they did so were common) while pursuing their different missions in their distinctive ways.

The thirteenth century brought yet another revolution: the arrival of the friars, new mendicant (the word means "begging") orders that had started on the continent, spread with startling speed, and were focused not on maintaining houses of prayer and seclusion but on outreach to the laity—especially the growing and increasingly sophisticated urban laity, an emerging social force that had received much attention at the Lateran Council of 1215. The Order of Preachers, or Dominicans, first appeared in England in 1221, the year that its founder, the Spaniard Dominic, died. When the Friars Minor or Franciscans followed three years later, their founder Francis of Assisi was still alive. Both orders emphasized poverty and simplicity of life along with helping ordinary people to live Christian lives in a world of towns and cities. They proved popular wherever they settled, though in doing so they often attracted the unfriendly attention of the secular clergy—the diocesan and parish priests who belonged to no order.

Soon there were Dominican and Franciscan houses for women, and still other orders of friars, Augustinians and Carmelites, also arrived from the continent. Both within the oldest Benedictine houses and among the more recent arrivals, the old struggle over how best to live the religious life went on as ever. The problem was perhaps most acute among the Franciscans. We have already encountered the Friars Observant, especially favored by the royal family until they refused to accept Henry VIII's annulment suit and his claims to be supreme head. They called themselves "observant" to distinguish themselves from those Franciscans who, in their opinion, were no longer sufficiently faithful to the precepts of their founder. Such splinterings were far from unusual, and they were hardly evidence of decay. They were evidence, rather, that the monastic impulse had not grown cold—that people drawn to the religious life still regarded themselves as on a quest that had to be taken seriously.

The English church that Henry inherited was, at least in part because of its monastic element, scarcely less diverse than the broader society of which it was part. Monasticism reached across the whole culture, from humanist scholars at Oxford and Cambridge to Charterhouse hermits growing vegetables outside their cells, from abbots in the House of Lords to friars ministering to the poor in the filthy streets of London and solitary Cistercians tending sheep on the windswept moors of Yorkshire. Vitality was probably lowest where monasticism was oldest, in some of the hundreds of Benedictine houses that dotted the landscape. All the religious orders had lost devastatingly large numbers of their members in the Black Death of the fourteenth century, but the ranks of the Benedictines were especially slow to refill. Because new kinds of opportunities were emerging in the lay world, and also because the most adventurous spiritual seekers now had so many other options, their appeal was not what it once had been. Increasing amounts of Benedictine land were being worked by tenant farmers, who generally found monks to be better land-lords than their counterparts among the nobility if only because they were less desperate for cash, and the monasteries were showing an in-creasing tendency to allow their tenants to become freeholders. Some sort of adjustment of the place of the Benedictines in the life of the na-tion was obviously advisable and becoming increasingly likely.

But it would be claiming too much to say that even the Benedictine rule had arrived at the point of exhaustion. That was proved by the will-ingness of some of the leading Benedictine abbots to die rather than surrender to Henry's demands. It is proved in the twenty-first century by the fact that Benedictine houses are again prospering in England and have been doing so since they ceased to be illegal.

12

"We Will All Die"

The full viciousness of the new regime that Henry and Cromwell had brought to perfection by the end of 1534 is not to be seen in the execution of the Nun of Kent, the destruction of the Friars Observant, or the fate of John Fisher and Thomas More. What was done to them was, if horrible, at least understandable. Elizabeth Barton, by ignoring friendly warnings not to meddle in politics in a dangerous way at a dangerous time, had made her own ruin all but inevitable. The Observants, if as innocent as Barton of anything that could reasonably be construed as a capital crime, had certainly gone out of their way to challenge the king and provoke his wrath. The stature of Fisher and More, two of the most esteemed Europeans of their time, made their refusal to acquiesce in the royal supremacy not only gallingly frustrating but an incitement to anyone else inclined to resist. There were reasons for destroying such people.

Nothing of the kind can be said in the case of John Houghton, a man who by his own choosing was so obscure as to be practically invisible, offered Henry all the loyalty that any other king of England had ever required of his subjects, and asked for nothing except that he and the men who had chosen him as their leader should be left alone. If Barton and the others were victims of judicial murder—and they were—Houghton's murder was of a singularly atrocious kind. His story is a vivid demonstration of the lengths to which Henry and Cromwell were prepared to go, the depths to which they were willing to descend, to break the will of England.

Houghton, when the Act of Succession became law, was in his late forties and his fourth year as prior, elected head, of the London monastery of the Order of Carthusians. This order, unique in the austerity of its rule, had been founded in a remote valley of the French Alps late in the eleventh century for the purpose of permitting its members to live both in community and as hermits. These two aims, if apparently contradictory, were achieved with impressive success. In four and a half centuries Carthusian houses were established all across Europe, so that by the sixteenth century there were more than two hundred. The order had been invited into England by Henry II as part of his effort to show contrition for the murder of Thomas Becket, and by the time of Henry VIII it had nine English houses. These were known as Charterhouses, their inhabitants as Charterhouse monks—an Anglicization of the name of the order's motherhouse at La Grande Chartreuse in France. The Carthusians were remarkable in never departing from their original rule and so never giving rise to reformist offshoots. In the sixteenth century, in England as elsewhere, they preserved a way of life focused on solitary prayer, contemplation, study, and work. Their daily routine remained identical in every detail to that established by their founders. Even a century and a half after Henry VIII, Pope Innocent XI would say of the Carthusians that they were *numquam reformata, quia numquam deformata:* never reformed because never deformed.

John Houghton, the son of a family of gentry or near-gentry in Essex, earned a bachelor's degree at Cambridge University as a young man and, to the intense disappointment of his parents, decided to take holy orders rather than embark upon the kind of career likely to raise the family's fortunes. Obliged to leave home, he lived with a parish priest while continuing his studies (eventually he would receive three degrees from Cambridge) and at around age twenty-five was ordained into the secular priesthood—meaning that he was a member of the local diocesan clergy, the source of most parish priests. In his late twenties, feeling himself called to something more demanding, he entered the London Charterhouse. Here, apparently, he was content. Like his brother monks he lived alone in a "cell" of three small rooms (one for storage, one for study and sleep, the third for prayer) adjacent to a small walled garden for growing flowers and vegetables. There was one meal a day in winter—always meatless, with each monk cooking foodstuffs delivered to his door—and two in summer, the diet limited to bread and water on Mondays, Wednesdays, and Fridays. The monks said daily mass alone in their cells but gathered twice a day for worship in common. Like all monasteries, the Charterhouses were required to be financially self-sufficient, and work of some kind was a prescribed part of the daily routine. For most Carthusians this meant making, by hand, scholarly and devotional books for sale. Sundays and the major feast days of the liturgical calendar were special: the monks had mass and a meal together, afterward meeting in chapter to conduct the business of the house and enjoy a period of free conversation.

It was a life stripped down to essentials. Only the roughest cloth was used as clothing and bedding, no silver or gold ornaments were permitted aside from the chalices in which the bread and wine of communion were consecrated, and monasteries were kept small to avoid the complications and distractions of managing large institutions. It was a life that could make sense only to men prepared to sacrifice everything in pursuit of spiritual experience, but the number of such men was not insubstantial in England and on the continent in the late Middle Ages. The London Charterhouse had an abundance of young members in the time of John Houghton, a number of them from noble families. Thomas More, at the start of his career, had thought long and seriously about giving up the law and joining the Carthusians, finally and with real regret deciding that he was not suited to celibacy. As late as 1534 Sir John Gage, a member of Henry VIII's council described by Charles V's ambassador as "one of the wisest and most experienced in war of the whole kingdom," resigned his post as vice-chamberlain and became a Carthusian.

Houghton had entered the order two decades before Gage, progressing in the customary way through a year as a postulant and two or three years as a novice. He then would have taken "simple" (nonperpetual) vows of poverty, chastity, and obedience, and later the "solemn" vows that bound a man for life. Almost nothing is known, naturally, of his first dozen years as a Carthusian, years spent in training and solitude, but it is clear that he won the respect of his superiors and peers. In 1523 he was made sacristan of the London Charterhouse, with responsibility for the vestments and paraphernalia used in worship services. Three years after that he was elevated to procurator, supervising the monastery's business dealings with the outside and managing its little corps of lay brothers, nonpriests who performed the labor needed to keep the establishment in good working order. He must have become known beyond London, because in 1531 the monks of the house of Beauvale in Nottinghamshire elected him prior. Later that same year, however, he returned to London after receiving word that his former associates had unanimously elected him prior there. Years later one of the monks of the London Charterhouse—a man who was still alive because under threat of death he had sworn the supremacy oath—recorded his memories of Prior Houghton. He was "short, with a graceful figure and dignified appearance; his actions modest, his voice gentle, chaste in body, in heart humble, he was admired and sought after by all, and by his community was most loved and esteemed. One and all revered him, and none were ever known to speak a word against him. . . . He governed rather by example than precept, and his subjects were influenced as much by the fervor of his preeminent sanctity as by the burning exhortations he addressed to them in their chapter. . . . Once at least each month, in his exhortation to the religious, he would cast himself upon his knees before them and with tears bewail his shortcomings, and ask pardon of his brethren."

It is hardly surprising, considering the nature of their rule, that the men of the Charterhouse did not follow the example of the Friars Observant in raising objections when King Henry cast off his first wife and took a second. The friars were a preaching order whose mission took them into the public arena and engaged them with the issues of the day. By contrast the Carthusians, modeling themselves on the desert fathers of the first Christian centuries, avoided any such engagement. They would have been content to allow the storm over the king's great matter to blow itself out at a distance.

No such thing was possible, however, under a monarch who felt entitled to the active support of everyone in the kingdom and was determined to have it. In April 1534 two of Thomas Cromwell's agents called at the London Charterhouse and demanded to see the prior. They told Houghton they wanted his signature on the succession oath. Houghton, in the most inoffensive way imaginable, declined to sign, saying simply that the king's matrimonial affairs were the king's business and had nothing to do with the Charterhouse or its monks. This was not the response the royal commissioners were looking for—their assignment was to get the agreement of everyone they visited—and so they demanded to meet with the house's full chapter of monks. The result was a community discussion in the course of which Houghton said more than he had ventured to say earlier: that he could not see how the king's marriage to Catherine, having been approved by the church and continued for so many years, could now be judged invalid. When the assembly expressed its agreement, Houghton and the monastery's procurator, Humphrey Middlemore, were taken away under guard.

For a month the two were kept in the Tower under the harsh conditions that were becoming standard for clerical prisoners—neither warmth nor bedding nor sanitation, scarcely enough food to sustain life—but at length they were visited by Archbishop Lee of York and Bishop Stokesley of London and persuaded, apparently after much discussion, that if royal marriages were not a monk's business they were also not something that a monk should sacrifice his life over. Having accepted this line of reasoning, and having indicated their willingness to encourage the other members of their community to accept the oath, Houghton and Middlemore were allowed to return home.

Back at the Charterhouse, Houghton told his fellows that he believed signing the oath would save neither him nor them for long—weeks in prison left him with no illusions about what lay ahead. Their response was to argue that in that case there was no reason for any of them to sign. Their resolve weakened, however, when the king's commissioners not only returned but brought with them the lord mayor of London, a company of armed men, and the threat that if they did not sign they would all be taken into custody. Houghton, Middlemore, and fourteen others signed with little or no delay, and the rest signed a day later. In doing so, however, they tried to create for themselves the same kind of loophole that the bishops had earlier attempted when faced with King Henry's demands, attesting that they accepted the Act of Succession "so far as it was lawful."

In the months that followed, the Carthusians, like other religious communities across the kingdom, were kept under constant pressure: those men who seemed most likely to yield were sent off in pairs to be interrogated and preached at by senior churchmen who had accepted the king's claims. The passage of the Act of Supremacy, bringing with it a new and even more demanding oath, sealed the fate of those unwilling to comply. The men of the London Charterhouse understood this from the start. When Houghton lamented that he didn't know how to save them, they replied that all of them should prepare to die together so that "heaven and earth shall witness for us how unjustly we are cut off."

"Would indeed that it might be so, so that dying we might live as living we die," Houghton replied. "But they will not do to us so great a kindness, nor to themselves so great an injury. Many of you are of noble blood, and what I think they will do is this: me and the elder brethren they will kill, and they will dismiss you that are young into a world which is not for you. If therefore it will depend on me alone—if my oath will suffice for the house—I will throw myself for your sakes on the mercy of God. I will make myself anathema, and to preserve you from these dangers I will consent to the king's will. If, however, they have determined otherwise—if they choose to have the consent of us all—the will of God be done. If one death will not suffice, we will all die."

From Houghton's perspective, that is, a forced return to the outside world was more to be dreaded than death. He was prepared either to take an oath he did not believe or to sacrifice his life if in either way he could save his brothers, but he did not expect any such solution to prove possible. According to the sole surviving account of what was happening inside the London Charterhouse at this time, the other monks agreed that escape was improbable and began to prepare themselves for death. There was one exception: a monk who wrote to Cromwell to acknowledge the royal supremacy and beg release from his vows, complaining that "the religion is so hard, what with fasting and with the great watch, that there is not six whole monks within this cloister but that they have one infirmity or other." Such eager surrenders were rare. It is surely ironic, considering the accusations of laxity that in due course would be leveled against all the orders, that from the beginning of Cromwell's campaign the harshest punishments were meted out to those houses where the strictest rules were most faithfully observed. And that the only complaint known to have been made against

Houghton by one of his own monks was that discipline was *too* strict under his leadership.

While waiting for the next display of kingly power, Houghton was visited by two other Carthusian priors, Robert Laurence of Beauvale and Augustine Webster of Axholme. No doubt they too were expecting the worst, and it would have been natural for them to look for direction not only to London but specifically to Houghton, who since 1532 had been "visitor" of the order's English province and therefore its senior member. For reasons unknown (possibly they thought that by taking the initiative they could demonstrate their wish to be cooperative, or perhaps Laurence and Webster had taken up Houghton's idea of trying to sacrifice himself for the sake of the community) the three decided not to await the return of the king's commissioners but to go and see Cromwell. There was, however, no meeting: as soon as he learned of their arrival, Cromwell had his visitors taken to the Tower and locked up. In the days that followed, they refused to take the oath and were joined in their confinement by a fourth prisoner, Richard Reynolds, a monk of Syon, the Bridgettine order's only English establishment. Reynolds was a noted humanist scholar, said to be the only English monk conversant in Latin, Greek, and Hebrew. He had helped to make Syon one of England's leading centers of Renaissance learning, and his order like the Carthusians and Friars Observant was noted not only for its high standards but for its long advocacy of church reform. Thus Syon, like the London Charterhouse, had been singled out by Cromwell for special attention, and that attention had focused on Reynolds because of his renown. Under questioning he had said that he "would spend his blood for the king" but could not deny that the pope was head of the church.

On April 28 the four priests were indicted for refusing the supremacy oath. They pleaded not guilty at the start of their trial, which did not go smoothly for the authorities. The jury declared itself unable to find the defendants guilty because, following as they did the dictates of their consciences and not seeking to persuade anyone to agree with them, they could not have been acting maliciously—"maliciously" being the word that Cromwell had had to insert into the Treason Act to get Parliament to approve it. The judges then instructed the jurymen that none of this mattered: that to refuse the oath was, ipso facto, to act maliciously. Even after this the jury continued to balk, so that finally Cromwell had to make an appearance and batter the members into submission with threats. On May 4 the four convicted men—joined now by a fifth, a parish priest named John Hale who was a friend and neighbor of Reynolds's—were tied to hurdles (flat rectangular forms made of wood and similar to sections of fence) and dragged from the Tower to Tyburn Hill, the place of execution for traitors. There they were given a final offer of pardon in return for swearing the oath, and all refused.

Remarkably, all were dressed in clerical garb; until now it would have been unthinkable to execute a priest in the habit of his vocation—or for that matter, to execute a priest without first degrading him from his clerical status. Even more remarkably, among those in attendance were Henry Fitzroy, Duke of Richmond, the king's illegitimate son; Queen Anne's father Thomas Boleyn, Earl of Wiltshire, and his son, George Lord Rochford; the mighty Thomas Howard, Duke of Norfolk; and in fact virtually the entire royal court including the council. This must have happened at the king's instructions, and its purpose was almost certainly to discourage expressions of discontent from the large crowd that an occasion of this kind was sure to attract. It is possible that the king himself was present, though in disguise: five horsemen whose faces were covered with visors arrived on the scene, and when one of these visors fell open it revealed the face of Norfolk's brother, an intimate of King Henry's. As the five approached the killing ground, the members of the court deferentially stood aside.

Houghton died first, and in keeping with custom he was allowed to speak before doing so. "I call almighty God to witness, and all good people, and I beseech you all here present to bear witness for me in the day of judgment, that being here to die, I declare that it is from no obstinate rebellious spirit that I do not obey the king, but because I fear to offend the majesty of God. Our holy mother the church has decreed otherwise than the king and the Parliament have decreed, and therefore rather than disobey the church I am ready to suffer. Pray for me and have mercy on my brethren, of whom I have been the unworthy prior." It was later reported that the king was angry with Norfolk, Wiltshire, and the other nobles because none of them had offered any response. But as he probably knew—he certainly knew if he was present—the mood of the crowd had been hostile not to the men being executed but to their being killed. It might have been dangerous to try to belittle Houghton in the moment before his death.

Perhaps because so many distinguished guests were on hand to be edified and impressed, the usual work of butchery—an interrupted hanging, followed by emasculation, evisceration, and the rubbing of a still-beating heart in the victim's face—was carried out with exceptional energy that day. Reynolds was last to die, offering encouragement to the others as they climbed the scaffold, and before presenting himself for execution he asked the crowd to pray for the king. He like the others was quartered, his head and the sections of his body put on display around London. One of Houghton's arms was nailed above the entry to his monastery, a warning to everyone associated with the place. In the weeks that followed, four more monks and lay brothers of the London Charterhouse would die at Tyburn, among them the procurator Humphrey Middlemore and a man named Sebastian Newdigate who before entering religious life had been a member of the royal court. In the subsequent months fifteen would be starved to death in prison; iron collars around their necks, their feet in shackles, they were chained to upright posts in such a way as to be unable either to sit or lie down and left to slowly die. A new prior, one friendly to the king's cause, was introduced by Cromwell to replace Houghton. With armed force he imposed a new regime that made it impossible for the monks to follow their rule and transformed their monastery into a prison. They were allowed to do almost nothing except listen to sermons delivered by preachers sent by Cromwell and wait for their fate to be decided.

It had been arranged, on the morning of Houghton's execution, that Thomas More would be visited in the Tower by his daughter Margaret, who had long been asking him to accept the oath of supremacy and so save his life. From a window, and obviously not by coincidence, the two were able to observe the condemned priests as they were taken off to be killed. It was all part of the continuing effort to use every tool at the Crown's disposal—terror, persuasion, the promise of a swift return to royal favor—to induce More and John Fisher to submit. This latest gambit worked no better than the others. It became an occasion for More, not to lose his resolve, but to offer comfort to the young woman to whom, of all his large family and circle of friends, he was closest. "Lo, dost thou not see, Meg, that these blessed fathers be now as cheerfully going to their deaths as bridegrooms to their marriage?" he asked.

> Wherefore thereby mayst thou see, mine own good daughter, what a great difference there is between such as have in effect spent all their days in a strait, hard, penitential, and painful life religiously, and such as have in the world, like worldly wretches, as thy poor father hath done, consumed all their time in pleasure and ease licentiously. For God, continuing their long-continued life in most sore and grievous penance, will no longer suffer them to remain here in this vale of misery and iniquity, but speedily hence taketh them to the fruition of his everlasting deity. Whereas thy silly father, Meg, that like a most wicked wretch, hath passed forth the whole course of his miserable life most sinfully, God thinking him not worthy so soon to come to that eternal felicity, leaveth him here yet still in the world, further to be plunged and turmoiled with misery.

He wanted his daughter to see his own death, which pretty clearly was not far off, as a deliverance, even a cause for celebration.

It is fair to say that the king did not want More's death and did not want Fisher's. What he wanted was their submission, their acknowledgment before the whole Christian world that from the beginning of his conflict with Rome he had been right and the two of them had been wrong. But if he could not have that he would take their lives instead, as yet another warning to anyone who had not paid sufficient attention to the fate of the Observant Franciscans and the Charterhouse priors. And by May 1535 his patience was wearing thin. A long procession of eminent churchmen had been sent to reason with his two most famous prisoners—at least half a dozen bishops are known to have called on Fisher—but all their arguments and commentaries upon ancient texts had accomplished nothing. The conditions of More's and Fisher's confinement, as well as the state in which More's household had to live, had been made progressively worse until by winter the aged Fisher was literally begging for help, declaring that he had neither enough clothes nor sufficient food to keep himself alive. But harshness, too, had produced no results. The prisoners continued to refuse to submit, but continued also not to do or say anything that would allow the Crown to condemn them to death. Under repeated questioning—they were always interrogated separately, just as they were kept apart in the Tower—they refused to express any opinion of the Act of Supremacy. Fisher was straightforward in his refusal: not even the Act itself, he said again and again, required any man to reveal his innermost thoughts. More was more careful if no less consistent. Because he had been attainted, he said, he no longer enjoyed the protection of the law and so had no reason to concern himself with it. "Now I have in good faith discharged my mind of all such matters," he said, "and neither will dispute kings' titles nor popes'." It was a sterile, agonizing standoff for everyone involved.

The new pope, Paul III, unwittingly broke the deadlock with an announcement that, when it reached England on May 20, astounded everyone and pleased no one: John Fisher had been named to the College of Cardinals, becoming the first Englishman since Wolsey to be so honored. Paul was a reformer, among the first pontiffs to recognize that the excesses of the Renaissance were not merely wrong but intolerable. In putting together a list of men to be made cardinals he had selected candidates known for scholarship, for exemplary personal conduct, and for upholding high standards in all areas of ecclesiastical life. Fisher was an obvious choice in every respect, a charismatic figure known across Europe for his theological writings and life of simple virtue. The pope is said to have believed that King Henry would be pleased to see the mentor of his youth, a man he himself had described as one of the ornaments of England, honored with a cardinal's red hat. If so, he was incredibly ill informed. It seems more plausible that he hoped by singling Fisher out to give him some measure of protection against the royal wrath, but even here any such thoughts would have been badly mistaken.

Henry interpreted the news from Rome as an intentional provocation. He took the announcement as an insult to his own man Thomas Cranmer, who as England's primate would, under ordinary circumstances, have been made a cardinal long before any mere bishop of Rochester. He warned that the pope could send Fisher a hat, "but I will take care that he have never a head to wear it on." Fisher, for his part, was reported to have told the man who brought him news of his appointment that if the red hat were lying at his feet "he would not stoop to pick it up, so little did he set by it." There is no reason to doubt the sin-

cerity of those words, or that Fisher could have uttered them. He was
the antithesis of Thomas Wolsey, never in the course of his long life
showing the slightest interest in personal advancement or political
power. Nor is it possible to doubt that the king meant what he said. The
pope's initiative settled the fates of Fisher and More alike.

Though further interrogations failed to draw anything new out of
Fisher, in June, enfeebled by two years of imprisonment under conditions that almost seemed calculated to kill, he was put on trial for treason. His conviction was a foregone conclusion, the judges and jury
having been handpicked by Cromwell and the king, but for purposes of
propaganda it was important to make the proceedings seem as legitimate as possible. The Crown's best weapon was its key witness, the
lawyer Richard Rich. Now in his late thirties, Rich had risen to become
solicitor-general by attaching himself to Thomas Audley, himself such
an unfailingly dependable servant of the Crown that Henry had made
him first speaker of the House of Commons and then, after More's resignation, chancellor. Rich's testimony was, after all the long months during which the Crown had repeatedly tried and failed to induce Fisher to
express himself on the supremacy, nothing less than a bombshell. He
told the court that when the king sent him to meet with Fisher, the
bishop told him that he "believed in his conscience and by his learning
knew that the king neither was nor by any right could be supreme head
in earth of the church of England."

What was perhaps even more surprising, Fisher did not challenge the
truthfulness of Rich's testimony. He erupted with the furious indignation that had been characteristic of him for years now, ever since the
king had begun claiming that his marriage to Queen Catherine was not
valid, but his anger here was aimed less at what Rich was saying than at
his daring to say it in court. Rich, it turned out, had in his visit to the
Tower told Fisher that he had been instructed by the king to ask for the
bishop's opinion of the Supremacy Act, and to promise that nothing he
said would be used against him in court or otherwise. He had added,
Fisher told the judges, that the king sincerely wanted to know what he
thought "for the great affiance [trust or confidence] he had in me, more
than in any other." There had followed—again according to what Fisher
told the court—an explicit suggestion that Henry, after taking Fisher's
position into account, "was very like to retract much of his former do-

ings and make recompense for the same, in case I should so advise him."
To all this Rich had added his own promise not to repeat anything Fisher
told him to anyone except the king. Fisher had responded as any honest,
trusting, and even moderately courageous subject would have under
such circumstances. For the first time since coming under suspicion, at
the king's request and for the king's sake, he unburdened himself. In
doing so he committed treason.

It is impossible to know anything about the characters of the two
men involved in this exchange—or for that matter, of Henry VIII—and
doubt Fisher's account. This is all the more true because even Rich himself, who was building a phenomenally successful career on a willingness to do and say whatever was likely to be most pleasing to those more
powerful than himself, never challenged what Fisher had said. And because Fisher, who to his dying day never lost a profound if exasperated
respect for Henry as king and an equally deep affection for him personally, would certainly have responded to even an indirect appeal from him
for guidance. He may have had little opportunity to get to know Richard
Rich or to learn what kind of man he was. He would have been reluctant to think any man capable of making the kinds of pledges that Rich
made not only on his own behalf but on the king's and then breaking his
word in the most destructive way imaginable.

"What a monstrous matter is this!" Fisher cried.

> To lay now to my charge as treason the thing which I spake not until
> besides this man's oath, I had as full and sure a promise from the king,
> by this his trusty and sure messenger, as the king could make me by
> word of mouth, that I should never be impeached nor hurt by mine
> answer that I should send unto him by this his messenger, which I
> would never have spoken, had it not been in trust of my prince's
> promise, and of my true and loving heart towards him, my natural
> liege lord, in satisfying him with declaration of mine opinion and con-
> science in this matter, as he earnestly required me by this messenger
> to signify plainly unto him.

Rich, accused not only of disgracing himself but of suggesting disgraceful behavior on the part of the king, might well have responded by
calling Fisher a liar. Instead he accepted Fisher's version of what had

transpired between them, probably in order to keep the Crown's case intact. Rich and Fisher were together in testifying that the bishop had—regardless of his reasons, whether or not he had been deceived—denied the supremacy. That was enough; it gave the king's judges all they needed. Tacitly accepting that Henry had, in effect, promised Fisher immunity, they set aside Rich's assurances to the bishop as making no difference. Every other argument that Fisher offered in his defense was likewise swept aside. Inevitably (the jurors understood that they had no choice if they valued their own liberty and livelihoods) he was convicted, sentenced to death, and returned to the Tower. Perhaps because of his wretched physical condition, perhaps because the king still felt some of his old affection, Fisher was told that he would merely be beheaded, not subjected to the horrors that had been visited upon the Carthusians.

June 22, the day of his execution, found him prepared and at peace. He was awakened at five A.M. and told that this was the day he had been expecting—that he was to be killed at ten. His response was to ask to be left to sleep longer. When he arrived at Tower Hill, the scaffold on which he was to die was still under construction, so that he had to spend an hour on muleback, waiting for the preparations to be completed. The assembled crowd was large and, being sympathetic to the old man, markedly subdued. Before putting his head on the block Fisher asked for the prayers of the crowd, telling them that though up to this point he had remained unafraid, he feared that his faith might fail him at the last moment. He asked the people to pray for their king, too, and to love and obey him, "for he was good by nature."

When it was all over, Fisher's head was set atop London Bridge. A story was circulated—an expression of the esteem in which he had been held—that every day that head grew pinker and healthier and more lifelike. He was the first English bishop ever to be condemned in a judicial proceeding and put to death by authority of the Crown. There had been no death remotely like his since Thomas Becket's murder more than three centuries before. England was shocked by it. Europe was shocked. Henry and Cromwell were now at liberty to turn their attention to Thomas More, who was still in the Tower and still refusing to share his thoughts with anyone.

BEST SELLERS

THE EXECUTION OF JOHN FISHER AND THE IMPRISONMENT
of Thomas More electrified not only England but all of Western Christendom, and for a reason that was entirely novel. The two men were phe-
nomena of a type that had only recently appeared on the world stage:
famous living authors, and therefore international celebrities. The books
they had written, and the books written about them and sometimes
against them, had spread through Europe's fast-growing reading public
with a speed that would have been impossible just a few generations
earlier. They had created the kind of sensation that only the news of the
day can generate.

It was all part of the revolution sparked by the invention of the printing press—of movable and reusable type, one of the most world-altering
technological breakthroughs in history. By the time Henry decided to
discard Catherine of Aragon, printing was Europe's leading growth industry. The new ability to mass-produce long texts at low cost was transforming everything: education, religion, the economy, the very character
of civilization. It was affecting everyday life more dramatically and profoundly than the automobile would in the twentieth century, or the Inter-
net in the twenty-first. It had so accelerated the movement of new ideas,
and so magnified the impact of those ideas, that all Europe was left almost literally dizzy. At a time when being educated meant reading Latin,
a controversialist like Martin Luther—or like Fisher or More—could become famous from Vienna to Lisbon in a matter of months.

Difficult though it is to measure something as amorphous as fame at
a distance of four and a half centuries, Fisher at the time of his death was
probably better known than More. He had been early to involve himself
in the religious disputes that evolved into the Reformation, and his deep
learning and the firmness of his opinions made him a formidable advocate. His book *Assertionis Lutheranae confutatio* appeared in 1523, just

six years after Luther first raised his voice against Rome, and was so widely reprinted and held up so well under rebuttal that it came to be regarded as *the* standard statement of orthodoxy. Within the next two years Fisher produced two additional responses to Luther—both were published in Cologne rather than England, an indication of Fisher's international reach—and they were followed in 1527 with a treatise on the Eucharist that would have a formative effect on Catholic thinking for many years. All this work had the enthusiastic approval of Henry VIII, but the attention it received explains why Fisher's subsequent objections to the king's divorce and claim to supremacy brought such wrath down upon him. His researches had placed him among the leading authorities on the history of church doctrine, and his flagrant refusal to accept the king's interpretation of that history was genuinely dangerous. There was no way that the man Henry had become by the 1530s could have found Fisher's resistance anything other than intolerable.

More's fame was of a different character than Fisher's, if no less likely to cause trouble when he declined to approve Henry's innovations. Outside England it was based mainly on his "novel" (as it is sometimes anachronistically described) *Utopia,* which he began writing in 1516 while on a diplomatic mission to Flanders and spending much time with his friend Erasmus. Written in Latin, the description of a visit to an imaginary island, the book *appears* to function on two levels: as a satirical commentary on contemporary life, and also as More's vision of how society (even a non-Christian society, one lacking revelation and therefore obliged to depend upon natural law for guidance) might best be organized. However, it is so complex, containing so many intentional ambiguities and possible red herrings (the name of the character who brings news of Utopia translates as "dispenser of nonsense") that critics and scholars still disagree about where More was being serious, where he was joking, and what the whole thing actually means. It definitely expresses a yearning for a simpler, less materialistic society than Tudor-era Europe—much the same kind of yearning, interestingly, that would be characteristic of the kinds of evangelical reformers whose rejection of the Roman church later horrified More. There is no private property in Utopia, the laws are so straightforward that the legal profession does not exist, and all people do manual work and wear the same plain clothing. The book also expresses the reverence for tradition and order, the almost obsessive fear of disunity and disruption, that later would turn its author into a determined persecutor of those people whose beliefs and practices he regarded as heretical: premarital sex is punished with enforced lifelong celibacy in Utopia, adultery with enslavement.

Surely More must have been joking in making it a capital crime to discuss politics anywhere except in Utopia's government buildings (one way to eliminate tedious conversations!). And it is curious, in light of his later history, that although belief in the immortality of the soul is mandatory (because essential to mortality) on the island, unbelievers are not punished but converted through instruction. More appears to have written the book for his amusement and that of his friends rather than for publication, and when Erasmus published it in Louvain in 1516 he did so without the author's knowledge or consent. It was a huge success from the start, establishing the thirty-eight-year-old More among the best-known writers of the day. Some of the book's most sensitive elements—its discussion of why kings are so inclined to start pointless wars, the suggestion that republics are the best-governed states—may explain why More, though he revised *Utopia* before republishing it in Switzerland in 1518, never translated it into English or allowed its publication in England. The elusiveness of its meaning foreshadows his later behavior when, under attack by the king, he refused to explain himself to anyone. In any case it was nothing that *Utopia* said but simply the fame it had brought to its author that drove Henry VIII to the belief that he had to make an example of More one way or another.

Printing's effects on the lives and careers of Fisher and More were nothing compared to what they did to and for Martin Luther. Without the magnifying power of the press, the disputes that Luther triggered might never have become anything more than what Clement VII called them: a dreary argument among monks. It can almost seem that printing arrived just in time to serve Luther's purposes; the last of the ingredients that made it possible fell into place only shortly before his birth. Astonishingly, paper (which originated in China and long remained the secret of Arab producers) was never seen in Europe until the twelfth century and was not produced there until the thirteenth. And although movable type first appeared in China by the eleventh century and in Europe three centuries later, no one knew how to produce raised letters that were hard or durable enough to make mass production possible. Only in the fifteenth century did the goldsmiths, silversmiths, and jewelers of Germany and the Rhineland take up the challenge, slowly developing the alloys and production methods with which Johannes Gutenberg was able to produce his magnificent two-volume Bible in 1455. That was only twenty-eight years before Luther's birth, and, as great an achievement as the Gutenberg Bible was, it was just the beginning. (For one thing, a single copy cost as much as a common laborer could earn in three years.) But from that point the refinements came one after another at a quickening pace. By 1517, when Friar Martin posted his complaints about papal indulgences on the door of Wittenberg Cathedral, the technology of printing was very nearly as advanced as it would remain for the next several centuries. Luther the writer proved to be as prolific as he was powerful, churning out books with almost unbelievable frequency, shifting from Latin to the vernacular and shaping the German language at least as much as Thomas Cranmer with his Prayer Book would soon be shaping English. Much of Europe was hungry for his words, and now it was possible to deliver them quickly wherever they were wanted.

13

"Preserve My Friends from Such Favors"

On Thursday, July 1, 1535, dressed in a plain robe of the coarsest wool, his once clean-shaven face covered by a long gray beard, filthy after long confinement and leaning heavily on a staff, Thomas More emerged from the Tower of London like some terrible vision out of the Old Testament. A week had passed since the killing of John Fisher, and now it was More's turn to stand trial for high treason. He was led under guard through the capital's busiest streets to the seat of government at Westminster—put on display, in effect, so that the people could see yet again the price of failing to believe what the king believed.

At Westminster More was taken before a panel of eighteen judges, among whom were Thomas Cromwell, Chancellor Thomas Audley, the dukes of Norfolk and Suffolk, and Anne Boleyn's father and brother. No longer able to stay on his feet as he had through the innumerable interrogations to which he had been subjected during his imprisonment, More accepted the offer of a seat. Promised release if he would affix his signature to the oath of supremacy, he thanked the gentlemen and politely declined. He then listened as the indictment was read aloud. It was ridiculously long, piling item upon item and burying each in a heap of explanatory verbiage, but essentially it boiled down to four charges: that More had committed treason by refusing during interrogation to acknowledge the king's supremacy, by conspiring with Fisher while both were prisoners, by describing the Act of Supremacy as a double-edged

sword that killed either the body or the soul, and finally by telling
Richard Rich—that name again—that the act was not legitimate.

More would have understood, even more clearly than Fisher, that this
was a show trial, the outcome of which could not have been more certain. In defending himself, therefore, he focused not on trying to save his
life—he could have entertained no hope in that regard—but on creating
an indelible record of the absurdity of the proceedings and his reasons
for declining to swear as ordered. His best weapons were the power of
his own mind and the fact that his case really *was* being handled in an
outrageously unfair manner. One by one he was able to dispose of the
charges. He invited his accusers to show that he had ever uttered a word
in opposition to the Act of Supremacy, and they were unable to do so.
He asked for evidence of any conspiracy between Fisher and himself
and was shown none. He acknowledged having described the Supremacy Act as a sword that would destroy the soul of anyone who
falsely swore to it—swore without believing it to be true—but repeated
that he had never spoken against it. He turned the judges' attention to
the fact that even under the king's new laws it was not possible to con-
strue silence as treason. On point after point the prosecution was
stymied.

Which left Richard Rich as the Crown's last hope not of convicting
More—his conviction remained inevitable—but of making the trial
seem something less ignoble than a lynching. What Rich had to say was
similar in significant respects to his testimony in the Fisher trial. Again he
told the court of having visited the defendant in the Tower, and of a conversation that culminated in a statement—an undeniably incriminating
statement—of opposition to the Act of Supremacy. There were important differences this time, however. Rich said that on June 12 he had gone
to the Tower not with a message from the king but simply to take away
the last of More's personal belongings, his books and writing materials.
(Obviously this had been done as part of the steadily intensifying effort
to make life in prison unbearable. Until deprived of the means to do so,
More had devoted his empty hours to composing two books, devotional
works titled *A Dialogue of Comfort Against Tribution* and *On the Sadness of
Christ.*) While waiting for More's things to be bundled up, supposedly
just to pass the time, Rich had engaged the prisoner in a kind of lawyerly
word game. Suppose, he had said, that Parliament declared that I,

Richard Rich, were king. And suppose Parliament declared also that it would be treason to deny that I were king. Would you then agree that I was king? More said that he would, because Parliament had the power to declare who was king of England. Then he offered a question of his own. How would Rich respond if Parliament declared that God was not God and made it treason to say otherwise? Would he accept that? Rich replied that he would not—that "no parliament may make any such law."

This was Rich's account of the first part of the conversation, and More never disputed it. What happened next, however, has been a puzzle ever since. According to Rich's testimony, he threw another question at More—a question that the surrounding circumstances loaded with all-too-obvious significance. What, he claimed to have asked, if Parliament declared the king to be supreme head of the English church? What would More say to that? Rich swore that More replied that Parliament could do no such thing, because England was forever part of the Christian community that had always recognized the bishop of Rome as its head. Such words were clear and certain treason as Parliament had defined treason in 1534—assuming that More spoke them.

But at this point More's story diverges radically from Fisher's. Whereas Fisher never denied saying the things that Rich had reported him as saying, complaining instead that he had opened himself in response to the king's request and under a promise of confidentiality, More vehemently denied having said anything to incriminate himself. There is of course no documentary evidence to establish who was and was not speaking truthfully. Two potential witnesses—the men who were packing More's books while he and Rich had their exchange— were called to testify but claimed to have paid no attention to the conversation. (It would be understandable if they had no wish to get involved in such a foul and dangerous business.) Be that as it may, More was unquestionably the more credible witness. He knew that he faced certain death, nothing could be more obvious than his determination to prepare himself for a "good" death, and for a man of his convictions lying under oath would have been tantamount to self-damnation. Nor is it easy to believe that a man as intelligent and careful as More, a man of his skill in the law, could have fallen into such an obvious trap. More himself asked his judges if they found it credible that he would have allowed himself to be drawn by Richard Rich, of all people, into revealing

thoughts that he had been keeping from the whole world, even from his
own family, from the beginning of his troubles.

"Can it therefore seem likely unto your honorable lordships," he
asked,

> that I would, in so weighty a cause, so unadvisedly overshoot myself
> as to trust Master Rich, a man of me always reputed for one of so lit-
> tle truth as your lordships have heard, so far above my sovereign lord
> the king or any of his noble counselors, that I would unto him utter
> the secrets of my conscience touching the king's supremacy—the
> special point and only mark at my hands so long sought for? A thing
> which I never did, nor never would, after the statute thereof made, re-
> veal either to the king's highness himself or to any of his honorable
> counselors, as it is not unknown to your honors, at sundry several
> times sent from his grace's own person unto the Tower unto me for
> no other purpose. Can this, in your judgments, my lords, seem likely
> to be true?

Regardless, he was that same day found guilty. Before sentence was
passed, he requested and was granted the customary right of a convicted prisoner to address his judges, the usual strategy at this point
being to argue that there should be no punishment because the conviction had been illegitimate. Being a good lawyer, More did exactly this,
saying that the acts of Parliament that had brought him before the
bench were "directly repugnant to the laws of God and his whole
church." But he did so in a way that offered not the slightest possibility
of saving him from execution. He was speaking now not to the men
who had judged him but to posterity, hoping to put himself on record
forever. He said that no layman, not even a king, could be supreme head
of the church even in a single country. He said that England was one
part of the great thousand-year-old community of Christendom, and
that it could make no laws contrary to the ancient understanding that
bound that community together. He spoke for an ideal that was even
then passing out of existence. When he had finished he was condemned
to die, exactly as he and everyone present had known he would be from
the start of the day's proceedings.

Later he was informed that the king, as a special favor, had ordered him like Fisher to be beheaded rather than hanged, drawn, and quartered. "God preserve all my friends from such favors," he said cheerfully. On the Tuesday following his conviction he was awakened early and informed that he was to die at nine o'clock. He was advised that the king wished him to say little before dying. He said he was grateful to be so informed, because although he had planned to say nothing that would displease the king, he had intended to speak at some length. "I am ready," he said, "obediently to conform myself to his grace's commandments." When his hour came round, he found himself too weak to climb the stairs of the scaffold unassisted. "I pray you, master lieutenant," he told the man in charge, "see me safe up, and for my coming down, let me shift for myself." Hoisted to the chopping block, he kissed the executioner, telling him that "thou wilt render me today the greatest service in the power of any mortal." He asked the crowd of onlookers to bear witness that he was dying "in and for the faith of the Catholic Church," and that he died "the king's good servant, but God's first." His last words came as he lowered himself to the floor, placed his head on the block, and moved his beard out of the way. The beard had committed no treason, he said, and did not deserve to be cut in two. His head joined Fisher's on London Bridge.

Cromwell now turned his attention to one of the main pillars not only of the church but of English society as it had evolved through the Middle Ages, the more than eight hundred monastic institutions that dotted the landscape from the cliffs of Dover to the Irish Sea. In January he had been given, as an addition to the offices he already held, that of vice-regent, first "for the sole purpose of undertaking a general ecclesiastical visitation" but later and more broadly as "vicar-general and principal commissary with all the spiritual authority belonging to the king as head of the church, for the due administration of justice in all cases touching the ecclesiastical jurisdiction and the godly reformation and redress of all errors, heresies and abuses in the said church." It was not only a lofty commission but an improbable one, conferring virtually absolute authority over the practices and beliefs of the church in England on a man with no background in theology, canon law, or related disciplines and no experience in ecclesiastical administration aside from the financial work done years earlier for Wolsey. The king had demonstrated the fact of his supremacy, the extent to which the church was

now subordinate to the civil government and the civil government to his
every whim, by placing Cromwell above every clergyman including the
archbishop of Canterbury, every nobleman including even the dukes,
and every other officer of the Crown including the lord chancellor. To
drive home the point, he next suspended by royal edict all the traditional
powers of the bishops—the authority to ordain priests, for example, as
well as to administer the ecclesiastical courts and probate wills. The
bishops were required to petition the Crown for permission to resume
their work, and by doing so they would acknowledge that they derived
their authority solely from the king. As a final insult, the bishops were
told that their petitions were being granted not because they were essential to the proper functioning of the church but because the vicar-
general was unfortunately unable to do everything himself. That the
lords of the church submitted to this humiliation virtually without complaint shows what they had learned from the examples of Fisher and
More: to resist was to die, to protest was to die, even to do nothing was,
if the king wished it, to die.

Whether any action on Rome's part might have made a difference is
a moot question, because Rome did not act. In the aftermath of Fisher's
execution, members of the papal court had demanded that Pope Paul
do *something*. A bull was drawn up giving Henry ninety days in which to
admit his errors and either appear in Rome personally or send representatives. The penalties for failing to comply were to be weighty if theoretical: excommunication, loss of the English crown, loss of the right of
Henry's descendants by Anne Boleyn to inherit the crown, the withdrawal of all clergy from the kingdom, a papal order for Henry's subjects to rebel, and more. But the pope, when the bull was ready for
publication, thought better of it. He realized that the only men in Europe who might conceivably back it up with force were the emperor
Charles and Francis of France, and that neither was likely to prove able
(or for that matter willing) to do so. He realized also that to issue such a
document under current circumstances could only underscore the im-
potence of the papacy and expose it to ridicule. Thus it was locked away.
The new pope remained, as far as anyone in England could tell, as passive as his predecessor Clement.

There was a second reason, one more substantial than a symbolic
demonstration of the king's might, for suspending the powers of the

bishops at precisely this time. The Reformation Parliament, in taking from the bishops their ancient responsibility to make occasional visits of inspection to the monastic houses, had placed a new and potent weapon in the king's hands. Visitation was now the Crown's business, which meant it was Cromwell's, and no man of the new vice-regent's vitality, ambition, and determination to please the king could have been given such an opportunity without finding use for it. By the time of More's death, Cromwell was ready to move against the religious orders and their houses. Aside from the monks and nuns living in those houses, the people most likely to object were those men who until recently had regarded the monasteries as theirs to oversee, to protect, and sometimes to exploit: the bishops. Suspension of their authority deprived them of even an historical basis for protesting: what had traditionally been regarded as their rights were no longer rights at all but privileges conferred by the king. The requirement that they ask the Crown to restore their ability to function made it indelibly clear to the bishops themselves, to the whole of the church including the religious orders, and to anyone else inclined to take an interest that none of them had any rights except those the king might choose to grant them.

Commissioners appointed by Cromwell were dispatched to make formal visitations to religious houses across the kingdom and to the two universities, Oxford and Cambridge, which were still so focused on the education of the clergy by the clergy as to be essentially religious establishments themselves. What Cromwell and the king intended in undertaking this program of visitation has been a matter of controversy ever since. Students of the subject who approve of what Henry VIII did to and with the church have tended, understandably, to argue that the visits were necessary and well intended. On the most practical level their stated purpose was to find out what the various monasteries owned and owed and what their annual income amounted to, so that the government could determine how much they should be required to pay under the new statute of First Fruits and Tenths. From a loftier perspective they were intended to search out and eradicate the many and supposedly horrible abuses of which the church's most radical critics had long been complaining.

Other factors, too, help to explain why Henry and Cromwell turned their attention to the monasteries as soon as their grip on the church was assured. The old religion was still a force to be feared: no student of Henry VIII's reign will deny that in the 1530s and for decades afterward the break with Rome was incomprehensible where not outright repugnant to very large numbers of the English people. The religious houses were symbols and instruments of a way of life that the population had not rejected even if the king had. If few of the leaders of those houses had thus far shown much inclination to follow the Friars Observant and the Carthusians to violent deaths, neither were many of them overly careful to conceal their dislike of what the king was doing. Thus they were natural, conspicuous targets for anyone determined that there should be no restoration of the connection with Rome—and exactly that determination was shared by everyone from Cromwell to Queen Anne, from Cranmer to the dukes of Norfolk and Suffolk. The more Lutheran or Protestant of the reformers (the word *Protestant* was just then being born in Germany) wanted the monasteries condemned as cesspits of hypocrisy, sexual deviancy, and general moral corruption. They saw them as unconnected to the true spirit of Christianity, and therefore to require elimination.

Cromwell was aware that the church—the monasteries perhaps most obviously, but the dioceses, colleges, hospitals, and other clerical institutions as well—owned a great deal of land and controlled the revenues generated by that land. He had seen this firsthand while in Wolsey's service, where he had been among the first Englishmen to taste the fruits of shutting down religious houses and seizing their assets. And it happened that the mid-1530s were a singularly hard time financially for the English nation and its government. The grain harvest failed almost completely in 1535 (people said it had been raining almost without stop since the killing of the Carthusian priors), and this was but the latest in a series of seriously lean years. Thousands were literally on the verge of starvation, and in June riots broke out in London over the scarcity and price of wheat. The people who farmed the king's lands were unable to pay their rent, owners of land were unable to pay their taxes, and the treasury was so empty that officers of the Crown went without their meager pay. The men responsible for guarding Catherine of Aragon reported being unable to keep her household supplied with food. The king, meanwhile, remained as financially insatiable as ever, spending freely on his varied pleasures and seemingly oblivious to the suffering of his subjects. No one in Cromwell's position could have been unmindful of the immense sums of money represented by the church whose master he now was. Nor was he unaware of the religious eruptions taking place in Germany, or of how Germany's elites were gorging on the property of the church. On the other hand, no one could have cared less than Cromwell and his master about the extent to which church revenues were used for the benefit of the population, or how important the benefactions of the monasteries became when conditions were as hard as they now were.

However appropriate it may have been for the Crown to examine the monasteries, however noble the motives of the king and Cromwell may conceivably have been in launching their program of visitations, as executed that program was a sordid affair. The men Cromwell chose for the job were largely a brutish lot, bent not on informing themselves about the state of the monasteries but on collecting or even fabricating as much negative information as possible as quickly as possible and hurrying it to court. It soon became clear that nearly their only aim was to give Cromwell what he had made clear he wanted—a quick harvest of money in the short run, a basis for harvesting vastly greater amounts later—so that they, in their turn, could be rewarded with a share of the spoils. Several of them became hugely wealthy in just a few years. The details of how they succeeded are almost comic in what they reveal about the malice and greed driving the whole project, tragic in their consequences for hundreds and ultimately thousands of blameless people.

Monastic visitations, whether by the local bishop or by officials of the order to which a particular house belonged, had traditionally been painstaking affairs in which residents and their superiors were interviewed separately about their daily routine, their perceptions of the orderliness of the community or its lack thereof, their questions, suggestions, problems, and complaints. Reports of misconduct or lapses of discipline were investigated to establish their accuracy and seriousness, and eventually the results of all this became the basis of an overall evaluation—a report card, in effect—that prescribed the changes that the visitors regarded as desirable or necessary. Follow-up visits ensured that corrective action was actually taken. The visits by Cromwell's people in 1535 and early 1536 were different: hurried and cursory, with all the emphasis on tallying alleged misdeeds, no exploration of the accuracy of what was reported, and no attempt at correction as opposed to condemnation. Two of the most active and prominent visitors, Richard Layton and Thomas Legh, traveled more than a thousand miles and supposedly visited 121 houses in two months—more than fifteen miles and two monasteries per day, on average. They carried with them eighty-six "articles of inquiry" (questions to which they were supposed to get answers everywhere they went) and twenty-five injunctions or rules to which every house was being required to subscribe. Obviously none of this could be done with even minimal care or thoroughness in the time available.

But it was not their purpose to be thorough or careful. Their mission was to make trouble, blacken reputations, and spread fear. Some of the injunctions could only have been intended to weaken the houses visited and make the maintenance of discipline impossible. It was ordered, for example, that any residents of religious houses under the age of twenty-four, and any who regardless of their current age had taken their vows before the age of twenty, should be discharged into the world whether that was what they wished or not. This had a devastating impact on the manpower (or womanpower) of many houses, the smaller ones especially, and it became a nightmare for individuals unprepared to be sent out into society and wanting nothing except to remain in the communities that had long been their homes. Some of the discharged men were given or at least promised small payments of money and, in the case of the old and infirm, small pensions. Discharged nuns, on the other hand, were given only gowns before being sent away. Those not forced to depart were encouraged to do so voluntarily (the number who agreed to do so appears to have been very small) and—in a step surely calculated to undercut good order and discipline—were told that if they had problems with their superiors they could appeal directly to Cromwell. Any costs incurred in connection with such appeals were to be paid by those same superiors. Another injunction forbade anyone to leave or enter a monastery without the permission of the royal commissioners. When used to stop all traffic in or out—and some of the commissioners used it in exactly this way—this could prevent a monastery from conducting essential business or even supplying its members with food. The new restrictions were rendered all the more odious by the introduction of preachers selected by Cromwell and Cranmer for their eagerness to propound ideas that the residents of the monastic houses were almost certain to find repellent.

The results of all this were sometimes as ridiculous as they were ruinous to the houses. Increasingly, Cromwell received letters from monks complaining not of immorality in their houses but rather of the strictness with which the rules were observed. He encouraged complaints of almost any kind and bestowed favors on those who complained. "Thanks for excusing my getting up for matins at midnight," John Horwoode, a monk of the Benedictine abbey at Winchcombe, wrote to him. "The abbot says this has given cause to some murmurs and grudging among the convent. The truth is, I do not like the burdens and straightness of religion, such as their accustomed abstinence, the 'frayer' (recreations), and other observances of the rule." Before the start of the visitation program, William Fordham, a monk of the priory of Worcester, had been removed as procurator on grounds of extravagance and dishonesty. When he and a former subprior who also had lost his position because of misconduct appealed to Cromwell, the viceregent responded (one can imagine his glee) by putting the two in charge of the house over the protests of the other monks and throwing the prior in prison on a charge of treason. When Chancellor Audley could find no basis for putting the prior on trial, it was decided to let him rot in confinement. Complaints were rare—surprisingly so, considering the rewards that Cromwell was prepared to bestow on anyone willing to help stir up trouble—but their nature was ironic all the same. A frenzied hunt for evidence of monastic laxity more frequently produced evidence that discipline was often so strict as to offend the less zealous religious.

Among the unstated objectives of the visitations was to harass the superiors, making their lives so unpleasant that finally they would give up and voluntarily surrender their establishments to the Crown. There is no reason to think that Eustace Chapuys, Charles V's ambassador to England, was misunderstanding the situation when, in September, he sent the emperor his report on what was happening: "Cromwell goes round about visiting the abbeys, making inventories of their goods and revenues, instructing them fully in the tenets of the new sect, turning out of the abbeys monks and nuns who made their profession before they were twenty-five, and leaving the rest free to go out or remain. It is true they are not expressly told to go out, but it is clearly given them to understand that they had better do it, for they are going to make a reformation of them so severe and strange that in the end they will go, which is the object the king is aiming at, in order to have better occasion to seize the property without causing the people to murmur." Chapuys was an alien at the English court of 1535, a man known to be hostile to Henry's whole religious program and to represent an emperor who was equally hostile. That even he knew not only what was happening but why, and that he knew it long before Henry made his real intentions explicit, indicates rather strongly that the king's and Cromwell's objectives, if they were secret at all, must have been the worst-kept secret in England.

In any case, Cromwell's hopes of bullying the heads of the religious houses into giving up came to almost nothing. By the end of the winter of 1535–36, in spite of incessant interference, threats of worse to come, and promises of pensions for those religious who agreed to depart, only five monasteries had gone out of existence. All five were poor, tiny establishments forced to yield to the hard fact that, after the expulsion of some of their members and the financial exactions of the Crown, they simply had no way of surviving. Still, the visitations had been far from a waste of Crown resources. The government had been able to intrude itself deeply into the internal affairs of every monastery in the kingdom. One house after another had seen the number of its residents reduced, with few except the aged left behind in some instances, and almost all had been weakened financially. In a number of cases it had proved possible to remove superiors unfriendly to the work of the visitors and to inject new leaders of Cromwell's choosing. Every such change had been another assertion of royal mastery, and as such had deepened the demoralization of men and women who were finding it increasingly difficult to believe that they were going to be permitted to continue living in the old way. Cromwell and his men, meanwhile, had taken a first big step down a road that promised to lead them to great wealth. Cromwell had long since shown himself to be expert at extracting money from the people with whom he did business. Now he was able to apply his skills on an immeasurably expanded scale. Money fell into his coffers from terrified abbeys and priories hoping to buy their way out of destruction, from people eager to buy their way into the leadership of abbeys and priories and thereby gain control of their assets, and from his own agents as they moved across the country shaking down their victims and taking care to send their master a share of the booty.

Most important for the long term, the visitations led to the creation of documents that Cromwell could offer to the king and Parliament as proof of the horrifying state of monasticism in England. That this report had been assembled with impossible haste, that it was the work of men interested only in negative findings, that it had involved no serious effort to distinguish fact from fiction—none of this was given the slightest attention. Nor was there any acknowledgment that in some cases the truth had been grossly distorted; masturbation was classified as "sodomy," for example, and when nuns admitted to having illegitimate children no effort was made to determine whether they had borne those children before entering religious life or after.

The fact that the visitors had been able to turn up evidence of *possible* immorality among only a tiny percentage of the monastic clergy was absolutely irrelevant as far as Cromwell was concerned. He had his report in hand—not a coherent report in any serious sense, but a jumbled assortment of mainly vague and unsubstantiated accusations—and it was up to him alone to decide what it actually meant. Whatever he decided, neither Parliament nor the bishops would be likely to disagree. He had planned to recall Parliament late in 1535, but widespread sickness related to continuing famine made a postponement necessary. When Parliament did reconvene, he would be ready to use it for a new and far more ambitious attack on the monastic houses. The report on the visitations, crooked though it was, would be his weapon.

One other event of 1535 merits attention. A group of zealous religious reformers arrived in England from the continent that year. They were Anabaptists, regarded as dangerous radicals even by the Lutherans because of their rejection of infant baptism and much traditional doctrine. They must have traveled to England in search of refuge, their movement having come under intense persecution in Germany, Switzerland, and elsewhere. Immediately upon arrival, however, they were taken into custody. The fourteen of their number who refused to re-nounce the tenets of their sect were promptly burned at the stake. Obvi-ously it was not sufficient in Henry VIII's England to be anti-Rome. Safety was going to require being anti-Rome in whatever way Henry himself decided to find acceptable.

POPES

WHAT IS CALLED THE RENAISSANCE PAPACY WILL STINK IN the nostrils of history to the end of time. Its story is a litany of violence and deceit, of greed and pride and murderous ambition—finally of a corruption that reached such depths as to defy belief. It is an embarrassment to every Catholic who knows about it, a gift to anyone wanting to believe that the Catholic Church really is the Whore of Babylon.

However, it had essentially nothing to do with Henry VIII's destruction of the old church. Tudor England was too far away to be much affected by or even very aware of it, and in any case the worst was already over when Henry came to the throne. By the time he was killing the likes of John Fisher and launching his attack on the monasteries, a new era of reform was dawning in Rome itself.

The papacy had touched bottom when Henry was a child, during the dozen years when the Spaniard Rodrigo Borgia ruled as Pope Alexander VI. A man so vile that when he died in 1503 the priests of St. Peter's Basilica refused to bury him, Alexander had begun his career as the nephew of an earlier Borgia pope thanks to whom he became a bishop, a cardinal, and finally vice-chancellor of the whole church. (He really was Calixtus III's *nephew,* by the way; the word was not always an oblique way of referring to a pope's illegitimate son.) Once he was pope himself, Alexander devoted his reign to advancing the fortunes of the favorites among his numerous bastard children, the most notorious of whom were his son Cesare (a ruthless adventurer who became archbishop of Valencia at age seventeen, and for whom Machiavelli wrote *The Prince*) and his oft-married daughter Lucrezia, rumored though never proven to have been a skilled poisoner and to have committed incest with her brother. Alexander tried to turn vast expanses of church property in central and northern Italy into private domains for his sons, not hesitating to start wars for this purpose or to involve Spain, France,

Venice, Milan, and Naples. At one point he was in such serious trouble that he appealed to the Ottoman Empire, which by that time posed a threat to the very survival of Christianity in eastern Europe, for help. His rather mysterious death, sometimes said to have been the result of an accidental poisoning by his son Cesare, came as a relief to everyone except his offspring. His successor refused to have masses said for him on grounds that it was blasphemous to pray for the damned.

If Alexander's reign was the worst, it differed from what came just before more in degree than in kind. The degradation of the throne of St. Peter had begun in the fourteenth century, during the seventy-three years when seven consecutive popes, all of them French, resided not at Rome but in Avignon and were under the control of the kings of France. This was followed by the Great Schism, four decades during which there were never fewer than two popes, each with his own court and college of cardinals. By the time the Council of Constance resolved this mess and reestablished a single pope at the Vatican, the reputation both of the papacy and of the city of Rome (its population down to twenty-five thousand) was in ruins. From that point, however, the popes began to rebuild their economic and political power, steadily increasing the size of the Papal States and making themselves major players in the cutthroat world of Italian politics. (They were less assiduous in attempting to rebuild their moral authority.) Each new pope tried to outdo his predecessor in restoring the Eternal City to its former splendor, in the process making the papal court Europe's leading source of patronage for artists and the new humanist learning.

The negative aspects of all this success were evident by the reign of Sixtus IV, which began in 1471. Sixtus had risen from modest beginnings to become a Franciscan friar, a university lecturer, minister-general of his order at age fifty, a cardinal at fifty-three. At the time of his election he was regarded as a reformer, so that great things were expected of his reign, but he devoted himself instead to power politics and to making his relatives rich. Though he had no children (like some other Renaissance popes he was probably homosexual), he went to outrageous lengths to advance the interests of his family, the della Roveres. He was implicated in a plot not merely to defeat but to exterminate the rival Medicis of Florence. (In fairness it must be acknowledged that there is no proof that Sixtus himself approved the committing of murder.) Though the scheme fell short of its objective, it did result in the stabbing death, in Florence's cathedral, of the Medici whose then-still-unborn son would one day have the misfortune of serving as Pope Clement VII when Henry VIII sued for his annulment. Perhaps Sixtus's greatest achievement was arranging the marriage that brought the Dukedom of Urbino into the possession of the della Rovere family, his greatest shame that he permitted Ferdinand of Aragon to launch the Spanish Inquisition. He started work on the Sistine Chapel, which is how it got its name.

Nothing much changed under Sixtus's successor, the ludicrously misnamed Innocent VIII. He was yet another assiduous nepotist, marrying the eldest of his numerous illegitimate children to an illegitimate daughter of Lorenzo the Magnificent of Florence and raising Lorenzo's thirteen-year-old son, Giovanni, to the College of Cardinals as part of the deal. (The boy would grow up to become the first Medici pope, Leo X.) Innocent was followed by the monstrous Alexander VI, of whom enough has already been said, and then by Sixtus IV's nephew Giuliano della Rovere, who as Julius II presided from 1503 to 1513 over what is often called the Renaissance papacy's golden age and in fact was, at a minimum, a gilded age. Della Rovere had been Alexander's bitter enemy— so much so that he spent the latter's papacy in exile—and upon becoming pope himself he made it his first priority to recover the papal territories controlled by Cesare Borgia and his brothers. That accomplished, Julius went on to make war on a much grander scale, organizing the so-called Holy League against France, inviting England to join, and thereby giving young Henry VIII a supposedly religious reason to pursue his dreams of military glory. As a ruler Julius was an epic figure: warrior, builder, patron of great artists. As a religious leader, he was perhaps the last of Rome's sick jokes.

Julius's death brought an end to the worst of the outrages. Leo X, the onetime thirteen-year-old Medici cardinal, was elected in 1513, and though he possessed none of the majesty of his predecessor he was also not a bad man. He raised the quality of the College of Cardinals (one of his appointees was the respected Lorenzo Campeggio, who much later would be sent to England to judge King Henry's annulment suit) and even tried without success to convene a council for the purpose of effecting reforms. It was during his eight-year reign that the Lutheran revolt erupted in Germany, which is one reason his death resulted in the elec-

tion of a scholarly and almost saintly Dutchman, Adrian VI, who died
before being able to accomplish anything (and would prove to be, incidentally, the last non-Italian pope for more than four hundred years).
Next came another Medici, Clement VII, the intelligent, conscientious,
but also indecisive and unlucky pontiff whose whole reign turned into a
stalemated struggle with problems among which the English king's wish
to be rid of his wife was far from the most difficult or dangerous. If
Clement solved none of those problems, he also never disgraced his office. He had been a champion of reform long before becoming pope and
recognized the need for reform on the largest possible scale, but he declined to call a general council of the church out of fear that such a body
might become yet another threat to papal authority.

The 1534 election of Alessandro Farnese as Pope Paul III must have
been a troubling development for at least some reformers. Early in his career Farnese had been a protégé of Alexander VI, who made him a cardinal in 1493 when he was only twenty-five, and almost his first major act
upon becoming pope was to bestow red hats on two of his own grandsons, both of them barely out of childhood. After that appalling start,
however, he changed course, making the papacy not only friendly to the
reform cause but its driving engine. He set remarkably high standards for
his subsequent appointments, looking for men of unquestionably good
character, impressive intellectual credentials, and a demonstrated commitment to the purging of abuses. It was he who added John Fisher to the
College of Cardinals in 1535, and he would do the same to Henry VIII's
cousin Reginald Pole a year later. Pole was also named to, and became a
conspicuously active member of, a commission responsible for identify-
ing areas where reform was most urgently needed. Paul had begun his
reign believing that it was still possible to close the rifts that in less than
twenty years had shattered the unity of Western Christendom, and unlike
Clement VII he saw a general council as a possible way of achieving reconciliation. In this he was perhaps naïve: when he announced plans for
a council to meet at Mantua, the German Protestant states declared that
they would attend no assembly held in Italy under papal auspices. A
council remained one of his highest objectives, however, and with the
support of the emperor Charles he would continue to try to convene one.

Paul definitely thought, in the early going, that reconciliation with
England was still possible. His years as dean of the College of Cardinals

had persuaded him that Henry VIII was well disposed toward him—the impression was probably not wrong when originally formed, Cardinal della Rovere being rich in the skills of diplomacy and Henry at first eager for friends at the papal court—but he appears never to have understood the island kingdom of the distant north. He even believed, evidently, that Henry would welcome his decision to make John Fisher a cardinal. News of Fisher's execution set him straight soon enough, and the killing soon afterward of Thomas More left no room for doubt. Obviously Henry would never voluntarily reconnect with Rome on anything resembling traditional terms, and henceforth Paul would shape his English policy accordingly.

14

All but Godlike

At the start of 1536 Catherine of Aragon, hidden away at Kimbolton Castle far from London, was on her deathbed. She asked that her daughter be permitted to visit, but though the two had not seen each other in years, the king once again refused. He had been as unsuccessful in getting Mary to accept his supremacy and her illegitimacy as he had been in persuading Catherine of those two things, and perhaps he feared that if the two met they would strengthen each other's resolve. Possibly he was motivated by nothing more calculating than a mean-spirited desire to punish his onetime queen by denying even her dying wish. Certainly his current queen could have had no argument with Henry's refusal: understandably, Anne regarded the very existence of Catherine and Mary, now a marriageable woman of twenty, as a threat to her own position and the futures of her daughter Elizabeth and the additional children she expected to bear. She had had Mary sent away from court and placed in the custody of her—Anne's—aunt, who pestered her daily with demands that she stop claiming that she was a royal princess and her little half-sister was not.

No longer strong enough to take pen to paper, Catherine dictated a last letter to the man she continued to regard as her husband. She touched on many subjects, gently calling Henry to account for having "cast me into many calamities, and yourself into many troubles," forgiving him for everything and asking God to forgive him also. She asked him to be good to Mary, and to provide the three ladies remaining in her service with dowries so that they could marry, and her servants with a year's pay. "Lastly, I make this vow," she said, "that mine eyes desire you above all things. Farewell." A few days later she was dead, an aged, worn-out, heartbroken woman just three weeks past her fiftieth birthday. An autopsy revealed that she apparently had been in good health except for a growth, "completely black and hideous," on her heart. Centuries later pathologists would conclude that this growth was a secondary cancer, a reflection of the apparently undetected sarcoma that must have been the actual cause of death. But in 1536, inevitably, a rumor traveled through England to the effect that Henry had had her poisoned. Catherine had asked to be buried at one of the houses of the Observant Franciscans, but thanks to her husband no such houses remained. Three days after her death he decided that she should be buried at Peterborough Cathedral. Her tomb was decorated with the arms of Spain combined with those of Wales rather than England. She could be honored as Princess of Wales, but not as queen of anything.

Henry was reported to have shed a tear or two upon reading Catherine's letter, but to be so jubilant when this was followed by news of her death that he dressed in yellow with a white feather in his hat and ordered up a banquet and a tournament in celebration. He and Anne—she too was festively adorned in yellow—brought little Princess Elizabeth to court that day and ostentatiously showed her off. To her parents she must have seemed an augury of still better things to come: her mother was once again pregnant. Anne and the king would have been ecstatic, Henry because once again he could look forward to the arrival of his long-yearned-for son, Anne because by giving birth to the next king of England she could make herself secure.

Ironically, the death of Catherine left Anne more vulnerable than she had been before. In the eyes of the Roman church Anne was the king's mistress rather than his wife, whereas Henry was now a widower, free to wed whom he chose. If he put Anne aside, he would be free to take a Hapsburg bride or a Valois bride or whatever bride he preferred. And he was obviously no longer as enchanted with Anne as he had been before their marriage. For months now he had been openly flirting with one of Anne's ladies-in-waiting, Jane Seymour. Anne, quick to notice, must have wondered if history might be repeating itself. In her anger and fear she had lashed out both at Henry, whose complaints about his wife's flaming temper were taking on a sharper edge, and at the apparently un-offending Jane. Henry, remembering the restraint with which Catherine had carried herself when faced with evidence of a romantic entangle-ment involving her husband and one of her ladies, could not have been pleased to hear of "much scratching and by-blows between the queen and her maid." But none of that mattered compared to the fact of Anne's latest pregnancy. If she could bring this child to term, if it proved to be male and survived, she would have nothing to fear from any woman in England and little to fear even from Henry himself.

But it was not to be. On January 29—the day of Catherine's burial—Anne miscarried a fetus that appeared to be in its fourth month of devel-opment, and to be male. Anne of course was deeply, wretchedly, almost hysterically unhappy, but when Henry visited her bedchamber he dis-played more self-pity than concern for his wife. According to one story, she tried to arouse his sympathy by telling him that the miscarriage had been triggered by the force of her love: six days before, he had been un-conscious for two hours after a hard fall from his horse, and Anne is sup-posed to have claimed that her fear for his life had caused her to lose the child. An alternate story has it that Anne went into labor after discover-ing Henry with Jane on his knee. Whatever the truth, the end of the pregnancy was the end not only of the marriage but of Anne. She now became a victim of history, of domestic and international politics, and of course of her husband.

Much more was in play now than Anne's failure to produce a son or the king's latest infatuation with one of the ladies of his court. Anne was also dangerously exposed because, for the first time, she was seriously at odds with Thomas Cromwell. What separated the two was the question of the monasteries: not whether to continue the attack on them, be-cause she as an evangelical was no more sympathetic to the religious houses than he was, but what to do with the riches that the attack was making available. Parliament, obediently accepting the king's assur-ances that Cromwell's visitations had shown the smaller monasteries to be sinkholes of degeneracy sexual and otherwise, passed in March a bill authorizing the seizure and closing of all religious houses (the bill said they were to be "converted to better uses") with annual revenues of less than £200. All the larger and richer houses, the "great and solemn monasteries," were spared on the grounds that "(thanks be to God) religion is right well kept and observed" by them. Obviously it was implausible that all the smaller establishments were so corrupt as to be beyond saving while all the larger ones were above reproach, but targeting only the weakest allowed Cromwell to win the acquiescence of those abbots of great houses who sat in the House of Lords. As for the lay lords and the Commons, quite apart from their fear of the king, they could be brought along by the twofold hope that the liquidation of the smaller monasteries might spare them from being taxed and possibly even enable them to share in the spoils. Cromwell, responsible as he now was for paying the bills of a financially irresponsible monarch, naturally intended to claim the property and income of the monasteries for the Crown (which would, of course, make it possible to divert some part of the resulting windfall into his own hands and those of his henchmen). Queen Anne, more nobly if naïvely, proposed that the money in question, once it had been cleansed of papist corruption, should continue to be used for religious or at least quasi-religious purposes—for education and charity. The stakes were high, and feelings were correspondingly intense on both sides. One result, a fateful one for the queen, was that Cromwell now had a positive reason to fear her continued influence over Henry. The most powerful man in England after the king thus became the enemy of a queen who already had too many enemies—all those numberless people who harbored resentments over how Catherine had been rudely discarded and Mary was even now being shabbily treated. Cromwell had chosen a good issue over which to break with Anne and her party. Where the disposition of the wealth of the church was concerned, he could be confident of his free-spending king's support.

Internationally, too, events were unfolding in ways that seemed almost calculated to leave Anne alone and vulnerable. The greatest danger to Henry was the possibility that Francis of France and the emperor Charles V would put their differences aside, ally themselves with the pope, and launch a military crusade aimed at driving the English apostate from his throne. This was not inconceivable: Charles was an ardent Catholic who might easily be persuaded to see such an undertaking as his duty if it had any real chance of success, and Francis was ambitious and restless enough to be drawn into almost any adventure that carried the promise of gold or glory. England's great need—Henry's desperate need—was to keep Charles and Francis apart. The best way to accomplish that was to enter into an alliance with one of them so as to neutralize both with a single stroke.

He could hardly have been luckier in this regard. For nearly eight years Francis had been biding his time, waiting for France to recover its strength sufficiently for him to avenge the humiliations inflicted after the battles of Pavia and Landriano. By the spring of 1536 he felt ready. Charles having sailed off to North Africa to attack the Turkish stronghold of Tunis, Francis invaded and overran part of the Hapsburg dominions in northern Italy. Charles returned to find that he had good reason to repair his relationship with England, and he was pleased to learn that Cromwell was receptive. The old obstacle, Henry's divorce of Charles's aunt Catherine, had been removed by Catherine's death; though Charles had apparently found it necessary to be mortally offended by the insult done to his mother's sister, he was too much of a realist and in 1536 too badly in need of friends to allow policy to be determined by what had been done once upon a time to his insane mother's dead sister. Now the problem was on the English side: it was Henry's insistence that everyone, not just everyone in England but *everyone*, recognize his marriage to Anne. In the case of Charles, this was asking too much. He could only have seen such a step as compromising his honor.

But Henry was no longer as devoted to Anne as he once had been. He was definitely less disposed to put his throne at risk for her sake. Perhaps his marriage was not something the whole of Christendom must be made to accept but a problem, a source of danger even, a barrier standing between himself and safety. He suspected that Anne's miscarriages, like Catherine's, must be signs of divine displeasure. Knowing that God could not be unhappy with him, he reasoned that Anne or the marriage must be the cause of the trouble. He began to complain that Anne had somehow bewitched him into marrying her "by means of sortileges [sorcery] and charms." He ordered the same churchmen who had provided him with grounds for annulling his first marriage to find reasons for annulling the second. Henry Percy, who years earlier had been in love with the young Anne Boleyn and would have married her if not for Wolsey's interference, was asked to testify that he and Anne had been bound together in a precontract of marriage that rendered her ineligible to marry the king or anyone else. Percy's refusal put an end to what might have been an easy solution, but it freed Cromwell to pursue a more ambitious course. He saw a way not only of ridding the king of another marital problem but of fortifying his own position by eliminating a whole power bloc, the court's Boleyn party.

He was able to make his move early in May: Anne was arrested on charges of adultery and locked in the Tower. Accused with her were five men: a court musician, three members of the king's inner circle including a knight who had long been one of Cromwell's rivals for royal favor, and Anne's own brother. She could not possibly have been guilty; her alleged lovers were offered pardon if they would confess, but only one did so and he had probably been tortured. Nor could Henry possibly have believed her guilty, unless he had sunk so deep into paranoia as to be out of touch with reality. That is unlikely: Henry was vicious by this point, but far from insane. Anne's destruction is adequately explained by Cromwell's opportunism, her husband's weariness with her, possibly his wish to punish her (it was revealed at her trial that she had ridiculed his sexual performance), and the changing international landscape. At times during her imprisonment (nothing could be more understandable) she broke down in fits of hysterical laughter or weeping, but during her farce of a trial she displayed regal composure and firmly maintained her innocence. On May 19, in the moment before being beheaded, she called upon Jesus to "save my sovereign and master the king, the most godly, noble and gentle prince that is." George Boleyn and the other accused men, the one who had been promised mercy for confessing included, had been executed two days before. Thomas Boleyn had been excused from sitting as a judge at his children's trials (their uncle the Duke of Norfolk presided and passed sentence), but he lost his position as Lord Privy Seal (Cromwell took the title for himself) and withdrew permanently to his country home.

Anne just missed out on the distinction of being the first queen of England to be executed; on the day of her death she was no longer Henry's wife and therefore not queen. Shortly after her arrest Henry had instructed the infinitely flexible Archbishop Cranmer to nullify the marriage. Even for Cranmer, this must have been an unwelcome assignment. It was he, after all, who had at the king's behest undertaken to review the two royal marriages and solemnly proclaimed the first to have been invalid and the second to be sound and true. Now he had to undo his own work. He went dutifully through the necessary motions, summoning Anne and inviting Henry to appear before him and offer, if they wished, reasons why their union should not be annulled. At the appointed hour a representative of the king presented arguments not in support of the marriage but against it. Two men claiming to represent the queen confessed themselves to be unable to answer such a convincing case, and all asked for a speedy judgment. Two days after Anne was found guilty of treason—an event celebrated with a pageant on the Thames, where "the royal barge was constantly filled with minstrels and musicians"—Cranmer declared that she was not married to Henry and never could have been, because of the king's relationship with her sister Mary. His master was content. The child Elizabeth, like her half-sister Mary, was now illegitimate. Henry was once again a bachelor with no legitimate offspring, free not only to marry but to generate children who would have an uncontestable right to succeed him.

He wasted no time. On the morning following Anne's execution, after a short delay that allowed Cranmer to issue a dispensation permitting Henry to marry Jane in spite of the fact that both were descendants of King Edward III and therefore distant cousins, it was announced that the two were betrothed and would be wed on May 30. Once again Henry was besotted with a bride-to-be. He had established Jane in apartments at Whitehall, with her brother Edward Seymour and his wife quartered nearby to act as chaperones when Henry made his frequent visits. The Seymours were a vigorous and ambitious clan—Jane had many brothers and sisters—and by captivating the king she had created thrilling opportunities for all of them. She herself was an intelligent woman in her late twenties, not beautiful but experienced in the ways of the court, modest in her demeanor and far more submissive than the temperamental Anne had ever been. As a longtime lady-in-waiting she had witnessed the fall not only of Anne but of Catherine before her, and she had seen the Boleyns raised high by their king only to be destroyed. She could not have been unaware of what dangerous waters she and her siblings would have to navigate when she became queen, and one can only wonder how she felt about having been singled out in this extraordinary way. Certainly her bridegroom was not, in physical terms, the stuff of which dreams are made. The onetime golden young king had become grossly overweight, afflicted with chronic headaches and stinking ulcers of the thigh and leg.

With Catherine and Anne both dead and Henry truly and entirely unattached for the first time in a quarter of a century, there was no longer any reason—any matrimonial reason, in any case—why Henry and his kingdom should not be reconciled with the papacy and the universal church. The marriage to Jane presented no problem at all: it was a valid union by anyone's reckoning, and Jane herself was known to be, in her quiet way, more drawn to the old religion than to the reformist party that the Boleyns had so energetically championed. Jane even, as the suppression of the smaller monasteries got under way, attempted to intervene with her husband on the monks' behalf, drawing back when Henry warned her that her predecessor had not benefited from injecting herself in matters that were none of her affair. Pope Paul and Charles V were not only hopeful that Henry could be brought back into the fold but expectant that it was going to happen. Both were prepared to make it as easy for Henry as possible. Paul was prepared to forgive and forget such inconvenient matters as the killing of Cardinal-designate John Fisher.

Which simply went to show that neither understood what kind of man Henry had by now turned into, or where things stood in England in the summer of 1536. Henry had taken immense risks in claiming supremacy over the church, and his success had been profoundly satisfying to his unfathomably needy ego. He would have seen little reason to relinquish any substantial part of all that he had won even if other factors had not complicated the situation. Foremost among those factors was the suppression of the monasteries and the seizure, by and for a Crown that desperately needed money, of their lands, revenues, and treasures. The information gathered by Cromwell's visitors indicated that 372 religious houses in England and another 27 in Wales—somewhat more than half of all the monastic institutions in the kingdom—had annual revenues below £200 and so were subject to liquidation under the statute enacted by Parliament in March. A new Court of the Augmentations of the Revenues of the King's Crown was established to manage the torrent of income that soon followed, and the administration of that court was entrusted to a man who would show himself capable of exploiting its full potential on the king's and Cromwell's behalf and also on his own: the same Richard Rich whose testimony had provided legal cover for the killing of Fisher and More. By April fat trunks were being hauled into London filled with gold and silver plate, jewelry, and other treasures accumulated by the monasteries over the centuries. With them came money from the sale of church bells, lead stripped from the roofs of monastic buildings, and livestock, furnishings, and equipment. Some of the confiscated land was sold—enough to bring in £30,000 in the first two years—and what was not sold generated tens of thousands of pounds in annual rents. Taken all together, it was a tremendous boost to the Crown's revenues, though as great as it was it failed to close the deficit. The longer the confiscations continued, the smaller the possibility of their ever being reversed or even stopped from going further. The money was spent almost as quickly as it flooded in—so quickly that any attempt to restore the monasteries to what they had been before the suppression would have meant financial ruin for the Crown. Nor would those involved in the work of suppression—everyone from Cromwell and Rich to the obscure men whose work it was to strip the monasteries bare and haul away what they contained—ever be willing to part with what they were skimming off for themselves.

Parliament's suppression bill had reserved to the king the power to allow any religious houses of his choosing to continue in operation. In practice this power rested with Cromwell as vicar-general, and in his hands it became another potent tool for self-enrichment. Desperate to save their houses by any possible means in spite of being offered pensions in return for cooperation, the heads of scores of abbeys and priories offered to pay not to be shut down. In many cases they had nothing to offer except the very treasures that would be confiscated if their houses were seized, or whatever money they could raise by leasing or borrowing against the land that was their chief support. The Crown stood to gain nothing by accepting such payment rather than taking possession of everything; Cromwell and his people, by contrast, stood to profit tremendously. The number of houses that survived in this way was surprisingly large—more than a hundred, ultimately—and the extent to which the king's men benefited was no less impressive.

All the same, the suppression was disruptive on a painfully large scale. The number of monks and nuns expelled from the seized houses was probably on the order of two thousand, and taking into account servants, dependants, and tenants makes it likely that as many as ten thousand people were displaced. It is impossible to believe, on the basis of the available evidence, that all or most or even a substantial minority of the closed houses were morally corrupt, unable to sustain themselves financially, or of no use to the broader society. In the archives there survive many letters written from members of the gentry to Cromwell and his agents, explaining why some establishment should not be destroyed and begging that it not be. "We beseech your favor," one such letter states, "for the prior of Pentney, assuring you that he relieves those quarters wondrously where he dwells, and it would be a pity not to spare a house that feeds so many indigent poor, which is in a good state, maintains good service, and does so many charitable deeds." Interestingly, the same prior who was defended in these terms had earlier been singled out for particularly harsh criticism in the visitation reports that preceded the suppression. Similarly, a letter asking mercy for the priory at Carmarthen in Wales asserted that its revenues exceeded £200 per annum, but that the total had been understated by the visitors in order to make suppression possible. This same letter describes the Carmarthen house as well built and in good repair, and the conduct of the twelve monks living there as impeccable. It adds that "hospitality is daily kept for poor and rich, which is a great relief to the country, being poor and bare . . . alms are given to eighty poor people, which, if the house were suppressed, they would want . . . [and] strangers and merchantmen resorting to those parts are honestly received and entertained whereby they are the gladder to bring their commodities to that country." Such documents provide a more objective picture than the reports of Cromwell's agents of the true state of the smaller monasteries and their role in the life of the kingdom. The appeals of the writers, however, were less effective than cash payment in determining which houses were closed and which were allowed to continue.

The appeals of the monks, begging not to be thrown out, were ignored except where enough gold could be found to touch the consciences of the king's commissioners. The suppressions proceeded with such speed that by early July 1536 Ambassador Chapuys was writing that "it is a lamentable thing to see a legion of monks and nuns, who have been chased from their monasteries, wandering miserably hither and thither seeking means to live; and several honest men have told me that, what with monks, nuns and persons dependent on the monasteries suppressed, there were over twenty thousand who knew not how to live." Chapuys's number may have been high, but the picture he painted was accurate. A new kind of pauperism was being created across England as a direct consequence of the actions of the king. It was a pauperism for which, with the disappearance of the monasteries, there could be no adequate relief. It would plague the reigns of Henry's children. As the government began to seek remedy by punishing the paupers themselves, yet another dimension would be added to the horrors of the age.

The response of the religious orders to the destruction of their houses was almost uniformly passive. They were, after all, communities of monks and nuns, not of politicians or soldiers, and they were receiving no support from their bishops or even from the larger, more influential houses. A striking exception occurred in late September in the north. As the four men charged by Cromwell with shutting down monasteries in Northumberland approached the town of Hexham, they found armed men blocking their way. The townsfolk had turned out to stop them, and had turned the local monastery into a fortress. The monks inside, informed that the commissioners had been sent in the king's name to execute the bill of dissolution, replied that "we be twenty brethren in this house and we shall die all, or that ye shall have the house." The visitors withdrew and did not return. Hexham was left in peace—for the time being. The fact that this act of defiance had taken place in the north would soon prove symptomatic of that whole region's hostility to the king's program.

Henry had other things to concern himself with than a small community of recalcitrant monks and their supporters in a distant corner of the kingdom. For many months, through his court chaplain, he had been badgering his young cousin Reginald Pole to provide a written statement of his position on the annulment of his first marriage and, especially, the supremacy. Pole was still on the continent, buried in the studies to which he had been allowed to return after infuriating the king and alarming his own family with his refusal to take Henry's side. During his absence the king had grown more confident than ever that no intelligent, informed, and open-minded person could possibly fail to see the irrefutability of his claims, and he had not stopped thinking of young Pole. By 1537, apparently, he was sure that Pole's years of reading and reflection must have brought him around. He sent him books refuting the idea of papal primacy (such works were being written in great numbers by clergymen eager to win the attention of the king), learned that he had begun researching and writing a book of his own on the question, and was eager to see the result. Winning over Pole would be a victory, a vindication, of international consequence.

But the fruit of Pole's labors, a work that he titled *De Unitate Ecclesiastica,* turned out to be the opposite of what Henry expected. Assuming the role of Old Testament prophet, casting the king as a tyrant in desperate need of being saved from the consequences of his own errors, Pole expressed himself recklessly, in terms that could hardly have been better chosen to offend a man of Henry's immense pride. After comparing Henry not only to Richard III—the archfiend in the Tudor version of English history—but to the emperor Nero as well, Pole charged that he "did not merely kill, but tore to pieces all the true defenders of the old religion in a more inhuman fashion than the Turk." Henry's actions, he said, made a mockery of his papal title Defender of the Faith, and without quite saying so explicitly he suggested in unmistakable terms that Henry's actions were so repellent to his own subjects as to make a revolt likely if not inevitable. Compared with this invective, Pole's scholarly denial that any secular ruler could claim to be supreme head of the church even within his own realm was familiar almost to the point of being merely tiresome. If at any point there had existed a real possibility that Henry might opt to settle his differences with Rome, Pole's little work (which he had not had printed, claiming that it was intended for the king's eyes only) ended that possibility absolutely. Pole's mother and brothers, when they learned of what he had done this time, denounced his actions as "folly." Though Henry took no action against them, he lashed out in other directions.

No longer satisfied merely to make the life of his daughter Mary a hell of humiliation and deprivation, he sent representatives to her place of confinement with a demand that she do what her late mother had taught her to regard as unthinkable: take the oath of supremacy and, the crowning blow, acknowledge that she herself was illegitimate. Mary refused, was threatened, and refused again. The screws were tightened further. The woman who was her closest friend, almost the last companion she was still permitted, was taken away to the Tower. Two men suspected of being sympathetic to her were purged from the Privy Council, and Cromwell himself began to fear that he was going to suffer for efforts he had made earlier to reconcile father and daughter. He wrote to Mary, calling her "an obstinate and obdurate woman, deserving the reward of malice in the extremity of mischief." He provided her with a draft letter that he suggested she transcribe in her own hand and send to her father; it recognized Henry as supreme head, repudiated the pope, and described her parents' marriage as "incestuous and unlawful." Rumors reached Mary of the king's intention—what better way to increase the pressure on a daughter with little fear for herself?—to move not only against her but against everyone regarded as friendly to her. Finally even the one man of any importance who had remained unflinchingly loyal to her and her mother, her cousin Charles's ambassador Eustace Chapuys, urged her to submit. And so she copied out Cromwell's draft word for word, signed it, and sent it to her father. In doing so she abjectly denied her own deepest beliefs, but she was not utterly crushed: later, when ordered to give up the names of those persons who had encouraged her to resist the king's demands, she said she would die before doing any such thing. Still later, sufficiently rehabilitated to be permitted to dine in her father's company, she heard him jokingly rebuke members of his council because "some of you were desirous that I should put this jewel to death." This revelation of just how close she had been to losing her life caused her to faint.

When Lord Thomas Howard, half-brother of the Duke of Norfolk, neglected to obtain royal permission before contracting to marry Lady Margaret Douglas, the king's sister Margaret's daughter by her second husband, Henry chose to interpret this, absurdly, as an attempt on Howard's part to make himself king of England. Howard was attainted for treason, and along with his bride-that-might-have-been he was imprisoned in the Tower, where he would remain until his death. (Lady Margaret survived to become the mother-in-law of Mary, Queen of Scots, and so paternal grandmother of England's King James I. Unlike Henry—who, one suspects, would be deeply chagrined if he knew—she is therefore an ancestor of all the subsequent kings and queens of England down to the present day.)

Henry used his expanding powers not only to blight lives but to bend

England's unwritten constitution into bizarre shapes. A new Act of Succession, pushed through Parliament without difficulty, voided the statute that had declared Anne Boleyn to be the king's only wife and their descendants to be the only legitimate heirs to the throne. Now Jane Seymour was the only wife, her (as yet unborn) children by Henry the sole line of succession. In a truly extraordinary step, one without precedent in law or tradition, Parliament bestowed upon the king the power, if he left no legitimate children, to name as his heir and successor "such person or persons in possession and remainder as shall please your Highness." At the same time the definition of treason was again broadened to make it easier to ensnare anyone bold or mad enough to follow the examples of Fisher and More. Now it became a capital crime not only to reject the new Succession Act but to remain silent when asked for an opinion. The act also provided—whoever thought this up must have smiled at his own ingenuity—that anyone who attempted to repeal it would be guilty of high treason by virtue of having done so.

The 1530s being a period of such astonishing religious ferment, with Protestantism taking firm root on the continent and splintering into sects virtually all of which found adherents in England, it was inevitable that Henry would set about to impose his will in the realm of dogma and doctrine. His confidence in himself as England's one source of truth, and his determination to cast aside the old connection to Rome, were accompanied by an equally strong determination to make all his subjects not only believe but actively profess exactly what he believed. This presented no small number of challenges. Being essentially conservative in his approach to questions of dogma, Henry was repelled by such defining Protestant beliefs as justification by faith alone (a rejection of the notion that individuals could improve their chances of salvation through prayer and good works). Likewise he was infuriated by the reformers' rejection of purgatory and transubstantiation (the belief that, in the mass, the bread and wine of the Eucharist become the flesh and blood of Jesus). But many of the people who at various times were closest and most important to him—Cranmer and the Boleyns among others—gradually came to embrace the very ideas that Henry himself most abhorred. From the time of his break with the papacy until the end of his life, Henry had to walk an often fuzzy and crooked line between Roman Catholicism and an evolving evangelical Protestantism. In doing so he had to remain mindful that there were politically powerful forces on both sides of that line. On the whole he was skillful at playing the factions off against one another, balancing conservative (but not necessarily Roman) Catholic interests against the evangelicals, allowing the two sides to neutralize one another to his advantage. But in the strictly religious dimension, in his efforts to explain what he wanted his people to believe and get them to believe it, he was not only less successful but ultimately a nearly complete failure. His problems in this regard began in the summer of 1536 with the issuance of the so-called Ten Articles, officially the work of convocation but really an expression of Henry's thinking at the time, the first in what would become his increasingly confusing efforts to tell England what to believe and how to worship. The Articles were wordy and ambiguous, and at points they were nearly self-contradictory in dealing with the issues that most sharply separated Catholic doctrine from the various Protestant and evangelical subgroups. Even today scholars disagree as to whether and to what extent they show Henry to have been holding to a firmly conservative line or leaning in a radical direction.

About one thing there can be no uncertainty. Henry wanted everyone in his kingdom to agree on religion, and he expected agreement on his terms. This is unmistakable in the preface to the Ten Articles, which states that it is the king's responsibility to assure "that unity and concord in opinion, namely in such things as doth concern our religion, may increase and go forthward, and all occasion of dissent and discord touching the same be repressed and utterly extinguished." Shortly after the Articles were published, Cromwell issued a set of injunctions ordering the clergy to preach and promote them in their Sunday sermons. At the same time, however, he forbade the churchmen to say anything about such inflammatory subjects as images, miracles, and relics—popular aspects of the old religion that the evangelicals despised as superstitious. No doubt this enforced silence was partly a reflection of Cromwell's (and the king's) reluctance to stir up unnecessary trouble. But it may have been rooted also in uncertainty on Henry's part about what he himself currently believed. He was determined to have uniformity, but he was not in every case sure what uniformity should entail. In shattering the consensus on which the old religion had been based, he had let a whole flock of doctrinal genies out of the bottle. To expect all of them to reassemble in a new bottle of his choosing was to expect a great deal, all the more so as Henry remained unclear about what he wanted the shape of that bottle to be.

Where Henry knew what he wanted, however, he had little difficulty translating his wishes into civil law and church doctrine. His all-but-godlike status under the new dispensation was captured vividly on the title page of a new translation of the Bible. The woodcut drawing that the court artist Hans Holbein created for this page under Cromwell's direction has as its dominant figure not God the Father or Jesus Christ, not the prophets of the Old Testament or the apostles of the New, but Henry VIII. He is shown seated center stage on his throne, the sword of justice clutched firmly in his right hand, passing the Sacred Scriptures to a cluster of bishops kneeling not before their creator but at the feet of their king. The dedication offered to that king by the new Bible's translator—"He only under God is the Chief Head of all the congregation and church"—is so modest by comparison with the illustration that one wonders if Henry found it disappointing.

But the real world had not been abolished. It lurked in the background mainly, but occasionally it intruded into the world of Henry's making with a reminder that the king was *not* God and could not bend *everything* to his will. In July his sixteen-year-old son Henry Fitzroy, Duke of Richmond, the possible successor on whom he had doted and lavished honors and riches, died of tuberculosis. And the months were passing without any sign that Queen Jane was with child.

And then the kingdom itself, to all appearances so submissive, so worshipful of its great ruler, suddenly exploded.

THEY WERE WHAT THEY ATE

SIXTEENTH-CENTURY EUROPE WAS A WORLD IN WHICH conspicuous consumption really mattered. It wasn't just that wealth meant power—has there ever been a society in which that wasn't true?—but that wealth had to be *seen* to be believed. Emperors and kings, nobles and bishops, landowners and merchants all understood that they could never be more important than they were able to *appear* to be. Appearance was reality. Only a man rich enough to *look* rich could expect to be taken seriously in the great marketplace of patronage and influence.

Hence all the emphasis, in England as elsewhere, on wearing extravagantly expensive clothes, and living in extravagantly grand houses, and trying to win friends by giving extravagantly costly gifts.

And on eating—more important, on serving—extravagant quantities of extravagantly expensive food. In dining as in all things, it was an age of excess for everyone who could afford it.

The roots of all this went back to early feudal times, if not further. When society was utterly dominated by the warlords, a man's importance was a function of the amount of land he controlled and the number of fighting men his land could support. To be of the highest importance, one needed a large following of lesser nobles, knights, and soldiers, a great hall in which these subordinates could be sheltered, and food and drink for all of them. If the Norman kings and barons fed their liegemen with deer and wild boars that they themselves had killed in their own hunting parks, that simply added to the aura of power that stayed with them everywhere they went.

None of this changed under what historians call the "bastard feudalism" of later centuries, when the old sacred oaths of loyalty to an overlord came to matter less than how much cash a man could raise and how big a following he could *buy*. Leaders were still expected to main-

tain and feed extensive households, and to receive and feed steady
streams of guests, and to do so in a style that made a statement. Those
lesser men who aspired to rise, to establish themselves as leaders, naturally tried to do the same. If the amounts of cash required could be
painfully, even dangerously high (they inevitably were, food being much
more expensive relative to income than it is today), that had to be accepted as part of the cost of doing business.

The most conspicuous consumers of all were the kings. Their responsibilities made an extensive administrative apparatus necessary, so their
courts had to be larger than those of even the greatest nobles. They also
had to surpass even their mightiest subjects in grandeur; anything less
would have compromised their dignity and raised questions about the
reality of royal power. Even Henry VII, that supposed miser, expended
huge sums to impress England and the world with the splendor in which
he lived. Following the French example to which he had been exposed
during his years in exile, he established a personal bodyguard of uniformed "gentlemen pensioners" and put his pages, grooms, and other
staff in green and white livery. His court became the setting of elaborate
rituals, processions, and ceremonies, with much bowing, scraping, and
genuflecting whenever royalty appeared. Hospitality remained, as it had
been for the Plantagenets, a central element in Tudor ostentation: as
many as seven hundred people would dine simultaneously in Henry
VII's great hall (the royal family sitting apart on a raised gallery), and on
the most special occasions as many as sixty different dishes might be
served.

In the next generation the young Henry VIII's hunger for grandeur and
indifference to cost raised court and kitchen to levels previously unimag-
ined. Most of the royal household was managed by a lord steward whose
annual budget was, at least in peacetime, the largest in the kingdom. His
225 subordinates (virtually all of them men, incidentally; the Tudor
"serving wench" is a mythical figure) staffed not only enormous kitchens
but such satellite operations as the bakehouse, pantry, saucery, spicery,
wafery, confectionery, scullery, boiling house, and scalding house. The
sheer numbers of people being fed made all this necessary; the record
survives of a single day when, though the royal household was smaller
than usual because temporarily in Calais rather than in England, it consumed six oxen, eight calves, forty sheep, a dozen pigs, 132 chickens,

seven swans, twenty storks, thirty-four pheasants, one hundred ninety-two partridges and an equal number of cocks, and many other things. Waste and pilferage were inevitable in an operation of such enormous dimensions and occurred on a scale commensurate with the quantities being prepared. Effective financial management was somewhere between difficult and impossible, and as Henry added more and more embellishments—eventually he employed sixty court musicians, compared with five in the reign of his grandfather Edward IV—the household sometimes teetered on the brink of being completely out of control.

At court as elsewhere, what one ate was largely a function of one's position in the social pyramid. As the list of things cooked one day in Calais indicates, courtiers like other people of wealth and prominence subsisted to an extraordinary extent on meat and poultry, which may have made up as much as eighty percent of the elite diet. The harvest (and eating) season for fruit and vegetables was short in England, it was difficult to import most such produce, and in any case ancient medical authorities including Galen had pronounced it unhealthful. People of means could afford to keep and butcher livestock throughout the winter and thus had year-round access to fresh meat. Where preservation was necessary it was accomplished through drying, smoking, or immersion in granular salt or brine. Salt was expensive, however, and so was used only with varieties of fish and meat that had demonstrated a capacity for surviving the preservation process in a reasonably appetizing state and were therefore regarded as "worth their salt." Cod from the abundant fisheries of recently discovered Newfoundland was an increasingly important example.

The Crusades had long since exposed western Europe to the spices and condiments of the East, and by the sixteenth century the trade in commodities ranging from pepper, cinnamon, cloves, nutmeg, ginger, saffron, and caraway to cardamom, coriander, mustard, and garlic was a major element in international commerce. By Tudor times, as a result, recipes like the following for stew had become possible:

Take a necke of mutton and a brest to make the broth strong and then scum it cleane and when it hath boyled a while, take part of the broth and put it into another pot and put thereto a pound of raisins and let them boyle till they be tender, then strayne a little bread with the Raisins and the broth

all together, then chop time, sawge and Persley with other small hearbes
and put into the mutton then put in the strayned raysins with whole prunes,
cloves and mace, pepper, saffron and a little salt and if ye may stew a
chicken withall or els sparrowes or such other small byrdes.

Other culinary delights, including some that would soon transform
European cuisine, were beginning to arrive from the New World. Among
them were corn and sweet peppers, potatoes and tomatoes, turkey and
peanuts and vanilla, and still other things so familiar today that their absence is almost unimaginable. In the lifetime of Henry VIII, however,
most such commodities remained unknown. Chocolate and coffee,
when they first arrived, were used for medicinal purposes only. Potatoes
were not seen in England until almost a century after Henry's death.

The high price of spices and other exotic foodstuffs was one reason
for the so-called sumptuary laws that were first introduced in England in
the fourteenth century and, with frequent revisions, would remain in
effect for hundreds of years thereafter. These laws, difficult to enforce,
were a somewhat oblique attempt to limit costly imports and thereby reduce the outflow of capital. Another of their purposes was to preserve
class distinctions by prohibiting the unworthy from presuming to imitate
the lifestyles of their betters (for a time only high nobles were allowed to
wear fox fur, for example), and they could become remarkably detailed
in what they prescribed. In 1517, probably at the direction of a Thomas
Wolsey eager to emphasize his superiority over everyone in England except the royal family, it was decreed that whereas cardinals could be
served nine dishes in the course of a single meal, dukes, archbishops,
marquesses, earls, and bishops were to have no more than seven each,
and nobles below the rank of earl a mere six. Gentlemen with annual incomes of between £40 and £100—was there ever a time when such
careful attention was paid to exactly how much money a man had?—
were to receive only three. Pains were taken, at banquets, to seat people
in precisely the right order of precedence, and the most eminent guests
received not only the most but the costliest dishes. Table manners were
better than is often supposed today, and for the most practical of reasons.
Guests wore the most expensive clothing that the law and their purses or
credit permitted, with laces and ruffles not only around their necks but
on their cuffs as well, and they had no wish to carelessly spoil costumes

that sometimes cost more than a laborer could earn in years. Forks were still exotic, rarely seen, and when dining out people knew that they were expected to bring their own knives and spoons. Even high nobles expected to share the dishes they were served with at least one person of equal rank.

Such was the life of the elite and near-elite only, and it would be a mistake to suppose that it had any connection with the lives of the common people. With food as with so many things, the mass of the population lived in virtually a parallel universe, one in which spices and sugar were so expensive as to be unattainable and even meat and salt were rarities. A working family's typical meal might consist of dark bread made of rye or barley rather than more expensive wheat flour (often a slab of this bread would be used as a "trencher" or edible dinner plate), cheese or the whey that is a by-product of cheese-making, a "pottage" or soup of oats or barley, perhaps a portion of curds or whatever fruits or vegetables happened to be in season. Though vitamin deficiencies were commonplace, especially in winter and early spring, and though crop failures could lead to malnutrition, outright starvation was almost unheard of except in the far north during the worst years. Perhaps the ultimate irony—the term "poetic justice" comes to mind—is that except in times of exceptional shortage, the diet of the plain folk was much more healthful than that of their meat- and sugar-devouring masters. Possibly that explains why so many of the Tudors were so worn out and sick at such early ages. Elizabeth, the longest-lived of them, was notably abstemious in her diet.

15

Rebellion and Betrayal

The story of how Henry VIII extracted himself from the most dangerous crisis of his life by lying to his subjects and betraying honest men who had put their fate in his hands is essentially the story of Robert Aske.

A lawyer and fellow of Lincoln's Inn in London, Aske was one of several sons in a modestly distinguished family in the north of England. His father, a landowning knight, was related by marriage to the mighty Percy clan. His maternal grandfather had been a baron, and Robert himself, early in his career, had served as secretary to the Percy who was then Earl of Northumberland. He was thirty-seven years old early in October 1536, when he set out from his Yorkshire home for London and the opening of the autumn term of the royal court at Westminster. It was a routine business trip of a kind that Aske had been making at this same time of year almost since boyhood, first as a student and then as a practicing attorney, and he had no reason to expect anything out of the ordinary. If he had started several days earlier, he would in all likelihood never have left the smallest mark on history.

Upon crossing the Humber River into Lincolnshire on or about October 4, Aske found himself in the midst of something extraordinary. Just two or three days before, a spontaneous protest had erupted in the town of Louth and begun spreading across the county. The trouble was triggered by reports that a group of royal commissioners was approaching

and was not only shutting down monasteries but confiscating the treasures (chalices, processional crosses, and the like) of parish churches.
The situation was developing with startling speed: by the time Aske arrived on the scene, some of the commissioners had been taken prisoner
by the protesters and set free after being given a list of demands that
they were to deliver to the king. The people wanted an end to the suppression of monasteries, punishment of Thomas Cromwell's notorious
henchmen Legh and Layton, an end to the subsidy recently levied by
Parliament, and the removal from office of Cromwell, Thomas Audley,
Richard Rich, and a number of bishops including Cranmer. The demands made no mention of the king's claim to supremacy—to object to
that was to commit treason—but obviously they arose out of opposition
to the entire royal program of ecclesiastical reform. That the impulse
behind the uprising was essentially religious and deeply conservative
was underscored when the people of Horncastle near Louth raised a
banner that was soon adopted wherever the rebellion spread. It showed
the eucharistic host, a chalice, and a figure of Christ bearing the five
wounds of the crucifixion.

Aske, who would have been recognizably a member of the gentry,
was taken into custody by the protesters. This was in no way unusual: in
its origins the rising was an eruption of the pent-up fears and frustra-
tions of the common people—to the extent that the initial outburst at
Louth had a leader, that leader was a shoemaker named Nicholas
Melton—and from the start the participants displayed a desperate hope
of recruiting men educated enough to articulate their case and respectable enough to get a hearing from the authorities. Wherever such
men fell into the hands of the demonstrators, they were threatened with
hanging if they refused to swear "to be true to almighty god to christ's
catholic church to our sovereign lord the king and unto the commons of
this realm so help you god and holy dam and by this book." It was a
rough way of finding leaders but surprisingly effective. And the rebel
oath, innocuous enough when considered without context, would have
been heavy with significance for the people of Lincolnshire—and no
doubt for the king and his people, too, when they learned of it. It acknowledged not just the church but the *Catholic* Church, the king but
none of his lieutenants. When coupled with the demands that the
demonstrators had already sent south and would be repeating many

times in the months ahead, the words of the oath lost all ambiguity. They were a call for a full restoration of the old ways and the removal and punishment of those—the king alone excluded—who had undertaken the work of destruction. There is nothing surprising about the exemption of the king from criticism; anything else would have been astounding. In a society where the person of the king was quasi-sacred, at a time when the idea that the king derived his authority from God was winning wide acceptance, the humanly natural inclination to blame unpopular measures not on the sovereign himself but on his counselors and deputies was becoming more pronounced than ever.

The fact that a number of the individuals who were coerced into taking the oath quickly and voluntarily became prominent in the rising is one indication of the extent to which people at all levels of society, gentry and nobility included, were in sympathy with its aims. Aske made himself one of the most prominent of all, galloping about Lincolnshire to help spread word of the movement. Within days the rebels had tens of thousands of men in the field and took possession of the city of Lincoln. Divisions, however, soon appeared. The common folk were eager to push on toward the south, where they would have greatly outnumbered the few thousand troops that nobles loyal to the king were finding it possible to muster. But the gentry among them, perhaps mindful of how much they stood to lose in an unsuccessful contest with the Crown, insisted on waiting for Henry's response to their demands. That response, when it came, was chilling. The king denounced Lincolnshire as a "brute and beastly" place (he had never seen it, never in his life having visited the north), ridiculed the rebels for presuming to offer advice on how to rule, and ordered them to hand over their leaders and return to their homes. Failure to comply would result in "the utter destruction of them, their wives and children." Behind all this was the threat—to the rebels it would have appeared to be the imminent threat—of an attack by the forces of the king. The dukes of Norfolk and Suffolk and the Earl of Shrewsbury were all known to be assembling troops, and though they were experiencing severe difficulties—not least the unwillingness of many of their own liegemen to suppress a rebellion the aims of which they heartily supported—the rebels were probably unaware of any of this. Suffolk, who was closest to Lincoln, found himself unable to muster more than a thousand men. He would have been overwhelmed if the rebels, at least sixteen thousand of whom carried weapons of war, had advanced without delay. But the rebels had delayed and thereby lost their momentum, their leaders were quarreling confusedly among themselves, and for all they knew they stood on the brink of annihilation. Frightened and discouraged, they disbanded and began to head for home. Their rising had collapsed without encountering serious opposition.

Aske, meanwhile, had crossed back into Yorkshire, where the population was now aware of what was happening on the other side of the Humber and itself beginning to boil over. He threw himself into introducing some measure of order and organization where otherwise there would have been chaos, persuading the towns through which he passed to take no action until they received a signal from him—the agreed signal being the ringing of the church bells. When on October 10 the signal went out and the Yorkshire rising began, Aske issued a proclamation stating that its purpose was "the preservation of Christ's church . . . and to the intent to make petition to the King's highness for the reformation of that which is amiss in this his realm." He declared himself "chief captain" in his part of the county, and by October 16, the day on which ten thousand armed rebels entered the city of York, they were using the name that he had given their movement: the Pilgrimage of Grace.

As word of what was happening spread, people all across the north began to join in. The movement quickly became bigger than it had been before the collapse in Lincolnshire, with perhaps as many as thirty thousand rebels advancing southward toward the royal stronghold of Pontefract Castle. On October 20 the castle's garrison surrendered without a fight. The pilgrims had with them Edward Lee, the archbishop of York, though whether he had joined or was a prisoner is not clear. Most were mounted and armed, and as they moved on to Doncaster they encountered the Duke of Norfolk at the head of a force that they outnumbered by nearly four to one. Aske, by now established as the movement's spokesman and public face, found himself in an immensely strong position. There was every reason to think that if his men attacked they could roll over Norfolk's eight thousand troops and be on the outskirts of London within several days. Meanwhile King Henry, whose situation was far more dangerous than he understood, was cursing the pilgrims as "false traitors and rebels" and demanding that his nobles attack and destroy them without delay. From start to finish he regarded the Pilgrimage as an unforgivable insult to his dignity as monarch. He despised the participants and was interested in nothing but revenge.

But Norfolk, the man on the scene, had to deal with reality. The pilgrims sent him a new but not-much-changed version of the same demands originally presented in Lincolnshire: no more closing of monasteries, the removal of Cromwell and Cranmer and Rich, et cetera. Norfolk met with their representative on Doncaster Bridge and offered a deal: he himself would take the pilgrims' demands—which they were now calling "articles"—to the king along with two of their representatives, who would be allowed to explain themselves to Henry in person. Meanwhile the armies on both sides were to disband. Norfolk, aware of how weak his position was and that many of his own soldiers were not to be relied upon in this extraordinary situation, was stalling for time and hoping that somehow the rebels could be talked into withdrawing without a fight, perhaps even into disbanding as had happened in Lincolnshire. He had the king's grudging permission to agree to whatever the rebels asked, but only for the sake of delay. There was never any thought, certainly not on the king's part, of actually *keeping* whatever promises might have to be made. The pilgrims were appropriately skeptical. They agreed only to meet again with Norfolk early in December, after he had returned from conferring with the king, warning that they would not do even that unless their safety were guaranteed.

On December 2 Aske and other Pilgrimage leaders assembled at Pontefract to prepare for another round of negotiations. In the intervening weeks the rank and file had grown restless—just keeping so many thousands of men fed would have been impossible except for the willingness of farmers across the north to contribute livestock and other foodstuffs to the cause—and Aske had had his hands full holding them together. At Pontefract he was again the most conspicuous member of the leadership (some historians suggest that he was to some extent a front man for more important personages who preferred for their own safety to maintain a low profile), drawing up a new and more comprehensive set of articles for presentation to Norfolk and, through him, to the king. As before there was much emphasis on reversing the religious reforms of the past several years, strengthened now with an explicit call for an end to the separation from Rome, and a number of striking new items were added. The pilgrims wanted the legitimacy of Henry's daughter Mary restored, the statute that allowed the king to choose his successor repealed, and a new Parliament summoned to meet not at Westminster as usual but in the north—specifically at York or Nottingham. Their articles went into considerable detail where the proposed Parliament was concerned: they called for less royal involvement in the selection of the members of Commons, less control over the business of Commons by officers of the Crown, and more freedom of speech for members. Finally they demanded a full pardon for everyone involved in the rising.

It was a startling document. If implemented, it would have reversed virtually everything that Henry had accomplished since first deciding to divorce Catherine. By weakening his grip on Parliament, it would have moved England closer to democracy than it had ever been, or would be for centuries. It illuminates as nothing else does the depth of northern unhappiness with the innovations of the 1530s and popular awareness of just how completely the king and his men—Cromwell in particular—had not only the machinery of government but the law itself under their control. For Henry, of course, the articles were an abomination, an insult, a gross and unforgivable violation of his rights. To a man like Norfolk, too, a proud exemplar of the old warrior nobility, they were an affront, a despicable attempt by presumptuous commoners to overturn the natural order.

But even now, more than two months after the first explosion at Louth, Henry and Norfolk and the nobles allied with them had been unable to assemble nearly as many men as the pilgrims still had under arms at Doncaster. The king's position was not unlike that of Richard III in 1485, when he attempted to rally his kingdom for what should have been the easy task of crushing the invasion of the first Henry Tudor. Richard had issued his call, but not enough men had responded because not enough wanted to save him. Now it seemed possible that, if the pilgrims marched, much of the kingdom would not only do nothing to impede them but might join them in bringing the second Henry Tudor to heel. Thus the king, despite being toweringly indignant, had no choice but to accept Norfolk's insistence that there was no possibility of defeating the "traitors" by direct attack. It remained necessary to stall. And so on December 6, when a delegation of thirty Pilgrimage leaders (ten knights, ten esquires, and ten commoners) met with Norfolk as agreed, the duke accepted every demand. A new Parliament would be summoned, and once in session it would take up the pilgrims' articles. Meanwhile no more religious houses would be closed, and those that the Pilgrimage had restored would be allowed to continue. The pilgrims themselves would be pardoned in return for returning peaceably to their homes.

At first blush this was a tremendous victory, but among the pilgrims there was skepticism. Doubters pointed out that the promised pardon did not apply to those involved in the Lincolnshire rising, that Norfolk had said nothing about when or even where the promised Parliament would meet, and that nothing had been put in writing except the *promise* of a pardon rather than the pardon itself. Under such circumstances, some argued, it would be madness for them to lay down their arms. Aske saw things differently. For him it was inconceivable that the king would not be as good as his word, would not honor promises made to loyal subjects who wanted only to free him from evil subordinates. When the promise of pardon was read aloud, Aske, to show his comrades that this was good enough for him, tore from his tunic the badge of their movement (like the banner, it depicted Christ and his wounds) and declared that he was captain no more and henceforth would wear no insignia except his king's. It was effective theater: the other pilgrims removed their badges, the banners were furled, and within a few days a huge rebel army had melted away to nothing.

Then came the strangest episode of the entire affair. Aske received a letter from the king, inviting him to spend Christmas at court because "we have conceived a great desire to speak with you and to hear of your mouth the whole circumstance and beginning of that matter [the rising]." The letter repeated Norfolk's assurances of "our general and free pardon, already granted unto you." Aske accepted—such an invitation was an almost unimaginable honor—and found himself treated with stupefying friendliness all through his visit. At Henry's request he wrote an account of the Pilgrimage, receiving from the king's hands the gift of an expensive coat. When he returned to the north, he did so in the conviction that Henry was his ally, supporter, and friend. In the next few months he would repeatedly show himself to be the supporter and friend of a king who had concealed his hatred under a blanket of hospitality and was now waiting until it became safe to exact his revenge.

None of the other pilgrim leaders had been exposed to the king's charm, and few were able to share Aske's enthusiasm. What they saw, rather, was that a new year had begun and nothing was being done to put into effect any of the promises made at Doncaster. Cromwell and Cranmer and the other officials of whom the pilgrims had complained all remained at their posts, the Crown continued to collect its ten percent of every kind of church revenue (though this, too, was among the things the pilgrims wanted stopped), and government troops were being moved north to fortify strongholds. Aske wrote to warn his new friend the king that feelings were again running high, asking Henry "to pardon me in this my crude letter and plainness of the same, for I do utter my poor heart to your grace to the intent your highness may perceive the danger that may ensue; for on my faith I do greatly fear the end to be only by battle." When he learned that former pilgrims were planning to attack Hull and Beverley, which were under royal control, Aske vainly begged them not to proceed and urged others not to join them. When the attacks failed and their leaders had been captured, Henry sent him a letter of thanks. Scattered and uncoordinated outbreaks of violence continued, each one sapping whatever strength and cohesion the remaining fragments of the Pilgrimage still had, and when eight thousand Westmorland men tried to take the city of Carlisle and failed miserably, it became clear that the movement was exhausted. Norfolk was able to move his troops into pilgrim territory, impose martial law, and begin a program of summary executions that quickly took scores and then hundreds of lives. Those monks who had returned to their suppressed monasteries at the invitation of the pilgrims were singled out for especially harsh treatment.

So, inevitably, was Robert Aske. With the north subdued, Henry was free to remove the mask of conciliation. Aske and other Pilgrimage leaders, members of the nobility among them, were arrested and put on trial in York. Norfolk, in a nice touch of sadism that brings to mind his own prominent role in the trial and sentencing of his niece Anne Boleyn, arranged to have Aske's brother put on the jury. The defendants were found guilty on two counts of treason, first for conspiring to deny the king his "dignity, title, name, and royal state . . . of being on earth the supreme head of the English church," second for trying to force the king "to summon and hold a parliament and convocation." Aske pointed to the fact that he had been pardoned both by the king and by Cromwell and had done nothing to oppose either of them since his pardon, but that counted for nothing. The convicted men were transferred to London, where they were condemned to death. Most of them, along with two abbots and three priors caught up in Norfolk's dragnet, were hanged, drawn, and quartered at Tyburn. Aske alone was hauled back to York and hanged there, not by rope but in a tangle of chains around his body so as to make his death a slow agony of exposure and dehydration. His body was kept on public display until nothing remained but bones. The population was paralyzed with fear, the king more firmly in control than ever.

Henry's triumph was capped with glorious news: Queen Jane was pregnant. The joyful couple departed on a celebratory summer progress, keeping well clear of the north in spite of a pledge Henry had made to show himself to his subjects there. It was left to Norfolk to complete the subjugation of the northern counties, and to Cromwell to resume the destruction not only of the smaller monasteries but, more broadly, of anyone refusing to align himself with the new English church. In May, the month of Aske's death, the Crown's choice as new prior of the London Charterhouse formally recognized Henry as supreme head and signed the house over to him. Twenty of the house's monks and lay brothers, broken by the two years of harassment that had followed the execution of John Houghton, gave up their resistance. The ten who refused were chained up in Newgate Prison and left to starve in their own filth. By mid-June half of them were dead, and by September only one remained alive. The sole survivor was then moved to another place of confinement, where he clung to life so tenaciously that at last he had to be butchered. With that single exception, however, Henry and Cromwell were able to eliminate the last of the Carthusians by allowing them to perish slowly, horribly, and in deepest obscurity, avoiding the kind of anger that would have resulted from the public execution of such transparently innocent men.

One of the most striking aspects of King Henry's reign, his determination to make all of his subjects change their beliefs exactly as he changed his, became more painfully awkward with the passage of time. Complete uniformity would have been unachievable under any circumstances during the decades of Henry's rule; even if he had remained

Roman Catholic and wanted his subjects to do the same, the ideas of Luther and the other continental reformers would have attracted English adherents and made doctrinal strife unavoidable. But Henry had compounded the discord in breaking with Rome, accelerating the process by which his subjects came to be divided into a multitude of contending sects, and his subsequent insistence on conformity made the situation impossible. By the time of his third marriage three religious factions were numerous or influential or both. One—the only one acceptable to the king—was made up of those many people who welcomed or at least had no objection to the break with Rome but wanted to retain their traditional beliefs and practices (the sacraments, for example, and the idea of purgatory). Another, probably larger, stood by the entire conservative package including the leadership of the pope. Finally, definitely smallest in numbers but afire with the zeal of the continental Reformation, was the circle for whom the whole of the old religion was superstitious nonsense that had to be swept aside in order for a simpler, purer Christianity based on the inerrancy of the Bible to become possible. To arrive at a single set of doctrines acceptable to all three of these groups would have been impossible, and the king's inextinguishable hopes of imposing uniformity, after he himself had done so much to create division, were both ironic and doomed. His efforts in that direction would have been pathetic if they had not also been so tragically destructive. They were yet another reflection of Henry's infantile belief in himself as a flawlessly wise ruler.

Late in 1536, annoyed that the dissemination of his Ten Articles had failed almost completely to settle the many roiling questions about what England was now supposed to believe, Henry turned the problem over to the bishops, instructing them to produce a more comprehensive, less ambiguous set of answers. But the bishops themselves were divided. At one extreme were men like Stephen Gardiner of Winchester, John Stokesley of London, and Cuthbert Tunstal of Durham, conservatives who almost certainly regretted the break with Rome and hoped to retain as much of the old ways as possible. At the other end of the spectrum there stood, for example, Hugh Latimer of Worcester, who went so far in his rejection of tradition that even other militant reformers accused him of heresy. The debates in which the bishops tried to decide how to carry out the king's instructions were long and contentious and never came close to achieving agreement. The result of the bishops' labors, a document whose official title was *The Institution of a Christian Man,* was less a thought-through compromise or a coherent response to the many questions stirred up by the establishment of an autonomous national church than a semidesperate packing together of incompatible, sometimes conflicting positions.

But the king had demanded action, and the bishops had done as well as anyone should have expected considering the depth of their differences. Most of them wanted to satisfy the king, certainly; they were all too aware of what could befall any cleric who failed to do so. But on both sides of the doctrinal gulf were men prepared to fight if perhaps not to die in defense of their beliefs. In the absence of specific royal guidance, with nothing to fall back upon but their own divergent convictions and their impressions of what Henry was likely to find acceptable, ultimately they had little choice—unless they could find the courage to do nothing—but to give everyone some voice in what they finally produced. When they finished in mid-July, no one could be entirely comfortable with what had been accomplished. Though the *Institution* was in many respects conservative—upholding, for example, the validity of all seven sacraments, whereas the earlier Ten Articles had specifically recognized only three—the most conservative bishops were neither satisfied that it was conservative enough nor confident of how the king would react to it. The evangelicals hated much of it; Latimer wrote to the king to protest that the *Institution* should not be printed until cleansed of Catholic "old leaven." It was offered to the king and Cromwell as a working draft, and accompanied by a timorous request that they review it and decide whether the bishops could tell the world that it had royal approval. They got no answer. When it appeared in print in September, it contained a most peculiar preface in which the bishops abjectly "confess that we have none authority either to assemble ourselves together for any pretence or purpose or to publish any thing that might be by us agreed on and compiled." This preface asked the king to approve or amend what the bishops had done as he saw fit. Printed with it was a curious message from the king himself, declaring that he had not found time to read the book but had merely "taken as it were a taste of it." From that day to this *The Institution of a Christian Man* has been better known as the Bishops' Book, an unofficial title that makes clear that

it should not be taken as a guide to the beliefs of the supreme head of
the Church of England because, according to the head himself, he had
little idea of what it contained. How anyone could have regarded such a
work as worth printing, how anyone could have expected it to be of the
slightest value even to subjects eager to be scrupulously faithful to the
royal theology, surpasses understanding. Perhaps Cromwell or Henry
assumed it must be close enough to the king's truth to be of some use
for the time being.

When he did read it at last, some three months after publication, the
king was not at all happy with what he found. Much of it was obviously
calculated to please and surely must have done so. The bishops had explicitly denied the supremacy of the pope and asserted that of the king,
declared the king to be accountable to God only, and warned that nothing could justify rebellion against him (a reflection of the fact that they
completed their work shortly after the failure of the Pilgrimage of
Grace). The only legitimate way of seeking relief from political oppression, their book said, was to ask God to change the monarch's heart.
Henry entered more than 250 comments in the margins of his copy.
Many of these were challenges and objections that led him into a debate
with Archbishop Cranmer, who had used his influence as primate to inject his own increasingly evangelical views into the text. In the end, of
course, Henry's opinion was the only one that mattered. No doubt to
Cranmer's intense disappointment, a new edition was prepared with all
passages that referred favorably to justification by faith expunged. The
new version also affirmed belief in the real presence of Christ in the Eucharist. Such changes were inevitable considering the king's conservative approach to almost all questions of doctrine, but in 1537 he was also
affected by what the Pilgrimage of Grace had revealed about popular attachment to the old religion. He had been given reason to proceed carefully in separating the mass of his subjects from the faith in which they
had been raised.

Some of Henry's changes rose out of that contempt for almost everyone except himself that had become an integral part of his character.
The Bishops' Book as first published had asserted that God sees all men
as equal; the king inserted a clarification to the effect that equality must
be seen as "touching the soul only," whatever exactly he might have
meant by that. A passage about the duty of Christians to attend to the

needs of the poor was amended to exclude from charity those "many folk which had liever live by the graft of begging slothfully"—easy words for a man who since adolescence had been able to regard the wealth of all England and Wales as his to do with as he wished and had rarely in his adult life been obliged to do anything he didn't want to do. Because Henry kept a court astrologer, he deleted astrology from the bishops' list of superstitions to be shunned. He also deleted a passage stating that rulers have a duty to "provide and care" for their subjects, and changed a warning that rulers in forcing their subjects to obey must act "by and according to the just order of their laws" so that it applied only to those acting in the ruler's name, not to the ruler himself. Some of Henry's changes were difficult even for Cranmer to swallow. What the archbishop found particularly irksome was the king's rewriting of the First Commandment (where, in an absurd anachronism, he inserted the name "Jesu Christ") and the closing words of the Lord's Prayer. That Henry felt no hesitation in changing such ancient and supposedly divine texts is perhaps the most striking evidence we have of the heights to which his arrogance could rise, his exalted view of his own place in the hierarchy of the living and the dead.

Between the first appearance of the Bishops' Book and the point where Henry found time to undertake its improvement, there occurred an event that he himself would have considered among the greatest of his life and reign. At two in the morning on October 12, after a labor of more than two days, Queen Jane gave birth to a healthy son. Henry was not present for the birth, having fled days before to his residence at Esher to escape an outbreak of plague. Upon receiving the news he rushed back to Hampton Court, ordering celebrations that soon had bells ringing from every church tower in England and the guards at the Tower firing two thousand rounds of artillery. Henry was said to have wept when he held his son for the first time. Almost exactly ten years had passed since he first undertook to rid himself of Catherine of Aragon, and at last, at forty-six, he had his heir. Amid great precautions aimed at keeping the plague out of the palace, the boy was baptized on October 15. He was given the name Edward, less in honor of his grandfather Edward IV than because he had been born on the eve of St. Edward's Day. His godfathers were Thomas Cranmer and the dukes of Norfolk and Suffolk. His godmother was his half-sister, the recently humbled and rehabilitated Mary. The baptismal oil was carried by the four-year-old Elizabeth. She in turn was carried in procession by Queen Jane's brother Edward Seymour, who, being now the uncle of a future king, was shortly made the Earl of Hertford.

The celebrations continued, but two days after her son's christening Jane was taken ill and soon was in gravely serious condition. Henry departed on a long-planned hunting trip—it was, after all, the start of the season—but returned to court on the evening of October 24 after receiving word that his wife had hemorrhaged and was not expected to live. She died that midnight of causes that can never be known with certainty. It has often been stated that a cesarean section had been performed to save her child after two days and three nights of fruitless labor, but this cannot be the case; a cesarean meant certain death in the sixteenth century, and though it is hardly inconceivable that the court physicians would have sacrificed Jane to save their master's heir, in the days following Prince Edward's birth Jane was expected to recover and appeared to be doing so. A more plausible explanation is that she died because part of the placenta had been left inside her womb after she gave birth. By a sad irony, midwives of the kind who assisted at almost all deliveries in Tudor times, and who were well schooled in such practicalities as removal of the placenta, had been excluded from the royal birthing chamber. Only physicians of the loftiest reputation had been permitted to attend the queen. The state of academic medicine being what it was in the sixteenth century, such worthies probably knew less about the realities of childbirth than any experienced midwife. Henry left Hampton Court and went to Windsor Castle. Three weeks later, when the queen's embalmed body arrived at Windsor for interment, he moved again, this time to Whitehall. It would be ungenerous to doubt that his grief over the death of his wife was as great as his joy over the birth of a son, but his recovery appears to have been swift. In rather short order he was reported to be in good spirits—"in good health and merry as a widower may be"—and to be scheming with Cromwell about where to find his next wife.

One would have thought that Henry might be a satisfied man by this point. He was definitely the most feared, and arguably the most powerful, king in the history of England. Not only the government but the church were his to command. His word was law, almost literally, and his word was religious doctrine as well; no noble or bishop would have dared to contradict him. And now at last, on the threshold of what in his time was old age, with a lifetime of self-indulgence taking its toll on his mighty physique, there was a male heir to the throne. Suddenly it was at least possible that the Tudor dynasty, which just recently had passed its fiftieth anniversary, might have a future. A lesser man than Henry might have decided that, having done as much as any of his predecessors and far more than most, he had done enough. A better man might have decided that he had shed enough of his subjects' blood.

But Henry was Henry, nothing better and nothing less, and he was far from satisfied. The Pilgrimage of Grace, in bringing to a halt the closing of monasteries in many parts of the north and making it possible for some of the expelled monks and nuns to return to their houses, had given rise to rumors that members of the various religious orders had encouraged and even helped to lead the rebellion. (The possible truth of such stories remains beyond reach. Nothing in the way of conclusive evidence exists one way or the other.) That had given the king and Cromwell an excuse to resume and broaden their attack on monastic establishments generally. The closing of the smaller houses was soon completed, and the attention of the agents of the Crown was turned to the larger, richer houses. Parliament having passed no law that permitted confiscation of establishments whose income exceeded £200 per annum, the royal commissioners reverted to using fear and greed to extract "voluntary" surrenders. This proved to be difficult in places, but usually not impossible. Over all the houses there hung the memory of those the Crown had already killed. Such memories were freshened by the execution, between March and May 1537, of the uncooperative abbots of Kirkstead, Barlings, Fountains, and Jervaulx, the prior of Bridlington, and an unknown number of the members of their communities. It is hardly surprising that, learning of these killings and finding themselves exposed to the questions, accusations, insinuations, threats, and promises of Cromwell's commissioners, most of the houses gave up the struggle. No decision could have been more rational: those who signed most speedily received promises of pensions—very handsome pensions in the case of the senior officers of the largest houses, along with new positions and sometimes even grants of land—while the only possible result of refusal was a death that could do nothing to stop the suppression process. The surrendered lands and buildings became the property of the Crown. So did everything inside the buildings—the accumulated treasure of the centuries. All the money flowed into the Court of Augmentations, from which Richard Rich parceled it out under Cromwell's direction.

In March 1538 the leg ulcers that by now were making Henry's life an intermittent agony began to block the flow of his blood. There may have been a clot in his lungs as well; he became unable to speak, barely able to breathe. For a week and a half he lay near death. But then, with a speed that surprised his physicians, it all passed, and he was up and active again. He had eight years and eight months more to live. They would be memorable years—as eventful as those that had come before. They would be extravagantly wasteful, they would be bathed in blood, and they would bring military and financial disaster.

THE SPORT OF KINGS

THE FATHER AT LAST OF A HEALTHY AND LEGITIMATE BABY boy, father also of a new national church that (if somewhat confused doctrinally) was free of any connection to Rome, Henry VIII found himself free to turn to fields still unconquered. It was almost inevitable that he would look exactly where he had looked when seeking to demonstrate his greatness at the start of his reign nearly three decades before: across the English Channel. The old dream of winning glory on the fields of France had never stopped burning in his breast.

But that dream had been a foolish one even in 1509, and it made no sense at all three decades later. Henry had succeeded his father at a time when it was all too easy for English kings to look down on the ruling house of France. Louis XII, product of the dynasty that had ruled France for some six hundred years, was entering his second decade as king then, and though not yet fifty he had already, much like Henry VII of England, slipped into a premature old age. After two marriages he remained sonless, and because France's Salic law prohibited daughters from inheriting the throne, he seemed destined to be the last of his branch of the Valois line. When younger he had conquered much of Italy, but his successes there gradually came to nothing as his armies were driven out of both Milan in the north and Naples in the south.

The whole dynasty seemed to be in the last stages of entropy. Louis had come to the throne only because his predecessor, the Charles VIII who as a boy-king in the 1480s had been an admiring supporter of the first Henry Tudor's invasion of England, died at twenty-eight (killed by striking his head against the stone lintel of a castle doorway) without sons, brothers, male cousins, or uncles. The family tree was so bare that the royal genealogists, in their search for an heir, had to explore branch after barren branch before finally declaring that the only grandson of a younger brother of Charles's great-grandfather should be crowned as

Louis XII. Louis as it happened was himself not only sonless but without brothers or uncles, so that his heir was a second cousin once removed, the boy Francis of Angoulême.

It must have seemed almost a joke, therefore, when in 1515 the Holy Roman emperor renounced the betrothal of his young grandson Charles of Hapsburg to Henry VIII's sister Mary, and Cardinal Wolsey retaliated by arranging the princess's marriage to King Louis. Mary was eighteen, an elegant and accomplished young woman of exceptional beauty. Her bridegroom, though a good man much loved by his subjects, was in his fifties and seriously decrepit, toothless and crippled with gout. If the courts of both kingdoms recycled tired witticisms about the dangers for old men of taking desirable young wives, in this case they were vindicated. Louis was dead within weeks of the wedding. It was said that he had been danced to death. "Danced," perhaps, was a euphemism.

At the time of his death Louis was actually the youngest of the continent's leading royal figures. Old Ferdinand of Aragon, embittered by the failure of his dynastic ambitions, still occupied the crown of Spain at sixty-three, and the fifty-six-year-old Maximilian of Hapsburg was in his third decade as Holy Roman emperor. Henry of England, after six years on the throne, continued to stand alone as the one youthful, conspicuously virile crowned head. All that changed abruptly, however, when Louis XII's successor stepped onto the world stage. In Francis I, France had a monarch even younger than Henry (he was only twenty) and in every way his equal: tall and powerfully built, brimming with intelligence and vitality, ambitious to expand French power and to make his court a magnet for the leading intellectual and artistic figures of the day. (He would entice even Leonardo da Vinci to leave Italy for France.) Francis opened his reign by making himself the kind of authentic military hero that Henry had hoped but failed to become with his earlier invasion of France, attacking Milan and achieving an astonishing victory over a supposedly invulnerable force of Swiss mercenaries. Almost overnight he supplanted Henry as the most glamorous figure in Europe, and there flared up between the two kings a rivalry that would not be extinguished until the pair of them died only weeks apart. It was a contest of massive egos, fueled by resentment, jealousy, and pride. Ruthless in the pursuit of their own aggrandizement and indifferent to what that pursuit cost others, they would make war on each other so often, entering and break-ing alliances so easily, that the military and diplomatic history of their reigns is a confused blur, far too complicated for brief description.

Henry and Francis met for the first time in northern France at what came to be known as the Field of the Cloth of Gold. This happened in 1520, a year after the death of Maximilian vacated the office of Holy Roman emperor. Both regarded themselves as uniquely well suited to wear the most venerable crown in Europe, and so both had put them-selves forward as candidates in opposition to Maximilian's grandson Charles. But Charles, who by this time had inherited Spain and its vast dominions from his maternal grandfather Ferdinand, and Burgundy and the Low Countries from his father Philip the Handsome, had the advan-tage of being German like the secular and ecclesiastical princes who elected emperors. He increased this advantage by borrowing heavily enough to distribute even richer bribes than Francis. (Henry, though in earnest, was never seriously in the running financially or otherwise.) The 1520 meeting was supposed to be a kind of summit conference—Fran-cis, anticipating war with Charles, was hoping for an English alliance—but it turned into something both more remarkable and less productive. Throughout most of June the two kings put on a competitive display of wealth and splendor on a scale never seen in Europe before or since. In Henry's entourage were most of England's nobility, most of the hierarchy of the church, more than five thousand men and women in all, along with nearly three thousand horses. Cardinal Wolsey's party included twelve chaplains, fifty gentlemen, and 237 servants, Catherine of Ara-gon's nearly twelve hundred people in total. Huge, ornate temporary palaces were constructed for the occasion by both sides, man-made fountains flowed with wine, and the days and nights were filled with jousts, tournaments, musical and theatrical entertainments, and feasting. Henry, sadly for himself, precipitated the best-remembered event of the whole gathering by jovially challenging Francis to a wrestling match and promptly getting himself thrown; it was a humiliation from which he never quite recovered. When the festivities were finished, nothing had been accomplished except an agreement under which Henry's little daughter Mary was pledged to one day marry Francis's equally little el-dest son. Francis hoped that this would lead to the alliance that he craved, but it did nothing of the kind. In short order Mary's parents promised her to her cousin Charles, and he rather than Francis became England's ally.

A fourth young dynamo entered the picture in the same year as the Field of the Cloth of Gold when Suleiman the Magnificent became sultan of the Islamic Ottoman Empire, which had already conquered a substantial part of southeastern Europe and was threatening to take more. From his capital at Constantinople he would cause much trouble over the following decades, but almost exclusively for the unfortunate Charles. Among the Christian monarchs it was Francis who proved the greatest cause of instability, largely because Italy was for him what France never ceased to be for Henry: a field of dreams, the setting for conquests endlessly envisioned but rarely achieved. French and Hapsburg armies fought in Italy from 1521 to 1525, with England providing Charles with substantial financial support up to the point where his forces achieved their great victory at Pavia and Francis was hauled off to Madrid as his prisoner. Henry saw Pavia as a gateway to the fulfillment of his dreams, an opportunity to eliminate France as a major power. Charles, he proposed, should help himself to great expanses of southern and eastern France while he, Henry, became king of what remained. The emperor, however, was a sensible fellow with little interest in conquest and less in glory, seeking only to hold on to what he had inherited. In any case he was virtually bankrupt by this time. He therefore declined to cooperate, which so disgusted Henry that he soon broke with Charles altogether and allied himself instead with France and the Papal States.

Reversals of this kind went on year after year. In the aftermath of Pavia, England, France, and the pope remained at war with Charles until the emperor's aunt and Francis's mother negotiated a separate peace that left England suddenly and frighteningly isolated. In 1530 the widowed Francis went so far as to marry Charles's sister Eleanor, though not even that could slake his thirst for conquests in Italy. By 1536 he and Charles were again at war over Milan, but two years after that they agreed to a truce so alarming to Thomas Cromwell that, in his desperation to find Protestant allies, he arranged King Henry's marriage to Anne, the sister of the Duke of Cleves. Nothing was ever really settled, and there continued to be no basis on which a lasting peace could be constructed. Francis remained as fixed as ever on the dream of driving the Hapsburgs out of

Italy, and to accomplish that he showed himself willing to become the ally not only of Germany's Protestant states but of the sultan Suleiman. Charles for his part remained determined to surrender not a yard of his patrimony.

All this was of incalculable value to Henry as he broke with Rome and embarked upon the destruction of England's monasteries. If a real peace had been possible between Francis and Charles, a crusade by the continent's Catholic powers to return England to the old faith might have become feasible as well. Certainly that was what Pope Paul III hoped for once he understood that Henry was never going to be coaxed back into the fold.

Henry should have been thankful to be left alone. He should have been content to leave the continent alone. But even now, with so much accomplished, it was not in his nature to be satisfied, and the very existence of Francis of France seems to have caused him torment. Though their two kingdoms were no longer even remotely equal in size, wealth, or strength—after the absorption of Brittany and Burgundy and other provinces, France's population was six times England's—for Henry the thought of being inferior in anything was unendurable. Early in his reign, in the Loire valley, Francis had started construction of the Château de Chambord. Twenty years later, in the late thirties, it was still under construction, on the way to its eventual total of 440 rooms, 365 fireplaces, eighty-four staircases, and more than a dozen different *kinds* of towers. Six months after the birth of his son, Henry decided that such a flagrant display could not go unanswered. He undertook a project specifically intended to surpass Chambord. The result was the stupendous Nonsuch Palace, the largest building ever seen in England up to that time, utterly unnecessary because not far distant from Hampton Court or Richmond or Greenwich or Whitehall or others of Henry's many residences, so ornate with its hundreds of feet of high-relief sculptures of gods and goddesses and emperors and kings all surmounted by huge representations of Henry himself and the child Edward that after £24,000 had been spent it would still not be nearly finished.

Nor was that enough. Henry could never be satisfied, probably, so long as Francis remained alive and securely in possession of his throne. He would continue to wait, to watch for the opportunity to show himself the greater man.

16

The Last of Henry

It was January 27, 1547, and the ulcers on King Henry's thighs were once again alarmingly inflamed. Clogged veins had swollen his legs until the skin seemed about to split, old open sores filled his bedchamber with an atrocious stench, and the royal body was jolted at unpredictable intervals by electric stabs of pain. This was the third such episode in less than a year; with a single brief remission it had been going on for more than a month, and this time Henry really *was* dying. At age fifty-five he was an old man at the end of his strength, bald, wrinkled, and gray-bearded, unable to read without spectacles, so grotesquely fat that he could no longer climb stairs and even on level ground had to be rolled about on chairs fitted with wheels. His physicians were cauterizing the ulcers with red-hot irons, adding to his agony. His many other afflictions—the headaches, the itching, the hemorrhoids—now seemed trivial by comparison.

He was, essentially, alone. Even his wife Catherine Parr, who had been twice widowed before becoming the king's sixth bride and was an experienced and solicitous nurse, had been sent away before Christmas and not summoned back to court since. His children—Mary, in her late twenties now and still unmarried, Elizabeth, who was just entering adolescence, and the child Edward—also were kept away. No one had access to the king except his physicians and the gentlemen of his privy chamber, who were busy fending off questions about his condition and denying that he was seriously ill or even, as some believed, already dead. On January 16, during a temporary resurgence of some of his old vitality, Henry had been strong enough to meet with the ambassadors of his old friends and enemies Francis of France and the emperor Charles, and that had put the rumors to rest for a while. The world, however, had seen nothing of him since then.

Though Henry's physicians didn't know *why* he was dying, exactly, it was obvious to all of them that he could not last long. The breakdowns had been coming with increasing frequency in recent years, the periods of recovery progressively shorter and less complete. His once-powerful constitution was so overburdened with problems (thrombosed varicose veins, possibly infected bones, possibly, too, a condition called Cushing's syndrome that would explain both his distended torso and face and his savagely irrational behavior) as to be in a state of general collapse. Whatever the facts of his condition—a condition far beyond the reach of sixteenth-century medical science—no one who could get close enough to the king to tell him that his life was at an end, to suggest that perhaps he might want to prepare himself for death, was willing to do so. Even now Henry was too dangerous to be trusted. Just eight days earlier he had had put to death, on a flimsy charge of treason, young Henry Howard, Earl of Surrey and son and heir of the Duke of Norfolk. In addition to being a poet of considerable brilliance, the originator of what would come to be known as the Shakespearean sonnet, Surrey had been arrogant and reckless. But he was not a traitor by any reasonable definition of the term. Even less was his father the duke a traitor, but now he, too, after an often hard life of service to the Crown, was in the Tower awaiting execution. Small wonder that none of the men huddled in the king's bedchamber dared to tell him the one thing that might, in his extremity, have been of some use to him. Long before, Henry had made it a crime to foretell the king's death. People had been punished severely on charges of having done so. And so Henry lay in solitude among the deep pillows of his great bed, while his retainers hung back and left him alone with his thoughts.

He had no shortage of things to think about. If he suspected that he was dying—and he surely did, having spent the last of his strength making arrangements for the management of the kingdom after he was gone—his thoughts would have turned inevitably to the old question of the succession. Prince Edward, the heir whose birth had been made possible by so many deaths, was still only nine years old. He was a bright child, perhaps exceptionally so, and like his half-sisters he gave every evidence of worshipping his mighty father. But he was a frail reed on which to hang the future of the dynasty—years before, when the boy was sick with fever, the court physicians had warned that he was not likely to live long—and far too young to take a role in governing or even protecting his own interests. Henry would have wished that the boy were older and more robust, or that he had a brother or two. His thoughts might have turned to the efforts he had made to produce more sons even as his potency ebbed away. To the three marriages he had contracted after the death of Jane Seymour—marriages that had cemented his reputation as England's bluebeard while at the same time making him the laughingstock of Europe.

There was sweet, dull Anne of Cleves, "the mare of Flanders," to whom he had betrothed himself sight unseen in 1538 when France and Charles were allied against him, an invasion of England seemed not only possible but likely, and a marital connection with the Protestant princes of Europe (of whom the Duke of Cleves was one) seemed the only safe haven. The marriage was a fiasco from the start; Henry found his bride so unappealing, her big, slack body so repellent, that though for a while he shared her bed he never attempted consummation. A pretext was found for having the marriage annulled, and Anne, who had no wish to return to the continent, was contentedly pensioned off with two handsome houses, a staff appropriate to her new station as the king's "sister," and an annual stipend of £500.

There had followed the far greater catastrophe, the profound public humiliation, of Catherine Howard. The nineteen-year-old niece of the Duke of Norfolk and first cousin of Anne Boleyn, petite and vivacious if rather mindless, Catherine had been dangled before the king like a juicy morsel by courtiers who thought that if they could draw him into marrying her the consequences would be good for the whole sprawling Howard clan, good for the religious conservatives, and bad for the brothers of Jane Seymour, evangelicals who had been prospering mightily since the birth of their nephew Prince Edward. Henry rose to the bait with a speed that must have astonished the anglers. His infatuation with Catherine became obvious well before the end of his marriage to Anne of Cleves, and he made her his wife eighteen days after the Cleves marriage was annulled. He was enchanted with the girl, lavished gifts on her, proudly put her on display during his annual summer progress. But there was much, sadly, that Henry did not know. Catherine, whose ne'er-do-well father had been absent through much of her childhood and died before she was brought to court, had had an undisciplined upbringing in the crowded household of her stepgrandmother the Dowager Duchess of Norfolk. She brought to her position as maid of honor to Anne of Cleves a good deal more sexual experience than the king would have found acceptable had he been aware of it. Trouble probably was inevitable from the day she was married, through no choice of her own, to an obese and diseased man some thirty years her senior, and when it came it came in squadrons. Soon after becoming queen, in an act of astounding recklessness, Catherine appointed her lover Francis Dereham to be her private secretary, later transferring her favors to a young gentleman of the king's privy chamber named Thomas Culpeper. In due course she was found out and reported, and the end of her story was similar to that of Anne Boleyn except that this time the queen was guilty. Dereham and Culpeper both were executed in December 1541, the latter receiving the mercy of a simple beheading but Dereham subjected to the protracted horrors reserved for traitors. The foolish and unfortunate Catherine was beheaded the following February. With her died her friend and accomplice in deceit Lady Jane Rochford, who on an earlier occasion had saved her own neck by providing damning testimony against her husband, George Boleyn. The king showed far more grief, for far longer, than he had after the death of Jane Seymour. Probably it was not grief so much as chagrin at having been cuckolded before the eyes of all Europe.

Why Henry would choose to marry yet again must remain a mystery. There could have been little chance of his becoming a father at this point, but hope may have sprung eternal in a man so proud. And Henry, in his increasingly brutal and self-defeating way, had always been hungry for affection. In any case marry he did, and wisely this time. Catherine Parr, who made little secret of being motivated by duty rather than love in accepting the king's proposal, was an attractive thirty-one-year-old widow of great dignity and self-possession. She proved skillful at adapting herself to her husband's moods and maintaining a pleasant household not only for him but for all three of his children—the first and only time that Henry's offspring were ever together even intermittently in something resembling a normal family home. But Henry proved a dangerous partner even in her case, at one point not only professing outrage at her evangelical beliefs but issuing a warrant for her arrest and dispatching guards to search her quarters and take her to the Tower. He soon changed his mind, however—if the whole episode was a kind of malicious practical joke, it was not the first time he had toyed cruelly with people close to him in this way—and as the queen learned to keep her theological opinions to herself domestic tranquillity was restored. The fact that she was kept at a distance throughout the painful final weeks of Henry's life, however, suggests that there must have been rather severe limits to whatever intimacy the two had achieved. In any event there was little about his marital history that Henry could have considered with satisfaction as he approached his final hour on earth. He could sentimentalize only about Jane, who had done him the supreme favor of bearing a son and then dying before he could lose interest.

Nor is he likely to have wanted to give much thought to the subject of money. No ruler in the history of England had reaped a bounty of gold to compare with Henry's, and yet somehow it had all ended with the economy of the kingdom in a parlous state and its government virtually bankrupt. And there had been absolutely no reason why things *had* to end up this way: it had all been Henry's doing, and he had done it for no better reason than the satisfaction of his own appetites and the demands of his swollen ego. The floodgates had opened wide in the aftermath of the Pilgrimage of Grace, when the campaign began to bully and bribe the inhabitants of the larger religious houses into surrendering their lands and possessions (and to kill them when neither bullying nor bribery would suffice). The climax of that campaign came in May 1539 with Parliament's passage of the Second Act of Dissolution, which declared all the church property confiscated since 1536 (when the smaller houses were condemned) and all the church property to be confiscated in the future to be lawfully the property of the Crown. This statute remedied an awkward legal flaw in the surrenders signed by the leaders of the larger houses: those leaders were not the owners of the monasteries they headed and had no right to give them away. It speeded the completion of the greatest redistribution of English land and wealth since the Norman Conquest in 1066. The whole suppression worked to the direct and immediate advantage of the king, who rather abruptly became richer than any other monarch in Christendom. By the spring of 1540 not a single monastic establishment remained in existence in England or Wales. Hundreds if not thousands of the monks and nuns expelled from them had become itinerant beggars, wandering from village to village in search of work or charity. The number of England's schools, hospitals, and institutions for the care of the aged and indigent had undergone an abrupt collapse from which it would not recover for centuries.

At the same time that all this was happening, Henry ordered the destruction of the shrines that had long been objects of veneration and destinations for pilgrims not only from England but the whole Christian world. The most famous of these was the fabulous tomb of Thomas Becket at Canterbury Cathedral, where for many generations wealthy visitors had been leaving offerings of jewels, gold, and silver. It was targeted for liquidation not only because of the immense treasure it contained (a treasure that had itself become a kind of tourist attraction, visible behind iron bars) but also because the man it honored had been murdered for defending the liberties of the church in defiance of an earlier King Henry. A farce was played out in which an order was issued for Becket, who had been dead for 370 years, to appear in court and face charges of rebellion and treason. When after thirty days he had not appeared, a trial was held at which the saint was represented by counsel appointed by the king and, upon being found guilty, was sentenced to have his bones burned and scattered. Not coincidentally, the court ordered also that the treasures of Becket's tomb should go to the Crown. The valuables hauled away from the tomb filled twenty-four wagons—this in addition to two chests so laden with precious gems that "six or eight strong men could do no more than convey one of them." Similar if less awesome troves were gathered up elsewhere. Particularly disgraceful was what happened at Winchester, where, in the course of looting the ancient shrine of St. Cuthbert, the king's agents broke open the coffin and scattered the bones of the most heroic figure in all of English history, the only English king ever to be called "the Great," the ninth century's genuinely courageous, good, and wise Alfred, King of Wessex. The loot from all these tombs went of course into the royal treasury.

Quite apart from the colossal sums that flowed into the king's coffers from the shrines, and ultimately dwarfing them, was the £140,000 in rent generated annually by the monastic lands that now came into the king's possession. Parliament, in being asked ("instructed" would be a better word) to approve Henry's appropriation of possibly as much as five percent of all the rental income in the kingdom, was told that this would make wondrous things possible. The king would be able to rule—even to wage war—without ever having to levy taxes. He would be able to expand the ranks of the nobility (an exciting thought for wealthy and ambitious families), increase spending on education, and advance religion by creating and endowing eighteen new bishoprics. This was Cromwell's great plan: to make the Crown financially independent and Parliament very nearly irrelevant. If carried out, it could have changed English history by giving future kings an endowment sufficient to support all the operations of their governments for any number of generations.

Nothing of the kind came to pass. Instead Henry ran through his windfall with a speed that defies belief. Almost as soon as the church lands fell into his hands he began selling them, in some cases even giving them away to a fortunate few. In the last eight or nine years of his life he divested himself, and his heirs, of land with a value of approximately £750,000. There were political advantages in this: by giving the most powerful families a share of the monastic spoils, and by allowing other families to become powerful from feasting on the pillage, he created a potent constituency with the strongest possible reason for supporting what he had done. Most of the sold lands went for prices approaching fair market value, rather than being deeply discounted or given away. If Henry had husbanded his receipts, they could have not only given him unprecedented and potentially permanent autonomy but also funded at least some of the good things promised to Parliament. But instead he squandered it, almost literally threw it away, creating a legacy of financial neediness that would cripple his successors for a hundred years and finally contribute to the collapse of the monarchy under his great-great-grandnephew King Charles I.

Catherine of Aragon—bright, well educated, virtuous, pretty, and in every way the perfect royal bride—would suffer grievously when her husband turned his affections elsewhere.

Kunsthistorisches Museum, Wien

Henry VII, the cunning first Tudor monarch, an enigma even to his contemporaries, took one great gamble, pulled it off, and spent the rest of his life consolidating his winnings.

V&A Images,
Victoria and Albert Museum

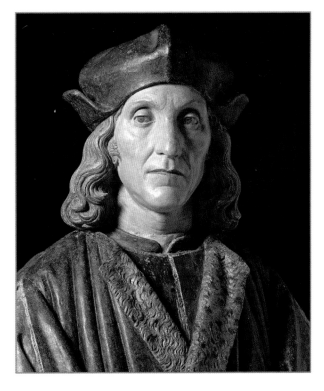

Pope Clement VII, caught between his desperate need to keep the friendship of England and the weakness of Henry VIII's divorce case, maddened the king with years of delay.

Pope Clement VII (1478-1534) c.1526 (oil on canvas) by Sebastiano del Piombo (S. Luciani) (c.1485-1547) Galleria Nazionale de Capodimonte, Naples, Italy/ Giraudon/ The Bridgeman Art Library

Anne Boleyn, elegant, sharp-witted, sharp-tongued, and ambitious, enchanted the king— until finally he accused her of ensnaring him with witchcraft and had her executed.

© National Portrait Gallery, London

Henry VIII, in this early miniature, is more pudgy than potent—not half as impressive as in the image that would be created for him years later by the more flattering Hans Holbein.

Henry VIII, c.1525-27 (bodycolour on vellum on card) by Lucas Horenbout or Hornebault (fl. 1534-44) Fitzwilliam Museum, University of Cambridge, UK/ The Bridgeman Art Library

Thomas Cromwell was the most remarkable figure of the Tudor era, a self-made man who rose to the heights of power only to be killed by the king he had served brilliantly.

Thomas More, who said he was "the king's good subject but God's first," paid with his life for persisting in distinguishing between the two.

Bishop John Fisher, one of the best known and most respected churchmen in Europe, was first imprisoned, then betrayed, and finally killed by the king whose mentor he had once been.

Keeping up appearances: Henry VIII hung this grandiose portrait of himself not in public but in his privy chamber, perhaps as a reminder of the heroic image he wanted to project.

© National Museums Liverpool

Harsh reality? This vastly less idealized, probably vastly more accurate picture of the king shows him as a quasi-monster approaching the end of his long and bloody reign.

© National Portrait Gallery, London

Beautiful and doomed, the boy-king Edward VI rejected the new church his father had created, supporting instead a second, more radical English Reformation.

Queen Mary I, in trying to turn back history, might have succeeded if she had not died at age forty-two after only five years on the throne— or if her pregnancies had been real.

Thomas Cranmer, a restless searcher after theological truth, persecuted people not only for beliefs that he himself had once proclaimed compulsory but for rejecting doctrines that he also thought untrue.

Philip of the House of Hapsburg, distrusted in England because of his Spanish roots, secretly repudiated the terms of the contract that wed him to his "aunt," Queen Mary.

Edward Seymour, Duke of Somerset, rose swiftly under his nephew Edward VI to a position of supreme power that he lacked the political skill—or perhaps the strength of will—to retain.

The young Queen Elizabeth I, at the start of her reign, could be portrayed as a quite normal, if richly attired, human being (as in the Clopton portrait of 1558, shown here).

© National Portrait Gallery, London

The later Elizabeth was transformed by her artists into an otherworldly Faerie Queen— the faintly godlike, faintly grotesque figure portrayed in the Ditchley portrait of 1592.

© National Portrait Gallery, London

William Cecil, Elizabeth I's right hand for forty years, accumulated such colossal wealth that two branches of his family were planted in the high aristocracy.

Robert Dudley, Earl of Leicester, in the third generation of his family to rise high in the service of the Tudors and pay a price for doing so, was the only man Elizabeth ever loved.

Mary Queen of Scots, a prisoner throughout the two decades preceding her execution at age forty-four, was not allowed to examine the evidence used to condemn her.

Whom the gods would destroy they first raise high: Robert Devereux, Earl of Essex, began his career as Queen Elizabeth's last great favorite and ended with his head on the chopping block.

He squandered his riches at home first, spending half a million pounds on building in the 1540s, much of it on coastal fortifications but as much as £170,000 on the construction, expansion, and unending improvement of his many palaces. (Even Hampton Court, which grew to more than a thousand rooms with luxurious sleeping accommodations for three hundred guests, was dwarfed by Nonsuch Palace, which was still a work in progress when Henry died, would never become an important royal residence, and in the space of a few generations would disappear from the landscape almost without leaving a trace.)

But what ruined the Crown financially was Henry's resumed pursuit, as the 1530s ended and his mastery of church and state seemed complete, of military glory. As in the first years of his reign and again in the 1520s, he made war on both France and Scotland, and as before, there was no real point in attacking either. As before, he accomplished nothing of consequence, did nothing to enhance his reputation at home or abroad, and aggravated problems that would torment his successors. Even in their most farcical aspects, Henry's last international adventures were painfully like his first. They began in 1543, when Francis of France and the emperor Charles—who five years earlier had signed a meaningless ten-year truce and then, with equal lack of seriousness, pledged that neither would enter into additional alliances without the other's consent—once again went to war with each other and began to court England. Henry, who had no good reason to involve himself in this sterile old quarrel and many good reasons to stay out, nevertheless entered into a treaty with Charles by which both promised to invade France in the following year. Henry did in fact lead an army into France in July 1544—his deplorable physical condition made him less the army's leader than a cumbersome part of its baggage—but predictably he and Charles neither cooperated nor even attempted to coordinate their operations.

Within two months Charles was making a separate peace with Francis, ending whatever chance Henry might ever have had of accomplishing anything. The conflict with Scotland was equally confused, confusing, and intermittently ridiculous. In 1542 Henry insisted on making a major issue of the kinds of skirmishes that had long been routine in the borderlands that separated the two kingdoms, demanding that the Scots acknowledge him as overlord of their king. The death of his

his nephew King James V after the English victory at Solway Moss in that year (Henry did not participate) opened up the possibility not only of peace but of union between the two countries. In 1543 Scotland's infant queen was betrothed to little Edward, Prince of Wales, as part of the Treaty of Greenwich, but the Scots were soon repelled by England's "rough wooing." In each of the following two years an angry Henry sent armies under the late Queen Jane's brother Edward Seymour not only to invade Scotland but—these were Seymour's specific instructions—to cause as much mayhem as possible. One result was an outlandish amount of death and destruction. Another was the raising of Scottish hatred of the English to a pitch rarely seen before. The Scots turned to France for support, and the stage was set for the marriage of their queen into the French royal family. In the end the only result of Henry's aggressive policy was the cementing of a French-Scottish alliance.

The French and Scottish campaigns cost England, in the five years leading up to Henry's death, the stupendous total of more than £2.2 million—this at a time when the Crown's customary revenues (those exclusive of the money from the monastic suppression) were in the neighborhood of £200,000. Just the three-month incursion into France in 1544 cost £586,000, and the subsequent defense of that campaign's one trophy (the city of Boulogne, which had little real value to England, and which in any case the English had no chance of holding on to permanently) cost another £426,000. The war against Scotland, conducted at Henry's insistence with gratuitous and self-defeating savagery, consumed £350,000, and the building up of an English navy took another £265,000. England had never seen spending on this scale. In almost any previous reign the burden imposed on the king's subjects would have sparked resistance, even revolt. So cowed were the people by the 1540s, however, that Henry had little difficulty in matching his unprecedented spending with unprecedented taxation. Almost literally, he pulled out all the financial stops.

Students of the subject have calculated that as early as 1535, with Wolsey and Cromwell showing the way, Henry had accomplished the amazing feat of taking in (and just as quickly spending) more tax revenues than all his predecessors combined. But in the following dozen years the Crown would take in more than twice as much again—and again we are speaking of taxes only, the riches taken from the monasteries not included. From 1540 to 1547 Parliament approved six of the traditional payments known as "fifteenths and tenths," a percentage of the value of movable property. Each of these grants yielded approximately £29,000. During these same years Parliament also approved three "subsidies," each requiring the clergy to give the Crown 20 percent of their income for three successive years and the laity to pay an annually increasing percentage of the value of their real and personal property. Nor was this all, or even nearly all. In 1542 Henry borrowed £112,000 from his wealthier subjects (everyone known to have an income of at least £50 received a letter informing him of how much he was expected to "lend"), and two years later Parliament declared the king free of any obligation to repay any such debts incurred since the start of 1540. Next Henry demanded and got something that Richard III had abolished because of its unpopularity and even Wolsey had been unable to revive because of parliamentary opposition: a so-called "benevolence," a gift to the Crown that in this instance totaled £270,000. Two London aldermen dared to object. One was required not only to join the war against Scotland but to take with him a troop of soldiers raised at his own expense; soon captured, he had to pay a hefty ransom to secure his freedom. The other was simply sent to prison, where he remained for three months until being allowed to purchase his release. Throughout all this Henry was also borrowing from continental moneylenders. Foreign loans totaled some £272,000 in all, at interest rates of up to 14 percent. Much of this debt remained unpaid at the time of Henry's death.

Even this was not enough to keep the Crown solvent. Something more was needed, and it was found in the most underhanded device available to the governments of the time: a systematic debasement of the coinage. As early as the reign of Henry VII, England had, in a legitimate response to a lowering of the value of continental currencies, occasionally and by modest amounts decreased the amount of silver or gold in its coins. In 1544, however, the royal mint began mixing more and more base metal into the coinage, not to keep in step with the Europeans but as a way of skimming off wealth. Soon its coins were only half gold or silver, and not long after that they were two-thirds base metal. Henry reaped £373,000 by this expedient, which caused his cash-strapped last chancellor, Thomas Wriothesley, to gratefully describe the royal mint as the regime's "holy anchor." Few outside the government had reason to celebrate. Prices rose some 25 percent in the last two years of the reign, and the increasingly dubious value of the coinage became an embarrassment to Englishmen trying to trade abroad.

The cumulative effects of Henry's changes were profound. If the old vision of a society in which wealth brought obligations had never come close to fulfillment, now even the ideal was dying. Stability was replaced by plunder, the institutions of government became the tools of the plunderers, and their aim, when it was not to pull in still more plunder, was to make sure that no one threatened the bounty that Henry's revolution had funneled to them. There is no better measure of the kind of England that Henry had created than a statute passed by his Parliament at the instigation of his ministers just months after his death. Under this law, anyone who "lived idly and loiteringly for the space of three days" could have the letter V (for vagabond) branded on his chest and could be required to spend two years serving whoever had reported him (or, presumably, her). Those impressed into bondage in this way were entitled to nothing more than bread and water, could be made to wear iron rings around their necks, and were legally obliged to do whatever work their masters ordered "however vile it might be, by beating, chaining or otherwise." Any who made themselves unavailable to their masters for two weeks or more were to have an S (for slave) burned into their faces and their two years of bondage extended into a life sentence. Further offenses could result in execution. No such law would have been conceivable in England between the coming of Christianity and the last years of Henry VIII's reign. It was a classic case of punishing the victim, singling out for final humiliation the very people left most helpless by the pillaging of institutions that for centuries had attended to the needs of the weak and the destitute. It was too outrageous to be tolerated even by the new oligarchy for more than a few years, but it expressed in extreme form something of the spirit of the age. In a sense it was the zenith of Henry's achievement, the highest expression of the new values that were growing out of the ruins of the old order.

In the years between the failure of the Pilgrimage of Grace and Henry's death, the ancient understanding that there were and must be limits on royal power even in the secular sphere, slowly hammered out during centuries of conflict, was crushed underfoot and left behind. The possibility that anyone other than the king might possess rights or powers not deriving from the king became something that no one dared mention. The king's word literally became law as early as 1539, when a Proclamations Act gave royal pronouncements the same force under the law as statutes passed by Parliament, prescribed imprisonment and fines for anyone failing to obey them, and made it high treason to flee England to escape punishment. This was such an extreme expansion of the power of the Crown that even the craven Parliament that Cromwell had put in place balked, but passage was secured by amendments which forbade the use of proclamations to override statutes already on the books, confiscate private property, or deprive subjects of life or liberty. There followed, within weeks, a fresh delineation of exactly which religious beliefs were now acceptable through an Act for Abolishing Diversity of Opinion. This law, better known as the Six Articles, prescribed the death penalty and confiscation of all possessions for anyone denying transubstantiation, the real presence of the body of Jesus in the Eucharist. It also, remarkably, forbade the extending of mercy to anyone willing to withdraw his denial. It was somewhat less harsh in meting out punishments for the denial of other things that the king was determined to make everyone believe (that it is·not necessary to receive communion under the two forms of bread and wine, that priests must not marry and vows of chastity are irrevocable, that private masses are acceptable and confession to a priest necessary for forgiveness). The penalty in connection with these doctrines was merely imprisonment and loss of property for first offenders; a second conviction was necessary for the death penalty to be imposed. Archbishop Cranmer, who almost certainly did not himself believe in the Six Articles at this point in the evolution of his theology, responded by quietly shipping back to Germany the wife whose existence he was at this point still keeping secret from the king.

Despite the increasing severity of the penalties for dissent—sanctions more far-reaching and inflexible than anything previously seen in England—uniformity remained unattainable. One wag compared Henry, with his insistence on rejecting Rome while preserving nearly every Roman Catholic practice and dogma, with someone who has thrown a man off a high tower and then commanded him to stop halfway down. The middle ground that Henry wanted all of England to occupy really was, in practical terms, as impossible as that. On the continent, in

Switzerland especially, reform had already moved far beyond anything that Henry was prepared to tolerate, and increasing numbers of England's reformers wanted to follow the Swiss model. There was no way, in a society where the old consensus had been shattered but faith was still taken so seriously that Parliament engaged in lengthy and passionate debates on transubstantiation, to get everyone to believe what the king told them to believe and to conduct themselves accordingly.

Henry's insistence on making his truth the universal truth led him deeper and deeper into futility and frustration. Even one of the centerpieces of the English Reformation, the delivery to the people of a Bible written in their own language, is a case in point. Such a Bible had been one of the supreme objectives of English reformers long before Henry was born, and nothing was more important to Luther and those who followed him than their conviction that true Christianity was to be found not in the rules and teachings of the church but in Scripture, especially the New Testament writings of the evangelists Matthew, Mark, Luke, and John. (Hence the name "evangelicals" for those reformers who went furthest in rejecting church tradition.) The early radicals had regarded as an outrage the banning of the translation of the New Testament produced by William Tyndale in the 1520s, scornfully brushing aside the hierarchy's contention that it objected not to translation as such but to Tyndale's ideologically motivated distortions (his use of "congregation" rather than "church," for example, and of "senior" rather than "priest"). Brushed aside, too, were the warnings of orthodox theologians that the Bible is an elusive work, easily misinterpreted by readers with little understanding of its linguistic and historical roots. In England as on the continent, the Reformation arrived on a wave of enthusiasm for Scripture as the one doorway to enlightenment and salvation. In 1538, as part of the enforcement of his second set of injunctions for the clergy, Cromwell ordered every parish church in England to obtain a copy of his so-called Great Bible (which was mainly Tyndale's translation and long afterward would provide more than 80 percent of the text of the King James Version). It became government policy to make the Bible directly accessible to every literate man and woman in England.

But Henry soon found the translated Bible an obstacle to uniformity. Readers found the interpretation of many passages open to debate;

many of them naturally began interpreting such passages in whatever way they themselves thought best, and inevitably their conclusions did not always agree with the truth according to Henry or Cranmer or anyone else in a position of authority. Translation launched the English church into diverging assertions of what Scripture does and does not say and hence into a bewildering array of sects. Henry, witnessing the start of this process, was offended by it and undertook to stop it in his usual way: by ordering it to stop or else. Thus in 1543 he drew out of Parliament an Act for Advancement of True Religion, the operative word being "true." True religion was to be preserved by removal of the Tyndale translation, condemned now as what the more conservative of Henry's bishops had persuaded him that it was: "crafty, false and untrue." Henceforth only clergymen were to read the Bible aloud in public, only nobles and gentlemen were to read it to their families, and only male heads of households, gentlewomen, and ladies of noble birth were to read it even in solitude. It was not to be opened by "prentices, journeymen, serving men of the degrees of yeomen or under, husbandmen nor laborers," and any caught doing so were to be jailed for a month. By such means the king sought to separate people "of the lower sort" from their "diverser naughty and erroneous opinions" and save them from "great division and dissension among themselves." The impact of this act on the lower orders is, at a remove of nearly five centuries, impossible to judge. Evangelicals, for the most part, maintained a prudent but resentful silence and bided their time. They took comfort in Henry's marriage to Catherine Parr, who saw to it that reformers of decidedly Protestant inclination were appointed as tutors to Prince Edward and Princess Elizabeth or otherwise provided with employment or patronage.

The king meanwhile soldiered on with the thankless and unending task of showing his people the way to salvation, to all appearances unaware that he could have spent his time more productively by trying to herd cats. Almost simultaneously with the Act for Advancement of True Religion he approved the issuance of what came to be known as the King's Book (its official title was *The Necessary Doctrine and Erudition of Any Christian Man*), an attempt to correct the flaws of the Bishops' Book and lay out yet again a system of beliefs that in most respects was Roman Catholicism purged of what even many conservative reformers often saw as superstition. The conservatives were generally pleased, the evangelicals unimpressed, and nothing really changed. The results were the same on Christmas Eve 1545, when Henry surprised Parliament by addressing it for what would prove to be the last time. Angrily, even tearfully, he complained of the divisions within the clergy, where "some be too stiff in their old Mumpsimus, others be too busy and curious in their new Sumpsimus." Somewhat oddly, considering that he was demanding an end to discord, he urged his listeners to report preachers of "perverse doctrine" to him and his council, saying that he was "very sorry to know and hear how irreverently that precious jewel, the word of God, is disputed, rhymed, sung and jingled in every alehouse and tavern." He found much to complain of that day, and he complained at length, but any who were moved by his sincerity could do little in response and nothing happened as a result. The man who had done more than anyone to make the religion of England a changeable and changing thing, to create and magnify confusion and division, was now very nearly begging his subjects to somehow come together as a united and happy fellowship of faith. If his lament was touching, it was also a bit ridiculous.

Not that the old man was to be scoffed at. To the contrary, at the time of his Mumpsimus speech, with only a little more than a year to live, he remained as murderous as ever, a hardened killer ruling by terror. There was no sure safety for anyone except of course his son and heir—not for his own relatives, not for strangers or those who had served him longest and best, not for reformers or conservatives. The whole last decade of his life was studded with the slaughter of men and women of every stripe, often in the most terrible ways that the technology of the time could make possible.

A representative sampling of Henry's reign of terror might well begin with the story of John Forest, who in the happier days of the 1520s had been a prominent member of the Observant Franciscans, Catherine of Aragon's confessor, and therefore connected to the royal family. He was among the first of the friars to speak out against the king's plan to divorce Catherine and marry Anne Boleyn, and he may already have been in prison by the time Fathers Peto and Elston challenged Henry in the Franciscan church at Greenwich. Later, however, he took the oath of succession, thereby escaping the grisly fate of his compeers, and was allowed to withdraw to the north of England. Still later it was reported that he was claiming to have sworn the oath "with his outward man, but his inward man never consented thereunto." This is plausible in light of the fact that in 1538, for reasons unknown, he was again taken into custody and returned to London for execution as a heretic. What makes Forest's killing noteworthy is the way it was turned into a kind of horrible joke. His death sentence came at the time when Cromwell was shutting down religious shrines and pilgrimage destinations all across England. It happened that at one of these shrines, Llandderfel in Wales, a wooden statue called Darvel Gadarn, an object of veneration from time immemorial, had recently been seized and was slated for destruction. There was a legend about Darvel Gadarn: one day, it was said, the statue would set a forest on fire. This gave someone a bright idea of the kind that no doubt appealed powerfully to officials with a broad enough sense of humor. Darvel Gadarn was hauled from North Wales to London for the burning not of *a* forest but of *John* Forest. On the day of his execution the friar, bound in chains, was suspended above a pyre on which lay the statue. Hugh Latimer, probably the most radical of Henry's bishops, preached a sermon at the end of which he offered to release Forest if he would acknowledge the royal supremacy. When Forest refused, the fire was lit, and for two hours he was slowly broiled until dead. He would remain the only papist executed for heresy rather than treason, and therefore burned rather than hanged. The less theatrical executions at about the same time of the abbot of Woburn and the prior of Lenton, both of whom had refused to sign over their houses, could pass almost unnoticed.

If fidelity to Rome could bring on a terrible death, so too could the rejection of things Roman. In the same year that Forest perished, John Lambert, a Cambridge-educated priest who had long been associated with the radical evangelicals and had been in trouble with the authorities even before Henry's break with Rome, was accused of having heretical opinions concerning, among other things, "the sacrament of the altar," the Eucharist. He appealed to the king, with consequences that must have gone far beyond anything he could have hoped for or feared. Henry decided to turn the case into another of his show trials, a demonstration of his mastery of theology. The great hall at York Place was transformed into a theater for the occasion, with scaffolds erected for onlookers and the walls hung with tapestries. When the trial opened on the morning of November 16, Henry presided from a high throne surrounded by phalanxes of nobles, bishops, judges, and scholars. He was resplendent in a costume of white silk, a kind of corpulent angelic vision. One can only imagine what poor Lambert must have thought, escorted into the center of this display of power and subjected to interrogation by such luminaries as Archbishop Cranmer (who, there can be no doubt, shared many of the beliefs that had brought Lambert to this pass), half a dozen bishops, and finally, most terrifyingly, the king himself, who as the day wore on took an increasingly prominent part in the proceedings.

Lambert was afforded no counsel, but he defended himself and his opinions heroically through hours of hard questioning. The climax came late in the day when, asked yet again to declare whether he believed that the bread and wine of the altar really were transformed during the mass into the body and blood of Christ in spite of undergoing no change in appearance, texture, or taste, Lambert replied that he believed it in the same way that Augustine of Hippo, one of the fathers of the church, appeared in his writings to have done. The king jumped on this.

"Answer neither out of St. Augustine, nor by the authority of any other," he demanded, "but tell me plainly whether thou sayest it is the body of Christ or nay."

"Then I deny it to be the body of Christ."

"Mark well!" said Henry. "For now thou shalt be condemned even by Christ's own words. *Hoc est corpus meum* [here is my body]."

And condemned meant condemned. When in the end Lambert simply abandoned the fight and threw himself on the king's mercy, Henry responded with contempt. He ordered Cromwell to declare the verdict, and the verdict was guilty. Six days later Lambert was dragged—literally dragged, shackled to the traditional hurdle—through the streets of London. Then he too was burned to death. Every sycophant at court praised and thanked the king for the brilliance of his performance.

The year ended with a final outburst of savagery that had only a tangential connection to religion but rose more directly out of the old questions about whether Henry, and his father before him, were rightfully kings of England. At the time of the Pilgrimage of Grace, the pope, having already made the king's cousin Reginald Pole a cardinal though he was not yet an ordained priest, had sent him north to see if the revolt might have inclined Henry to return to the Roman fold or, failing that, if Francis of France and the emperor Charles might be disposed to join forces for an invasion of England. Pole's mission came to nothing—by temperament he was a professional student, sometimes ineffectual in practical matters and sufficiently aware of his limitations to avoid politics—but news of it finished whatever affection Henry had retained for his troublesome young kinsman. It also inflamed his long-smoldering distrust of the entire Pole family. He saw an opportunity to accomplish something that he probably had long desired: the extermination of his remaining Yorkist cousins.

Reginald Pole's elder brother Sir Geoffrey was arrested and interrogated. He must have been a weak man; terrified, he tried to save himself by telling his captors whatever he could about ways in which members of his family had shown themselves to be unfriendly to the new church and therefore disloyal to their king. The evidence he provided was thin stuff, a secondhand account of vague idle talk about unhappiness with the current state of affairs and a longing for the old ways, but in the hands of Cromwell and the king it became sufficient for the arrest of Geoffrey and Reginald's eldest brother Henry, Lord Montague, who as the senior male member of the family and grandson of a brother of Edward IV and Richard III had a claim to the crown that he had never been foolish enough to pursue. Arrested with him were Henry Courtenay, Marquess of Exeter, who like Henry VIII was a son of one of Edward IV's daughters, and his twelve-year-old son Edward, Earl of Devon. Into the Tower they all went. The charges against them were worse than dubious—the Poles and the Courtenays alike had remained loyal to Henry through the various disturbances of the mid-1530s—but their royal blood doomed them all the same. On December 6 Montague and Exeter were beheaded, and the executions of others accused of involvement in the supposed Pole conspiracy went on until in the end sixteen people were dead. Montague's little son, who had been sent to the Tower with his father, was never seen again and is assumed to have died in confinement. Margaret Pole, Countess of Salisbury, the Pole brothers' mother and onetime governess of the king's daughter Mary, was arrested soon after Montague's execution and, after long days of questioning in which nothing could be found to suggest that she might be guilty of anything, attainted of high treason. Exeter's widow, too, was imprisoned and attainted.

It went on in this way year after year, killing following gratuitous killing and every death ugly in its own new way. In the months following the attack on the Poles, as the last and largest of England's religious houses were pulled down and their valuables carted off to London, the abbots of the three great Benedictine monasteries at Colchester, Glastonbury, and Reading became the last to refuse to submit. No one could have been surprised, after what had already transpired, to see them arrested on charges of treason and condemned without trial. But their ends were shocking all the same. The eighty-year-old Abbot Richard Whiting of Glastonbury, a man so far above reproach that even Cromwell's commissioners had praised him and his house at the end of their first visit, was not merely executed. After a debilitating period of imprisonment in London he was returned to his monastery, dragged prostrate to the top of Glastonbury Tor, a conelike geological freak that is the highest promontory in its region, and there put to death along with two of his brother monks. His body was quartered, with the four parts put on public display in the towns of Wells, Bath, Ilchester, and Bridgwater. His head was mounted atop the entrance to the abbey. Henry, keeping his scales balanced, was at this same time having evangelicals imprisoned and burned for failing to conform to the Six Articles.

The year after that, as if in confirmation that what goes around comes around, even Thomas Cromwell was abruptly stripped of his offices and put to death. Contrary to what has often been asserted, he did not die because he had used a deceptive painting by Hans Holbein to trick the king into marrying a miserably homely Anne of Cleves. He died, rather, because he had become too closely identified with the evangelical party in England and the Protestant cause in Europe, and because the collapse of the latest alliance between Francis of France and the emperor Charles gave Henry a choice of Catholic allies and made Cromwell not only expendable but a diplomatic liability. Henry dispensed with him because he thought he no longer needed him, and because he thought he would be better off without him. The endlessly useful Richard Rich (he was *Sir* Richard now, on his way to becoming Lord Rich) testified against his longtime master with effect as deadly as his earlier contributions to the destruction of Fisher and More. He quoted Cromwell as saying that he was prepared, if necessary, to fight for the evangelical cause even in defiance of the king. It is not easy to believe that the wily Cromwell would have said any such thing within Rich's hearing, but the standards of evidence were even lower in his case than in Fisher's or More's because he had no actual trial. Interestingly, at the moment of his arrest, Cromwell pulled off his hat and angrily flung it to the ground. It was the exasperated gesture of a gambler learning that he had made a bad bet, a trickster tricked. There would be no more opportunities to roll the dice.

In the days before his death Cromwell begged Henry for "mercy, mercy, mercy," and just before being executed he professed to having always been a good Catholic. (He could not have meant a good *Roman* Catholic.) It was not long before Henry realized that he *did* need Cromwell, and that in executing him he had deprived himself of as effective a chief minister as any monarch could ever have hoped for. Characteristically, he blamed the loss not on himself but on Cromwell's enemies at court—men and women who had in fact wanted to see the secretary ruined but would have been powerless to accomplish any such thing without the king's active cooperation. Throughout the 1540s Henry would pay and pay again for having extended that cooperation.

Two days after Cromwell's execution the prominent evangelicals Robert Barnes, William Jerome, and Thomas Garrett were all burned at the stake for heresy, and three distinguished Roman Catholics were hanged, drawn, and quartered for treason. All these deaths remain shrouded in mystery. As with the abbots and Cromwell, there had been no trial, no presentation of evidence, no defense; the king was now simply killing whomever he chose without taking the trouble to explain. The atrocities went on and on. Some, such as the 1541 execution of the seventy-year-old Margaret, Countess of Salisbury, the mother of the Poles, were small affairs barely deserving notice except for their brutality.

The countess, whose father, brother, and son had been murdered by Edward IV, Henry VII, and Henry VIII respectively, and whose small grandson had disappeared while in prison, was obviously guilty of nothing. All her life she had been a loyal if independent-minded member of the royal family, though her early support of Catherine of Aragon had caused her to be dismissed from court and the defection of her son Reginald to the old religion had brought trouble down on the entire family. When brought to the chopping block, Margaret refused to cooperate. "No," she said, "my head never committed treason. If you will have it,

you must take it as you can." Her death became a grotesquely protracted affair. The executioner had to chase her around the scaffold,
slashing at her awkwardly with his blade until at last he had "literally
hacked her head and shoulders to pieces in a most pitiful manner."

Some of the atrocities were on a vastly bigger scale. In late 1543, after
the Scots repudiated the Treaty of Greenwich and the betrothal of their
infant queen to Prince Edward, Henry sent Edward Seymour on an unnecessary and ultimately counterproductive invasion. Seymour's orders
were to annihilate every man, woman, and child wherever resistance
was encountered, which was likely to mean wherever English troops appeared. Every place of habitation was to be destroyed "so that the upper
stone may be the nether and not one stick stand by another." Seymour
questioned these instructions, sensibly thinking that an approach with
less resemblance to genocide might be more conducive to long-term
peace. When told to proceed as ordered, he did so with such diligence
that most of Edinburgh was reduced to rubble and the countryside
around was scoured clean. The following year, when Seymour again
crossed into Scotland, his orders were the same as before: to carry out a
program of wholesale and indiscriminate destruction. This time he demolished sixteen castles, seven major abbeys, five towns, and 243 villages, killing uncounted hundreds or thousands of Scots. Henry, still not
satisfied, ordered the execution of several Scottish hostages whom he
had been holding for more than two years and gave his support to a plot
(which succeeded) to assassinate the Cardinal Beaton who had long
been the leader of the most anti-English faction in Edinburgh. This last
he did secretly, however, "not misliking the offer" of the men who volunteered to murder Beaton, thinking it "good they be exhorted to proceed," but regarding such a project as "not meet to be set forward
expressly by his majesty."

This was the Henry who, on January 27, 1547, having been told at last
by a brave gentleman of his privy chamber that he was dying and asked
if he wished to confess, replied that he was confident that his sins would
have been forgiven even if they were far greater than in fact they were.
Again he was asked if he wished to see a confessor. He said perhaps
Cranmer, safe old Cranmer, but not quite yet, not until he had slept
awhile. He drifted into a sleep that became a coma, so that later, when
his gentlemen tried to rouse him, they were unable to do so. Cranmer

was summoned and came in a hurry, taking the king's hand and trying to talk with him but getting no response. Finally he asked Henry to signify his faith in Jesus Christ by squeezing his hand. The king, Cranmer said later, squeezed hard and died.

Something very big had come to an end. It was time for the aftermath, whatever that might prove to be. As for Henry, perhaps his best hope was that he had been wrong all along and the evangelicals right, and all that was needed to save his soul was the gift of faith. No doubt he himself would have been willing to be judged by his works, but it might not have been a good bet.

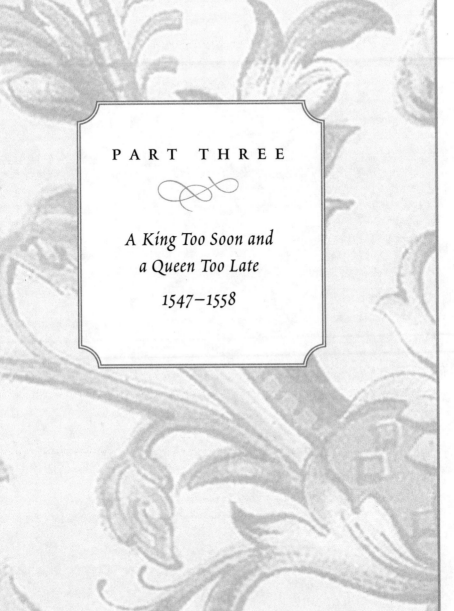

PART THREE

A King Too Soon and
a Queen Too Late

1547–1558

17

A New Beginning

With the death of Henry VIII, the supreme headship of the church in England, the authority to decide what every man and woman in the kingdom was required to believe about God and salvation and the nature of ultimate reality, passed to a nine-year-old child. Little Edward Tudor, upon becoming King Edward VI, was recognized by church and state alike as the one person empowered by God to resolve conflicts over doctrine and practice that divided the most powerful and learned of his subjects.

It would have been a challenging situation under the best of circumstances. England's experience of being ruled by boys had been mercifully limited but not very happy. Even in the days before the Crown was responsible not only for the government but for a fractured and fractious church, it had been an experience of struggles for power punctuated with betrayal, bloodshed, and disorder. In the late 1540s, under the circumstances that Henry had created with his jumble of innovations, rule by a child-king was a recipe for trouble, little better than an absurdity. With a restless population kept quiet only by the threat of armed force, and with court and church divided into factions that hated each other mortally, the chances that Edward's minority could be passed without serious difficulty must have seemed slim indeed.

The church of Henry's making was, at the time of his death, emphatically not Roman Catholic but just as emphatically not Lutheran (the king having made it a capital crime to follow Luther in denying free will or believing in justification by faith alone). The new theology contradicted itself so boldly on so many points as to border on incoherence: in the King's Book of 1543, for example, Henry had forbidden the very use of the word *purgatory*, but then in his will he made provision for thousands of masses to be said for the repose of his soul (which could only have benefited if it were in something like purgatory). The result was confusion, contention, and division on a scale without precedent.

The main points of dispute were familiar by now. They ranged from free will to justification by faith, from whether the eucharistic bread and wine were literally the body and blood of Jesus Christ (Henry and Luther had both affirmed this, but increasingly influential Swiss theologians denied it and were winning over Englishmen as eminent as Archbishop Cranmer) to whether religious statues and pictures should be destroyed as idolatrous and practices that had been at the center of English religious life for a millennium should be banned as superstitious. Disagreement was almost boundless, debate smoldered just below the surface of public life in spite of Henry's readiness to condemn anyone who disputed his truth, and the dangers of the situation were compounded by the fact that so many people believed the questions at issue to be matters of eternal life and death. People in every camp, if not always prepared to die in defense of their positions, were prepared to kill to prevent others from luring the population into the fires of hell.

In the final weeks of Henry's life, as the various organs of his huge body began to malfunction and he became incapable even of rising from his bed, he had focused the last of his strength on arrangements for holding the kingdom together until his son grew old enough to take charge. Someone, or some group, was going to have to manage the kingdom in Edward's name, probably for almost a decade. Finding such a person would not be as simple as it had been in similar situations in the past. The royal family was small: Henry had no brother or uncle entitled by blood to rule on the boy-king's behalf, and his only adult child, Mary, the former princess, remained illegitimate in consequence of the annulment of her parents' marriage. Mary's legal status would have made her an unsuitable candidate to serve as regent during her half-brother's minority even if Henry had trusted her on the supremacy, which he rightly did not.

The central contest continued to be between the traditionalists, who wanted the religion of their ancestors regardless of whether they secretly accepted the leadership of the pope, and the evangelicals, a diverse party united by its contempt for the old church and a determination to restore what its adherents believed to have been the purity and simplicity of earliest Christianity. Henry, whether by craft or good luck, had since his break with Rome been able to maintain a balance between the two sides, dividing the highest offices of church and state between them while leavening his own conservative pronouncements on doctrine and dogma with enough reformist measures to keep both sides insecure. The traditionalists, the most prominent of whom were by the mid-1540s Thomas Howard, Duke of Norfolk, and Stephen Gardiner, bishop of Winchester, undoubtedly represented by a wide margin the greatest part of England's population. Though evangelicals hostile to the old ways had been prominent at court at least since the days of Anne Boleyn, King Henry's conservatism had always required them to tread carefully and appear more conservative than they actually were. This had become more true than ever after Thomas Cromwell began to fall out of favor; it was then that Henry lost his appetite for religious innovation and made it a crime punishable with death to reject Catholic orthodoxy in favor of the Lutheran beliefs he despised. By the early 1540s it must have seemed inevitable that, if Henry ever made provision for the governing of England after he was dead and before Edward attained his majority, he would reinforce the position of the traditionalists. Even if he made no such provision, conservative dominance after his death must have seemed practically certain. Most of England's clergy, most of the bishops included, belonged to the traditionalist camp. So did most of the population, the nobles, and the gentry. On their side they had the law of the land: the Six Articles, with which Parliament had upheld the real presence and clerical celibacy. On their side, too, they had the King's Book, which to the horror of the evangelicals had affirmed the traditional creed and all seven of the Catholic sacraments. As a final bulwark they had Henry's heresy laws, which made it a capital crime not to believe as the king believed.

Thus the evangelicals could preach as they believed only at the risk of their lives. Even if they had been left free to express themselves, they would have been a tiny and scorned minority almost everywhere except at the universities and in London and southeastern England, and even in those places they remained a minority, though not such a tiny one or nearly so scorned. Remarkably, however, from the start of Edward's reign they assumed a position of such complete dominance that with astonishing speed the official religion became more radically evangelical and reformist than Henry could ever have intended or imagined. And it was Henry, improbably enough, who had made this possible. How did it happen? The answer is almost certainly not to be found in anything like an end-of-life shift in the king's thinking in favor of justification by faith or any of the other foundation stones of evangelical thought. It lay, more likely, in the fact that in the last years of his life Henry was a solitary and profoundly lonely man.

Henry was alone as only a man can be who is feared by nearly everyone with whom he has contact, who believes that he alone has the truth on every subject of real importance so that there is no need to converse or listen but only to pronounce, and who has cast away or even destroyed one after another of the people to whom he had been closest earlier in his life when he was still capable of being close to anyone. At the end of his life he was no longer capable of any such thing. He exalted his little son as the jewel of England but rarely saw him. If he dined with his daughters, they sat not at the same table as their father but beneath him, and at a distance. He had threatened the life of his sixth and last wife, Catherine Parr, for her reformist religious views and summoned neither her nor any of his children to be with him for his last Christmas or the beginning of what would turn out to be his last year.

Still, the very fact that he had married Catherine despite being far along in his physical decline is suggestive of neediness, and the marriage was significant even if it produced no offspring and in all likelihood was never consummated. Catherine like Anne Boleyn before her was a fervent evangelical, and as the king's wife she was able to take a hand in the education of his children. Thus was the child Edward placed in the care of tutors who began the process by which he became an evangelical of an exceptionally militant bent. Thus, too, Queen Catherine's brother William Parr, an elegant gentleman of deficient judgment but like her a supporter of religious reform, was made Earl of Essex (the same title that Cromwell had been given not long before his death) and joined the increasingly influential evangelical faction on the Privy Council, the innermost circle of royal advisers.

The king's neediness helps to explain the survival, almost alone among the men who had been important in church or state when Henry was still married to Catherine of Aragon, of Thomas Cranmer. Cranmer's religious views had never meshed well with Henry's, really, and for years he had to conceal the fact of his marriage from a king who to the end of his life insisted on a celibate clergy. But Cranmer became and was able to remain archbishop of Canterbury because no matter what happened, no matter what the king demanded, he was always compliant. Though he had his own beliefs and his own agenda for reform, and though those beliefs became increasingly radical with the passage of the years and he became increasingly ambitious in pursuit of his agenda, the side of himself that he allowed the king to see was unfailingly submissive. He lived in a style reminiscent of Wolsey's, with four palaces and a small private army, but he was unfailingly careful never to do anything that might be construed as a challenge to royal authority. Thus Henry found it possible to trust Cranmer as he trusted no other man, perhaps even, in a way, to love him. And thus the senior bishopric of the English church remained in the hands of a confirmed enemy of the old religion, a man who in his innermost being utterly rejected many of the things that the conservatives, his royal master among them, believed most strongly. Cranmer was infinitely easier to work with, to manage, than the most prominent of the conservative bishops, Stephen Gardiner. Gardiner was *too* conservative, too proud, too firm in his beliefs ever to coexist comfortably with a ruler as self-willed as Henry even though the two of them were never far apart in doctrine. Gardiner came as close to displaying a mind of his own as it was possible for a bishop to do while retaining his position (and staying alive) in the England of the 1530s and 1540s. He never seemed as dependable as Cranmer made himself appear. And so it was almost inevitable, when Henry began to plan seriously for the succession, that Gardiner would be dismissed and Cranmer would prosper.

The same sort of dynamic worked to the advantage of other men whose religious opinions had little in common with Henry's. The excellent family connections that had brought Jane Seymour to Henry's

court as a lady-in-waiting first to Catherine of Aragon and then to Anne
Boleyn also created opportunities for her brothers Edward and Thomas.
The elder of the pair, Edward, was about thirty-five years old when his
sister became queen and had been in royal service almost from childhood. He had had some success, being knighted while with the English
army in France in 1523 and later becoming master of horse to King
Henry's illegitimate son the Duke of Richmond, but he was still a mere
esquire of the body when his sister was chosen as the king's third bride.
The marriage changed his life completely. In 1536, the year of the wedding, he was made a gentleman of the privy chamber—one of the privileged few with free access to the king's private apartments—and raised
to the nobility as Viscount Beauchamp. The following year, the year of
Prince Edward's birth and Jane's death, he was made Earl of Hertford
and given a number of coveted offices including a seat on the Privy
Council.

Little is known of whether Edward and Jane Seymour had a close relationship—before her death she showed herself to be attached to the
old religion, while he was strongly inclined in the other direction—but
in any case her death did nothing to interrupt his rise. He retained the
confidence of the king, who, when he resumed his wars in 1544, appointed Seymour lord lieutenant in the north and gave him an army
with which to invade Scotland. Seymour proved a capable commander,
hesitantly at first but then energetically carrying out the king's instructions not only to capture Edinburgh but to lay waste to it and everything
surrounding. Later that same year he was with Henry at the capture of
Boulogne, which he was rumored to have made possible by bribing the
commander of the French defenders. In 1545 he was in command at
Boulogne, routing a superior French force that attempted to retake it.
He then returned to Scotland, where he conducted a scorched-earth
campaign even more devastating than the one of the previous year. In
1546, yet again in command at Boulogne, he negotiated a treaty under
which England was to retain possession of that city until 1554 and then
allow the French king to buy it. By this point it was clear that Henry had
come to rely heavily on his brother-in-law in war and diplomacy, and
that Seymour was not unworthy of the king's confidence.

Henry had another reason to put his trust in Seymour. Born a commoner though with a tincture of royal blood, Seymour could never pos-

sibly aspire to the throne. He owed his place in the world, his title and position and the wealth he was rapidly accumulating, entirely to the fact that he was uncle to the Prince of Wales, who of course had no uncles on the paternal side. Seymour had every reason to want Edward to live and prosper, and everything to lose if Edward were to die or somehow be removed from the throne. In searching for someone who seemed capable of managing the kingdom during his son's minority, of waging war if necessary and holding the government together, Henry had to look no further than to Seymour. Best of all, it was not necessary to fear that in a crisis Seymour would subordinate his nephew's interests to his own. Seymour could never become a Richard III. He could help himself, save himself from the enemies that his rapid rise and his unfriendliness to the conservatives had inevitably created, only by preserving the child. The interests of the two were inextricably intertwined.

It was much the same in the case of the leading lay conservative, the leader of one of the last of the grand old noble families that for centuries had possessed so much land and had at their command so many armed men as to make them an effective counterweight to royal power. Thomas Howard, Duke of Norfolk, was seventy-three in 1546, still tough and vigorous though nearly old enough to be the father of a king supposedly dying of old age, and he had spent his long life serving the Tudors at home and abroad, in peace and in war. Grandson of the Duke of Norfolk who had died fighting on the side of Richard III at Bosworth Field in 1485, son of the Howard who was restored to the Norfolk title after destroying a Scots army at Flodden in 1513, he himself had led his father's vanguard at Flodden and had gone on to serve as lord lieutenant in Ireland and commander of English armies in the north and in France. His shrewd if unscrupulous management of the Pilgrimage of Grace may very well have saved King Henry from ruin. Though the Howards like the Seymours (and, for that matter, like a number of noble and gentry families) had a touch of royal blood from generations back, and though Norfolk's first wife had, like Henry VIII's mother, been one of the numerous daughters of Edward IV (she died young, and none of their four children survived), the family had no plausible claim to the throne and no illusions on that score. Three times in the space of a decade, marriages had created the possibility that the Tudors and the Howards would be permanently linked by blood. Norfolk's daughter

Mary had been wed to Henry Fitzroy, the king's bastard, but that had come to nothing as a result of Fitzroy's early death. King Henry's disastrous marriages to two of Norfolk's nieces, Anne Boleyn and Catherine Howard, had served as persuasive reminders of the dangers of aspiring too high. As an ambitious but sensible dynast, Norfolk would have been content to remain first among the peers of the realm and a faithful servant first of Henry and then of his son.

That did not, however, turn out to be possible. To the Seymours and other "new men" around the king—men who had not inherited their high places, but had been elevated to them in consequence of winning Henry's favor—Norfolk was like Gardiner a rival, an obstacle, and a threat. Both had to be neutered, removed if possible, if the Seymour faction were to achieve and maintain control. From about 1544 events began to turn in the Seymours' favor. Norfolk found himself criticized by the king for not conducting his military operations more aggressively in France. (He replied, not unreasonably, that he had been given neither the men nor the munitions to accomplish what Henry demanded.) Edward Seymour, at almost the same time, was ravaging Scotland and delighting the king with his reports of devastation. Two years later, in the last year of Henry's life, Norfolk's son Henry, Earl of Surrey, was replaced by Seymour as commander of the garrison at Boulogne. Upon negotiating his settlement with the French, Seymour returned to court, where he found himself in higher favor than ever with the failing king and therefore easily able to win the friendship of the most well placed of the evangelicals. Among them were William Paget, the king's principal secretary; Queen Catherine and her brother Essex; second gentleman of the privy chamber Anthony Denny; and—most fatefully for the long term—a hitherto obscure soldier named John Dudley, recently elevated to the Privy Council and to the post of lord high admiral. Even conservatives as prominent as Thomas Wriothesley, the new lord chancellor, sought to establish good relations with Seymour as they saw which way the political winds were blowing, and with what force. Seymour's importance even before the death of the king is apparent in the fact that the Privy Council began holding its meetings at his home rather than at any of the royal palaces.

Norfolk and his son Surrey found themselves elbowed aside by the very men who wanted to persuade the king that the entire Howard clan was not to be trusted. The enmity between the two groups was bitter and had deep roots: as early as 1537, Surrey, then only about twenty, had been taken into custody for striking Edward Seymour, who that very year became King Henry's brother-in-law and a viscount with a place on the council. This happened at Hampton Court Palace, and the prescribed penalty for such an act of violence on royal premises was loss of the right hand. Surrey, whose hopes for a military career hung in the balance, was saved by the intervention of Cromwell. As recently as 1546 an argument around the Privy Council's table had ended with Seymour striking Bishop Gardiner, who as a leading conservative was linked to the Howards, in the face. Two years before that, with the council increasingly under Seymour domination, the bishop's personal secretary and nephew, Germaine Gardiner, had been put to death after being charged with denying the royal supremacy. Much more than political advantage was at stake here, obviously. These were men who hated and feared each other intensely and had good reason to do so.

No one was more intense than Surrey, who shared his father's high pride in their family's ancient lineage (actually far more ancient and noble in the female than in the male line, the Howards themselves being rather recent upstarts who had married well) and his disdain for the new men by whom they saw themselves being supplanted. What he lacked, tragically, was the political savvy, the craftiness, that had made it possible for his grandfather to erase the stigma of having fought on the wrong side at Bosworth Field and finally claw his way back to preeminence among the noble families of England. Surrey was brilliant—an accomplished classicist, a poet of very nearly the highest order—but also arrogant and reckless almost to the point of madness. He had an obsessive, anachronistically medieval conception of personal honor. His lifelong pursuit of military glory had been punctuated with pridefully self-destructive acts; his striking of Edward Seymour, whom he was incapable of accepting as an equal, much less as senior in rank, was merely a remarkably vivid example.

With the king visibly failing and increasingly susceptible to their suggestions, Seymour and his following saw an opportunity to finish off their rivals. They ensnared Gardiner in a clumsy but effective trap, telling the king that the bishop had refused a request that he exchange some properties belonging to his see of Winchester for lands belonging to the Crown. It is understandable if Gardiner had in fact been reluctant to agree to such a deal—trades advantageous to the Crown had become a subtle way of plundering the dioceses—but it is unlikely that he would have flatly refused. Gardiner himself protested that he had simply expressed a wish to discuss the matter with the king. In the end he had to submit an apology and surrender his seat on the council. If there had ever been any chance that he would figure in the king's plans for the management of the kingdom after Prince Edward succeeded, that chance was now lost. He did, however, survive. He remained not only free but bishop of Winchester.

The Howards were not so fortunate. On December 12 father and son were confined in the Tower amid rumors that they had been planning to seize control of the government in the event of the king's death, planning to abduct Prince Edward, and other, similar nonsense. When in January 1547 they were charged, however, it was for no such offense. Surrey was accused of committing high treason by using the heraldic emblems of Edward the Confessor, a Saxon monarch whose reign had preceded the Norman Conquest, and thereby staking a claim to the crown. Norfolk was charged with being aware of his son's treason and failing to report it. When put on trial, Surrey defended himself vigorously and at length, pointing out that his ancestors had displayed the same arms that were now alleged to be treasonous and had experienced no difficulty as a result of doing so. It was by no means clear that the jury was prepared to convict until Secretary Paget brought word that the king demanded a guilty verdict. Surrey was beheaded six days later. Thereafter Norfolk, in an effort to save himself, sent the king a letter of submission in which he pleaded guilty to "keeping secret the acts of my son, Henry earl of Surrey, in using the arms of St. Edward the Confessor, which pertain only to kings." It did no good. Norfolk was attainted by Parliament, so that he had no opportunity to answer the charges against him, all his possessions became the property of the Crown, and the king could order his execution whenever he wished. On January 26 Henry signed the necessary order, which was to be carried out the next day; but when the sun rose on January 27, Henry was dead and the council became afraid to proceed. The old duke, a pauper now, paced his cell waiting to learn his fate.

Henry's Third Succession Act had authorized him to appoint a Regency Council to govern if his son inherited while still a child. Many of the king's last hours of consciousness were spent in consultation first with his secretary Paget, then with Paget and Edward Seymour, and finally with a wider circle to decide who would be named executors of his will and the new king's regents. Gardiner and Norfolk were out, absolutely. So was anyone too closely associated with either of them—the bishop of the new see of Westminster, for example, because he had been "schooled" by Gardiner, whom Henry described as being of "so troublesome a nature" that if he were included no one would be able to control him. The Regency Council was by no means uniformly evangelical; Henry ensured a measure of balance by appointing such figures as Cuthbert Tunstal, the bishop of Durham who, a decade and a half before, had made himself a nuisance with his objections to the royal supremacy. But when all the names had been filled in, the list was dominated on the clerical side by Archbishop Cranmer and bishops affiliated with him, and on the lay side by Seymour and his cohorts. The evangelicals had won the last throw of the dice, the one that decided the long contest for control of policy that the whole final decade of Henry's reign had turned into.

Under the terms of Henry's will, the sixteen members of the Regency Council were to be equals and all decisions were to require approval of the group as a whole. If this is really what Henry intended, he was being exceedingly unrealistic: his arrangement left not only the council but the kingdom in desperate need of a chief executive. Edward Seymour recognized this need and put himself forward to fill the void, and his friends on the council were so quick to support him that the public learned of his appointment as lord protector of the realm and governor of the new king's person almost before they knew that the old king was dead. It is not certain that this was a usurpation; Charles V's ambassador reported seeing a letter bearing King Henry's signature that bestowed the duties of lord protector upon his brother-in-law.

Nor is there any way of knowing whether Seymour and his cohorts were, as they claimed, simply carrying out the king's wishes when they made it almost their first matter of business to heap rewards upon themselves. Henry's will instructed his executors to make good on any promises that he had made before his death, and when the Regency Council sought to find out what was intended by this, it could turn only to the three of its own members who had been most in the king's company during the last weeks of his life: Anthony Denny, William Paget, and Seymour himself. They reported that "the king, being on his death-bed put in mind of what he had promised, ordered it *to be put in his will* [emphasis added], that his executors should perform everything that should appear to have been promised by him." They then went on to provide details. What they disclosed was, if a true statement of Henry's intentions, an act of extraordinary generosity on the part of a king who knew all too well that he was leaving his son an empty treasury, heavy debts, and ruined credit. If it was not true, Seymour and the others were thieves on a breathtaking scale. Certainly it is reasonable to suspect that the whole thing had been fabricated for their benefit. The statement that Henry was on his deathbed when he added to his will instructions for the carrying out of his promises is not easily squared with the fact that the will itself was almost certainly completed and signed weeks before he died and well before he or anyone else had reason to think that death was imminent. But the entire record of the king's final weeks—of what he actually did and said, and when he did and said it—is an impossible tangle of contradictions and ambiguities.

What is certain is that, well before Henry's body was put to rest, the closest associates of his last days declared that among the "unfulfilled gifts" he would have bestowed if he had lived were new titles for them and their friends. Thus, supposedly in keeping with the king's wishes, Edward Seymour was elevated from Earl of Hertford to Duke of Somerset, William Parr from Earl of Essex to Marquess of Northampton, and Seymour's henchmen John Dudley and Chancellor Wriothesley to the earldoms of Warwick and Southampton respectively. Six knights, Thomas Seymour, Richard Rich, and Paget among them, were made barons, and to all these men and to others besides (Cranmer, for example, who as a clergyman could not receive a title, and Anthony Denny, who for some reason got no title) there were munificent disbursements of money and land. The new Duke of Somerset—we will use that name for Edward Seymour henceforth, to distinguish him from his brother Thomas Lord Seymour of Sudeley—did best of all. He was given four manors previously belonging to the Diocese of Lincoln, seven from the Diocese of Bath and Wells, and tracts of church land at Westminster on which he would soon begin building the magnificent Somerset House with stones hauled in from ruined monasteries. He was also granted the incomes of the treasurership of one cathedral, the deanship of another, and prebends (chapter memberships) at six others. Overall this splendid payday transferred lands generating income of £27,000 annually to private hands, nearly half in the form of gifts for which the recipients paid nothing. If these benefactions were in fact expressions of the late king's wishes and not merely an act of plunder by which Somerset enriched himself and rewarded his allies, they did in fact accomplish the second purpose as well as the first.

There was trouble all the same. Thomas Seymour was as ambitious as his elder brother, he would soon show himself to be every bit as ruthless, and now he was unable to see why he—no less an uncle of the king than Somerset—should not have a more important part in the new regime. Somerset, in addition to being lord protector and governor, had taken for himself the offices of high steward, great chamberlain, lord treasurer, and earl marshal. Thomas Seymour regarded it as an indignity that he was only a baron, and that his only office—aside from his seat on the council—was that of master of ordnance, a job he had been given more than two years earlier, when King Henry was still alive and active. He argued that the posts of protector and governor should not be held by one man, and that he, by virtue of his blood relationship with the king, should have one of them. Somerset refused but attempted to appease his brother by surrendering the office of great chamberlain (a lucrative one involving custodianship of royal lands) to John Dudley, the new Earl of Warwick, who in turn resigned the office of lord high admiral in favor of Thomas Seymour. But Seymour was not at all satisfied, turning his attention and energy not to his new naval responsibilities but to securing the kinds of honors to which he thought himself entitled. Later in the year, when Somerset and Dudley went north to resume the war on the Scots, Seymour remained behind in London to make mischief in his brother's absence and pay court to Dowager Queen Catherine, with whom he had had a budding romance years before until the king took an interest in the lady.

A more pressing problem emerged in the person of Thomas Wriothesley, lord chancellor and new Earl of Southampton. During the last half-decade of Henry's reign Wriothesley had been one of the chief instruments through whom the king discouraged religious innovation and tried to achieve a national uniformity based on the kind of conservatism set forth in the Six Articles. He himself was as conservative a major figure as was to be found on the Regency Council, and though he had offered no objections to Somerset's appointment as lord protector (his share in the "unfulfilled gifts" must have helped to make him cooperative), soon thereafter he began to make a nuisance of himself. He insisted that there should be no significant departures from the terms of the late king's will and that no religious reforms should be undertaken until the new king reached his maturity and could act in his own right. What gave particular offense was his insistence that Somerset must—as had been stipulated when he became lord protector—take no action without the approval of a majority of the council.

Somerset had no intention of accepting any of these strictures, but he quickly ran up against a complication. Wriothesley, as chancellor, had custody of the king's Great Seal, without which no order that Somerset might issue or have issued over the king's signature could be binding. And, being a strong-willed politician who knew how to use the powers of his office to good advantage, Wriothesley would allow no use of the seal in matters of which he did not approve. The solution proved to be relatively simple. Judges subservient to Somerset declared Wriothesley guilty of having abused his office. (The charge was transparently trumped up; Wriothesley was technically guilty, but only of the previously acceptable practice of delegating judicial responsibilities that his duties at court left him with no time to perform.) He was stripped of his office and placed under arrest. The newly ennobled Richard Lord Rich, ready as always to do whatever was required by whoever was in power, was dispatched to collect the seal. Somerset then used the seal to stamp and thereby make official a letter of patent, signed by his nephew the king, by which he was given the power to appoint and remove members of the Privy Council, into which the Regency Council was now absorbed. He also empowered himself to assemble the council (or just as important, decline to assemble it) "as he shall think meet . . . from time to time."

This was all Somerset needed to begin exercising the authority of a king. He secured Rich's appointment as chancellor, thinking that this would ensure his control of the Great Seal. He began to live in royal fashion, ordering that two gold maces be carried before him wherever he went. That his rule would be less savage than Henry's was signaled when Wriothesley was freed, excused from paying the heavy fine that had been levied against him, and allowed to keep most of the winnings of his long career at court. He was even allowed to return to the council where, while taking care not to go so far as to put himself at risk, he continued to resist the majority's efforts to shift the church in a markedly evangelical direction.

At the center of all this turmoil, sometimes seen but almost never heard, was the small figure of King Edward VI. He was a solitary figure: a boy who had never known a mother, had grown up worshipping a distant father who appeared to be the mightiest man in the world, and had spent most of his life in a household separate from those of his father and two half-sisters. Though Catherine Parr appears to have been an attentive and even affectionate stepmother, soon after Henry's death her attention was drawn in other directions. Edward was a lad of above-average intelligence (all the Tudors were that), if not necessarily the prodigious genius that some of his tutors and courtiers claimed. He was also an exceptionally conscientious child, so serious about the rigorous course of study to which he was subjected from the earliest possible age and his responsibilities as a great king's heir that in learning about his upbringing one begins to wish for more evidence of play, and playfulness. Probably it would have been better, if only for Edward himself, if he had been less obedient to the learned men who were always on hand to direct his development into a great, good, and wise ruler worthy of his father. If he had been given more time and space in which to be a child.

His coronation, the first of a king of England in nearly four decades, was an outsize event, grandiose but rather sadly overwhelming for a child to have to endure alone. It was preceded, three weeks after Henry's death and just days after his embalmed corpse had been lowered into a crypt beneath the floor of St. George's Chapel at Windsor Castle, by a four-hour parade during which the new king, dressed in cloth of silver and gold and mounted on a horse draped with satin and pearls, was put on display for the people of the metropolis. The next day, February 20, Edward entered Westminster Abbey at the center of a vast procession, a bishop flanking him on one side and an earl on the other, the long train of his crimson robe carried by John Dudley, William Parr, and his uncle Thomas Seymour. There he was anointed king. The ceremony was conducted according to a formula that had been used on every such occasion since 1375. Cranmer, however, in his capacity of master of ceremonies, had introduced changes underscoring the new powers that Henry VIII had gathered to the Crown and the fact that for the first time in history a new king was becoming not only head of state but also head of the church. A traditional promise to respect the laws and liberties of the English people was expunged from the coronation oath; henceforth the king would decide which laws and liberties to grant and which to deny. "Peace and concord" were promised to the church and the people but not, as in the past, to the clergy; now it was for the king to decide whether the clergy deserved peace. Somerset and Cranmer together placed three crowns in succession on Edward's head—one each for England, France, and Ireland, Henry VIII having been the first English king to fashion himself king of Ireland. Then all the bishops and nobles came forward in pairs to pay homage, lowering themselves to their knees and swearing in unison to be loyal. Finally Cranmer delivered a sermon that he addressed not to the whole assembly but to Edward alone. The boy was told that nothing he had just sworn should be interpreted as limiting the right that God had bestowed on him to rule in whatever way he thought best. There was a half-concealed message in this, and it was unmistakably evangelical: the king was not bound by law. Emphatically he was not bound by such laws as Henry VIII's Six Articles. To the extent that the king was bound by anything, Cranmer said, he was bound by a duty that was primarily religious, and religious in an evangelical way. It was, "as God's viceregent and Christ's vicar, to see that God be worshipped and idolatry be destroyed; that the tyranny of the bishop of Rome be banished and images be removed." Cranmer, who by this time had abandoned whatever belief he might once have had in transubstantiation, then went through the elaborate motions of the traditional solemn high mass.

He had placed a heavy burden on the shoulders of a boy of nine, one that many normal and healthy boys might have cheerfully ignored. But the melancholy fact is that Edward regarded such matters with a solemnity that would have seemed more fitting in a pious cleric deep into middle age. His early education, under the supervision first of his stepmother Catherine Parr and then, from age six, of Archbishop Cranmer, had provided intense exposure to evangelical doctrine along with inoculation against what he was taught to see as the monstrous absurdities of the old religion. Cranmer placed him in the hands of scholars as accomplished and committed as any that evangelical England had produced up to that time. Hugh Latimer, who in 1539 had lost his position as bishop of Worcester because his insistence on radical reform had put him too far out of step with Henry's orthodoxy, was brought to court soon after Edward became king. From a special pulpit installed for the purpose, he delivered hour-long sermons that Edward dutifully watched from one of the windows of his privy chamber, taking detailed notes. The boy embraced what he was taught, forming firm opinions on immensely complex subjects at a prodigiously early age. It is more pathetic than impressive to see him, at age ten, producing under the approving eyes of his tutors a lengthy treatise in which he considers the claims of the pope to headship over the church and concludes not only that these claims are invalid but that the bishop of Rome is "the true son of the devil, a bad man, an Antichrist and an abominable tyrant." By this time he was certain, as he would remain for the rest of his life, that the religion of his father with its seven sacraments and toleration of images and purgatory and free will was nearly as great an abomination as Roman Catholicism itself. If he rebelled, it was against the traditionalism of his dead father, not against his own mentors.

All of which was entirely acceptable to his uncle Somerset, most of whose supporters in the court and council were zealous reformers genuinely committed to the evangelical cause. The coronation of the new king had been a thrilling event for these people, promising an outlet for their contemptuous opinion of the old dogmas and an opportunity to cast off the dead weight of the past in favor of something cleaner, something capable of remaking the world. They wanted a religious revolution vastly more ambitious than anything Henry VIII had attempted, a replacement of idols and false sacraments and empty superstitious practices with the direct authority of Scripture. If they also had a hearty appetite for whatever riches it might still be possible to extract from the church, that did not mean they were necessarily less than sincere in their convictions.

They faced formidable obstacles—so much so that, in spite of controlling the person of the king and the principal levers of power in both

state and church, they continued to think of themselves as a beleaguered and even oppressed minority. Virtually all the laws and pronouncements of Henry VIII were against them: the Six Articles, the
King's Book, and the heresy statutes that put their lives at risk at least
theoretically every time they gave voice to what they believed. Most of
the people of England, even most of the clergy, had no liking for their
ideas. Throughout the first year of the new reign, therefore, they had to
proceed carefully. They began the process of imposing their theology
on the kingdom, but always with an eye to keeping their adversaries off
balance. When accused of preaching what was unlawful, they replied in-
genuously that they were merely saying what the late king had believed
at the time of his death but had not lived long enough to express in law.
To complaints that they were advocating change of a kind that should
not be attempted before Edward came of age, they responded in tones
of innocence that they were doing no such thing—that they accepted
the Six Articles as the law of the land and recognized that heresy remained a capital crime. Meanwhile they were actively carrying out their
revolution, but by such small steps that it was difficult for the traditionalists to know where to lay down a challenge. Even as they advanced
their agenda, the evangelicals continued to insist that they wanted nothing more than peace and continuity and the unity of the church.

That they actually wanted nothing of the kind first became plain in
August 1547, seven months after the old king's death, when Somerset
sent official "visitors" to every diocese. These representatives of the
Crown delivered to the bishops a set of sermons to be read in every
church every Sunday. This was provocative: the sermons were the work
of Cranmer, who by now had abandoned any pretense of believing
what he had professed during the reign of his master Henry, and their
content was in direct contradiction not only to Henry's Articles but to
what an overwhelming majority of the clergy and indeed the population still believed. Even more provocatively, the visitors had oral instructions that went far beyond their written commissions, and in pursuit of
those instructions they launched a campaign—shocking to most people
in every part of the country—of physical destruction. Magnificent
stained-glass windows, an irreplaceable part of England's medieval
legacy, were condemned as idolatrous and smashed to bits. The same
thing happened to statuary, to paintings, and to the ancient adornments

of church buildings everywhere. Whole libraries of Latin works, even the library of Oxford University, were put to the torch. Barbaric as such acts may seem today, to the radical evangelicals they were something to be celebrated, a necessary step in freeing England from a filthily papist past.

For Stephen Gardiner, the disgraced bishop of Winchester, all this was too much to be borne. Protesting that the Cranmer sermons contradicted the doctrines of the English church as established by Parliament under the late king, he accused the archbishop of contradicting what he himself had claimed to believe when Henry was alive. For this he was thrown into prison; clearly the evangelicals no longer saw any point in trying to seem conciliatory. Neither Somerset nor Cranmer could afford to have Gardiner at liberty to rally the forces of tradition when a new Parliament was called later in the year. The evangelicals had big plans for that Parliament—plans that Gardiner was likely to oppose to his last breath.

First, however, Somerset wanted to deal with Scotland, which had been almost an obsession for him since his two invasions in the closing years of Henry's reign. Scotland at this time was in a state approaching civil war, with an evangelical faction friendly to England fighting a Catholic, pro-French faction for control of Edinburgh and custody of Queen Mary, still a child of four. Somerset assembled an army of twenty thousand men, many of them mercenaries recruited at great cost from distant parts of Europe, and started north with John Dudley as his second in command. They crossed the River Tweed early in September, and on the tenth day of that month they met and destroyed the Scottish defenders at the Battle of Pinkie, a rout that ended in the slaughter of nearly ten thousand Scots. Edinburgh remained in the hands of England's enemies, however, and Somerset surprised those enemies and his own followers by declining to exploit the tremendous advantage his victory had given him. Instead he allowed his troops four days of pillaging and then hurried back to London.

He was now England's greatest living military hero in addition to having control of the Crown, Parliament, and the church. England was his to do with as he chose. It was also his to lose. Everything now depended upon his ability to manage what fate and his own boldness had put into his hands.

INSTRUMENTS OF POWER

THE REGENCY COUNCIL THAT HENRY VIII HAD CREATED TO manage England until the boy Edward grew up was a new variation—the latest of many variations—on an old, old theme. The rulers of England had always had councils, weak kings no less than strong ones all the way back to Saxon times, but the makeup and importance of those councils had varied drastically from one reign to the next. The idea of the royal council was a kind of blank slate on which each generation was free to write as it chose according to its own circumstances.

Why councils at all? Because history offers no examples of leaders of nations, even tyrannical leaders of nations, who were able to survive without finding competent advisers and listening to them, sharing some portion of their power with *somebody* and accepting the fact that, no matter how much they may have wanted to do everything themselves, that was simply impossible. For many hundreds of years, until the evolution of more modern instruments of government, royal councils were the best mechanisms available for dealing with that reality.

Even that flinty old killer William the Conqueror, after he crossed over from Normandy in 1066 and by brute force turned the whole of England into his personal property, immediately put a council in place. The most important men in the kingdom sat on it—the bishops, the half-civilized warlords who were William's tenants-in-chief—but everyone understood that it was the *king's* creature and existed to do his bidding. That would remain the rule for more than half a millennium, and England would depart from it only when something was deeply, seriously wrong. When the king was insane, for example, or otherwise unable to maintain control. Or when he was, like Edward VI, simply too young to take command.

The earliest Norman councils did everything: executed the king's orders, heard and passed judgment on complaints and appeals, settled disputes, and offered as much advice as the king was willing to take. But as the population grew and the economy developed and society grew more complicated, such a workload became unmanageable. Various functions were spun off one by one—an exchequer to manage the Crown's money, courts for the handling of different kinds of cases—and turned into governmental departments. One function, however, was never spun off: that of advising the king, of having a voice when policy was being decided. That was what made a seat on the council a prize. Always in principle and almost always in fact, being a councilor meant having access to the king, being able to speak directly with the king, having a chance to influence the king and win his favor.

The value of this access fluctuated, increasing at times to the point where councils became more powerful than the monarchs they formally served. This happened late in the fourteenth century, after Richard II came to the throne as a half-grown boy, and again in the fifteenth during the reign of Henry VI, the half-brother of Edmund and Jasper Tudor, who became king as an infant and even when grown was too weak a character to take back control of the council from magnates who were using it to bend the government and the judicial system to their own advantage.

Under the Tudors, the flexibility of government by council was put to new tests and not found wanting. In the course of his twenty-four-year reign the wily Henry VII appointed upward of 150 men to his council, but his doing so was an exercise in public relations intended to win the support of different interest groups—merchants, lawyers, soldiers—by allowing them to think that they were represented at the highest level. Real power was limited to an inner circle of perhaps a dozen men, many of them officers of the royal household and therefore the king's dependents, and council meetings were typically attended by only between six and ten members. Henry VII used the council's adaptability to devise a quick and simple solution to one of the most serious problems inherited from the Yorkists: England's sclerotic, cumbersome, and too-often-corrupt courts of law. He resurrected the council's aboriginal judicial function, encouraging subjects to bring their suits to it with the promise of receiving an impartial hearing at tolerable cost. Thus the councilors' traditional meeting place, the room at Westminster called the Star Chamber because of the decorations on its ceiling, became a famous and, for a long time, a respected source of royal justice. The lord chan-

cellor, as the Court of the Star Chamber's presiding officer, would gradually be so burdened with its caseload that he was unable to function as
the king's chief minister as in the past and became what he is today:
Britain's senior law officer.

We saw earlier how young Henry VIII, when he first became king,
had no interest in the routines of administration and so left the business
of governing in the hands of his father's councilors, and how this ended
when Thomas Wolsey became chancellor and drew the reins of power
into his own hands. Throughout the decade and a half of Wolsey's ascendancy the council sank into unimportance, a development much
resented by those nobles and others who felt excluded from decision-
making. The workaholic Wolsey performed the considerable feat, never
to be repeated by his successors, of simultaneously overseeing both the
entire government *and* the courts, continuing to preside at sessions of
the Star Chamber and giving high priority to improving the delivery of
justice to ordinary subjects. On the negative side, he displayed an occasional tendency to use the Court of the Star Chamber as an instrument
of discipline, a political weapon with which to punish people perceived
as enemies. A century on, under the next dynasty, this tendency would
become so pronounced that hatred for the court finally caused it to be
destroyed.

Another action of Wolsey's that merits attention in this connection is
his unprecedented capture of all the royal seals, the coinlike bas-relief
carved figures that, when pressed into a blob of hot wax, certified the au-
thenticity of documents such as grants, writs, warrants, subpoenas, and
correspondence. In becoming chancellor, the cardinal had automatically taken custody of the king's Great Seal, which since its origins in
pre-Conquest times had become so essential to the operations of government that its removal from the chancery at Westminster was forbidden.
This had led to the creation of what was called the Privy Seal; it was
smaller, simpler (it showed the king's arms rather than his picture), lawfully transportable, and so useful to the peripatetic monarchs of the Middle Ages that by the early fourteenth century its official keeper was one
of the court's most important members. As administrative machinery was
erected even around the Privy Seal, again the need arose for something
simpler. Hence the signet, at first a "secret" seal, which was kept by the
king's secretary and by the advent of the Tudors was even more impor-

tant than the older, grander seals in the origination and authentication of important documents. It is a measure of Wolsey's unprecedented power that he became the first minister ever to achieve control of all three seals and thus of every item of official business.

It was however Thomas Cromwell, not Wolsey, who broke the patterns of the past and found genuinely new uses for old institutions including the council. He was content to allow Thomas More and then his own protégé Thomas Audley to occupy the office of lord chancellor and disappear into its judicial responsibilities. Instead he transformed the unencumbered position of king's principal secretary into a power base from which he made himself chief executive and, on the king's behalf, managed everything from the treasury to the church, from diplomacy to military affairs. Though Cromwell was far too canny to ignore the seals—as secretary he had possession of the signet, and in 1536 he took over the office of Lord Privy Seal from the ruined Thomas Boleyn—he demanded obedience on the basis of his own signature and by doing so allowed the use of seals to become an almost empty formality.

It was however in his use of the Royal Council that Cromwell displayed the full reach of his political genius. Wolsey had treated the council much as he treated Parliament: as a nuisance to be ignored when possible, bullied when necessary. Cromwell, by contrast, saw that the council, like Parliament, could be shaped into a tool of enormous value. In the mid-1530s he carved out of Henry VIII's excessively large and essentially useless council what would become one of the principal institutions of government: a *Privy Council* of purposely limited size (only nineteen members in the beginning and thereafter never many more than that). This new council was no longer too big to function but did have enough size to carry an important load of work. And it was, most importantly, a *working* council: each of its members brought either influence or special expertise to the table, and various members were put in charge of various activities—always, of course, under Cromwell's careful supervision—almost like a modern cabinet. In selecting the membership Cromwell strove for, and to a considerable extent achieved, a balance of power among the leading factions. Cranmer sat as representative of the religious reformers, Gardiner and Tunstal for the conservatives. There were members of the ancient nobility—the Duke of Norfolk, the Earl of Sussex—and of families recently raised to the peerage. Among the commoners were representatives of the old landowning gentry and men (solicitor-general Sir Richard Rich being once again among the favored) who had risen from obscure origins to positions of prominence in the royal service. Together they formed an instrument beautifully engineered to perform exactly as Cromwell, and the king, desired.

When Cromwell fell and no one emerged to take his place, the Privy Council simultaneously grew in importance and became the cockpit within which the factions suddenly found themselves free to fight for dominance. And fight they did, with the results we saw in the last chapter: by the start of Edward's reign, chiefly as a result of King Henry's choices, the evangelicals had overcome long odds and routed the conservatives. Norfolk was in prison, Gardiner was in prison, and Tunstal and his kind had been utterly marginalized. The kingdom and the future were in the hands of the new and evangelically inclined nobility of whom Edward Seymour had made himself chief. The power of that new nobility, in turn, was rooted in the council.

18

England's Second Reformation

Despite the Duke of Somerset's great victory at Pinkie—it might be just as fair to say *because of* that victory, or because of Somerset's failure to follow up on his success—Scotland remained as big a headache as it had ever been. The death of Henry VIII had been followed, just weeks later, by that of his old friend and rival and enemy Francis I. In his final days, enfeebled by syphilis and wandering miserably from palace to palace in search of a peace that he seemed unable to find, the king of France had displayed not only a willingness to come to terms with the English but a kind of paternal solicitude for the child who now wore England's crown. At the end he seemed accepting even of the Treaty of Greenwich, by means of which Henry had provided for the marriage of Edward VI to Mary, Queen of Scots, and the eventual union of England and Scotland.

Francis's son, Henry II, was far less amenable. He saw what his father would have had no difficulty seeing when he was younger and more vital: that a Scotland unfriendly to England was a precious asset, a back door through which to threaten the English whenever they came out of their front door to threaten France. Henry disavowed the Greenwich agreement, and when the Scots asked for his help after Pinkie he sent shiploads of fighting men. His troops were soon making life a misery for the forces that Somerset had positioned in Scottish lowland garrisons, and his fleet took the five-year-old Scottish queen to France, where she was soon betrothed to the heir to the throne and Henry could proudly declare that "France and Scotland are now one." Fighting continued in the border country between England and Scotland, but the whole situation had been turned into a humiliation for England and especially for Somerset, whose judgment was inevitably brought into question.

But Somerset clung stubbornly to his idea of controlling Scotland by maintaining a string of fortresses there, and in doing so he destroyed any possibility of coming to grips with the financial and economic problems inherited from Henry VIII. The magnitude of his blunder is evident in a few numbers. In the six years following Henry VIII's death, a total of £335,000 was raised through parliamentary taxation, but during just the first three of those years Somerset's government spent £580,000 on its campaign to subdue Scotland—£350,000 on manpower alone. Somerset found it necessary to import mercenaries—nearly 7,500 of them, by common reckoning—from Ireland, Spain, Germany, and Italy, even from Hungary and Albania. The treasury being empty and the Crown deep in debt when Somerset became protector, financing his wars (not only in Scotland but also in France, where the virtually useless city of Boulogne could be defended only at great expense) was totally beyond the Crown's capacity. Thus the duke found himself unable to reverse Henry's debasement of the coinage and in fact was driven to worsen the problem, skimming £537,000 from the mint in four years. The hundreds of thousands of additional pounds needed to meet the government's obligations were secured through the plundering of pockets of church wealth that had remained untouched until now (more about that shortly), extensive sales of Crown lands, and further borrowing at the high rates of interest that lenders demanded because of the sorry state of the treasury and the shriveling value of English coins.

Another problem that the lord protector encountered, one far less avoidable than the conflicts with Scotland and France but at least as dangerous, was the kingdom's ever-more-serious division along religious lines. Statistical precision is impossible, but at midcentury perhaps 20 percent of the population of London was in some meaningful sense evangelical, while the new religion had scarcely penetrated many other parts of the kingdom. Though radical reformers from Cranmer down had the approval of the Somerset faction and were therefore increasingly influential in the setting of Crown policy, and though the dispersion of the monastic lands was creating a new landowning gentry class that would have felt threatened by any move in the direction of Rome, the Pilgrimage of Grace had demonstrated the dangers of imprudently aggressive reform. The fall of Norfolk and Gardiner—both remained in prison—had sealed the ascendancy of the evangelicals, who responded to their victory not with satisfaction but with redoubled determination to rid the kingdom of papistry. Having supported Edward Seymour when he set out to make himself protector, governor, and duke, they now demanded to be repaid. And what they wanted was the dismantling of all the legal defenses that King Henry had erected around traditional doctrine. One of Somerset's greatest challenges was to maintain the support of his radical allies without sparking a reaction akin to the Pilgrimage of Grace.

He proved unequal to the task. What he lacked above all was firmness—the ability to face his problems cleanly and decisively, lay down clear policies, and thereby secure the acquiescence if not the active support of people who might themselves have preferred a different course. He appears to have believed that it was possible to be all things to all people. As a result, he left uncertainty in his wake and allowed difficulties that might have been dispatched quickly to linger and grow worse.

His brother Thomas was quick to exploit his weakness. In the first weeks of the protectorate, smarting from Somerset's failure to bestow upon him offices and honors commensurate with what he saw as his deserts, the fortunate but sullenly ungrateful Baron Seymour of Sudeley set out to advance himself through matrimony. According to various reports he set his sights on Princess Mary (now a mature woman and unlikely to have any interest in an upstart evangelical), on Princess Elizabeth (barely more than a child, quite young enough to be impressed), and even on poor Anne of Cleves, now living quietly on her estates and enjoying her status as a peripheral member of the royal family. He found, however, that his best prospects lay with the Dowager Queen Catherine Parr, whom he probably would have married years earlier if the king had not swept her up first. Catherine for her part was eager enough: childless after three marriages (all of them to men much older than herself), yoked most recently to a fat, sick, and prematurely aged king whose every word and act was overhung with menace, she must have seen in the virile, wolflike Seymour a last chance for something like a normal life. Soon he was paying secret visits to her residence, arriving late at night and slipping away quietly before sunrise.

When Somerset learned of his brother's activities, he reacted angrily, declaring that neither of them was a suitable mate for the daughters or widows of kings. The council, too, found the proposed marriage to be unthinkable. But Seymour had been currying favor with his nephew the king, supplying him with money—as much as £40 at a time—with which he could confer gifts on the preachers, musicians, and other retainers to whom he wished to show favor. At Seymour's direction, Edward wrote a letter worded, cleverly, to suggest that he was *asking* Catherine to take his uncle as her husband—not only expressing his approval but allowing the queen to believe that if she agreed she would be doing her sovereign a favor.

Under this canopy of royal protection the wedding was allowed to take place, but it solved little. Soon the Seymours' wives—one a duchess and wife of the lord protector, the other a former queen but now the spouse of a mere baron—were squabbling over which should have precedence at court. Seymour, insatiable, took control of his bride's considerable wealth and tried to resist when she was ordered to return the jewels that Henry had given her during their marriage. He also began scheming to take from his brother the title of governor of the king's body, and again he was able to make the king his accomplice. This led to his being called before the council and accused of plotting to overthrow the government. He refused to recognize the council's authority until threatened with arrest, at which point his nerve failed him and he acknowledged that he had in fact done wrong.

His brother the duke, who might have spared both of them much future grief by seeing to it that Seymour was thoroughly chastised, instead not only forgave him but arranged for his income to be increased by £800. It is understandable if the younger brother came away from the episode believing that, almost whatever he did, the consequences would turn out to be greatly to his advantage. He was soon back at his old tricks, looking for ways to make himself more important and his brother less. When he and Catherine, who was now pregnant, took Princess Elizabeth into their household, Seymour was soon raising eyebrows by entering the girl's bedchamber when she was still in her nightclothes and engaging in intimacies that went at least as far as playful slaps on her backside. The onetime queen, told of these high jinks, made light of them, but a storm erupted when she found the pair embracing. The rumor mill said that Seymour regretted marrying the king's widow when he might have had a bride of royal blood. It said, too, that Elizabeth was not averse to her host's advances.

When Parliament convened late in 1547, Somerset and the council presented it with a legislative agenda that was largely religious in content and aimed primarily at dismantling Henry VIII's church. The Act of Six Articles, which the late king had labored to make a definitive statement of his theology, was repealed outright, as was the Act for Advancement of True Religion, which had offended the evangelicals by curtailing freedom to read the Bible. Also expunged were every one of the many felonies created during Henry's reign, every one of his heresy laws, every treason law passed in the two centuries since the reign of Edward III, and the act that had given royal proclamations the force and legitimacy of parliamentary statutes. It was a thorough housecleaning, but it is not plausibly interpreted as a birth of religious liberty. Its effect was to free Cranmer and his fellow evangelicals not merely to preach and worship as they wished but to suppress all beliefs and practices of which they disapproved. One crucial piece of Henrician orthodoxy remained intact: it was still a capital crime to deny that the king was supreme head of the church.

But with the evangelicals now dominant, the young king supportive of everything they were doing, and England becoming a haven for continental reformers who would have risked their lives by entering the kingdom during the previous reign, supremacy now meant much more than separation from Rome. Now it was a tool to be used in the destruction of almost everything that remained of the old religion. Cranmer, confident of the backing of the lord protector and the king, forbade ceremonies that had been part of community life in England for so long that to most people they seemed eternal: the carrying and blessing of candles on Candlemas Day, for example, and of ashes on Ash Wednesday and palms on Palm Sunday. King Henry himself had inveighed against religious images—statues, pictures, whatever—where these were deemed to have become objects of worship, but few such images had been destroyed. Cranmer now ordered their wholesale removal. It was one of the earliest outbreaks of Puritanism in England, though the word *Puritan* had not yet been coined.

The most notorious act of the Parliament of 1547, one that Henry probably would have admired, transferred to the Crown two of the few repositories of church wealth not already expropriated: the endowments of chantries (small chapels that over the centuries had been established in almost incalculable numbers for the purpose of offering prayers for the dead) and the assets of guilds, fraternal associations of individuals and families designed to provide benefits such as burial insurance and funding for schools and charitable activities. By any reasonable reckoning the property of the chantries—much of it income-generating land—was private. If prayers for the dead made no sense to people with no belief in purgatory, the Crown's claim on the money that generations of donors had provided for the saying of such prayers (as Henry VIII himself had done, on a characteristically lavish scale, in anticipation of his own demise) made even less. To argue that the property of the guilds did not belong to their members, or that the existence of the guilds was not of significant benefit both to their members and to the community, was equally implausible. The confiscation bill, when presented to Parliament, was defended as a way of making funds available for education, the relief of the poor, and the support of vicars and preachers. What had already happened to the wealth of the monasteries made such arguments so utterly incredible that even Cranmer objected at first, but when he saw which way the political winds were blowing he swiftly fell silent. The government was desperate for cash as usual, everyone from the lord protector down to the lowliest member of Parliament was eager for a share in fresh spoils, and cities that objected vigorously were bought off with promises of special exemption.

And so the bill passed. Commissioners rushed out to gather the gold and silver plate belonging to the chantries and deliver it to the mint to be melted down, blended with base metals, and thus converted into still more of the debased currency with which the government was—just barely—fending off bankruptcy. Much chantry and guild land went the way monastic land had gone earlier: into the possession of the Crown, then out again either to buyers or to those influential enough to claim such munificent gifts. All this was accomplished by the same Parliament that, as noted earlier, enacted a statute providing for the branding and enslavement of anyone found guilty of vagrancy. The English Reformation was hardening into the shape that would one day cause G. K. Chesterton, in his *Short History of England,* to call it "the revolt of the rich." The target of this revolt was not established authority but the common people, the poorest definitely included.

Once Parliament had finished its business, the authorities deemed it safe to release Stephen Gardiner from prison. But the bishop refused to behave himself; the abrupt swerve toward evangelicalism that began with the new reign had exhausted his considerable reserves of malleability. After his release he remained such an outspokenly disgruntled critic of this latest religious settlement that he was called before the council, of which he had long been a leading member. There he was ordered to appear outside St. Paul's Cathedral on an appointed day and, in the presence of King Edward, deliver a sermon expressing his acceptance of the latest official orthodoxy. He was given a script and invited to use it instead of drafting his own, but he refused. Invited to show his text to the council before delivering it, he again refused, promising however that he would deal with the subjects that the council had prescribed. He was admonished to say nothing that could be considered controversial, but his sermon when he delivered it proved to be exactly what the council least wanted: an explanation of the traditional understanding of the mass and the Eucharist—possibly the first time in his life that Edward had been exposed to such ideas. The young king must have been horrified by such compelling evidence that the Antichrist had not yet been expelled from England.

Gardiner, accused of disobeying his instructions, replied that what he had said could not possibly be considered controversial because it expressed the beliefs of their late, great king and in fact was exactly what Cranmer himself had often preached during Henry's life. Cranmer, outwitted, was no more amused than the king. Gardiner was sent back to prison, this time to stay. The number of bishops who followed his lead was surprisingly large in light of how he had been treated and how few had followed John Fisher less than two decades before; the innovations introduced under Somerset's protectorate proved to be too radical even for many who had accepted the separation from Rome. Edmund Bonner was stripped of the see of London and joined Gardiner in prison. The bishops of Chichester, Durham, Exeter, and Worcester also were removed. Their dioceses, before successors were appointed, were stripped of much of their income.

But blood was no longer flowing. The English reign of terror was, at least for the time being, at an end. This has to be attributed to Somerset, who with all his faults (which were numerous and serious enough) was utterly lacking in the bloodthirstiness of the late king. He was scarcely less proud or greedy than Henry, and he became increasingly autocratic as problems pressed in on him, but he was never viciously and rarely unnecessarily cruel. This is perhaps the most attractive feature of his complex, almost inscrutable personality. It may also—one hesitates to say such a thing, because it can seem to excuse the enormities of Henry VIII's reign—have been the most serious of his weaknesses. He lacked the toughness that his situation required.

He may also have lacked the needed intelligence. This would explain the tenacity with which he persisted in his bellicose approach to Scotland, where there was nothing to be gained after the removal of the child Mary Stuart to France, and his determination not to allow the French to have Boulogne in spite of the ruinous cost of defending it. It would also explain his fumbling and ill-conceived efforts to deal with England's economic problems, notably the growing discontent over high inflation and declining wages. Somerset took a simplistic view of the economy, believing that the worst of its ills were rooted in the practice of enclosures, which had first become a cause of unrest long before he was born. Wolsey and Cromwell among others had attempted to stop them, but the profits of the wool and cloth trade made conversion difficult to resist and political power lay in the hands of those who owned the land.

Somerset decided to give it another try. He sent out commissioners to enforce the laws against enclosure and to look for evidence of corruption in their enforcement. Some of these commissioners were evangelists of a crusading bent, men committed not just to law enforcement but to creating a new and ideal England in which the pursuit of money would be replaced by brotherly love. Though they accomplished little or nothing in practical terms, the speeches in which they condemned the greed of the rich excited hopes and inflamed resentments among the common folk. This had different effects at different levels of society.

Among the working poor, whose livelihoods were being jeopardized by changes in rural life of which the enclosures were just one aspect, Somerset came to be known as "the good duke," the champion of the oppressed. There were scattered riots and attacks on property by mobs who thought their actions would be approved by the lord protector. The nobility and gentlemen farmers, the greatest of whom owned tens of thousands of sheep, naturally took a drastically different view. They were alarmed by the disturbances and angered by the protector's role in fomenting them. They were angered, too, by a new tax on sheep and wool—a government attempt to encourage a return to the growing of crops. If the duke's motives were noble, if he was really motivated by a desire to relieve the suffering of the rural poor, his actions were ineffectual. If on the other hand his intention was to make himself widely popular, he was successful in the most immediate sense but ultimately deeply foolish. The same gestures with which he was winning the affection of the impotent were costing him the trust of the classes with real power, the ones he needed in order to survive. Those classes would not have been impressed by expressions of sympathy for the peasantry under any circumstances, but when such expressions came from an upstart duke who was using his position to make himself the greatest private landowner in England, they could only snort in derision. Somerset was certainly vulnerable on that score. Ownership of a "manor"—the term refers to an estate of indeterminate size, originally large enough for the support of a feudal lord and his retinue—was generally sufficient to put a family well up among the gentry. Somerset, in just a few years as protector, helped himself to more than two hundred manors.

A kingdom broken into religious factions was now in danger of class warfare as well—or so it seemed, at least, to many of those with most to lose—and Somerset responded as indecisive men in positions of authority often will: by trying to please everyone. Arriving at some new kind of unity continued to appear as necessary as it had under Henry VIII, though that goal would remain unachievable as long as the government tried to enforce beliefs that most of the population found incomprehensible if not repugnant. Cranmer was instructed to bridge the gap between the conservatives and the radicals by doing something that no one could possibly have done in mid-sixteenth-century England—produce "one convenient and meet order, rite and fashion of Common

Prayer" that everyone in the kingdom could accept. It was probably in-evitable that the result—the first version of the Book of Common Prayer, a volume of prayers and church services so ambiguous in its treatment of controversial questions that no one was satisfied but not even the conservatives could find reason to reject it outright—led to ran-corous debate among the bishops and in Parliament. (The very fact that the conservatives were *not* grievously offended evidently persuaded the evangelicals that what Cranmer had produced could not possibly be ac-ceptable.) Unity, in any case, was not achieved. Cranmer's prayers (beau-tiful compositions by one of the supreme masters of English prose) were embedded in a new Act of Uniformity, but the fact that they were in English rather than Latin ensured a skeptical reception in many places. Stiff penalties for failure to use the new service added resent-ment to the brew. An uneasy sense that all the old ways were under di-rect attack by people determined to force a religious revolution was heightened by passage of a statute making it lawful for clergymen to marry.

All the chickens came home to roost in 1549. The protector's brother Thomas, who had learned nothing from his earlier escape from the con-sequences of his own recklessness, now intensified almost to the point of insanity his efforts to advance himself at Somerset's expense. When his wife, the former Queen Catherine, died shortly after giving birth in September 1548—inevitably it was rumored that he had poisoned her—Seymour turned his attention back to King Edward's half-sister Eliza-beth. Meanwhile he was taking a cut of the profits of the pirates that it was his duty as lord high admiral to suppress, conspiring with the vice-treasurer of the royal mint to divert a steady stream of gold and silver into their own pockets, and trying so indiscriminately to buy allies that his activities inevitably became widely known. The council had no choice but to respond. Summoned, Seymour declined to appear until a more "convenient" time, thereby making his arrest inevitable. When six weeks of investigation and the interrogation of numerous witnesses re-sulted in a bill of attainder charging him with thirty-three counts of high treason, he haughtily refused to defend himself. In March he was beheaded. Somerset had freed himself of his most relentless enemy, but not necessarily of a terribly dangerous one; Seymour had been too undisciplined, his ambition and resentment too wildly unfocused, to pose a lethal threat. It would have been wiser of the protector to put him in prison and keep him there, or perhaps to exile him. By executing his own brother (or perhaps only by not stopping the council from having him killed, we don't really know), this man who had ended Henry VIII's bloodbath gave his critics an excuse to complain that he no less than the old king was capable of killing anyone. Such a perception could not have alleviated the distrust and fear that he had already aroused among the gentry and the nobles.

None of which might have mattered if the kingdom had not suddenly convulsed in a series of spontaneous uprisings. These were widespread and uncoordinated, communication across long distances still being little more advanced than it had been in the time of the Caesars, and most of them subsided or were put down without leaving much record of their exact cause, who led them, or what they were intended to achieve. Wiltshire, Sussex, Surrey, Hants, Berkshire, Kent, Gloucester, Somerset, Suffolk, Warwick, Essex, Hertford, Leicestershire, Worcester, Rutland—these and other counties experienced violent outbreaks of discontent in May 1549. After a period of quiet, trouble then broke out in Oxfordshire, Norfolk, Devon, and Cornwall. In all these places except Oxfordshire, where enough of the government's Italian mercenaries happened to be on hand to help the local authorities restore order and send a dozen ringleaders to the gallows, the threat quickly assumed dangerous proportions.

In Devon in the far west the trouble has been known ever since as the Prayer Book Rebellion. On Whitsunday (the feast of Pentecost, when the priest traditionally wore white vestments), in obedience to the new Act of Uniformity, the vicar of the church at Sampford Courtenay used Cranmer's new Book of Common Prayer instead of following the customary Latin liturgy. This provoked nothing worse than grumbling at first, but discontent somehow turned overnight into hot anger, and on Monday the townsfolk demanded celebration of the old rites. Resentment must have been smoldering throughout the region, because as word of what had happened spread, people from distant places began converging on Sampford Courtenay. Within a few days a ragtag army of ten thousand had formed and was on the march. An experienced soldier named Humphrey Arundel, a member of a landowning family with no liking for the evangelical reforms, made himself its leader. Lord John

Russell, upon arriving at the head of a body of government troops, realized that he was hopelessly outnumbered and did what the Duke of
Norfolk had done at Doncaster when faced with the Pilgrimage of
Grace: he offered to negotiate. The insurgents presented a list of demands, all of which dealt with religious issues. They wanted a restoration of the Latin Mass, Henry VIII's Six Articles, images in church, and
at least two abbeys in every county. Perhaps most remarkably, and
demonstrating that even in the most remote corners of the kingdom
there could be detailed understanding of England's doctrinal struggles
and the personalities involved, they demanded that Reginald Pole be
brought home from exile and given a place on the Privy Council.

Archbishop Cranmer, when these demands reached London, wrote a
lengthy response that expressed contempt for the rebels and their presumption in addressing such weighty questions. Somerset issued a series
of proclamations. He offered a pardon to every rebel who submitted to
the Crown. He declared that the lands and other possessions of any
rebels who declined to submit could become the property of any loyal
subject who chose to seize them, that anyone responsible for an unlawful assembly was to be put to death, and, rather curiously, that his commissioners were to proceed with the undoing of illegal enclosures while
seeing to it that they themselves were free of guilt. There was no reason
to think that enclosures had been a significant factor in the rising. The
attention that Somerset gave them at this juncture raises questions
about whether he understood what was happening in the west country,
or whether he was sufficiently focused on crushing this challenge to the
council's authority to satisfy men of property. In any event he was lucky.
Instead of advancing eastward into counties where they would almost
certainly have been able to attract recruits, the rebels laid siege to the
city of Exeter, where the Crown's garrison troops held them immobile
for forty days. When a royalist force made up largely of Somerset's German and Italian mercenaries arrived on the scene at last, the rebels were
forced to break off their siege and then were crushed in a series of increasingly lopsided battles. In the end nothing remained but a panicky
mass of fleeing peasants. As many as four thousand men were dead by
the time it was all over, most of them killed in combat but the last executed. A striking feature of the whole episode was the extent to which

the Crown had to use foreign mercenaries to save itself from its own subjects.

Far to the east, in Norfolk, an even bigger rebellion was playing itself out almost within striking distance of London. As if to illustrate the breadth of the problems facing the Crown, this one rose out of complaints completely different from those that had sent the west up in flames. As in Devon, a trivial incident had mushroomed into a general uprising, and this time not ten but twenty thousand men joined. Their demands, like those of the Prayer Book rebels, were essentially conservative, expressive of a yearning to get back to what once had been, but here the focus was economic rather than religious. An extraordinary figure named Robert Kett, a wealthy tanner and landowner, though fifty-seven years old and a grandfather, had not only joined the rebellion but made himself its leader and spokesman. He announced a number of demands: an end to enclosures (a much bigger issue here than in the west country, obviously), a rollback of rents, freedom for bondsmen or serfs (of whom there were few in Norfolk by this time), punishment of corrupt officials, and the replacement of incompetent priests and royal councilors "who confounded things sacred and profane and regarded nothing but the enriching of themselves with the public treasure, that they might riot in it during the public calamity." The last demand was, all too clearly, a challenge to the authority of the council ruling in King Edward's name. When the rebels were offered pardon if they would disperse, Kett replied indignantly that pardons were for criminals, not for subjects loyal to their king. With that, the rebels left themselves with no alternative to a fight to the finish, which is what Kett's Rebellion became.

Somerset, who had preparations for another invasion of Scotland under way at this point, sent William Parr, the late Queen Catherine's brother and now the Marquess of Northampton, to Norfolk with a mixed force of English and Italian troops. Parr, no soldier, made the mistake of leading his men into Norwich, then the largest city in England after London, where the narrow streets made it impossible for them to mass against the rebels. They were bloodily driven out. Somerset meanwhile was increasingly isolating himself, refusing to confer with the other members of the Privy Council and sending out signals that confused rebels and loyalists alike. With one proclamation he condemned destruction of the hedges with which formerly common lands had been enclosed, and with the next he promised pardon to those who committed such acts so long as they expressed sorrow for their deeds. New local risings continued to erupt—in Kent, in Surrey, in Sussex—and increasingly the violence was directed at the property of the wealthy. When Somerset cried out in near-hysteria that the demands of the rebels were "fair and just," his fellow councilors concluded, not unfairly, that he was cracking under pressure.

Norwich remained the epicenter of the crisis, so dangerous by now that Somerset had no choice but to call off his Scottish campaign and summon to center stage the next great figure in the Tudor saga, John Dudley, Earl of Warwick. The reader will recall that at the beginning of the reign of Henry VIII, when the young king and his councilors were eager to dissociate themselves from the unpopularity of Henry VII, the lawyers Edmund Dudley and Richard Empson had been attainted and executed on a ridiculously implausible charge of having plotted to seize control of the government. Their real offense—which probably involved no violation of the law, was largely if not entirely aimed at the acts of bona fide lawbreakers, and certainly was done with Henry VII's knowledge—was to have been their royal master's all-too-visible instruments as he went about the hard business of extracting money from the most prosperous and powerful of his subjects. Edmund Dudley, whose professional and political skills propelled him into the speakership of the House of Commons and a seat on the Royal Council, had accumulated an impressive fortune as reward for his services. He had also boosted his social status by marrying a viscount's daughter. Attainder meant that all the fruits of his success were confiscated by the Crown, so that his widow and their three sons and one daughter, of whom the six-year-old John was the eldest, were ruined.

But just a year after Dudley's execution, his widow entered into an advantageous second marriage with Arthur Plantagenet, an illegitimate son of King Edward IV. A half-brother of Henry VIII's mother, Elizabeth of York, Plantagenet was such an amiable soul that, in spite of being more than twenty years older than the new king, he became one of his closest companions. In short order Edmund Dudley's attainder was posthumously revoked, perhaps a tacit admission that he had never been guilty but more likely an easy way of enriching King Henry's bastard uncle: the part of the Dudley estate that remained in the Crown's possession was awarded not to the dead man's widow or children but to Plantagenet. For reasons unknown to history, the boy John became the ward not of his stepfather but of a soldier and courtier named Edward Guildford. At some point in early adolescence he was admitted to court as a page, a humble first step on the ladder of royal service but one that was naturally much coveted. In due course he made the acquaintance of another young courtier-in-training, Edward Seymour, the future Duke of Somerset.

The lives of the two were intertwined from that point. Both participated in King Henry's invasion of the continent in the early 1520s, and both were knighted in France in 1523. Thereafter Dudley began to advance more rapidly than Seymour in spite of being younger by four years. His success may have been owing at first to the prominence at court of both his stepfather Plantagenet (who by the time of the French war was Viscount Lisle and a member of the council) and his onetime guardian and then father-in-law, Guildford. Later, however, the talent he displayed in martial arts including jousting, one of the king's favorite pastimes, would have brought him to the fore. By 1524 he was an esquire of the body, an honor that Seymour did not achieve until 1531, and in 1534 he became a member of Parliament. He and Seymour were among the first courtiers to affiliate themselves with evangelical reform, becoming associates of Cromwell in doing so. That they were more than casual acquaintances is suggested by the fact that, in 1532 or thereabouts, Dudley signed as guarantor of a loan taken out by Seymour.

The door to wealth and power opened wide for both of them in 1536, but from then on, thanks to his sister Jane's marriage to the king, it was Seymour who took the lead while Dudley followed doggedly in his tracks. When Seymour became an earl and member of the Privy Council, he helped to secure Dudley's appointment as vice-admiral with responsibility for driving pirates from the English Channel. When Seymour took command of King Henry's invasion of Scotland, Dudley assumed the key supporting role of warden-general of the Scottish marches. But Dudley was far more than a mere sycophant riding the crest of his friend's good fortune. In the chronicles of the time he seems to pop up everywhere: as envoy between the king and the Duke of Norfolk during the Pilgrimage of Grace, delivering to Henry the terrible news of Catherine Howard's confession, negotiating treaties, commanding troops. Wherever he was sent, he was effective. In 1543 Dudley (himself a viscount by now, having been given the title vacated by the death of his stepfather) was made lord high admiral and a knight of the garter, and he joined Seymour on the Privy Council. No one could doubt that he had earned these honors. Nor could anyone have been surprised when, after Henry's death, Dudley joined with Seymour in dominating the executors of the king's will, became Earl of Warwick when Seymour made himself Duke of Somerset, and commanded the frontline troops when Somerset again attacked Scotland. In alliance with Cranmer, who looked after their interests where the church was concerned, Somerset and Dudley had control of nearly everything.

But by the summer of 1549, with Kett's rebels in possession of Norwich and disturbances continuing to erupt in many places, it was all in danger of falling apart. Somerset's behavior became more and more erratic, his leadership more and more confused. He appeared to be sinking into a paranoia that made it impossible for him to trust even his oldest allies. In a pair of mistakes either one of which might have been enough to doom him, he distanced himself both from William Paget, the canny master of court politics who had steered him through the first days of the protectorate, and from Dudley. He had refused to restore Dudley to the post of lord high admiral, an assignment Dudley loved and took seriously, after the execution of Thomas Seymour left it vacant. He had forced Dudley to give up Warwick Castle, a demand that made no sense unless he regarded the new Earl of Warwick as too untrustworthy to be left in possession of such a mighty stronghold. Dudley by now was himself an immensely wealthy landowner—that followed more or less automatically from political success in the Tudor kleptocracy—and so had much to lose. Like his whole class, he was alarmed by the rebellions and convinced that Somerset was encouraging and condoning them.

It may have been distrust that caused Somerset to send the inexperienced William Parr rather than Dudley to put down Kett's Rebellion, but whatever the reason it was another of the duke's mistakes. Parr's ignominious expulsion from Norwich left Somerset with no alternative to Dudley unless he were willing to take command himself, which would have destroyed the image that he had built for himself as the special friend of the people. And so Dudley advanced on Norwich with an army of some eight thousand men, a quarter of whom were German cavalry. His performance there confirmed his reputation for courage and resolution and his image as a charismatic commander. Upon arrival he offered the rebels pardon in return for their abandonment of the struggle, and when they refused he attacked, penetrating the city's outer defenses. The city fathers of Norwich, fearful that if the rebels bested Dudley as they had Parr they would go on a rampage of destruction, implored him to take his campaign elsewhere. Instead he gathered his lieutenants and in a moment of high drama kissed his sword, made the sign of the cross, and swore to fight to the death rather than surrender or withdraw. When his subordinates took the same oath, the spines of the townsfolk were stiffened and the fighting resumed. Step by bloody step Dudley's men bludgeoned Kett's out through the city gates and into open country. The rising ended with the last of the rebels surrounded and shouting defiance at a final offer of pardon. They didn't believe the offer to be genuine and said they would rather die fighting than on the gallows. Dudley, in probably the noblest act of his life, rode forward to tell the rebels face-to-face that if they would lay down their arms he would personally guarantee their safety. They decided to believe him, and Dudley was as good as his word. Kett was executed, inevitably, and so were ten other rebel leaders, but that was the end of the killing. When the landowning gentlemen of the neighborhood said they wanted revenge, Dudley asked if they intended to do their own planting after their tenants had been exterminated.

When Dudley returned to London, he was the hero of the governing class, the one man who had proved capable of restoring order. Somerset by contrast, though the rural peasantry continued to revere him, was so discredited in the eyes of the elite, so alienated even from a majority of the Privy Council, that he found it necessary to leave the capital and withdraw with his nephew the king to Hampton Court. There ensued a power struggle of great complexity. After first and briefly allying himself with the religious conservatives, Dudley embarked on a purge of those same conservatives as soon as he no longer needed them, thereby freeing himself of a connection that the young king could never have found acceptable. The turmoil continued for months, with many twists and turns. In October Somerset was deprived of the protectorship and became a prisoner in the Tower. Four months later he secured a pardon by confessing on his knees that he had abused the powers of his office. Still later he was readmitted to the council, and eventually he achieved such an advanced state of rehabilitation that his daughter Anne was married to Dudley's eldest son. Like his late brother, however, Somerset proved incapable of being satisfied. He wanted to be lord protector again, and with that in mind he plotted a marriage between King Edward and another of his daughters, a girl bearing the name of her aunt Jane Seymour. Dudley could not possibly trust him; in practical terms it was becoming difficult even to permit him to remain alive. Dudley arranged to have himself elevated to Duke of Northumberland in October 1551, which put him on an equal footing with Somerset at the apex of English nobility, and a few days later Somerset and his wife and most powerful allies all were arrested. Somerset was charged with having committed treason by planning to capture or murder Dudley, and of having feloniously involved others in his plot. He was tried in the House of Lords and somehow found guilty of the felony but not of treason. The outcome was inevitable in any case: early in 1552 he was beheaded on Tower Hill before a crowd of thousands of his lowborn admirers. The execution was a scene of immense tension, with the onlookers appearing to be on the verge of turning on the authorities.

Thus the king, in early adolescence now, lost a second uncle to the headsman's ax. As with the first of those losses, there is no record of his having been affected emotionally to even the smallest extent. It is not clear that Edward had much capacity for affection, which is understandable in light of how little he appears to have received in the course of his young life and how many of the people to whom he might have been close had gone to their graves. Two of the closest friends of his childhood, the sons of the Duke of Suffolk and the woman he had married after the death of King Henry's sister Mary, had been carried off by the sweating sickness. Another had been sent off to study in France. Of his two half-sisters, he appears to have been closer to Mary, who was old enough to be his mother, but as he matured Edward came to regard even her with a prim and prudish disapproval. Mary insisted on remaining a papist, after all, and therefore, sadly, was damned. Nothing Edward said, nothing he did to pressure her, could deflect Mary from having the old Catholic mass said regularly in her private quarters. That had to be a cause of deep distress to a boy schooled to be very serious about his role as supreme head, and to take nothing so seriously as his duty to show everyone in England the way to the true religion.

John Dudley, now the Duke of Northumberland and rapidly becoming the richest man in England thanks to an appetite for church and Crown lands no less voracious than Somerset's, knew that he needed the king's favor in order to maintain his place. He was adroit at winning that favor and at keeping it. He dared make no claim to the title of lord protector—that had never been held by anyone outside the royal family—but he adopted and made good use of "lord president of the Privy Council." He invited the king to attend council meetings, seeing to it that he was briefed in advance on matters to be discussed and even given words to say at the appropriate times (words that the boy, always conscientious, would memorize for delivery). In so doing he encouraged Edward to believe that he was not merely participating in the governance of the kingdom but beginning to *rule*. At the same time, Dudley embraced the increasingly Calvinistic theology of the king and his tutors. It would be unfair to accuse Dudley of adopting whatever beliefs were most certain to please the king; he had been, as we have seen, a member of the evangelical faction before Edward was born. Still, he was a man of action, and his proper arena was that in which power, not ideas, was in play. It is not impossible that he would have become a conservative if doing so would have helped him to maintain control of king and council.

Be that as it may, King Edward was a sincerely fervent evangelical, and Dudley, by displaying his own fervor in the same cause, found it possible to have things almost entirely his way. And he was never as feckless as Somerset in the exercise of his power. He gave up Boulogne, and though many Englishmen thought the terms he accepted from the French were humiliating, doing so was vastly wiser than continuing a struggle that the kingdom could not afford and could gain nothing from. Peace with France brought peace with Scotland, too, and after a final, desperate devaluation of the coinage (the Crown remained in terrible financial condition), Dudley began taking painful steps to restore it to respectability. The conservatives were required to absorb blow after blow: the venerable Cuthbert Tunstal was losing not only his bishopric but his freedom, the altars were being torn out of every church, and a revised and unmistakably Protestant Book of Common Prayer was made compulsory while attendance at mass became unlawful. But justifications for such acts seemed in good supply. To the victors go the spoils, after all. And there was no reason to think that the conservatives wouldn't have been just as vindictive if given the chance. Religious tolerance remained inconceivable: in sixteenth-century Europe almost no one could imagine a kingdom surviving while its people were separated into camps with incompatible beliefs.

Dudley had achieved everything that an Englishman not of royal blood could ever have imagined achieving. He was rich beyond the dreams of avarice, he was so powerful that no one dared challenge him, and he had five fine and faithful sons to whom to pass on what he was building. And if it all depended on the goodwill of the king, he had every reason to expect that the king, if properly handled, would continue indefinitely to be Dudley's fine and faithful instrument.

It was all perfect. And from the point in the spring of 1552 when the king was briefly bedridden with measles and smallpox, it was all doomed.

CALVIN

WHEN EDWARD VI BECAME KING, MARTIN LUTHER HAD
been dead for thirteen months and the Lutheran part of the Reformation
had largely run its course. After changing the world, the former Friar
Martin had withdrawn into a relatively quiet life as the father of a growing family and a writer of biblical commentaries. In the last decade of his
life he was tortured by constipation, hemorrhoids, and kidney stones,
plagued by the scandal that had erupted when he endorsed bigamy, and
increasingly consumed by a virulent anti-Semitism. (Three days before
his death he preached a sermon urging the expulsion of the Jews from
Germany.) His theology, having conquered half of Germany and all of
Scandinavia, had been overtaken on the cutting edge of the religious
revolution by newer varieties of Protestant belief.

Edward became king, therefore, at the point where a second generation of evangelical thinkers, based in Switzerland rather than Germany,
was making itself heard. Its increasingly dominant member was a
Frenchman living in Switzerland, John Calvin, one of history's most
paradoxical figures. In assuming the leadership of a revolt against the
authority of the Roman church, Calvin came to claim for himself more
power than any Renaissance pope had ever dared to do. He not only declared himself to be something very like the infallible head of a one true
church of his own devising—any lunatic might have done that, and one
or two of the sixteenth century's more interesting lunatics did—but
through willpower, sheer force of intellect, and unshakable integrity he
largely made good on that claim. In the little city of Geneva, a place not
particularly friendly to reform, he constructed a regime that came about
as close as anything in Europe ever had to an enduring totalitarian theoc-
racy. In laying down the rules by which the people of Geneva (and, by
implication, the whole Christian world) were to live, and more important by articulating a rationale for the validity of those rules, he made

himself one of the most influential theologians in history. In places as remote from his home base as Scotland (where his disciples transformed
not only the church but the culture) and England (where his teachings
triggered the Puritan movement), it was Calvin more than Luther who
defined what it was to be Protestant. The reach of his ideas is evident
in the fact that from 1550 to 1650, a century that encompassed the careers of Shakespeare and other writers of gigantic stature, Calvin was England's most published author. This happened although Calvin never set
foot in England, rarely showed more than passing interest in its affairs,
and was reviled by an Anglican church that persecuted his followers and
attempted to suppress his teachings.

Both in background and in temperament, Calvin was profoundly different from Luther. He was trained in the law rather than in theology, and
much of his impact was rooted in a lawyerly impulse to systematize, to
impose order on what can sometimes seem the *dis*order, the emotional
excess, of Luther's attacks first on the abuses of the church and then on
some of its doctrines. Born in 1509 (the family name was Cauvin, Latin-
ized as "Calvinus" when young Jean began putting his ideas in writing),
he was raised by a devoutly Catholic mother but came of age in a France
that was being shaken apart by the disputes that Luther had ignited. He
was drawn to the cause of reform while still a student in Paris, where he
began acquiring the mastery of Latin, Greek, and Hebrew that would
make him one of Europe's most formidable Scripture scholars. The beliefs that he adopted at this early stage were, not surprisingly, almost
identical to what Luther was then preaching. Thus he agreed with
Luther's view that original sin had so damaged the human soul as to
make it impossible for anyone to *merit* salvation and that man was therefore entirely dependent upon a divine grace that cannot be earned. Like
Luther, he repudiated most of the traditional sacraments (all, in fact,
except baptism and the Eucharist) along with the practices (celibacy,
fasting, pilgrimages, and indulgences, for example) that the Catholic
Church had long offered as ways of winning divine favor. Throughout his
public life Calvin displayed a hatred of Rome at least as intense as
Luther's, but he never descended to the kind of childishly scatological
rhetoric with which the German reformer defaced so much of his own
writing. (Thomas More and others, to their own everlasting shame, answered him in kind.)

Theologically, Calvin soon went beyond Luther. He is best known for making explicit something that had remained implicit in Luther: the conclusion that, because fallen man has no free will and can do nothing to win salvation or escape damnation, some are predestined to be saved while others are predestined for hell. The saved are the *elect,* in Calvin's system. Though they can be recognized by their acceptance of divine truth, their love of the Eucharist, and their upright conduct, these are not the *means* by which they achieve salvation but rather a *sign* of election. Calvin's notion of "double predestination"—of some being marked for damnation just as surely as others are fated for salvation—has too often been regarded as the centerpiece of his theology. It is said to have made his God a kind of insanely cruel monster and to explain the severity of the regimen that Calvin imposed upon Geneva. In fact, however, Calvin regarded predestination as logically inescapable but otherwise beyond human understanding and in practical terms not of great importance. It was his followers who, after his death, moved predestination closer to the center of "Calvinist" belief. Calvin's own view was that the idea of predestination should make it possible for believers to set aside their anxieties about earning salvation and put their trust in the mercy of a gentle, compassionate divine father (who was also, Calvin suggested, a loving mother). Calvin was generally disinclined to take a passionate interest in theological questions that consumed many of his contemporaries but seemed to him to have little practical value in addressing the needs of the elect. He finessed one of the most contentious of issues, for example, by declaring that Christ was really present in the Eucharist but only in a "spiritual" sense, and letting it go at that. He regarded the heart as more important than the intellect in establishing a right relationship with God.

What separated Calvin from the Lutherans most radically, at least in terms of practical consequences, was his approach to the governance of the church as well as—church and state being inextricably connected in his system—the civil society. Luther, in renouncing the traditional church, had discarded Catholic belief in a priesthood endowed with special authority and unique sacramental faculties. In its place he offered a "priesthood of all believers," and while acknowledging the church as a legitimately distinct element of society, he emphatically subordinated it (especially after the Peasants' War) to civil authority. For

Calvin, by contrast, the church and its clergy retained a unique authority, with not only the right but the duty to reshape the world in such a
way as to make it a fit habitation for the elect. Hence one of the defining
characteristics of Calvinism (and the Puritanism to which it gave rise in
England): a zealous commitment to making the world a fully realized
part of Christ's kingdom. Curiously, people who believed they could do
nothing to alter their eternal destinies nevertheless dedicated themselves
to making everyone in the world conduct themselves in a holy manner
as Calvin defined holiness. This was a matter of duty, and its aim was not
to save souls but to protect the elect from the doomed.

Calvin's whole career was an expression of commitment to a Christian reordering of society. He came early to be certain not only that
Catholicism was a gross perversion of the gospel—his contempt for the
old religion appears at times to border on the pathological—but that he
himself, by reading Scripture correctly, had found in it truths that European Christianity had either intentionally suppressed or, more charita-
bly, remained blind to for more than a thousand years. Among his
recovered truths were highly specific instructions as to how the church
and the community of believers should be organized and managed. It
was of course extraordinary, his conviction that virtually all of Christendom had been grievously in error almost from the beginning and that he
alone was free of error. On its face it was outlandish. But in the theological confusion of the sixteenth century, Calvin's impregnable self-
confidence and the clarity of his ideas brought him an eager audience.

Most of his core ideas were already in place when, in 1536, Calvin
happened to make an overnight stop in Geneva and was persuaded to
remain there and join the embattled local forces of reform. He quickly
showed himself to be the most unhesitating and uncompromising of cru-
saders, answering disagreement with scorn and demanding that everyone in the city either assent to his beliefs or face excommunication and
expulsion. During his first months in Geneva he published the first edition of his *Institutes of the Christian Religion,* which as it evolved would
become arguably the most important single work in the history of Protestantism. When after two years he insisted that the city council submit to
the authority of the clergy—to *his* authority, in effect—he found that he
had overreached. Now it was he who was sent into exile.

Geneva remained a religious cockpit, however, and the most ambitious of its reformers soon were yearning once again for strong leadership. In 1541 Calvin was invited to return. He did so on very nearly his own terms, demanding that the council enact and enforce his Ecclesiastical Ordinances, and from that point until the end of his life twenty-three years later he outmaneuvered one after another of his adversaries until Geneva became the Sparta of Protestant Europe. His rules were not only given the force of law but declared "holy doctrine"—infallible, or something not easily distinguished from it. The regime that he imposed was democratic in the sense that church members chose their pastors, but once chosen, those pastors, working with and through lay elders, were able to rule virtually unchallenged. Eventually Calvin's consistory, an ecclesiastical court presided over by the pastors, was empowered to investigate and discipline anyone in the city. Not only drunkenness, gambling, and sexual promiscuity but dancing, singing outside church, swearing, and failing to attend sermons became crimes. Catholic practice, of course, was absolutely forbidden. Punishments ranged from reprimands and public confession to beatings, banishment, even execution. In a five-year period toward the end of Calvin's career, fifty-eight Genevans were sentenced to death, seventy-six exiled.

Calvin became a major force in England's religious evolution without really trying to do so. Many of the evangelicals who could not accept Henry VIII's quasi-Catholic Church had taken up exile in Geneva, where Calvin's mind and personality powerfully affected their beliefs. When they flooded back into England after Edward VI's accession, they carried a white-hot Calvinist fervor with them. They formed the nucleus of what would become a potent new element in English national life. They sparked a movement that knew what it wanted, knew that it was right, knew that its opposition was damnably wrong in the most literal sense, and was not inclined to compromise.

19

A Revolution and a Coup

E dward Tudor was fifteen and a half years old when, on the second day of April 1552, he suddenly fell ill. His physicians were of course concerned, especially when it became clear that he had not only measles (a dangerous disease into the twentieth century) but smallpox to boot. The men who were ruling in the young king's name had reason to be more worried than the doctors. If Edward died, everything they had achieved, both for themselves and for their faith, would be at risk. If he were followed on the throne by his half-sister Mary, next in line under Henry VIII's final arrangements, they could expect little better than disaster. However, the boy's recovery was swift and soon seemed complete, and in short order everyone was breathing easier.

On the brink of manhood now, Edward was taking an increasingly conspicuous part in the management of the kingdom. Under the indulgent tutelage of John Dudley, Duke of Northumberland and lord president of the Privy Council, he gave every evidence of developing into a formidable monarch. He had the Tudor intelligence, and like his father and sisters he was being given the rigorous training in languages, the classics, and theology that Renaissance Europe deemed appropriate to royalty. From early childhood he had been schooled in a very particular view of the world and his place in it, and he embraced everything he was taught: that his authority came directly from God, so that he was accountable to no living person; that God had given him dominion over the English church no less than over the state; that as God's vicar he had a solemn responsibility to establish true Christianity throughout his realm; and that the only true Christianity was the evangelical faith of his godfather Cranmer and his tutors. Having been raised and educated by passionate anti-Catholics who scorned tradition—even his stepmother Catherine Parr believed that God had chosen her to be Henry's sixth queen so that she could do her part in fending off the dark forces of superstition—he was a firm believer in justification by faith, in predestination, and in other things that his father had never ceased to abominate. Things that Henry had never stopped believing, on the other hand, were now Edward's abominations. And he displayed the eager combativeness of the incipient Puritan—a determination to engage the world and transform it into God's kingdom. Francis van der Delft, the Catholic ambassador of the doggedly Catholic Charles V, reported dryly that "in the court there is no man of learning so ready to argue in support of the new doctrine as the king, according to what his masters tell him and he learns from his preachers."

In fact, however, by 1552 Edward was no one's mere puppet. As early as 1550, barely in adolescence, he had delighted his mentors and horrified the court's remaining conservatives by demanding the removal of any invocation of the saints (veneration of saints having become an obnoxious vestige of the old religion) from the consecration oath taken by new bishops. By that time, too, Edward was objecting to the masses being said in his sister Mary's household, refusing to agree when his advisers suggested that it would be better to turn a blind eye to such practices than to provoke the wrath of her cousin the emperor. The mass was sinful, Edward insisted, and if he tolerated sinfulness he himself would sin. England's second Reformation was thus now fully under way, and it had no advocate more enthusiastic than the young king himself. It was in every respect a revolution from above, driven by a council whose conservative members had been either purged or politically neutered. With the power of the Crown at its back, it was gathering momentum in spite of having feeble support in the population or even the clergy at large. The narrowness of its base is suggested by the fact that the Canterbury and York convocations of the clergy were never asked to approve or even express an opinion about the changes being made. They were not regarded as trustworthy.

The revolution's main driver was Cranmer, whose changing beliefs had by this time carried him beyond the Lutheranism of his earlier years and to the more radical austerities of Swiss, and specifically Calvinist, reform. He achieved perhaps the greatest triumph of his career in 1552, when Parliament passed the Second Act of Uniformity and thereby mandated the use of his reworked (by himself) Prayer Book. If the earlier 1549 edition, issued before the evangelicals were sufficiently entrenched to disregard conservative opposition, had been an equivocal thing, a stopgap that satisfied no one and that exasperated the most ambitious of the reformers, the revision, or rather its adoption by Parliament, signaled the all-but-total victory of what now could be called the English Protestant church. Services cleansed of all vestiges of tradition—prayers for the dead, any mention of saints, the old familiar music and clerical vestments—became compulsory for laity and clergy alike. Harsh penalties were imposed: six months imprisonment for being present at any service not in conformity with the new law, a year for a second offense, life for a third. In other ways, too, Parliament brought to an end the liberality that had marked the beginning of the new regime (a pro forma liberality that in practice had been extended to the evangelicals only). Once again it was made treason to deny not only the royal supremacy but any prescribed article of faith. More positively, the provisions by which Henry VIII had permitted treason convictions on the basis of testimony from a single witness, prevented defendants from facing their accusers, and prescribed the death sentence for any first offense were expunged by Parliament. Henceforth the death penalty could be imposed for a first offense only if the treasonous statements were expressed in "writing, printing, carving or graving." Treason by spoken word was punishable by imprisonment and loss of possessions for first and second offenses, with a third conviction required for execution. Edward's regime, if not exactly a national liberation, continued to be not nearly as bloody as his father's.

The revolution proceeded apace, receiving fresh impetus from the many reformers who had come hurrying from the continent after the death of Henry (who would have had many of them killed for their beliefs). Seven of Henry's bishops were replaced with men of solidly evangelical credentials—men who impressed king and council with their

zeal to make England a fitting home for the elect. The Dudley administration launched yet another assault on what remained of the church's
wealth, confiscating most of the endowments of the dioceses and destroying the last of the guilds and chantries. Such raids served an array
of purposes. The government's financial state remained dizzyingly precarious, and Dudley and his cohorts welcomed opportunities to funnel
fresh revenues into the treasury while skimming off a share for themselves. The most radical of the reformers would have been pleased not
merely to reduce the bishops to penury but to rid the church entirely of
its traditional structures, bishops and dioceses included. These, too,
were regarded as vestiges of the old Roman decadence.

The religious landscape was growing more complicated by the year.
Cranmer's difficulties were compounded by the fact that the uniformity
he hoped to establish at any given time was always based on what he
himself happened to believe at that time, and his beliefs were endlessly
developing. Thus he repeatedly found himself demanding that everyone
believe what he himself had previously denied, and forbidding beliefs
that he had previously held to be compulsory. There were of course no
longer any avowed *Roman* Catholics in positions of importance in the
central government or the national church, and anyone conservative
enough to try to retain the old forms without the old connection to
Rome was rendered voiceless when not purged. It was the radicals,
therefore, who now presented the most serious challenge to consensus.
Their beliefs differed bewilderingly; the innovations with which Martin
Luther had rocked Europe just three decades before could seem conservative if not reactionary when compared with the ideas more recently
imported from Geneva and Zurich. Confusion was inescapable, and discord followed inevitably in its wake. When Cranmer introduced his revised Prayer Book, the fiery Scottish preacher John Knox (trained in
Geneva and a protégé of Dudley, who had given him employment as a
royal chaplain) complained loudly because it did not ban the old practice
of kneeling to receive communion. Though Cranmer was archbishop of
Canterbury and Knox by comparison was scarcely more than a nonentity, there followed a struggle for royal approval during which Edward
himself intervened to postpone the issuance of the new service. Cranmer finally prevailed, at least to the extent that worshippers were in-

structed to kneel, but he was obliged to insert into the Prayer Book a so-called Black Rubric explaining that the practice was a gesture of respect, not a worshipping of bread and wine.

It is hardly surprising if many men and women, faced with endless surprises and reversals and disagreements, witnessing the abandonment of one aspect after another of the church in which they had been raised, simply lost interest in religion. That this was happening is suggested by the Second Act of Uniformity, which deplored the emptiness of pews and compelled regular attendance at approved services. But it was too late for Parliament, or any archbishop or king, to restore uniformity on any basis. England had become a religiously divided nation and would remain one until, after four more centuries, it became essentially post-Christian.

John Dudley, soon after Somerset's fall, had made himself a kind of father figure for Edward, coaching him and encouraging his involvement in governance of church and state. At first Edward was most active in religious matters—delaying, as we have seen, issuance of the 1552 Prayer Book—and always his aim was the acceleration of evangelical reform. Always he acted in the conviction that he was charged by God to lead the people to the truth, and always he was applauded for this by Dudley and Cranmer in spite of the fact that those two worthies were often at odds with each other. In affairs of state, too, Edward gradually became not only active but important. By 1553 he was signing the Crown's financial warrants not only with but in place of the council. Though it would be saying too much to claim that he was actually *ruling,* certainly he was receiving a thorough preparation for the responsibilities of kingship. His apprenticeship, reinforced by his intelligence and immense self-assurance and an education probably more rigorous than that received by any English king before or since, suggested that a remarkable career lay ahead.

The soldier Dudley broadened Edward's daily regimen to include the kinds of martial exercises in which his own sons were being trained, skills needed to make him a warrior-king in the ancient tradition. The boy underwent instruction in horsemanship, jousting, archery, hunting, and the latest weaponry, and though he had inherited little of his father's strength and vitality he appears to have responded with enthusiasm. If it is idle to wonder about what sort of man Edward might have become, it

is nonetheless irresistibly interesting. What he revealed of himself suggests that he would have ruled as flamboyantly as his father: while still
little more than a child he showed a passion for gambling, lavish dress,
and other extravagances. In true Henrician fashion he spent outlandish
sums to acquire some of the costliest gems to be found on the continent
even as his government struggled to stave off insolvency. He appears to
have been like his father, too, in taking no interest in whatever misfortunes—hunger resulting from failed harvests, outbreaks of plague or the
sweat—might be afflicting his subjects. Perhaps his least attractive characteristic was his apparent conviction, which could easily look like prig-
gishness anchored in arrogance, that he possessed not only the authority
but the wisdom to manage the lives of his elders. He not only attempted
to prevent his sister Mary from hearing mass but admonished her to refrain from dancing, an innocent pleasure that that thwarted and unhappy spinster must have badly needed. When his schoolmate Barnaby
Fitzpatrick went off to study in Paris, Edward sent him hectoring letters
cautioning him to avoid not only Catholic observances but the company
of women. On the other hand, he displayed no thirst for blood; so far as
is known, the fact that neither Somerset nor Dudley killed a single conservative for resistance to reform was perfectly acceptable to the king.

As for what the future might bring—for Edward VI it brought almost
nothing. What sixteenth-century medical science could not know was
that at some point in childhood or early adolescence he had contracted
tuberculosis. The infection had been confined inside the healthy tissue
of his lungs but not eliminated, and his brief illness of April 1552
amounted to a sentence of death because measles destroys the immune
system's ability to keep latent tuberculosis in check. As the year proceeded he continued with his studies, continued to pursue the military
exercises that Dudley had introduced, and continued to participate in
the work of the council and the formalities and festivities of what remained a fairly splendid Renaissance court. But he was slowly, inexorably, invisibly dying. He had never been an impressive physical
specimen (an Italian physician named Hieronymus Cardano, upon
meeting him, reported that he was "of a stature somewhat below the
middle height, pale-faced with gray eyes . . . rather of a bad habit of
body than a sufferer from fixed diseases" and "carried himself like an old
man"), and in the course of growing up he had occasionally been seri-

ously ill with diseases including malaria. Overall, however, through most of 1552 he seemed healthy enough and even engaged in jousting for the first time. Eventually, it became evident that something was wrong. By year-end a chronic cough and increasing weakness were making it obvious to all, the king himself included, that something was *seriously* wrong. He continued to deteriorate through the first months of 1533, then experienced a remission that sparked hopes of a recovery, and finally relapsed so severely that in the first week of June both he and his councilors were advised that death was now not only inevitable but likely to come soon.

He makes a melancholy picture: this solitary boy, his father and mother and stepmothers all long dead, separated by religion from the one sister to whom he appears to have had a strong bond of affection, faced with oblivion just as a life of limitless possibility was opening before him. It is difficult to comprehend, today, the extent to which his life as a juvenile king in an almost fantastically formal court had cut him off from normal human interaction. Not even Edward's sisters could speak to him without first kneeling, and when either of them dined "with" him, she had to sit not at the same table but off at a distance, on a low cushion. His food was served by nobles and gentlemen who were obliged to kneel before placing their offerings on the table. All this went far beyond the protocols of even the French court, where serving was done by pages rather than mature men of high rank, and where even the pages had only to bow rather than kneel. Everything reinforced in Edward the sense that he was a being apart, existing on a plane beyond the reach of ordinary humans. Eventually some suitable marriage might have brought him companionship. Though his early betrothals—first to Mary, Queen of Scots, and then to a French princess—had come to nothing, and though a nearly bankrupt English Crown no longer could play as weighty a role in continental affairs as it had during his father's prime, Edward was still as marriageable a young bachelor as any in Europe. Now, however, none of that meant anything. There would be no marriage, no fourth generation of Tudor kings . . . no companion.

Facing the end, the certainty that he could hope for nothing in this world, Edward turned his attention to what would happen after he was gone. In all of England and Wales hardly anyone could have been more passionately devoted to the cause of religious reform, more certain that the Protestant revolution being carried out during his reign was a triumph for divine truth and that a reversal of that revolution would be a disaster worse than war or plague. But under the terms of his father's last will, the throne was to pass next to his sister Mary, who in Edward's presence had proclaimed herself ready to die rather than abandon her Catholic faith. The affection that Edward had always shown for Mary did not keep him from recoiling at the prospect of a Catholic queen. Thus was he moved, as his life began to ebb away, to search for a way to pass the crown to someone other than Mary and also other than his other sister. (Elizabeth, whatever her religious inclinations, was burdened with the same liability as Mary: though Henry's will recognized her as third in line to the throne, she like Mary remained illegitimate under a statute that Parliament had never repealed. Thus if Mary were to be set aside on grounds of bastardy—probably the best available way of denying her the crown—Elizabeth, too, would be disqualified.)

Edward needed an heir of royal blood and impeccable legitimacy. At least as important, because this was the point of everything he was setting out to do, his heir must be solidly Protestant. But the condition of the Tudor family tree in 1553 was such that, to find someone who satisfied all three criteria, he was going to have to stretch the law in awkward ways.

The first problem was the curious fact that, among the descendants of Henry VII then living in England, Edward was the only male. As a result of the early deaths over two generations of several Scottish princes, the only surviving product of his aunt Margaret Tudor's marriage to King James IV of Scotland was the young Mary, Queen of Scots. Henry VIII, perhaps because Margaret's offspring were foreigners and perhaps out of pique with her irregular marital history, had excluded her entire branch of the family from the succession. Had he not done so, Edward would have found Mary unacceptable anyway. She was reputed to be almost as fervent a Catholic as he was an evangelical. Nearly as bad, she was not only living in France but betrothed to the heir to the French throne.

This left the fruit of the love match between Henry VIII's younger sister Mary and Charles Brandon, Duke of Suffolk. Four children had been born of this union, two sons and two daughters, but the boys had both died in childhood. When Mary herself died at age thirty-seven, she was survived only by the girls Frances and Eleanor, who were married to Henry Grey, Marquess of Dorset, and Henry Clifford, Earl of Cumberland, respectively. Eleanor Clifford was dead by 1553, but she and her sister between them had four living children, the eldest just reaching maturity. All, as it happened, were female: Frances's daughters Jane, Catherine, and Mary Grey, and Eleanor's daughter, Margaret Clifford. (The Grey sisters, incidentally, were granddaughters of one of the sons that Elizabeth Woodville had before her marriage to Edward IV.)

If Frances or any of her children or Eleanor's one child had been male, Edward would have had no difficulty in selecting his heir. The absence of a single male among them, however, complicated matters considerably. Throughout the thousand-plus years of post-Roman English history, there had been only one attempt to place a female claimant on the throne, and that had led (back in the twelfth century, when King Henry I died leaving only a daughter) to years of disorder and war. A pair of documents survives showing the steps by which the dying Edward groped toward a solution. In the first, a draft in Edward's own hand, he proposes leaving the throne of England to "the Lady Fraunces's heirs masles" first (Frances was still in her mid-thirties, possibly still capable of producing a son), then to the male heirs of Frances's daughters beginning with "the Lady Jane's" because she was the eldest. The problem was that none of the Grey girls had heirs male or otherwise—Jane was only sixteen, her sisters scarcely more than children. According to this first plan of Edward's, after his death the throne would have to remain vacant until someone in the Grey family gave birth to a boy. And what if one of the younger sisters had a son before Jane? Would the succession remain in abeyance until Jane either bore a son or grew too old to do so?

It was impossible. Edward in his next draft removed Frances from the succession—there is no evidence that she objected—and with a few strokes of his pen outlined an almost outlandishly ambitious new plan. The deletion of an apostrophe and a single letter turned "Jane's" into "Jane," and the words "and her" were inserted immediately thereafter. Now the crown was to pass not to the male heirs *of* Jane Grey but to *"the Lady Jane and her heirs masles."* (Edward was of course highly literate, but spelling was a kind of free-form creative art in the sixteenth century.)

Thus did a doomed youth put his mind at rest. The Greys were confirmed evangelicals. In their hands his church, his legacy, would be safe.

But there was a joker in the deck, one that added a bizarre dynastic twist to the king's plan and continues to complicate historians' efforts to understand why the situation unfolded as it did. Shortly before Edward's remission ended and the imminence of death became undeniable, a flurry of grand marriages and betrothals had been arranged by John Dudley. His youngest daughter was wed to the son and heir of the Earl of Huntingdon, who was of royal blood through the Pole family and an ally worth having. The duke's brother Andrew Dudley was betrothed to Margaret Clifford, who was thirty years his junior but, as we have seen, a possible heir to the throne. The two younger Grey sisters were likewise dispensed to the advantage of the Dudleys: Catherine was affianced to the son and heir of the Earl of Pembroke, who owed his title and much of his wealth to his alliance with the Dudleys, Mary to the son of a somewhat lesser notable. Each of these unions served to tighten the duke's connections to important families and factions—sources of support that might become a matter of life or death in case of serious trouble. Even when taken together, however, they were trivial in comparison with the wedding that formed the centerpiece of the celebrations that spilled out into the streets of London from John Dudley's grand residence. On May 25 Lady Jane Grey, heir presumptive according to King Edward's still-secret plan, was married to young Guildford Dudley (he was in his late teens, though his year of birth is not certain), fourth among the duke's five sons.

Even if King Edward had not been dying, the wedding would have been a coup for the Dudleys. Quite apart from her royal blood, Jane as the eldest daughter of a sonless duke was a great dynastic prize. At one time she had been considered a possible bride for the king himself; probably they would have been a good match, being not only of almost exactly the same age but physically attractive, superbly educated, and devotedly evangelical. The Duke of Somerset, during his time as lord protector, had made preliminary arrangements to marry his son to Jane, but that opportunity was lost with the Seymour party's fall from power. John Dudley's success in bringing the girl into his family, combined with the altering of the succession, set the stage for Dudleys—possibly Guildford himself, certainly any son that he and Jane succeeded in producing—to be kings of England. The question of whether the scheme originated with Edward or with the duke remains unresolved. Whatever the case, both were entirely committed to the project and had excellent reasons to be so. For the king it meant that the gospel could be preserved in England for all time—that his short life and shorter reign would have vast and eternal value. For the duke it meant not only deliverance from his many enemies—and the gruff Dudley, for all his courage and ability, was disliked by almost everyone except his own family and his king— but the opportunity to continue ruling England indefinitely through a daughter-in-law whom he undoubtedly expected to be the pliant instrument of his will.

Poor Edward, who could only listen from his deathbed as news was brought of the nuptials of the young woman who under other circumstances might one day have become his bride, was by June in a desperately bad state, weak and racked by fits of coughing, needing stimulants to remain focused. He knew that no scribbled statement of his desire to bypass his sisters in favor of Jane could be depended upon to alter the succession. Something more formal, more official, was needed. On June 12 he revealed his thinking to a group of the court's legal officers, explaining why he regarded it as impossible to allow Mary to succeed him and instructing them to draw up whatever documents they deemed necessary to make Jane incontestably his heir. Two days later, in reporting to the Privy Council as the king had ordered them to do, the lawyers complained that if they followed Edward's instructions they would violate Henry VIII's final Succession Act and thereby commit treason. John Dudley, infuriated at being blocked in this way, arranged for the lawyers (among whom were the solicitor-general and attorney-general) to meet again with an equally dissatisfied king. They told Edward that the succession, having been established by statute, could not be changed except through passage of a new statute. This was a trenchant argument—a measure of the extent to which Parliament's role in the making of law was taking firm root even in the midst of the Tudor autocracy—but entirely unacceptable to Edward, who could have no confidence of living long enough for a Parliament to be summoned and put through the necessary paces. He declared that he wanted the matter settled immediately by execution of a deed that the next Parliament could ratify when it met in September, and he tried to assuage the fears of the lawmen by assuring them that it could not possibly be treason to obey a living king. After a good deal of bullying by various lords and members of the council, Sir Edward Montague, chief justice of the Court of Common Pleas, agreed to comply on two conditions. He wanted a written commission authorizing him to act—a document bearing the imprint of the Great Seal. And he wanted, in advance, a pardon freeing him from any future charge of treason. When this was granted, all the lawyers fell into line.

One last thing could be done, short of parliamentary ratification, to give a patina of legitimacy to Edward's plan. The deed that Montague and the others now hastened to complete for the king's signature could be endorsed by every personage of importance in the kingdom. The collection of signatures, and of the seals of the individuals doing the signing, therefore became a matter of urgency. Generally there was little difficulty: the Privy Council and Crown offices had, over the preceding few years, been packed with men of Dudley's choosing, and there remained few bishops or nobles with reason, doctrinal or financial or otherwise, to want the throne to pass to an adherent of the Roman church. Cranmer proved more difficult than most, complaining that he could not sign without violating the oath he had sworn to Henry VIII. Ultimately, however, he showed himself to be as willing to conform to the will of the son as to that of the father. His signature became the last of the 101 affixed to the formidable document declaring Jane Grey to be Edward's rightful heir.

It came none too soon. The bright and earnest young king, as yearned-for a prince as had ever been born in England, was at the end of his resources. His final days, horrible to behold, must have been far more horrible to undergo. "He has not the strength to stir, and can hardly breathe," the imperial ambassador reported. "His body no longer performs its functions, his nails and hair are falling out, and all his person is scabby." Another courtier reported that the king's body was riddled with "ulcers," probably a reference to bedsores. In any event he was no longer capable of anything more than waiting, preparing, and perhaps hoping for death. The fulfillment of his last great wish was going to depend, and depend entirely, on John Dudley.

Dudley understood that, no matter how many signatures and seals were affixed to a piece of vellum, success was not assured. He controlled the government and all its instruments, but by this point it was a weak government not only financially but militarily, the sorry state of the treasury having made it necessary to disband the mercenary troops, Italian and German mainly, used in suppressing the risings of 1549. Dudley himself was a charmless, graceless figure, resented at court for his rough style and for having risen so high after beginning as the son of an attainted traitor. (In all of England there were currently only three dukes, one of whom had been languishing in prison since before the death of Henry VIII, and Dudley was the first in history without even a trace of blood connection to the royal family.) To the common people he had always seemed a distant and threatening figure, the bad duke who had destroyed their friend the good Duke Somerset and crushed them for seeking redress of their grievances. Nothing if not practical and hardheaded, Dudley is unlikely to have harbored many illusions about the number and quality of his friends.

The central issue, however, proved to be not Dudley's popularity but the strength of Lady Jane's claim versus that of Mary Tudor. Jane was in fact a person of rather lofty character for a sixteen-year-old, dignified, serious about serious matters, to all appearances utterly without personal ambition. But few people outside the court had ever heard of her, and almost no one knew anything about her. It was hard to believe—it was inconceivable, actually—that her sudden emergence as monarch was going to be greeted with widespread enthusiasm. Mary, by contrast, had been born and raised a public figure, a mighty king's eldest daughter and therefore generally recognized as the rightful successor once his only son was gone. She was a woman against whom no bad thing could be said except by those who regarded her religion as intolerable. Great sympathy had been aroused by the humiliations to which she and her mother had been subjected over a quarter of a century. She was a formidable threat to everything Edward had planned, and would have to be dealt with.

Edward's sufferings came to an end on the evening of July 6. He died in the arms of a Dudley son-in-law, Sir Henry Sidney, who later reported that the "sweetness" with which the king had surrendered his spirit "would have converted the fiercest of papists if they had any grace in them of true faith in Christ." Before losing the ability to speak, Sidney said, Edward "made a prayer to God to deliver this nation from that un-

charitable religion of popery, which was the chiefest cause for his election of the Lady Jane Grey to succeed before his sister Mary . . . out of
pure love to his subjects, that he desired they might live and die in the
Lord, as he did." The death was kept secret while Dudley made his
arrangements to transfer the crown to his daughter-in-law. The Tower
of London and Windsor Castle were put on alert, the Privy Council was
assembled in the Tower, lords lieutenant in every part of the kingdom
were instructed to be ready to muster their forces, and warships were
deployed in the Channel to intercept any vessel attempting to carry
Mary away. A Dudley daughter was dispatched to escort Lady Jane (not
yet informed of the king's death) from Chelsea (where she had gone to
recover from what she believed to have been an attempted poisoning) to
Syon House (which had been a great abbey until seized by Henry VIII,
briefly became the property of Lord Protector Edward Seymour, and
now belonged to the Dudleys). John Dudley himself, at the head of a
delegation including the late Queen Catherine Parr's brother and three
earls, called on Lady Jane there and informed her on his knees that the
king was dead and had named her as his successor. Jane, by her own
later account, thereupon fell to the floor and began to weep, protesting
that she was unprepared for and unworthy of the crown. In due course
she was persuaded to accept God's will and vowed to do her best. The
next day, July 10, Jane's elevation was proclaimed throughout London
along with a declaration that neither Mary nor Elizabeth could inherit.
Three reasons were given: Henry VIII's daughters were bastards under
the law, were merely half-sisters to the king, and might, if either became
queen, jeopardize England's autonomy by marrying some foreign, possibly Catholic, prince. The first and second arguments were, if they had
an impact at all, counterproductive: the denial of Mary's legitimacy was
widely offensive, and not to the conservatives only. Jane was escorted to
the Tower amid the celebratory firing of cannons and such other fanfare
as Dudley and his associates could arrange. Behind the scenes, however,
there were early signs of discord: when Dudley advised his daughter-in-
law to declare her bridegroom king of England, he was immediately rebuffed. The crown, Jane declared with a firmness that must have taken
her father-in-law aback, was "not a plaything for boys and girls." In the
great scheme of things it was a minor setback; at worst, it meant that the
crowning of a Dudley king might have to be postponed a generation.

The duke had already overreached himself and was lucky to have been refused. People were reacting with sullen surprise to the news that someone called Jane was their new queen. Many would have been outraged to learn that a son of the unpopular upstart Dudley was being foisted off on them as king. In the streets of London the lack of enthusiasm for the new regime was painfully obvious. There were no cheers or demonstrations, no spontaneous lighting of bonfires, none of the effusions of joy with which the citizenry customarily welcomed the advent of a new reign. Still, Dudley's position, and Jane's, seemed unassailable. Dudley controlled the levers of power. He had even received assurances of support from Henry II of France, eager to help if he could to keep a cousin and protégé of Charles V from the English throne. Charles's representatives in London, meanwhile, were reporting glumly that the English capital, government, and treasury were all in Dudley's hands, that Queen Jane had already been officially recognized, and that Mary's chances of reversing this fait accompli were virtually nil.

Mary, however, had ideas of her own. Convinced that she was the rightful queen, willing to believe that it was her destiny to restore the true faith to her homeland, she had no intention of surrendering. She and Elizabeth had been at their country seats as Edward entered his final decline, keeping themselves as informed as they could about his condition. When they received instructions to come to the king at Greenwich, both sensed danger. Elizabeth claimed to be too ill to travel. Mary set out from her residence at Hunsdon, but proceeded so slowly that in two days she covered barely five miles and at the end of the second day was still at Hoddesdon on the outskirts of London. She would have entered the capital the next day, placing herself at the mercy of Dudley and the council, but during the night someone sent a message informing her of the king's death. Within minutes, with members of her household struggling to keep pace, she was galloping off northward, away from London and toward her Kenninghall estate in East Anglia. Since her reconciliation with her father a decade before, she had been the owner of extensive East Anglian properties, and the local population was friendly. Dudley dispatched two of his sons, Henry and Robert, to find Mary and deliver her to London, but when the latter arrived at Hunsdon he found her gone. Word soon reached London that fighting men by the hundreds were rallying to Mary, and that she was receiving substantial financial support as well. When she moved on from Kenninghall, she and her followers were refused admittance to Norwich, a city that had fresh and painful memories of what was likely to happen to those who defied John Dudley. The town of Framlingham, however, threw open its gates.

In short order Mary found herself in command of tens of thousands of armed men. As word spread of what was happening, impressive demonstrations of support spread from London up the Thames valley into Oxfordshire. The fleet deployed to keep her from escaping across the Channel returned to port and declared for her. Still, Dudley continued to have the advantage. When Mary sent a messenger to the council demanding recognition as queen, an order to the lords lieutenant, supposedly from Queen Jane but actually written by Cranmer, instructed them to ignore any appeals from the "bastard doughter to our said dearest cousin and progenitor great unkle Henry the eight of famous memory." When the clergy were told to preach against Mary, none did so more energetically than Nicholas Ridley, evangelical bishop of London. The congregations he addressed listened impassively while word reached the capital of the growing numbers of volunteers gathering around Mary in East Anglia.

Dudley knew that it was essential to confront Mary and disperse her supporters before things got out of hand. His troops, however, were all in or near London, and among his associates there was scarcely a man who was both capable of leading an army into battle and entirely trustworthy. By the same token he had no one he trusted to hold his party together in London if he went off to fight. He tried to send the Duke of Suffolk, Queen Jane's father (not much of a soldier, but unlikely to defect), but she would not allow him to go. In the end Dudley had no choice except to assemble such troops as he could muster—not more than a few thousand probably—and lead them out of the city himself. Before departing he sent word to the nobles to join him as quickly as possible with as many men as they could muster.

Both in East Anglia and in the capital, Dudley's situation quickly fell apart. He proceeded to Cambridge and from there toward Framlingham, but as his troops advanced they encountered increasing demonstrations of the population's hostility. He reached Bury St. Edmunds in a state of thorough demoralization and, finding no support there, decided to turn back. In London, meanwhile, a frightened council had broken up into bickering factions and finally dissolved. On July 19 a number of the leading councilors, among them the earls of Shrewsbury, Bedford, and Arundel and the same Earl of Pembroke to whom Dudley had given Lady Catherine Grey as a daughter-in-law, broke ranks and declared for Mary. Jane's own father pulled the cloth canopy of royalty from above his daughter's head, announced that Mary was queen, and fled. Jane herself, nine days after being proclaimed queen, quietly withdrew to Syon House.

John Dudley's years as the most powerful man in England ended with a whimper. His army having deserted and his cause lost, he stood alone in the market square at Cambridge and tearfully declared Mary Tudor his queen. In a forlorn attempt to demonstrate a joy he cannot have felt, he threw his cap into the air. The next day he was taken to London surrounded by guards who were needed less to keep him from escaping than to protect him from angry crowds.

Two weeks later, accompanied by her sister Elizabeth and Anne of Cleves, Queen Mary I entered London. This time the expressions of joy were loud and long and genuine.

THE MAKING OF MARY

WHEN THE FIRST WOMAN EVER TO RULE ENGLAND TOOK
the throne in 1553, she was already a tragic figure. For a quarter of a
century she had been immersed in betrayal, loss, and grief. Her life had
been blighted first by the egotism of a father who was quite prepared to
destroy her, then by a young half-brother who regarded it as his sacred
duty to save her from her own deepest beliefs and, when that could not
be arranged, to save England from her.

It was all doubly sad because Mary's life had begun so brilliantly.
From earliest childhood she had been an ornament of the English court,
a pretty little golden-haired princess doted on by her parents and by
every noble, churchman, soldier, and diplomat eager for her parents'
favor. Her father would carry her about, proudly showing her off. Her
mother had raised Mary as she herself had been raised: to become the
wife and partner of a monarch. It was impossible to doubt that she
would become exactly that. She was betrothed to the eldest son of Francis of France at age two, and to her cousin Charles V at five (when the
emperor was twenty-one). Later there were discussions of her possible
marriage to her Scottish cousin James V, to other princes of France, to a
son of the Duke of Cleves, and to Francesco Sforza, Duke of Milan. One
by one these possibilities faded as international alliances came and
went, but there seemed no cause for hurry. Quite the contrary: the
French ambassador, in reporting on the eleven-year-old Mary, told Francis that though she was "admirable by reason of her great and uncommon mental endowments," she was also "so thin, sparse and small as to
render it impossible for her to be married for the next three years."

Meanwhile she continued to prepare for whatever great match lay
ahead. She was tutored not only by leading English scholars but by respected humanists from the continent, and she wrote and spoke Latin
fluently by age nine. She was equally proficient in French, shared her fa-

ther's love of music and dance and learned to play several instruments, and under her mother's watchful eye was given a solid grounding in the classics and theology. In the Tudor pattern she was a dutiful child, eager to please, and throughout the first decade of her life she had no reason to think that either of her parents would ever want her to be anything other than a faithful and obedient daughter of Holy Mother Church. In England as in all of Europe's greatest royal houses, conventional Catholic piety was taken for granted as integral to being female and royal.

At age ten Mary was set up with her own court at Ludlow Castle, the very place to which Catherine of Aragon and her first husband had been sent shortly after their marriage—the place where Prince Arthur met his early death. There Mary became a figurehead under whose banner a council of Cardinal Wolsey's appointees managed Wales and the marches that bordered it. This was to be the beginning of her apprenticeship in government. It also made her, in effect if not by official proclamation, the first *Princess* of Wales. It was a signal that, in spite of the signs of favor that her father had recently showered on his illegitimate son Henry Fitzroy, *she* was his heir and rightful successor.

When Mary was recalled to court a year and a half later, however, she found everything changed in alarming ways. Her father and Wolsey, unhappy about the dominance that Charles V now enjoyed on the continent in the aftermath of his victory over the French at Pavia, were considering a treaty under which Mary would become the wife not of Francis I's son but of Francis himself. Queen Catherine could only have been appalled, not only because of her wish for friendship between England and her imperial nephew but also because Francis, a thirty-three-year-old widower with voracious and wide-ranging sexual appetites, was hardly the husband that any loving mother would have chosen for her not-yet-grown child. Francis, in any case, had no interest in waiting for a girl who was still years short of the age at which cohabitation would become permissible under church law. Mary was betrothed to his second son, the Duke of Orleans, instead. Assuming that Mary was informed of any of this, she is unlikely to have taken it seriously; the volatility of her father's relationship with Francis made this latest arrangement as implausible as those that had come before. (In fact, Francis would eventually repudiate his treaty with England and marry Orleans—the future King Henry II—to Pope Clement's niece Catherine de'

Medici, who in the fullness of time would join the ranks of France's most remarkable and ultimately tragic queens.)

It was not the bartering over possible marriages that caused life to turn dark for Mary, but the unmistakable evidence that her parents' union was breaking down. By the spring of 1527, when she returned from Ludlow, the king was not only far advanced in his obsession with Anne Boleyn but raising questions about the validity of his marriage. In July Henry informed Catherine that they had never been married, and from that moment the two of them were at war. Mary regarded her mother as entirely innocent and grievously wronged, but like Catherine she was unable to blame Henry. Anne became the villain, responsible for the unhappy wreck that the royal family had become, and her understandable inclination to see Mary as a rival for Henry's affection, and therefore as a mortal threat, was soon inflamed. As Mary entered adolescence, she found herself spurned by her father. Her mother, who had always been devoted and would remain so through all the misfortunes now descending upon them, was sent away, she and Mary forbidden to see each other. As Henry's rejection of wife and child broadened into an attack on the church that both parents had always taught Mary to revere, the magnitude of the disaster must have become literally incredible in her eyes. Anne for her part became so ferociously hostile, swearing that Mary would be either reduced to servility or given to some lowborn husband, that people loyal to Mary feared for her life. Her health, which had always been good, began to fail under the strain.

In 1533, with the king's marriage to Anne and the birth of their daughter Elizabeth, a separate household was established for the newborn at Hatfield House some seventeen miles from London. Mary's household was shut down, and she was ordered to become a maid of honor to her infant half-sister. She was told also that she herself, being illegitimate, was not a princess and never had been and must stop using the title or expecting others to use it in addressing her. Mary accepted none of this; to do so would have seemed a gross betrayal of her mother. She said disingenuously that she did not understand what princess she was supposed to serve, dryly noting that "Madame de Pembroke" (a reference to the title that Henry had conferred on Anne before their marriage) could have no child of such exalted rank. The situation at Hatfield proved to be intolerable not only for Mary but for Anne, who visited with some frequency. Mary's stubbornness sparked quarrels; most of the temper appears to have been on Anne's side, while Mary maintained a coldly insulting disdain. Things only grew worse when Anne, attempting to make peace, offered to intercede with the king on Mary's behalf if she would recognize her as queen. Mary replied that she recognized no queen except her mother. Anne retaliated in pettily vindictive ways, confiscating Mary's clothing and jewelry. A low point was reached when the household was moving temporarily to another place so that Hatfield could be cleaned and aired out at the end of winter; Mary refused to go unless acknowledged as princess. In the end she had to be forcibly stuffed into a cart and hauled, complaining, away.

Henry held himself aloof from this latest mess of his own making, refusing to see Mary when he visited Hatfield, which he did rarely. One of the most poignant scenes of the whole Tudor story took place at the conclusion of one of his visits. On the morning of his departure, happening to look up as he mounted his horse, the king saw Mary alone on a terrace at the top of the house. She was on her knees, hands clasped before her, gazing down at her father in silent supplication. He touched his hand to his cap in salute, but rode away without saying a word. He was angrier with Mary than she knew, seething at her refusal to accept her reduced state. Still scarcely more than a child, adoring her father as daughters are naturally inclined to do, she continued to lay all the blame for her troubles on Anne. Like her mother she clung to the barren hope that her father would recover his senses and return to his family.

This grotesque battle of wills went on unresolved for two and a half years; Mary fought back against what she could see only as malicious humiliation, and Anne was unable to avoid regular confrontations with an implacable little stepdaughter whose actions—whose very existence—were a challenge to her and her child's place in the world. Their drama unfolded against a background of historic events: the bishops' surrender of their ancient rights, the resignation of Thomas More, the start of Henry's judicial murders. When Parliament's passage of the first Act of Succession required everyone in the kingdom to take an oath acknowledging Anne as queen and Elizabeth as heir and both Catherine and Mary refused, Henry let it pass. Possibly he wished, out of some residuum of affection and respect, to spare them the penalty for high treason. It is at least as likely that he was simply being sensible. Nothing in the world would have been more likely to provoke his subjects than the trial or attainder—never mind the execution—of the admired woman most of them still regarded as their queen and her dutiful young daughter. The terms of Mary's confinement were, however, made even more stringent. She was allowed no visitors except, occasionally, Charles V's longtime ambassador Eustace Chapuys. By 1535 she and Chapuys were aware of rumors that the Boleyn party were planning to have her and her mother killed. (There is no evidence that any such thing was planned, but even the ugliest rumors had to be taken seriously now that Henry was killing old friends for refusing to accept his supremacy.) Soon Mary, her nerve failing along with her health, was begging Chapuys to help her escape to the continent. Nothing came of this, in part because Mary became too ill to flee (her physicians reported that she was immobilized by "grief and despair"), in part because the emperor Charles, short of money as usual, had no wish to assume responsibility for providing Mary with the kind of household appropriate to the princess that he himself declared her to be.

The death of Catherine early in 1536 brought fresh grief; even at the end Henry would not allow Mary to visit her mother. The political situation, however, was unaffected by the passing of the old queen (who was all of fifty when she died). It was her daughter, not she, who had a claim to the throne and therefore constituted a challenge to the new queen's security. Everything did change four and a half months later, however, with the nullification of Anne's marriage followed by her beheading; now the child Elizabeth was no less a bastard than Mary. Suddenly everything seemed open to negotiation and rearrangement. With no woman living who could claim to be his wife, Henry was free not only to marry whomever he chose but to do so with the blessings of the church; a healing of the breach with Rome had become entirely possible. The pope expected this to happen, as, probably, did Mary. Henry, however, appears never to have considered compromising the supremacy that he had taken such extreme measures to achieve. He wed Jane Seymour without so much as a nod in Rome's direction and proceeded with the consolidation of his power over the church. Nor did he display any interest in reconciliation with his eldest child.

It was left to Mary to seek an end to their estrangement. She began by approaching Cromwell, now the king's right hand, who replied that nothing would be possible until she showed herself willing to extend to her father the obedience that was his right. Cromwell meant, by this, that Mary must acknowledge that her parents had never been married and that Henry was supreme head of the church. Mary, however, chose to put an easier interpretation on his words, taking them as an invitation to assure her father in general terms that she remained his faithful and loving daughter. She wrote directly to the king, asking him "to consider that I am but a woman and your child, who hath committed her soul only to God, and her body to be ordered in this world as it shall stand with your pleasure." She assured him of her willingness to submit to him in all things "next to God."

Clearly she had little understanding of who her father was at this stage—of how convinced he was that the only way to be faithful to God was to be submissive to him. She must have had no understanding of how little the destruction of Anne Boleyn had done to soften his attitude toward anyone who resisted. Her three words "next to God" acted on Henry like a red cape on a bull. Instead of answering Mary's letter, he sent the Duke of Norfolk and the bishop of Chichester to where she was now being kept, at Hunsdon. They demanded to know whether she accepted the Act of Supremacy and her own illegitimacy. In refusing both points, Mary made herself doubly guilty of high treason. The climactic struggle between father and daughter was joined, throwing Mary into a situation vastly more dangerous than the worst of her earlier experiences.

The king and Cromwell had all the advantages, and they used them to full effect. What Cromwell wanted was not Mary's death, with its incalculable political risks, but her surrender. Therefore, though he removed members of the Privy Council suspected of being sympathetic to her, at the same time he brushed aside the demands of other members that she be brought to a trial that could only end in her conviction. And though some of her oldest and closest friends were arrested and questioned, this was done not in the expectation of learning anything but simply for the purpose of frightening Mary and anyone inclined to support her. Finally, three weeks after her first hopeful letter to the king, she broke, signing the articles of submission that Cromwell had prepared for her. Thereby she repudiated not only the Roman church but, in a real sense, her mother. Anyone inclined to judge her for this act should remember that

she was almost totally isolated, threatened not only with her own destruction but that of her most faithful friends, and barely twenty years
old.

It was perhaps King Henry's most grotesque victory, grotesque not
only because he achieved it over his own helpless child but because he
seems to have crushed, very nearly to have extinguished, her spirit. Chapuys would claim, in his dispatches, that Mary had yielded without
reading the articles of submission, that her motive had been to save not
herself but her friends, and that she was prostrate with guilt over having
compromised herself so deeply. Other evidence suggests that her surrender was very real and very nearly complete. A letter of effusive thanks to
Cromwell for saving her life gives no hint of being anything but sincere.
The same is true of Mary's letters to the emperor Charles and his sister,
the regent of the Netherlands; she told them of having been shown by
the Holy Spirit that the pope had no authority in England, and that her
parents' relationship had been incestuous. It is possible that she wrote
such things in the expectation that her correspondence was being intercepted by Cromwell; there is no way of being certain.

One thing only indicated that the autonomy of Mary's person had not
been utterly destroyed. Ordered to provide the names of those who had
advised and supported her in her refusal to submit, she not only declined but said she would die before betraying her friends in any such
way. At this point Cromwell—or was it Henry?—decided that the game
was at an end, that nothing could be gained by further intimidation or
new demands. Though not legitimated, Mary was restored to favor.
Henry visited her in company with his bride Jane Seymour, invited her
to begin spending time at court, and significantly increased her allowance. The household at Hatfield House was expanded and reorgan-
ized so that Mary's standing was equal to Elizabeth's.

By late 1536—the time of the Pilgrimage of Grace, which she did
nothing to encourage or support—Mary was spending a great deal of
time in her father's presence. She established an affectionate relationship
with Queen Jane, who was close to her in age and of similarly conservative religious leanings. The birth of Prince Edward in October 1537 came
as an immense relief to Mary: the existence of a male heir reduced her
political importance to an extent that she can only have welcomed after
so many years of tension. It must also have encouraged hopes that the

king might remove the cloud of illegitimacy from over her head. (In fact Henry, in futile pursuit of an understanding with France, offered at about this time to legitimize Mary in order to make possible her marriage to yet another prince of France's royal house.) Jane's death appears to have been at least as hard a blow for Mary as for Henry, but it did nothing to disturb her status at court. On the contrary, during the two years that the king remained unattached Mary basked in his favor, emerging as the most important female personage in England. His next wife, Anne of Cleves, came and went too quickly to present difficulties. Even during her father's marriage to Catherine Howard, Mary remained a significant presence at court. In Catherine Parr Mary found another friend; the fact that the two women became close in spite of Catherine's evangelical convictions is suggestive of the extent to which Mary was, at this point, unwilling to make an issue of religious differences.

A development of greater importance than Henry's sixth marriage was the new Act of Succession of 1543. It stated that if Edward died without offspring the crown was to go first to Mary and "the heirs of her body" and then, if Mary, too, died without issue, to Elizabeth and her descendants. This act became law without any effort to legitimate either Mary or Elizabeth (the king's marriages to their mothers remained null). It meant—bastardy always having been a barrier to succession—that for the first time in history an English king was claiming the right to *choose* his successors. Though it must have seemed improbable, in 1543, that not one of Henry's three offspring would leave a child to carry on the dynasty, the act made provision for such an eventuality by giving his Grey and Clifford cousins a place in the order of succession. It is ironic, in light of what history held in store, that the descendants of Henry's elder sister Margaret were excluded altogether. It is only through Margaret that today's royal family is related to the Tudors at all.

King Henry's death at the start of 1547 appeared at first to improve Mary's position. Now she was not only first in line to the throne but financially independent. Under the terms of her father's will she inherited property generating an annual income of nearly £4,000, which made her wealthier than anyone else in England aside from the new king and perhaps two or three members of the high nobility. For the first time in her life, and she was entering her thirties now, she did not have to look to the treasury for her support. The fact that much of her property was concentrated in East Anglia, having been taken from the Howards when Henry attainted the Duke of Norfolk and had the Earl of Surrey executed, gave her a base not far from London. She had always had a good relationship with the boy Edward, so the start of his reign appeared to presage good fortune.

The good times in Mary's life were always brief, however, and now as before, the question of religion brought trouble. It began with the Privy Council's determination, under the Duke of Somerset's leadership, to push ahead with innovations that the late king had consistently rejected. A decade had passed since Mary's acceptance of her father's supremacy. Since then she had shown herself to be consistently, almost surprisingly comfortable with the church that Henry had brought into existence—a church that conformed in most respects to Catholic tradition. In this she was no different from other leading conservatives, bishops such as Gardiner, Tunstal, and Bonner, and nobles such as Norfolk until his calamitous fall. If a definite settlement of disputed questions had not been achieved under Henry, a fairly solid truce had. It might have endured for years more, might have hardened into something permanent, if the evangelicals led by the increasingly heterodox Thomas Cranmer had not begun campaigning for further change, and if they had not received the full support of Protector Somerset, the council that he headed, and the boy-king himself. We saw earlier how Cranmer, just months after Henry's death, issued for the use of the entire clergy a book of homilies, sermons, that propounded the archbishop's acceptance of Lutheran dogma including justification by faith alone. This was, according to the Act of Six Articles passed by Parliament at Henry's direction in 1539 and still in effect at the time of his death, heresy pure and simple. Not surprisingly the book met with much resistance and much complaint. Some of the more prominent objectors—Gardiner, Bonner, old Tunstal—soon found themselves in prison and deprived of their offices.

Mary, not only of royal blood and popular with the people but heir presumptive to the throne, presented the reformers with a delicate challenge. Without questioning the royal supremacy—doing so would have made her no less a heretic than the evangelicals—she protested that Cranmer and his faction were violating the law of the land, trampling on the terms of her father's last will and testament, and imposing innovations that could not possibly be acceptable until her brother reached his majority and became capable of leading the church. When Parliament changed the law, nullifying the Six Articles and other obstacles to reform, she again took the position that it had no right to do any such thing during the king's minority. By 1549, when the new reign's first Act of Uniformity replaced the mass with Cranmer's service and ignited the Prayer Book rebellion, Mary protested more vehemently than before and received from the council a letter advising her to be "conformable and obedient to the observation of his Majesty's laws." Her response dripped with contempt. She told the councilors that the Act of Uniformity was "a late law of your own making for the altering of matters of religion, which in my conscience is not worthy to have the name of law."

For much of the next four years she was virtually at war with the government whose head she would become in the event of Edward's death. With the fall of Somerset and the rise of John Dudley, things grew so much worse that Mary once again believed she was going to have to flee to the continent to save her life. Charles V sent three ships to rescue her by dark of night; at the last moment, though frightened and confused, she decided that duty required her to stay in England. She became the most conspicuously defiant champion of the old ways. Ordered to travel to London and present herself to the king and his council, she entered the city at the head of an entourage of some 150 friends and retainers, every one of whom displayed either a rosary or some other forbidden symbol of the old faith. Ordered by Edward to conform, she reduced him to tears by replying that she would die first. Several of the senior officers of her household, upon refusing to try to persuade her to abandon the mass, were thrown into prison. When representatives of the king arrived to inform her that she would no longer be permitted to hear mass (the delegation was headed by Baron Rich, now lord chancellor and a very wealthy man, the same Richard Rich whose perjured testimony had facilitated the killing of Thomas More and John Fisher two decades before), she dismissed them scornfully.

The conflict ended in a standoff. The law against the saying or hearing of mass continued in effect, but no effort was made to enforce it in Mary's case. Eventually she was even able to resume her visits to her brother, spending time with him amicably as long as both avoided the subject of religion. It was clear to everyone, however, and to Edward more than to most, that in all of England there was no enemy of his evangelical establishment more dangerous or determined than his heir. Nothing could be less surprising than Edward's decision, when he knew that his life was ending, to prevent Mary from succeeding him. Or Mary's commitment, once she had stopped Dudley from putting Jane Grey on the throne, to destroy the Edwardian Reformation root and branch.

20

Another New Beginning

From the hour she entered London as queen, Mary Tudor faced a daunting array of challenges. She had to take charge of a government most of whose senior members—both those who were now her prisoners and those still in office—had actively opposed her succession. She had to assume the headship of a church whose primate publicly condemned her as a heretic and had supported Jane Grey to the end. The treasury she had inherited was not only empty but deep in debt, her kingdom too enfeebled by financial mismanagement to play a weighty role in international affairs, her people confused and divided by three decades of religious convulsion.

Of course she had an agenda of her own and her own priorities. She wanted a regime, a religious settlement especially, that accorded with her view of what was true and false, what right and wrong. To accomplish this she was going to have to decide who were her friends and who her enemies, who could be trusted and who could not. She had had almost no training in government, had in no way been prepared to rule. And, being a thirty-seven-year-old virgin whose heir was both the daughter of her mother's great enemy and obviously on the evangelical side of the religious divide, she had good reason to want to produce a child. But she had little time in which to do so—her biological clock was approaching sunset.

When she arrived at the Tower, which in keeping with tradition was to be her residence until her coronation, Mary was welcomed by a rather pathetic little collection of eager well-wishers. One was the old Duke of Norfolk, an octogenarian now, who had remained a prisoner since narrowly escaping execution at the end of Henry VIII's reign. Another was Stephen Gardiner, who had risen high in Henry's service only to lose his seat on the council, then the Bishopric of Winchester, and finally his freedom. Still another was young Edward Courtenay; like his cousin Mary he was a great-grandchild of King Edward IV, and he had literally grown up in the Tower after being locked away at the time of his father's execution fifteen years before. For them and for others, Mary's arrival meant deliverance from what otherwise might have been confinement until death. And for all of them, release meant more than liberty. The bishops deposed during Edward's reign were soon restored to their sees. Gardiner was not only restored but became chancellor. Norfolk was given back much of the Howard family patrimony and his place on the council. Courtenay was made Earl of Devon and, because of his royal blood and his family's conservative credentials, found himself put forward as a possible husband for the queen. If they were not all her friends, strictly speaking, at worst they were the enemies of her enemies. That was not nothing.

Mary was generous even with those who obviously were her enemies—at least with most of them. The whole sprawling Dudley connection—John, Duke of Northumberland, his brother Andrew, all five of his sons, his daughter-in-law Jane Grey and Jane's father the Duke of Suffolk—were in custody along with various of their supporters and allies. Most were put on trial for treason, convicted (the guilt of the accused being, for once, certain beyond possibility of doubt), and attainted. But only the duke and two obscure henchmen were executed. Jane and her husband Guildford Dudley, though under sentence of death, were kept in the Tower in comfortable circumstances, as were Guildford's brothers John, Earl of Warwick, Ambrose, Robert, and Henry. Suffolk was, somehow, released without being charged. Thomas Cranmer, who after initial hesitation had thrown himself fully behind Dudley's attempted coup, was merely confined to Lambeth Palace, the archbishop of Canterbury's London residence. He was permitted to preside at King Edward's funeral ceremony and to use the reformed rites in doing so. Mary declared that she "wished to constrain no man to go to mass" or to "compel or constrain other men's consciences." A proclamation informed her subjects that nothing would be done to alter the Edwardian settlement until a Parliament was assembled to address the question. When that old champion of reform John Dudley faced the crowd that had gathered to witness his execution, he professed himself to be a Catholic who prayed for England's return to the old faith. (He could hardly have meant the *Roman* Catholic faith, but possibly he was hoping to win favor for all the members of his family whom Mary had in custody.) The conservatives must have thought that a reversion to the traditional ways was going to be accomplished without great pain: Dudley's conduct would have encouraged them to believe that the evangelical movement was made up entirely of self-seeking opportunists prepared to abandon their heresies as soon as pressure was applied.

The evangelicals for their part, having had things almost entirely their way since the last months of Henry VIII, remained fiercely committed to expunging every trace of Catholicism from English life. This was true of no one more than of Cranmer, who seemed to grow more radical by the month. By 1553 he had had ready for Parliament's attention his Code of Ecclesiastical Constitutions, a revision of canon law that, if enacted, would have made it heresy to believe not just in papal supremacy but in transubstantiation (described as "repugnant to the plain words of scripture") and *not* to believe in justification by faith alone. Anyone accused of such offenses was to be tried in the church courts, excommunicated upon conviction, and given sixteen days in which to recant or be turned over to the civil authorities for execution. John Dudley, who blamed Cranmer for the frequency with which evangelical preachers were offending the rich and powerful by criticizing their ongoing seizures of church property, had taken his revenge by blocking action on Cranmer's code in the House of Lords. He then discredited the proposal—cleverly gave Parliament a reason to reject it—by allowing it to be published under a demonstrably false claim that it had the approval of the Canterbury Convocation.

In all likelihood Dudley was able to thwart Cranmer only because by this point the young king was on the brink of death. Almost certainly the code would have become law—Dudley might not have dared even to raise objections—if Edward had remained strong enough to give it vigorous support. It accorded perfectly with his revulsion against

Catholic doctrine and his belief that it was his responsibility to transform England into Christ's kingdom on earth. Cranmer's attempt to re-
vise canon law shows that he was no less willing than the most radical
reformers on the continent to use the state's power over life and death
to stamp out error and spread the gospel. It is impossible to doubt that
Edward would have gone along with him.

Cranmer was understandably bitter after Mary became queen. Not
only had everything that he still wanted to achieve suddenly become impossible, but the stupendous gains of the past half-dozen years were in
imminent danger of being undone. News reached him of one setback
after another. Even Elizabeth, in whom the evangelicals had invested so
much hope, was reported to be attending mass with her sister the
queen, establishing a chapel in her home, even ordering from the continent a chalice, a cross, and other things useful only for engaging in the
ceremonies of the papists. Cranmer exploded in rage when informed
that a mass had been celebrated in his cathedral church at Canterbury
and, worse, that it was said to have been done with his approval. His
printed denial dripped with invective, condemning the mass as a concoction of the pope, that arch-persecutor of Christ and true religion. He
asked for an opportunity to demonstrate to the queen herself that the
mass was blasphemy and that the church as purified during her brother's
reign expressed the authentic spirit of Christianity. This got him a summons to appear before the council, followed by commitment to the
Tower. Neither he nor anyone else can possibly have been surprised.
Cranmer had not only been conspicuous among those proclaiming Jane
Grey queen, he had contributed part of his personal security force to the
army with which Dudley had set forth from London to confront and
capture Mary. Now he was accused also of "spreading abroad seditious
bills, and moving tumults to the disquietness of the present state," and
his guilt was again obvious.

From the start of Mary's reign, however, the attention of council,
Parliament, court, and even the kingdom at large was focused at least as
much on the question of the queen's marriage as on religious issues.
Mary appears to have had little if any personal interest in taking a husband. There was nothing in her past to suggest that she had ever had
strong romantic inclinations, or that she was a particularly sexual creature. In the 1530s, at the nadir of her fortunes, she had expressed the

hope of entering the religious life, possibly in Spain. By 1553 she seemed
a settled, satisfied, and distinctly middle-aged spinster, an amiable creature who enjoyed music and dance and gambling for small stakes and
shared her father's and brother's taste for jewelry and costly dress, but
was no more inclined than she had been in youth to engage in flirtations
or dalliances. It was a long time since she had had great value on the international marriage market, an equally long time since she had given
evidence of wishing for a spouse or children.

But she had been raised and educated to be not a ruler but a consort
to some male monarch. And now, contrary to everyone's expectations
including her own, she found herself an unmarried female monarch in a
world that scarcely knew what to make of such an anomaly. Her situation seemed unnatural to almost everyone—certainly to Mary herself. It
seemed contrary to nature that any woman, even a queen, should not be
subordinate to some man. The universal question, virtually from the
first day of her reign, was not *whether* she should marry but *whom*.

It is understandable if Mary herself, so alone and vulnerable for much
of her life, welcomed the thought of a partner with whom to share the
unfamiliar burdens of rule. It is no less understandable if she wanted a
child—and not for sentimental reasons, but as the one sure way of ensuring that England would not fall back into the hands of the evangelicals after her death. If she could find a partner capable of compensating
for her lack of political experience and skill, so much the better. But
what was truly essential was that her husband be a religious conservative—certainly a Catholic, preferably a Roman Catholic. That narrowed
the field of candidates. One obvious possibility was Mary's cousin Reginald Pole, who as a young man had broken with Henry over the divorce,
observed from abroad as the king destroyed one of his brothers and executed another and finally had his mother killed as well, and now was a
cardinal of the church (though not an ordained priest and therefore not
under a binding vow of celibacy). Pole was so well respected as a person,
a scholar, and a reformer-from-within that in 1549, while doing nothing
to advance his own candidacy, he had come within two votes of being
elected pope. He had only one disadvantage, but it was a decisive one:
seventeen years older than Mary, Pole had no intention of marrying her
or anyone else. In fact he was opposed to Mary's taking a husband, see-

ing more clearly than most that whoever she chose, whether English or foreign, was going to present her with serious political problems.

Another possibility was another of the queen's cousins, that same Edward Courtenay, now the Earl of Devon and endowed with estates consistent with his new rank, who had come to manhood as a prisoner in the Tower. Among Courtenay's advantages was the fact that his mother, the widow Gertrude, Marchioness of Exeter (Henry VIII had had her husband killed), happened to be one of Mary's oldest, closest, and most faithful friends. Courtenay was a quarter of a century younger than Pole, a decade younger than the queen. His mother, not surprisingly, thought he would make a splendid consort, and the fact of his royal blood won him the support of most of the experienced politicians on the council, Chancellor Gardiner among them. These men believed, as did virtually everyone in those days, that no woman should attempt to rule without a husband. They believed also that popular opinion would be far more accepting of an English husband than of any foreigner. Gardiner had another, more personal reason for supporting Courtenay. During their years as fellow prisoners they had formed a close relationship, one that apparently caused the bishop to regard the youth as a kind of surrogate son and blinded him to the defects in Courtenay's character.

The list of possible foreign husbands was extensive and included the king of Denmark and the heir to the throne of Portugal. When Mary sought the advice of her cousin the emperor Charles—she had been taught by her mother to trust her Hapsburg kin, and all her life looked to them for guidance and support—he briefly considered offering to marry her himself. Mary made it clear that she would welcome such an offer (the two had, after all, been engaged when Mary was a small child); Charles was a widower (not for the first time), and though she had not seen him in decades he had, at long distance, come to seem not only a protector but a kind of father. But he was Pole's age, and thoroughly world-weary after a lifetime of struggling to hold together his vast but ramshackle and perpetually threatened empire. He had the good sense to rule himself out. But rather than forgo the advantages of a firm and lasting alliance with England, even perhaps of adding England to a Hapsburg patrimony that already included Spain and the Netherlands and much of Germany and Italy and the New World, he offered his son Philip.

Immediately Philip became, with Courtenay, one of the two leading candidates. He also became a bone of contention inside the English court. Favored by most of Mary's female intimates and the men who had been officers of her household in the bad old days before her brother's death (several of those men now sat on the Privy Council despite being political innocents), Philip was opposed by Gardiner and most of the council's other old hands. These seasoned professionals, several of whom had sat on Edward VI's council and been followers of John Dudley right up to the point where the effort to enthrone Jane Grey collapsed, understood the impact of the anti-Spanish propaganda that had begun with Henry VIII and grown steadily more intense as the Reformation proceeded under his son. Many of the people alive in England in 1553 had been taught from childhood that Spain was the handmaiden of the Antichrist. Philip, though a Hapsburg, was a *Spanish* Hapsburg, and many of Mary's subjects were certain to find him hard if not impossible to accept.

Mary was unpersuaded, perhaps in part because she had little confidence in some of the men who warned her of danger. A number of her advisers remained on the council only because they were too influential, too dangerous, to be put aside. Everything in her experience disposed her to want an alliance with the Hapsburgs. When she was shown a portrait of the blond and blue-eyed Philip—no doubt one of the portraits that showed off the legs of which he was so proud—this inclination turned into infatuation.

In fact Philip had much to recommend him, and not just his family connections. At twenty-six he was already a significant figure on the world stage, intelligent and serious-minded and an experienced junior partner in the management of his father's immense (and at times unmanageable) domains. Like his father a widower (his first wife had been a Portuguese cousin), he had a young son and so was obviously fertile. If he was known to dally with women to whom he was not married, he never did so as recklessly as young Courtenay, who had begun to run wild almost as soon as he was released from prison. In any case, such dalliance was neither unexpected in royalty nor easily condemned in a healthy young man whose wife had been dead for eight years and whose chances for remarriage were circumscribed by the political schemes of his father the emperor. The Hapsburgs had for centuries been masters of the advantageous marriage; it was how they had extended their empire into the Netherlands, Spain, and elsewhere. It would hardly have been reasonable to expect the men of the family to be entirely satisfied with wives chosen for reasons of territorial expansion. As for Mary, no daughter of Henry VIII could have been deeply shocked by the thought of discreet sexual adventuring on the part of royal males.

Courtenay, whose good looks and aristocratic bearing had made a favorable initial impression in the days just after his release, was soon showing that fifteen years in prison had left him desperately eager for the pleasures of the flesh. Arrogance and dissolute behavior soon cost him all but his most indulgent supporters, mainly his mother and Gardiner. The queen, who had little difficulty in taking Courtenay's measure, appears never to have seriously considered marrying him. English and Spanish diplomats were put to work on constructing the terms of a Hapsburg marriage, while Mary turned her attention to other concerns. Arrangements got under way for the first Parliament of the new reign, and for a coronation ceremony to be conducted beforehand, so as to avoid any suggestion that Mary's possession of the crown was dependent on parliamentary approval. The coronation, a lavish affair, took place on October 1 with Gardiner presiding in place of Archbishop Cranmer. Mary took an oath that avoided any mention of the reforms of the preceding reign and omitted all the words with which the boy Edward, at his coronation, had laid claim to supremacy over the church. Two days before, in an even more forceful demonstration of her determination to break with the recent past, Mary had gathered the members of her council in the Tower. Lowering herself to her knees, she had spoken earnestly, almost tearfully of the *duties* rather than the powers of monarchs, and of her wish to fulfill those duties to the limits of her strength. The episode suggests the depth of Mary's wish to rule well and wisely, and her lack of confidence in her own abilities. It is impossible to imagine her father, or her brother even at age nine, assuming such a posture or uttering such words.

Philip, meanwhile, was coming to terms with the prospect of taking as his wife a woman eleven years his senior, a woman he was accustomed to calling his aunt. He had been exploring a marriage to yet another Portuguese princess (his mother as well as his first wife had come from the royal house of Portugal, the Hapsburgs being almost suicidally

insensitive to the dangers of inbreeding) when Europe was surprised to
learn that Mary Tudor had emerged from the turmoil following her
brother's death in firm possession of the English throne. It seems improbable that the emperor Charles, in offering his son to Mary, was motivated primarily by the hope of adding England permanently to the
family business. He was aware of Mary's age and the chronically troublesome state of her health; the likelihood of her producing healthy
children would have seemed less than impressive. Beyond that he already possessed more of Europe and the Americas than he and his son
together could properly manage even with the help of various kin, and
the England of the 1550s seemed to Charles and Philip alike (not entirely without reason) a poor, half-civilized island of distinctly secondary
importance perched off one of Europe's less attractive coasts. But the
marriage offered important advantages all the same. It could eliminate
the danger of England's entering into an alliance with Spain's archen-
emy, the king of France. The south coast of England formed the northern edge of the English Channel, the nautical highway that connected
Spain to the Hapsburgs' Low Countries possessions and was bounded to
the south by France. Charles, after decades of fending off ambitious rivals, after recurrent wars that had cost him much and gained him nothing, after the failure of all his attempts to stamp out the Reformation in
Germany, was worn down and heartsick. He was beginning to dream of
passing his burdens to his son, of devoting whatever remained of his life
to a preparation for death. The English marriage could help to make this
possible. In all of Europe there were few economic relationships more
important than that between England and the Netherlands, and Hapsburg—meaning Spanish—rule of the Netherlands was far from popular.
But if Philip married the queen of England, if he himself became England's king, he could at a single stroke be transformed from an alien op-
pressor to an asset valuable to the Dutch. The delicate process of
passing the crown of Spain (and with it possession of the Netherlands)
from Charles to Philip might be vastly simplified. That alone was
enough to make the marriage appealing.

Ten days after Mary's coronation Philip's formal proposal of marriage arrived at her court. Within the month, with Parliament in session,
Mary informed the council of her decision to accept. The news proved
to be as unpopular as Pole and Gardiner had feared: England did not

want a foreign king, least of all a Spanish one. Parliament sent a delegation to the queen, expressing its unhappiness with her plans and begging
her to reconsider. Her peremptory refusal—her anger at Parliament's
presuming to intrude into a matter as personal as matrimony, its effron-
tery in supposing that she might subordinate the interests of her subjects to the promptings of her heart—soon persuaded an assortment of
disaffected and unstable hotheads that only desperate measures could
save England from becoming an appendage of the Hapsburg empire.
Mary had made the first great mistake, indeed the seminal blunder, of
her reign. She had put herself at odds not only with some portion of
England's ruling elite but with many of her people.

A marriage treaty still needed to be hammered out, one that would
settle the specific terms of the union. Mary had sufficient acumen to as-
sign the negotiations to Stephen Gardiner, who, as the highest-placed
opponent of the match, could be depended upon not only to drive a
hard bargain but, once he had satisfied himself, to have maximum credibility in bringing other skeptics around. Parliament meanwhile, perhaps chastened by the queen's anger, proved cooperative in other
matters. By repealing Henry VIII's Succession Act of 1534 it restored the
validity of the marriage of Mary's parents, thereby making her once
again legitimate. The most recent and aggressive definitions of treason
were likewise repealed, so that treason became once again what it had
been in the fifteenth century: an overt action, not just something *said*.
All nine Edwardian reform statutes, Cranmer's acts of uniformity and
the legalization of clerical marriage included, were swept away. Essentially the church was returned to what it had been at the time of Henry
VIII's death, and in some respects to what it had been under Henry VII.
Praemunire crimes were abolished, along with felonies that had not
been violations of the law until Henry VIII made them so.

Ambitious as all this was, Mary and Gardiner were proceeding with
caution. They had separated the question of Mary's legitimacy from the
religious issues, specifically from the issue of supremacy. Nothing had
been done to bring the supremacy under discussion and thereby to
alarm at least the more moderate reformers. (About the radicals nothing could be done. They of course had been alarmed and offended since
it first became plain that Mary had won the throne.)

Nor was anything done or said to indicate that the new regime was so much as thinking about the one subject even more explosive than the marriage: the church land that had been seized by Henry and his cohorts in the 1530s, had since then been given to favorites or sold and broken up and sold again, and now was in the hands of noble and gentry families in every corner of the kingdom. Gardiner had warned Mary not only that there was no possibility of returning this property to the church, but that any move in that direction would spark a reaction so violent as to wreck any possibility of progress on other fronts. The emperor Charles and his son, who had come to regard it as one of their purposes in life to heal the schism in England if they could not do so in Germany, agreed so completely that they successfully pressured Pope Julius II to assent as well. They were opposed, however, by Cardinal Pole, whom the pope had ordered to England as his legate and was now in the Low Countries awaiting permission to cross the Channel. Pole, after decades of exile from his home country, had no understanding of how alien the notion of papal supremacy now was to many Englishmen, or of how the dispersion of the church lands had given rise to a whole new class that would go to war before surrendering the foundation of its wealth and influence. He found himself stalled just a short voyage from home. The Hapsburgs wanted him kept away until Philip was safely married to the queen—Charles wrongly feared that if given the opportunity Pole might claim the bride for himself—and Gardiner wanted no trouble over the land question. Parliament, both of its houses dominated by exactly the kinds of men who had prospered mightily from the dispersion of the church land, was relieved to find that Mary was doing nothing about the subject. It remained distrustful, however, and would continue to be so.

Before year-end Gardiner was able to disclose the contents of a completed marriage treaty. It was, from the English perspective, a thoroughly favorable arrangement: Gardiner had been able to use the Spanish ambassadors' understanding of English public opinion to extract extraordinary concessions. If Mary and Philip had a son, the treaty stated, he would be heir not only to England but to Philip's possessions in Germany, Burgundy, and the Netherlands. Philip's son Charles, then eight years old, was acknowledged as heir to Spain and the Hapsburg holdings in Italy and the New World, but if he died without issue that entire empire would go to the English heir as well. If on the other hand

Mary died without issue, Philip was to have no claim to the English crown or, for that matter, to anything in England. Mary and any children that she might bear were not to leave England without permission of Parliament, thereby ensuring that the children would be English in their upbringing. Though Philip was to be styled king of England he was to assist Mary in ruling, not rule himself. Nothing was to be done to alter the laws or customs of England, and England was not to be involved in the Hapsburgs' wars.

Opponents of the marriage could hardly have hoped for more, but nevertheless news of the agreement was received without enthusiasm. People grumbled that words on paper meant nothing, because the Spanish could not be trusted, and that if Mary did have a son he would grow up to rule not England but a far-flung assortment of domains of which England would be only a part. There was grumbling on the continent, understandably, where some thought too high a price was being paid for a union of little real value to anyone except the English and perhaps the Dutch. Philip himself, when he learned the details of what his father's representatives had promised, was aghast. To him the agreement seemed insulting. He secretly signed a document repudiating the treaty on grounds that he had not been consulted about its terms and therefore could not be bound by them. Thus what should have been seen as a diplomatic victory for England became instead a shaky foundation upon which to erect a lasting understanding.

Disclosure of the treaty's terms, which remained subject to approval by Parliament, did nothing to stop secret plans for simultaneous rebellions in several parts of England. These plans—it is not clear where they originated—had been in preparation since shortly after the queen's refusal to be deflected from the marriage. The aim of the plotters also remains unclear and was probably a confused mixture. They certainly wanted to stop the wedding, probably hoped to depose Mary (though a proposal that she should be assassinated had been rejected), and possibly intended to replace her by marrying Elizabeth to Courtenay and crowning them together. The risings were scheduled for March 1554 and were to take place simultaneously in four places: Devon in the west, Hereford and Leicestershire to the north, and Kent near London. The hope, evidently, was that a government that had no standing army would find it impossible to deal with so many irruptions at the same time. But by January Gardiner had learned that trouble of some kind was brewing. He had his protégé and onetime prison-mate Courtenay brought in for questioning. Whatever Courtenay knew he quickly revealed, and when the plotters saw that their secret had been disclosed they decided to act without further delay. Everywhere but in Kent the results were disastrous—or pathetic. In Devon the ringleaders ran for their lives as soon as they saw that no one was willing to rise with them, and the attempt in Hereford fizzled almost as quickly. In Leicester Jane Grey's father the Duke of Suffolk, the only nobleman among the plotters, foolishly put himself at the head of a rebellion that likewise came to nothing. On the run, he tried to hide in a hollow tree but was found out by a sharp-nosed dog and taken to the Tower in chains.

In Kent, however, it was a different story. There the rising was led by a cabal of disaffected country gentlemen with substantial military experience, a history of association with King Edward's regime, and hopes of gaining much if Mary's government could be overturned. Prominent among these men was Sir Thomas Wyatt, son of a famous poet and courtier of the same name. He had been involved in the plotting as early as November and was able, when the rising went off prematurely, to quickly assemble several thousand fighting men. That was a force quite big enough to challenge the queen—it soon swelled to fifteen or even twenty thousand—and with it Wyatt began advancing on London. He was met at Rochester by troops mustered in London and commanded by the aged Duke of Norfolk, who found himself first outnumbered and then neutralized by the defection of a substantial portion of his army.

It was a genuine emergency. The capital was virtually undefended, the queen in real danger of losing the crown that she had won scarcely half a year before. The imperial ambassador offered to request troops from the continent, while many of Mary's councilors urged her to flee. Once again she was saved by her own courage. She refused the offer of foreign military support and refused also to leave London. Instead she put her faith in her subjects, and her fate in their hands. She went to the Guildhall, one of London's great gathering places, and in an impromptu speech addressed a gathering of citizens assembled by the lord mayor. She denounced Wyatt and his fellow conspirators, accusing them of wanting not only to prevent her marriage but to usurp the authority of the Crown and use it for their own narrow purposes. Scepter in hand, she declared her confidence that her subjects would never allow the rebels to prevail.

"As for this marriage," she said, "ye shall understand that I enterprised not the doing thereof without the advice of all our Privy Council. Nor am I, I assure ye, so bent to my own will, or so affectionate, that for my own pleasure I would choose where I lust, or needs must have a husband. I have hitherto lived a maid; and doubt nothing, but with God's grace I am able to live so still. Certainly, did I think that this marriage were to the hurt of you my subjects, or the impeachment of my royal estate, I would never consent thereunto. And I promise you, on the word of a queen, that if it shall not appear to the Lords and Commons in Parliament to be for the benefit of the whole realm, I will never marry while I live. Wherefore stand fast against these rebels, your enemies and mine. Fear them not, for I assure ye I fear them nothing at all." It was as splendid a moment as any in the history of English royalty. Mary departed to shouts of approval, and within hours more than twenty thousand men had volunteered to defend her and the city. By the next morning Wyatt, because he had failed to attack while the city lay open to him, was doomed to defeat. His followers, faced with the defiance of the queen's defenders, began to melt away. He proceeded nevertheless, penetrated to St. James's Palace and beyond, and again caused a panic that only Mary's resolution prevented from turning into a headlong flight of the entire court. Finally, on the morning of February 7, what remained of the rebellion fell apart. Wyatt threw down his sword and surrendered. It had been a near thing, but when it was over Mary found her position strengthened. The fact that Wyatt's early success had not caused the rebellion to spread, and her fresh demonstration of courage, were enough to put heart into the queen's friends and discourage further plotting. For the second time in half a year Mary had been tested, as had the loyalty of the kingdom, and neither had been found wanting.

As always in such matters, the rebellion left a residue that had to be cleared away. Wyatt of course was executed for treason, along with a number of the other ringleaders. The Duke of Suffolk, having again betrayed Mary in spite of the leniency that she had extended to him after the fall of John Dudley, also went to his death. Far less inevitably, his daughter Jane and Jane's husband Guildford Dudley were executed as well. They had had nothing to do with the rebellion, but it was not unreasonable for the authorities to fear that if the pair remained alive they would serve as a rallying point for the discontented. In all some 480 men were convicted of treason, but fewer than a hundred died. The others were pardoned, in most cases without so much as being fined. Mary's government took far less vengeance than that of Edward VI had done five years earlier in dealing with risings that never challenged his right to the crown.

Restrained as they were in meting out punishment, however, the queen and her chancellor made a mistake that would prove to have poisonous consequences. Faced with the confused aims and conflicting grievances of the rebel leaders, they chose to conclude that the rebellion had erupted not chiefly in opposition to the Spanish marriage (such a conclusion would have been uncomfortable in light of Mary's determination to proceed) but in the hope of restoring the evangelical church. Their willingness—possibly it was eagerness—to believe that Protestantism had given rise to treason made it easy to go a step further and conclude that Protestantism *was* treason, to equate religious dissent with sedition. This could help to explain the execution of Jane Grey and her husband: if evangelicals were irreconcilable enemies of Mary's regime, they were likely to try again to put Jane on the throne. Such thinking would lead Mary and her associates to acts that echoed the outrages committed by Henry VIII and foreshadowed further atrocities in the next reign. It was profoundly misguided, there being no conclusive evidence that the objectives of Wyatt and his cohorts were mainly religious at all. Not only when put on trial but before and during the revolt, many of them had professed to be Catholic.

Elizabeth and Courtenay presented a particularly difficult problem. Courtenay certainly had been aware of the conspiracy before it became known to the government; after telling Gardiner everything, he had declared his support for the queen and even participated—though in a characteristically ineffectual and even cowardly fashion—in the battle with the rebels. Equally certainly, Wyatt had written of his plans to Elizabeth, but if she replied she did so orally or her letters were destroyed. After the collapse of the rebellion she along with Courtenay was confined in the Tower, but relentless questioning failed to draw anything incriminating out of her and evidence of her involvement remained circumstantial and thin. The imperial ambassador argued for her execution, warning that her very existence made her a danger to the queen, a focus not only for evangelical subversion but for a French king so desperate to prevent the union of England and Spain that he was encouraging sedition wherever he could find it. It certainly lay within the power of the Crown to have Elizabeth done away with, but Mary and Gardiner refused. Ultimately Elizabeth was sent to the royal estate at Woodstock, where she prudently did everything possible to satisfy her sister that she was a sincere and observant Catholic. Courtenay, too, was released. He was sent traveling on the continent, undoubtedly in the hope that at such a distance he would be less able to make a nuisance of himself. The French ambassador, though he had encouraged the rebellion and even promised that his king would support it with troops, was likewise set free after brief confinement.

Mary had won. She was free to enter upon what would prove to be the golden part of her reign, probably the best months she had experienced since childhood. That it would end so soon and so badly is the saddest part of her story.

SCHOOLING AND THE SCHOOLS

ONE OF THE FEW ENDURING MYTHS ABOUT THE SHORT, sad, and largely forgotten reign of Edward VI is that it brought a new birth of education to Britain, an explosion in the number, availability, and quality of schools. The myth finds support in the fact that a number of England's oldest and most prestigious private schools proudly bear Edward's name and claim to have been founded with money provided by the Crown.

The truth, as usual with Tudor myths, is neither so simple nor nearly so edifying. A great many of the so-called Edward VI schools were not started or endowed but re-endowed during their namesake's time on the throne. Many in fact were merely the survivors of the pillaging of church and community property that made the Tudor era not a boon to education but rather the interruption of a long, slow process of educational expansion. That process had begun before Edward's father was born (St. Paul's School, which would set the standard for grammar schools across England, began in the same year Henry VIII became king), and it would not recover its momentum until years after the boy-king himself was dead.

Throughout the Tudor era education remained what it had long been in England: a thing available, at least beyond a rudimentary level, to only a tiny part of the population. It had begun, of course, as an enterprise of the church; instruction had always been one of the functions of the monasteries and the parish clergy. In 1179 the Lateran Council in Rome had ordered every bishop to establish an institution to train clergy for his diocesan chapter, and the resulting "cathedral schools" had joined the monasteries as places where young clerics could become literate and be prepared for university. Outside the church there was, for centuries, almost no such thing as an educational establishment and no need or demand for one. The elite families were obliged to do little more, in occupational terms, than manage their lands. To the extent that their male offspring aspired to anything beyond more wealth and more power, it was usually to become warrior-knights of the kind idealized in tales of medieval chivalry. The nobility sent their sons to each other's castles to be trained in the martial arts, to learn to comport themselves in a manner appropriate to their status, and to make the kinds of connections that could pay dividends later in life. Hence the desire to find places in the homes of the most important people possible, and the supreme value, at the court of the young Henry VIII, of being good at jousting and other aristocratic games. Though education was gradually coming to seem relevant, the barely literate could still flourish in high society.

For the great mass of people, at the end of the Tudor period no less than at the beginning, education beyond some basic reading and perhaps writing instruction from the local parish priest was simply not an option. The only available careers, at the bottom of the social pyramid, were agricultural labor and domestic service, and that was literally as far as opportunities went. For families of greater but still modest means, the best road to prosperity often led through apprenticeships. Such a family could, upon payment of a bond, enter a son (or even, in relatively rare cases, a daughter) into an indenture contract that provided a years-long course of training in the household of a skilled specialist in some craft or trade. Apprentices were usually between ten and fourteen years old at the start of their training, which lasted about seven years during which they received food and lodging but little or no pay and were pledged to remain unmarried and avoid drunkenness, gambling, and other forms of misbehavior. ("Fornication within the house of his said Master hee shall not commit," an apparently representative indenture reads, "matrimony with any woman dureinge the said tearme hee shall not contract.") Upon completing his apprenticeship and a further year or so as a journeyman working for pay, the new carpenter, tailor, cordmaker, tanner, butcher, barber, baker, or whatever would become free to join a guild and set up shop as a master of his specialty. The guilds regulated competition (limiting the number of shops in a particular area and the amount of work that any member could undertake, for example), monitored quality and maintained standards, provided assistance to the sick or unemployed, and supported local charities. Their aim was a stable, almost static marketplace in which every competent participant was protected and no individual was allowed to get too far ahead of the rest.

Before becoming old enough to enter an apprenticeship, a child might (or just as possibly might not) spend a few years in a petty school or "dame school," basically a kind of day-care facility, usually operated in the home of some literate member of the community, where some degree of instruction in the basics of religion as well as reading (but usually not writing) English was available. Girls attended such schools, but this was as far as they could go with education outside the home. Sons of the most prosperous and ambitious families could proceed to grammar schools rather than into apprenticeships, and that was where education turned serious. The entry age for grammar school was seven, generally, and those who completed the full course remained for about seven years. Their lives, during those years, appear to have been positively hellish. Grammar school pupils, like all children through the Middle Ages and the Renaissance, were regarded as miniature adults and therefore capable of adult behavior, and all but the most exceptional schoolmasters subjected them to iron-hard discipline. The school day started at six in the morning—seven during the dark months of winter—and continued until about five P.M. The heart of the curriculum was instruction in Latin, supplemented with religion and arithmetic and sometimes a smattering of Greek, and though the older pupils were supposedly exposed to such classic authors as Ovid, Cicero, Virgil, and Horace, most of their time was devoted (books being expensive and therefore scarce except in the most generously funded establishments) to memorization and recital by rote. Unsatisfactory performance was met with lashings with birch canes or similar instruments. This was the routine year-round, the only breaks occurring at Christmas and Easter and lasting just two and a half weeks.

Latin was emphasized so heavily because it was the language of the universities and therefore synonymous with academic achievement, and because it was what the teachers knew. Because in most schools all age groups were together in a single large room (most had only a single master plus, sometimes, an assistant or "usher"), all the chanted recitations must have created a constant racket. Even the exercises in English would present special challenges for today's students. The alphabet in use in England in the sixteenth century had only twenty-four letters: *u* and *v* were the same letter (the first was used in the middle of a word, the second at the beginning), as were *i* and *j* (*j* being used as the capital form of *i*). Though other letters were used exactly as we use them today, in the handwritten form of four and a half centuries ago they would be indecipherable to the modern reader. A long-since-forgotten symbol that was almost but not exactly the letter *y* represented the same sound as *th* (as in "ye olde chandlery" or whatever). Roman numerals were much more commonly used then than now, and the last in a series of Roman *i*'s was written as a *j*: thus "King Henry *viij*." Spelling was freely improvised and would remain so until someone presumed to publish a guide to the subject in 1558.

From about the mid-fourteenth century on, families of means showed increasing willingness not only to subject their sons to the grammar school regimen but to make significant financial sacrifices in order to do so. Their reasons were perfectly rational: in a developing economy where subsistence farming was no longer an inescapable fate for nearly everyone, opportunities were opening up in commerce, government, and other fields but were available only to the educated. And though the use of English for official purposes was no longer as unusual as it once had been, being properly educated still meant being at least somewhat proficient in Latin. Grammar schools were therefore portals to advancement, increasingly in demand and increasingly common, and some were even operated under secular auspices with lay rather than clerical teachers. Seventeen such schools are known to have been in operation in the county of Gloucestershire at the time of the dissolution of the monasteries, and there is no reason to think that an untypical number. London, where there had been only three in 1440, would have fifteen by 1660, each able to accommodate a hundred pupils on average. This two-hundred-year emergence of a national educational system was not accelerated but temporarily reversed by the two decades that began with Henry VIII's attack on the monasteries and ended with the death of his son. Where schools were allowed to survive, they did so less often as a result of increased support from the Crown than because patrons of particular institutions had enough wealth or influence, either at court or in their own home districts, to save them from destruction.

The universities began a profound process of change during those same decades, in large measure because the most privileged families started wanting their sons to become "gentlemen" according to the emerging fashion. Gentlemen were still expected to have basic military skills—swords and daggers continued to be essential elements of their attire and were not always left sheathed—but under the new code it was no longer enough to be able to fight and hunt and hawk. No doubt in part because of the example set by the Tudors in providing even their daughters with superb educations, any young man hoping to make his mark at court knew that he was going to need more than a passing acquaintance with Latin if not other ancient languages and with subjects ranging from rhetoric to theology, from philosophy to astronomy. Boys from the best families continued almost without exception to be educated by private tutors rather than at grammar schools, but in increasing numbers they were entering Oxford or Cambridge at the customary age of fourteen or fifteen. In the fifteenth century Oxford's Magdalen College became the first to open its doors to the sons of "noble and powerful personages" even if they were not preparing for careers in the church—so long as their fathers paid well for the privilege. By the middle of the sixteenth century a few years at Oxford and Cambridge were a familiar rite of passage for the well-born young. Problems arose, inevitably, as the quasi-monastic serenity of the universities was invaded by rich young aristocrats whose interest in the life of the mind was easily overwhelmed by the opportunities for mischief that their new freedom put in their way. Some of the fun-seekers went, no doubt wisely, to London's Inns of Court instead, the inner sanctum of the English legal profession. There they could find an education recognized as fully equal to that available at the universities, along with the advantages of being situated in the capital with all of its bawdy temptations.

21

And Another Early End

Within weeks of the collapse of the Wyatt Rebellion, Parliament approved the treaty that laid out the terms under which Mary was to become the wife of Philip of the House of Hapsburg. On July 19 the bridegroom arrived. Aware of the extent to which the marriage was disliked by Mary's subjects high and low, he conducted himself with care. He made a great display of bringing with him chests supposedly loaded with treasure, was ostentatiously generous with Mary's council and court, and let it be known that the costs of supporting his princely household would be paid out of his coffers and not the queen's. Though he spoke no English he used his considerable charm, brought to a high polish in some of the most elegant courts in Europe, to ingratiate himself with England's elite. "His way with the lords is so winning," one of the Spanish grandees who had accompanied him to England reported in words that may have been a better reflection of his hopes than of reality, "that they themselves say they have never had a king to whom they so quickly grew attached."

At the same time Philip was making a dazzling impression upon his wife-to-be. But how much of his bonhomie was a facade? And what might it have cost him to appear more delighted with his situation than he possibly could have been? He had been compelled by duty to move to a damp and chilly northern island, not many of whose inhabitants were at all happy to see him, and now he was obliged to conduct himself impeccably night and day while making preparations to marry an older cousin. He had left behind on the continent an aging father who was sinking into a morbid depression, perhaps even the mental illness that had caused Philip's grandmother, Catherine of Aragon's sister Joanna the Mad, to be kept in confinement most of her long life. He had put the Channel between himself and the various nerve centers of the sprawl-ing Hapsburg family business, an empire that was beset with enemies, stumbling endlessly from crisis to crisis, and desperately in need of care-ful management. England must have felt like exile to Philip, like a distrac-tion from more important matters. Even his displays of generosity—his lavishing of gifts on English courtiers and his pointed refusal to use a penny of Mary's funds for his own purposes—were a painful pretense. In fact Philip was the financially hard-pressed junior partner in an insol-vent international enterprise, and every gold coin that he bestowed on England was needed elsewhere. "If the English find out how hard up we are," one of his retainers wrote, "I doubt whether we shall escape with our lives."

Philip did his duty, however, and six days after his arrival he and Mary were wed in a grand public ceremony in which both were robed in cloth of gold. There was no coronation for Philip—Parliament refused to con-sent to that—but henceforth he was to be addressed as king. The mar-riage treaty granted him that dignity, and to remove any doubts about his entitlement to it, his father had had him declared king not only of Naples but, rather absurdly, of Jerusalem as well. And in fact he soon found himself functioning as something very like a king. From the start of their life together, Mary gratefully relied on Philip for guidance, sup-port, and even leadership. Members of the council, even those opposed to a foreign marriage, found their dislike for the interloper overridden by their preference for dealing with a male rather than a female monarch. It seemed more *natural*.

With the wedding celebrated and the marriage presumably consum-mated, the Crown no longer had any need to keep Reginald Pole out of England. At the urging of the Hapsburgs, Pope Julius signed a bull relin-quishing all claim to the English church's alienated lands, at the same time instructing Pole, in his capacity as legate, to issue a general dispen-sation to all the current holders of those lands. Pole also absolved of schism a number of the conservative bishops who had accepted the royal supremacy under Henry VIII but lost their posts under Edward VI, so that they could now be restored to the good graces of their Catholic queen. Late in November he set foot on his native ground for the first time in two decades and was escorted from Dover to a barge waiting at Gravesend by eighteen hundred mounted men including court officials, bishops, and representatives of the nobility. These worthies presented him with an act of Parliament that repealed the attainder passed against him in the time of Henry VIII. His arrival at Westminster was made a great occasion, one that in pomp and solemnity almost rivaled Mary's coronation and wedding. The cardinal was met by Chancellor Gardiner upon disembarking from his barge, by Philip at the gate of the palace, and finally, at the top of the stairs, by the queen. The four of them then set about accomplishing what Mary and Philip had already declared to be the purpose for which the new Parliament had been summoned: reconciliation with Rome.

Pole was at least as burdened as Mary by the religious struggles of the past quarter century, most of his family having been obliterated by Henry VIII, and he brought to his new duties a weighty array of assets and liabilities. On the positive side he was a man of high moral character, blameless in his personal life, a leader in ecclesiastical reform. He had long been a major figure at the papal court, serving (among many other assignments) as one of the pope's representatives at the first meeting of the reformist Council of Trent in 1545. He probably would have been elected pope in 1549 had he condescended to show any real interest in the office. (He took the lofty view that no one should become pope who actively wished to do so.) Instead he declined an opportunity to be chosen by acclamation, and when the matter came to a vote he fell short by the thinnest of margins. He was committed to correcting the abuses of the Renaissance church generally and in England in particular, and in his pursuit of change he emphasized education for the laity and high standards of conduct and learning for the clergy at all levels.

He would have been a superb leader of the national church in more settled times, but in some ways he was ill suited to the England of the 1550s. He no longer understood his homeland (not appreciating, for example, the extent to which Protestantism had taken root in London), and he misjudged his cousin the queen. Not having been on hand to observe Mary as she faced down Dudley's attempted coup and then

Wyatt's Rebellion, he underestimated her strength and courage. He looked not to Mary but to her husband for support, counsel, and leadership. In so doing he made it easier for skeptics to regard him less as an Englishman than as part of Philip's Spanish faction. The effects would be profoundly negative where Pole's (and Mary's) aspirations were concerned: many in England and Rome alike would come to think that opposition to Philip, and to Spain, required opposition to Pole as well. Nor would the Catholic cause be helped, in the long term, by the mild-mannered Pole's increasing determination to find and root out heresy as he and his church defined it. In this he was no different from an overwhelming majority of his contemporaries, his evangelical adversaries included, but he would have been more effective if he *had* differed.

During Mary's reign as in the time of her father and brother, much of the population retained its attachment to the old church and was prepared to welcome its return. Thus Mary and her husband and advisers had little difficulty in seeing to it that the House of Commons was dominated by members who supported their agenda. The Parliament that convened in August 1554, two months before Pole's return, showed no hesitation in cooperating with the new regime—and with the cardinal, too, once he was on the scene. In a great flurry of activity that began at the end of November and continued into 1555, Parliament turned back the calendar to the days when Henry VIII was still a favorite of the pope's. Its two houses (and the convocation of the clergy as well) asked the Crown to petition Pole for a restoration of the ancient connection to Rome. Yet again great care was taken, first by Parliament in its entreaty and then by the queen and Pole in their response, to make clear that there could be no question of restoring the church's lost property; obviously this remained an issue of the most extreme sensitivity. Thereafter a committee representing both houses drafted, and the Lords and Commons approved, a kind of omnibus bill reversing every piece of legislation passed since the end of the 1520s for the purpose of destroying the authority of the pope in England. At the same time Parliament restored heresy laws that dated back to the reigns of Richard II, Henry IV, and Henry V and had been nullified by the Edwardian reformers. This would be momentous in its consequences. It opened the way to an attack on Cranmer and other evangelicals that would end by blackening Mary's name forever.

It was all quite astonishing. The schism, the Reformation, had been reversed with almost no resistance and no shedding of blood. The old faith had been restored, and because people on all sides of the question regarded this as either a profoundly joyous or a profoundly deplorable development, it is worthwhile to recall what, exactly, it entailed. It meant that the bishop of Rome, the pope, once again had the authority to correct heresy; implicit in this was the acknowledgment that the pope (or the papal administrative machinery), rather than the queen, had the right to decide what constituted heresy and who was or was not a heretic. It meant also that the pope had the authority not to choose England's bishops, but to confirm the Crown's choices and veto nominees it deemed unacceptable. It meant that the pope could dispense clergymen from the prohibitions against nonresidence and multiple benefices, set aside the canon law's proscription of certain kinds of marriage, and hear appeals of the decisions of the English ecclesiastical courts. Even when taken together, these powers do not add up to a great deal unless one subscribes to the distinctly modern idea that *no one* has the right to impose religious uniformity. Certainly the pope's authority infringed very little on the prerogatives of any monarch who did not claim, as Henry VIII and Edward VI did, to be the highest arbiter of divine truth. Nor did it have much to do with the everyday lives of ordinary people. For Mary, however, the restoration of the old ways was the greatest achievement imaginable. It appeared to justify all her sufferings and losses, to have made everything worthwhile. That her husband and the churchmen he had brought with him from Spain had participated actively in making it happen added to the sweetness of what she had accomplished.

The culmination came that same autumn with the discovery, confirmed by her physicians, that Mary was pregnant. This was announced to the people and publicly celebrated, and when the queen first felt the child move in her womb she ordered Te Deums to be sung in thanksgiving. Every dream she could ever have had for herself or for England had come to pass. She sat on the throne; she had a husband whom she admired, trusted, and loved; the faith that she had struggled so long to maintain was once again the faith of her countrymen; and now—climactic miracle—there was going to be an heir. Surely God had saved her for this transcendent destiny, and surely it was incumbent on Mary to behave magnanimously in response to so much divine bounty. Already in October John Dudley's widow, after months of begging, cajoling, and bribing anyone who would listen to her and had access to Mary and Philip, had won the release from the Tower of her four surviving sons (one of whom died soon after being freed). Mary even allowed herself, or so it was said, to be dissuaded by Philip from sending Elizabeth to a convent in Spain. The queen continued to look skeptically on her sister's demonstrations of fidelity to the old religion, and time would show that she was right to do so even if she was acting less on the basis of hard evidence than in response to intuition. Philip, on the other hand, had good reason to want Elizabeth to remain in England and succeed to the throne if Mary died without issue. The most obvious alternative to Elizabeth was the other Mary, the young queen of the Scots, who soon would be marrying the heir to the French throne. The thought that a queen of Scotland *and* France might also inherit the throne of England was at least as intolerable from the Hapsburg perspective as Mary's choice of Philip had been to the French.

The period of her pregnancy was the pinnacle of Mary Tudor's life. It did not last long, and the drumbeat of discord, frustration, disappointment, and loss soon resumed. The first thing that went wrong was that the evangelicals proved far more persistent than the conservatives had ever supposed they would dare to be. Protestant preachers who had not fled to the continent when Mary became queen not only publicly condemned transubstantiation, free will, the restored Latin liturgy, and the sacraments but mocked the Crown and challenged the legitimacy of everything it was doing. There were physical assaults on conservative clergy, and pamphlets attacking Mary and her husband and their church poured into England from Europe, often with the assistance of the king of France. Though the dissenters were a diverse lot, divided among themselves on sometimes arcane points of doctrine and practice, to the queen and council they had the appearance of a monolithic threat. Some of the priests who had come with Philip from Spain, including the friar who was now Mary's confessor, urged the necessity of suppressing these heretics and stopping the spread of their sedition.

Action was made possible by Parliament's restoration of the heresy statutes, and targets were available in the form of those evangelicals who had been conspicuous in supporting Jane Grey and preaching against the return to traditional orthodoxy. Several such figures were already in custody, and in January 1555 six of them were brought before a court of bishops with Stephen Gardiner presiding. One of the six recanted, another asked for time to consider his position, and after a day of debate on the all-too-familiar old issues (the mass, justification by faith, and the rest) the remaining four were declared excommunicated. In accordance with traditional practice they were then handed over to the civil authorities for disposition—which meant for killing. The first to die was a preacher named Rogers, who was burned on February 4 and thus became the first of the Protestant martyrs to lose his life to Marian persecution. Within days it was the turn of John Hooper, who had been made bishop first of Gloucester and then of Worcester in the last few years of Edward's reign and was so Calvinist in his opinions (condemning, for example, the wearing of traditional clerical vestments) that he was often at odds even with Cranmer. All four died heroically, scorning invitations to save themselves by abjuring their beliefs. When another six were brought before the court, found guilty of heresy, and excommunicated, they, too, showed themselves to be unafraid to die.

And so began that sustained policy of killing that is the only thing for which Queen Mary I is generally remembered today—the long series of ugly events that earned for her the ineradicable title Bloody Mary. Exactly how it happened, and who exactly was responsible for starting and continuing it, remains one of the mysteries of the Tudor Age. What is clear is that it was controversial even within the court and council. It has been depicted as a transplanting of the Spanish Inquisition, but in fact it differed from Spanish practice in crucial respects and some of the most prominent Spanish churchmen in Philip's household regarded it with horror. On the day after the second group of prisoners was convicted and passed on to the government, Philip's confessor Alfonso de Castro, at a mass attended by the queen and king and other dignitaries, condemned the execution of heretics as contrary to the teachings of Christ and far less likely than patient instruction to keep heretics from attracting followers or suffering damnation. His words (would he have dared to utter them in such a setting without Philip's knowledge and approval?) led to a suspension of trials and executions alike. But little more than a month later it was discovered that yet another rebellion was being plotted, this time in East Anglia. The capture of another ring of would-be rebels added to the court's sense of danger and made it easy to dismiss restraint as a contemptible sign of weakness. Magistrates across the kingdom were instructed to be on the alert for heresy, and to hand unrepentant suspects over to their local bishops for examination. The trials and executions resumed.

It was long and widely believed that Gardiner was a driving force, even *the* driving force, behind the burnings. In fact little evidence supports this notion, and much puts it in doubt. After presiding at the first trial and thereby involving himself in the condemnation of Rogers, Hooper, and their associates, Gardiner handed the direction of the court's activities over to Edmund Bonner, the restored bishop of London, and took no further part in them. He came to see the executions as unproductive if not inherently wrong. Another figure sometimes singled out as the villain of the story, Cardinal Pole, was indeed fixated on the dangers of heresy, but that he regarded wholesale killing—or any killing—as the answer to those dangers is quite another matter. There is food for doubt in the fact that, when Pole became archbishop of Canterbury, the burnings came to an abrupt and permanent halt in that jurisdiction.

Bonner of London has always been seen as an especially eager killer, but his guilt is no longer so clear as it once seemed. After the resumption of the trials and burnings, the queen's aged treasurer William Paulet complained to the council that the bishops were not displaying enough zeal in taking action against those suspects brought to their attention. At his urging the council reprimanded Bonner specifically, directing him to be more diligent. Under pressure of this kind not only Bonner but other bishops swallowed whatever reluctance they may have felt to take action against those courageous or cranky enough to stand firmly for their departures from orthodoxy. Ultimately the blame must be left at the feet of the queen, who cannot be excused from a charge of fanaticism in spite of being neither cruel nor vengeful (she was quite the opposite) in other areas of her life and reign. Disappointingly little is known of her role in the campaign of persecution, and even less is known of what she thought of it all. The results in any case were famously repulsive and naturally destructive of Mary's reputation, her legacy, and the cause that she had put at the center of her life. Something on the order of three hundred individuals were executed before it all ended, an overwhelming majority in the area of southeastern England centered on London. Most were obscure commoners, tradesmen, and craftsmen, incapable of posing a threat to church or state or even the leadership of their home communities.

How aware most people were of the killings, or how deeply or even if they were horrified, is unknown. The burnings were a vile spectacle in any case, and as they went on month after month they fed the evangelicals' hatred of the regime. It became easy to depict Mary's church as synonymous with oppression—worse, with oppression from abroad—and difficult to defend it or the queen herself. A darkness descended upon the reign, one that must have been connected in some deep way to the sufferings of Mary's life—the hatred that she must, at some level, have felt for her father—and would continue to the end. To the extent that Mary thought she was serving Rome, she would soon find herself repaid in strange coin indeed.

At the start of 1555, however, all that lay in the future. For the time being, with her husband at her side and the birth of their child approaching, Mary felt free to think expansively, to pursue new goals in fields not yet explored. She decided to try her hand at peacemaking. The Crown no longer possessed the resources that had permitted Henry VIII and then Somerset to make war on the continent and join in European games of power, but the games went on, wasting lives and treasure as profligately as ever. Perhaps not surprisingly the earnest Mary, devoid of dreams of conquest or personal glory, began to hope that she might be able to bring the adversaries together and help them arrive at a lasting concord. The result was a conference at Gravelines, on France's Channel coast, where neither France nor Spain proved willing to compromise its territorial claims. The meetings cost England a good deal of money and ended with nothing accomplished. Mary had experienced her first failure as queen.

Worse soon followed. Just weeks after the formal reunion with Rome, the death of Pope Julius set in motion a sequence of events that would magnify to an almost preposterous extent the price that Mary paid for having chosen a Hapsburg spouse. Julius had been a throwback to the most notorious pontiffs of the Renaissance, wallowing in luxury, enriching his relatives, and elevating to the College of Cardinals the adolescent whom he had almost certainly made his lover. The excesses of his reign hardened the determination of reformers to bring such scandals to an end. After a period of confusion, during which a reformist pope was elected but died after three weeks in office and Reginald Pole was twice more a leading candidate despite being far away in England and uninterested, the octogenarian Cardinal Giovanni Pietro Caraffa took office as Paul IV. For the emperor Charles and his son Philip, this was a serious setback. The Caraffas were among the leading families of Naples, one of the most important of the Hapsburg possessions in Italy (the emperor, remember, had made his son king of Naples in preparation for the latter's marriage to Mary), and this part of his background dominated the new pope's view of international affairs. Like most Neapolitans he hated the Hapsburgs—a long tour of duty as nuncio in Spain had done nothing to improve his opinion—and though he had no ambition to become pope, he was provoked into accepting election by the efforts of the imperial agents in Rome to defeat him. His supporters saw in him a severely self-denying ascetic, a man whose way of life could not have contrasted more sharply with that of Julius III. One of his most conspicuous characteristics, admired by some cardinals but troubling to others, was a burning hostility to anything that smacked, to him, of heresy, and an inclination to condemn as heresy any idea not clearly rooted in the scholastic philosophy of the Middle Ages. It was possible to see him as either a selflessly holy or a disturbingly hard man. Whether out of holiness or hardness, he was unwilling to compromise or curry favor even with his colleagues at the papal court.

The improbable election of such an impolitic man reflected the cardinals' sense of how desperately necessary it now was to put the church back on the path of reform. In any case it meant trouble for the Hapsburgs and their position in Italy, and Philip and his father knew it. It meant trouble for Pole, too, though in the beginning that must have been less obvious. Both Pole and Caraffa had been prominent in Rome for many years, and both had been active in trying to work out a consistent line of response to the teachings of the Lutherans and evangelicals. In the course of all this, however, the two had become something other than friends. Caraffa, in fact, had come to suspect that the amicable Pole was so willing to arrive at a friendly resolution of such questions as justification by faith as to be flirting with heresy himself. His distrust was compounded, inevitably, by the fact that Pole was now associated with the despised Philip in England. If there was a tinge of fanaticism in Paul's character, however, he was no maniac. Shortly after his election he issued a general condemnation of the confiscation of church property. But he understood that his position could have unwelcome consequences in England. Therefore he neutralized it by issuing a bull declaring that the religious houses suppressed by Henry VIII no longer existed even in a legalistic sense, that they were and would remain legally distinct from any new houses established under Mary, and that such new houses therefore had no claim to what had been taken from the old. In this way he reinforced Mary's position on the land question, the position that Pole, too, had been brought around to accepting. On the surface, all remained well between England and Rome. Though the pope was seeking to ally himself with France against the Hapsburgs, he was, for a while, able to keep his efforts concealed.

For a while, therefore, the worst of Mary's problems had almost nothing to do with pope or church. They were painful problems all the same, and they carried with them painful consequences. By June, after increasingly embarrassing postponements of the date on which her child was likely to be born, it had become clear that she was not expecting at all. There is no way of knowing what her supposed pregnancy was all about—whether she miscarried, or had been swollen by a tumor, or had allowed a desperate longing for an heir to deceive herself and her eager-to-please physicians. Whatever the case, Mary's hopes fell with a smash, and gone with them was the possibility that some son of Philip's might make England a Hapsburg kingdom. Philip began to chafe at being kept in England, and he had compelling reasons to depart. His father was in increasingly fragile health and more eager than ever to rid himself of his burdens. The Hapsburg dynasty now had no future in England, the Spaniards continued to be regarded as interlopers, and because Philip was continuing to pay all the expenses of his household the whole enterprise was becoming not only pointless but seriously wasteful. Mary, however, was almost pathetically devoted to Philip, as eager to depend on him as she once had been to have his father's guidance. When in September he left England, she sank into sorrow. The harvest had failed, turning 1555 into a year of hardship across England and of outright famine in some districts.

Once on the continent, Philip found himself sinking into his family's quagmire of problems. He had been regent of Spain (strictly speaking, of the still-distinct kingdoms of Aragon and Castile) since before his move to England, and now his father made him regent of the Netherlands as well. To Mary's appeals that he return to England, he replied that he could do so only if formally crowned as king—something that (as he undoubtedly understood) Parliament would never allow. When Parliament met in the month after Philip's departure, it showed itself to be less ready than in the past to conform to the Crown's agenda. The session was marked by almost childish conflicts; at one point Commons was locked inside its chambers because of its refusal to approve one of the queen's bills, and at another it locked itself in to avoid having to take action it didn't want to take. At the heart of the squabbling was money. Mary made her first request for a tax levy since becoming queen and was granted only part of what she asked. She had more success in restoring some of the former revenues of the church, winning agreement mainly because the money in question was the approximately £60,000 per year that the government still received from lands seized by Henry VIII and not subsequently sold or given away. In a sense, therefore, the restoration would cost the gentry and the nobility nothing. Even so, Mary was able to win agreement only by arguing that, having repudiated the supremacy, she could not in good conscience keep money that had been diverted to the Crown on the basis of that supremacy. Mary and Gardiner wanted to introduce legislation barring Elizabeth from the succession—they continued to believe her complicit in Wyatt's Rebellion and possibly other plots as well, and had reason to believe that her sympathies lay with the reformed religion—but were held back by the fear that such a move would be not only doomed to failure but dangerous. Enough ill feeling had been aroused by the October executions of former evangelical bishops Hugh Latimer and Nicholas Ridley to make it obvious that there were limits to how far the government could safely go. Questions of religion aside, Elizabeth was the daughter of a king who had placed her in the line of succession. Her claim to the throne, therefore, was widely seen as incontestable.

November brought a weighty loss. Gardiner, having exhausted himself in the effort to extract from a recalcitrant Parliament the resources needed to keep a virtually bankrupt government afloat and allow a threadbare church to recover some of its strength, fell ill and in a short time died. With his death there passed from the scene, and from the royal service, a man whose experience reached far back into the reign of Henry VIII and whose political skills, if not those of a Wolsey or a Cromwell, were unmatched by any living councilor. There was no one to replace him—no one, at least, in whom the queen was prepared to put her trust. Increasingly, in dealing both with Parliament and with foreign governments, she looked for advice only to that little circle of political neophytes that had formed the nucleus of her household before her brother's death. And it, too, was being diminished by mortality. An ever more solitary queen assumed Gardiner's burdens herself and soldiered on, hoping that her husband would return and begging him to do so. Reginald Pole had so completely won Philip's confidence while the two were together in England that Philip regarded him as a kind of unofficial regent and expected him to look out for the interests of the Crown, and Mary, too, had high confidence in the cardinal. But Pole's position was still that of legate, and he was so occupied with the needs of a gravely damaged church that when the queen attempted to make him chancellor, both he himself and the pope objected—no doubt for very different reasons. His emphasis, not surprisingly in a man who from the beginning of his career had wanted only a life of scholarship, was on raising the quality of the clergy through education while also improving the education of the laity. He also explored reconciliation with the evangelicals, if not on the most generous terms; "heretics" were welcomed back into the church so long as they repudiated all the ecclesiastical legislation enacted between 1529 and the death of Edward VI, and married priests could retain their posts only if they put away their wives.

During his years in exile Pole had consistently pointed to the grim consequences of clerical misconduct, accusing the clergy of much responsibility for the disruptions that became the Reformation. He now brought those same ideas to bear upon England by convening, in the closing weeks of 1555, a synod of the clergy at Westminster. This gathering, by the time of its adjournment in February, approved an agenda called the Twelve Decrees aimed at rebuilding the church. Every diocese was to establish a seminary for the training of parish clergy, and the laity, too, were to be made more knowledgeable through the dissemination of a new prayer book (one very different from Cranmer's, of course), new catechisms and books of homilies, and an English translation of the

Bible. Bishops were to be held responsible for maintaining high standards of clerical conduct and for seeing to it that income and expenditures were carefully managed. The criteria that Pole set for the selection of bishops were, if anything, unrealistically high under the prevailing circumstances. The candidates that he chose were of impressive moral character and in many cases had the kinds of exceptional scholarly credentials that he found appealing. But candidates of this kind were not abundant after a generation of turmoil, and vacancies were not filled quickly. Undoubtedly Pole's ideas could have had a major impact if fate had granted him the time required for their implementation. But throughout the kingdom the church was so lacking in resources that only York was able to get a seminary up and running.

And that was not the worst of it. Far away in Rome the new pope was stewing. Determined to drive the Hapsburgs out of Naples, he had continued to pursue an understanding with Henry II of France. Ordinarily Henry would have welcomed the pope's overtures, and in fact he agreed at one point to enter into an alliance that was for the time being to remain secret. But when Philip offered a five-year truce, the French king, his treasury as empty as Mary's and Philip's, grabbed at it eagerly. An exasperated pope was left to fend for himself, and to seethe with anger over reports of Cardinal Pole's putative willingness to come to an accommodation with the heretics of England. Europe was entering one of those periods when the complexities of its politics matched its instability. Charles V abdicated the crowns of Aragon and Castile in Philip's favor, at about the same time reluctantly allowing his brother Ferdinand to succeed him as Holy Roman emperor because the princes of Germany rejected Philip as unacceptably Spanish. Philip, free for the moment of war with France but experienced enough to expect Henry II to resume hostilities as soon as he found the means to do so, returned to Spain to attend to his long-neglected duties there. Meanwhile he had to manage at very long distance his possessions in the Netherlands, Italy, and America. To compound his difficulties he was in conflict now with his uncle Ferdinand, who as new emperor had both possessions and ambitions in Italy. It is hardly surprising if England, and his wife the English queen, seemed of less than the highest importance.

Mary's perspective was of course entirely different. With Gardiner gone, dissenters were becoming increasingly bold in deploring the Spanish marriage, the reunion with Rome, and Mary's whole regime. They accused the queen of being more Spanish than English in her loyalties and of scheming to deliver England permanently into the hands of the Hapsburgs even if she and Philip failed to produce a child. In March the authorities uncovered a plot—originally encouraged by Henry of France, though he lost interest when discovery might have jeopardized his treaty with Philip—to overthrow Mary and put Elizabeth on the throne. Though a number of the conspirators were captured and executed, their leaders (including Sir Henry Dudley, a freebooting soldier and distant cousin of John Dudley, the late and unlamented Duke of Northumberland) remained at large in France. Efforts to trace the plot down to its roots ended in frustration. Elizabeth, who may or may not have been a party to it, was extricated from danger when Philip sent orders that she was not to be questioned or investigated. As in the aftermath of Wyatt's Rebellion, he was acting less as the uncrowned king of England than in the interests of the Spanish Crown. Again his concern was that if Elizabeth perished—and Mary would surely have been satisfied to see her die *if* she could be proved guilty of treason—the next in line to the throne would be Mary, Queen of Scots.

During the investigation of the so-called Henry Dudley conspiracy, with the court feeling itself under threat both from subversives at home and exiles abroad, Thomas Cranmer was burned for heresy. His execution was the most notorious event of Mary's reign, one that cast no credit on any of the people involved, Cranmer included. From the time when his compeers Latimer and Ridley went bravely to their deaths, Cranmer had begun denying the evangelical beliefs that he had devoted himself to imposing upon all of England. He repeatedly renounced the idea of royal supremacy and took upon himself responsibility for all the religious troubles that England had undergone since his consecration as archbishop of Canterbury. He went so far as to beg the pope for forgiveness, declaring that he deserved not only death but eternal punishment. In doing so he repudiated his own entire career and gave his enemies a propaganda victory of tremendous potential value. But Mary and her advisers snatched from the jaws of that victory an even greater defeat. Instead of being satisfied with Cranmer's surrender and allowing him to fade away into obscurity, they pushed ahead with plans for his execution. When the hour of his death arrived, seeing that he no longer had anything to gain or lose, Cranmer declared that all his recantations had been lies told in the hope of saving his life and that in fact he recanted nothing. Famously, when the fire was lit, he is supposed to have held his right hand in the flames—can anyone who has ever scorched a finger with a kitchen match believe this story?—while telling onlookers that it must be punished first because it had written the lies. Be that as it may, the drama of his last moments established Cranmer as chief among those martyred in the English Protestant cause. Others were being burned at this time, but few were known to the public. Many of the evangelical clergy had fled abroad—first to Lutheran Germany, where they were unwelcome because of their departures from Lutheran theology, and then to Switzerland, where they were embraced. Those members of the gentry who could not contain their hatred for Philip and Spain went mainly to France, where they received royal support except during those intervals when Henry II found it advantageous to suspend his hostility to the Hapsburgs and therefore to Mary.

The most recent of those intervals came to its inevitable end in July 1556. Paul IV was still hoping to draw France into his ancestral feud with the Hapsburgs, and now at last he found Henry ready to be drawn. An alliance was agreed under the terms of which, once the Spanish had been expelled from Italy, one of Henry's sons would become king of Naples (evidently the pope was willing to accept foreign rule of his home city so long as it was not *Hapsburg* domination) and another would become Duke of Milan. Philip retaliated by ordering his viceroy the Duke of Alba to invade the Papal States. When the pope found himself without the means to defend Rome, he offered, unhappily, to make peace. That might have been the end of the trouble, but then Henry II sent an army under the Duke of Guise into Italy with orders to support the pope, and all the adversaries found themselves at sword's point yet again. Predictably, the pope was enraged with Philip—so enraged that he excommunicated him, declaring him a "son of iniquity" and ordering the eviction of every Spaniard in Rome and the withdrawal of every papal legate from the territories of the Hapsburgs. Having been installed as archbishop of Canterbury just days after Cranmer's death (he had finally been ordained), Pole was not required to leave England. This fresh rupture, however, gravely compromised his ability to proceed with reform. His work of rejuvenating the church, the Westminster synod included, came shuddering to a halt.

Mary was caught in the middle. She appears to have had little difficulty deciding that, at least in this matter, her loyalty was owed to her spouse. Her inclinations were reinforced in January 1557 when Henry of France opened a new front in his conflict with Philip by attacking the Flemish city of Douai, a Hapsburg possession. Mary had previously warned the French against an action of this kind, reminding them that Douai had been covered by a 1543 mutual defense treaty between Henry VIII and Charles V and asserting that the treaty remained in effect. The French king, who like his father Francis loved to fish in England's as well as Spain's most troubled waters, was predictably unimpressed. As far as he was concerned, Mary's connection to the Hapsburgs meant that she and her kingdom were France's enemies. It was the pope's willingness to challenge Hapsburg rule in Italy that had caused him to rush troops to Italy, and it was because those troops were now stymied that he had turned his attention to Flanders, where he could open a new front against the Hapsburgs.

Philip, his resources stretched thin, desperately needed English help, and as Mary's consort he thought himself entitled to it. In March he crossed the Channel, received a rapturous welcome from his adoring wife, and set about trying to secure the use of English ships, naval bases, and troops. Mary was fully on his side but prudently looked to her council to make the necessary commitment. This presented Philip with a challenge of the first order: most members of the council wanted nothing to do with his war, largely if not entirely because the treasury was so deplorably short of funds. In opposing Philip, they could point to the part of the marriage treaty stating that England was not to be drawn into Spain's conflicts. Even Pole, despite the trusting relationship that he had formed with Philip, was opposed to helping him against the pope. All his life Pole had demonstrated, and repeatedly proved his willingness to suffer for, a keen sense of obligation to Rome. He was not prepared to change now, but neither did he wish to be disloyal to Mary or her husband. And so he withdrew from politics, declining to attend council meetings or even to meet with Philip. He received scant thanks. On April 29 the pope issued an order for Pole to return to Rome for unexplained reasons that were universally understood to involve accusations of heresy. The absurd process was now under way by which, in the space of not many months, Pope Paul would make himself the implacable enemy of the very people who had restored the Catholic Church in England.

Philip might never have received English help if not for an act of pure folly. Among the young rakehells and soldiers of fortune who had gone into exile in France after Mary won the crown was her twenty-four-year-old relative Thomas Stafford, who had inherited royal blood through both his father and his mother, regarded himself as entitled to the Dukedom of Buckingham (which had belonged to his family until his grandfather was executed by Henry VIII), and was an ardent Protestant in spite of being a nephew of Cardinal Pole. Lured by fantastic visions of glory, and drawing on mysterious sources of support that probably included Henry of France, Stafford came ashore at Scarborough in the north of England on April 25 at the head of a mixed force of English, French, and Scottish followers who numbered at least thirty but no more than a hundred. Taking possession of a poorly defended and half-ruined castle, he issued a proclamation calling upon the people of England to join him in deposing Mary and establishing a protectorate. So far as is known, he failed to attract a single recruit. Stafford was in custody within four days of his landing, and before the end of May he was, to little public notice, executed for treason. At court his adventure was interpreted as the latest French outrage. It brought the council around to supporting Philip and the queen.

As preparations got under way for assembling an army and transporting it to the continent, efforts were made to dissuade the pope from recalling Pole. The English ambassador in Rome begged the pope to reconsider, Mary and Philip sent appeals of their own, and at last even the diffident Pole wrote to say that the feeble state of the church in England required the presence of *someone* authorized to represent Rome. All of it availed nothing or less than nothing. It appears, rather, to have thrown Pope Paul into a fresh rage. He placed one of Pole's oldest friends and fellow reformers, Cardinal Giovanni Morone, under arrest on a variety of heresy charges of the kind that probably would have been brought against Pole himself had he been in Rome. Like Pole, Morone had lost the trust of the archconservatives with his willingness to deal with the Lutheran reformers on respectful terms and acknowledge that not all blame for the breakup of the church lay on the Protestant side. The pope made malicious use of Pole's letter by replacing him as legate with Friar William Peto, the same Observant Franciscan who decades before had denounced Henry VIII to his face for seeking to discard Catherine of Aragon. Peto was now back at his old monastery at Greenwich—Mary herself had restored it—and was serving as confessor to the queen. The situation deteriorated into a ridiculous tangle. Pole, loyal as always, would have traveled to Rome as ordered but was forbidden to do so by Mary, who insisted that he was entitled to defend himself in England. Peto, eighty years old and in bad health, protested that he was neither able nor willing to serve. The nuncio bringing official notification of Peto's appointment was intercepted at Calais and prevented from crossing the Channel, and his mission was soon rendered pointless by Peto's death. The pope wanted to declare that Philip was no longer legitimately king of anything but was dissuaded by cooler heads. He contented himself with refusing to transact any business with the English church. Mary's (and Pole's) nominations for vacant bishoprics were ignored, and the number of vacancies mounted.

After three consecutive crop failures and widespread hunger, a weakened population was being ravaged by an influenza epidemic that would in a few years claim hundreds of thousands of lives. Nevertheless an army of seven thousand men was somehow pulled together, and by July it was on the continent ready to join Philip's thirty thousand Spanish, German, and Flemish troops in the war with France. Philip, too, was back on the continent, but neither he nor the English army was on the scene when, in September, the main Hapsburg force inflicted a devastating defeat on the French at St. Quentin. Fully half of the French army was killed or taken prisoner, and upon receiving the news, the pope abandoned his hopes for Italy and signaled his willingness to make peace. Henry II then ordered the army that he had sent to the pope's assistance to return home and asked its commander, the Duke of Guise, to find some way to avenge the shame of St. Quentin. When around the turn of the year Mary announced that she was once again pregnant, no one including her husband paid serious attention. Philip sent congratulations, but they were little more than a formality. It was, after all, nearly six months since he had last seen her.

January 1558 brought the crowning calamity of Mary's reign: the loss of Calais, the last of England's once-vast holdings on the European mainland. The Duke of Guise, having received reports of the sorry state of Calais's defenses from French ambassadors passing through the town after their expulsion from England, knew that no one would expect a midwinter assault. He positioned his army in such a way as to appear to be preparing a move against St. Quentin, wheeled it around for a surprise advance on Calais, and extracted a surrender from its garrison so quickly that neither Philip nor the English had any chance of responding. Though the loss would prove to be of no strategic importance—the English figured out in time that holding Calais had produced no benefits commensurate with the costs—it came as a shock to England's nascent national pride and a humiliation for Mary. Philip, inevitably but unfairly, was blamed. He had warned the council in advance of Guise's offensive and offered to provide Spanish troops for the defense—an offer that was rejected because of groundless suspicions that Philip wanted Calais for himself. Afterward, when he offered to match whatever number of troops England made available to retake Calais, he was again rebuffed. A sense of things coming to an end, a miasma of something like death, was beginning to hang over Mary and her court. A Parliament was called but quickly prorogued after showing itself unwilling to help the government with its financial problems, and by May the queen was no longer talking of an expected child.

Mary was ill that month, and again in August, and yet again in October. In September Charles V died, removing whatever small hope Mary might still have had of Philip's return to England. Finally, knowing that Reginald Pole, too, was seriously ill, resigned to her own impending death and to the certainty that she would be succeeded by her half-sister, she sent a maid of honor to Elizabeth with a letter in which she asked for three things. First, that upon becoming queen she, Elizabeth, would deal generously with the members of Mary's household. Second, that she would repay the debts that the Crown had incurred under Mary's Privy Seal. And third, that she would continue to support the church in the form that Mary had reestablished. Elizabeth had only recently repeated her assurances that she was a believing Roman Catholic, politely complaining of the queen's difficulty in accepting her word on that score. There was no opportunity for her to do so again. On the morning of November 18, Mary quietly expired while hearing mass from her bed. Pole died hours later. The English Counter-Reformation was dead too.

Mary at the end was worn out and thoroughly defeated. She seemed somehow to have lived for a long time, and her reign, too, seemed to have lasted too long and to have grown sterile. It is startling to realize that at the time of her death she was all of forty-two years old, and had ruled for only five years.

PART FOUR

Survivor

1558–1603

22

Yet Another New Beginning

It is an hour or two past midnight on March 24, 1603. In the deepest recesses of Richmond Palace the fireplaces are ablaze, the light from shoals of candles dancing in the drafty air. In the shadows at the rear of the palace's innermost chamber Queen Elizabeth lies in bed, her face turned to the wall. Her physicians have made it known that she is dying. Everyone with access to the court has come to bear witness to a momentous event.

Despite the hour the atmosphere is electric: the death of the monarch is certain to bring enormous changes—good things for some, disappointment for others. People bundled up in hats and furs whisper together in little clusters, disperse, gather again in new combinations: the grieving and the hopeful, the worried and the merely curious. Among them is Sir Robert Carey, the queen's cousin, the ambitious grandson of Anne Boleyn's sister Mary. Like the others he keeps his face stern and his voice low, but he is excited and impatient and struggling not to show it. A fast fresh horse awaits him outside, and he has arranged to have other horses posted all along the four-hundred-mile route from Richmond to Edinburgh. He is determined to give himself a leg up with the next regime by being the first to inform the king of Scotland that Elizabeth is dead at last, and that England is now his.

Tudor medicine being the tangle of butchery and superstition and sterile tradition that it is, not even the doctors have any real idea of why the queen is dying. A bronchial infection that has turned into pneumonia, perhaps. Possibly streptococcus, or the failure of some vital organ. Whatever the root cause, it appears to have been aggravated by depression; one thing even her physicians can see is that Elizabeth has been seriously depressed for months. It is possible that she has been poisoned—that she has, inadvertently, poisoned herself. For forty years, ever since smallpox nearly took her life and ravaged her fine fair skin, she has refused to leave her privy chamber without first having her face, neck, and breast caked with the most prized cosmetic of her day, a mixture of white lead and vinegar known as ceruse or spirits of Saturn. Even painters who use brushes to apply white lead not to their own skin but to walls often fall victim to poisoning. That Elizabeth has remained vigorous to such an age while living under a thick coat of such a toxic concoction is little less than astonishing.

By the standards of the day her age is ripe indeed. Ninety-four years have passed since her father Henry VIII became king, 118 since her grandfather won the crown at Bosworth Field. Elizabeth herself, next to Henry VII the Tudor who overcame the longest odds in coming to the throne, has reigned for four and a half decades. This is nearly twice as long as the first Henry Tudor, nearly a decade longer than the second, nine times as long as either her brother or her sister. Her next birthday would be her seventieth.

Longevity in fact is the dying queen's supreme achievement, and that is fitting. Longevity, survival, is all she ever really aspired to. There is no reason to believe that at any point she had high dreams for her kingdom, her people, or herself. Like her father she has always been a master of political theater, creating a jewel-encrusted image with which to awe the whole world and concealing herself behind it. But even in fabricating the persona of Gloriana, the strong, wise, and good Virgin Queen, even in projecting that persona in every direction near and far, she has been driven by defensive impulses—by the determination to make herself *seem* strong, invulnerable, indispensable. Always the aim was to preserve her life and her rule and the status quo. If it is possible to argue that she never accomplished much else, she has unquestionably accomplished that. Therefore she has succeeded in everything that mattered to her— no small achievement for any ruler. In the process, simply by staying in power as the earth made forty-five trips around the sun and forces beyond anyone's control swept over her kingdom, she has also presided over much of England's evolution into a modern nation-state. This is the ultimate irony of her story, because there rarely was a monarch who wanted change less.

One wants to know, as Elizabeth draws her last breaths, what she has been thinking during these strange final days. Her decline began with a refusal to speak, to eat, even to sit down until at last she was too weak not to. Then, seated on cushions with a finger in her mouth, she passed days and nights gazing blankly at the floor or something beyond the floor, locked in a stony solitude. Only when she had lost all power to resist or even complain was she finally put to bed. Has she been asking herself if it was worthwhile, the long drama that is now drawing to a close? Does she wish she had played her part differently? Does it seem enough, looking back, that she has survived this long? Does the price she paid seem acceptable—or to have been necessary?

All we will ever know is what the people attending her take the trouble to record. That is not much, and it has no certain meaning, but it does not suggest a spirit at peace. When begged to get some sleep by the faithful old Earl of Nottingham, longtime commander of her navy and husband of another of her Boleyn cousins, Elizabeth answers that if he saw what she sees when she closes her eyes he would suggest no such thing.

She is a pathetic spectacle, all the more so because throughout her reign she has been vain to the point of childishness. Almost inevitably for someone who has lived this long at a time when dentistry is still little more than a sideline for barbers, she has lost a good many of her teeth and those remaining are mostly black. For forty years she has been concealing the loss of hair suffered when smallpox nearly carried her away, but now, with the end obviously at hand, it is pointless to worry about whether the latest wig fits properly or if it is even in place. As for hygiene, suffice it to recall that bathing is considered unhealthful in the sixteenth century, that it is scarcely practical even for royalty during the dark chill months of an English winter innocent of central heating, and that winter was not over when the queen began refusing to have herself attended to even in accordance with the minimal standards of the time.

If her last moments taste of bitterness, nothing could be more understandable. From 1603 she looks back on eighteen years of uninterrupted foreign war, and on an interminable domestic bloodletting rooted first in the revolution begun by her father and then in the decisions that she herself took in attempting to manage her father's (and her brother's, and her sister's) legacy. Her wars have accomplished little, almost nothing on the whole, and they have laid up much trouble for her successors. Unlike her father's wars they were undertaken not in pursuit of glory but because she believed they would enhance her security, but like her father's they have been financial catastrophes. At a time when the Crown's ordinary revenues still total little more than £200,000 annually, England since 1585 has spent some £2 million to keep a war of rebellion going in the Netherlands, even more to suppress rebellion in Ireland, and untold hundreds of thousands in France and on the high seas. The question of whether all this trouble was avoidable has no simple answer, but there can be little doubt that much and perhaps most of it need never have happened. Even the most glorious event of the reign, the defeat of the Armada in 1588 (a victory owed as much to the weather as to England's doughty sea dogs), drained the treasury of £160,000 and would never have been necessary if Elizabeth had not persisted in goading her onetime protector and brother-in-law King Philip of Spain until finally his forbearance was exhausted.

The effects on the people of England have been very real and painful. Nearly two decades of war have seriously disrupted trade, especially with the crucial Low Countries markets, and thereby given rise to serious unemployment. Ferocious inflation has combined with falling wages to drive living standards to their lowest level since the mid-1300s. This has led to food riots and crimes of desperation, and then to an almost vicious crackdown by frightened local authorities: in 1598 one hundred and twenty-five sentences of death were pronounced by courts of assize in the London area, nearly double the number of just two years earlier. Repeated crop failures have made everything worse. Anyone disposed to believe that nations prosper or suffer according to whether their rulers enjoy divine favor—and such ideas remain common at the dawn of the seventeenth century—would find it easy to argue that heaven has turned its back on Elizabeth Tudor. She is in every way a spent force, and her people are ready to be quit of her.

To a remarkable extent—one all the more striking in light of how deeply the two sisters always differed, and the determination of the younger to set herself apart from the elder—Elizabeth's reign has followed much the same trajectory as Mary's. Both, upon becoming queen, were welcomed enthusiastically by most of their subjects, England being quite as weary of Mary and her Spanish connection in 1558 as it had been of Edward's evangelical regime in 1553. Both went on to enjoy a middle period of popularity and success (Mary's was measured in months, Elizabeth's in decades), and both ended in exhaustion and disillusion (the dark times having lasted well over ten years in Elizabeth's case). If Mary was fated to become a largely forgotten figure, remembered as "bloody" when she was remembered at all, and if Elizabeth by contrast came to be celebrated as one of history's heroines, the difference is largely traceable to factors unconnected to the character of their reigns. No historian today could dispute that Mary was a capable and conscientious queen, or argue that her government killed or tortured or imprisoned as many people as Elizabeth's. She devoted herself to what she perceived (rightly or wrongly) to be the interests of her subjects, and she might have achieved her objectives if she had reigned even half as long as Elizabeth. The process of winnowing the facts has taken four centuries, but it is clear by now that Mary was the more ambitious of the sisters—that she aspired to much more than her own survival, certainly—and that the reason for her failure may be nothing more mysterious (or shameful) than the fact that at the time of her death she was twenty-eight years younger than Elizabeth would be at hers.

This is not to say, of course, that Elizabeth accomplished nothing. She achieved two very big things that had eluded her father, brother, and sister: a settlement of the question of what England's established church should be and do and believe, and a degree of internal stability not seen in a very long time. From the end of the 1560s until the end of Elizabeth's life, and then for decades beyond that, not a single armed rebellion of even marginal seriousness occurred in England or Wales. Such a protracted period of peace had not been seen since before the Wars of the Roses, and if Elizabeth and her ministers don't deserve credit for that then no one in history should be given credit for anything. Likewise, by 1603 everyone understood what acceptance of the Church of England entailed, and most of the population was conforming. Where persecution was concerned, Elizabeth had differed from her brother and sister only in (much like her father) striking out in two directions simultaneously, both at the shrinking part of the population that still clung to the old religion and at the growing part that demanded rejection of every vestige of the pre-Reformation church. If she continued to meet resistance from both directions, after the first decade of her reign it posed no serious threat.

Still, both the settlement and the stability were bought at a price that Elizabeth herself was careful to avoid paying. Just below the surface of the uniformity her government imposed, England continued to be troubled by the religious conflicts that her father had first put in motion. The actions she took in managing those conflicts are unintelligible unless seen as part of Elizabeth's obsessive focus on her own survival. She declined to address virtually any question of religion that could be passed along to posterity, and to avoid trouble in the near term she ignored growing pressure for adjustments of the religious arrangements put in place at the start of her reign. The bill would come due two generations on, with an explosion that not only permanently weakened the monarchy but actually, for a time, obliterated it. If that was at least partly Elizabeth's doing, however, she took pains to keep it from being her problem.

The England whose queen Elizabeth became late in 1558 was probably not yet halfway along the road from being one of the most devotedly Catholic nations in all of Christendom to one of the most ferociously anti-Catholic. Though of course we have no data on popular religious sentiment as of the start of her reign, much if not most of the population unquestionably continued to be attached to traditional forms of worship, though not to the notion of papal supremacy. Protestantism of the severely Calvinist variety that the evangelicals had attempted to establish during Edward's reign, by contrast, remained a minority movement even in London and those other places (Cambridge University and various seaports, most notably) where it had struck the deepest roots. Despite the setbacks of the Marian interlude, the evangelical movement remained fervently militant and continued to attract adherents who felt impelled to propound their beliefs in writing and in the pulpit. It was becoming economically formidable as well, finding fertile recruiting ground among the mercantile families of London and other commercial centers as well as those that had risen to the top of the rural gentry thanks to the dispersal of church and Crown lands. Inevitably, the wealth of these rising classes was translating itself into political power.

The regime that Elizabeth inherited was Roman Catholic neverthe-less, with the Marian state and church tightly intertwined. In a reversion to long-standing practice, Mary had chosen as her chancellors first Bishop Stephen Gardiner and then, after Gardiner died and Cardinal Pole begged off, Archbishop Nicholas Heath of York. Maintaining the status quo might seem to have been the path of least resistance for Eliz-abeth, especially as Mary's arrangements were in no way objectionable to a majority of her subjects. Elizabeth herself had, albeit without great success, tried continually to convince her sister that she was a faithful daughter of Holy Mother Church. In fact, though, the choices facing Elizabeth when she became queen were not at all simple. Quite aside from her own convictions, she had compelling reasons, from the day of Mary's death, to undertake the fourth religious revolution (or counter-revolution) to be visited upon England in the space of three decades. Practically all of her active political support lay on the Protestant side, and she had been careful to maintain contact with the evangelical community all through the years when many of its members were pre-tending, for the sake of their positions and possibly their lives, to be or-thodox Catholics. She had gone to great lengths, always being as surreptitious as she could, to encourage the Protestants to see her as one of their own, which she undoubtedly was. The Protestants were given good reason to expect that as queen she was going to overturn the Catholic establishment; if she had ignored this hope the Protestants would have been justified in feeling betrayed, and Elizabeth might have found herself without any dependable base of support. To the Catholics, she had always been the bastard child of a schismatic king's heretic concubine. Queen Mary herself suspected that Elizabeth was the illegitimate daughter not of Henry VIII but of Mark Smeaton, the court musician who had been among those executed on charges of adultery with Anne Boleyn. Certainly both England's Catholics and Rome would have accepted Elizabeth as queen if she had left the Marian church in place—most of her Catholic subjects did so even after she set out to ex-terminate their church—but it is not difficult to understand why a wary new queen, taught in a hard school to be cautious about trusting any-one, had no interest in putting her fate in the hands of the Catholics.

What she *did* have in mind, at least at the opening of her reign, is not entirely clear. So many potent forces were in play, and in conflict, that it has always been difficult to sort out how much of what happened accorded with Elizabeth's own wishes and how much was imposed on her by circumstance. Essential as it was that she not fail the Protestants who had made her their champion and their hope, she also had to avoid alienating the still-powerful (and still-popular) Catholic party so completely as to provoke it into defiance. An exquisitely delicate balancing act was required, something similar to the one performed by the evangelicals just after the death of Henry VIII, and for an inexperienced monarch not yet twenty-five years old this was an imposing challenge. Elizabeth navigated her way through it with the skill of a master (there is no sure way of knowing, really, how much of "her" policy was actually the work of her canny secretary William Cecil and her other friends on the council), dashing no hopes while keeping everyone uncertain. In the beginning she placated the conservatives by punctiliously observing the established Catholic formalities, not interfering with the saying of mass even at court until a new Parliament could be summoned. Elizabeth herself attended Christmas mass at the end of 1558, some three weeks before her coronation, though when the celebrant followed an ancient practice that the Protestants had long condemned and elevated the consecrated communion host above his head, she exited the church in a theatrical flourish of indignation. She also refused to be escorted, in traditional fashion, by the Benedictine monks whom Mary had restored to residence at Westminster Abbey. In such ways she made it plain that she shared the evangelicals' revulsion at papist "idolatry" and their scorn for monasticism. No one could doubt where her sympathies lay, but she shrouded her political intentions behind a cloud of ambiguity and left the conservatives with reason not to despair.

The coronation took place on January 15, 1559. Elizabeth spent £16,000 of Crown money on it, a stupendous amount, and the city fathers of London were induced to contribute similarly impressive sums. She was crowned by Owen Oglethorpe, a junior bishop from the distant and unimportant Diocese of Carlisle. He was the newest of Mary's bishops, and though definitely a conservative, he had throughout his career shown a tendency to bend when put under pressure. Elizabeth chose him to do the honors at least in part because Pole of Canterbury was dead and Heath of York claimed to be too unwell to attend, but she may also have been demonstrating her disdain for the whole Marian hierarchy and what it represented.

Weeks before the coronation, in an unmistakable sign of the direction of her thinking, Elizabeth had overhauled the Privy Council. Here she was dealing with real power, not symbolism, and everything she did must have been gratifying to the evangelical camp. Within hours, literally, of learning of Mary's death, the new queen was summoning the council to meet and reshaping it by adding new members and removing more than she added. In short order it shrank from thirty members to nineteen: ten Henrician conservatives (men who accepted the royal supremacy but otherwise were inclined to traditional orthodoxy), nine evangelicals of an Edwardian-Calvinist stamp, no Roman Catholics, and remarkably, no clergy from any faction. The Protestants could take particular satisfaction in the appointment of Cecil as principal secretary, the position from which Thomas Cromwell had taken control of Henry VIII's government many years before, and of Nicholas Bacon to replace Archbishop Heath as chancellor. Cecil and Bacon, married to sisters, were members of families that had been Tudor loyalists since the start of the dynasty (or even earlier: Cecil's grandfather, when scarcely more than a boy, had joined the future Henry VII on his march to Bosworth Field). Both were ardent evangelicals whose careers had been in eclipse throughout the Marian years, though Cecil even more than Elizabeth had gone to almost ridiculous lengths to pretend to be a faithful Catholic, showily fingering rosary beads whenever he thought someone with access to the queen might be watching. Both would make plain that they regarded persecution of Catholics—even the torture of Catholics—a necessary means of purging the kingdom of superstition, sedition, and division.

The Protestants could have found no reason to object to the favors that Elizabeth began showering on her few living relatives, mainly the remnants of her mother's family, the Boleyns. Among the first to benefit was her cousin Henry Carey, son of Anne Boleyn's sister Mary and her husband, William Carey. (Actually Henry may have been Elizabeth's half-brother; the uncertain date of his birth makes it possible, though not probable, that he had been conceived when Mary Boleyn was Henry VIII's mistress.) He was raised to the peerage as Baron Hunsdon and granted lands that, by generating some £4,000 annually, vaulted him into the ranks of the richest men in England. This was an extraordinary gesture on Elizabeth's part; throughout her life she would remain deeply reluctant to create new peerages, and the wealth bestowed on Carey was badly needed by her government. Carey's older sister Catherine (more likely than her brother to have been King Henry's child) was made a lady of the queen's bedchamber, a high honor that Elizabeth would bestow on only about two dozen women in the course of her long reign. Catherine's husband, Francis Knollys, upon returning from exile on the continent, was given a comparable honor: a seat on the Privy Council. Still another Boleyn cousin, Sir Richard Sackville, also joined the council. Though Knollys and Sackville were not ennobled, both would use the queen's favor to put their families on courses that would lead to the former's son becoming a baron and the latter's an earl. With appointments like these the queen was able to surround herself with people who were entirely dependent on her for their positions, had impeccable Protestant credentials but no plausible claim to the throne, and so could be counted upon to remain absolutely loyal.

One other of the queen's first appointments must be noted here: the selection of the dashing young Robert Dudley as master of horse. Though he was not put on the council—not yet—Dudley's new position was highly visible and rather glamorous, and his selection was clear and early evidence of the unique place he held in Elizabeth's affections. He was the younger of the only two surviving sons of the John Dudley who as Duke of Northumberland had destroyed himself by attempting to put Jane Grey on the throne, and so he was also the grandson of the Edmund Dudley who lost his head at the start of Henry VIII's reign. Thus for the third time in as many generations a young member of this irrepressible clan won a place close to the throne, and for the second time it was happening in spite of the previous generation's failure and deep disgrace.

Dudley, like almost everyone singled out for preferment, was allied with the evangelical camp. With his four brothers he had spent the first months of Mary's reign as a prisoner in the Tower. (Elizabeth was confined there at the same time, though there is no evidence of their having been in contact.) After his release he had withdrawn to a life of obscurity on his father-in-law's estates in East Anglia. His sudden emergence as a highly visible member of the new regime formed part of a pattern that must have seemed to ensure a swift and thorough triumph for the Protestant cause. But then January 25 arrived, Elizabeth's first Parliament assembled at Westminster with the convocation of the clergy in session as well, and it became obvious that the way ahead was not in fact going to be easy.

The new House of Commons, many of its members chosen as usual for their willingness to accept the guidance of the Crown, showed itself from the start to be a potent engine of religious reform. Under Cecil's direction, and in collaboration with Protestant divines newly returned from the continent, it raised questions about whether the late Queen Mary's religious legislation could be considered valid in light of her repudiation of the royal supremacy. It began pushing for a restoration of all the powers that Henry VIII had taken for himself, and of King Edward's Protestant church. But it met with resistance from a surprising number of directions. A struggle developed in which the Crown, the bishops and clergy, the Protestants of the Commons, and conservative and reform factions in the House of Lords all tried to advance their own agendas. Over a period of months the terms of the conflict remained in flux, with the advantage appearing to shift from party to party. Elizabeth and Cecil, as they threaded their way through endless complexities, had to face the possibility that moving too emphatically in an anti-Roman position could bring papal condemnation down upon their heads, and with it the danger of a Spanish-French crusade. Likewise the queen's Catholic subjects, if pushed too hard, might be driven—might even be led by disgruntled conservative nobles—into armed rebellion. Elizabeth's relations with Parliament at this early stage are best understood not in terms of any attempt on her part to achieve some specific set of religious objectives but rather as one aspect of her broader struggle to maintain a balance between two contending parties: a fearful conservative majority that the queen and her ministers neither liked nor trusted, and an energized Protestant minority bent on domination. The government's goal, if only for the time being, was to win acceptance of a purposely ambiguous status quo.

The Privy Council opened the legislative bidding early in February by introducing bills with an aggressively Protestant slant: if enacted they would officially recognize the queen as supreme head, require all members of the clergy to swear an oath acknowledging her supremacy, and abolish Catholic worship in favor of the Edwardian Prayer Book. Commons not only approved these proposals but toughened them, but the Lords (with a conservative core consisting mainly of the Marian bishops) deleted restoration of the Prayer Book and merely authorized Elizabeth to take the title of supreme head *if* she chose to do so. Archbishop Heath objected even to this, taking the line (which even few women would have challenged in the sixteenth century) that the very idea of a female being head of the church was preposterous. Convocation, meanwhile, was putting itself at odds with queen, council, and Commons by voting to uphold a fully orthodox set of Catholic beliefs, including the bishop of Rome's supremacy. While all this was transpiring, word arrived that England's emissaries to a peace conference at Cateau-Cambrésis in France had succeeded in ending Mary's and Philip's war on the continent. This was important news. It stopped up a painful drain on the royal treasury. At least as significantly, by demonstrating the willingness of France and Spain to enter into a treaty with England, it eased concerns that both countries might refuse to acknowledge Elizabeth's legitimacy as queen. International recognition of the new regime, by immediately lessening the danger of a Catholic crusade, strengthened Elizabeth's domestic situation. She took the opportunity to pause and reconsider her options, adjourning Parliament with nothing resolved.

Her willingness to do as much for the Protestants as she could without putting herself at risk became obvious. What was called an official "discussion" was arranged, ostensibly to give representatives of the conservative and evangelical camps an opportunity to air their views on the future of the church, and any doubts about which side the government favored were put to rest when the leading spokesmen for the Catholic side, the bishops of Winchester and Lincoln, were immediately afterward thrown into prison. This had the considerable advantage, from the Protestant perspective, of removing two staunchly conservative votes from a closely divided House of Lords as the climax of the legislative dispute drew near. When Parliament reconvened on April 3, both houses took up a revision of a supremacy bill that recognized the queen as supreme *governor* rather than *head* of the church, once again separated England from Rome, and re-repealed the heresy laws that Mary's Parliaments had restored. This bill encountered serious opposition in the Lords and might have been defeated there if the old bugbear having to do with possible restitution of church lands had not been resurrected to alarm the lay majority one last time. A uniformity bill outlawing the mass in favor of a somewhat watered-down version of the Edwardian Prayer Book (verbal abuse of the pope was deleted from the worship service) passed even more narrowly after being opposed not only by all the bishops but by eleven lay lords including, rather embarrassingly for the Crown, two members of the Privy Council. Thus yet another new English church was born. It was unmistakably a Protestant church, possibly more emphatically Protestant than Elizabeth herself thought prudent. The new legislation had been softened to avoid extinguishing the last hopes of the Catholics, however, and so it served the queen's chief purpose: it avoided a crisis. Before going further, the government was going to have to weaken the Catholics.

One way to undermine the Catholic party was to eliminate the Marian bishops, and the legislation of 1559 made that possible. Thanks to the breakdown in relations between Mary and Philip and Pope Paul IV, ten of the kingdom's twenty-seven bishoprics were now vacant. A remarkable number of the remaining bishops were aged and infirm, and with Pole dead and Heath of York wanting to avoid conflict the hierarchy was essentially leaderless. Moreover several of its members—including Cuthbert Tunstal of Durham, who had been bullied into submission by Henry VIII early in the divorce dispute and was now in his mid-eighties—had lived through all the turmoil of the past thirty years and survived by bending under pressure. Elizabeth, not unreasonably, expected that some and possibly all of these men would do the sensible thing and once again repudiate the connection with Rome. She found, however, that almost to a man they were unwilling to make Cranmers of themselves by changing their allegiance yet again. Only Anthony Kitchen of Llandaff in Wales took the uniformity oath. Every one of the others, even those who in the past had shown themselves willing to go wherever the winds of fortune blew, stood fast. One resigned, two died in the months following the passage of the new Uniformity Act, and by the end of the year all the others had been expelled from their offices and either imprisoned or placed under house arrest. This time, however, there would be no executions. Elizabeth was not burdened with her father's terrible need for capitulation or his willingness to kill anyone who failed to capitulate abjectly. Determined to put her regime in the sharpest possible contrast to her sister's, she understood that a resumption of executions would have been entirely counterproductive.

Having decapitated the Marian church, the queen found herself at liberty to fill twenty-six bishoprics with men of her own choosing. This proved to be no simple matter. The most impressive candidates, the men who had departed for the continent rather than conform during Mary's reign and thereby achieved heroic stature in the eyes of the English Protestant community, had during their years of exile broken up into quarreling factions. The most important factions were the one centered at Frankfurt under Richard Cox, who had been tutor to Prince Edward before Henry VIII's death and chancellor of Oxford University afterward, and the one at Geneva under the Scotsman John Knox, who had declined a bishopric when Edward was king. Though they had become enemies while in exile, both Cox and Knox were rich in the kinds of credentials that should have brought success under the Elizabethan settlement.

Unfortunately for himself and his followers, however, during the closing months of Mary's reign Knox had written and published a document with an eye-catchingly dramatic title: *The First Blast of the Trumpet Against the Monstrous Regiment of Women*. This was, in essence, a vitriolic attack on three Catholic rulers: Queen Mary of England; the Frenchwoman Marie of Guise, who was ruling Scotland in the name of her daughter Mary Stuart; and Margaret of Hapsburg, Philip of Spain's half-sister and his regent in the Netherlands. Knox's tract excoriated the three for everything he found loathsome about their regimes—their "regiments," in the diction of the time. He had, however, couched his argument in such broad terms that it easily could be understood as (because in fact it was) a condemnation of rule by women as contrary to nature and therefore "monstrous." Elizabeth, who in a fantastically bad stroke of timing for Knox became queen just months after its publication, interpreted it in exactly this way. Not only Knox but those associated with him, even that most seminal of Protestant theologians John Calvin, became personae non gratae in England precisely at the moment when their version of Christianity was once again finding acceptance there. Luckily for Knox, a political-religious coup soon gave the Scots evangelicals control of the government and church in Edinburgh, enabling him to return home and proceed to the next stage of his momentous career as a crusading Puritan and anti-Catholic polemicist. From there he would try without success to persuade Elizabeth that *The First Blast* had never had anything to do with someone as obviously favored by God as she was. Cox meanwhile returned to England, secured for himself the lucrative see of Ely, and resumed his interrupted campaign to purge Oxford of conservative theology; he had the satisfaction of seeing one member after another of his old Frankfurt circle appointed to positions of importance. If not as radical as the Genevan Calvinists, the Coxians, too, were strongly inclined to the austerity that would soon be given the name Puritan. They were just as disposed to look on the old church with horror and only somewhat more willing to enter into alliances of convenience with Protestants less uncompromising than themselves.

The stage seemed set for the triumph of Cox's party. Elizabeth, however, showed herself to be unwilling to let that happen. Whatever her innermost motives—fear of the consequences of going too far, perhaps, or a personal theology capacious enough to make room for her father's kind of conservatism—she was soon obstructing her own new bishops. The nominee for Canterbury, Matthew Parker, was the choice not of the queen herself but of Secretary Cecil and Chancellor Bacon, and he was not one of the evangelical heroes returning from exile, having spent the Marian years staying as inconspicuous as possible at home. He had only the narrowest base of support, therefore, and even before his consecration (an honor, it must be acknowledged, that he tried to escape) he found himself at odds with Crown and Parliament. The point of conflict was a piece of legislation called the Act of Exchange, an attempt to allow the government to enrich itself at church expense (yet again) by taking possession of property belonging to the many vacant bishoprics and promising revenues from tithes in return. The Protestant clergy had as much reason as their Catholic predecessors to object to this latest plundering of their resources, and Parker, to the queen's indignation and the discomfiture of Cecil and Bacon, put himself at the head of the objectors. There ensued a long series of conflicts between Crown and church, and increasingly between different groups of Protestants, that made a misery of Parker's tenure as archbishop and a confusion of the council's efforts to manage the church. The queen went to sometimes

outlandish lengths to extract money from the dioceses while staying
within the letter of the law. She allowed the Diocese of Ely to remain
without a bishop for nineteen years after Cox's death. Bristol remained
vacant for fourteen years, Chichester for seven. There were arcane but
bitter conflicts over such questions as what churchmen should be required or permitted or forbidden to wear in the performance of their
ceremonial duties.

As angrily as they could contend among themselves, the Protestants
rarely had difficulty in uniting to expunge from the kingdom their despised common enemy: the Catholic Church and those of their countrymen who persisted in its beliefs and practices. Here again, however, with
what must have been baffling frequency, they found themselves unable
to get the expected level of cooperation from the queen. Out of the
eight thousand priests in England, no more than three hundred were removed from their positions between 1560 and 1566 for failing to confirm
to the Act of Uniformity. This number, certainly a small fraction of the
conservative clergy, can reasonably be taken as a measure less of concord than of Elizabeth's unwillingness to press the issue. In 1561, after
the recently elected Pope Pius IV called the Council of Trent back into
session after a years-long adjournment and invited England to send representatives, an alarmed Cecil, horrified by the thought of intercourse
between Canterbury and Rome, ginned up enough supposed evidence
of Catholic sedition to persuade Elizabeth not only to spurn the invitation but to intensify the harassment of practicing Catholics. The persecution was relaxed as soon as the danger of English participation in the
council was past, and two years later, when an increasingly aggressive
Parliament made it a capital offense to refuse twice to take the supremacy oath, the queen quietly ordered Parker to see to it that no one
was asked a second time. When convocation adopted the Thirty-Nine
Articles as a definition of current English orthodoxy, she saw to it that
the language was kept general enough that Catholics would not have to
repudiate either it or their beliefs. Repeatedly over the first decade of her
reign she vetoed legislation intended to increase the difficulties of being
Catholic while functioning more or less normally as a member of the
English nation.

Nothing in this should be taken as suggesting that Elizabeth was in
some way a crypto-Catholic, or that she entertained any thought of es-

tablishing a new kind of country in which fundamentally different belief systems would be permitted to coexist. She was not only Protestant but militantly Protestant, and no more capable than her contemporaries of imagining that any nation could tolerate multiple faiths without weakening itself fatally. But her highest objective remained her own security, not the pursuit of any agenda religious or otherwise. For more than ten years she remained content just to inconvenience her Catholic subjects, trying to make them gradually decline in numbers and finally—or so it was hoped—disappear. She was likewise content to keep in place a national church whose doctrines and practices were thoroughly acceptable to very few people except herself, a Protestant church from which increasing numbers of her most passionately Protestant subjects felt utterly alienated.

THE COUNCIL OF TRENT

THE RELIGIOUS AGENDA WITH WHICH ELIZABETH BEGAN her reign, her hope of slowly extinguishing the old church by a process of neglect that was far from benign but also stopped short of lethal persecution, was complicated by an improbable development: the emergence of the Roman Catholic Church, even before Elizabeth became queen, as the most ambitiously reformist element in the whole expanding universe of Christian sects. The energy with which Rome began to address the problems, failures, and doctrinal questions that lay at the root of the Reformation had become a challenge for Protestants of all stripes even before Henry VIII's death. As the resulting changes made themselves felt in England, they decreased the likelihood that Elizabeth's government was going to be able to win over its Catholic subjects simply by making their attachment to Rome an embarrassment and an inconvenience.

What made the difference was the Council of Trent, itself one of the most remarkable developments in the history of Christianity. Its results, for better or worse, were nothing less than momentous. That it happened at all, considering the obstacles that stood in its path from beginning to end, struck many of its participants as little short of miraculous.

Councils had been a central element in the development of Christianity almost from its origins, a way of settling disputed questions by referring them to conclaves of church leaders from every part of the believing world. The eighteen councils that had been convened before Trent, more than one per century on average, had played an essential role in deciding what was required for church membership, which texts were and were not authoritative, what was doctrine and what heresy. Though conflicts had arisen over whether councils or popes had primacy, and though the part played by councils in causing schism in the fourteenth century had caused them to be viewed with deep skepticism thereafter, the fundamental idea of councils as a means by which God could reveal himself to the faithful continued to exert a strong pull. Luther himself, at the start of his rebellion, had demanded that a council be called to pass judgment on what he was teaching. Though scarcely a year later he was declaring that councils had no power to decide questions of faith, by then some of his followers and some defenders of the old orthodoxy were looking to a council as possibly the only hope of preserving unity.

For two decades and more, as the reform movement sprouted more and more branches under the leadership of Zwingli, Martin Bucer, Calvin, and others, multiplying the ways in which tradition was being rejected, Rome failed to respond in anything resembling a systematic fashion. Even within the old church, there was more than a little doctrinal ambiguity—uncertainty about questions that the theologians had never attempted to answer definitively because they had never before seen a compelling need to do so. By the time Henry VIII embarked upon making himself head of his own church, it was generally the Catholics more than their enemies who thought a council desirable and even necessary. They were driven, at the start, by three impulses: to effect a reconciliation by which Christian Europe could be made whole once again, to clarify disputed doctrines, and to address the abuses that even the most conservative churchmen were no longer able to ignore. When it became clear that there could be no reconciliation, that rebellion was hardening into an array of alternative churches that were never going to be defeated or won over, the other two reasons came to seem more urgent than ever. The Roman church was not going to be able to defend itself until it became definitive about what it stood for, and it was not going to be able to command respect until it dealt with (which meant acknowledging) its own failings. The papacy having become so controversial, only a council could confer sufficient legitimacy on whatever the church decided to do. But every specific proposal for the holding of a council was met by objections from one quarter or another.

The political difficulties long seemed insurmountable. In 1523, at the Diet of Nuremberg, the rulers of Germany's newly Lutheran states issued a demand for a "free Christian council"—insisting also that it be held in Germany. Rome rejected the idea on the grounds that such a council would be national rather than ecumenical and therefore could not represent the entire church. Charles V not only supported Rome's position but forbade the holding of a council anywhere within his domains. By 1530, however, conditions had changed and both sides seemed ready: Charles and Pope Clement VII were agreed that a council should be called, and the Lutheran princes were repeating their demand for one. But when the pope sent invitations, it became obvious that although everyone professed to like the *idea* of a council, there was insufficient agreement on practicalities for any real progress to be made. The Germans found Clement's conditions insulting—understandably so, as he had insisted that the Protestants return to the old communion pending the results of the proposed council—and rejected his summons in scornful terms. Henry of England responded equivocally, neither agreeing to participate nor refusing outright. Francis I did likewise, complaining that his bishops could not possibly travel in safety while his country and the empire were at war but actually fearing that a council, if somehow successful in healing Germany's divisions, would make the emperor stronger. The situation drifted until 1534, when Clement died and Alessandro Farnese became Pope Paul III.

The new pope declared almost immediately that he, too, wanted a council—that he regarded a council as the only way of dealing with the crisis facing the church—but at first he seemed just as blocked as his predecessor. Paul was a paradoxical figure, one who gave the Protestants many reasons to remember what they had long found despicable about Rome. In many ways he was a classic Renaissance pontiff—a member of the high Roman aristocracy, extravagant in his spending, scandalously devoted to the advancement of the children whom he had produced early in his career and those children's children (among whom were two grandsons elevated to the College of Cardinals while still in their teens). He was also a ferocious hunter of heretics, the founder, in fact, of the Roman Inquisition. But with all this he was absolutely convinced of the need to reform the church. When in 1536 he called for all patriarchs, archbishops, bishops, and abbots to gather at Mantua the following year, the negative responses of the Lutherans, the king of France, and others— even the Duke of Mantua objected—did not deter him. His proposal, like those of Clement VII, became entangled in the conflict between France and the Holy Roman Empire, England's defection, and the fears of many cardinals that a council could only lead to further trouble. But he continued to push, and the emperor continued to support his efforts in general terms while often disagreeing on the details. After a good many more years of frustration and intrigue, a council finally opened in December 1545 in the city of Trent, an Alpine site that is now Italian but at the time lay within the borders of the Hapsburg empire.

It was, in the beginning, an unimpressive affair. Presided over not by the pope but by three cardinals serving as his legates (one of them was Reginald Pole), its opening session was attended by only one additional cardinal (who was also the bishop of Trent), four archbishops, twenty-one bishops, five heads of religious orders, forty-two theologians, and nine canon law scholars. This was scarcely enough for the council to claim to be representative of the church as a whole; France, England, and virtually all of Protestant Europe had declined to take part. Those present required three sessions and a good deal of acrimonious debate to get past preliminary questions of procedure. Finally in March 1546, having decided who would be allowed to vote (the religious orders were given a single vote each) and that questions of reform and of doctrine would be addressed simultaneously, they were ready to turn their attention to substantive issues. Over the next year, in the course of seven more sessions separated by intermissions during which the theologians and lawyers prepared reports on the matters to be considered next, the number of participants gradually increased and the amount of business completed went far beyond what anyone could have expected at the start.

The initial focus, naturally, was on those points where the German and Swiss Protestants had mounted their most damaging attacks on the old doctrines. Luther's assertion of justification by faith was debated on fully one hundred occasions, at the end of which council members approved an immensely detailed decree (it included sixteen chapters) to the effect that justification (salvation) is achieved not regardless of the individual's actions or beliefs but when man actively cooperates with divine grace. Thus free will was affirmed and predestination condemned. This set the pattern by which the council would proceed from then on, rejecting beliefs that made Protestant theology distinctly Protestant, upholding doctrines that the Protestants had repudiated, and drawing upon Scripture, tradition, and the writings of the church fathers to explain why. In its first months the council also affirmed—with sometimes laboriously detailed explanations—that both the Bible and tradition are sources of revelation; that all seven of the original sacraments are valid; and that the so-called Latin Vulgate version of the Bible (largely developed by Saint Jerome in the fourth century from Greek and Hebrew sources) is an authoritative text. The council's first major action with regard to practice and discipline was to declare that bishops must reside in their sees, thereby ending the "pluralities" long enjoyed by (for example) Cardinal Wolsey.

Perhaps because it was coming to grips with issues of the greatest sensitivity and highest importance, the council continued to grow in size and in credibility. By its ninth session the number of voting participants had more than doubled to include nine archbishops and forty-nine bishops along with the heads, or generals, of an increased number of orders. At the same time, however, the political divisions that had originally made it impossible to convene a council remained a formidable obstacle. After two years the pope found it necessary to shift the meetings to Bologna, where progress slowed to a crawl and finally stopped altogether with his death in 1549.

The council entered its second major period in 1551 under Pope Julius III, who as a cardinal had been its first president. This phase lasted only one year, during which the members met in six sessions. In that time they issued a comprehensive decree of eight chapters on the Eucharist or communion, once again affirming and systematizing traditional doctrine including the real presence. By now the council was giving substantial attention to the correction of abuses, issuing far-reaching rules on clerical discipline and the powers and responsibilities of bishops. This work was barely completed when, in 1552, the Protestant Maurice of Saxony launched a military attack on Charles V that made Trent so unsafe that once again the proceedings had to be adjourned. They remained in abeyance not only until Julius's death in 1555 but through the subsequent reign of Paul IV, who used his office to push an ambitious program of administrative reforms but (possibly because of his hatred of the Hapsburgs, very nearly the only royal supporters of the council) had absolutely no interest in seeing work resume at Trent or elsewhere.

The next pope, Pius IV, announced his intention to reconvene the council almost as soon as he was elected but quickly ran up against complications old and new. Many German states repeated their refusal to participate and their condemnation of what had been done thus far; the new Holy Roman emperor Ferdinand I demanded that an entirely new council be assembled in some city other than Trent; the French continued to complain and to stay away; and there was no possibility of involving Elizabeth's new regime. When Pius went ahead anyway and the council's members gathered in Trent early in 1562, the problems persisted. Bishops from France arrived for the first time that November, but their presence was very much a mixed blessing: they tried, though without success, to get the council to reconsider its earlier prohibition of pluralities. Despite much turmoil and intrigue, the nine sessions of this last of Trent's three periods led to a grand culmination. New decrees laid out rules of conduct for religious men and women of all types and at all levels from cardinals to lay brothers, and it was agreed that every diocese must establish seminaries for the education of its priests. Church doctrine was set forth in detail on subjects ranging from matrimony to the veneration of saints, from purgatory to the necessity of an ordained priesthood. The council even dealt, finally, with the issue that had triggered the Lutheran explosion: indulgences. To the scorn of Protestants, it affirmed the pope's authority to issue indulgences but ruled that they must never be sold or made conditional on the giving of alms. The council's last decrees were approved by 215 participants, among whom were six cardinals, three patriarchs (leaders of non-Roman rites that accepted the pope as head of the universal church), twenty-five archbishops, 167 bishops, seven abbots, seven generals of orders, and nineteen absent dignitaries voting by proxy. They closed the council on a note of jubilation, confident that their church had been put on a new course. Through their work that church had repudiated the Reformation conclusively, had explained its doctrines more systematically and comprehensively than ever before, and had made a repetition of the lapses and abuses of recent history all but impossible. Pius IV confirmed the council's decisions in the year of life that remained to him, put sanctions in place to enforce compliance, and introduced further reforms of his own that would be carried still further by his successors.

From start to finish the council had taken eighteen years and spanned the reigns of five popes. Its members had spent more than four years actively engaged in their deliberations, with much work ongoing between the twenty-five formal sessions. Those who rejected the very idea of a universal church headed by the bishop of Rome naturally dismissed the results as flawed and exclusive at best, as yet another abomination per- petrated by the Whore of Babylon at worst. Even some within the Catholic community saw the council as an overreaction, one that went too far in giving conclusive answers to difficult questions and made the church too rigidly triumphalist in its claim to be the sole source of reli- gious truth and salvation.

What cannot be doubted is that the council contributed mightily to stopping the unraveling of what remained of Catholic Europe. From the point at which its work was concluded, Protestantism made few geo- graphic gains of any significance. In the four and a half centuries since then, except with limited and short-lived exceptions, the kind of internal disorder that had made the council necessary never recurred. There has never been another pope whom any reasonable person could accuse of moral corruption in the mode of the Renaissance papacy. Almost cer- tainly, Trent made the transformation of England into a thoroughly Protestant nation a more difficult challenge, a bloodier process, than it otherwise would have been.

23

The Succession, Again

Religion was not the only great question pressing in on the new queen. Another, just as thorny in its very different way, cried out for an answer almost from the first day of Elizabeth's reign. It was a question that, like the future of the church, was resurfacing with undiminished force every time one Tudor monarch died and was succeeded by another. It was the matter of the succession.

At the start of Elizabeth's reign, as for a long time thereafter, the solution appeared to be matrimony. In the main line of Tudor descent, now that Henry VIII's only son and elder daughter were in their tombs, no one remained but this one young woman. There were cousins of royal blood, the few living descendants of Henry VIII's two sisters. But the most senior of these cousins had been born in Scotland and absorbed into the French royal family and was a Roman Catholic, making her suspect in the eyes of many Englishmen and absolutely unacceptable to the evangelicals. The others were the Protestant younger sisters of the late Lady Jane Grey and therefore objectionable, although no more so than Elizabeth herself, to the Catholics. The Tudor family tree remained a worrisomely thin organism, and if Elizabeth were to die childless the result was sure to be confusion and could be civil war. If on the other hand Elizabeth married and had children—at least one son, preferably, to end this awkward business of female rulers—the problem would disappear.

That the queen would follow her sister's example and take a husband seemed inevitable. To the extent that Mary's decision had become a source of trouble, the problem lay in her choice of the Spanish Philip. His status as ruler of Spain and the Netherlands and so much else made him an alien in the eyes of many of his wife's subjects, and not the evangelicals alone. But if Mary had not married Philip, those same subjects would have expected her to marry *someone*. The five years between Mary's accession and Elizabeth's did nothing to alter the universal conviction that it was unnatural for any woman not to be subordinate to some man (even nuns were "brides of Christ"), or for a queen to rule alone. Elizabeth herself, though she never forgave John Knox for his attack on *The Monstrous Regiment of Women*, never challenged this belief. She took the position, rather, that though her reign was a departure from the natural order of things, God had permitted it as a necessary means of restoring the gospel in England and preserving the kingdom's autonomy.

When Elizabeth took the throne she was an attractive young woman, with the fair skin and red-blond hair of the Tudors, her mother's dark eyes and slim body, and more than a dash of the Boleyn sexual magnetism. The men who dominated her first Privy Council thought themselves to have been blessed by God with a Protestant monarch, and naturally they hoped that she would become the progenitor of a long line of rulers of her religious persuasion. All this focused them on finding a marital answer to the succession question. For Elizabeth, the prospect of marriage was nothing new. As a king's daughter and the sister of a king and a queen, she had occasionally been in play on the market for royal brides, though in her case even more than in Mary's, illegitimacy had had a dampening effect on her value. We have seen Philip II, from the time of his arrival in England, protecting Elizabeth as a counterweight to Mary, Queen of Scots. He tried at one point, during his time in England, to marry her to his kinsman Emmanuel Philibert, Duke of Savoy. Elizabeth herself could see no advantage in such a match: the duke was little better than a displaced person of high distinction, having lost his ancestral lands to France, and he labored under the additional disadvantages of being Catholic and related to the Hapsburgs. Her lack of enthusiasm contributed to keeping the negotiations from getting serious, and shortly after she became queen Philip offered to marry her himself. She gave him no answer while consolidating her position—getting a new administration up and running, making preparations for her first Parliament. Rather than pressing the issue, Philip betrothed himself to a continental Elisabeth, a fourteen-year-old daughter of the king of France.

In February 1559, just two weeks after Elizabeth's coronation, a select committee of the House of Commons (it was "select" in the sense of being essentially a creature of the Privy Council) presented her with a formal request that she marry without undue delay. That such a step was taken so early in the reign is a good measure of how important the issue seemed to senior members of the new government. Elizabeth's not-unfriendly response to this intrusion into an otherwise intensely personal matter demonstrates that she, too, understood the question to be one in which her council, the Parliament, and indeed the nation had a legitimate stake. New candidates for her hand, meanwhile, were soon sending emissaries (and rich gifts) to explore the queen's availability. Among the suitors were King Erik XIV of Sweden and two young princes of the House of Hapsburg, sons of the emperor Ferdinand I and cousins of Philip of Spain. Efforts were made to arrange for one of the Hapsburg candidates, the archduke Charles, to travel to England, but when Elizabeth would not commit to the betrothal in advance of his visit the project collapsed. The fact that any Hapsburg would be a Catholic was a difficulty but obviously not an insuperable one. What mattered was finding a husband who could save England from being threatened, as seemed possible at this juncture, by an alliance of France and Scotland, or even *Spain* and France and Scotland.

Events with momentous consequences for England were meanwhile taking place in France. King Henry II arranged a lavish celebration both of the Treaty of Cateau-Cambrésis—under which France, Spain, England, and Scotland all were pledging to bring their war-making to an end—and of his daughter's marriage to Philip II. Henry participated in the jousting that was part of the festivities and suffered a slow, painful death (lingering in agony for ten days) after a sliver from an opponent's lance entered his eye and exited through his ear. He was succeeded by his eldest son, who took the throne as Francis II. The change proved to have far-reaching consequences in spite—or because, really—of the fact that Francis II was a frail and feeble fifteen-year-old and utterly incapable of taking charge. His accession meant that his bride of less than a year, Mary Stuart, the queen of Scotland and Catholic heir presumptive to the crown of England, was queen of France as well. Mary, now seventeen years old, had been raised in France while her mother, Marie of the House of Guise, one of France's most powerful families, remained in Scotland as regent. The bond between France and Scotland grew all the closer as young King Francis fell under the domination of his bride's uncles, the Duke of Guise and his brother Charles of Lorraine, a cardinal. Both countries were effectively under Guise control.

The contract under which the child Mary Stuart had been betrothed to Francis specified that if the couple had a son he would inherit France and Scotland as a single unified kingdom. For England this was an intolerable prospect, one that lifted the girl Mary to a position of stupendous geopolitical importance. But for Philip the situation was even more ominous: if Mary went on to succeed her cousin Elizabeth—such a development was far from impossible, considering the high mortality of the time and the fact that the queen of Scots was the younger of the two by almost a decade—he would be in grave danger. His Spanish base would be separated from his possessions in the Netherlands by a wall of hostile kingdoms extending from the islands north of Scotland to France's Mediterranean coast. The English Channel, the nautical highway connecting Spain and the Netherlands, would become a gauntlet lined on both sides by the seaports of his rivals. From Elizabeth's perspective, Philip's worries had a brilliantly positive aspect: they meant that Spain, with its vast European and global empire, needed the friendship of England at a moment when she, too, was urgently in need of friends. As long as Mary Stuart remained queen of France, there could be no possibility of a French-Spanish crusade to pull Elizabeth from her throne. As in Mary Tudor's reign, the existence of Mary Stuart gave Philip all the reason any king could have needed to want Elizabeth to survive.

The French-Scottish union would remain conditional, however, until Mary gave her husband a son. And no such thing was in the cards. Francis II, so unlike the vital and virile grandfather whose name he bore, lost his tenuous grip on life after only a year on the throne, almost certainly without having consummated his marriage. His death broke the power of the Guises over the government of France, and when his ten-year-old brother took the throne as Charles IX, control passed into the hands of their mother, Catherine de' Medici. The tall and rather beautiful Mary Stuart found herself an entirely superfluous second dowager queen, no longer wanted at a court that had been her home since childhood but was now dominated by the enemies of her Guise relatives.

Mary had little choice, really, except to return to the one place where she really was queen. But Scotland, too, had recently been convulsed by radical change and was no longer the kind of kingdom that her mother had struggled for years to preserve for her. Marie of Guise, not long after becoming regent, had found herself embroiled in a civil war with a party of Scottish noblemen, the "lords of the congregation," who were determined to install a Protestant government and establish a Protestant national church. Under the leadership of radical reformers such as John Knox, who had returned from the continent by ship after being denied permission to travel overland across England, evangelicalism had become popular and potent in Scotland's lowlands. Its adherents seethed with hatred for a Roman church that, long used as a source of spoils by the Scottish elite (King James V, Mary's father, had secured lucrative bishoprics for several of his illegitimate sons while they were still boys), had descended to levels of corruption never approached in England. Outnumbered and lacking in resources, despised for her foreign origins in spite of being honest, courageous, and by no means a mere agent of her French kinsmen, Marie of Guise had fought a protracted defensive action that might have been successful if not for two strokes of profoundly bad luck. Her health began to decline precipitously—she was dying, probably of heart disease, though still in her early forties—and England abruptly intervened on the side of the Protestant lords.

England's involvement was entirely the doing of William Cecil, Elizabeth's secretary and de facto minister-in-chief. He saw early what his royal mistress had difficulty seeing at all: that Scotland's internal divisions offered an unprecedented opportunity to drive out the French, establish Protestantism in the only kingdom with which England shared a border, and so turn an ancient enemy into a pacific neighbor if not an actively grateful friend. This was an enormous risk for Cecil, one in which failure could have meant ruin, because he had to labor to get the queen's assent (threatening to resign at one point) and in doing so took on full responsibility for the intervention's success. Elizabeth thought the chances of success small and the costs likely to be painful. But the

death of Marie of Guise in June 1560 doomed the Catholic cause in
Scotland and cleared Cecil's path. The result was a new Treaty of Edinburgh, a triumph for the Scottish rebels, for Knox and his newborn
Church of Scotland, and not least for England. When the young widow
Mary returned from France in 1561, it was to a Scotland profoundly different from the one in which she had been born nineteen years earlier. It
was under the control of people who reviled her religion and her French
associations, had no intention of allowing her to be more than a figurehead, and made her no more welcome than she had been in France in
the eight months since her husband's death. She faced a challenge beyond anything Elizabeth had experienced in England.

Elizabeth, meanwhile, was growing steadily more adept at dancing
around the subject of marriage when discussion could not be avoided altogether. One need not be Sigmund Freud to find reasons for her lack of
interest. She was, after all, the daughter of a queen whose marriage had
brought her to the block, the stepdaughter of another queen executed
by a wrathful husband and of two queens who died as a result of giving
birth, and the sister of a queen who had accepted it as her destiny to
marry and paid a high price for doing so. She had seen her own reputation dangerously compromised when, still a mere girl, she became resident in the home of the newly married Catherine Parr and was
subjected by Catherine's husband to advances that were obliquely sexual at least. She had good reason to see matrimony as a dubious portal
to fulfillment, or to safety.

And there was another factor at play. Not surprisingly for a healthy
and unmarried woman of twenty-five whose position exposed her to
the flattering attentions of some of the cleverest, most privileged, and
best-educated men in Europe, Elizabeth was in love. Her choice of objects would provide one of the most sustained and dramatic narrative
threads in the long story of her reign and an eventful chapter in the saga
of that most astonishing of Tudor-era families, the Dudleys. She had
fixed her affection, her passion, on her master of horse, Robert Dudley—"Rob" to her—a son of the late and not-much-lamented Duke of
Northumberland. The simple animal attraction was understandable:
Dudley was handsome and young and distinctly virile, with a fine education, the kind of sophistication and polish that only an upbringing at
court could produce, and experience as a fighting man. (As a youth he

was with his father at the crushing of Kett's Rebellion, and in 1557 he participated in the siege of St. Quentin, where his brother Henry was killed in his presence.) He and the last of his brothers, the three-years-older Ambrose, were accepted as leaders by the circle of soldiery that had originally coalesced around their father. They would have impressed any monarch, male or female, as living symbols of military potency.

Having grown to manhood during the years when his father was rising to become the most powerful man in England, Robert Dudley was intimately familiar with the royal household and not intimidated by any of it. He would eventually claim, not implausibly, to have known Elizabeth before she was eight years old, and he appears to have been the sort of boy who would have effortlessly impressed almost any younger girl (he was older than Elizabeth by about a year), however exalted her parentage. It is likely that, along with Elizabeth, he became a beneficiary of the scholarly establishment put in place for the education of the boy-king Edward VI. At any rate he emerged with the attainments—proficiency in French, Italian, and Latin, for example—that were among the fruits of royal life for the third generation of Tudors. He became a gentleman of Edward's privy chamber, an honor that any ambitious young Englishman would have hungered for, and from an early age was accustomed to the company of the richest, most powerful people in the kingdom. He even, before his father's fall, sat as a very young member of Parliament.

Beyond all this, and quite aside from the possibility that early in life the two had formed a bond of which we have been left no record, Elizabeth had reason to regard Dudley as a kindred spirit. Although the Duke of Northumberland died professing himself a Catholic, all his offspring embraced evangelical Protestantism. The male Dudleys who had not been executed were still being held in the Tower when Wyatt's Rebellion led to Elizabeth's confinement there. The experience, which for Elizabeth and Robert alike included the very real possibility of execution, gave them a profoundly memorable experience in common. Both were ultimately saved by the intercession of Philip after his arrival from Spain, Elizabeth as a safeguard against Mary Stuart, Dudley and his brothers because of their stature among England's warrior elite and Philip's wish for influential friends. Both remained deep in the political wilderness, however, as long as Queen Mary remained alive. The properties bestowed on her in her father's will had made Elizabeth rich, and during Mary's reign she was an inherently important personage as heir presumptive, but her life was quiet except for those moments of near-terror occasioned by official suspicion that she was involved in plots against the queen. Dudley, his conviction for treason set aside thanks to Philip's intervention, settled into the peaceful existence of a country gentleman.

Mary Tudor's death was a deliverance for the Dudleys almost as much as for Elizabeth. Ambrose and Robert were given military appointments that made them figures of some importance at court, the former as master of ordnance and the latter as master of horse. They received other signs of favor; in Robert's case these included knighthood in the exclusive Order of the Garter, the lieutenantship of Windsor Castle and, to fatten his purse, a license to export wool without paying duty. (Later he would receive a more important license to import sweet wines.) Their sister Mary, the wife of the courtier Sir Henry Sidney, became a lady of the queen's privy chamber, her husband president of the council responsible for governing the territories bordering Wales.

It became obvious at court that Elizabeth had a singularly strong liking for Robert's company and was conspicuously unwilling for him to be absent. Inevitably, quite possibly without anything improper transpiring between them, a whiff of scandal began to emanate from their relationship and give rise to backstairs talk. There can have been no gossip of a possible marriage, however, because for almost two years after Elizabeth became queen such a thing was literally impossible. It would have been problematic for the queen to marry even the noblest of her subjects; such a union would have seemed demeaning to the Crown and would have carried with it the danger of dividing court and country into the husband's allies and rivals. For Elizabeth to marry a member of the Dudley clan would have provoked resentment among the more ancient noble families. But that was not the worst of it. The fatal fact was that Dudley was married. In 1550, in what would appear to have been a love match because it brought no political and little financial advantage to the bridegroom or his family, John Dudley had allowed Robert to marry a girl named Amy Robsart, only child of a respectable but unimportant East Anglian landowner. It was on his father-in-law's properties that

Robert had passed the years after his release from the Tower, living happily enough with Amy so far as is known but having no children. When the Dudleys were restored to royal favor, Amy was not brought to court with them. Her health may not have been good, and Robert undoubtedly understood that the queen would not have welcomed reminders that he had a wife. Dudley did visit Amy for a while, but with decreasing frequency and finally not at all.

But then came an earthquake. On the evening of September 8, 1560, Amy Robsart Dudley was found dead in her country home in Berkshire. An investigation followed, to the extent that such a thing was possible in the sixteenth century, but the result was a meaningless ruling of "death by misadventure." Amy's neck may or may not have been broken. She may or may not have had breast cancer. The possibility of suicide was raised, but her servants insisted that she never would have taken her own life. Naturally a suspicion of murder arose, and inevitably that suspicion focused on the husband. But Dudley had incontrovertibly been at Windsor on the day of Amy's death, having just returned from accompanying the queen on one of the "progresses" by which, every summer, she displayed herself to her subjects. The death was, and has remained, an impenetrable mystery. It also proved to be of immense political importance. It freed Dudley to marry the queen. But at the same time it spread over both of them the dark question of whether they had somehow conspired to eliminate the one person who stood between them. People were not slow to note that, at the time of her death, Amy had not been visited by her husband in more than a year. And that Dudley, who now became sole owner of his late father-in-law's holdings in land, neither attended his wife's funeral (that was actually not unusual at the time) nor arranged for the kind of memorial customarily created when a member of a prominent family died. Gossip turned to scandal, not only across England but in Europe. People eager to believe that Anne Boleyn had been a slut were easily persuaded that her daughter was a slut as well. Even people close to the queen—even Cecil, her trusted secretary—encouraged the foulest of the rumors in hopes of making the marriage impossible.

THE FALL AND RISE OF ENGLISH THEATER

WHEN ELIZABETH BECAME QUEEN, TWO VERY DIFFERENT kinds of theater were alive and well in England. One was old and religious in impulse and tightly woven into the lives of the people. The other was new and boisterously secular and more than a little disreputable. Both were regarded, from Elizabeth's first days on the throne, as serious problems—as threats to domestic peace if not to true religion, to the morals of the community if not to the efficient functioning of the economy. Over the next forty years the government would systematically suppress the old kind until finally, despite dogged popular resistance, it was extinguished. By the end of the Tudor era the new kind, in spite of a state censorship so strict as to amount almost to persecution, would be emerging as one of the supreme achievements of English cultural history.

Drama, like so much of life in England, had its roots in the early Middle Ages. It made its first, almost childishly simple appearance no later than the tenth century, in the form of little scenes from Scripture acted out by priests and worshippers inside their parish churches. Over the next few centuries these performances grew larger and more elaborate, finally spilling out of the churches and being taken over by the guilds. Three types evolved: mystery plays, in which stories from the Bible were acted out; miracle plays, based on incidents from the lives of saints; and finally morality plays, forerunners of modern drama, in which characters representing good and evil struggled to win the soul of some Everyman. (Mystery plays, by the way, took their name not from the Latin word *mysterium*, meaning "secret," but from *misterium*, meaning "occupation" or "trade." The name reflected the importance of the various occupational guilds—of silversmiths or bakers or carpenters or whatever—as sponsors, underwriters, and producers of dramatic performances, especially in the cities and larger towns.)

Ultimately, and without losing their religious content and purpose, such productions became a major form of popular entertainment and communal celebration. Whole cycles of plays were developed; some cycles included as many as twenty-five or even fifty separate tableaux (enactments of the Genesis account of creation, say, or of Jesus raising Lazarus from the dead). The sets for these miniplays would be mounted on wagons called "pageants," which could be wheeled from place to place in sequence so that in the course of a day spectators could see an entire cycle without having to move. It was not unlike the passage of floats in a parade. The cycles became central to observances of the major events in the liturgical calendar: Christmas of course, but also Twelfth Night (January 6, the feast of the epiphany), Candlemas (February 2), Holy Week with its culmination in Easter, Whitsun (the seventh Sunday after Easter), the feast of Corpus Christi (the Thursday after Trinity Sunday), and Hallowtide at the beginning of November. Schools, too, put on regular theatrical productions—which must have been a hugely welcome break from the tedious recitations that formed the core of classroom instruction—as did the universities and the Inns of Court.

As in any society where even simple forms of theater thrive, some individuals found themselves prepared to sacrifice security and stability in order to spend their lives performing. Tiny companies of professional players began to form and to scratch out a living by traveling from place to place. These groups would put on shows wherever they were allowed to, occasionally finding employment in the universities' Christmas productions or at the courts of the great nobles or even the king. Thus did the professional actor first emerge in post-Roman Britain. With him, inevitably, came nonreligious dramatic works. Few early examples have survived; those available to us tend toward the crude, rude, and unrestrainedly vulgar, but they are also funny enough in their Three Stooges slapstick way and sometimes surprisingly accomplished in character development. One of the oldest survivals, *Gammer Gurton's Needle,* is believed to have been written as late as the 1550s but to be one of the first comedies ever written in English. This dating, if correct, puts the play little more than a generation before the start of Shakespeare's career and marks the beginning of a period of astonishingly rapid artistic development.

At the beginning of Elizabeth's reign, in any case, the mystery, miracle, and morality plays were still a central, much-loved element in En-

glish community life, and professional theater was becoming increasingly popular both in London and in every place where local authorities
would permit touring companies to put on shows in exchange for
money. The new queen's council, its evangelical members especially,
was uncomfortable with theater of any variety and decided almost
before doing anything else that limits had to be imposed. The main problem with the religious plays was their traditional—meaning Catholic—
content. As for the newer, more secular performances, the Puritans
believed that, even if their content was not idolatrous or superstitious,
they wasted time that could better be devoted to work or prayer. Secular
theater suffered also from a growing perception on the part of the ever-
more-respectable middle classes that the kinds of people who engaged
in it were distinctly undesirable. Such opinions were not entirely unfair.
Plays were presented, usually, in neighborhoods where rents were cheap
and houses of prostitution and bear-baiting pits were leading forms of di-
version.

Officialdom's first response was a 1559 proclamation to the effect
that no plays were to be presented anywhere unless licensed either by
the mayor of a city or town or by a titled nobleman. The sternest of the
Puritans undoubtedly would have preferred simply to ban all theater
outright, but this was rendered impossible by the inconvenient fact that
drama had established itself at court. Those responsible for providing
amusements for the queen and her courtiers were learning that hiring a
company of players to perform works already written and rehearsed was
easier—and vastly less expensive—than developing new entertainments
from scratch. Queen and courtiers, for their part, responded enthusiastically to theatrical performances—to the best of them at least.

Theater continued to be regarded as intrinsically disreputable, however. The Privy Council observed it through narrowed eyes, imposing increasingly firm controls. Eventually it limited the authority to license
companies to the titled nobility, in part, no doubt, because nobles were
far fewer in number than mayors and judicial officials and more easily
monitored and subjected to pressure from the Crown. But another reason must have been the fact that England's increasingly well-educated
nobility found pleasure in quality theater, displayed a willingness to support it, and would not have accepted its elimination without complaint.
By the 1560s the Earl of Leicester, the same Rob Dudley who stood first

among Elizabeth's favorites, was sponsoring one of the most successful companies. This weighty endorsement was given even more force by Dudley's status as a prominent evangelical.

As the 1560s proceeded, men more puritanical than Dudley were moving into positions of leadership in cities and towns including London. Such men were repelled by the traditional religious theatricals so loved by their neighbors, and they refused to issue licenses except for scripts cleansed of all vestiges of the old religion. Finally they refused to license the productions altogether, and though resistance was widespread and persistent it was itself unlawful and ultimately fruitless. Cycles tailored to the feast of Corpus Christi were still being performed in Kendal in the north in the late 1580s, and in distant Cornwall even in the 1590s, but by the end of the century they were gone. The tradition they expressed was fading. Henceforth the story of English theater was the story of secular drama exclusively. And it, far more than the old religious plays, was concentrated in London.

The capital was becoming the biggest city in Europe; by the end of the century it would have 200,000 residents, four times as many as in 1500. It was a boiling, brawling cauldron of tradesmen and nobles, clerics and domestic servants, sailors and soldiers, idlers and whores and fortune-seekers from every corner of Europe, most of them hungry for entertainment and many with at least a penny or two to spare. Such a place was a magnet for the traveling companies of actors that, as they put on performances in the courtyards of inns and other rented spaces, found themselves attracting large and lucrative audiences. Necessarily, such performances were almost invariably presented in daytime, and naturally they attracted the sorts of people who were free in the daytime—prostitutes, sailors, and other visitors in search of a good time, workers willing and able to slip away from their jobs. The city fathers, appalled, appealed to the council to purge London of such decadence and refused to issue licenses. The theater people responded by moving to downmarket suburbs beyond the reach of city law. Respectable England's attitude toward the whole phenomenon is apparent in the name of the bill with which Parliament, in 1572, sought to impose order: An Act for Punishment of Vagabonds. Now licenses could be granted only by nobles or two "judicial dignitaries of the realm." In due course the lord chamberlain was made responsible for approving dramatic works—which meant banning any play of which he disapproved—and the stationers' guild for preventing the printing of banned works.

None of this even dented the popularity of the theaters. Audiences continued to grow, and venues grew with them. Impresarios stopped renting space and began to build theaters instead; these were ramshackle affairs at first but soon were more substantial, and by the 1580s the largest could hold three thousand people. Admission was a penny in the large roofless amphitheaters, twopence if you wanted a place to sit, while more exclusive indoor performances might charge as much as sixpence per seat—a sum beyond the means of most people. The revenues thus generated were more than sufficient to encourage the construction of increasingly impressive theaters. The frequency with which many people went to the theater created a voracious market for new material, and the licensing restrictions tended to concentrate the best talent in a small number of companies. For many such reasons London's theatrical world not only expanded but grew more accomplished at an extraordinary pace. Its leading figures became almost respectable. Queen Elizabeth herself became patron of a company in 1583, and in 1594 the lord chamberlain was authorized to select two companies to perform within London itself. By then young Shakespeare had been on the scene for five years, having come up to the city from Warwickshire in the hope of making his way as a writer. The hunger for talent was so strong, and the rewards for exceptional talent so great, that when the grand Globe Theatre was built on the south bank of the Thames in 1598, Shakespeare would be one of its five principal shareholders.

24

A Torrent of Miseries

The intrigues surrounding a possible marriage of Elizabeth to Rob Dudley grew weirder and weirder. Henry Sidney, Dudley's brother-in-law and a courtier close to the queen, soon was approaching the Spanish ambassador about a possible deal in which Philip II would support the marriage and England would once again be reconciled with the Roman church. The context in which this astounding scenario was discussed—with Dudley, Cecil, and the queen herself all involved—was predictably complex. In 1559 the combative Pope Paul IV, that great hater of Hapsburgs and heretics, had died and been succeeded by Pius IV, a placid soul in comparison with his predecessor and more inclined to seek an understanding with schismatics than to condemn them out of hand. It would have seemed distinctly likely that this new pope would be receptive to an arrangement that had the endorsement of the king of Spain and promised to heal the breach with England. Pius was just then making preparations to reconvene the Council of Trent. He intended to invite England, hoping (against hope, one might think) to bring it back into the fold as a partner rather than a rival in reform.

Other parts of the background were the aforementioned deaths of Marie of Guise and young Francis II of France, Mary Stuart's demotion from queen consort to widow and dowager, and the consequent unraveling of the connection between France and Scotland. These developments had, from the Spanish perspective, put Mary's claim to the throne of England in a new and more attractive light. Philip II began exploring the possibility of making Mary the wife of one of his Austrian cousins, or even his own son by his first marriage, the boy Don Carlos. Such a union would have transformed the Queen of Scots, once such a threat to Hapsburg interests, into an immensely useful asset. In dangling her own possible marriage to Dudley in front of Philip, Elizabeth may have merely been attempting to draw his attention away from Mary Stuart. This seems a stretch, however; Elizabeth certainly understood that Philip was capable of pursuing both matters simultaneously, and the notion that Philip could reconcile England and Rome only by abandoning the idea of bringing Mary into the Hapsburg family makes very little sense. The whole affair remains cloaked in mystery, as do the motives of the participants. The negotiations were conducted in such deep secrecy that they remained unknown to the world until the nineteenth century, when the historian J. A. Froude turned up the evidence while examining Spain's diplomatic correspondence.

The idea that Elizabeth was merely playing a diplomatic game is undercut by what is known of Cecil's reaction to the negotiations. He wrote to a confidant that he was, for reasons left unspecified but almost certainly having to do with the proposed marriage, so unhappy with the state of affairs at court as to be considering resignation. At the same time he was continuing to try to disrupt the proceedings by discrediting Elizabeth and Dudley, telling the Spanish ambassador that the two had planned Amy Robsart's death. These would not appear to be the actions of a man who knew his mistress to be pretending. They are more understandable if Cecil genuinely feared that the queen might be willing to abandon the Protestant cause in order to marry the one man she wanted as a husband. If somehow he was acting in collusion with the queen, the two were playing a game so deep and devious as to be incomprehensible.

What appears to have happened, in the end, is that Cecil frightened Elizabeth into calling the whole thing off. He announced that his agents had uncovered a Catholic conspiracy against the Crown, made some dramatic arrests including that of a fugitive priest, and claimed to have evidence of Catholic perfidy so outrageous as to destroy any possibility of a restored relationship. The queen was persuaded, on the basis of evidence that at a distance of four and a half centuries looks distinctly flimsy, that she could expect no loyalty from her Catholic subjects and that large numbers of Protestants were prepared to rise if she turned her back on them. The papal nuncio responsible for delivering an invitation to Trent was prevented from crossing to England. Though the affair ended with scarcely a whimper, it marked a watershed in Elizabeth's life. It would be a good many years before she again regarded an offer of marriage as anything more than an opportunity to manipulate and deceive. Dudley would remain her beau ideal, the most important person in her life, but for both of them the hope of marriage had burned down to dead ash. As it became clear that no great royal unions were in the offing and Mary Stuart made preparations for her return to Scotland, the French queen mother Catherine de' Medici urged the pope to excommunicate Elizabeth. Philip, no longer cast in the incongruous role of enemy of the papacy, persuaded him to do nothing.

Some months later Elizabeth was struck down by smallpox, one of the world's great killers until modern times, and became so ill that she was not expected to live. Council and court were made more painfully aware than ever of how difficult a predicament they would be left in if she died without a spouse, a child, or a designated successor. When she emerged from unconsciousness, still in mortal danger, she asked her councilors to appoint Dudley lord protector of the realm with an income of £20,000 annually, a sum sufficient to support him in the most munificent style. The request was poignantly romantic and utterly without foundation in reality; the council would never have agreed to anything of the kind. Even if it had consented for the second time in little more than a decade to deliver the whole kingdom into the safekeeping of a Dudley—an improbable development to say the least—Robert's elder brother would have been the more logical choice. Ambrose by now had been made Earl of Warwick, the title held by John Dudley until he became Duke of Northumberland, while Robert remained a commoner. The comparison was in any case meaningless; only a delirious Elizabeth could have imagined that her council would surrender control to either of the brothers.

The disease passed but left its mark. Elizabeth's face was badly scarred, and patches of her scalp were left permanently bare. It was a melancholy turn of events for a woman not yet thirty who had always been both attractive and vain. Hardheaded political survivalist though she was, for the rest of her life she would be pathetically susceptible to any sycophant who praised her for a beauty she no longer possessed. It was in a sense doubly cruel that council and Parliament now resumed their appeals for her to marry. But from this point forward the business of finding an acceptable consort and inducing Elizabeth to assent took on a perfunctory character. Fresh attempts were undertaken from time to time, but even those making the effort were never terribly hopeful. The queen herself barely pretended interest unless she could see some diplomatic advantage in doing so. The period after her recovery brought a revival of the candidacy of the Hapsburg archduke Charles, younger brother of the newly elected emperor Maximilian II. Cecil's support for this possibility shows once again that the desire for an heir could override even the strongest antipathy toward Rome. The pressure was for a while so intense that Elizabeth came close to agreeing. In the end she was saved less by her own unwillingness than by the refusal of the emperor to compromise Charles's freedom to practice his religion after taking up residence in England.

Eventually the council's focus shifted from trying to get the queen to marry to the presumably more straightforward task of designating her successor. Here again, however, Elizabeth balked. She did so in spite of the fact that her refusal multiplied the dangers of disorder in the event of her death. And so as the life of her cousin Mary Stuart became one of the most dramatic (and also melodramatic and tragic) in the history of English royalty, it also became heavy with significance for everyone who feared and everyone who desired a restoration of the old religion.

Mary, from the day of her arrival in an Edinburgh that she had not seen since age six, a city now ruled by militant Calvinists with no desire for her return, was herself enmeshed in questions of marriage and succession. Like Elizabeth she was probably a virgin, she, too, would leave behind a chaos of contending factions if she died childless, and almost any husband she chose was certain to bring a baggage train of complications trailing behind him. At first she showed impressive political adroitness, especially for a twenty-year-old dealing with enemies more powerful than herself in what was, essentially, a foreign country. With very nearly no trustworthy advisers to guide her, she accepted the settlement that had delivered Scotland's government and church into Protestant hands. She refused, however, to ratify Cecil's Treaty of Edinburgh, because doing so would have involved relinquishing her claim to the throne of England. Using the little power that remained to her, she established religious toleration as Crown policy—the first time that any such thing had ever been attempted in the history of the British Isles. The dignity and restraint with which she handled herself began to erode the distrust with which many of her subjects had received her in 1561 and to build up a store of goodwill.

Mary had no reluctance to marry, and the English court naturally took an interest in her intentions. In 1564, in a bizarre twist that nevertheless made a good deal of sense from the English perspective and offered practical advantages to Scotland as well, Elizabeth offered Mary as bridegroom none other than Robert Dudley, who was made Earl of Leicester to enhance his suitability. Mary replied that she could agree only if recognized as Elizabeth's heir, but Elizabeth would promise only that Mary and Leicester, once married, would be permitted to live at the English court. That was the end of that. It was also the end of the best part of Mary Stuart's life. She now plunged headlong into a sea of troubles from which she would never emerge.

While the Dudley proposal was still in negotiation, a young cousin of Mary's named Henry Stuart, eldest son of the Earl of Lennox and known as Lord Darnley, had arrived at the Scottish court. Like Mary, he was a grandchild of Henry VIII's sister Margaret, who had married twice more and borne a daughter after the death of King James IV. Also like Mary, therefore, he was a blood member of the royal families of both kingdoms; in the event of Mary's death, in fact, he would have had a strong claim to the Scottish throne. He had grown up in England and become a familiar figure at Elizabeth's court, his father having had to flee Scotland after supporting Henry VIII's failed invasions of the early 1540s. On at least two occasions in his youth, undoubtedly at his father's bidding and for the purpose of winning favor for the family if not specifically for himself, Darnley had traveled to France and met the Queen of Scots there. For reasons that remain obscure, Elizabeth eventually took up the Lennox cause, encouraging Mary to admit her kinsmen back into their homeland and restore their confiscated lands. Mary eventually agreed, her reasons, too, being less than clear, and the consequences were momentous. She was soon smitten with Darnley, who was not yet twenty, and with rather unseemly haste they married. Of the many costly mistakes that Mary would make in the course of an epically difficult life, this was by far the worst, the precipitating blunder from which a torrent of miseries would flow.

Objectively, the marriage offered Mary so many advantages that when news of it reached England Elizabeth was deeply angered. Darnley's bloodlines were so good as to strengthen not only Mary's hold on the crown of Scotland but her claim to that of England as well. Formally he was a Catholic, which was important to Mary, but his beliefs, if he had any, were elastic enough to have allowed him to function comfortably at Elizabeth's court; he was not likely to offend the Protestant lords of Scotland with displays of the faith they despised. The marriage was doomed, however, and its flaw was Darnley himself. He was vain, arrogant, and weak, not merely immature but deeply, dangerously foolish. His wife discovered this soon enough, but by the time she did so she was pregnant. The sequence of calamities that ensued requires attention here because of its bearing on the Tudor succession, but could be dealt with in detail only in a different kind of book. Much of what happened remains open to interpretation; who actually did what, and why, is largely shrouded in mystery.

It began, the worst of it, grotesquely. Mary had a private secretary, a strutting and self-important little Italian named David Riccio who had first come to her court as a musician in search of employment. He alienated the Edinburgh nobles by limiting their access to the queen. (Riccio had many of the same powers as Elizabeth's secretary Cecil, but gave no evidence of comparable intelligence or skill.) The disaffected lords had no difficulty in convincing Darnley (now the Duke of Albany but disgruntled because Mary would not make him her co-ruler) that his wife and the gnomish Riccio were lovers. They drew him into a scheme in the execution of which he and a little gang of retainers burst in on Mary and Riccio while they, in company with a court functionary, were innocently having supper. Riccio was dragged out of the room, stabbed dozens of times, and thrown down a flight of stairs. Mary was six months pregnant, and the conspirators may have hoped to shock her into premature labor so that the child would die and she with it. That didn't happen, and early that summer she gave birth to a healthy boy who was given the name of a long line of his royal forebears: James.

There was more, and worse, to come. Almost a year after the Riccio murder, Darnley himself died in spectacular fashion when the house in which he was sleeping was blown up. It was later determined that Darnley was not killed by the explosion but subsequently strangled. Three months after that Mary eloped with James Hepburn, Earl of Bothwell, an alpha male who had earlier been an important source of support in her struggles with the Scots lords and was probably responsible for killing Darnley; the two were married, surprisingly, in a Protestant ceremony. That is one version of the story and for a time it was the only version anyone heard. Another version, more credible when all the known facts are thrown onto the scales, is that Mary was abducted by Bothwell, acquiescing in the marriage only because he had raped her. Within a few months she was the prisoner of the Protestant lords, who tried to get her to repudiate the Bothwell marriage but were unable to do so, probably because she was pregnant. Told that if she refused to abdicate in favor of her infant son she would be executed, she yielded (though later she would say that she did so only after being secretly advised that an abdication coerced under threat of death could never be upheld as valid). A miscarriage of twins followed, then a nervous breakdown, an escape from prison, defeat in battle, and a flight into England that ended with Mary becoming Elizabeth's prisoner. She was subjected to a ludicrously unfair judicial inquiry in which she was confronted with the now-notorious "casket letters," messages to Bothwell that implicated her in the murder of Darnley but were almost certainly artful forgeries. She was, by this time, all of twenty-five years old.

The year when Mary entered England, 1568, also brought the dynastically important death of Catherine Grey. As the younger sister of Jane Grey and the eldest surviving granddaughter of Henry VIII's sister Mary, the Lady Catherine had a claim to the throne and was the favorite of many Protestants. But she, like her elder sister before her and her younger sister after, learned what a poisonous legacy Tudor blood could be. In law, because King Henry's last will had excluded the Scottish branch of the family from the succession, Catherine's claim appeared to be better than Mary Stuart's. But when, early in Elizabeth's reign, Catherine wanted to marry Edward Seymour, son of the brother of Queen Jane Seymour who had become lord protector after Henry's death, she came up against a statute prohibiting the marriage of anyone of royal blood without the queen's permission. Catherine and her young beau, fearful that approval would be denied, wed in secret and in doing so committed treason. Elizabeth was furious when she learned of this (it was characteristic of her to go into a rage whenever someone close to her married) and had the newlyweds confined in the Tower. Catherine was pregnant by then and gave birth to a son while in prison. Afterward the lieutenant of the Tower allowed the couple to see each other in secret, with the result that Catherine had a second son and any hope of receiving the queen's forgiveness was destroyed. Catherine was still in custody, though no longer in the Tower, when she died. Because her marriage was found to be invalid—that was Elizabeth's doing too— her sons were officially illegitimate and not eligible to inherit the throne. Meanwhile the third Grey sister, the misshapen little Lady Mary, had disgraced herself not only by marrying without permission but by choosing a commoner husband, a widower more than twice her age. That union was broken up before it produced offspring. Thus one of the highest hopes of the Protestants, that the last of the Tudors might be followed by one of the evangelical Grey sisters or a child of one of them, was extinguished.

Attention turned all the more intensely back to Mary Stuart, now almost the only living member of the royal family aside from Elizabeth herself and the mother of a son, albeit a son in the custody of his mother's enemies in Scotland. Even as a prisoner Mary was strongly supported—not as a rival to Elizabeth necessarily, but as her rightful heir—by two factions. One was headed by the leaders of the most powerful ancient families of the north of England, Thomas Percy, the seventh Earl of Northumberland, and Charles Neville, the sixth Earl of Westmorland, and included the large part of the northern population that continued to practice the old religion. The other was based at court, took its strength from those councilors and courtiers who resented the dominance of Secretary Cecil, and looked for leadership to Thomas Howard, the fourth Duke of Norfolk (whose sister, not incidentally, was married to Westmorland). He was the grandson of the duke who had narrowly escaped execution at the time of Henry VIII's death and spent Edward VI's entire reign in the Tower of London.

The next chapters in the Mary Stuart story were as rich in drama as everything that had come before, but their details are less important for present purposes than their results. Percy and Neville secretly allied themselves with the Norfolk faction, took fright when a suspicious Elizabeth summoned them to court, concluded that they had no choice except to fight or flee, and therefore hastily raised the standard of rebellion. They certainly hoped to free Mary and to restore Catholic practice, but whether they aspired to remove Elizabeth from the throne is unclear. In any case their rising was so ill prepared and ineptly managed as to be put down quickly and without great difficulty, the earls finding it advisable to abandon their supporters and escape into Scotland. Before that happened, however, they dispatched to Rome a request that Pope Pius bless their undertaking, send support, and declare Elizabeth excommunicated. By the time this appeal reached Rome the revolt was already over, but Pius had no knowledge of this and was being assured that the people of England were eager to cast off their heretic queen and inhibited only by the fear that rebelling against an anointed ruler would be a grievous sin. Pius issued a bull expelling Elizabeth from the church, absolving her subjects of the obligation of loyalty, and providing grounds in canon law for her fellow rulers to attack and dethrone her. It was perhaps in response to the excommunication that the collapse of the northern rising was followed by some eight hundred executions—extraordinarily savage vengeance for a movement that had petered out before becoming dangerous or even notably large. In fact, the revolt soon proved to have brought immense benefits to the Crown. The centuries-old quasi-independence of the northern nobility came to an end from which there would be no return—the Percys and Neville were only the most prominent of the proud old families ruined—and the administration of the north was put in the hands of officers of Elizabeth's choosing.

The excommunication of England's queen was perhaps understandable after ten years in which to be a Catholic in England was very nearly to be an outlaw, and in which Elizabeth and her council had consistently responded with contempt to overtures from Rome. It was a monumental blunder nevertheless, by far the greatest mistake made by either side during the long conflict between the Tudors and the popes, and England's Catholics paid a high price for it. Immediately their situation was

made desperate: they were left with no alternative except to choose between their church and their queen. Overnight it became plausible for
the authorities to claim that refusal to take the oath of supremacy really
was an act of treason, a declaration of loyalty to foreign enemies committed to making war on England. Intense persecution followed swiftly,
beginning with the execution of the bold character who had posted the
bull of excommunication outside the bishop of London's residence.
New legislation followed also—a Treasons Act increasing penalties for
denial of the supremacy, for example, and an Act Against Papal Bulls.
For the radical Protestants who were just now coming to be known as
Puritans, these new opportunities to attack Catholics could not have
been more welcome. They were exasperated, therefore, when Elizabeth
refused to go as far as they wanted, blocking the implementation of
statutes that would have made it a crime not to receive communion
under the auspices of the Church of England. It was still her hope that
she could gradually, with the sustained application of judicious amounts
of pressure, nudge Catholicism toward extinction while avoiding a repetition of anything as alarming as the revolt of the northern earls. At the
same time, she was refusing to allow the Puritans to reshape her church
to fit their agenda, which was becoming so radical as to include demands for the elimination of bishops. She thereby alienated the Puritans
to such an extent that they began to regard themselves as outside the established church, to spurn that church as beyond hope of reform, and to
direct their energies toward the building of a power base in Parliament.
Thus there emerged three major and irreconcilable religious groupings:
the Catholics, the Puritans, and an approved church the doctrines and
practices of which were determined, essentially, by the queen alone.
Only the second two had access to political power, Catholics having
been barred from the House of Commons as early as 1563 and the practice of their faith now being unlawful and subject to increasingly harsh
sanctions. The Puritans, too, though growing in numbers and clout, felt
excluded and persecuted. Out of these divisions came conflicts and
grievances that would poison the life of the kingdom for centuries.

Looming over it all, a living symbol of unresolvable conflict, was the
forlorn figure of Mary, Queen of Scots. She was Elizabeth's prisoner
though England had no legal grounds for holding her, to the Protestants

she was little better than the Whore of Babylon personified, and yet as Elizabeth grew older she remained—a horrible thought for many—the only plausible heir to the throne. In her person the problem of religion and the problem of the succession merged to become a quandary for which there appeared to be no answer.

THE TURKS

IT IS EASY, IN THINKING ABOUT THE INTERNATIONAL POLITICS of the Tudor century, to overlook the fact that there was another major player besides the Hapsburgs, the kings and queens of France and England, and a papacy that at various times became involved as referee, cheerleader, or freelance utility infielder.

Easy, but a serious mistake. Because throughout the entire period a fourth force was at work, one more aggressive, more dangerous, and more powerful overall than any of the others. It was the Islamic empire of the Ottoman Turks, which at midcentury reached the zenith of its six-hundred-year history, controlled eastern Europe south of the Danube, and directly or indirectly was affecting the destinies of all the Christian powers. The fields of force that it projected, like some vast dark star at the edge of the universe of European nations, are a major reason why Elizabethan England was able to preserve its autonomy in spite of being smaller and weaker than France or Spain and potentially a pariah kingdom in the aftermath of its withdrawal from the old church. By sapping the strength of its principal rival, the Hapsburg empire, Ottoman Turkey contributed importantly to the survival of Protestantism across much of northern Europe.

When Elizabeth became queen, the Ottomans either ruled directly or controlled through puppet regimes not just Turkey but Greece, Serbia, Bulgaria, Romania, and much of Hungary. And that was only the European segment of their dominions, which also encompassed Egypt and Algeria and other strongholds in North Africa, Syria, Palestine, Iraq, the Arabian Peninsula, and some of the most important islands in the Mediterranean. They had been ferociously expansionist since their first emergence among the Turkic-Mongol peoples of Anatolia in the thirteenth century, and generation after generation they had consistently demonstrated their ability to outfight formidable adversaries on land and at sea. In 1453 they captured Constantinople, which had remained the capital of the Eastern Roman Empire and of the Orthodox Church for centuries after Rome itself fell, turning it into the principal metropolis of the Islamic world. And because they were Muslims with entirely non-Western cultural roots, their success in pushing northward and across and even beyond the Balkans was seen, not without reason, as a mortal threat to European civilization itself.

The tenth and greatest of the Ottoman sultans, Suleiman I, was in the thirty-ninth year of his reign when Elizabeth began hers. To his subjects he was Suleiman the Lawgiver, having in the course of his awesomely fruitful career rewritten his empire's entire legal code. Europe called him Suleiman the Magnificent, a title he richly deserved. Like his forebears, he was above all a soldier, having personally led campaigns that crushed a revolt in Damascus, captured Belgrade in Serbia and Buda in Hungary, taken much of the Middle East from the shah of Iran, expelled the Knights Hospitalers from the island of Rhodes, and twice laid siege to the Hapsburg capital of Vienna. But he was also much more than a soldier: an accomplished poet and goldsmith, a lifelong student of philosophy with a particular devotion to Aristotle, the guiding patron of a remarkable efflorescence of Islamic art, literature, and architecture. Impressive and even admirable as he was, however, he should not be sentimentalized. At the heart of his regime—of the entire Ottoman enterprise—lay something worse than barbarism. Suleiman's father, Selim I, himself a great conqueror who nearly tripled the size of the empire in only eight years as sultan, cleared the way for his favorite son to succeed him by killing his own brothers, his brothers' seven sons, and all four of Suleiman's brothers. Suleiman, decades later, would watch through a peephole as his eldest son and heir, a young man much honored for his prowess in war and skill as a governor, was strangled by court eunuchs to make way for a different, younger, and (as time would show) totally worthless son. Fratricide on a grand scale became standard Ottoman practice; each new sultan, upon taking the throne, would have all his brothers and half-brothers murdered and those members of his predecessor's harem who happened to be pregnant bundled up in sacks and thrown into the sea. Conquered peoples were treated little better. Eventually the viciousness of the regime would lead the whole empire to shocking depths of cruelty and degeneracy and finally, in the First World

War, to collapse. But through much of the sixteenth century, under Suleiman, it appeared to be almost invincible. The possibility that it might break through into central Europe, and continue onward from there, not only seemed but was terrifyingly real.

The threat fell first and most heavily on young Charles Hapsburg, who became the seventeen-year-old king of Spain in the same year that Cairo fell to the Turks. By the time he was elected Holy Roman emperor two years later, the Turks had taken Algiers from Spain, the trade routes of Venice and the other seafaring cities of the Italian peninsula were in danger of being cut off by Turkish raiders, and the southern Hapsburg kingdoms of Naples and Sicily were under direct threat. Francis I was king of France by then and Suleiman was about to become sultan, and for the next three decades they and Charles (the three had been born within six years of each other, and all came to power between 1515 and 1520) would be locked in an almost continuous, endlessly complicated struggle. Henry VIII, from his safe haven on the far shore of the English Channel, would join the fray and withdraw from it as the mood struck him and the state of his treasury dictated.

Despite the size of his empire, Charles V usually found himself on the defensive, with Francis repeatedly trying to pry away substantial chunks of Italy and Suleiman both pressing northward out of the Balkans and seeking to clear the Mediterranean of European ships. Charles's successes were almost always limited and his defeats were occasionally serious, but when the number and strength of his adversaries are taken into account (Germany's increasingly numerous Protestant states were soon joining forces to oppose him), he merits recognition as one of the great commanders of the age. When Francis launched an attack on Milan in 1525, Charles not only destroyed his army but took him prisoner. But just a year later, with Charles occupied elsewhere, Suleiman invaded northward, inflicted a ruinous defeat on the Hungarians, and seized territories that the Hapsburgs regarded as theirs by ancient right. Next came Suleiman's 1529 siege of Vienna, which Charles and his brother Ferdinand were barely able to lift after both sides suffered heavy losses, followed by the sultan's attempt to take the island of Malta from the same order of crusader knights from whom, some years earlier, he had taken Rhodes. Emboldened by his success in saving Malta and killing thirty thousand Ottoman troops in the process, Charles decided to carry the war into enemy territory. He crossed to North Africa and, at Tunis, succeeded in expelling Suleiman's client regime and installing one of his own.

The contest seesawed back and forth year after year, as Charles and Suleiman traded blows along the Danube and in the Mediterranean but neither could gain a decisive advantage. For a time Henry of England joined with Charles against Francis, later switching sides and finally turning away from the continent to focus on Anne Boleyn and his conflict with the church. One development that shocked many Europeans, who saw in it a betrayal of all Christendom, was Francis's entry, in 1536, into an alliance with Suleiman and the Turks. Once again he was grasping at Milan, though he like Charles was very nearly at the end of his financial resources. An important side effect was that Henry VIII was left alone and unthreatened as he completed his break with Rome and fattened on the wealth of the church. Under other circumstances a crusade against England's schismatic king by the Catholic powers of the continent might have been at least possible. Under the circumstances actually prevailing in the mid-1530s, nothing of the kind could be seriously considered. Neither Charles nor Francis was in any position to make trouble for England. Either would have been grateful for Henry's active friendship.

In 1538 Suleiman's great admiral Khayr ad-Din, called Barbarossa by Westerners because of his red beard, defeated the Hapsburg navy in a battle so conclusive that it made the Turks dominant in the Mediterranean for the next thirty-three years. In 1541, as Charles tried and failed to restore Algiers to Spanish control, Suleiman resumed offensive operations in the north. He had sufficient success to impose a humiliating peace on the Hapsburgs: Archduke Ferdinand was obliged to renounce his claim to the throne of Hungary and to become a Turkish vassal, pledging to pay an annual tribute for the portion of Hungary he was permitted to retain. In 1542 Charles and Francis were once again at war, and when the French king asked Suleiman for assistance, the sultan cheerfully agreed. He dispatched a fleet of one hundred galleys, warships powered by oars, to France's south coast, permitting them to pause along the way to pillage Charles's kingdoms of Naples and Sicily and the city of Nice, also a Hapsburg possession. On all fronts, Suleiman appeared to be gaining in strength.

Fortunately for Europe, Suleiman like Charles had multiple enemies and more than the conflict between their two empires to deal with. By the late 1540s the shah of Iran had recovered much of the power that had been shattered by Suleiman's father thirty years earlier, and was making himself troublesome. From 1548 to 1550 Suleiman waged war on the shah, and must have been taken aback to find himself making little headway. He settled in for a time at his sumptuous Topkapi Palace, indulging in the pleasures of the court and involving himself in domestic-dynastic intrigues. (It was during this interlude that he had his son Mustafa murdered, so that the son of the Russian slave girl he had made his wife could become heir.) In 1554 he returned with his army to Iran, finally securing a peace in which he received Iraq and eastern Anatolia but relinquished any claim to the Caucasus. By this time his old ally Francis, along with the distant Henry of England, had been dead for seven years. The emperor Charles, spiritually and physically exhausted, was beginning the process by which, over the next two years, he would give the crown of Spain to his son and that of the Holy Roman Empire to his brother and retire to a monastery. Suleiman alone—older than any of the others except Henry—remained vigorous and actively in command. His enemies were not free of him until 1566, when, at age seventy-two, he suddenly died. At the time, he was leading an army northward to Hungary, making ready to reopen the war there. We can only guess at what Europe may have been spared by his passing.

After Suleiman the Ottoman dynasty went into an abrupt decline. His successor, for whose sake the splendid young Mustafa had been eliminated, was a drunkard who reigned in a stupor for eight years before falling in his bath and fracturing his skull. *His* successor specialized in copulation, fathering 103 children in his twenty years as sultan, and every Ottoman ruler after him proved to be utterly incompetent or deeply degenerate or both. The empire, however, was slower to decay; its administrative machinery would wind down only gradually over the next three centuries. To the end of Elizabeth's reign it would remain a formidable presence.

A major turn in Europe's favor came just five years after Suleiman's death. In 1571, off the western coast of Greece, the Ottoman navy met the forces of Christendom in what was, for the latter, a desperate last stand. On the Turkish side were 222 galleys supported by numerous smaller vessels and carrying some thirty-four thousand soldiers. Opposing them was a smaller fleet contributed by members of what called itself the Holy League: Venice, Spain, Naples, Sicily, Sardinia, the Knights of Malta, the Papal States, and such places as Genoa and Savoy.

It was the last major battle ever fought entirely with ships powered by oarsmen, one of the biggest naval battles in history, and according to some historians the most important since Mark Antony lost the Battle of Actium in 31 B.C. and his rival Octavian became master of Rome as the emperor Augustus Caesar. When the Battle of Lepanto was over, all but forty of the Turkish galleys had been captured or destroyed, perhaps twenty-five thousand Turks had been killed or captured, and ten thousand Christian slaves had been freed. The league, by contrast, had lost only twenty galleys and thirteen thousand men. It was not the end of the Ottoman Empire, not even the end of the empire as a great power, but it did bring the empire's mastery of the Mediterranean to a permanent close. The momentum of Turkish expansion was not yet entirely exhausted—the capture of Cyprus and recapture of Tunis still lay ahead—but the Ottomans would never again be quite the threat they had been in Suleiman's time, and they had been deprived of the vast opportunities that a victory at Lepanto would have opened to them.

The commander of the Holy League fleet was the twenty-four-year-old Don John of Austria, Charles V's illegitimate son by a Bavarian girl of common stock. Second in command, himself only twenty-six, was Alessandro Farnese, great-grandson and namesake of Pope Paul III, son of Charles V's illegitimate daughter Margaret, future Duke of Parma. The two, though scarcely more than boys, had changed the course of history. We will encounter both in connection with another of the great conflicts that shaped the Tudor century.

25

Actions, Reactions, Provocations

It would be fatuous to deny that Pope Pius V, in excommunicating Elizabeth, intended to destroy her. Or that he hoped to recruit the leading Catholic powers for a crusade aimed at removing her from her throne.

Nor were such hopes ridiculous. Three decades before, the Pilgrimage of Grace had exposed the unpopularity of Henry VIII's religious innovations and left hanging the question of what a rising might accomplish if given strong enough leadership and sufficient encouragement and support. The rebellions of Edward VI's reign, and the ease with which Mary I had overcome John Dudley's attempted coup, bolstered the credibility of those wanting to make Rome believe that Elizabeth's regime, if given a firm shove, might fall almost of its own weight.

As for the idea of involving France and Spain, here again hope was not entirely without a footing in reality. Though Pius V had become pope with little experience in politics and even less in diplomacy (it is a measure of how rapidly the church was changing that he had grown up in poverty and spent much of his life as a Dominican friar known for austerity), he was not naïve enough to expect kings to sacrifice their thrones on the altar of religion. But in Philip of Spain he had an ally who genuinely believed that if he could save England from the Protestants he would save her people from eternal damnation. And Pius could hope to find support at France's Valois court if he could point to practical advantages of removing the English queen.

Thus it is entirely understandable that Elizabeth and her council went to great lengths to prevent a Catholic combination from forming. If they can be faulted, it is for going too far with their meddling in continental affairs, thereby helping to bring into existence something very like what they most feared. The worst of their mistakes was to overreact, bringing down upon England hardships that might and even should have been avoided.

For in fact their position was less dangerous than they understood. Under any circumstances it would have been difficult in the extreme for France and Spain, locked in a struggle for European domination that was already half a century old, to join forces for any shared purpose involving sacrifice and risk. They had already shown themselves to be incapable of organizing a common defense even against the Ottoman Empire, which unlike England posed a threat to the very survival of their civilization. And that was only half the story. The Reformation had come to France by this time, giving rise to conflicts that were draining away the kingdom's power. Yet another new phenomenon, nationalism, had come at the same time to the Spanish possessions in the Netherlands, sparking a rebellion that Philip would need all the resources of his sprawling empire and all the gold being stripped from the New World to keep from overwhelming him. France and Spain alike—though France more than Spain—rarely ignored an opportunity to exploit and worsen the other's problems and to ally themselves with England whenever it seemed advantageous to do so. Neither was easily drawn into fantasies of returning England to the universal church by force of arms. Philip, though more the idealist than Marie de' Medici, understood from personal experience that, in the almost forty years since Henry VIII's break with Rome, the number of Englishmen likely to see any sense in fighting to repair that break had shrunk severely.

The brilliant success of Elizabeth's first international adventure, the 1560 foray into Scotland, served to encourage further enterprises more distant from home. An opportunity came just two years later with the eruption of France's first religious war, which pitted Calvinist Huguenots against the regime headed by the queen dowager Catherine

de' Medici in the name of her sickly and ineffectual second son, the adolescent Charles IX. It was easy to argue that England could both help itself and do God's work by becoming involved on the Protestant side,
and the Dudley brothers, ambitious and eager for action, argued exactly
that. Intervention could frustrate Philip of Spain, who was supporting
the royal Catholic party in the hope of building a lasting alliance. At the
same time it could undermine the Valois by enhancing the strength of
their internal enemies. Conceivably it could lead to the recovery of
Calais, which would be a tremendous propaganda coup for Elizabeth, a
demonstration of the superiority of her rule to that of her late sister.

William Cecil, who by pushing the Scottish incursion to its conclusion had laid at the feet of his queen an achievement of genuine strategic importance, was not enthusiastic about making war on France. As a
committed Protestant he naturally favored the Huguenots, but he was
not as confident as the Dudleys that providing assistance required going
to war with a kingdom whose population was several times that of England. The queen, however, approved the sending of an expeditionary
force. She disappointed Robert Dudley, who wanted command, by selecting his brother the Earl of Warwick instead. He was to land his
troops at, and take possession of, the port of Le Havre—the English
called it Newhaven—on the Normandy coast. The plan, from that point,
was to win the gratitude of the Huguenots to such an extent that they
would exchange Calais for Le Havre. Exactly how this was to be accomplished appears to have been left rather vague.

All did not go according to plan. Ambrose Dudley showed himself to
be an effective enough leader, maintaining order and discipline in his little army under difficult conditions and establishing good relations with
the inhabitants of Le Havre. But his instructions from the queen made
it impossible to achieve anything. Throughout the first two months following his arrival in France, Dudley remained under orders to take no
action. Then, when the opposing French sides surprised him by making
peace, the earl was ordered to hold on to Le Havre until a trade for
Calais could be arranged. This led—a crowning absurdity—to his erst-
while allies joining forces with the Catholics to drive him out. After several months of standing their ground in spite of the inadequacy of Le
Havre's defensive works, the English were so ravaged by plague that
Dudley was left with no choice but to surrender. A final, tragic chapter

was added when the remnants of his expeditionary force returned to England and brought the plague with them. In the subsequent Peace of Troyes, England abandoned forever its claim to Calais. Robert Dudley, as responsible as anyone for putting the whole debacle in motion, was rewarded with appointment to the Privy Council. Perhaps because Elizabeth's refusal to part with him had spared him exposure to the hardships of the campaign, his appetite for war was undiminished. Cecil, whose responsibilities made him acutely aware of the strain the affair had put on the treasury, would henceforth be incapable of mustering much enthusiasm for sending armies across the Channel for any purpose.

Cecil was not averse, however, to tweaking the tail of the despised king of Spain whenever he found opportunities to do so without excessive risk. This tendency became increasingly pronounced, in fact, as the first decade of Elizabeth's reign approached its end and Cecil persuaded himself that France and Spain were preparing a great joint invasion. About this he was consistently, demonstrably wrong—a rare and even weird miscalculation by one of the most astute, careful, and successful politicians of the age. Above all it was a misreading of the king of Spain. Perhaps Cecil could not understand Philip, could think only the worst of him, simply because his contempt was so deep. Probably he had no idea that Philip had concluded, during his years as England's uncrowned king, that it was an alien and treacherous place and best left alone. At this stage Philip was, despite his religious convictions, almost desperately eager for England's friendship, and if he could not have that he wanted her neutrality. He had more than enough other matters demanding his attention, more than enough other uses for resources that never seemed sufficient to his needs, and little reason to be confident that he stood to gain anything by deposing Elizabeth and replacing her with Mary, Queen of Scots. Cecil might have benefited from remembering how supportive of Elizabeth Philip had been both before she became queen and during the uncertain early days of her reign. He might have asked himself if conditions had changed enough to turn Philip into an actively aggressive foe. Instead he allowed his concerns to grow into something akin to paranoia, and to drive him—and with him England—into dangerously provocative actions that could serve no significantly good purpose and for which there was absolutely no need.

A particularly dangerous temptation came within Cecil's grasp late in 1568, when a fleet of Spanish ships traversing the Channel en route to the Netherlands found itself threatened by pirates and took refuge in English ports. The fleet's commander had good reason for wanting to avoid capture: he was carrying a fortune in gold and silver that Philip had borrowed from his Italian bankers and was sending to the Low Countries to pay the troops he had stationed there. Cecil, when he became aware of what had fallen into his clutches, did not hesitate. He ordered the money seized and locked away. The Spaniards, needless to say, were outraged. Philip's governor in the Netherlands, the tough old Duke of Alba, responded by seizing English trade goods. England retaliated in its turn, and the dispute escalated until there was a real danger of war. Alba, however, had a turbulent region on his hands and so dispatched envoys with instructions to make themselves agreeable to the English. Cecil for his part wanted nothing less than outright war, and gradually the situation was defused.

The Privy Council then fell into an angry dispute over what Cecil had done. A substantial number of its members, Robert Dudley prominent among them, accused him of having recklessly put England in danger. There followed a contest over whether he should retain his position as secretary and with it his control over what information was allowed to reach the queen, what business was brought before the council, and how the council's decisions were translated into action. This became the decisive crisis of Cecil's long career. It ended with Elizabeth intervening so decisively on his behalf that it was no longer possible to doubt that he enjoyed her full confidence. He became and would remain unassailably secure. Not coincidentally, by protecting him the queen implicitly endorsed his policy of harassing the Spaniards by almost every possible means while pretending innocence. She and her government were turning a benignly blind eye to the raids that freebooters like John Hawkins and his cousin Francis Drake, privateers destined to rank high among the immortals of the Elizabethan age, were making on Spanish ports and shipping. It seemed an ideal arrangement: Cecil and even Elizabeth herself not only provided the pirates with a secure home base but helped to finance their voyages in return for a share of the profits. When Spain protested they claimed, unconvincingly, to know nothing and to be unable to do anything. Philip's restraint through years of this undeclared naval war is the strongest possible indication of just how badly he wanted to avoid conflict.

Soon it was again France's turn at center stage. The end of the 1560s brought a resumption of the increasingly bitter and bloody conflict between the Huguenots and the Catholic government in Paris. (It might be appropriate to speak of the *ostensibly* Catholic government, the young king Charles showing at this point more inclination to accept the counsel of the Protestant leader Admiral de Coligny than that of his mother, Catherine; the alignments were rarely not confusing.) These wars were dangerous because of the pull they inevitably exerted on other countries: Spain was always drawn to what Philip judged to be the Catholic side, England to the Calvinists. The latest round of hostilities ended in 1570 with the Peace of St. Germain, but on terms that offered little hope of lasting amity. Catherine de' Medici agreed, over the objections of Philip, to the marriage of her daughter Margaret to the bride's royal cousin Henry of Bourbon, more widely known as Henry of Navarre. The Guises, still the driving force behind Catholic militancy in France, were not alone in complaining that such a marriage would be an outrage: Navarre was a Protestant and therefore judged to be no fit spouse for a princess of the blood. The Huguenots, by contrast, rejoiced; Navarre would be next in line to the throne if (as must have seemed possible by this time) none of Catherine's diminishing supply of sons produced a male heir, and a Valois bride could only strengthen his claim. Elizabeth and Cecil were untroubled by the prospect of peace. They were content to be relieved of the obligation to support the Huguenots financially, and ready to try to wedge themselves between Spain and France by building a friendly relationship with the Valois. Their first steps in this direction gave rise to a possible new way of solving England's festering succession problem. King Charles's heir presumptive—his heir, that is, if he died without a son—was his brother Henry of Anjou, not yet twenty years old. Elizabeth being in her late thirties now, negotiations of a possible marriage got under way with some sense of urgency on the English side: those still hopeful that the queen might have a child knew that, for such a thing to happen, she would have to act soon.

Elizabeth probably had as little interest in marrying now as at any point in the preceding decade; she allowed the talks to proceed simply to distract the French from rapprochement with Spain. Anjou definitely had no interest, speaking contemptuously of his prospective bride as a "public whore" and (after being told that varicose veins were causing her to limp) as "an old creature with a sore leg." If somehow the two had married, the consequences could only have been disappointing for both sides. Anjou was more militantly, aggressively Catholic than Elizabeth was Protestant. His irregular personal behavior, including a passion for extravagantly lavish, sometimes shockingly feminine attire and a refusal to engage in hunting or the other customary pastimes of male royalty, had won for him the epithet "Prince of Sodom." His very appearance would have stunned Elizabeth's court and mortally offended every Puritan in England. As for his breeding potential, he would live a good many years more but never have a child in or out of wedlock.

The following year, 1572, brought convulsions that would briefly make an Anglo-French marriage alliance seem more plausible but then drive the two countries apart. In March the conflict between the people of the northern Netherlands and their Spanish masters erupted into open revolt. In short order four provinces made themselves functionally independent under the leadership of William of Orange (William of Nassau if you prefer, or William the Silent), a onetime Catholic and protégé of the Hapsburgs who had gone into exile and become a Calvinist in reaction to Spanish demands for the surrender of what the Dutch regarded as their inalienable liberties. Elizabeth, for obvious reasons, always regarded loyalty to the sovereign as a sacred duty of all subjects everywhere, and so now as in other, similar situations she found it difficult to support or even condone rebellion. At first England's ports were closed to the seafaring Dutch renegades. But the temptation to create trouble for Philip once again proved irresistible, all the more so when the rebels demonstrated that they were not going to be easily suppressed. Soon the English authorities were coyly noticing nothing as Protestant volunteers and money began streaming out of the country in aid of the revolt. The French, too, could find nothing objectionable in a war that soaked up so much Spanish manpower and treasure, and they saw new reason to make common cause with England. In April the two countries entered into the Treaty of Blois, by which they pledged to assist each other if either were attacked. The Duke of Anjou having conclusively removed himself from contention for Elizabeth's hand, a new candidate emerged in the person of his younger brother Francis (at birth he had been given the name Hercules), the Duke of Alençon. He was sixteen years old; Elizabeth was thirty-nine.

August was when it all blew up. The explosion came in Paris on the feast of St. Bartholomew, and it was horrific. From all around France thousands of Huguenots, many of them people of considerable wealth and social standing accompanied by their private security forces, had gathered in the capital to celebrate the wedding of their champion and hope for the future, Henry of Navarre, to the sister of a childless king. The city was electric with tension between the visitors, who continued to parade through the streets long after the wedding was over, and the local population. Four days after the ceremony there was an attempt on the life of the Protestant leader Admiral de Coligny, who, to the indignation of powerful Catholics including the Guises, had been readmitted to the national governing council as part of the reconciliation between the contending factions. Coligny escaped with relatively minor gunshot wounds, but on the third day of his recuperation one of the Duke of Guise's ruffians burst into his room, pulled him from his bed, stabbed him to death, and threw the body out the window. The killing was like a spark put to gunpowder. There followed days and then weeks of wholesale butchery; Protestants were hunted down first in Paris and then in other cities as well. The generally accepted best guess puts the number of dead in the neighborhood of ten thousand, and the total may very well have been higher. Who exactly was responsible, and why the slaughter was carried to such extremes, remains unclear. That the Guises were responsible for the killing of Coligny cannot be doubted. The involvement of Catherine de' Medici, and through her of her son King Charles, is likewise beyond dispute; she appears to have been frightened into thinking that the Huguenot leadership had to be eliminated to abort an investigation that would have revealed her approval of the original assault on Coligny. The Duke of Alba may have encouraged the attack on Coligny because the admiral had been urging French support of the Dutch rebels and appeared to be winning the young king's agreement, but we have no conclusive evidence that any of these people intended a massacre. More likely the original plan was to eliminate Coligny only, and the scheme was broadened to include a number of his associates only after the failure of the first attempt on his life stirred up fears of reprisals, a damaging investigation, or even a coup d'état. But the people of Paris were Catholic and poor, they had been experiencing hardship that year as a failed harvest inflated the price of food, and their resentment had been inflamed by the spectacle of so many prosperous Protestant outsiders, some of them guarded by armed men, ostentatiously showing themselves off in the streets. Catholic preachers were warning of a Protestant takeover, no doubt in inflammatory ways, and apparently some of their listeners took the news of the first killings as license to go on a rampage. Within a few days the disorder had spread to Rouen, Lyon, Orleans, and Bordeaux, and in all these places royal orders for it to stop were ignored.

The religious divisions of France were even more hateful than those in England and obviously much more dangerous. Open war had erupted between the contending parties three times in the previous decade, with much criminality on both sides. That the 1572 calamity began on the feast of St. Bartholomew was probably not a coincidence. On the same day three years earlier, in the south of France, Henry of Navarre's mother, a woman whose contempt for the old religion made the evangelicals of England seem models of toleration by comparison, had ordered the execution of a company of Catholic nobles who had surrendered after receiving assurances that their lives would be spared. The young Duke of Guise, if in fact he ordered Coligny's murder, was undoubtedly spurred less by theology than by a hunger for revenge: the admiral had earlier been responsible for the killing of Guise's father. In France the Reformation was becoming a sordid chronicle of atrocities and reprisals, treachery was by no means exclusive to either side, and the complications were almost as endless as the provocations. What matters here is that the massacre of 1572 horrified the Protestants of England, seemed to provide rich justification for their insistence that Catholicism had to be extinguished, and made it impossible for Elizabeth even to feign interest in marriage to any son of Catherine de' Medici.

In that same year the increasingly discontented, increasingly unmanageable Puritans began bullying Elizabeth to destroy Thomas Howard, fourth Duke of Norfolk. Son of the Earl of Surrey whose execution was one of the last acts ordered by Henry VIII, grandson of the duke whose life was saved only by Henry's death, great-grandson of the earl who restored the family's fortunes by crushing the Scots at Flodden, and great-great-grandson of the duke who died fighting for Richard III at Bosworth, this latest Norfolk was a somewhat feckless individual who lacked the strength to resist being drawn into dark schemes that he could neither control nor, probably, understand. Secretary Cecil had put him on the council in 1564 as a conservative and presumably manageable counterweight to Robert Dudley, who also became a member that year and was obviously not going to be managed by Cecil or anyone else. Things did not work out as Cecil planned, however. Instead of helping to neutralize Dudley, Norfolk joined him in trying to get Cecil dismissed after his seizure of the Spanish king's gold. He also opposed the secretary's policies with respect to Mary Stuart, aid to the French Huguenots, and the harassment of Philip II. He had given Cecil no reason to support him—or even, in a pinch, to do anything to save his life.

What made Norfolk a prime target of the Puritans was his involvement with Mary, Queen of Scots, and a faintly asinine (unless he was instead profoundly devious) Florentine banker named Roberto di Ridolfi. After Mary became a prisoner of the English Crown, a group of courtiers (including, somewhat oddly, Robert Dudley) hatched the idea of neutralizing her as a threat to Elizabeth and at the same time solving the succession problem by marrying her into the English, and Protestant, nobility. Norfolk, a youngish widower who as the only duke in the kingdom was its premier noble, was an obvious possibility. And he was immediately, if foolishly, interested. Most of the Puritans, uncomfortable with anything that might even tend to legitimate Mary as heir, were so hostile to the proposal as to cast Norfolk into the role of mortal enemy. William Cecil, as always, was opposed to anything that might lead to Mary Stuart becoming queen of England.

The marriage scheme became, in ways far too arcane to be unraveled here, intertwined with the revolt of the northern earls. Norfolk, as a result, fell into deep disfavor at court. It is at this point that Ridolfi enters the story. A busybody who had first come to England as a moneylender, much too restless a spirit to be satisfied with dabbling in the currency markets, he began intriguing in so many directions that in due course he became a paid informant of the French and Spanish governments and the pope's "secret nuncio." Like Norfolk he got into trouble in connection with the northern rising, and for a time he was in custody and under interrogation by Cecil and the head of Elizabeth's intelligence service, Francis Walsingham. After his release Ridolfi appears to have made it his mission to win papal approval for the marriage of Mary Stuart and Norfolk and, probably, to arrange a good deal more than that. He began weaving a web of conspiracy that extended from the English to the Spanish court, from Mary's place of confinement to Rome and the Netherlands. In 1571 he crossed to the continent, traveling from place to place presumably to make arrangements for a Spanish invasion to occur simultaneously with a rising of England's Catholics, the marriage of a liberated Scots queen to Norfolk, and Elizabeth's removal. In actuality it was all talk—no one was doing anything serious in preparation for either an invasion or a rebellion—and almost all of it came from Ridolfi himself. He was so free in telling everyone who would listen about his plans that there has hung over him, ever since, the suspicion that when Cecil and Walsingham had him in custody, they may have bribed or blackmailed him into becoming their agent. Certainly no agent provocateur could have done more to lure Norfolk and others into incriminating themselves, or to make certain that nothing about his scheme was truly secret. Cecil was fully aware of what Ridolfi was up to: Grand Duke Cosimo de' Medici of Florence even sent him a warning immediately after being visited, and confided in, by Ridolfi. Norfolk was arrested and put on trial for treason. Slanted in favor of the prosecution as all treason trials were in those days—the accused were allowed neither legal counsel nor any opportunity to prepare a defense—in this instance guilt was undeniable, and the duke was quickly sentenced to death. For four months, however, the queen refused to approve his execution. Parliament and council, meanwhile, badgered her relentlessly to allow Mary Stuart to be condemned as well. To this she absolutely would not agree. Her unwillingness to see even a deposed queen put to death was even more powerful than her reluctance to kill dukes. Though Norfolk had to be sacrificed at last, Mary was too valuable a prisoner to be dispensed with. So long as she remained alive, England's Protestant subjects would have strong reasons for wanting Elizabeth to remain alive as well. And of course Elizabeth may have felt compassion for her fallen cousin, who was passing her life as a prisoner in spite of having been charged with no crime.

TORTURE

IT IS A MISTAKE TO ASSUME, UPON BECOMING AWARE OF how extensively Henry VIII and Elizabeth I used torture to terrorize their subjects and extract information about real or imagined enemies, that they were simply continuing a standard practice of the English Middle Ages.

They were doing nothing of the kind. Though inflicting physical pain on captives to achieve some political purpose goes back further than recorded history, and though it was certainly not unknown in England before the Tudors, it was never legitimized by law there or allowed to become accepted practice. English rulers never used torture as an instrument of state in anything approaching a systematic way until Henry VIII and Thomas Cromwell began doing so in the mid-1530s. Half a century later, when Elizabeth surpassed her father in the intensity and frequency of the tortures inflicted on people perceived to be a threat to her survival and even began to torture people because of their religious beliefs, the population was so repelled that after her death such practices soon fell into disuse and in due course were banned—forever, as it turned out—by Parliament.

Being an inherently loathsome thing—church leaders condemned its use from the earliest centuries of the Christian era—torture inevitably required Elizabeth and her henchmen to employ singularly odious men. Not much is known about her first principal torturer, a member of Parliament called "Rackmaster Norton," but whatever atrocities he may have been capable of must have been almost trivial compared to those of the man who replaced him in 1572, Richard Topcliffe. A Yorkshire landowner who appears to have won Elizabeth's favor early in her reign or possibly even earlier, Topcliffe was not only a dutiful torturer but an eager one—a sadist to the point of psychosis. Having begun his public career as a kind of intelligence agent for Francis Walsingham, who entered royal service as an associate of the queen's secretary William Cecil and rose to secretary himself when Cecil became lord treasurer, Topcliffe distinguished himself first as a hunter of fugitive Catholics and then as an interrogator of the people he captured. He was so passionate in his hatred of Catholics and all things Catholic that there appear to have been no limits to what he was willing to do; in devising new ways of inflicting pain he was always confident of doing God's work. The relish with which he approached his duties—he participated personally in the disemboweling and quartering of condemned men in spite of the fact that there was no need for him to do so—made him so useful to Cecil and Walsingham (not to mention the queen) that he was permitted to install a torture chamber in his Westminster home. Though by no means the Crown's only torturer (the Tower of London's warders or "Beefeaters" customarily operated such machinery as the rack, the scavenger's daughter, and the iron maiden, while gentlemen merely did the questioning), he easily established himself as the leading practitioner of his dubious trade. He wrote with a kind of pornographic glee of the mastery required to push victims up to but not quite across the threshold of death, comparing the prolongation of unbearable agony to a skilled lover's ability to sustain sexual ecstasy.

A number of the best-known priests to fall into the Crown's hands in the 1580s and early 1590s, the Jesuit poet Robert Southwell among them, spent long periods in Topcliffe's custody (some were apprehended by Topcliffe himself) before finally being put to death. If challenged about his methods and the validity of confessions made under torture, he always replied—not truthfully, it is clear—that his objective was always to obtain information, not mere confessions. No one was ever tortured, he absurdly claimed, whose guilt had not already been established beyond doubt.

Two stories, one nightmarishly horrible and the other merely disgusting in a sardonically amusing way, reveal as much as any normal person could ever want to know about Topcliffe's character. The first happened in 1592, when he had been pursuing Southwell without success for six frustrating years. His search led him to the home of a family named Bellamy, several of whose members were already in prison (two would die there, and a third would be executed) on suspicion of harboring priests. Somehow he learned that one of the daughters of the household, Anne

Bellamy, supposedly had information about Southwell's plans. When the girl would tell him nothing, Topcliffe made her his prisoner, but instead of using the usual instruments of torture he adopted a method that must have been vastly more painful and infinitely humiliating. He raped her repeatedly until at last, broken, she gave up her secret (which was that Southwell had promised to return to the Bellamys' house on June 20, in order to say mass). Southwell was captured as a result. He was tortured on thirteen separate occasions, first at Topcliffe's home and then in the Tower. After refusing to answer questions even about the color of his horse—he feared that anything he said might compromise the people who had sheltered him—the priest was taken to Tyburn to be hanged, drawn, and quartered. When Anne Bellamy found that she was pregnant, Topcliffe was able to avoid disclosure of what he had done by forcing her to marry his assistant. One can only speculate as to what sort of bridegroom a torturer's assistant must have been. Nothing is known of what finally happened to the girl, one of history's forgotten victims.

The second Topcliffe story involves another of his assistants, one Thomas Fitzherbert, whose family were landowning Catholics. Topcliffe and Fitzherbert concocted a scheme for making a tidy fortune quickly. Fitzherbert would accuse his father, his uncle, and a man named Bassett of treason, thereby providing an excuse for their arrest. Topcliffe would then torture the three to death, Fitzherbert would inherit their property, and the two of them would split the proceeds. All went according to plan, apparently, until Fitzherbert refused to pay up. Amazingly, Topcliffe then had the temerity to go to court, explaining the nature of the bargain and suing Fitzherbert for £5,000. In defending himself, Fitzherbert complained that Topcliffe had not done his part: that Bassett was still alive, and the father and uncle had died not of torture but of a fever contracted in prison. Even more amazingly, thanks no doubt to his excellent connections at court, Topcliffe won the case instead of being arrested for conspiracy to commit murder or worse. Fitzherbert was obliged to surrender his inheritance.

One would like to think that the queen knew nothing of such matters and little of what was being done in her name. Where Topcliffe is concerned, unfortunately, it is not possible to believe anything of the kind; the records make clear that the torturer had ready access to Elizabeth over a great many years, that at least some of his foul work was done with her knowledge and possibly at her direction, and that he was well rewarded for his labors. He wrote of being encouraged by Elizabeth, quoting her as complaining about "sundry lewde popishe beasts." He always claimed that he acted not on Walsingham's or Cecil's authority but on that of the queen herself, and that he was accountable to her only. This is not implausible, though it is not likely that Topcliffe ever had to bypass either Cecil or Walsingham in the performance of his duties; those two shared a fear and hatred of Catholics that, if not pathological like Topcliffe's, certainly gave them no reason to interfere with his work. Perhaps it was thanks to Elizabeth that Topcliffe was given a seat in the House of Commons, that Crown and local officials always treated him with more deference than the offices he held warranted, and that he was set free after Burghley had him arrested for appearing to threaten members of the Privy Council. He was always treated generously. When the queen decided for some reason that the bumbling patricide Fitzherbert should have his inheritance after all, Topcliffe was given a generous grant of Crown lands to compensate him for his loss.

It is hardly surprising that historians wishing to emphasize the glories of Elizabethan England have rarely given much attention to the career of Richard Topcliffe. He is nearly as forgotten as Anne Bellamy, though in his own lifetime he became all too well known. At the time of his death—like that other reptilian arch-villain Richard Rich, he died in his bed, an old and wealthy man—he was everywhere reviled. His own nephew had by then changed his name to escape the ignominy of being a Topcliffe.

26

A Horrific Tangle—
And War at Last

By the early 1570s the Puritans had grown significantly in numbers and in economic and political clout. They were not only unsatisfied, however, but increasingly discontented. At the same time that they were trying and failing to pressure the government into killing Mary Stuart, some of the more adventurous among them surreptitiously printed and distributed a First and then a Second Admonition to Parliament. These were bold, even treasonous complaints about how far the church had, under the Elizabethan settlement, departed from the gospel and from true religion. They reflected John Calvin's absolute rejection of everything that the English reformers had retained from the time before Luther's revolt, and they expressed the conviction that even the office of bishop was an abomination little less repulsive than the papacy itself. The authors of the Admonitions declared that in the pure first years of the Christian era the communities of the faithful had been led by deacons and elders, not by bishops, and that fidelity to Scripture and to Christ himself required a return to that aboriginal system. This was, in England, the genesis of Presbyterianism. Because it challenged the legitimacy of the church that Elizabeth had established upon becoming queen, it was taken as a challenge to Elizabeth herself. Her reaction should have surprised no one. Those responsible for publication of the Admonitions became hunted men, finally having to flee to the continent. They continued, from exile, to produce pamphlets condemning the Rome-ish corruptions of the Elizabethan church. That church became a dangerous environment for clergy of Calvinist-Presbyterian inclination, but their beliefs continued to spread.

Meanwhile the government's program of killing Roman Catholicism through a slow process of discouragement, through harassment and disdain rather than murderous persecution, was not working out as hoped. The lifeblood of Catholic practice was the sacraments, and that loftiest of sacraments, the Eucharist, was not possible in the absence of a priest empowered to consecrate the bread and wine. Elizabeth and Cecil were not being foolish in expecting that, deprived of its priests, the Catholic community would atrophy, especially if at the same time it were punished in large ways and small and repeatedly accused of being disloyal to England and the queen. But eliminating the priesthood turned out to be considerably more difficult than it must at first have seemed. Among the Catholics purged from the English universities after Elizabeth ascended the throne was Oxford's proctor William Allen, already well known as a scholar and administrator though not yet quite thirty years old. Like many of his academic coreligionists Allen drifted back and forth between England and the continent in the early 1560s, eventually deciding to become a priest and fixing his attention on the large numbers of onetime Oxford and Cambridge teachers and students who were now as adrift as he was. Many of these men had been drawn to the Catholic Low Countries, particularly to the universities at Louvain and Douai. It was at the latter that, in 1568, Allen found the financial support to start Douai College, a seminary where the faculty and all the candidates for the priesthood were English.

It is not clear that Allen began with the idea of developing a cadre of missionary priests to be sent back into England. His goal, rather, seems to have been to keep the intellectual life of the English Catholic community intact in preparation for a time when it would once again be welcome at home, and to engage the Protestant establishment in disputation while preparing a Catholic translation of the Bible. His college, in any case, attracted so many exiles that soon it was filled beyond capacity, and other seminaries were established elsewhere, most notably in Rome. As the students completed their studies and were ordained, some naturally yearned to return home and minister to the priest-starved Catholics of England. Such requests were granted, and the first of the young "seminary priests" slipped quietly across the Channel in 1574. As soon as the authorities became aware of their presence, the hunt was on. Inevitably the likes of Cecil and Dudley and Walsingham saw the products of Allen's school as spies and instruments of subversion and wanted the queen to see them in the same way. Certainly the priests were a threat to the policy of trying to bleed English Catholicism dry with a thousand tiny cuts; almost from the moment of their arrival they infused fresh vitality into a community that was supposed to be dying. The first to be caught, Cuthbert Mayne, was a Devon farmer's son who had taken two degrees at Oxford and become a Church of England chaplain before converting to Rome. He had then departed for Douai, where, in his early thirties, he enrolled in Allen's seminary. Within months of his ordination he was back in the west of England and, under the patronage of a wealthy Catholic landowner, taking on the public role of steward in order to travel the countryside and deliver the sacraments. Captured inside his patron's house by a posse of more than a hundred men, he was charged with six counts of treason, convicted, and offered a pardon in return for acknowledging the queen's supremacy. Upon refusing, he was made an object lesson in how religion was once again a matter of life and death in England. He was hanged, cut down alive, and thrown to the ground so violently that one of his eyes was put out. He was then disemboweled, castrated, and quartered. By hanging him as a traitor rather than burning him as a heretic, the government was able to deny that it was returning to the Marian persecutions. In Mayne's case as with the hundreds of priests who would follow him to the scaffold, the queen and her council maintained the fiction that they were killing Englishmen not for their beliefs but for seeking to deliver their homeland into the hands of foreign enemies.

As the suppression of Catholics entered a new, more desperate phase, so, too, and almost simultaneously, did the conflict with the Puritans. By the mid-1570s the queen had run out of patience with the practice known as "prophesying," which was not a matter of making predictions but simply of preaching with a pronouncedly evangelical slant rather than staying within the boundaries prescribed by the Book of Common Prayer. Somewhat oddly for a Protestant of her time, Elizabeth throughout her reign displayed a strong distaste for preaching and a determination to retain many of the trappings—clerical vestments, for example, and crucifixes—that growing numbers of her subjects were coming to regard as insufferable carryovers from the age of superstition. Such issues generated more and more heat as the 1570s advanced, until finally Edmund Grindal, the archbishop of Canterbury, was suspended for refusing to suppress prophesyings as the queen ordered. Canterbury remained an unoccupied see for years, and at times it must have appeared that Elizabeth was the head of a church of which she herself was almost the sole completely faithful member. It was her good fortune to have two sets of adversaries, the Puritans on one side and the Catholics on the other, who feared and despised each other far too much ever to combine against her. (Grindal, for example, had pleaded with the queen to stiffen the penalties for attending mass.) It also continued to be her good fortune to have the Queen of Scots as her most likely successor. So long as Mary Stuart drew breath, not even the most radical Protestant could possibly wish Elizabeth harm. The church that had taken shape under her direction was a peculiar and even improbable concoction of rather uncertain identity, no more Lutheran than Calvinist or Catholic. For the time being it was able to hang in a state of suspension easily mistaken for stability between the other contending parties.

In order to sell the story that the priests coming into England were the agents of a foreign enemy, England needed to *have* such an enemy. Though the pope would always be the ideal all-purpose bogeyman, no one could take him seriously as a military threat. The same was true of the Holy Roman Empire now that it was detached from Spain, run by a separate branch of the Hapsburgs, and fully occupied by intractable internal problems and external enemies as potent as the Turks. That left France and Spain, and so many factors made Spain the more compelling choice that not even the memory of the St. Bartholomew's Day massacre could neutralize them for long. After the massacre, the Valois regime nominally headed by Charles IX made an effort to capture the Huguenot stronghold of La Rochelle and, upon failing, sensibly gave up on anti-Protestantism as the cornerstone of its domestic policy. Like England, it turned its attention to the most significant thing then happening in northern Europe: the ongoing revolt of the Dutch against Spanish rule, and Spain's difficulty in bringing that revolt to an end. England and France alike were eager to contribute what they could to exacerbating Spain's troubles. And England had a good story to tell in explaining its involvement: it could claim to be protecting the Dutch from the Roman Church (the *Spanish* Roman Church, specifically) and its Inquisition. England and France were also drawn together by the simple realization that it could be disastrous for either of them if the other became an ally of Spain's. The 1574 death of King Charles at twenty-four did nothing to change the dynamics of the situation. He was succeeded by his nearest brother, the flamboyant Duke of Anjou, who as Henry II became the third of Catherine de' Medici's sons to inherit the throne. There remained one more brother, the young Duke of Alençon, who now assumed the Anjou title but is usually referred to as Alençon to keep him distinct from his brother. There was resumed talk, not particularly serious on either side, of marrying the young duke, disfigured by smallpox and bent by a spinal deformation but nearly twenty years old now, to the forty-one-year-old Elizabeth. Each side played the game in the faint hope that the other might attach more importance to it than it deserved.

Philip, meanwhile, was sinking deeper into the quagmire created by his rebellious Dutch subjects, and England and France were being drawn in with him. Philip had received from his father Charles V, thanks to the fifteenth-century marriage of Charles's Hapsburg grandfather to the only daughter of the last Duke of Burgundy, a region of seventeen provinces, much of it reclaimed tidal plain, known for obvious topographical reasons as the Low Countries or—what means the same thing—the Netherlands. The rebellion had started in response to Philip's efforts to impose a Spanish-style autocracy on the northernmost provinces, an almost fantastically prosperous center of trade and manufacturing where the Reformation had taken a strong hold and provided particular reason for resentment of Spanish interference. It had then spread southward as a newly appointed governor, the Duke of Alba, clamped down not only with harsh new taxes but with a reign of terror in which thousands of people, Protestants and Catholics alike, were brutally put to death. Militarily Alba was successful, bringing all but two of the provinces under control in years of hard fighting, but the savagery of his methods made reconciliation impossible. His successor Requesens tried to negotiate with the leader of the rebels, William of Orange, but resumed military operations after his overtures were spurned. In spite of crippling financial problems—Philip's government was essentially bankrupt—Requesens, too, began to have some success, but he died in 1576 with the job of reconquest still incomplete. Much of what he had achieved was thereupon undone when his troops, finding themselves unpaid, went on a rampage of looting and vandalism. Their targets, necessarily, were the only provinces accessible to them: the ones still loyal to, or at least under the control of, Spain. Thus even the most Catholic sectors of the Netherlands were given good reason to hate the outsiders.

At this juncture, with his position in the Low Countries seemingly almost lost, Philip was rescued by the fact that his father, the emperor, had, in the course of his long career, produced illegitimate branches of the Hapsburg family tree on which grew a pair of genuinely brilliant figures. First among them was Philip's younger (and illegitimate) halfbrother Juan, known to history as Don John of Austria, a charismatic, even heroic character who in his youth had run off to pursue a military career in spite of being steered toward the church by both Charles and Philip. When he became governor-general of the Netherlands in 1576, Don John was almost thirty and not only a seasoned veteran of the Turkish conflict but the victor of the great Battle of Lepanto. He didn't want the Dutch assignment but accepted it with the thought that it might give rise to an opportunity to fulfill an old romantic fantasy: that of invading England and liberating Mary, Queen of Scots. The situation he found himself in was very nearly unmanageable, but after two years he was making such good progress that William of Orange, in desperate straits and without hope of getting assistance from England, invited the Duke of Alençon, still under consideration as a possible spouse for Elizabeth, to become leader of the rebellion and, by implication, ruler of the Netherlands. Alençon was utterly unqualified to take command of anything, but he was eager to make a place for himself in the world and attracted by the possibility of carving a kingdom out of the Netherlands. The Dutch of course had no real wish to accept such an unprepossessing specimen as their chief but as brother and heir to the king of France he carried with him the implicit promise of substantial help. He eagerly accepted Orange's invitation, discovered that there was no serious chance of getting meaningful assistance from his brother the king, and leaped to the conclusion that nothing could satisfy his needs more quickly and completely than a successful courtship of the English queen. Discussion soon resumed through diplomatic channels, and when word came from England that Elizabeth would never consent to marry a man she had not seen, Alençon made preparations to cross the Channel.

Don John, though continuing to progress inch by painful inch closer toward the defeat of the rebellion, was physically and mentally exhausted by the struggle and chronically short of essential resources. When in October he contracted typhus and died, his loss must have seemed another lethal setback for the Spanish cause. But before expiring he had nominated as his successor yet another product of Charles V's extramarital adventures. This was Alessandro Farnese, a son of Charles's bastard daughter, great-grandson of his namesake Pope Paul III. Farnese was almost exactly Don John's age, had been raised and educated with him as well as with King Philip's son Don Carlos, and had been second in command both at Lepanto and in the Netherlands. Usually remembered as the Duke of Parma, a title he would not inherit from his father until ten years after becoming governor-general in the Netherlands, he was no less gifted a soldier than Don John and a canny diplomat as well. Building on what Don John had accomplished, he began to coax the southern and central provinces (which would remain Catholic and evolve long afterward into Belgium, Luxembourg, and France's Nord-Pas-de-Calais) back into the Spanish camp. The seven northern provinces—the future Holland—proved however to be too strong and too determined for Farnese to overpower them. And so the war went bitterly on, poisoning northern Europe.

Influential members of Elizabeth's council, Robert Dudley among them, were not satisfied with merely assisting the Dutch rebels financially and leaving the military glory to Orange and his countrymen. Elizabeth, however, was still as wary of continental wars as she had been since the Le Havre debacle of a decade and a half before. She was sensitive to the costs of such wars and the unpredictability of the results. She had learned how difficult it was to manage seekers after glory, men convinced that where war was concerned it was absurd to take orders from any woman, even a queen. She sent money to Orange, but only in amounts calculated to keep him from putting himself completely under French domination. A strong French presence in the Low Countries, with their proximity to England across the narrowest part of the Channel, was less unattractive than Spanish dominance there, but not by a wide margin.

From this point forward the Dutch revolt, the religious divisions of France and England, and nagging uncertainty about the English succession all became impenetrably intertwined. The elfin little Duke of Alençon arrived in England, and to the amazement of her court, Elizabeth gave every appearance of being smitten with him. She was easily old enough to be his mother, and there was something pathetic in her infatuation with this youth whom she playfully called her "frog." As it dawned on people that marriage was not out of the question, council and court separated into factions. Elizabeth meanwhile made clear that this time she regarded her choice of a husband as no one's business but her own. When a loyal subject named John Stubbs published a statement of opposition to the much-talked-of marriage, both he and his printer had their right hands chopped off.

Robert Dudley was opposed, too, and probably for a multitude of reasons. He wanted to make war in the Netherlands, but he was sure that he and not the absurd Alençon should be the commander. To this wish were added his evangelical leanings, and a consequent dislike of the idea of a Catholic consort for the queen. But Dudley had kept his antipathy for Catholics within bounds when other possible husbands were under discussion, and this time more personal factors undoubtedly were in play. In 1578, after years of widowhood during which he had lived at the queen's beck and call and lamented the fact that because neither he nor his brother Ambrose had children the Dudley line seemed doomed to end with them, he had impregnated the beautiful Lettice Knollys, daughter of the veteran privy councilor Sir Francis Knollys and widow of the Earl of Essex. The two were secretly married—secretly because Dudley knew what the queen's reaction would be—and when Elizabeth learned she was angry and hurt. She arranged to complicate Dudley's life financially by withdrawing certain remunerative favors, but he was allowed to remain at court and soon was restored to his old place as favorite. His bride, already the mother of several children by her first husband, gave birth to a son who was christened Robert. But she was forbidden to appear at court. (The boy, Lord Denbigh, would be the last child born legitimately into the Dudley family and would die at age three.) All this could well have injected an element of spite into Dudley's reaction to the queen's marriage plans.

By the early 1580s Elizabeth's uncertainties, hesitations, and ambiguous policies had enmeshed her in a tangle of political, military, and religious conflict. In 1585 it all finally blossomed into a war that would consume the last eighteen years of what increasingly looked like an overlong reign. Much of the trouble grew out of the determination of the government's most influential and militant Protestants—Cecil certainly, but even more his protégé Francis Walsingham—to make the queen believe that the survival of Catholicism in England posed a threat not only to domestic peace but to her very life. As early as 1581 Walsingham was asking Lord Hunsdon, Elizabeth's cousin and one of the men to whom she had entrusted the management of the north after the revolt of the earls, to amend his reports so as to give a darker—and to the queen more alarming—appraisal of the loyalty of the region's still-numerous Catholics. In that same year Parliament, with Cecil ennobled as Baron Burghley and dominating the House of Lords while continuing to control the Commons through his agents, passed bills making it high treason for a priest to say mass and condemning anyone attending mass to life imprisonment and confiscation of property.

This was more than Elizabeth was prepared to approve, and the penalty for "recusancy" was reduced to a fine of £20 per month—a sum so impossible for most subjects as to be no different from confiscation. The queen's efforts to find a middle ground, to avoid being so soft on the old religion as to outrage the evangelicals or persecuting the Catholics so savagely as to leave them with nothing to lose, resulted in a policy that sometimes seemed incoherent. An innovation called "compounding," which permitted Catholics to elude the statutory penalties by purchasing what amounted to a license to practice their faith, was soon followed by a royal proclamation declaring all the priests entering England to be traitors regardless of what they did or refrained from doing. Life became increasingly difficult for Catholics, but the Puritans complained that it was not being made nearly difficult enough. As the queen refused to approve the most draconian of Parliament's anti-Catholic measures, the conflict between her church and her growing numbers of Puritan subjects became chronic and deeply bitter. When the archbishop of Canterbury whom she had suspended years earlier died in

1583, Elizabeth was able at last to appoint a primate, John Whitgift, whose views accorded with her own. He soon began a program aimed at purging the clergy of Puritans and suppressing Puritan practices. The Elizabethan church, therefore, was soon waging religious war in one direction while Elizabeth's government did so in another.

And the fighting in the Netherlands dragged wearily on. Philip II's financial problems had eased in 1580 when the king of Portugal died without an heir and he, as the son and onetime husband of Portuguese princesses, successfully laid claim to that crown. This gave him control of the Portuguese fleet and the vast overseas empire that went with it. The following year, when the so-called United Provinces under William of Orange formally repudiated Spanish rule, Philip had the wherewithal to respond by putting more resources into the capable hands of his governor-general and nephew Farnese. The result was a sequence of successes for the Spanish army and calamities for the rebellion, all of it deepening the difficulties of the English. The little Duke of Alençon, whose dalliance with England's queen had advanced to the point where a betrothal was announced by both parties only to founder on the old religious obstacles (how could even the queen's husband be allowed to hear mass at the Elizabethan court?), went off to try his hand as leader of the rebellion. He showed himself to be even more inept than his worst critics had expected, and died of a lung ailment not long after returning to France a thoroughly discredited figure.

In that same year, 1584, William of Orange was assassinated by an apprentice cabinetmaker eager to strike a blow for the Catholic faith, the Guises allied their Catholic League with Spain, Farnese took the city of Antwerp from the rebels, and English policy lay in ruins. Philip meanwhile was repeatedly being goaded by the raids of Francis Drake and other English pirates—if *pirates* is the right word for thieves who found financing at the English court and were welcomed as heroes when they returned from their raids—on ports and treasure fleets from the coast of Spain to the New World. Now he appeared to be near victory in the Low Countries, and if he achieved his aims there the English had given him an abundance of reasons to turn his army and navy on them. When Drake, on a 1585 West Indies voyage financed by Elizabeth and Robert Dudley and others, burned and looted Cartagena and Santo Domingo and other Spanish ports and brought his ships home loaded with booty, it was the last straw for Philip. He ordered work to begin on the assembly of a great fleet and the planning of an invasion of England.

For Elizabeth and her council it was a nightmare scenario, though undeniably they had brought it on themselves. They had provoked the Spanish king's open enmity at last, and had done so in such a penny-pinching way as to leave their rebel clients virtually at his mercy. The prospect that Philip might soon subdue the Low Countries was, under these circumstances, vastly more frightening than it had been when the revolt began. And so at last there seemed no alternative except to do exactly what Elizabeth had never wanted to do: send troops. Robert Dudley was delighted, especially when he was ordered to take command. He was well into his fifties by now, however, and his experience of war was decades in the past and not really extensive. But his enthusiasm was such that he took on a ruinous load of personal debt to cover his expenses—Elizabeth was not going to pay a penny more than she was forced to—and once in the field he found that he was neither receiving satisfactory support from home nor able to outwit or outfight his seasoned Spanish adversaries. The arrival of English troops was sufficient to avert the collapse of the rebellion but not sufficient to produce victory; the result was the further prolongation, at greatly increased cost, of a conflict that offered vanishingly little hope of a truly satisfactory outcome. England's intervention had persuaded Philip, meanwhile, that he could never recover his lost provinces—might never again know peace within his own domains—unless England was humbled. The invasion that he had in preparation began to seem not just feasible but imperative.

Overt war with Spain provided a new basis for portraying England's Catholics as agents of a foreign enemy and therefore as traitors. Suppression, along with the hunting down and execution of missionary priests, intensified. Inevitably, persecution further eroded the number of practicing Catholics, but at the same time, it gave rise to a cadre of young fanatics desperate enough to plot against the queen's life. This development—like Philip's anger a direct outgrowth of the government's actions—was the best possible news for Francis Walsingham with his network of spies, torturers, and agents provocateurs. It gave him new evidence to draw on in making Elizabeth believe that it was necessary to do more to exterminate the old religion. None of the most notorious and supposedly dangerous plots against Elizabeth had the slimmest chance of success, and Walsingham himself probably actively encouraged at least one of them in order to entrap gullible young true believers. He may even have concocted the last of the conspiracies (the so-called Babington Plot, which led to Mary Stuart's confessing to planning an escape and being accused, but not really proved guilty, of assenting to Elizabeth's assassination) in order to get a deeply reluctant Elizabeth to approve Mary's execution. Historians have often argued that the need to eliminate the Queen of Scots is demonstrated by the fact that after she was beheaded in February 1587 there were no more plots against the queen's life. But it is possible that, once Mary was dead, Cecil and Walsingham no longer saw any need to put such plots in motion, nurse along the ones that they discovered, or exploit their propaganda value when the time was ripe for exposure.

What is often depicted as the apotheosis of the Elizabethan Age, the turning point at which the wisdom of everything the queen had done was made manifest and the way was cleared for England's emergence as the greatest of world powers, came in the third week of July 1588. It was then that Philip's mighty Armada came plowing up the Channel into England's home waters, found Drake and Elizabeth's other sea dogs waiting, and was put to flight. It was indeed an escape for England, even a victory, though it was accomplished as much by weather and Spanish mistakes as by weapons. But it changed very little and settled nothing. It was less a culmination than a bright interlude, and it led only to the fifteen years of trouble and decline that would be the long final third of Elizabeth's reign.

THE PUNISHMENT OF THE INNOCENT

TUDOR ENGLAND WAS A WORLD IN WHICH THE RICH GOT richer while the poor got not only poorer but much, much more numerous. Twenty years into Elizabeth's reign she had so many seriously poor subjects, and the situation of many of them was so desperate, that figuring out what to do with them had become one of the challenges of the age.

There were many reasons why the condition of ordinary English families deteriorated precipitously during the Tudor century: the destruction of an ecclesiastical social welfare system that for centuries had reached out from the monasteries and parish churches into every corner of the kingdom; the ongoing enclosure of arable land and the expulsion of the people who had long farmed it to make way for sheep; an unprecedented concentration of wealth in the hands of a gentry class that was only a tiny part of the population; and a toxic mix of economic forces that caused real wages to fall decade after decade even as prices relentlessly rose.

Added to all this was the emergence of a new set of social values—call it the Protestant ethic—that encouraged the prosperous to equate wealth with virtue and to regard the destitute as responsible for (even predestined to) their predicament. An older worldview in which society was expected to provide a place for everyone, in which the poor were believed to have a special relationship with God and caring for them was supposed to be one of the primary moral obligations of every person, was inexorably passing away.

Poverty did not begin with the Tudors, obviously. Parliamentary statutes dealing with the homeless and unemployed had first appeared as early as the reign of King Richard II, late in the fourteenth century. Such persons were described as "vagabonds" even then, and if they were "sturdy vagabonds"—drifters capable of working—they were to be

put into the stocks wherever they were found and then ordered to go
back to where they had come from. Only the "impotent" were permitted
to beg—only, that is, the very young and very old and those otherwise
genuinely unable to earn a living—and they needed a license and were
forbidden to beg very far from home. In these first poor laws as for centuries thereafter, one of the government's chief objectives was to prevent
idlers from roaming wherever they wished.

Implicit in all this was the assumption that even the poorest could find
at least minimal subsistence in their home districts, and that appears to
have been generally true. That there were no new laws dealing with the
poor for almost a century after Richard II, and that when Henry VII revised the old law in 1495 he did so to ease the prescribed penalties,
seems a clear indication that poverty remained a negligible problem, for
the government at least, for a very long time. The introduction of new
measures in 1531 had less to do with Henry VIII's quarrel with Rome
than with the economic problems of the late 1520s, which had driven
streams of people out of their homes and onto the roads in search of food
and work. Soon thereafter, however, the expropriation of the resources
of the church destroyed the one traditional refuge of the English poor,
and poverty became a significant policy issue. What is striking about the
new laws that followed is the contempt for the poor that they reflect. This
was something new to English life. An inclination to treat poverty as an
offense deserving punishment came to dominate the Privy Council's actions.

From the early 1530s on, anyone judged to be a vagabond was to be
not merely put in stocks but given a public whipping before being driven
away. It was a curiously cold-blooded way to deal with people who no
longer had homes, could not find work, and could find no way to escape
starvation. But it set the pattern for what lay ahead: a national system of
laws and proclamations designed not to help the poor but to keep them
confined: to limit their mobility, increase their difficulties in entering a
skilled trade, force them to take any available work on whatever terms
were offered, and punish and humiliate those able to find nothing.
Everything was slanted to the advantage of the property-owning
classes—Parliament not only put limits on wages but made it a crime to
either demand or pay more—and only the immediate threat of civil un-

rest could on rare occasions force council or Parliament to intervene even briefly on behalf of workers or the unemployed.

A theme that runs through all the poor laws from the 1530s on is fear of the itinerant homeless. This was not irrational; people living on farms or in tiny villages had reason to be concerned when ragged strangers suddenly appeared, whether singly or in groups. It is no coincidence, therefore, that one of the most savagely repressive measures of the whole Tudor era was passed in 1547, a time when thousands of men had recently returned from the last of King Henry's continental wars. These were hardened cases, many of them, and penniless, and often resentful of the callous treatment that was the lot of soldiers in those days. Many of them had little option but to take to the highways, begging as they went, looking for work or, failing that, for something to steal. The scare that they put into the gentlefolk of southeastern England was a factor in Parliament's passage of a law unlike any other in the recorded history of England—one that prescribed branding for vagrancy and enslavement for those who failed to mend their ways. When this law was repealed after two years—it was simply too repulsive to be enforced or defended—whipping and expulsion once again became the standard punishment for poor people who showed up where they were not wanted.

As the years went by and unrelenting punishment failed to solve the poverty problem, local authorities and central government alike were slowly, grudgingly forced to the realization that some people were poor not because they were lazy but as the result of conditions beyond their control. It became impossible to believe that force alone was going to maintain public order. Thomas Cromwell seems to have understood this as early as the 1530s: he drafted a bill that would have required parishes to collect alms for the support of the impotent and assigned the able unemployed to public works projects supervised by "councils to avoid vagabonds." He was ahead of his time, however, and the bill never became law. Finally, in 1552, begging was banned completely, parishes were admonished to take up collections for the impotent, and so for the first time the helpless no longer had to fend for themselves. Five years later, during the reign of Queen Mary, a system was established to provide the unemployed and their families with materials—hemp, flax, wool— that they could fashion into items for sale and so support themselves.

With numerous short-term ups and downs, general conditions continued to deteriorate during Elizabeth's reign. The Statute of Artificers of 1563, while making contributions to parish poor boxes compulsory and thereby establishing the rudiments of a national tax system, went to new lengths to keep the poor in their place, in some ways quite literally. Upward mobility, already reduced by the disappearance of many schools, was further curtailed by a tightening of the property qualifications for apprenticeship. Responsibility for putting limits on wages was transferred from Parliament to the justices of the peace, but it remained unlawful to exceed those limits or even to ask for more than the law allowed. Nine years later Parliament put sharp new teeth into the punishment of vagabonds. The penalty for a first offense was now not whipping alone but also the boring of a hole into one ear—an ineradicable sign that one was not a respectable person. Second offenses were treated as felonies, and anyone found guilty of a third could be put to death. These provisions remained in effect for more than twenty years, but in 1576, with a conspicuous lack of enthusiasm, Parliament established a new category called the "deserving poor"—people who were not only able but willing to work, but could find no employment. The Marian practice of providing such people with raw materials to be fashioned into merchandise was revived, but in reviving it Parliament scornfully stated that its motive was not to help anyone but to assure that "rogues may not have any just excuse in saying that they cannot get any service or work." In the eyes of the governing elite, the poor remained a nuisance that unfortunately could not be ignored.

By the late 1590s the state of the economy had become so alarming that chaos seemed to threaten. Failed harvests, raging inflation, unemployment caused by war in the Netherlands, and a continuing decline in the standard of living combined to spark food riots in London and its environs in 1595, and in East Anglia, Kent, and southwestern England in the two following years. The capital and the roads leading into and out of it had become notoriously unsafe, with much of the trouble caused by soldiers returning from the continent. The authorities, in a panic, began cracking down ruthlessly on almost any sign of discontent. When an attempt at an uprising fizzled in Oxfordshire—only four men responded to the call, and upon finding themselves alone they returned to their homes—the Privy Council nevertheless demanded arrests. That led to some suspects being tortured (possibly to death in two cases), and to others being executed. The use of the death penalty rose sharply in many jurisdictions, provost marshals were commissioned to conduct sweeps aimed at clearing the roads of "base persons," and a statute of 1597 ordered that "dangerous rogues" were either to be banished from the kingdom or put to work as oarsmen on the queen's galleys.

As the century came to an end economic conditions improved somewhat, and social tensions lessened. But for an overwhelming majority of the men and women of England, the great Elizabethan Age was limping to a distinctly miserable conclusion.

27

The Last Favorite

I f the failure of Philip's great Armada was the zenith of Elizabeth's reign that it has so often been depicted as being, if it really did carry her to the heights of glory and provide proof of God's favor, she was not slow to return to the lower altitudes at which she had been accustomed to operate throughout the previous thirty years.

Her navy had barely broken off its pursuit of the fleeing Spaniards, in fact, when Elizabeth exposed her bred-in-the-bone selfishness, her cold indifference to the well-being of the subjects whose supposed love for her she and the royal propagandists endlessly celebrated as one of the wonders of the age. The commander of the Spanish fleet, upon abandoning hope of being able to land his troops on English soil, had decided not to run the gauntlet of the Channel in returning to his home ports but to take the much longer, presumably safer route all the way around England, Scotland, and Ireland. He therefore set a course for the north. The English kept pace with him as far as the waters off Scotland but then, being virtually out of ammunition and no better equipped than any of the ships of the time for long periods at sea, turned back south. It was well that they did. Plague was breaking out among the crews, and soon the ships were hauling into whatever havens they could find and unloading hundreds of desperately sick men. These were the heroes of the hour, the sailors who had saved their homeland from invasion, but now they were carrying deadly contagion. It is hardly surprising that they were not welcomed when they came ashore. What *is* surprising, not to say appalling, is the queen's failure to do anything to help them. Her admiral, Lord Howard of Effingham, wrote urgently of how "sickness and mortality begins to grow wonderfully amongst us, and it is a most pitiful sight to see, here at Margate, how the men, having no place to receive them into here, died in the streets . . . It would grieve any man's heart to see them that have served so valiantly, to die so miserably."

Howard was a court insider, not only a grandson of the Duke of Norfolk who had defeated the Scots at Flodden but the husband of one of Elizabeth's Carey cousins, and messages from him were not likely to be casually disregarded. He wrote the day before Elizabeth paid a visit to an encampment of her soldiers at Tilbury on the lower Thames, where nearly twenty thousand troops had been positioned to engage any Spanish force that might enter the river's mouth and attempt a landing. Here she supposedly delivered one of the greatest of her orations.

Characteristically, she focused her words on herself ("resolved in the midst and heat of the battle to live and die among you all") and her superiority to ordinary mortals ("I have the heart and stomach of a king, and of a king of England too"). This took place, if it *did* take place, fully one week after Howard broke off his pursuit of the Spanish and therefore even longer after the Armada had switched over from attack to escape. Possibly her main reason for going to Tilbury was that Rob Dudley was in command there—hating as she did to be apart from him at any time, she must have felt a particular need for his company in the middle of such a crisis; she and Dudley must both have known that the danger was now past, the enemy scattered. But it was an occasion for the kind of theater that Elizabeth loved, a gesture that cost nothing except a costume or two. (In pictures of her Tilbury performance, she is often shown wearing a metal breastplate and brandishing a sort of toy sword.) Trying to do something for the men who had saved her and were now dying in barns and sheds and gutters, by contrast, would have been both expensive and lacking in opportunities for drama. The admiral's appeal fell on deaf ears at least in part, apparently, because of the fact—an attractive one to Elizabeth and her hard-pressed treasurer Lord Burghley—that dead seamen were unlikely to demand back wages.

That was the worst of the government's conduct in the immediate aftermath of the Armada, but just barely. During the period when invasion seemed imminent, England's Catholics had rallied to the queen and volunteered to join in the defense. This behavior fit badly, of course, with what the Cecils and Walsinghams wanted Elizabeth and the nation to understand about the dangers of papist sedition. And so, rather than being mustered, Catholics were forcibly and humiliatingly disarmed. Between July and November twenty-one imprisoned priests, eleven Catholic laymen, and one woman were put to death. The Protestants needed little persuasion that these people were traitors and had to be eliminated.

Just a few weeks after Tilbury, Rob Dudley died unexpectedly while traveling from London to join his wife, his brother Ambrose, and Ambrose's wife (herself one of the ladies of the queen's privy chamber). He had been on his way to a period of rest in the country. The immediate cause of death appears to have been malaria, but Dudley's health had been undermined by the military campaign in the Netherlands, the difficulties of dealing with distrustful and sometimes resentful Dutch rebels, and the strain of being criticized by Elizabeth for almost his every move. His small son had died in 1584, he had mortgaged his estates and borrowed heavily from the Crown to help cover his expenses in the Low Countries, and in October 1586 his nephew Sir Philip Sidney, the apotheosis of the Elizabethan warrior-poet-gentleman, had died an agonizing death almost a month after being shot in the thigh in a skirmish at Zutphen. Quite apart from being the most important man in Elizabeth's life through the first three decades of her reign, the one man from whom she could scarcely bear to be separated, Dudley had sacrificed much, at least partly for her sake. He had never been disloyal, unless daring to marry after many years of enforced widowhood can be considered disloyalty. Elizabeth of course was genuinely hurt by his death, but on the practical level her response was once again frigid. She did nothing to relieve Dudley's widow, the despised Lettice, who was left to struggle alone with the ruinous financial consequences of her husband's service.

Dudley's death had broad consequences. It removed from the Privy Council one of the last influential members with a real attachment to the Puritan cause. Thereby it removed also one of the few remaining obstacles to the conservative program of the only prelate that Elizabeth ever appointed to her council, John Whitgift, archbishop of Canterbury.

Though theologically Whitgift was a Calvinist, in matters of church structure and practice he abhorred many of the positions taken by the radicals (their demands for the elimination of bishops, for example). He had the queen's full support in setting out to cleanse the church of radicals, and in undertaking a persecution of the Presbyterians that at times rivaled the ferocity of the hunt for priests: several men were executed for the publication of Protestant tracts. Whitgift himself was ridiculed in a series of widely distributed pamphlets by an anonymous radical who called himself "Martin Marprelate," and the Calvinists separated acrimoniously into rival camps with opposing notions of "sublapsarian" versus "supralapsarian" predestination. With the power of the Crown at his back Whitgift finally destroyed Presbyterianism as a significant element in the established church and drove it underground, where it continued to smolder menacingly and to grow in size.

By dying suddenly and earlier than might have been expected—he was about fifty-five—Dudley left behind a momentously unfinished piece of business: the preparation for public life of the youth whose patron and mentor he had become, Robert Devereux, the second Earl of Essex. It is a curiosity of history that, just as the Dudleys were dying out, the last member of the family to occupy a position of prime importance left a stepson who also, and with surprising speed, vaulted to prominence and power. Even more curious is the possibility, remote perhaps but nonetheless real, that young Essex was actually Dudley's son. His mother, Lettice Knollys, had married Dudley after the death of her husband Walter Devereux, the first Earl of Essex, but she appears to have been involved with Dudley many years before marrying him—even before her eldest son's birth. Intriguingly, Devereux and Dudley became enemies at about the time the boy was born, the rift between them is not explained by anything going on in politics at the time, and in spite of their bad relations Dudley became the child's godfather as well as his namesake. Walter Devereux died in 1576, deep in debt as the result of a failed scheme to establish a "plantation" of English settlers in Ireland. The pregnant Lettice married Dudley two years later, when the boy Robert was entering his teens, and from that point forward, regardless of whether they were connected by blood, the stepfather was advancing the stepson's career not only vigorously but far more speedily than was good for him.

Essex was a young man of high intelligence and authentic intellectual attainment; unusually for a nobleman of the time, he qualified for the M.A. at Oxford before ending his formal education. He was clever and quick and had exquisite manners, and because his mother was a granddaughter of Mary Boleyn he was related to the queen. He made a brilliant impression when Dudley first brought him to court and was quickly established among Elizabeth's younger favorites. In 1586, when Dudley departed for the Netherlands and command of the English expeditionary force, he took his stepson, barely twenty-one years old, with him as colonel-general in command of the cavalry (and therefore senior even to Lord Burghley's experienced soldier son, the forty-four-year-old Sir Thomas Cecil). A year later Dudley handed over to Essex the court position of master of horse, and among the younger men at court only the dashing Walter Ralegh could rival Essex in the competition for Elizabeth's attention and approval. Like his stepfather, and indeed like Ralegh, Essex wanted more than opportunities to dally with the queen. From the beginning he had a lofty sense of his place in the world and his destiny, and his rapid rise contributed to his expectation that great things lay ahead. He craved military glory and more: while still little more than a boy, he appears to have regarded himself as destined for a place second only to that of the queen herself. He was also desperately hungry for money, not because he was greedy—greed had no part in his makeup— but because both his father and his stepfather had left monstrous debts. At the Elizabethan court one could have little real power without a cadre of followers, and followers were not possible without the ability to reward. It is perhaps essential to Essex's tragedy that he was only twenty-three when his stepfather died. Dudley had lived just long enough to show him the view from the heights and to encourage his belief that he belonged at the pinnacle. But Dudley had not lived long enough to teach him anything of political wisdom—the need for shrewdness and cunning, patience and restraint. Most obviously Dudley had not taught the youngster what he himself knew best: how the mind of the queen worked, what flattery could accomplish with her, above all what she would and would not tolerate. Nearly alone in the world of high politics almost before he was fully grown, Essex had almost all the qualities necessary for the achievement of even his most extravagant ambitions. Some virtues he possessed in excess: he was courageous to the point of recklessness, and he had an exceedingly strict sense of honor. But of the craftiness that makes for longevity in the realm of power politics he had none. If he understood Elizabeth at all, he was too proud to exploit his knowledge.

The story of the last third of Elizabeth's reign is, to a remarkable extent, Essex's story. The war with Spain continued, the two sides alternately delivering blows that settled nothing; France was intermittently drawn in while continuing to be crippled by its religious divisions; and finally Ireland became, from the English perspective, the most important theater of operations. And at every stage, in military or governmental affairs and often in both, Essex was among the leading figures and at the center of the action. He eagerly pursued every opportunity that the queen's affection opened to him, but in the end he so overreached himself, so misjudged the queen and mismanaged his relationship with her, as to bring about his own destruction.

Early in 1589, just months after the failure of the Armada, plans took shape for a great counterstroke aimed at rendering the Spanish incapable of further offensives. A fleet was to be assembled and sent off to the Spanish ports on the Bay of Biscay, where it was to search out and destroy the forty-odd warships that were known to be undergoing repair after the disaster of the previous year. (All the other vessels that had made up the Armada had been lost in storms off Scotland and Ireland.) Upon completing that part of its mission, the fleet was to proceed out into the Atlantic and take possession of one of the islands of the Azores, establishing a permanent base from which England would be able to prey on the transport ships that regularly returned to Spain laden with the treasures of the New World. As ambitious as it was strategically, in broad terms the plan was not unrealistic; Philip's navy being in a state of ruin in 1589, its remnants were incapable of defending themselves or their ports. Just as encouragingly, the English counter-Armada was to be commanded by the redoubtable Sir Francis Drake, already a legend in his own time, and the thousands of soldiers crowded aboard Drake's ships would be led by probably the best English general of the time, Sir John Norris. These advantages were largely neutralized, however, by the financial realities that involvement in continental wars was once again imposing upon the government. Elizabeth had neither enough ships nor enough money to make the venture a success. The old pirate Drake was able to provide ships and money of his own, however, and he had the backing of speculators accustomed to reaping huge dividends by financing the privateers. Preparations moved forward, therefore, but not all the people involved had the same objectives. Queen and council, in contributing tens of thousands of pounds, were motivated primarily by the hope of breaking Spanish power beyond possibility of recovery. Drake and his syndicate were looking for profit first.

Elizabeth, now as reluctant to allow Essex to be absent from court as she had always been to part with Robert Dudley, forbade him to take part. But he had a young man's hunger for adventure, reinforced by a determination to prove himself and to share in the spoils that Drake seemed certain to bring home. He therefore invested in the expedition—invested by borrowing—and sometime after Drake and Norris had set out he sailed off to join them. The queen, when she learned of his departure, was furious. She sent orders for his immediate return, but was too late. The expedition turned out to be a disaster. The main assault force, instead of proceeding to the ports of Santander and San Sebastián where it would have found the core of the Spanish navy disabled and ripe for the picking, sailed instead to La Coruña. There, after destroying a single galleon, its sailors and soldiers were unleashed for weeks of drunken carnage that yielded almost nothing in the way of booty. When the fleet finally set out again, its destination was not the Azores but the Portuguese capital of Lisbon, which Drake and Norris had sworn to stay away from before being allowed to leave England. Drake had with him a pretender to the throne of Portugal who assured him that the city would rise up as soon as he appeared. Essex joined them en route—the ease with which he found them suggests that all of them had planned in advance to rendezvous in defiance of the queen's instructions—and was able to make himself conspicuous in an attack on Lisbon that was, by almost every measure, a fiasco. The long stop in La Coruña had provided the Portuguese with ample warning, there was no rising in support of Drake's claimant to the throne, and the English had brought none of the equipment needed for a siege. A halfhearted pass at the Azores proved equally fruitless, and by the time the thoroughly demoralized fleet limped back to England late in June some eleven thousand of the nineteen thousand men with whom it had set out three months earlier were dead, mostly from disease. The expedition had cost an estimated £100,000, half of which had come out of the royal treasury, and exactly nothing had been achieved.

Everyone associated with the venture was in disgrace, in some cases permanently. (Drake, for one, was never trusted by the queen again.) Essex's situation was especially dangerous because he had participated in direct disobedience of Elizabeth's orders. Nevertheless, he was rehabilitated with surprising speed. As total a failure as the attack on Lisbon had been, it had provided him with numerous opportunities to put his courage and gallantry on display. Upon arrival he had personally led an amphibious assault, wading through chest-high water onto a shore defended by armed enemies. He had challenged the Spanish governor to a duel (the invitation was declined), defiantly hurled a lance against the city's locked gates when the siege was obviously failing, and at one point thrown his own belongings out of his carriage to make room for wounded troops. He more than any other member of the expedition had covered himself with something like glory, his praises were literally sung back in England, and Elizabeth's anger must have been mixed with pride that her favorite had acquitted himself so well. And at court he had influential friends who were willing to speak up for him. Old Lord Burghley, who had taken a hand in Essex's upbringing and education after the death of his father, remained one of his defenders even though the earl was becoming a rival of his own son, Robert Cecil. Among Essex's other champions were his grandfather Sir Francis Knollys, still active on the Privy Council though nearly eighty years of age; his and the queen's cousin Lord Hunsdon; and Ambrose Dudley's wife, the Countess of Warwick, one of the longest-serving ladies of the privy chamber. Such support made it easier for Elizabeth to yield to her own powerful affection for the young hero. She not only allowed him to resume his place at court but conferred upon him the monopoly on sweet-wine imports that had previously belonged to his stepfather. This eased Essex's financial problems; renewed in 1593 and again in 1597, it would become essential to his ability to maintain himself as the leader of a significant political faction.

Among the more appealing aspects of Essex's character, and ultimately one of the key factors in his tragedy, was his unwillingness to be a courtier only, or to rely entirely on the queen's favor for advancement and the accumulation of wealth. He could have done well for himself and restored the fortunes of his family by remaining close to the throne and wheedling offices and other streams of income from the needy, aging woman who sat on it. But he was determined to be more and do more than that, and even after his escape from being buried in the ruins of the Lisbon expedition he continued to involve himself in matters that a more prudent man—a Cecil, say—might have left alone. Just days after his return from Portugal, the French wars of religion were ignited yet again by the assassination of King Henry III, who, in spite of being decidedly Catholic in his beliefs, was stabbed to death by a Dominican friar for having arranged the murder of three leading members of the Guise clan, including the duke himself. The last of Catherine de' Medici's sons being thus dead, the crown passed to their cousin, the Protestant Henry of Navarre, who duly became King Henry IV but met such fierce popular opposition that he was unable to enter Paris. One after another the major pieces on the northern European chessboard went into motion, some of them sensing opportunity, others danger. For Spain especially, a divided France whose Protestant ruler was too weak to impose order seemed extravagantly rich in possibilities, and it soon became known that Philip was preparing to intervene. The English had reason to be alarmed. A new expeditionary force was hastily assembled and, under the command of Essex's friend Lord Willoughby, sent across the Channel with a threefold mission: to assist Henry IV and his Huguenots, to discourage aggressive action on Philip's part, and to explore any avenues that might lead to the recovery of Calais. It all happened too quickly, and too soon after Lisbon, for Essex's participation to be possible. He considered Henry of Navarre a friend and ally, having since 1587 been sending him boyishly excited promises of support in the great struggle with the Roman Antichrist, and he followed events in France with passionate interest. At the same time, in cooperation with his sister Lady Penelope Rich (wife of the majestically wealthy grandson of the Richard Rich who had played such a villainous role in the reign of Henry VIII), Essex was secretly communicating with James VI of Scotland about the importance of an international Protestant alliance. He appears to have been calculating, more than a decade prematurely, that the aging Elizabeth and her closest, most trusted ministers were not likely to live a great deal longer. In encouraging the son of Mary, Queen of Scots to prepare for inheritance of the English throne, he appears to have been motivated at least as much by genuine religious zeal as by any wish to promote himself.

The Willoughby expedition ended soon and badly, more because of insufficient support and the diseases that invariably afflicted armies attempting to operate in wintertime than because of any failure on the part of its commander. Nothing had been accomplished that might prevent the Spanish from moving in; by early 1590 everyone could see that such a move was in fact impending; and clearly England was going to have to either do more or leave France at Philip's mercy. The result was two new theaters of conflict. An English force commanded by John Norris (Essex had begged for the assignment and been refused) was sent to Brittany in France's northwest to block the army that Philip had placed there. Almost simultaneously the governor-general of the Netherlands, the Alessandro Farnese who was now Duke of Parma, led a Spanish army from the Low Countries into Normandy. This last move was a boon to the Dutch rebels, easing the pressure on them just at the point where Parma appeared to be on the verge of victory. With the Spanish now in Brittany and Normandy, Henry IV (who was at war with his own country's Catholic League as well) faced the danger of being caught in a vise and crushed. Regardless of the fate of the Huguenots, for England it was unthinkable that the French Channel ports should fall into Parma's, and Philip's, hands. Yet another expeditionary force, this one responsible for dealing with Parma, had become imperative. Elizabeth asked Willoughby to take command once again. But both his health and his finances had been impaired by the campaign of the previous year—Willoughby, like Dudley before him, paid dearly for the privilege of fighting the queen's wars—and he begged off. He recommended that the assignment be given to his friend Essex, who was lobbying to the same purpose on his own behalf. The queen finally consented, if reluctantly, and once again the earl was eagerly off to war.

At about this same time, in another echo of the career of his stepfather, Essex secretly married Frances Walsingham Sidney, who was both the daughter of Elizabeth's recently deceased secretary and (what is likely to have mattered more to the romantic young earl) the widow of his late friend Sir Philip Sidney. Sidney had left his sword to Essex when he died; now Essex had his wife as well. The marriage would remain secret until the birth of the couple's son, news of which drove Elizabeth into the vengeful rage that had to be expected whenever one of her favorites or some member of the privy chamber became seriously involved in an affair of the heart. Essex was able to save himself from banishment only by pledging to keep his wife away from court. He was helped by the fact that his great rival Sir Walter Ralegh now impregnated and married one of Elizabeth's maids of honor. Ralegh had the worst of it by far: he and his bride were imprisoned in the Tower.

Essex's marriage was happy enough by all appearances, producing a number of children over the next decade, but it brought none of the political or financial advantages that a more calculating man might have sought in a wife. Sir Francis Walsingham had left a surprisingly modest estate aside from tens of thousands of pounds owed him by the Crown for expenses incurred in the performance of his varied duties—a debt that would remain unpaid to the end of Elizabeth's life. The banishment of Essex's bride meant that he could never possess that most valuable of political weapons, a spouse whose position at court enabled her to serve as an advocate and a trustworthy set of eyes and ears. Young Robert Cecil, by contrast, was newly and wisely married to a goddaughter of the queen and lady of the privy chamber, and he had had the good sense to get the queen's approval before marrying.

Ambrose, Earl of Warwick, the last of the Dudleys, died in 1590. The next year brought the death of one of Elizabeth's oldest and closest favorites and friends, Sir Christopher Hatton, a kind of tame Robert Dudley who had devoted himself so unreservedly to the queen's service that he never married or is even known to have considered marriage. He had been first brought to court because he amused the queen with his talent for dancing and theatricals, but as their friendship developed he was made a gentleman of the privy chamber; this was the rarest of honors, affording access to the innermost royal sanctum, a place otherwise off limits except to women. He also became a member of the Privy Council, then finally lord chancellor and chancellor of Oxford University. He receives scant attention in histories of the reign, perhaps because unlike the other men in Elizabeth's life he never provoked her to jealousy or anger and was unfailingly satisfied to do her bidding. His passing must have been a painful loss; one by one the people who had long been closest to the queen—ladies of the chamber as well as veterans of the council—were dropping away. Now only one was left, really—William Cecil, Lord Burghley, who was growing so feeble that increasingly he had to be carried about in a chair but still kept his hands on the levers of power. The circle around Burghley and Elizabeth was growing both younger and smaller. The question of who might ascend to Burghley's supreme position when he too died remained as unresolved as the royal succession. The most obvious possibilities were the dashing young favorites—Essex and even Ralegh in spite of his current eclipse. A somewhat darker horse was the distinctly unglamorous Robert Cecil. A faintly grotesque little man, bent of back and spindly of leg, Cecil was the antithesis of Essex, following his father's example in working quietly but tirelessly to make himself indispensable, patiently maintaining a focus on the big picture and the long term.

As 1592 opened, Essex appeared to have the advantage. In January he returned from Normandy, where his first experience of independent command had left a bitter aftertaste but done him no grievous political harm. The Normandy campaign is sometimes described as a farcical affair in which Essex marched his four-thousand-man army hither and yon to no purpose except to impress Henry IV and to no effect beyond the wasting of the queen's money. In fact it was a failure and an expensive one, but that Essex should be blamed is not clear. His instructions were to remain in France for only two months, and upon landing his little army at Dieppe he was to be met by and begin joint operations with Henry. The French king was not at Dieppe, however, so that to effect a union Essex had to move his troops a hundred miles in bad weather. He soon learned what Dudley, Norris, and Willoughby had learned before him about what it was to command an army in the name of Elizabeth Tudor: the queen, too far away to have much grasp of the realities on the ground, barraged him with instructions, criticism, and complaints. Also characteristically, she refused to provide enough troops or money to reap the benefits of her initial investment. Twice Essex hurried back to England to explain his situation and beg for more time and resources. He attempted repeatedly to put spirit into his demoralized and disease-ridden troops with daring attacks in which he exposed himself unnecessarily to danger. None of it was enough. By year-end he and Henry IV were bogged down in what seemed certain to be an interminable siege of the city of Rouen. Lashed by the queen's angry letters, annoyed to learn that while he was fighting in France Robert Cecil had been appointed to the Privy Council, he finally gave up and returned home. He had been shown something about the importance of being physically at court if one wanted to keep the queen's affection and influence her thinking. He had not, unfortunately for himself, taken the lesson sufficiently to heart.

WINNING BIG

THOMAS WOLSEY, THOMAS CROMWELL, EDWARD SEYMOUR, John Dudley, Thomas Cranmer—the history of the Tudor era is littered with the wreckage of more or less briefly brilliant careers. To rise too high or too swiftly, clearly, was to tempt the fates.

Slow and steady was the way to win the race. This is the lesson of the Cecils, who entered our story at its beginning, stayed in the background through two generations, and finally during Elizabeth's long reign not only attained the political, financial, and social heights but managed to entrench there two distinct branches of their family tree.

We noted in passing, in dealing with the first Henry Tudor's invasion of England in 1485, that among those who joined him on his march from Wales into England was a young man named David Cecil. Little is known of his background except that he appears to have been the son of a minor gentry family from the Welsh marches. After the victory at Bosworth Field he shows up in the records as a member of Henry VII's bodyguard, a yeoman of the chamber (which means he had access to the king's private quarters), and finally sergeant at arms (a kind of security officer with authority over others). He became a landowner, though not an important one, in Lancashire in the north.

This David Cecil used his position at court to secure an appointment for his son Richard as a page in Henry VIII's privy chamber. Richard in his turn rose to become a groom of the chamber and yeoman of the wardrobe, a position of sufficient respectability to permit him to make an advantageous marriage, get himself appointed to various offices in Nottinghamshire, and add to the landholdings accumulated by his father. Obviously he understood that the world was changing and the route to advancement was changing with it: though he brought his son William to court at an early age as page of the robes, the boy was later sent off to Cambridge University, an expensive undertaking. In six years at Cambridge young William, while somehow failing to take a degree, became proficient in Latin, Greek, Italian, French, and Spanish, thus making himself capable of dealing on equal terms with the Tudor court's elite. While still at university he married the sister of John Cheke, a rising star among England's classical scholars and a prominent young Protestant. Richard Cecil is not likely to have been greatly pleased with this marriage; union with the Cheke family offered no financial advantages and few if any political ones. Nevertheless, upon leaving Cambridge William was permitted to take up the study of law at Gray's Inn in London; obviously his father remained willing to invest heavily in his preparations for a career. The investment began to pay dividends as early as 1542, the year William became twenty-two. Thanks no doubt to his father's access to Henry VIII as well as his own attainments, William was not only appointed to the Court of Common Pleas but made a member of Parliament. His wife died the following year, having given birth to a son, and after two years of widowhood he married the eldest daughter of Sir Anthony Cooke, a leading courtier, humanist scholar, and educator. This marriage should have pleased Richard mightily; the Cookes, being exceptionally well connected, provided William with entry to the circle led by Edward Seymour, uncle to the little Prince Edward and leader of the evangelical faction at court.

Cecil, with his intelligence and education and understanding of court life, was soon noticed and put to use. He became secretary to Seymour—now the Duke of Somerset—in 1548. The following year he spent two months as a prisoner in the Tower in the aftermath of Somerset's fall, negotiating that crisis with all the skill that Cromwell had shown after the fall of Wolsey almost two decades before. In 1550 he became a member of the Privy Council, one of King Edward's two secretaries, and "surveyor" (general business manager) of Princess Elizabeth's estates. Having definitely arrived, he allied himself with Archbishop Cranmer and so impressed Lord Protector John Dudley that he was knighted.

The religious restoration that came with the accession of Mary I created grave difficulties for the evangelical party and everyone connected with Dudley, as we have seen, but Cecil does not appear ever to have been in danger. The queen respected him, he continued to sit in Parliament, and Cardinal Pole used him in diplomatic missions to the continent. In all likelihood he could have played a substantial role in the new regime, but he chose instead to withdraw to his estate at Wimbledon, maintaining contact with Elizabeth and like her going to occasionally ridiculous lengths (ostentatiously displaying his rosary beads, for example) to demonstrate that he was a faithful and practicing Catholic. Elizabeth was fortunate, when Mary died, to have close at hand an experienced politician who was also as dependable a friend as Cecil. In immediately appointing him her principal secretary, she was showing her basic good sense.

Cecil used his new position to take control of all communications to and from the queen and make himself head of the Privy Council and minister-in-chief. He and Elizabeth were, in important respects, a strangely matched pair. Cecil, once in power, showed himself to be a statesman of some vision, capable of formulating strategic objectives and acting decisively when presented with opportunities to achieve them. Elizabeth, with her focus on trying to maintain a stable status quo, on surviving, was chronically reluctant to make irrevocable commitments. The difference between the two became manifest almost at the beginning, when Cecil correctly saw his opportunity to drive the French out of Scotland but had to threaten to resign before the queen would allow him to act. This set the pattern for the next forty years: Cecil generally knew what he wanted to do next and why, and he repeatedly found it difficult or impossible to get a decision out of the queen. In no way, however, can the partnership be dismissed as a failure for either party. The shrewd and patient Cecil, himself a cautious man but able to take carefully calculated risks, learned to swallow his frustration and wait. In the end he accomplished more than a little. And Elizabeth got what she wanted: she survived, and rather handsomely.

Cecil had been born too late to get in on the great scattering of wealth triggered by the suppression of the monasteries, but his father had benefited in a small way, and during the reign of Edward VI both were able to buy up church lands at insider prices. He was already a fairly rich man when Elizabeth became queen, but the best was yet to come. In the aftermath of his great success in Scotland he was given the lucrative post of master of the Court of Wards and granted extensive tracts of land in Lincolnshire, Rutland, and Northamptonshire. Elizabeth also gave him licenses to trade in beer and cloth—licenses that he could then sell to eager merchants. For the rest of his life he was able to put himself first in line whenever royal largesse was being dispensed.

On the dynastic front, by contrast, things did not seem to be going particularly well for Cecil. In 1561 he sent his only son, Thomas, who was then nineteen years old, on a two-year grand tour of Europe, during which the youth was reported to be neglecting his prayers and studies to such an extent, and devoting so much time to gambling and sport, that his father threatened to have him forcibly confined. Actually Thomas appears to have been nothing worse than high-spirited and mischievous, his conduct intolerable only by the standards of his father and his strait-laced stepmother. After returning to England he was given a seat in Commons and married to a baron's daughter. (William Cecil was careful to find spouses among the nobility for all his children, thereby condemning one of his daughters to a disastrously unhappy marriage to an earl.) The court, and the whole world of politics, now lay wide open to Thomas Cecil. His father must have been disappointed when he showed himself to be less interested in life at court than in making a career as a soldier.

In 1563, after eighteen years of marriage, Mildred Cooke Cecil presented William with their first and only son, a boy who was given the name Robert. As with Thomas, however, paternity brought disappointment and worry: the child was not only frail but misshapen, with a humped back and feet that pointed outward; all his life he would walk with a crablike shuffle. Rather obviously, this boy was never going to be a soldier. His father must have feared that he might never prosper in the image-obsessed world of the court, either.

But William now had two heirs a generation apart in age, and it became part of his life's work to place both of them high among the elite. The age, as we saw earlier in connection with food, was one of conspicuous consumption, and of a growing gulf between rich and poor. All across England, families newly rich on church land were building lavish country homes; it was a way of showing off, of proving wealth and power, of staking a claim to aristocratic status. Probably it is only natural that William, as alert as his own father had been to what would be required for success in the next generation, now set out to build for his sons the grandest nonroyal palaces of the age. From his father he had inherited a Staffordshire estate stitched together from onetime monastic lands and an old manor called Burghley, and during Queen Mary's reign he had begun building a house commensurate with his new wealth. Upon the birth of his second son he had bought a property called Theobalds only about a dozen miles from London and begun building there as well, and as his fortune increased his plans for both places became more and more grandiose. Work went on at what was named Burghley House for thirty-two years, culminating in the late 1580s in the completion of the most stupendous of the so-called "prodigy houses" of the Elizabethan period. The house's main part had thirty-five major rooms on two floors plus another eighty more or less ordinary rooms, with east and west wings nearly equal in size, and it was all set in a park of ten thousand acres. The plans for Theobalds were expanded after Elizabeth paid a first visit in the 1560s and declared her intention to return. She visited ten more times between 1571 and 1594 (each visit cost the proud owner between £2,000 and £3,000—money very well spent), and each time she found the place more imposing than before. In the end it had five interior courts, the largest 110 feet on each side with a huge fountain of black and white marble as its centerpiece. The next largest was eighty-six feet square and abutted presence, privy, bed, and coffer chambers specially built for the queen. The land that Burleigh acquired around it eventually had a circumference of eight miles. When Elizabeth created him Baron Burghley in 1573, there could be no doubt about his having resources appropriate to his new rank.

And neither son proved to be a disappointment. Thomas got the military career he had wanted and distinguished himself, participating in putting down the revolt of the northern earls in 1569 and in an English foray into Scotland in 1573. He was knighted in 1575, went with Robert Dudley and the young Earl of Essex to the Netherlands war in 1585, and was wealthy enough to establish his wife and five sons and eight daughters in a prodigy house of his own at Wimbledon. Though Robert's disabilities could not be outgrown, and though he was educated at home rather than being sent to university, he grew up to be intelligent, hardworking, ambitious, and cunning. His father placed him in Parliament when he was twenty-one and arranged his marriage to a lady close to the queen. When Francis Walsingham died in 1590 and Elizabeth procrastinated in naming a replacement, William Cecil arranged for Robert to take up the duties of secretary without being able to give him the title.

The question of whether he or someone else would ultimately be appointed gave rise to much court gossip.

Ultimately the question was one of succession: who would take charge when Burghley was finally gone? Essex obviously regarded himself as entitled to do so. And it was he, obviously, whom the queen loved. But it was Robert Cecil whom she appointed to the council in 1591, when Essex was away in France. Nobody knew what to expect, which was exactly the way Elizabeth wanted it.

28

A Seat at the Table

The value of staying home, of keeping close to the queen and flirting with her and becoming as adept as Christopher Hatton at appearing to worship her as an unattainably perfect woman, was soon made plain to Essex. In just a year he was given a seat on the council. That made him a player at the table where policy was decided, and it did so at a time when great questions urgently needed to be answered. After Essex's departure from France, Alessandro Farnese had forced Henry IV to break off the siege of Rouen, which thus remained in control of France's Catholic League. But then Farnese suffered a wound that at first did not seem dangerous and abruptly died, not yet forty-eight years old. His passing cost Philip II possibly the best soldier-diplomat of his time. William of Orange's son and heir, the capable Maurice of Nassau, was able to nurse the Dutch rebellion back to vigor with the help of a continuing English military presence. In Brittany, at the same time, John Norris with his little army succeeded in fighting the Spanish to a standstill—an admirable achievement in light of the difficulties he had experienced in trying to get Elizabeth and Burghley to send him men and money. If Norris was a more effective beggar than Essex in addition to being the better general, he had the advantage of a mother who was a lady of the privy chamber. In any case, having accomplished far more than Essex ever had on the continent, Norris received typical Tudor thanks, returning home sick and seriously in debt only to be ordered against his will to depart again, this time with orders to crush a rebellion now boiling in Ireland. He was all soldier, gruff and charmless, and though his mother helped to shield him from taking all the blame for disappointments that were not his fault, she was unable to make the queen enjoy his company.

Thanks in part to the queen's approval, thanks as well to the force of his own personality and to Burghley's ability to wait patiently for conditions to ripen to the advantage of his son, Essex found himself not only taking an active part in the council's deliberations but second only to Burghley himself among its members. An informal division of labor was established: the lord treasurer continued his customary dominance over domestic politics and matters financial, while Essex, not yet thirty, was able to take charge of military and foreign affairs. This arrangement created the impression, and certainly encouraged Essex to expect, that when Burghley passed from the scene (surely he could not last long now!) he would be succeeded by the earl as minister-in-chief. The situation was not without difficulty, but it put Essex at odds less with Burghley than with Elizabeth. Essex made himself the council's great champion of the continental Protestants and therefore of his friend Henry of France. Like Dudley before him, he wanted an English war on Spain and on Spain's friends in France. Elizabeth, however, not only wanted but needed reduced commitments—and much less military spending. Burghley must have been pleased to remain on the margins of this debate. As treasurer, he was obliged to struggle with an increasingly restless Parliament to find the hundreds of thousands—ultimately the millions—of pounds needed to sustain a conflict that had metastasized from the Netherlands into France and was now threatening to worsen the situation in Ireland as well. However strong his sympathy for the beleaguered Protestants across the Channel, however convinced he may have been that Spain was too dangerous a threat not to be confronted, the old man cannot have been displeased to see Essex become the object of the queen's displeasure.

Essex had been on the council less than a year when Henry IV brought France's religious wars to an abrupt end by the simple but shocking expedient of becoming a Roman Catholic. His Huguenot followers, along with the Puritans of England, were of course horrified at such an utterly cynical conversion—"Paris is worth a mass," Henry famously declared—but the Catholic League dissolved in confusion mixed with relief. Even the Spanish were at first baffled. Soon the Spanish army was gone from Brittany, its presence there having been rendered pointless, and England was able to withdraw all its troops from the continent except for the small force supporting Maurice of Nassau in the seven Dutch provinces that he now controlled. There could be no general peace, however, so long as England remained engaged in the Low Countries. The relationship between England and Spain deteriorated further as Philip awoke to the possibility of repaying the English for the trouble they had caused him in the Netherlands by making similar trouble in Ireland. The limitations of religion as a determining factor in international relations were demonstrated afresh when Henry IV, securely in command in France as a result of his conversion, declared war on Spain and allied himself with England (thereby allying himself as well, if a bit obliquely, with the Dutch Protestants).

It was time once again for direct action against the Spanish homeland, which meant naval action, and Essex of course insisted on a prominent part. By 1596 he had been at home for several years and had been sharing power with Burghley for two. He was restless, satisfied neither that he was being adequately rewarded for his services nor that his abilities were being put to full use. The idealist in him had always found the artificial life of the court to be faintly contemptible, especially under an aged queen who persisted in wearing low-cut gowns, demanded to be wooed, and expected every man at court to pretend that she was still as fresh and desirable as a girl of twenty. What was real by Essex's romantically aristocratic code, what required genuine courage and sacrifice and provided a true test of a man's worth, was *war*. And England was in need of heroes: nearly a decade had passed since the death of Philip Sidney, and no comparably chivalrous figure had arisen to take his place. (Essex would have said he had not yet had a chance to do so.) In 1595 those old salts Drake and Hawkins had died on a wretchedly unsuccessful last voyage to the West Indies, where improved Spanish defenses had made their tactics obsolete. The time was ripe for new exploits and new men, and Essex set out to provide both. He partnered with Howard of Effingham, the admiral of what there was of an English navy, and Francis Vere, who had long and successfully commanded the queen's forces in the Netherlands, to find investors for an assault on the Spanish port city of Cádiz. Getting the queen's approval was difficult as usual, but when the assault force set out at the beginning of June it was formidable: more than a hundred ships carrying twenty thousand men. Howard commanded the fleet and Essex the troops, with Vere and Ralegh in prominent positions. (For all his faults, Essex was not petty or mean-spirited. Upon getting the upper hand in his long rivalry with Ralegh he had become generous, even serving as godfather to Sir Walter's son.) The Cádiz expedition turned out to be a stupendous success, one of the greatest achieved by either side in the course of this long and generally sterile war. The defenders were taken by surprise, some three dozen ships including several of Spain's finest fighting galleons were captured or destroyed, and to the profound humiliation of the Spanish Crown, Cádiz itself was occupied. Essex achieved his dream of becoming a national hero, leading the assault and putting the Spanish to flight. He wanted to fortify the city and make it a base from which to prey on the enemy's coast and shipping, and perhaps attack inland as well, but was overruled by Howard and the other leaders. They set Cádiz ablaze and sailed home in triumph, only to find upon arrival that Elizabeth was unhappy because so much Spanish cargo had been destroyed rather than brought to England. (Her complaint was justified: the English had carelessly given the Spanish admiral an opportunity to burn his ships rather than handing them over.) Essex was further chagrined to learn that in his absence Robert Cecil had been appointed secretary. Essex himself had no interest in the position; a less suitable appointment for a man of his restless temperament could hardly be imagined. But he was intensely jealous of the Cecils now, and in his quixotic fashion he had somehow decided that he was honor bound to deliver the job to William Davison, who had lost his place in the administration (as well as being sent to the Tower) when Elizabeth used him as a scapegoat, pretending that he was responsible for the execution of Mary, Queen of Scots. Her choice of Robert Cecil seemed to Essex both a gratuitous rebuke and confirmation that Lord Burghley was so committed to his son's advancement that he had to be considered a rival, even an enemy. As with his Normandy expedition of 1591, from which he had returned to find the younger Cecil seated on the Privy Council, Essex felt that he had gone abroad to perform services of real value only to see the finest rewards in the queen's gift bestowed upon the paper-shuffling time-servers at court. Something like paranoia began to fester in his mind and spirit. With each new slight or perceived slight his suspicions would grow more pronounced, generating helpless fury, for example, when Howard of Effingham was made Earl of Nottingham, placed above Essex in the hierarchy of nobility, and given sole credit (or so it seemed to Essex) for the success of the Cádiz venture.

That autumn, in an effort to take revenge for the destruction of Cádiz, Philip II sent another Armada to pillage the English coast. Even more quickly than its predecessor, this new fleet was dispersed by storms, so that once again it was England's turn to strike a blow. Essex, who had by this time stopped sulking and secured his own appointment as master of ordnance, began preparations for an expedition to be modeled on, but strategically more ambitious than, Cádiz. The original plan was to attack the Spanish port of Ferrol, where many of the ships involved in the abortive 1596 attack were known to have put in for refitting, garrison it as a permanent foothold on the Spanish mainland, and then proceed westward to the Azores for the purpose of intercepting that summer's treasure fleet from America. This time, however, nothing went smoothly. When Essex set sail in July he ran into viciously foul weather and had to return home. By the time he could set out again his army had been savaged by plague, so reduced in numbers that attacking a target as formidable as Ferrol was out of the question. Probably the entire enterprise should have been abandoned, but the fleet was manned and equipped, there remained every reason for confidence that the Spanish treasure convoy could be found and taken, and Essex badly needed a return on all the money he had invested not only in this venture but in the previous year's as well. So the flotilla charted a course for the Azores, where angry disagreements broke out between the earl and his vice-admiral, Ralegh, and the Spanish treasure ships managed to slip into the port of Terceira just hours ahead of the English. By the time Essex gave up hope of accomplishing anything and was making his empty-handed way home, the Spanish ships at Ferrol had completed their refitting and put to sea under orders to do to the English port of Falmouth what the English had done to Cádiz. With Essex still too far away to intercept them, the Spaniards faced almost no opposition. But once again Philip's plans were undone by storms that scattered those of his ships that did not sink and sent them struggling back toward home.

It had been a near thing all the same, and it put a scare into the English court. The fact that Essex's expedition had left the Spanish fleet not only intact but free to move unopposed against England increased Elizabeth's disgust at the failure of what would come to be called derisively, as though it had been a holiday excursion, Essex's "island voyage."

In the following year, 1598, Henry IV decided that he had had enough of a war that was bankrupting France and bringing severe hardship to many of her people. (The Dutch rebels, he observed sourly, could not expect all of northern Europe to be "miserable in perpetuity" for their sake.) Elizabeth was not pleased with his change of heart, troubled no doubt by the old fear that an end to hostilities could lead to an alliance between the Catholic powers. She decided to send an embassy to France in an attempt to change the king's mind, and it is rather surprising that her choice to head this mission was not Essex, an old friend of the French king's, but her secretary Robert Cecil. Possibly this was a measure of her displeasure with the earl after the disappointment of his Azores venture; just as possibly, she remained unwilling to allow her favorite to absent himself from court for months yet again. Essex for his part was undoubtedly mindful that he could ill afford to set forth on new adventures while leaving his enemies at court.

A deal was worked out: Essex agreed to take on the duties of secretary while Cecil was out of the country and pledged not to use the office for the benefit of himself and his friends or to the disadvantage of Burghley (who was in failing health and no longer much at court), Cecil, or any of their faction. During two months on the continent Cecil saw firsthand how severely war had ravaged northern France and how hungry the French were for peace. He saw, too, that the king was determined to make peace and abandoned the idea of changing his mind. Cecil found himself inclined to agree with the king; the status quo was difficult for England as well as for France, and he, unlike Essex, was prepared to let go the dream of destroying Spanish power on its home ground. He returned home in April to find that Essex had not only kept his word to make no mischief but had—much to the surprise of his detractors— done a competent job of managing the queen's affairs. If this had been the great test of his ability to function responsibly and effectively at the highest levels of administration, he had passed with distinction.

Cecil's return, however, brought a revival of the old half-submerged tension between himself and Essex and the two camps whose leaders they were. The strength of the Cecil party lay in the unchallengeable authority of its patron Burghley, who had enjoyed the queen's confidence longer than most of the courtiers of 1598 had been alive. Thanks to Burghley, it enjoyed a decided advantage in terms of ability to bestow offices and incomes on its friends. Essex on the other hand attracted, more or less by default, those upon whom Burghley (and therefore the queen) had declined to bestow favors: alienated and disaffected nobles and gentleman-adventurers who hoped that when Burleigh died the tables could be turned. Ultimately it would all depend upon Elizabeth, of course. The people who allied themselves with Essex put their hope less in his aristocratic flair or his not-quite-stable brilliance than in the simple fact that even after years of turbulence the queen remained in some deep way powerfully attached to him. Whether he was Rob Dudley reborn for her, or a surrogate son, or proof that she could still win the adoration of the most sublimely elegant young nobleman in the kingdom—there was no need to speculate about such things so long as whatever it was that bound the queen to her last favorite remained intact.

The bond was fraying, however. A month after Cecil's return from France, the inevitable happened: France and Spain signed the Treaty of Vervins, by which Philip II formally acknowledged Henry IV as rightful king of France and ended hostilities against him. The pact compromised, if it did not violate outright, the terms of the existing understanding between France and England. It came as a keen disappointment to those Protestants (Essex being the most prominent) who regarded themselves as locked in a war to the death with Spain and had no qualms about allying themselves with a Catholic French king for the sake of victory. It also—with consequences that would prove more fateful for Essex than for anyone else at court—freed queen and council to give the Irish problem the attention that it now urgently required.

Ireland had been a problem for centuries, not least because of its way of absorbing the Englishmen sent to subdue it and gradually turning their descendants into Irishmen. But the problem took on new dimensions when England became Protestant and added a new system of religious belief to the political control it had long sought to impose on its neighbor island. Ironies proliferated. The Irish, who if anything had been less loyally Roman Catholic than the English over the centuries,

learned from the 1540s to associate the Reformation with foreign oppression and to resist it ferociously, simultaneously embracing the old
religion with a devotion they had not previously displayed. And at the
very time when England claimed to be fighting in the Netherlands to defend the religious liberty of the Protestants, it found itself trying to impose its church on Ireland by main force. The Netherlands revolt had
been England's one great opportunity to threaten and torment Philip of
Spain, and Elizabeth's government had seized the opportunity. In the
1590s Ireland was Philip's best chance to play tit for tat, and though he
was perhaps slow to awaken to the possibilities, by 1598 he had done so.

At the end of June 1598 Elizabeth met with her councilors to discuss
the worsening of the English position in Ireland. Hugh O'Neill, Earl of
Tyrone, was mounting a rebellion bigger and better organized than
anything the Irish had previously managed, and, poor worn-out John
Norris having died on active service, the council was going to have to
dispatch a new commander to restore order. When the queen suggested
William Knollys, Essex's uncle, the earl interpreted this as an attempt to
weaken his position at court by removing one of his supporters. In reply,
no doubt in an arrogant and even disdainful tone, he proposed a member of the Cecil party. When the queen dismissed this suggestion as
ridiculous, a shocking scene unfolded. Essex turned his back on Elizabeth, an unthinkable breach of etiquette. Elizabeth stepped forward and
struck him across the head—hit him hard, apparently. Cecil then
clutched at the hilt of his sword, but regained control of himself before
doing anything more. He stormed out proclaiming that he would accept
no such insult from anyone, possibly even saying (historians have been
understandably hesitant to believe that even he was capable of such
words) that Elizabeth was "as crooked in her disposition as in her car-
cass." The witnesses must have looked on in stunned silence.

During the month that followed, while queen and council struggled
with the Irish problem, Essex stayed away from court in a deep, self-
destructive sulk. He was needed both as the council's acknowledged
military authority and in his capacity as master of ordnance, but he continued to ignore even summonses from the queen herself. Finally he
won the test of wills: Elizabeth appointed him earl marshal, which
salved his delicate ego by putting him once again above the Earl of Nottingham in order of precedence, and when she heard that he was ill she

dispatched her own physician. At last, like an indulged child, Essex was drawn back to court with flattery and favors—but not until, and largely because, an English army had been ambushed and massacred at Yellow Ford in the north of Ireland. That happened on August 14. Ten days earlier Burghley had died. Essex returned to court to find that he, and therefore the men whose patron he was, had missed out on the great redistribution of offices and honors that the lord treasurer's death had occasioned. The discovery heightened his already poisonous sense of alienation and grievance.

At this point Essex fell into a trap that may or may not have been of his own making. In the wake of the disaster of Yellow Ford, where half the English army had been left dead on the field, Tyrone and his rebels controlled nearly all of Ireland. Unless England decided to give up the fight—but that was unthinkable—*somebody* was going to have to take a new and bigger army across the Irish Sea. There could hardly have been a more dangerous assignment—Ireland was a notorious graveyard for English reputations and fortunes, those of Essex's own father included—and Essex knew that his departure would leave Cecil in control of almost everything, including access to the queen.

But he was England's leading living soldier, or regarded himself as such and was so regarded by many others, and no one in the kingdom had a stronger sense of noblesse oblige. If his queen needed him, he could not do other than serve. Hardly foolish enough to want the job, in effect he talked himself into it by finding every other candidate unacceptable. Whether Cecil and the earl's other rivals were nudging him on, and were doing so for the purpose of destroying him, it is impossible to say. By early spring 1599 thousands of troops had been sent to Ireland, but they still had no commander. What was perhaps inevitable happened on April 12: Essex was commissioned to depart for Ireland, not as a mere lord deputy but with the grander title of lord lieutenant, and there take command.

His fate was sealed.

A DIAMOND OF ENGLAND

EARLY ONE SUNDAY MORNING IN JULY 1581 A MAN NAMED George Eliot, who had once gone to prison for rape and homicide but was released by the queen's government to take up a commission as hunter of priests, arrived on horseback at the gates of a country house called Lyford Grange some miles south of Oxford. It was a casual visit, a sort of fishing expedition prompted by the fact that Lyford Grange was locally notorious as a center of underground Catholic activity, its owner currently in a London prison for refusing to repudiate the bishop of Rome. Eliot, earlier in his life, had been employed in Catholic households, even that of Thomas More's son-in-law. He had become adept at pretending to be Catholic himself, acquiring a knowledge of papist practice and a network of Catholic acquaintances that was proving useful in his new career. Happening to pass through the neighborhood on this Sabbath day, he had thought it worthwhile to stop at Lyford Grange on the off chance of snagging a fugitive priest.

Immediately upon arriving, Eliot began to suspect that something unusual might be afoot: a guard was on duty atop the house's watchtower, and the gates leading to its courtyard were barred. He was received warily at first, but when he called up that he had come to see the cook and asked for him by name, the guard left his post to fetch him. The cook, who had once worked with Eliot and believed him to be Catholic, welcomed him warmly and ushered him inside. Eliot and his assistant were given ale and invited to stay for a meal. With the assistant remaining behind in the kitchen, Eliot was led through several rooms to a large chamber where—no doubt to his delight—he found a mass in process before a congregation of several dozen men and women, among them two nuns in the habits of their order. When the service was concluded, a second priest went to the altar and began another mass. Eliot remained for it, and for what must have seemed to him an interminable sermon on the subject of "Jerusalem, Jerusalem, thou that killest the prophets." As soon as the mass was over, Eliot collected his assistant, gave thanks for the hospitality, said that he was now too late to remain to eat, and hurriedly departed. By early afternoon he was back with a force of armed and mounted men.

The house was searched all that day and into the night, and though many incriminating discoveries were made (rosaries and other forbidden religious objects, the habits out of which the nuns had changed upon learning of Eliot's return, even the wanted brother of Lyford Grange's owner), priests were not among them. The search resumed the following morning, but even stripping away paneling in a number of rooms failed to turn up anything more. The searchers, who had been reinforced the preceding night and now numbered about sixty (Lyford, obviously, was a sprawling and complicated structure), finally concluded that the priests must have been alarmed by Eliot's swift departure and made their escape before his return. Just as they were preparing to leave, however, Eliot's assistant noticed a tiny sliver of sunlight in a crack above a stairwell. Using a crowbar to pry an opening, he found not one or two but *three* priests lying side by side in a tight space along with a supply of food and drink. For Eliot it was a triumph, a bonanza. All the more so when it was established that among the three was the most notorious papist in all of England, a member of that alien and sinister new brotherhood known as the Jesuits, the infamous turncoat Edmund Campion. The following Saturday, his hands tied in front of him and his elbows behind and his feet bound under the belly of his horse, a sign bearing the words "CAMPION THE SEDITIOUS JESUIT" pinned to his hat, Eliot's prize was put on display in the crowded marketplaces of London. Then he was taken to the Tower and locked in the space known as the Little Ease, where there was no window and not enough room to stand erect or lie down at full length.

His capture was a coup for the government even more than for Eliot. Campion had been in England only a little more than a year, and during that time he had been only one of the dozens of priests moving in secret from one place to another. But his activities had made him an improbably prominent public figure, the most wanted man in the kingdom, an intolerable embarrassment for the government and its church. Not even Catholics could challenge the fact that, according to the statutes as they

stood in the 1580s, Campion was guilty of high treason. Now that he
was in custody, neither he nor anyone else could be in doubt about his
fate: he was a doomed man. As for what exactly he and his fellow priests
and the people who harbored them were guilty of, what kind of threat
they actually posed—understanding that requires an examination not
only of Campion's activities during the year before his capture and his
conduct afterward, but of his life before he became an outlaw.

He was born into very ordinary circumstances, one of several children of a London bookseller, but his talents set him apart from an early
age. He became a scholarship boy, his education financed by London's
Worshipful Company of Grocers, and was still in his early teens when
selected to deliver a Latin oration to Mary Tudor as she entered London
for her coronation. He was sent to Oxford at age seventeen, rose with
unusual speed to positions of prominence, and was a fellow and proctor
when, at twenty-six, he was chosen to deliver a formal address before
Queen Elizabeth during her visit to the university in 1566. The queen not
only noticed Campion but singled him out for praise. Her church being
in need of distinguished young candidates for advancement in the aftermath of the purging of the Marian hierarchy, this royal attention led to
Campion's being offered the patronage of both William Cecil and Robert
Dudley. He became Dudley's protégé—Dudley was chancellor of Oxford at the time—and was called upon to deliver orations on occasions
of state and at events including Amy Robsart's funeral (which must have
been an excruciatingly delicate affair for everyone involved). As part of
his preparation for the great things that clearly lay ahead, Campion took
holy orders as a deacon in the Anglican church in 1568. He must have
been suspected of leaning in the direction of Rome, however, because
as part of the government's reaction to the revolt of the northern earls
and the pope's excommunication of Elizabeth he came under pressure
to demonstrate his willingness to conform. Upon declining to do so he
was repudiated by the Grocers Company and departed for Ireland,
where he found influential patrons including the queen's deputy Sir
Henry Sidney and his son Philip and hoped to become involved in the
refounding of Dublin University. The stern measures enacted in England
in response to the queen's excommunication—it was made high treason
to "absolve or reconcile" anyone in accordance with the Roman rite, or
to be absolved or reconciled—were soon extended to the parts of Ire-

land that England controlled. The authorities were ordered to arrest anyone suspected of being Catholic. Campion, though not yet a professed
Catholic, once again came under suspicion and found it advisable to
move on. He quietly returned to England for a time, then crossed the
Channel. He traveled to Douai, where he was received into the Catholic
Church and entered the college that William Allen had established three
years earlier for the education of English refugees seeking to become
priests. Lord Burghley, upon learning of Campion's conversion, lamented
the loss of "one of the diamonds of England."

There followed a decade of study and teaching. In three years at
Douai—where the discussion of current politics, incidentally, was absolutely forbidden—Campion taught rhetoric while adding a degree in
theology to his two Oxford diplomas. He then proceeded to Rome,
where he requested and was granted admission to the young, phenomenally fast-growing Society of Jesus, the Jesuits. The order naturally not
having a presence in England, he was assigned to its Austrian province.
After another six years of preparation in Moravia, Vienna, and Prague, he
was ordained a priest, and in 1580 he was called back to Rome to join
the faculty of the English seminary recently established there. It happened that at just this time the Jesuits were being asked to send priests
into England, to join those who year after year were crossing the Channel after graduating from Allen's seminaries and one after another were
being captured and killed. The Dutchman who was then general of the
Jesuits hesitated before agreeing. He feared (with good reason, as time
would prove) that even English members of a religious order about
which England's people knew nothing except its evil reputation among
Protestants would be all too easily depicted as aliens, subversives, and
traitors. That they would, having joined an order founded by the
Spaniard Ignatius Loyola, be entering an England whose government
was relentless in depicting Spain not only as the nation's arch-enemy but
as the principal agent of the Antichrist. And that they were therefore certain to be accused of having come on a political mission. Campion is
said to have shared these concerns, and at no point in his career had he
shown the smallest interest in anything more than a life of quiet scholarship. Nevertheless, when it was finally decided that Jesuits would be
going to England—the general's agreement was probably inevitable, it
having been part of Loyola's vision that his men should go wherever they

were most needed—Campion along with another product of Oxford, the thirty-four-year-old Robert Persons, was chosen to be the first.

Campion and Persons were given highly specific instructions. Their purpose, the "preservation and augmentation of the faith of Catholics in England," was to be accomplished through the delivery of the sacraments exclusively. They were not to attempt to convert Protestants or engage in disputation. As with Allen's seminary priests, they were forbidden to give attention to political questions, to send reports on the English political situation back to the continent, or to permit anything to be said against Elizabeth in their presence. Their experience was harrowing from the start. The government was on the lookout for Campion even before his arrival, its agents on the continent having learned of his assignment, and upon landing at Dover he was detained and taken to the mayor for questioning. At first the mayor seemed inclined to disbelieve his claim to be a traveling merchant and to send him to London in custody, but in the end, somehow, Campion was let go. He reconnected with Persons, was taken into the care of the Catholic underground, and was never again out of danger.

Campion was a brilliant rhetorician, a master of Latin and English composition. It was his writing that made him the most talked-about man in England and the living symbol of the old church, the hero of his cause and a monstrously seductive liar to the enemies of that cause. The first thing that he wrote after reaching England, a short piece dashed off in half an hour, was a message to the Privy Council. Campion and Persons both wrote such messages. They did so at the request of a lay member of the underground, solely for the purpose of leaving behind, as they moved out of London and began their travels, a statement of their purpose in England that could be made public if they were captured and had no opportunity to explain themselves before being killed. In his statement, Campion defends his adherence to the old faith and asserts that he and his fellow missionaries seek only to preach the gospel and deliver the sacraments to England's Catholics. He asks to be given a hearing before the masters of the universities (to consider his theology), the kingdom's high judges (where the subject would be the legality of his actions), and the Privy Council (for a defense of his loyalty to the queen). The man to whom Campion entrusted the message, instead of holding it for use in case of capture as instructed, made copies and sent them to others. Soon it was being reproduced and circulated everywhere. To its Catholic readers, long without leadership and treated as criminals, it was an inspiration. To the government it was a tissue of lies woven as a cover for conspiracy. Wherever copies were found they were destroyed. It became known by the name given by those who scorned it: "Campion's Brag."

Later, while traveling in the heavily Catholic north, Campion produced a longer statement in response to the Protestant pamphleteers who were, under government auspices, flooding England with condemnations of the church of Rome. He titled it *Decem Rationes,* because it sketched out ten reasons why he believed as he did. It was printed by Persons at a secret press in the Thames valley and given wide distribution: dignitaries arriving for Oxford University's commencement exercises in June 1581 were shocked to find copies on their chairs. The resulting hubbub made Campion the personification of Catholicism in England, his elimination a matter of urgency for the Burghley administration.

The government disgraced itself with its treatment of Campion after his capture. After some days in the Little Ease he was taken to Leicester House, where his onetime patron Dudley and other officials questioned him about his actions before and after coming to England. Having heard him out, they told him they could fault him for nothing beyond his acceptance of Rome. "Which is my greatest glory," Campion replied. He was offered not only his freedom but preferment in the Church of England if he would change his allegiance. Upon declining—one is reminded of Reginald Pole at the time of Henry VIII's divorce—he was returned to the Tower. At the end of July he was stretched on the rack (evidently his fingernails were also torn out), his examiners trying to make him confess that he had taken the immense sum of £30,000 to Ireland to support rebellion there. He was tortured still more savagely some three weeks later, just before being put on display in a series of so-called "conferences" at which senior members of the Anglican clergy presented their positions on various theological and ecclesiastical questions, invited him to respond, and repeatedly interrupted his attempts to do so. In spite of having been given no opportunity to prepare and being allowed neither books nor pen and paper nor even a table or chair, Campion was sufficiently effective in rebuttal, and public revulsion at his

mistreatment was so strong, that a scheduled fifth session was abruptly
called off and the conferences brought to an end. He was then given a
third racking, saying later that he thought the man in charge, the sadist
Richard Topcliffe, had intended to kill him. (Asked how he felt after Topcliffe had finished with him, Campion replied, "Not ill, because not at
all.") Even three weeks later, when with other captured priests he was
brought to court to face charges of high treason, he was unable to raise
his right hand to take the required oath. One of his codefendants took
his hand, kissed it, and elevated it for him.

The trial was more of the same, a travesty no less outrageous than the
show trials of Henry VIII half a century before. Campion and others were
charged with having conspired, at Rome and later at Reims, to murder
the queen, encourage a foreign invasion, and incite rebellion in support
of the invasion. It was easily established that some of the accused had
never been in Rome or in Reims, and that some had never set eyes on
each other before being brought together in court. Such facts counted for
nothing, as did an absence of evidence that would have been laughable
under less appalling circumstances. Campion conducted the defense in
spite of his shattered health, and by all accounts he was once again impressive. He was helped by the fact that the Crown's witnesses were an
unsavory crew of demonstrably bad moral character, and by the prosecution's inability to provide corroboration of transparently perjured testimony. Though some observers naïvely thought it inconceivable that
such proceedings could possibly end in conviction, a finding of guilty
was never less than inevitable.

"In condemning us you condemn all your own ancestors—all the ancient priests, bishops and kings—all that was once the glory of England,
the island of saints and the most devoted child of the See of Peter," Campion told the court before he and the others were sentenced. "For what
have we taught, however you may qualify it with the odious name of
treason, that they did not uniformly teach?" When condemned to death
he began to lead the others in singing the Te Deum, the old song of
thanksgiving, and they continued to sing while being led away. He lay in
chains and in darkness for eleven more days, at the end of which he was
lashed to a hurdle and dragged through muddy streets to Tyburn. There,
as the implements of butchery were being made ready, one of the members of the Privy Council who had turned out to witness the event sug-

gested that Campion might best end his life by asking the queen's forgiveness.

"Wherein have I offended her?" Campion replied. "In this I am innocent. This is my last speech. In this give me credit—I have and do pray
for her."

Lord Howard of Effingham, no doubt thinking of Mary, Queen of
Scots, and suspecting that Campion was being as devious as all Jesuits
were supposedly trained to be, asked him just what queen it was for
whom he prayed.

"Yea," came the answer, "for Elizabeth your queen and my queen,
unto whom I wish a long quiet reign with all prosperity."

With that the cart on which he stood was rolled away, and Campion
fell to the end of the rope around his neck. In short order he was cut
down, and the executioner, knife in hand, began the horrible part of his
work. Throughout the four centuries since, the story of how Elizabeth
and her government were ahead of their time in wishing for religious toleration, of how they would never have killed hundreds of priests if those
priests had not persisted in seeking their destruction, has remained central to the mythology of the Tudor era. But Campion himself showed that
story to be a fable. He did so at his own trial, pointing out that not only
he but all the defendants, men whom the government supposedly believed had devoted their lives to the conquest of England by foreign
powers and the killing of England's queen, had been offered full pardons
in return for nothing more than attending Anglican services.

29

The Last Act

The England that the Earl of Essex left behind when he set out for Ireland bore all too little resemblance to the merry, prosperous, and even glamorous Renaissance kingdom that television and the movies persist in offering us as the glorious culmination of the Elizabethan age.

The country's economy was not only primitive by the standards of later times—that could go without saying—but provided most of its people with a lower standard of living than they had experienced not just in decades but in centuries. The royal treasury, which had never recovered from the profligate spending of Henry VIII, was chronically bare after a decade and a half of inconclusive and arguably unnecessary war. Five Parliaments had had to be called between 1586 and 1597 to vote the special subsidies (the double, triple, and even quadruple subsidies) without which the Crown's credit would have been ruined. Hundreds of thousands of pounds had been extracted from a church that no longer had anything approaching its pre-Reformation resources, and even all this was not nearly enough. Elizabeth and her council levied taxes whenever and wherever they thought it safe to do so, sold monopolies and licenses that gave special (not to say flagrantly unfair) advantage to a lucky few while burdening everyone else, and borrowed at home and abroad. As these measures too proved insufficient, attention turned to sale of the Crown lands that were the centerpiece of the queen's inheritance, assets that if husbanded could have ensured the security and autonomy of untold generations of her successors.

No one could remember a time when conditions had been so miserable for the population at large. The rise in taxes became particularly onerous as market conditions changed, reducing, for example, continental demand for English wool. This combined with the disruptive effects of war to increase unemployment and reduce incomes. Starting in 1594 there had been an unbroken sequence of wet summers leading first to crop failures, then to chronic and widespread hunger, and finally to rioting by the desperate poor and a savage response by frightened authorities. Prices of necessities soared, malnutrition increased the death rate, and the income of a common laborer had not bought so little since the mid-1300s.

The Tudor propaganda machine worked hard (underwriting and promoting the work of friendly poets and balladeers, for example) to keep the people mindful of how devoted their queen was to them and how much they presumably loved her. Her acts of charity, infrequent and niggardly as they generally were, were aggressively publicized. Behind the theatrics, however, there was ample reason for cynicism, and disillusion was widespread. The nobility became a minority as pampered as it was tiny and, by the meager standards of the day, fabulously wealthy. In 1534, at the dawn of the English Reformation, the average amount paid by holders of hereditary titles when Parliament voted a subsidy was £921, and fifteen nobles paid more than £1,000 each. The average declined to £487 by 1571 and would be down to £311 by 1601, when in all of England only one nobleman was assessed more than £1,000. This change—between Elizabeth's first Parliament and her last it amounted to a 38 percent drop—is especially striking in light of the 500 percent inflation experienced in England during the sixteenth century, and the increasing tax burden imposed on the rest of the population. Elizabeth's government remained fearful enough of the landowning magnates to be unwilling to risk offending them even when the Crown's need for revenue was urgent.

Subjects lacking the ability to retaliate when aggrieved, on the other hand, could count themselves fortunate if they were merely ignored. By the 1590s a long generation had passed since Queen Mary's brief restoration of the old religion, decades of officially prescribed preaching had persuaded increasing numbers of churchgoers that to be Catholic was to be pro-Spanish and therefore disloyal, and the fear of Catholic resistance with which Elizabeth had begun her reign was no longer necessary. A statute passed in 1593 took religious repression in new directions, forbidding Catholics to travel more than five miles from their homes and making exile the penalty for failure to pay the ruinous fines imposed on recusants—those refusing to attend Church of England services. There was some easing of pressure between 1595 and 1598, when England was allied with France in opposition to Spain. When Henry IV of France issued the Edict of Nantes, with its broad grant of freedom to the Huguenots, English Catholics briefly hoped for similar treatment by their government. Exactly the opposite happened, however: the government resumed the aggressive hunting down, torture, and killing of priests and the harsh punishment of anyone who harbored them. The regime was sufficiently secure by this point to be able also to complete its expulsion of militant Puritans from the established church and the destruction of Presbyterianism as an open expression of Puritan belief.

Elizabeth herself, from her position at the privileged center of a national network of misery and exclusion, continued to bend the economic, religious, and political life of the whole kingdom to whatever shapes seemed best suited to ensure her own safety. Approaching seventy now, she had already lived much longer than any other member of the dynasty and was still in good enough health to ride ten miles. At close range, however, she was a wretched approximation of Gloriana, the Virgin Queen celebrated in the poetry of the likes of Edmund Spenser and Philip Sidney. Even as a young woman she had been comically, almost childishly insecure about her appearance and desperately needful of praise. (At thirty, upon being told that Mary Stuart was taller than herself, she had exclaimed in jealous triumph that the queen of Scots was therefore obviously "too high—I myself am neither too high nor too low!") Forty years later foreign visitors were writing home of their encounters with a haggard crone, her wig off center and her face a stiff white mask of makeup, who persisted in dressing like a young woman, had lost so many teeth that she was impossible to understand when she spoke rapidly, but remained so hungry for flattery that when it was not offered freely she would call herself an old and foolish woman and wait eagerly to be contradicted. Insiders described the experience of serving an evil-tempered harridan, a thrower of shoes who could bear no signs of independence in the people around her. It took two hours of preparation every morning, the ladies attending the queen noted, before she was in a condition to be seen outside the privy chamber. Before receiving visitors she would stuff a perfume-soaked handkerchief into her mouth in the hope of taming her breath.

Four decades of painstakingly building and maintaining a theatrically regal persona, of projecting a manufactured image across not only her kingdom but all of Europe in order to compensate for being a female monarch in a world ruled by men, had reduced Elizabeth to the tiresome shabbiness of a trouper whose prime was long past. The show went on—her wardrobe at the end included 102 French gowns, 67 "round" gowns (dresses not opening in the front), 100 loose gowns, 126 kirtles or skirts, 96 cloaks, and more than two dozen fans—but it no longer carried much conviction. The audience, no longer impressed, was looking forward to the next act whatever it might turn out to be. The queen herself, however, not only showed no interest in removing herself from center stage but forbade her councilors to so much as raise the question of what, or who, might follow her final bow.

Throughout her reign Elizabeth had been careful to maintain her own authority by balancing faction against faction, party against party, at court and in council. Thus she had prevented any one group (William Cecil's circle, for example, or even that of Robert Dudley) from becoming dominant. Now, however, she appeared to have lost the energy for such calculations, or to have ceased to find them necessary. She was allowing her world to grow narrower; only eleven men remained on the Privy Council by 1597, all of them either aged associates of long standing or the sons of personages from the early days of the reign. Virtually all authority over the setting and execution of policy had been gathered into the hands of the Cecils. Perhaps she was satisfied that Robert Cecil, the careful and hardworking little son of Lord Burghley, was too much the bureaucrat ever to dare to threaten her authority, never mind her survival. No doubt she was confident that she had in him a chief of staff who, if even more attentive to the filling of his own pockets than his father had been, could be depended upon to manage the affairs of the Crown with sufficient care to free her of the burden of having to pay close and sustained attention. Elizabeth had never been willing to sacrifice for the sake of any grander goal than simply keeping herself on the throne, and Cecil was perfectly suited to making sure that she could do that with minimal difficulty. That she had little interest—no discernible interest at all, really—in what would happen to England's government or people after her passing became all too apparent as old age settled upon her. It was obvious in her willingness to sell off the assets of the Crown. It was even clearer in her failure to make a will or otherwise prepare for a transfer of power after her death, her refusal even in her final decline to so much as suggest whom she wished to succeed her.

This was the queen—irascible, distrustful, incorrigibly selfish—who sent the Earl of Essex off to Dublin. She sent him because she understood that an Ireland free of English domination could become a platform for her continental enemies. She understood too, however, that there was no money for another long war like the one that had still not ended in the Netherlands. She wanted, therefore, a quick and decisive victory, she wanted it on the cheap, and she was prepared to tolerate nothing less. Essex knew this from the start; his understanding of the queen's expectations, and of her certain reaction if those expectations were not met, is the only possible explanation for his later behavior. He was certainly capable of understanding that in taking on the Irish mission he was putting himself at mortal risk, and it was not paranoid of him to suspect that his rivals at court rejoiced to think that in going to Ireland he was embracing his own destruction. But by 1599 his situation was so bad as to justify desperate measures. Every mark of favor that the queen had bestowed on Burghley and then Cecil—putting them into the most powerful and lucrative positions, allowing them to share the royal bounty with their friends and supporters—had been another nail in the coffin of Essex's aspirations, another affront to his sense of entitlement. By 1599 he was the leader less of a faction on the Privy Council than of a gang made up largely of outsiders and misfits—men who shared his sense of being unfairly excluded and were therefore more disposed than they otherwise might have been to resent the status quo and seek opportunities to challenge it. He still had friends and family connections at court, but he consistently failed in his efforts to boost their careers. He tried repeatedly to win the office of attorney-general for his cousin Francis Bacon, for example, but never came close to succeeding.

It was long customary to interpret what happened to Essex in Ireland as the necessary consequence of arrogance, incompetence, and sheer foolishness. Such a verdict, however, is more easily delivered than defended. The earl encountered daunting obstacles almost from the day of his arrival in Dublin, and his conduct remained rational even as the pressures on him mounted. The Ireland that he entered was, and long had been, a cesspit of ethnic and religious hatred. Attitudes and behaviors that would endure for half a millennium were already in place: the English, seen inevitably as invaders and oppressors, regarded the Irish as not only uncivilized but barely human. The Reformation's success in England became a reason for its rejection by Ireland, giving both sides rich new reasons to despise each other. Rebellions had been brutally crushed in the 1570s and 1580s (at the same time that Essex's father, Walter Devereux, was coming to ruin with his failed effort to establish English settlements), only to be followed by the much bigger, better organized rising led by the charismatic, tactically adroit Hugh O'Neill, Earl of Tyrone. Tyrone's bloody victory at Yellow Ford had caused Irishmen to think that it might be possible to expel the English altogether.

By the time of Essex's arrival, Tyrone had under his command a larger, better-equipped and -led, more modern rebel force than any the English had ever encountered in Ireland. Essex for his part commanded the largest English army ever sent there: sixteen thousand foot soldiers and thirteen hundred horse. Nevertheless, the council responsible for the management of the English "pale" centered on Dublin, upon meeting with the new lord lieutenant, advised him that conditions were not yet right for a direct attack. Essex, seeing that he possessed neither the ships nor the draft horses that an offensive against Tyrone would require—the geography was such that in order to engage the Irish he would have to move his troops by water—wrote to the queen to request more of both. While waiting for a reply he moved part of his force through the northern counties of Munster and Leinster to relieve besieged garrisons, establish new ones, and so secure his rear against a rumored Spanish landing. (This move is sometimes characterized as a flagrant act of disobedience on Essex's part, but in fact he had requested and received permission for it before leaving England.) As time passed and Essex received little of what he had asked, he and the queen began an acrimonious exchange of letters. The earl's requests became complaints, and Elizabeth responded with angry demands that he get on with his assignment and stop squandering her money. Almost certainly it was the sharpness of the queen's words that caused Essex to launch an offensive that she would regard as too little too late and that he believed to be premature; he undertook it only because to refuse would be to risk recall and a disgrace from which there might be no recovery. And so in September, with the problematic weather of autumn beginning, he took his available troops, by now greatly reduced in number, northward into Ulster in search of Tyrone. The only alternative would have been to suspend operations until the end of winter, and it was inconceivable that Elizabeth would accept such a delay. (Maintaining Essex's army had cost £300,000 in the five months since his arrival in Ireland.) In the end he was unable to bring the rebels to battle. Instead he had to settle for a parley at a river crossing; the unarmed Tyrone sat on a horse that was belly-deep in midstream while Essex stood on the bank and the two talked for half an hour. They agreed on a truce, the details of which hardly matter because a furious Elizabeth repudiated the agreement as soon as she was informed of it. She sent off an order for Essex to remain where he was pending further instructions.

At this point, no doubt because he thought that Elizabeth's rejection of his truce meant that she had given up on him, something snapped in Essex. He lost control of himself and his destiny. Fear of the queen's wrath, certainty that Cecil and others must be encouraging the queen to be wrathful, news that in his absence Cecil had been given the lucrative mastership of wards that he himself had badly wanted—perhaps all these things together drove the earl to decide that unless he seized the initiative he was lost. He had already been talking recklessly of taking his army back across the Irish Sea to Wales and advancing from there to London and a showdown with the rivals who—or so he told himself— had gained control of the queen and needed only to destroy him in order to ensure their mastery of the kingdom. Such an undertaking would have been as difficult as dangerous, however, and Essex put it aside in favor of a headlong dash back to court and the mistress who had so often forgiven him in the past. He must have hoped that if he could see Elizabeth, talk with her and explain himself, all would be well.

And so on September 24 he sailed back from Ireland accompanied by only a small party of companions. Once across, he began the long, hard gallop across Wales, the marches, and the midlands to where the queen and court were gathered at Nonsuch Palace, the massive folly begun so many years before by Henry VIII. He arrived, having left a long string of spent horses in his wake, on the morning of September 28. Still filthy from what under happier circumstances might have been considered an epically heroic ride, he burst into the queen's privy chamber and found her neither dressed nor bewigged. She induced him to leave, promising that they could meet again an hour later, when both had had an opportunity to compose themselves. The day became a sequence of meetings in which Essex talked first with the queen, then with the queen and members of the council, finally with his fellow councilors only. Thus Elizabeth gradually extracted herself from a situation that she must have found intensely uncomfortable, leaving it to Cecil and others to question Essex about the conduct of his campaign in Ireland and the meaning of his disobedience.

The day ended with the earl under arrest and sinking into a state of physical and emotional collapse from which he would never entirely recover. Preparations were put in motion to try him for treason, but they were suspended when he became so ill that (much to Elizabeth's annoyance) his admirers had church bells rung in anticipatory mourning. His recovery was followed by a renewal of planning for a trial, but this time Essex saved himself by sending the queen a letter sufficiently submissive and repentant to drain off the worst of her fury. After a thirteen-hour hearing at which Essex found the strength to mount an eloquent defense against numerous charges of misconduct—a defense that inspired his followers and increased the popularity that the Cecil party found so threatening—he was "sequestered" from all his offices, meaning that until further notice he could neither perform their duties nor draw income from them. He was returned to house arrest under restraints that were gradually relaxed until at last, in August, his liberty was restored.

He had, by the narrowest of margins, been spared permanent imprisonment or worse. But he had not emerged undamaged. Indeed he was, in almost every sense, mortally wounded: his health shattered, his nerves in disarray, his political career at a dead end, and his financial position nearly hopeless. The conditions under which he was freed included a prohibition against his appearing at court; this destroyed any possibility that he might charm his way back into the queen's good graces, and shows just how great a danger he seemed to the Cecil party.

Theoretically, the way remained open for Essex to retreat gracefully to a life of rural retirement, but in practical terms not even that was possible. Like his stepfather Dudley, he had incurred unmanageable debts in the service of the Crown. Being left at the mercy of his creditors would mean the lowest depths of humiliation not only for the earl himself but for his wife and their children.

Essex's only hope—literally his *last* hope—lay in the income generated by his monopoly on imports of sweet wines. This "concession" must have seemed like something very close to family property by 1600: it had originally belonged to Dudley, and after bestowing it on Essex in 1589 the queen had routinely renewed it in 1593 and 1597. It was up for renewal yet again in 1601, but this time the decision was in no way routine. It put into Elizabeth's hands the power to save her onetime favorite, whom she had in so many ways encouraged to expect so much, or to crush him utterly. Any inclination that the queen might have felt to allow Essex to withdraw into dignified failure would have been discouraged by Cecil himself. Cecil had long since arrived at the conclusion that the only plausible successor to the aging queen was James VI of Scotland, and he knew that Essex in his younger days had taken pains to cultivate a friendly long-distance relationship with James on the basis of their shared Protestantism. The possibility that as king of England James might rehabilitate the fallen earl was both real and, from Cecil's perspective, ominous.

The decision therefore was to show no mercy, and it brought the Essex story to a swift, dramatic, and pathetic close. The final chapter opened with the queen's refusal to renew the sweet-wine concession, which left the earl with no way of extracting himself from his financial predicament. His London residence, Essex House (it had been Leicester House when owned by Robert Dudley), was by this point a gathering place for all the malcontents and adventurers who had not won places for themselves at the Cecil court and found all routes to advancement blocked as a result. Like Essex himself, those men were easily persuaded that Robert Cecil and his cohorts were not only their enemies but, because of their unwillingness to keep the struggle against Spain at a fever pitch whatever the cost, the enemies of England and Elizabeth and the whole Protestant cause. They had no difficulty believing that the queen had become the prisoner and the tool of self-serving schemers, and that those who knew the truth had a duty to free her. Essex with his medieval-romantic code of honor was particularly vulnerable to being seduced by such thinking, especially now that he was cornered. He embraced the delusion that if he rose against the council, the people of London would rise with him.

Robert Cecil was aware that Essex House had become a hotbed of sedition (though the "Essexians" would have denied being guilty of any such thing), and he had infiltrated the place with his agents. He could have moved early to arrest the ringleaders and scatter their followers, but that might not have been sufficient to ensure the earl's destruction. He waited until February 8, 1601, more than three months after the termination of Essex's monopoly, before sending a delegation of Privy Council members with a summons for him to appear at court for questioning. Essex panicked. After making prisoners of his visitors—itself an outrageous act, considering their eminence—he rallied his followers and took to the streets, proclaiming his loyalty to the queen and declaring that he had been forced to take up arms because of a plot against his life. At no point was there the smallest possibility of his succeeding, and within a few hours he was under arrest. Thomas Cecil, himself Lord Burghley now that his father was dead, commanded the troops that rounded up Essex and his companions and was made a knight of the garter as his reward. (The first Lord Burghley would have regarded his whole career as justified if he had witnessed this triumph of his two sons—both of whom would become earls during the next reign, and both of whom have descendants who are marquesses today.)

Essex, at the end of a trial in which he responded to charges of treason with icy contempt, was found guilty and condemned to death. The situation remained explosive, however. A member of Essex's circle managed to burst in on the queen and demand that she grant the earl an audience; his reward was immediate execution. Essex remained so popular a hero, however, that the council ordered the preachers of London to denounce him from their pulpits. He was beheaded not at Tower Hill, where crowds of his admirers might have gathered, but in one of the Tower's interior courtyards, in the presence of only a few witnesses.

The end of Essex was in a real sense the end for Elizabeth as well. There would be no more favorites; Walter Ralegh, once Essex's chief rival for the queen's affection, was again at court but, perhaps because he was alive and Essex was not, he was no longer doted on by the queen. Elizabeth showed a marked aversion to almost everyone known to have played a part in bringing Essex to ruin or to have denounced him after his fall, telling the French ambassador that she knew she had a share in responsibility for his death. War continued in the Netherlands and in Ireland; though Essex's successor in Ireland was slowly getting the upper hand over Tyrone, he was doing so in ways that ensured perpetual Irish hatred. The costs continued to be nearly insupportable. A Parliament summoned in 1601 was asked to vote a quadruple subsidy, one twice as onerous as the double subsidies extracted from its two immediate predecessors. The news that a Spanish force had been landed in Ireland made it impossible for members to refuse. They did, however, mount an unprecedented challenge to Elizabeth's view of her prerogatives, demanding an end to the monopolies that she had long been either selling to the highest bidder or (as with Dudley and Essex and their wine concession) giving to those she wished to enrich at no direct cost to herself. These monopolies were a burden on the public and had a distorting effect on the economy, and when Parliament first complained of them in 1597 the queen had promised corrective action but done nothing. This time Commons was determined, and when the queen resisted it began work on a bill that would have taken the matter out of her hands and possibly precipitated a crisis. Faced with this defiance, Elizabeth delivered a speech in which she claimed to be surprised to learn that the monopolies had caused so much unhappiness. She committed herself to their elimination. This has often been represented as a victory for the queen, a climactic demonstration of her political skill. Such a verdict is mystifying. She avoided a showdown by surrendering, abandoned a cherished prerogative at the insistence of Parliament, and established no precedent that did her or her successors the slightest good.

In spite of Parliament's approval of unprecedented subsidies, the state of the treasury remained so alarming that the government was selling not only great expanses of Crown land but the queen's jewels. Revenues from the land sales totaled some £800,000 over the last two years of the reign, and even that did not save the government from remaining hundreds of thousands in debt. That much if not all of this land was sold for less than fair market value is suggested by the behavior of Robert Cecil. In 1601 and 1602 he became the leading speculator in the kingdom, using £30,000 of his own money to buy up as much as possible of the property being sold by the government he headed and borrowing heavily to buy still more. Meanwhile he had quietly taken up Essex's old lines of communication with James of Scotland, positioning himself for the next reign by making himself the mastermind behind a transfer of power that the queen had never approved.

Death, when it came, was an enigmatic affair. Elizabeth remained in excellent health through almost all of 1602, continuing to ride, to hunt, and even on occasion to dance. But in December an abrupt decline began, and by the time she moved to Richmond Palace the following month she needed help dismounting her horse and could not climb stairs without the help of a walking stick. Her hands began to swell so badly that the coronation ring she had never removed in four and a half decades had to be cut off. (A second ring, one given to her by Essex, remained.) By March she was feverish, chronically unable to sleep, and unwilling to take nourishment or allow her physicians to attend her. We have already observed her strange final days: the long hours spent standing in a kind of semi-trance, the days and nights on the floor with her finger in her mouth, the final removal to the deathbed when she lost the ability to resist. Though it was later claimed that in her final moments she signaled her wish to be succeeded by the king of Scotland, the people who said so were the very ones who had arranged things that way.

Her passing was not nearly as lamented as legend would have us believe. One wonders what her grandfather would have thought of the dynasty he had started at Bosworth, of what it had wrought and how it ended. One wonders too what her father would have thought. Whether he possibly could have cared.

An Epilogue in Two Parts

The world, as is its way, got along perfectly well without the Tudors. England in particular—which is to say the thin but highly visible slice of the population that reaped the fruit of the Tudor revolution—did very well indeed, not least over the very long term. If it took two centuries to turn the descendants of looters and speculators into the ladies and gentlemen of Jane Austen's novels, for the lucky few the transformation process was as agreeable as it was prolonged. As for the mass of the people, their numbers, their poverty, and their power-lessness simply added to the comforts of the comfortable, providing a virtually limitless supply of desperately needy, all-but-free domestic and agricultural labor. Those unable to find work in the houses and fields of the gentlefolk would become the manpower—and womanpower and childpower—for the "dark Satanic mills" of the Industrial Revolution, which could never have proliferated as they did or been so staggeringly profitable without them. Those unable to do even that work would eventually populate the underworld described by Dickens in *Oliver Twist*.

The Tudor juggernaut left problems of ideology in its wake, but time dissolved most of them. First to go was the Catholic-Protestant split. When James VI of Scotland became James I of England, many of his subjects still retained an at least sentimental attachment to the old religion, and a considerable number took it more seriously than that. But before he had been king three years, the exposure of the Gunpowder

Plot—a plan by despairing and fanatically foolish Catholics to blow up the royal family and the entire Protestant establishment—quickly and permanently changed everything. Catholicism became indefensible, the long campaign to eradicate it accepted as not only justifiable but necessary. Anti-Catholicism became integral with British patriotism. (Catholics were long barred from the universities and from public office, and even today any member of the royal family who so much as married a Catholic would be removed from the line of succession.) Though the Catholic part of the population did not disappear entirely, it became tiny, peculiar, and politically irrelevant. The old religion became the hereditary foible of a minuscule minority of stubbornly eccentric noble and gentry families. Catholics continued to be persecuted, often with brutal harshness, but from now on the only religious differences that mattered would be among Protestants of various kinds.

Less easily settled was the conflict between the Tudor theory of kingship—Henry VIII's expansive view of the authority of the Crown—and the economic and political power that Henry's plundering of the church had bestowed upon a new landowning elite. When James and then his son Charles I persisted in claiming that they, like Henry, were accountable to God only, and when a Parliament now dominated by the gentry refused to agree, a showdown became almost inevitable. It came in the form of the years-long unpleasantness known as the English Civil War, the cutting off of King Charles's head, and Parliament's triumphal emergence as the most powerful institution in the kingdom. By the time all this was sorted out, England was beginning to assemble its global empire. It had begun its rise to a position of astounding preeminence in the family of nations.

Meanwhile the Tudors—not all the Tudors, but Henry VIII and Elizabeth—were not receding into the background as historical personages usually do. Instead they were showing themselves to be the two most durably vivid figures in the whole long saga of English royalty. Henry struck deep roots in the world's imagination as something more than, or at least other than, human, a kind of sacred monster: as pitiless as a viper, a killer not only of enemies but of the utterly innocent as well as of his own best servants and even his wives, but at the same time the magnificently manly centerpiece of Holbein's larger-than-life portraits. Though there was no way to deny his awfulness, throughout the

English-speaking (and Protestant) world it remained impossible to condemn him outright; to do so would be to bring into question the English Reformation and—what continued to matter most—the legitimacy of the people who now owned and governed the empire. No matter that three-plus centuries of Plantagenet rule had produced any number of stronger, braver, *better* kings. Henry had proclaimed himself greater than any of them, bought agreement where he could and coerced it when he had to, and resorted to murder if all else failed. What with one thing and another, the story he told about himself stuck. Every king before him was a pale and shadowy figure by comparison, and no later king ever rivaled his fame. The nature of that fame was deeply ambiguous, however, which is perhaps one reason why it continues to fascinate. Henry remained both sacred (to his beneficiaries certainly, and to all who regarded the Reformation as God's own work) *and* a monster. He has held the world's interest in part because of the question of how such a gifted and fortunate man could have committed such crimes. And because of the related, troubling question of how it is possible for such a thoroughly vicious character to be so . . . *attractive.*

With Elizabeth things are both simpler and more complicated. She is more understandable in ordinary human terms than her father, but at the same time her personality is no less opaque; it is often impossible to be confident that we know what she wanted, what she felt, or what (if anything) she intended in making (or refusing to make) particular decisions. Her image has been much more fluid over the centuries than her father's, and it is undergoing a profound change even now, more than four centuries after her death. Her reputation certainly got off to a fast start: upon becoming queen, she was exalted as the restorer and protector of true religion, and she was still a fairly young woman when the anniversary of her accession was made an official public holiday. But she disappointed and even alienated many of her most ardent early supporters (the proto-Puritans, for example), and the whole last third of her reign was a time of deepening general misery. By the end of her life most of her subjects were pleased to have seen the last of her, and to have what they regarded as the natural order restored in the person of a *male* monarch. But the Stuarts in their turn proved a disappointment too—a disappointment above all to the landowning gentry, whose agents in the House of Commons were unwilling to tolerate Henrician assertions of unlimited royal power. Praising Elizabeth, depicting her reign as England's golden age, became an effective if oblique way of cutting the Stuarts down to size. Her first biographer, William Camden, laid down the tracks along which Elizabethan historiography would run almost up to our own time. In volumes published first in Latin and then in English between 1615 and 1629, he depicted Elizabeth's reign as a half century of peace, prosperity, and true religion harmoniously achieved. It mattered little that the picture he painted could have been scarcely recognizable to anyone alive in England from 1559 to 1603. The figure of Elizabeth became sacred in its way, too, and thanks to the disregarding of certain inconvenient facts it was never nearly as dark as her father's. She became part saint and part goddess, the highest expression of what England was coming to see as its own quasi-sacred place in the world.

The pedestal on which she had been placed was given a vigorous shake in the nineteenth century by historical writers as esteemed (in their own time) as Macaulay and Froude, and by the better historian John Lingard, but it was too firmly planted to topple. To the contrary, these early challenges were followed by decades in which the study of Elizabethan England was dominated by scholars whose belief in the queen's greatness and the glory of her reign was little more qualified than Camden's had been three centuries before. Possibly in unconscious reaction to a decline in England's global stature, A. F. Pollard, A. L. Rowse, John Neale, and Conyers Read together erected a fortress of hagiography so formidable that for a time it must have seemed that there could never be anything more to say. Gloriana was not only greater than ever but evidently more secure in her greatness.

There is always something more to say when the subject is history, however; time passes and perspectives change. The chief vulnerability of the Pollard-Rowse-Neale-Conyers consensus was its close connection to the old Whig school of history, according to which everything that had happened was to be celebrated because all of it was part of the (divinely ordained?) process by which England had ascended inexorably to greatness. Membership in this school required believing that the English were fortunate—and had also always been grateful, most of them—to be rid of everything the Tudors had cast aside. Such a subjective judgment was by definition unprovable at best, and the work of a new generation of scholars has rendered it untenable. The cooling of ancient religious passions—the evolution of Britain into an essentially secular, post-Christian culture—has made a dispassionate examination of the past possible at last. The result has been—still is—a literally radical revaluation of Elizabeth, her reign, her times, and their meaning. One could cite many examples, but for present purposes one will stand in for all: Eamon Duffy's *The Stripping of the Altars*. This single book, since its first edition was published by Yale University Press in 1992, has made it impossible to responsibly assert that at the time of Henry VIII's revolution the English church was a decadent, moribund, obsolete, or obsolescent institution that had lost its central place in the everyday lives of the English people.

Elizabeth—and with her the whole Tudor story—looks very different today than she did half a century ago. She appears likely to change at least as much again when another twenty or fifty years have passed. The process is still at full flood. Whether or when it will end, whether and to what extent the popular image of the Tudors will be reshaped by all the fresh scholarship, we can only wait to see.

It is somehow impossible to resist ending on an admittedly minor note, by making a final visit to the amazing Dudleys.

Edmund Dudley had risen high in the reign of Henry VII only to be destroyed. His son John had risen even higher in the reign of Edward VI only to be destroyed also. One of John's sons was married to a queen of England (even if she was queen for only nine days), another had come close to marrying a much longer-lasting queen, but in the end it had all come to nothing. When we left them, the Dudleys appeared to have become extinct. The last of the line, Ambrose Dudley, Earl of Warwick, had a long marriage but no children. His brother Robert, Earl of Leicester—Elizabeth's beloved Rob—had died in 1588 and had been preceded to the grave by his little son Lord Denbigh, the only child of his late marriage to Lettice Knollys Devereux. (A very Dudleyesque footnote: Leicester had hoped to marry Denbigh to Arabella Stuart, a descendant of Henry VIII's sister Margaret. If James VI and I had died without children, Arabella Stuart would have had a strong claim to the English throne and the Dudleys might have had a *third* chance to become kings through marriage.)

But in fact the story was not over. In 1574, five years before the birth of Denbigh, Leicester had had a son with Lady Douglas Sheffield, a daughter of the queen's admiral Lord Howard of Effingham and therefore a royal cousin through the Boleyn connection. Lady Sheffield would later claim that she and Leicester had been married, but he would always deny this and she could produce no documentary evidence. (Possibly there had been a sham ceremony as part of an elaborate seduction scheme.) Leicester did, however, recognize the boy, whose name was Robert, as "my base son," enrolling him at Oxford as *filius comiti* or earl's son and providing for him in his will.

By the time of Elizabeth's death, this new Robert Dudley was in his late twenties and, having married very young, was the father of a family that would soon grow to include six daughters. He was a true Dudley—tall and handsome, skilled not only in handling horses and dogs and the sports of the aristocracy but at mathematics as well—who at age seventeen had been temporarily exiled from court for kissing the maid of honor who later became his wife. Shortly after Elizabeth died, taking her jealous resentment of any wives and offspring of the Earl of Leicester with her, Dudley asked the Court of the Star Chamber to affirm that his parents had in fact been married and that he was, therefore, rightful heir to the earldoms of Warwick and Leicester. Whatever the merits of his case (they have been in dispute ever since), a finding in Dudley's favor would have given rise to horrendous complications having to do with property already distributed to other heirs. (Among those other heirs were the Sidney family—Sir Philip Sidney, that most perfect of Elizabethan soldier-poet-courtiers, had a Dudley as his mother.) The court never ruled on Dudley's legitimacy or lack thereof, instead taking an easy way out by dismissing his suit on technical grounds, locking up the evidence, and forbidding him to pursue the matter further.

Dudley then requested and received King James's permission to go traveling. He departed for the continent, secretly taking with him his beautiful young cousin Elizabeth Southwell, who went disguised as a boy. In short order the pair reported from Lyon, France, that they had converted to Catholicism and married. It was one of the great scandals of the age.

Dudley and his bride proceeded to Florence, where he entered the service of the Medici grand dukes. His career there was long and distinguished: he became a respected authority on all things maritime—sailing to the New World, designing and building ships and harbors, writing books on navigation—while also developing a "curative powder" of some kind and receiving a patent for a silk-weaving machine. He and Elizabeth had half a dozen sons, a fresh crop of Dudleys but now named Carlo, Fernando, Cosmo, and the like. At that point we lose track of them. If there are still Dudleys in Italy today, it is easy to believe that they must be dashing figures, and having fabulous adventures.

Sources and Notes

Nothing could be easier, in connection with the Tudors, than the assembly of an impressively weighty bibliography. The available literature, even the fairly *recent* literature, is so vast as to bring the concept of infinity to mind. And few exercises could be of less real value to the general reader for whom this book is intended. What may have some value—at least in a book that is an attempt at synthesis, without any claim to plowing new ground in original source materials—is an indication of which works the author has found to be particularly useful.

As to source notes, to the extent that the facts of the Tudor story are knowable (many are not, and after more than four centuries it is unlikely that they ever will be) they have by now been sifted and settled by something like fifteen generations of scholars and writers. Many of the facts, often the most significant or just plain interesting, recur so frequently in the literature of the Tudor era that to give sources for them would (while requiring dozens of pages) be no less pointless than a comprehensive bibliography. The author of the current work has elected, therefore, to provide sources in particular cases only: for quotations that do not appear to have become widely familiar as a result of frequent previous use, and—what seems especially necessary—for those facts and opinions that are most likely to challenge the reader's preconceptions because they are most at variance with popular views of the Tudors. The resulting source notes appear below, along with citations of those books to which the author feels particularly indebted. Both things are arranged under headings corresponding to the four parts of this book.

In assembling and verifying the facts out of which his narrative has been constructed—dates and biographical details, for example—the author has relied heavily on one of the world's most awesomely comprehensive and authoritative resources: the sixty-volume 2004 edition of the *Oxford Dictionary of National Biography* (*DNB* in the notes below). Use has also been made of *The*

Encyclopaedia Britannica, and for the same reasons. Readers seeking to confirm statements of fact for which sources have not been provided, or to pursue additional information, are encouraged to begin by consulting those two works.

The Subject Overall

Studies dealing in depth with the reigns of all five Tudor monarchs have always been rare, at least in comparison to biographies of individual figures, and some of those that were once well known are now discredited and largely forgotten. Examples are the works of Macaulay and Froude, who survive as masters of style and of storytelling, but not of scholarship. An exception is the relevant part (volumes 4, 5, and 6) of John Lingard's *History of England* (New York: Publication Society of America, 1912). Though inevitably superseded in many details since it first appeared early in the nineteenth century, this remarkable work (pioneering in its use and sophisticated evaluation of original source material) remains a fruitful and broadly reliable guide to sixteenth-century England, rich both in facts and insights. Lingard is obscure today mainly because he has *always* been obscure. He was too far ahead of his time, replacing fable with fact more than a century before England was ready for so much objectivity.

Noteworthy among much more recent treatments of the whole dynasty are works by G. R. Elton, especially *England Under the Tudors* (Methuen, 1955) and *The Tudor Constitution* (Cambridge University Press, 1960); John Guy's *Tudor England* (Oxford, 1988); and Penry Williams's *The Tudor Regime* (Oxford, 1979). These are scholarly achievements of a very high order and immensely useful, though not well suited—or indeed intended—for a general audience.

PART ONE
An Excess of Good Fortune

In tracing the careers of the first two Tudor kings, the author has taken as his guide two biographies generally still regarded as the best on their subjects: S. B. Chrimes, *Henry VII* (University of California Press, 1972), and J. J. Scarisbrick, *Henry VIII* (University of California Press, 1968). G. W. Bernard's *The King's Reformation: Henry VIII and the Remaking of the English Church* (Yale University Press, 2005) provides a massive and magisterial overview of the first of the Tudor reformations.

Other notably good sources of the information and ideas presented in this section (and in several cases later parts of the book as well) include:

Duffy, Eamon. *The Stripping of the Altars: Traditional Religion in England, 1400–1580,* 2nd ed. Yale University Press, 2005.

Fraser, Antonia. *The Wives of Henry VIII.* Vintage, 1994.

Griffiths, R. A., and R. S. Thomas. *The Making of the Tudor Dynasty.* Alan Sutton, 1985.

Loades, David, ed. *Chronicles of the Tudor Kings.* Bramley, 1996.

———. *Henry VIII: Church, Court and Conflict.* National Archives, 2007.

Mackie, J. D. *The Earlier Tudors, 1485–1558.* Oxford, 1952.

Marius, Richard. *Thomas More.* Vintage, 1985.

Mattingly, Garret. *Catherine of Aragon.* Little, Brown, 1941.

Smith, Lacey Baldwin. *Henry VIII: The Mask of Power.* Houghton Mifflin, 1972.

Starkey, David. *Six Wives: The Queens of Henry VIII.* HarperCollins, 2003.

Williams, Neville. *Henry VII.* Weidenfeld & Nicolson, 1973.

Notes for Part One

PAGE

3   *But because we have no eyewitness accounts . . .* : Good if conventional introductions to the Battle of Bosworth appear in Griffiths and Thomas, *Tudor Dynasty,* and Michael Bennett, *The Battle of Bosworth* (Sutton, 2000).

9   *The detailed descriptions in countless books . . .* : The conventional understanding of Bosworth is seriously and responsibly challenged by Michael K. Jones in *Bosworth 1485: Psychology of a Battle* (Tempus, 2002).

31   *On top of all his other blessings . . .* : As Lawrence Stone observes in *The Causes of the English Revolution, 1529–1642* (Harper & Row, 1972), p. 88, the concept of the divine right of kings figured importantly in the thinking of radical (anti-Roman) religious reformers from William Tyndale onward. Henry VIII's exposure to and embrace of such thinking, and Anne Boleyn's role, is shown in Fraser, *Wives,* p. 145, among other sources.

33   *When the seemingly endless demands for new taxes . . .* : Popular resistance to the tax levies of the mid-1520s, and the shift of blame to Wolsey, is in Carolly Erickson's *Great Harry* (Simon & Schuster, 1980), p. 173.

46   *One of the mentors of Henry's youth . . .* : John Fisher's upholding of Henry's marriage to Catherine of Aragon is in Fraser, *Wives,* p. 139.

47   *Henry, clutching at straws, suggested . . .* : The question of how Leviticus should have been translated is an insuperable one for anyone lacking knowledge of Hebrew. Bernard, *King's Reformation,* p. 17, and others take the position that Henry's interpretation lacks merit. By contrast, Richard Rex in *The Tudors* (Tempus, 2002), p. 56, is more supportive.

47   *About this, too, he was proved wrong . . .* : Bernard, *King's Reformation,* p. 18.

50   *"No one would ever have taken her . . ."* : This quote, and the one on the following page about Henry being "struck by the dart of love," appear in the *DNB* entry for Anne Boleyn.

51   *In one of the many letters he sent her . . .* : *DNB* entry for Anne Boleyn.

51   *It is entirely possible* . . . : Bernard, *King's Reformation*, p. 7, provides reasons why Henry might have chosen to defer consummation of his relationship with Anne.

53   *"I close my eyes before such horror"* . . . : Scarisbrick, *Henry VIII*, p. 216.

55   *No easy solutions were open* . . . : The extent to which Clement VII had freedom of action in dealing with Henry's annulment suit is one of the unresolved and probably unresolvable questions of Tudor history. The ambiguities and contradictions of the pope's situation are explained in ibid., p. 197.

57   *Instead of congratulating her* . . . : Erickson, *Great Harry*, p. 199.

57   *To this group he delivered an address* . . . : Fraser, *Wives*, p. 155.

58   *When it came back to him* . . . : Erickson, *Great Harry*, p. 223.

67   *That Wolsey himself felt any compelling* . . . : While Scarisbrick, *Henry VIII*, p. 47, argues persuasively that Wolsey would have pursued very different policies had he aspired to the papacy, Elton, *England Under*, p. 84, says without offering much evidence that the cardinal wanted to be pope throughout all his years in high office.

70   *"Sir," she began in the accent* . . . : Fraser, *Wives*, p. 160.

72   *"No, my lord, not so"* . . . : Bernard, *King's Reformation*, p. 105.

73   *He felt obliged to do this* . . . : Loades, *Henry VIII*, p. 83.

74   *A considerable exercise of the imagination* . . . : Among the many good introductions to England in the sixteenth century are Penry Williams, *Life in Tudor England* (Batsford, 1964) and John Morrill, ed., *The Oxford Illustrated History of Tudor and Stuart Britain* (Oxford University Press, 1996).

74   *The great humanist scholar Erasmus* . . . : Penry Williams, *Life*, p. 104.

76   *The population, which in the year 1300* . . . : Loades, *Henry VIII*, p. 9.

76   *By 1485 the population was again growing* . . . : Guy, *Tudor England*, p. 10.

79   *"The people here are held in little more esteem* . . .": W. G. Hoskins, *The Age of Plunder* (Longmans, 1971), p. 105.

84   *"Inasmuch as ye, the fathers of the laws* . . .": Scarisbrick, *Henry VIII*, p. 238.

85   *"God forbid that he should die!"* . . . : Lingard, *History of England*, p. 4:537.

85   *On October 26, in conversing* . . . : Scarisbrick, *Henry VIII*, p. 246.

87   *As early as 1515 during a dispute* . . . : Elton, *England Under*, p. 107.

87   *"God hath made in every realm* . . .": Guy, *Tudor England*, p. 121.

88   *"This," he is supposed to have said* . . . : Mackie, *Earlier Tudors*, p. 352.

89   *Henry, whose opinion of himself* . . . : Smith, *Mask of Power*, p. 124.

90   *Genuine and legitimate power, More said* . . . : Marius, *Thomas More*, p. 365.

91   *The England of 1530 contained* . . . : Good introductions to the religious life of pre-Reformation England are Penry Williams, *Life;* Maurice Keen, *English Society in the Later Middle Ages* (Penguin, 1990); Francis Aidan Gasquet, *England Under the Old Religion and Other Essays* (G. Bell & Sons, 1912); and most important, Duffy, *Stripping of Altars.*

99   *Stern and unfamiliar penalties* . . . : Guy, *Tudor England*, p. 144.

101   *When he had heard Cranmer out* . . . : Scarisbrick, *Henry VIII*, p. 255.

103   *"Stop, sir," he said in French* . . . : Lingard, *History of England*, p. 4:545.

104   *Martin Luther himself, while insisting . . .* : Ibid., p. 4:549.

106   *According to one of his confidants . . .* : Ibid., p. 4:555.

106   *Henry, meanwhile, the bit in his teeth . . .* : Bernard, *King's Reformation*, p. 38.

111   *By the end of the reign this number . . .* : David M. Loades, *The Tudor Court* (Barnes & Noble, 1987), p. 185.

116   *At the same time he involved himself . . .* : The words about Wolsey being "persuaded from vainglory," and those on the following page about presumptuous sinister practices," are in Scarisbrick, *Henry VIII*, p. 239.

118   *"Father Abbot," he said upon arrival . . .* : Smith, *Mask of Power*, p. 107.

119   *Delay, long a source of frustration . . .* : Bernard, *King's Reformation*, p. 52, and Scarisbrick, *Henry VIII*, p. 291, explain Henry's gradually emerging desire for delay.

121   *In the message that conveyed their offer . . .* : Elton, *England Under*, p. 125.

121   *If they came from John Fisher . . .* : Marius, *Thomas More*, p. 379, says: "The saving words usually have been incorrectly ascribed to John Fisher. But their insertion seems to have been an effort by the government to soften the blow . . ."

122   *He blithely assured Tunstal . . .* : Bernard, *King's Reformation*, p. 180, and Scarisbrick, *Henry VIII*, p. 278.

123   *A letter signed by seventeen members . . .* : Scarisbrick, *Henry VIII*, p. 277.

124   *"This proposition cannot be counted as heretical" . . .* : Marius, *Thomas More*, p. 380.

125   *In a stroke of sheer good luck . . .* : Mackie, *Earlier Tudors*, p. 350.

127   *The comptroller of the king's household . . .* : Neville Williams, *Henry VIII and His Court* (Macmillan, 1972), p. 117.

135   *"God grant him a good conscience" . . .* : Bernard, *King's Reformation*, p. 75.

138   *"My lord," a surprisingly good-humored . . ."*: Lingard, *History of England*, p. 4:562.

139   *The supreme oddity, in any case . . .* : Elton, *England Under*, p. 131, suggests that the initiative lay with Cromwell rather than the king, while Bernard, *King's Reformation*, p. 60, takes the opposite position.

143   *Cromwell had pulled it off . . .* : The adherence of most of England to the old religion is accepted today by all of the most respected historians. See Elton, *England Under*, p. 109, and Scarisbrick, *Henry VIII*, pp. 241 and 328. Duffy, *Stripping of Altars*, provides an exhaustive demonstration of the vitality of the pre-Reformation English church.

144   *The churchmen were ordered to give . . .* : Mackie, *Earlier Tudors*, p. 355.

149   *In doing so he crushed whatever autonomy . . .* : Ibid., p. 749.

153   *Henry VIII on more than one occasion . . .* : Francis Aidan Gasquet, *Henry VIII and the English Monasteries* (John Hodges, 1889), p. 1:156.

153   *"I beseech your Grace to take good heed . . ."*: Derek Wilson, *In the Lion's Court* (St. Martin's Press, 2002), p. 339.

155   *From the start of the crisis . . .* : Bernard, *King's Reformation*, p. 173.

156   *"Well-beloved subjects," Henry told . . .* : Scarisbrick, *Henry VIII*, p. 299.

157   *Thus it was that May 15 became . . .* : Ibid., p. 300.

160   *It seems an exceedingly strange coincidence . . .* : Among fruitful one-volume

introductions to the Reformation both in England and on the continent are A. G. Dickens, *The English Reformation* (Schocken, 1968); James D. Tracy, *Europe's Reformations 1450–1650* (Rowman & Littlefield, 1999); John Bowker, ed., *The Cambridge Illustrated History of Religion* (Cambridge University Press, 2001); Geoffrey Woodward, *The Sixteenth Century Reformation* (Lion, 2001); and Gordon Mursell, gen. ed., *The Story of Christian Spirituality* (Hodder & Stoughton, 2001).

164   *Europe's leading humanist* . . . : Gasquet, *Henry and Monasteries*, p. 1:120.

167   *He had been drafting, presumably for delivery* . . . : Marius, *Thomas More*, p. 421.

173   *Knowing little of who Cranmer* . . . : Scarisbrick, *Henry VIII*, p. 310.

174   *Cromwell was ready with an answer* . . . : Elton, *England Under*, p. 132; Mackie, *Earlier Tudors*, p. 357; and Guy, *Tudor England*, p. 132.

174   *This happened on March 30* . . . : A detailed account of the oddities of Cranmer's installation ceremony is in Lingard, *History of England*, p. 5:6.

175   *By all accounts the news* . . . : Scarisbrick, *Henry VIII*, p. 313.

175   *But when he wrote to the king* . . . : Fraser, *Wives*, p. 190.

PART TWO
Monster

W. G. Hoskins's *The Age of Plunder* (Longmans, 1971) delivers what its title promises: a trenchant study of the price paid by the population of England for the innovations of Henry VIII. David Starkey's *The Reign of Henry VIII: Personalities and Politics* (Vintage, 2002) is rich in insights about the last two decades of Henry's life. Much detail about the end of the reign is to be found in Jesse Childs, *Henry VIII's Last Victim* (Jonathan Cape, 2006), and Robert Hutchinson, *The Last Days of Henry VIII* (William Morrow, 2006).

Notes

PAGE

181   *The first victim* . . . : The story of Elizabeth Barton is told in Scarisbrick, *Henry VIII*, p. 321, and in much greater detail in Bernard, *King's Reformation*, p. 87.

182   *It is not certain that these reported confessions* . . . : Fraser, *Wives*, p. 211, writes that Barton *"was said"* (italics added) to have recanted, and Bernard, *King's Reformation*, p. 94, refers to her "scaffold speech" as having been *"put into her mouth"* by an unfriendly writer.

184   *There Barton, perhaps because she was* . . . : Bernard, *King's Reformation*, p. 94.

186   *The act's assertion that Henry was to be succeeded* . . . : The 1534 Succession Act appears in its entirely in Elton, *Tudor Constitution*, p. 6.

186   *Conveniently, Parliament neglected to specify* . . . : Marius, *Thomas More*, p. 459.

187   *Cromwell continued to take care* . . . : Guy, *Tudor England*, p. 135.

195   *A special version of the succession oath* . . . : Bernard, *King's Reformation*, p. 157.

196   *The results of the visits were* . . . : Ibid., p. 157.

197   *Several were clearly unhappy* . . . : Ibid., p. 178.

199   *To be guilty of high treason* . . . : Elton, *Tudor Constitution*, p. 61.

200   *This probably explains the insertion* . . . : The intent behind the inclusion of "maliciously," and the word's significance for the king, are in Guy, *Tudor England*, p. 139, and Marius, *Thomas More*, p. 480.

200   *It was called the Act of First Fruits* . . . : The act is explained in Elton, *Tudor Constitution*, p. 42, and it appears in full on page 53 of the same book. The resulting increase in Crown revenue is detailed in Guy, *Tudor England*, p. 136.

200   *He was given a traditional levy* . . . : Taxation on the basis of "fifteenths and tenths" is explained in Mackie, *Earlier Tudors*, p. 353.

201   *The king's gambling, his many luxuries* . . . : Fraser, *Wives*, p. 211, and Hoskins, *Age of Plunder*, p. 208, provide details on Henry's spending on palaces.

202   *Even the most reform-minded of the bishops* . . . : Lingard, *History of England*, p. 5:51.

203   *Background: Monks, Nuns, and Friars*: An excellent introduction to the religious orders of England is C. H. Lawrence, *Medieval Monasticism* (Longmans, 1993).

209   *Nothing of the kind can be said* . . . : The story of the Carthusians is in Lingard, *History of England*, p. 5:39, and in much greater detail in Bernard, *King's Reformation*, p. 160. An entire chapter on the subject, with many of the statements about Sir John Gage and John Houghton and others in the pages that follow, appears in Gasquet, *Henry and Monasteries*, pp. 1:202ff.

216   *It is possible that the king himself was present* . . . : This and Houghton's words *"I call almighty God to witness"* are attributed to Eustace Chapuys in Gasquet, *Henry and Monasteries*, p. 1:224.

217   *"Lo, dost thou not see, Meg . . ."*: Marius, *Thomas More*, p. 491.

219   *"Now I have in good faith discharged my mind . . ."*: Bernard, *King's Reformation*, p. 145.

219   *The new pope, Paul III, unwittingly* . . . : Scarisbrick, *Henry VIII*, p. 328.

219   *He warned that the pope could send* . . . : Lingard, *History of England*, p. 5:40.

220   *He told the court that when the king* . . . : Bernard, *King's Reformation*, p. 123.

221   *"What a monstrous matter is this!"* . . . : Ibid., p. 124.

222   *He asked the people to pray* . . . : Ibid., p. 125.

228   *What Rich had to say* . . . : Ibid., p. 146.

230   *"Can it therefore seem likely . . ."*: Marius, *Thomas More*, p. 506.

230   *Being a good lawyer, More* . . . : Bernard, *King's Reformation*, p. 149.

231   *"God preserve all my friends . . ."*: Lingard, *History of England*, p. 5:45.

231   *In January he had been given* . . . : Ibid., p. 5:51, and Bernard, *King's Reformation*, p. 245.

233   *What Cromwell and the king intended* . . . : Mackie, *Earlier Tudors*, p. 376.

235   *The men Cromwell chose* . . . : The character, motives, and conduct of the monastic visitors are subjected to critical scrutiny in Bernard, *King's Reformation*, p. 254; Elton, *England Under*, p. 144; Lingard, *History of England*, p. 5:54; and Geoffrey Moorhouse, *The Pilgrimage of Grace* (Weidenfeld & Nicolson, 2002), p. 27. However, Bernard, *King's Reformation*, p. 247, argues that the original intent of Cromwell's visitations was entirely honorable.

236   *Two of the most active* . . . : Citing the reports and correspondence of the visitors themselves, Gasquet, *Henry and Monasteries*, p. 1:286, details the astonishing number of monasteries examined by Layton, Legh, and others in only a few weeks.

237   *"Thanks for excusing my getting up* . . ." : Ibid., p. 1:278.

237   *When Chancellor Audley could find no basis* . . . : Ibid., pp. 1:278–80.

237   *There is no reason to think that Eustace Chapuys* . . . : Ibid., p. 1:265.

239   *Nor was there any acknowledgment* . . . : Bernard, *King's Reformation*, p. 258.

247   *"Lastly, I make this vow* . . .": Catherine's words and the autopsy results are in Fraser, *Wives*, pp. 228 and 229.

248   *Henry, remembering the restraint* . . . : That and "Much scratching and by-blows" are in Carolly Erickson, *Anne Boleyn* (Macmillan, 1984), p. 242.

248   *According to one story, she tried* . . . : Henry's jousting accident is in Scaris-brick, *Henry VIII*, p. 485, the story of Jane Seymour on the king's knee in Fraser, *Wives*, p. 233.

248   *All the larger and richer houses* . . . : Mackie, *Earlier Tudors*, p. 376.

250   *He began to complain that Anne* . . . : Fraser, *Wives*, p. 233; Mackie, *Earlier Tudors*, p. 379.

251   *On May 19, in the moment before* . . . : Fraser, *Wives*, p. 257.

252   *Two days after Anne was found guilty* . . . : Neville Williams, *Henry VIII*, p. 146.

253   *The information gathered by Cromwell's visitors* . . . : Mackie, *Earlier Tudors*, p. 378, put the number of smaller monasteries at 399—372 in England and 27 in Wales—and estimated that 220 of these were eliminated in the first round of suppressions. Writing half a century later, Bernard, *King's Reformation*, p. 271, put the total at 419 and said 243 were dissolved.

254   *Some of the confiscated land was sold* . . . : Mackie, *Earlier Tudors*, p. 378.

255   *"We beseech your favor* . . .": This letter, and the appeal for the Carmarthan house, are in Gasquet, *Henry and Monasteries*, p. 2:34, giving Chapuys's reports as source.

256   *The monks inside, informed that* . . . : Gasquet, *Henry and Monasteries*, p. 2:37.

257   *After comparing Henry not only to Richard III* . . . : Bernard, *King's Reformation*, p. 220.

258   *He wrote to Mary, calling her* . . . : Lingard, *History of England*, p. 5:80.

258   *Still later, sufficiently rehabilitated* . . . : Neville Williams, *Henry VIII*, p. 152.

259   *In a truly extraordinary step* . . . : Mackie, *Earlier Tudors*, p. 381.

260   *Even today scholars disagree* . . . : Bernard, *King's Reformation*, p. 281, says

that the Articles expressed Henry's search for a "middle way." Elton, *England Under,* p. 153, says similarly that they were a "compromise" between the demands of conservatives and evangelicals. By contrast Guy, *Tudor England,* p. 179, emphasizes their "reformed" character, and Scarisbrick, *Henry VIII,* p. 399, their "Lutheran" content. But Mackie, *Earlier Tudors,* p. 382, notes that even Reginald Pole found little to object to in them.

260   *This is unmistakable in the preface* . . . : Bernard, *King's Reformation,* p. 277.

261   *The dedication offered to that king* . . . : Neville Williams, *Henry VIII,* p. 162; Penry Williams, *The Tudor Regime* (Oxford, 1979), p. 361.

262   *Sixteenth-century Europe was a world* . . . : See Alison Sim, *Food and Feast in Tudor England* (Sutton, 1997).

267   *The story of how* . . . : Succinct but detailed accounts of the Pilgrimage of Grace are in Bernard, *King's Reformation,* p. 293; Scarisbrick, *Henry VIII,* p. 339; and Lingard, *History of England,* p. 5:82. Moorhouse, *Pilgrimage of Grace,* is of course a much fuller account.

268   *This was in no way unusual* . . . : Mackie, *Earlier Tudors,* p. 387.

268   *Wherever such men fell into the hands* . . . : Bernard, *King's Reformation,* p. 306.

269   *The king denounced Lincolnshire* . . . : Scarisbrick, *Henry VIII,* p. 342.

269   *He would have been overwhelmed* . . . : Mackie, *Earlier Tudors,* p. 388.

270   *Meanwhile King Henry, whose situation* . . . : Scarisbrick, *Henry VIII,* p. 343.

273   *Aske received a letter from the king* . . . : Words from the letters exchanged by Henry and Aske are in Gasquet, *Henry and Monasteries,* p. 2:131.

277   *When they finished in mid-July* . . . : Extensive treatments of the *Institution* are in Scarisbrick, *Henry VIII,* p. 399, and Bernard, *King's Reformation,* p. 475.

277   *The evangelicals hated much of it* . . . : The bishops' groveling preface, and the message from the king, are in Scarisbrick, *Henry VIII,* p. 404.

278   *The Bishops' Book as first published* . . . : Henry's changes are in Scarisbrick, *Henry VIII,* p. 405.

280   *A more plausible explanation is* . . . : Chris Skidmore, *Edward VI: The Lost King of England* (Weidenfeld & Nicolson, 2007), p. 19.

280   *In rather short order he was reported* . . . : Erickson, *Great Harry,* p. 282.

281   *Such memories were freshened by* . . . : Mackie, *Earlier Tudors,* p. 397.

289   *His once-powerful constitution* . . . : Perspectives on Henry's health problems are in Smith, *Mask of Power,* pp. 15 and 264; Erickson, *Great Harry,* pp. 328 and 360; and Scarisbrick, *Henry VIII,* p. 485.

290   *But he was a frail reed* . . . : Smith, *Mask of Power,* p. 94.

292   *But Henry proved a dangerous partner* . . . : The story of the near-arrest of Catherine Parr is in Fraser, *Wives,* p. 388.

293   *A farce was played out* . . . : Lingard, *History of England,* p. 5:189.

293   *The valuables hauled away* . . . : Mackie, *Earlier Tudors,* p. 396.

294   *Quite apart from the colossal sums* . . . : Lingard, *History of England,* p. 5:97.

294   *He would be able to expand the ranks* . . . : Ibid., p. 5:99.

294   *In the last eight or nine years* . . . : Mackie, *Earlier Tudors,* p. 400.

294   *He squandered his riches at home first* . . . : Guy, *Tudor England*, p. 184.

296   *The French and Scottish campaigns* . . . : The financial figures in this paragraph are all from Guy, *Tudor England*, p. 192.

296   *Students of the subject have calculated* . . . : Lingard, *History of England*, p. 5:195.

297   *In 1542 Henry borrowed £112,000* . . . : The forced loans of this period are in Mackie, *Earlier Tudors*, p. 411. The financial consequences of the campaigns in France are in Elton, *England Under*, p. 198, and Scarisbrick, *Henry VIII*, p. 453.

297   *Next Henry demanded and got* . . . : Smith, *Mask of Power*, p. 244.

297   *Two London aldermen dared to object* . . . : Lingard, *History of England*, p. 5:193, and Mackie, *Earlier Tudors*, p. 411.

297   *Foreign loans totaled some £272,000* . . . : Mackie, *Earlier Tudors*, p. 413.

297   *Soon its coins were only half gold* . . . : Erickson, *Great Harry*, p. 352.

297   *Henry reaped £373,000* . . . : Smith, *Mask of Power*, p. 172.

297   *Prices rose some 25 percent* . . . : The inflation rate and the "holy anchor" quote are in Erickson, *Great Harry*, p. 353.

298   *Under this law, anyone who "lived idly* . . .": Hoskins, *Age of Plunder*, p. 106.

298   *Those impressed into bondage in this way* . . . : Lingard, *History of England*, p. 5:258.

298   *The king's word literally became law* . . . : Ibid., p. 5:129.

299   *The penalty in connection with these doctrines* . . . : Ibid.

301   *Thus in 1543 he drew out of Parliament* . . . : The Act for the Advancement of True Religion, with the condemnation of Tyndale's translation, is in Mackie, *Earlier Tudors*, p. 429, and Lingard, *History of England*, p. 5:159.

301   *It was not to be opened by "prentices* . . .": Guy, *Tudor England*, p. 194.

301   *Almost simultaneously with the Act* . . . : Scarisbrick, *Henry VIII*, pp. 399 and 407.

302   *Angrily, even tearfully, he complained* . . . : Mackie, *Earlier Tudors*, p. 433, and Lingard, *History of England*, p. 5:202.

302   *Still later it was reported* . . . : Bernard, *King's Reformation*, pp. 157 and 489.

303   *In the same year that Forest perished* . . . : Erickson, *Great Harry*, p. 294.

304   *"Answer neither out of St. Augustine* . . .": Smith, *Mask of Power*, p. 154.

305   *On December 6 Montague and Exeter* . . . : Erickson, *Great Harry*, p. 288.

306   *Contrary to what has often been asserted* . . . : Bernard, *King's Reformation*, p. 574; Guy, *Tudor England*, pp. 178 and 186; and Scarisbrick, *Henry VIII*, p. 376.

306   *The endlessly useful Richard Rich* . . . : Neville Williams, *Henry VIII*, p.195.

308   *"No," she said, "my head never* . . .": Lingard, *History of England*, p. 5:126.

308   *The executioner had to chase her* . . . : Fraser, *Wives*, p. 342.

308   *Every place of habitation was to be destroyed* . . . : Erickson, *Great Harry*, p. 334.

308   *This time he demolished* . . . : Data about the destruction in Scotland and the quote about Henry's "not misliking" the plan to assassinate Beaton are in Lingard, *History of England*, p. 5:184.

PART THREE
A King Too Soon and a Queen Too Late

The author is grateful to have been able to make use of:

Erickson, Carrolly. *Bloody Mary: The Life of Mary Tudor.* Robson, 1995.

Loades, D. M. *Mary Tudor.* National Archives, 2006.

———. *Two Tudor Conspiracies.* Cambridge, 1965.

MacCulloch, Diarmaid. *Tudor Church Militant: Edward VI and the Protestant Reformation.* Penguin, 1999.

Skidmore, Chris. *Edward VI: The Lost King of England.* Weidenfeld & Nicolson, 2007.

Wilson, Derek. *The Uncrowned Kings of England: The Black Legend of the Dudleys.* Constable, no date given.

Notes

PAGE

314 *The main points of dispute were familiar . . .* : Religious divisions as of the start of Edward's reign are examined in MacCulloch, *Church Militant*, pp. 2 and 63; Skidmore, *Edward VI*, p. 7; and Mackie, *Earlier Tudors*, p. 426.

315 *This had become more true than ever . . .* : The difficulties faced by the more ambitious reformers late in Henry's reign are addressed in Smith, *Mask of Power*, pp. 147 and 159, and Mackie, *Earlier Tudors*, p. 429.

315 *Even if they had been left free to express . . .* : MacCulloch, *Church Militant*, p. 59.

321 *Surrey, whose hopes for a military career . . .* : Mackie, *Earlier Tudors*, p. 420.

321 *They ensnared Gardiner in a clumsy . . .* : Scarisbrick, *Henry VIII*, p. 490.

322 *It was by no means clear that the jury . . .* : Mackie, *Earlier Tudors*, p. 422.

322 *Thereafter Norfolk, in an effort . . .* : *DNB* entry on Thomas Howard, third Duke of Norfolk.

323 *So was anyone too closely . . .* : Henry's rejection and distrust of Gardiner is in Erickson, *Great Harry*, p. 371.

323 *It is not certain that this was a usurpation . . .* : Lingard, *History of England*, p. 5:235.

324 *He was given four manors . . .* : *DNB* entry for Edward Seymour, Duke of Somerset.

325 *Overall this splendid payday . . .* : Guy, *Tudor England*, p. 199.

326 *He also empowered himself to assemble . . .* : Skidmore, *Edward VI*, p. 66.

327 *Edward was a lad of above-average intelligence . . .* : Skidmore, *Edward VI*, p. 62, and Lingard, *History of England*, p. 5:237.

328 *"Peace and concord" were promised . . .* : Skidmore, *Edward VI*, p. 61.

328 *It was, "as God's viceregent and Christ's vicar . . ."*: Lingard, *History of England*, p. 5:238.

329   *It is more pathetic than impressive . . .* : Skidmore, *Edward VI*, p. 149.

329   *The coronation of the new king . . .* : MacCulloch, *Church Militant*, p. 126, and Skidmore, *Edward VI*, p. 69.

330   *Even more provocatively, the visitors . . .* : Lingard, *History of England*, p. 5:251; MacCulloch, *Church Militant*, p. 70; and Skidmore, *Edward VI*, p. 89.

338   *In the six years following Henry VIII's death . . .* : The numbers in this paragraph are from Guy, *Tudor England*, p. 203.

338   *Statistical precision is impossible . . .* : Ibid., p. 204.

339   *According to various reports he set his sights . . .* : Skidmore, *Edward VI*, p. 71.

340   *At Seymour's direction, Edward wrote a letter . . .* : *DNB* entry for Thomas Seymour.

343   *Gardiner, accused of disobeying his instructions . . .* : Lingard, *History of England*, p. 5:264.

343   *The number of bishops who followed . . .* : Mackie, *Earlier Tudors*, p. 518.

344   *It would also explain his fumbling . . .* : Skidmore, *Edward VI*, p. 113, and Roger Turvey and Nigel Heard, *Edward VI and Mary* (Hodder Murray, 2006), p. 48.

344   *Though they accomplished little or nothing . . .* : Skidmore, *Edward VI*, p. 91.

347   *None of which might have mattered . . .* : Lingard, *History of England*, p. 5:285.

347   *In Devon in the far west . . .* : MacCulloch, *Church Militant*, pp. 43 and 119, and Guy, *Tudor England*, p. 208.

348   *As many as four thousand men were dead . . .* : Lingard, *History of England*, p. 5:289.

349   *An extraordinary figure named Robert Kett . . .* : The demands are in Turvey and Heard, *Edward and Mary*, p. 135; Kett's words are in Lingard, *History of England*, p. 5:290.

349   *With one proclamation he condemned destruction . . .* : Skidmore, *Edward VI*, p. 113.

350   *When Somerset cried out . . .* : The duke's concessions to the rebels are in ibid., p. 45.

353   *And so Dudley advanced on Norwich . . .* : Lingard, *History of England*, p. 5:290.

353   *After first and briefly allying himself . . .* : MacCulloch, *Church Militant*, p. 95.

355   *The conservatives were required to absorb . . .* : Lingard, *History of England*, p. 5:342.

363   *Francis van der Delft, the Catholic . . .* : Skidmore, *Edward VI*, p. 162.

363   *The narrowness of its base is suggested . . .* : MacCulloch, *Church Militant*, p. 163.

364   *He achieved perhaps the greatest triumph . . .* : Elton, *Tudor Constitution*, p. 396.

364   *Harsh penalties were imposed . . .* : MacCulloch, *Church Militant*, p. 141, and Lingard, *History of England*, p. 5:342.

364   *Once again it was made treason to deny . . .* : Skidmore, *Edward VI*, p. 82.

364   *Henceforth the death penalty could be imposed . . .* : Ibid.

364   *Seven of Henry's bishops were replaced . . .* : MacCulloch, *Church Militant*, pp. 96 and 154.

367   *He had never been an impressive physical specimen . . .* : Skidmore, *Edward VI*, p. 240.

370   *In the first, a draft in Edward's own hand . . .* : Ibid., p. 247, and Lingard, *History of England*, p. 5:357.

372   *Two days later, in reporting to the Privy Council . . .* : Lingard, *History of England*, p. 5:358.

373   *"He has not the strength to stir . . ."*: Skidmore, *Edward VI*, p. 255.

374   *He died in the arms of a Dudley son-in-law . . .* : Wilson, *Uncrowned Kings*, p. 226.

375   *The crown, Jane declared . . .* : *DNB* entry for Jane Grey.

377   *When Mary sent a messenger to the council . . .* : Mackie, *Earlier Tudors*, p. 527.

379   *Quite the contrary: the French ambassador . . .* : Loades, *Mary Tudor*, p. 26.

381   *She said disingenuously . . .* : Loades, *Elizabeth I*, p. 28.

382   *One of the most poignant scenes . . .* : Erickson, *Bloody Mary*, p. 118.

382   *When Parliament's passage . . .* : Loades, *Mary Tudor*, p. 41.

383   *Nothing came of this . . .* : This and *"grief and despair"* are in the *DNB* entry for Mary I.

384   *She wrote directly to the king . . .* : Loades, *Mary Tudor*, p. 47.

384   *Therefore, though he removed members of the Privy Council . . .* : Ibid., p. 48.

385   *Ordered to provide the names . . .* : Erickson, *Bloody Mary*, p. 242, and Lingard, *History of England*, p. 5:80.

386   *(In fact Henry, in futile pursuit . . .* : Loades, *Mary Tudor*, p. 52.

386   *Under the terms of her father's will . . .* : Ibid., p. 66.

388   *By 1549, when the new reign's first Act of Uniformity . . .* : Ibid., p. 75.

391   *Mary declared that she "wished to constrain . . ."*: Erickson, *Bloody Mary*, p. 309.

392   *When that old champion of reform . . .* : Lingard, *History of England*, p. 5:390.

392   *By 1553 he had had ready for Parliament's attention . . .* : Skidmore, *Edward VI*, p. 232.

392   *Anyone accused of such offenses . . .* : Lingard, *History of England*, p. 5:462.

393   *Cranmer exploded in rage when informed . . .* : This and the following statement about Cranmer *"spreading abroad seditious bills"* are in Lingard, *History of England*, p. 5:401.

394   *Pole was so well respected . . .* : Erickson, *Bloody Mary*, p. 389.

397   *Two days before, in an even more forceful . . .* : Ibid., p. 320.

399   *By repealing Henry VIII's Succession Act . . .* : Guy, *Tudor England*, p. 233.

400   *If Mary and Philip had a son . . .* : Mackie, *Earlier Tudors*, p. 537.

401   *Philip himself, when he learned . . .* : Erickson, *Bloody Mary*, p. 348, and *DNB* notes for entry on Philip II.

403   *"As for this marriage," she said . . .* : Lingard, *History of England*, p. 5:425.

404   *In all some 480 men were convicted . . .* : Loades, *Two Tudor Conspiracies*, p. 127.

404   *Not only when put on trial but before . . .* : Ibid., p. 16.

409   *London, where there had been only three* . . . : Penry Williams, *Life,* p. 129.

411   *"His way with the lords is so . . ."*: Erickson, *Bloody Mary,* p. 380.

412   *"If the English find out how hard up . . ."*: Ibid., p. 382.

416   *Mary even allowed herself* . . . : Loades, *Mary Tudor,* p. 168.

416   *Protestant preachers who had not fled* . . . : Erickson, *Bloody Mary,* p. 397.

417   *What is clear is that it was controversial* . . . : Lingard, *History of England,* p. 5:469.

418   *It was long and widely believed* . . . : Ibid., p. 5:464.

418   *Something on the order of three hundred individuals* . . . : Mackie, *Earlier Tudors,* p. 553.

422   *She had more success in restoring* . . . : Lingard, *History of England,* p. 5:494.

422   *Mary and Gardiner wanted to introduce* . . . : Loades, *Tudor Conspiracies,* p. 260.

423   *But Pole's position was still* . . . : *DNB* entry for Reginald Pole.

423   *This gathering, by the time of its adjournment* . . . : Mackie, *Earlier Tudors,* p. 555.

430   *Philip, inevitably but unfairly* . . . : Loades, *Mary Tudor,* p. 175; Guy, *Tudor England,* p. 248; Lingard, *History of England,* p. 5:521; Loades, *Mary Tudor,* p. 175, and Guy, *Tudor England,* p. 248.

430   *Elizabeth had only recently repeated her assurances* . . . : Lingard, *History of England,* p. 5:525, and Erickson, *Bloody Mary,* p. 480.

PART FOUR
Survivor

Though the enormous number of biographies of Elizabeth I continues to grow decade by decade, no single work is recognized as definitive. Three generations have brought a movement from J. E. Neale's *Queen Elizabeth I* (Jonathan Cape, 1934), regarded originally as authoritative but now as hagiographic, to gradually less worshipful and finally rigorously critical works. Biographies of value include:

Haigh, Christopher. *Elizabeth I,* 2nd ed. Longman, 1998.

Hibbert, Christopher. *The Virgin Queen.* Viking, 1990.

Loades, David. *Elizabeth I.* Hambledon & London, 2003.

Neale, J. E. *Queen Elizabeth I.* Pelican, 1960.

Smith, Lacey Baldwin. *Elizabeth Tudor.* Little, Brown, 1975.

Williams, Neville. *Elizabeth I.* Weidenfeld & Nicolson, 1972.

Notes

PAGE

437   *Her decline began with a refusal* . . . : An exceptionally detailed and vivid account of Elizabeth's last days appears in the opening pages of Evelyn Waugh's *Edmund Campion* (Little, Brown, 1946).

437   *When begged to get some sleep* . . . : Lingard, *History of England,* p. 6:647.

438   *At a time when the Crown's ordinary revenues* . . . : Elton, *England Under,* p. 362.

438   *Even the most glorious event of the reign* . . . : The cost figure is in Haigh, *Elizabeth I,* p. 138.

438   *Ferocious inflation has combined with falling wages* . . . : Data on living standards and death sentences are ibid., p. 166.

440   *Though of course we have no data* . . . : As noted above, Duffy's *Stripping of Altars* is an exhaustive demonstration of the lingering popularity of the old religion.

441   *Queen Mary herself suspected* . . . : Erickson, *Bloody Mary,* p. 346.

442   *The coronation took place on January 15* . . . : The cost figure is in the *DNB* entry for Elizabeth I.

445   *The Privy Council opened the legislative* . . . : Elton, *England Under,* p. 271.

446   *When Parliament reconvened on April 3* . . . : The change to supreme "governor" is in Hibbert, *Virgin Queen,* p. 92.

447   *A uniformity bill outlawing the mass* . . . : Elton, *Tudor Constitution,* presents the words of the bill on p. 401 and a brief discussion of it on p. 388.

447   *Thanks to the breakdown in relations* . . . : Loades, *Elizabeth I,* p. 134.

447   *She found, however, that almost to a man* . . . : Lingard, *History of England,* pp. 6:9 and 14.

449   *The point of conflict* . . . : Haigh, *Elizabeth I,* p. 47.

450   *She allowed the Diocese of Ely to remain without a bishop* . . . : Ibid., p. 49.

450   *Out of the eight thousand priests in England* . . . : Elton, *England Under,* p. 276.

450   *The persecution was relaxed as soon as* . . . : Haigh, *Elizabeth I,* p. 42.

460   *Elizabeth herself, though she never forgave* . . . : Hibbert, *Virgin Queen,* p. 67.

467   *Even people close to the queen* . . . : Haigh, *Elizabeth I,* p. 16.

473   *Henry Sidney, Dudley's brother-in-law* . . . : Milton Waldman, *Elizabeth and Leicester* (Collins, 1946), p. 103.

474   *What appears to have happened* . . . : Haigh, *Elizabeth I,* p. 16.

481   *It was perhaps in response* . . . : Elton, *England Under,* p. 298.

481   *It was a monumental blunder nevertheless* . . . : Ibid., p. 303; Lingard, *History of England,* p. 6:225; and Loades, *Elizabeth I,* p. 169.

482   *They were exasperated, therefore, when Elizabeth* . . . : Haigh, *Elizabeth I,* p. 38.

491   *The worst of their mistakes was to overreact* . . . : Elton, *England Under,* p. 279.

494   *The Privy Council then fell into an angry dispute* . . . : Wilson, *Uncrowned Kings,* p. 303.

495   *Anjou definitely had no interest* . . . : Hibbert, *Virgin Queen,* p. 181, and Lingard, *History of England,* p. 6:241, note 1.

498   *In that same year the increasingly discontented* . . . : Elton, *England Under,* p. 300.

500   *In actuality it was all talk* . . . : Loades, *Elizabeth I,* p. 176, and Smith, *Elizabeth Tudor,* p. 143.

507   *Somewhat oddly for a Protestant* . . . : Guy, *Tudor England,* p. 262.

508   *It was her good fortune to have two* . . . : Lingard, *History of England,* p. 6:328.

513   *Much of the trouble grew out of the determination* . . . : Smith, *Elizabeth Tudor,* p. 172; Haigh, *Elizabeth I,* pp. 122 and 149; and *DNB* entries on Francis Walsingham and Mary, Queen of Scots.

513   *As early as 1581 Walsingham was asking* . . . : Haigh, *Elizabeth I,* p. 76.

513   *An innovation called "compounding"* . . . : Loades, *Elizabeth I,* p. 234.

522   *Her navy had barely broken off its pursuit* . . . : Smith, *Elizabeth Tudor,* pp. 66 and 72.

523   *Her admiral, Lord Howard of Effingham* . . . : Howard's words are in Loades, *Elizabeth I,* p. 252.

523   *Here she supposedly delivered* . . . : Loades, *Elizabeth I,* p. 252, observes that the queen "is alleged to have made" the Tilbury speech.

524   *During the period when invasion seemed imminent* . . . : Hibbert, *Virgin Queen,* p. 220, and Lingard, *History of England,* p. 6:505.

524   *Between July and November twenty-one imprisoned priests* . . . : Lingard, *History of England,* p. 6:520.

525   *Though theologically Whitgift was* . . . : Elton, *England Under,* p. 428.

528   *When the fleet finally set out again* . . . : Drake's instructions, and the number of lives lost on the expedition, are in Guy, *Tudor England,* p. 349.

544   *Getting the queen's approval was difficult* . . . : Loades, *Elizabeth I,* p. 265, and Haigh, *Elizabeth I,* p. 142.

546   *The Dutch rebels, he observed sourly* . . . : The words in quotes are in the *DNB* entry for Robert Cecil.

548   *He stormed out proclaiming* . . . : The words in quotes are in the *DNB* entry for Robert Devereux, second Earl of Essex.

558   *Five Parliaments had had to be called* . . . : Loades, *Elizabeth I,* p. 292; Elton, *England Under,* pp. 362 and 461; and Haigh, *Elizabeth I,* p. 166.

559   *Prices of necessities soared* . . . : Haigh, *Elizabeth I,* p. 166.

559   *In 1534, at the dawn of the English Reformation* . . . : The numbers in this paragraph are from ibid.

560   *(At thirty, upon being told* . . . : Smith, *Elizabeth Tudor,* p. 73.

561   *The show went on—her wardrobe* . . . : Haigh, *Elizabeth I,* p. 90. Lingard, *History of England,* p. 6:657, says the number of the queen's gowns was in the thousands.

561   *She was allowing her world* . . . : The number of Privy Council members is in Haigh, *Elizabeth I,* p. 107.

563   *It was long customary to interpret* . . . : Loades, *Elizabeth I,* p. 274.

564   *He had already been talking recklessly* . . . : Lingard, *History of England,* pp. 6:597 and 600, and *DNB* entry on Robert Devereux, second Earl of Essex.

568   *Elizabeth showed a marked aversion* . . . : *DNB* entry for Robert Devereux.

568   *This has often been represented* . . . : Lingard, *History of England,* p. 6:629, suggests that the queen's "victory" lay in the fact that the royal prerogative on monopolies had not been positively surrendered.

568   *Revenues from the land sales totaled* . . . : Smith, *Elizabeth Tudor,* p. 203.

569   *In 1601 and 1602 he became the leading* . . . : Hibbert, *Virgin Queen,* p. 244; Elton, *England Under,* p. 411; and Guy, *Tudor England,* p. 396.

Index

About the Author

G. J. MEYER is a professional writer whose bylines have appeared in *The New York Times*, the *Los Angeles Times*, *The Boston Globe*, *Harper's*, and many other newspapers and magazines. While working for the *St. Louis Post-Dispatch*, he was awarded a Nieman Fellowship by Harvard University. He is the author of *A World Undone*, as well as *The Memphis Murders* (recipient of an Edgar Award for nonfiction) and *Executive Blues*. Meyer lives in England.